Harlem Renaissance Re-examined: A Revised and Expanded Edition

Edited by

Victor A. Kramer
and Robert A. Russ

The Whitston Publishing Company
Troy, New York
1997

Copyright 1997
Victor A. Kramer and Robert A. Russ

Library of Congress Catalog Card Number 96-61876

ISBN 0-87875-488-1

Printed in the United States of America

Harlem Renaissance
Re-examined

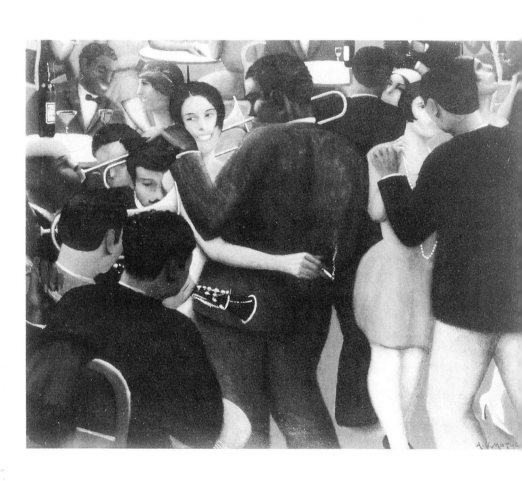

ACKNOWLEDGMENTS

The subsidiary paperback rights for this book have been granted by AMS Press, Inc. This completely revised edition is an expansion of *The Harlem Renaissance Re-examined*, Vol. 2 of the Georgia State Literary Studies Series. The revised and expanded version has been completely re-set and includes two new essays, a portfolio of photographs, and a chronology as well as a completely revised and updated bibliography.

For the permission to reprint the photographs of Cullen, Du Bois, Hughes, Hurston, Waters, and West, thanks is extended to the Estate of Carl Van Vechten, Joseph Solomon, Executor. Edward Steichen's photograph of Robeson is reprinted courtesy of Joanna Steichen. Further thanks for the photographs reprinted in this volume goes to Regina Andrews, Griffith J. Davis, and the Harold Jackman Countee Cullen Memorial Collection at Atlanta University.

Blues, a 1929 oil by Archibald Motley, Jr., was executed in Paris while he was there on a Guggenheim Memorial Foundation Fellowship. Born in New Orleans in 1891 and a virtual lifelong resident of Chicago, Motley has been termed America's first urban black painter. (Photograph courtesy of Archie Motley.)

The assistance of the English Department of Georgia State University; the expertise of Leigh Kirkland, who saw the book through its preparation as a camera-ready project; and the work done by several graduate students including Michael Newman, David Remy, and, especially, Petra Dreiser, is greatly appreciated. The new contributions by colleagues Carolyn C. Denard and Jane Kuenz have added to the usefulness of this edition.

The co-editor, Robert A. Russ, who did the bibliography for the first edition combed the original volume during the revision and proved to be invaluable as this second project unfolded.

LIST OF ILLUSTRATIONS

TABLE OF CONTENTS

INTRODUCTION TO NEW EDITION

VICTOR A. KRAMER

In 1938, when much we now call the Harlem Renaissance was overshadowed, even forgotten, because of the Great Depression, Zora Neale Hurston published a book dedicated to Carl Van Vechten, whom she called "God's Image of a Teacher." Her gracious gesture reminds us of how we learn and is a reminder of what was frequently sensed about the complexity of the Harlem Renaissance, a cultural blend now being intensely investigated by scholars of both races. Like any complex cultural movement in which persons learn from each other, the Harlem Renaissance (and its continuing study) must be seen as a series of inter-related events which reverberate down into our present consciousness. It is for such reasons that we return to this project with this expanded paperback edition.

Scholars know the surprising story of Zora Neale Hurston, long neglected and now being re-evaluated. We sometimes forget that the continuing process of re-examination is furthered because of the energetic intellectual and artistic curiosity of people like Hurston and Van Vechten and all the other artists examined in this book. As is clear from the figures examined here, as well as from the photographs added to this edition, which provide hints of the interplay between and among artists and black and white awareness, the phenomenon called the Harlem Renaissance will continue to spark the imagination of students and scholars.

It is especially appropriate as this book goes to press to mention the late Charles T. Davis, whose encouragement stood behind much of this continuing project. His 1970 University of Iowa N.E.H. Summer Institute on the Harlem Renaissance, which I attended, was a stimulus to the 1974 *Studies in the Literary Imagination* issue, which led to this revised study. A recent article about

Professor Davis (in the Spring 1991 *Mississippi Quarterly*) emphasizes his combination of the best of traditional scholarship along with a continuing and sustained awareness of his roots as Southern and Black. His scholarly career included investigations which ranged from traditional American writers to re-evaluations of neglected figures, including Jean Toomer, the subject of the essay by Davis included here.

This expanded book is meant as one more way of encouraging study and good teaching—the kind of work accomplished by Hurston, Van Vechten, and scholars such as Davis. We hope the paperback will encourage a new group of students as we move towards the twenty-first century, while continuing to demonstrate that the legacy of the Harlem Renaissance remains strong and provides additional possibilities for literary and cultural analysis in the future. The paperback edition of *The Harlem Renaissance Re-examined* adds a new essay by Robert A. Russ about Claude McKay, one by Jane Kuenz about George Schuyler, as well as an expanded bibliography, a group of photographs, a chronology, and an afterword by Carolyn C. Denard. It thereby extends the collaborative work which led to the publication of the original book in 1988 and provides considerably more information for scholars.

Victor A. Kramer
General Editor
Georgia State Literary Studies Series
(1986–1993)
1996

INTRODUCTION:

THE HARLEM RENAISSANCE RE-EXAMINED

The new and revised essays gathered within this book provide a systematic examination of many important aspects of that complex period called the Harlem Renaissance. In addition, because a dozen years have passed since the original collection was commissioned for *Studies in the Literary Imagination* (1974), much additional scholarly work about the Harlem Renaissance has been accomplished, and thus many new approaches for study of the Renaissance are reflected in the new essays included here. Subjects which may not have even seemed promising to scholars in the early 1970s have now yielded valuable results. All of this reflects the continuing scholarly process which advances while it builds on earlier work. When the first group of essays was written in 1973 and 1974, I sought to include examinations of the "major" figures involved in the Renaissance. Not all were covered then, and even with this book some still remain unexamined. This, too, suggests the complexity of a literary period which involves so many aspects of cultural and literary history.

The 1974 *Studies* issue sought to accomplish two things: it attempted to provide examinations about the Harlem Renaissance in relation to the most significant black artists, and it also sought to suggest some of the complexity of the relationships between white and black writers. In this expanded volume new studies reveal that both areas (black artists themselves, as well as the complex relationships between white and black), continue to generate valuable inquiries. In this book many more theoretical questions are also raised. Valuable new inquiries are possible because scholars have refined their approaches and sought out materials not readily available a decade earlier. For example, while male artists dominated the earlier collection, black women artists and work by women scholars take their rightful place in this book. This re-examination of the Harlem Renaissance, therefore, is much more complex and considerably more detailed than the 1974 collection of articles. While they provide a more complicated picture of "The New Negro," the essays within this book generally do not seek to provide definitive answers. At this stage, questions about such a complicated movement may be even more valuable than answers.

Much remains to be fully explored: how writers—white and black—developed art in the twenties; other relationships between writers and other artists who pursued the imaginative creation of the figure of the Negro during the Renaissance; the motivations of black writers who experienced considerable sociological, financial, and psychological pressures during this period. In his study, *Harlem Renaissance* (New York: Oxford, 1971), Nathan Huggins insists that "black and white Americans have been so long and so intimately a part of one another's experience that, will it or not, they cannot be understood independently. Each has needed the other to help define himself" (11). This book offers many new perspectives from which to view some of the complex interrelationships which made the era of the New Negro.

These essays often provide keys to how major writers like W.E.B. Du Bois, Jean Toomer, Countee Cullen, Langston Hughes, Zora Neale Hurston, and Sterling A. Brown formulated methods for writing about the black experience. Other essays demonstrate the importance of Renaissance themes for non-black writers who were, in various ways, attracted to ideas and images important during the period of the "New Negro." Eugene O'Neill, Carl Van Vechten, and DuBose Heyward each contributed a basic impetus to the Renaissance. As time passes and more distance is achieved, it has become easier to see the development of the black figure in our literature as an extremely complicated cultural movement. Black artists in the Twenties created their work clearly within an atmosphere which was to some degree created by others at the edge of the phenomenon we now call the Renaissance. Some of the essays included here examine the pressures which generated art in the midst of that complexity.

Many of the articles included in this collection make it clear that the complexity of the literary movement we label, retrospectively, as the Harlem Renaissance is due to the interactions of enormous numbers of forces. In the new essays commissioned for the book, aspects of patronage upon the careers of black artists, the complexity of Van Vechten's *Nigger Heaven* and its marketing, the many forces which contributed to the works of black women playwrights, the complexity of the art of Nella Larsen, Zora Neale Hurston, and Wallace Thurman, are examined. Understanding the Harlem Renaissance is, as indicated, a continuing project. Thus we are grateful for the new scholarly work which has prepared the way for the contributors to this book who now provide a new overview of Rudolph Fisher's fiction; or an interview with Dorothy West, whose career continues down to the present; a systematic examination of *Nigger Heaven*, which reveals that it is both a successful novel and, to an important degree, an anthropological study; a shrewd new appraisal of Zora Neale Hurston's work; as well as other new approaches.

It has been argued that the Renaissance was short-lived and without much effect, but it has been much more convincingly demonstrated that what the major black thinkers and writers accomplished in the Twenties was absorbed not only in America but in Africa by young writers like Léopold Senghor. Mercer Cook in *The Militant Black Writer in Africa and in the United States* (Madison: Univ. of Wisconsin Press, 1969) reminds us that "[s]peaking at Howard University on September 28, 1966, Senghor paid tribute to 'the pioneer thinkers who lighted our road in the years 1930–1935: Alain Locke, W.E.B. DuBois, Marcus Garvey, Carter G. Woodson.'" At the same time Senghor also said that he wanted "'to render well-deserved homage to the poets whom we translated and recited, and in whose steps we tried to follow: Claude McKay, Jean Toomer, Countee Cullen, James Weldon Johnson, Langston Hughes, Sterling Brown'" (12). Clearly, racial awareness in Africa at the present moment is related to the continuing currents of the Harlem Renaissance.

To say that the Harlem Renaissance is limited merely to the 1920s would be a great mistake. The critical writing of Du Bois, as demonstrated by Darwin Turner's essay here, early manifested an awareness of the possibilities of a black aesthetic. It is equally difficult to say just when the Harlem Renaissance ended. It might even be that its effects were still being strongly felt, and thus that it was still figuratively alive, as late as 1970, when Arna Bontemps spoke at the University of Iowa Summer Institute which I attended and which was organized by Charles T. Davis. It is true that Professor Davis's enthusiasm generated much of the work reflected in this volume. Further, a book like *Black Writers of the Thirties* (Baton Rouge: Louisiana State Univ. Press, 1973) by James O. Young stands as documentation that many of the ideas and artistic ideals of the Twenties were carried over into following decades. A writer like Langston Hughes developed the themes nurtured earlier into the refinements of his later career. Thus, the Renaissance has many links reaching down to the present.

The Harlem Renaissance may have been a disappointment in some ways; some careers did not develop as they promised, but we must remember this is always true of all artistic movements. This was the case with Cullen and Toomer, and probably others, but much was accomplished. For example, the important poet Melvin Tolson has stated that his writing of poetry was stimulated in the years after the Renaissance precisely because he had been inspired by the Harlem writers of the Twenties while he was a student at Columbia. Similarly, Sterling Brown's career is one which grows naturally out of the resurgence of interest in folk material which took place in Harlem after the war. Zora Neale Hurston's career is likewise still in the process of being re-evaluated, but we are beginning to see that hers was a much more sophisticated approach than frequently assumed in the past. The essays in this volume about her, about women playwrights, about white patronage, and the complexity of black–white relationships (good and bad) suggest some of the areas wherein still more work will be done by scholars in the future.

As an indication of the fact that the Harlem Renaissance will continue to require re-examination, I have asked Robert A. Russ to prepare a working bibliography which concludes the book. This bibliography takes note of the most significant scholarly work in relation to the writers treated in this volume. This working bibliography goes beyond Margaret Perry's earlier Harlem Renaissance bibliography (1982). We know that years hence many more valuable essays will become available, and still another bibliography will be assembled which will add to this work of the mid-nineteen-eighties as reflected both in the bibliography and in the many essays within this book.

II

To read such a diverse collection of studies as these of *The Harlem Renaissance Re-examined* is to be reminded of the complexity of American culture and of the pleasures of reading; yet it also is to be reminded of the challenges which so easily appear within a society which is so complex. Much more can and will be done in subsequent studies of the Harlem Renaissance. Especially, I sense that in the future younger scholars and still newer techniques of literary theory will make it possible for new generations of readers to profit from close attention to the many texts which were generated during the Harlem Renaissance.

What is implied, the subtext if you will, is where our attention must be placed in the future. These essays with their systematic re-examination of aspects of the Harlem Renaissance provide many ways to understand particular writers and issues, yet it seems to me that the emphasis in the essays remains (rightly so) on what these writers accomplished and how their art functions. Still unexamined are larger questions about culture and social issues which are implied.

Two basic concerns are frequently touched upon in these essays, yet none of the writers has time to investigate these questions as they relate to a larger social, cultural, even economic context. One concern is the cultural climate of the 1920s which made it possible for the explosion of talent we label the Harlem Renaissance to be recognized, and how the artistic energy of these many writers was successfully (or not so) channeled into the kinds of works examined in these essays. As we become more familiar with the circumstances which generated the life and work of those artists, we will see more clearly that biography, autobiography, history, economics, folklore, religion, philosophy, racial prejudice, and cultural interaction between blacks and whites are immensely complicated. Something never to be easily dismissed. And we also see, by looking carefully, that this complexity provides a lens for looking at other such cultural situations. Truly what might look like a stereotypical situation can be archetypal.

Another concern about which we are made more aware, but about which we still sense a need to experience more, is the realization that all of these writings— so assiduously re-examined—are the spirited overflow of the artistic discipline of individual artists. These artists have provided us with gifts to which we can frequently return. As Walter J. Ong has so eloquently written, the poet's cry is a dialectic of aural and oral objectives. The work of the artist is a complex combination of words which come directly from the heart of the speaker. This fact is, I suspect, sometimes overlooked as the interpreter seeks to explain what this or that poem or drama or story means. Ultimately the work may mean, yet it is performed and it is in the performance that the artist and reader derive their satisfaction. In the future, as more sophisticated readings are provided by feminist critics, Marxist critics, critics concerned about how works reflect parts of the culture which have generated them, we will, no doubt, see that within the art of the Harlem Renaissance lies a vast reservoir of material for our analysis of the culture beyond that art while there is great pleasure to be enjoyed.

The poet as prophet cries out and only much later do we fully hear.

This book is arranged in two parts: the first, "Theory and Questions," raises many of the fundamental questions which are going to be answered only little by little. Thus, W.E.B. Du Bois and Black women playwrights of the 1920s; the interaction of black and white characters and themes with Black and White writers generate all kinds of questions about the meanings implied in the art. This suggests why this book is arranged in two parts. The second, "Art and Answers," is mostly about individual artists and particular works. In these essays, scholars remind us that in all works of sustained accomplishment, the artist makes his work well because he enjoys what he is doing. Thus, in essays about Brown, or Hurston, or Hughes, or Larsen, or Toomer, scholars remind us that at the heart of the Harlem Renaissance is the artist's nostalgia for entertainment.

A Black artist in America is caught between a yearning for such nostalgia and the fact of a time present which may best be called alienation or frustration. How to build a work which is balanced between nostalgia and anger, between an ideal world and the reality lived which prods the imagination, is an extremely difficult chore. The essays in this book demonstrate that such an achievement is possible. Different artists accomplish this in different ways, and this is to remind us that our chore, ultimately, is to go back to the words, the songs, the texts, which they provide. When we do so, we can then continue to re-examine the Harlem Renaissance.

A PORTFOLIO OF HARLEM RENAISSANCE PHOTOGRAPHS

VICTOR A. KRAMER

These twelve photographs, selected from the Harold Jackman Countee Cullen Memorial Collection, housed within the archives of Atlanta University, represent many aspects of that era sometimes called "The New Negro," truly a renaissance in that a birth was possible because of a happy concatenation of events in the nineteen twenties. The rich collection from which these photographs are taken is a valuable resource which reflects the complexity of that era.

In a dozen photographs one can only catch glimpses of "The Harlem Renaissance," yet such glimpses can be extremely revealing. One definite suggestion in these selected photographs is the combination of strength and sometimes brooding dignity reflected in the faces of persons, such as Paul Robeson, within a movement which had its roots in the nineteenth century and earlier. Recognition of this fact also helps the observer to understand that in many ways what was begun in the nineteen twenties lives on into the present moment. Today we remain fascinated with the accomplishments of the Harlem Renaissance.

The photograph of W.E.B. DuBois, by Carl Van Vechten, included here is a striking portrait which illustrates my basic point. It was made in 1946. Similarly striking are the two concluding photos which make up this portfolio. They clearly reveal that what was born in the nineteen twenties flourished quite beyond those limited years. The vivid portrait of Dorothy West, also taken by Van Vechten in 1948, catches her vibrancy, something still beautifully evident in 1988, forty years later, when she came to Atlanta to speak upon the occasion of the publication of the first edition of this book.

In a related way, the photograph of Langston Hughes, included here as the last item, shows him with students in an Atlanta school in the nineteen forties and suggests the wonder of continuity. His poetry, as well as his spirit, reflected in this one photographic moment some decades removed from the Harlem Renaissance, is a life's work which has served as an inspiration for generations of readers. In these few photographs, then, we have glimpses of many artists (writers, poets, actors, singers) whose enthusiasm makes the Harlem Renaissance remain a living phenomenon, and thereby something we can profitably keep on examining.

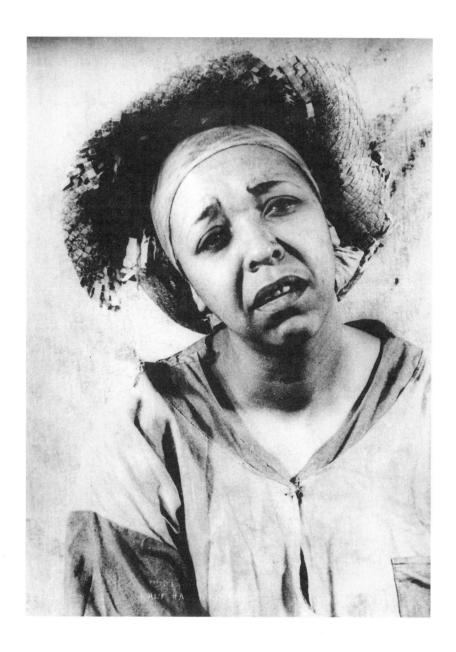

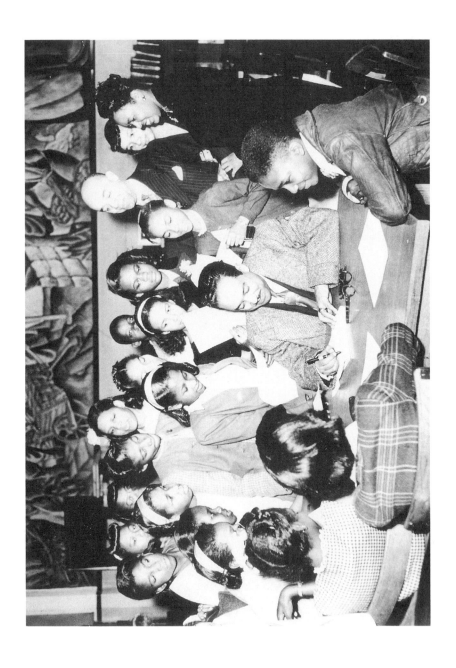

CAPTIONS

1. W.E.B. DuBois (Van Vechten Portrait), July 18, 1946.

2. Countee Cullen (Van Vechten Portrait), September 20, 1941.

3. Jules Bledsoe (Photographer Unknown), Inscribed to Cullen, 1928.

4. Jessie Fauset (Photographer Unknown), Inscribed "Souvenir de Votre Amie."

5. Paul Robeson (Photograph by Edward Steichen). In EMPEROR JONES costume.

6. Langston Hughes, Charles S. Johnson, E. Franklin Frazier, Rudolph Fisher, Hubert Delaney (From Metropolitan Museum "Harlem on My Mind" Exhibit: Courtesy Mrs. Regina Andrews), 1924.

7. Zora Neale Hurston (Van Vechten Portrait), April 3, 1937.

8. Langston Hughes (Van Vechten Portrait), 1937.

9. Ethel Waters as Hagar in MAMBA'S DAUGHTERS (Van Vechten Portrait), 1939.

10. Ethel Waters and Carl Van Vechten (Van Vechten Portrait), February 19, 1939.

11. Dorothy West (Van Vechten Portrait), May 17, 1948.

12. Langston Hughes with students at David T. Howard School in Atlanta (Photograph by Griffith J. Davis), circa 1947.

CHRONOLOGY OF THE HARLEM RENAISSANCE

ROBERT A. RUSS

Although the major historical and literary events of the Harlem Renaissance are generally placed between the years 1919 and 1929, I have expanded both ends of this range, especially the later years. The Depression had a devastating effect on all aspects of American society, including the publishing industry (and through it, of course, the writers of the Harlem Renaissance), but as can be seen, a significant number of the Renaissance writers could and did continue writing and publishing after 1929. Consequently, I have chosen to end this chronology at 1940 because with the publication, in that year, of Richard Wright's *Native Son* on the one hand and that of Langston Hughes' *The Big Sea* and Claude McKay's *Harlem: Negro Metropolis* on the other, we seem, simultaneously, to observe the beginning of a new era and the end of an old.

I am indebted to a large number of sources for information contained herein, but I would particularly like to acknowledge a debt to Jeffrey Stewart, who compiled a brief chronology of the Harlem Renaissance for the Studio Museum in Harlem's traveling exhibit "Harlem Renaissance: Art of Black America" in 1988, and to Bruce Kellner, whose book *The Harlem Renaissance: A Historical Dictionary for the Era* is an indispensable aid for the study of this period.

1917

Hubert H. Harrison's *The Negro and the Nation* published by Cosmo Advocates.

Three Plays for a Negro Theatre by Ridgely Torrence staged at the Garden Theatre, April 5.

James Weldon Johnson's *Fifty Years and Other Poems* published by Cornhill.

Harry T. Burleigh, composer, pianist, singer, awarded the Spingarn Medal for excellence in creative music, May 16.

East St. Louis, Illinois, Riot, June.

Oscar Micheaux's *The Homesteader* published by Western Book and Supply.

Silent Protest Parade in New York, July 27. Some 10,000 blacks parade down Fifth Avenue to protest lynchings and the East St. Louis Riot. Marchers include Du Bois and James Weldon Johnson.

Joel A. Rogers' *From Superman to Man* published by Lenox Publishing; reprinted, 1924.

The United States enters World War I. Joel Spingarn presses the War Department to establish an officers' training camp for blacks.

Julius Rosenwald Fund for Education, Scientific and Religious Purposes organized, October 30.

Most blacks and black newspapers support the war, as 365,000 blacks are drafted for military service. Blacks comprise 11% of troops sent overseas.

369th Black Regiment embarks for France, November.

Monroe Nathan Work's *Negro Year Book: An Annual Encyclopedia of the Negro* published by Negro Year Book Publishing (preceded by annual or biennial volumes, 1912, 1913, 1914–1915, 1916–1917, and followed by 1918–1919, 1921–1922, 1925–1926, 1931–1932, 1937–1938).

Edward A. Johnson, the first black representative, elected to the New York State Assembly, November 23.

Afro-American Liberty League founded.

Claude McKay publishes his poems in *Seven Arts*, probably the first work by a black writer in a white publication during the century.

Emmett J. Scott appointed special assistant to the Secretary of War.

1918

Joseph Seamon Cotter Jr.'s *The Band of Gideon and Other Lyrics* published by Cornhill.

Sarah Lee Brown Fleming's *Hope's Highway* published by Neale Publishing.

The French award the Croix de Guerre to the 369th Regiment and name it "Hell Fighters," April.

Kelly Miller's *An Appeal to Conscience* published by Macmillan.

Carter G. Woodson's *A Century of Negro Migration* published by Ames Press.

William Stanley Braithwaite, poet, literary critic and editor, receives Spingarn Medal for distinguished achievement in literature, May 5.

Walter White joins the National Association for the Advancement of Colored People (NAACP) staff.

Marcus Garvey incorporates the Universal Negro Improvement Association (UNIA) and begins publishing *Negro World*.

National Liberty Congress of Colored Americans petitions Congress to make lynching a federal crime.

The Messenger editors arrested for violation of the Espionage Act.

North Harlem Community Council founded.

Harlem Conservatory of Fine Arts founded.

First soldiers in American army to be decorated for bravery in France are two blacks, Henry Johnson and Needham R. Roberts.

1919

The 369th Infantry Regiment of Black American soldiers return from France and marches up Fifth Avenue to Harlem, February 17.

Father Divine starts his congretation in Sayville, Long Island.

Samuel Gompers of the American Federation of Labor delivers an address to the Federation's annual conference in which he vows to remove "every class and race distinction" from the movement.

U.S. Attorney General A. Mitchell Palmer launches "Red Scare" by creating a special division of the Justice Department, headed by J. Edgar Hoover, to combat and spy on blacks and radicals, including Marcus Garvey, founder of the Universal Negro Improvement Association (UNIA).

The National Association for the Advancement of Colored People (NAACP), founded in 1909, holds a conference on lynching after repeated incidents of lynching of blacks occur in 1918 and 1919 and government fails to enact sufficient legislation to stop the violence. The NAACP publishes *Thirty Years of Lynching in the United States, 1889-1918*.

Twenty-seven race riots occur between the "Red Summer" and end of 1919 as whites and blacks compete for postwar employment and blacks establish residence in major American cities.

The Southern-based Commission on Interracial Cooperation formed to fight racism.

W.E.B. Du Bois organizes the First Pan-African Congress at Grand Hotel in Paris, February 29–21, with representatives from the United States, the West Indies, and nine African countries, to lobby for the independent administration of Germany's African colonies.

Claude McKay, Jamaican emigré living in Harlem, publishes "If We Must Die" in *The Liberator*, a leftist journal.

Henry O. Tanner's works are exhibited in the *Group of American Artists* exhibition at the Knoedler Gallery in New York City. Show later tours other cities.

Richard Lonsdale Brown, a prominent black American artist, exhibits his work at the Ovington Galleries, sponsored by Miss Mary White Ovington and the NAACP.

Benjamin Brawley's *The Negro in Literature and Art in the United States* published by Duffield; reprinted, 1925, 1930.

The West Virginia Supreme Court rules blacks should be admitted to juries.

Joshua Jones' *The Heart of the World and Other Poems* published by Stratford.

Archibald K. Grimké, former U.S. Consul in Santo Domingo, author and president of the NAACP branch in the District of Columbia, receives the Spingarn Medal, June 27.

Robert T. Kerlin's *The Voice of the Negro* published by Dutton.

Walter Adolphe Roberts' *Pierrot Wounded and Other Poems* (translated from the French of P. Alberty) published by Brothers of the Book.

Membership of the NAACP approaches 100,000 despite attempts in some areas, such as Texas, to make it illegal.

Emmett Jay Scott's *Official History of the American Negro in the World War* privately printed.

Race Relations Commission founded in Chicago, September.

Brotherhood Workers of America founded, September.

Marcus Garvey founds the Black Star Shipping Line.

Dr. Louis Wright, first black staff member, appointed to the Harlem General Hospital.

National Association of Negro Musicians founded.

Associated Negro Press founded.

1920

A nationwide steel strike ends in complete capitulation of the workers and a major defeat for organized labor.

Postwar economic boom subsides, ushering in a deep recession.

W.E.B. Du Bois awarded the Spingarn Medal for achievements in scholarship, as editor of *Crisis*, and for founding and calling the Pan African Congress, June 1.

Marcus Garvey's militant UNIA holds its first annual convention at Madison Square Garden, August 1.

Eugene O'Neill's *The Emperor Jones*, starring black actor Charles Gilpin, performed for the first time by the Provincetown Players in New York, November 3.

The Howard Players, a student drama group at Howard University in Washington, D.C., performs Lord Dansany's *Tents of the Arabs* and Ridgely Torrence's *Simon the Cyrenian* at the Belasco Theatre. The run marks the beginning of the black universities' theater movement.

Meta Warrick Fuller's sculpture exhibited at the Pennsylvania Academy of the Fine Arts.

William Crogman and H. F. Kletzing's *Progress of a Race* published by Nichols.

Natalie [Burlin] Curtis's *Songs and Tales from the Dark Continent* published by Schirmer.

W.E.B. Du Bois's *Darkwater*, a collection of his poetry, addresses, and essays, published by Jenkins; reprinted by H. B. and Howe, 1930.

Hubert H. Harrison's *When Africa Awakes* published by Porro Press.

Walter Everette Hawkins' *Chords and Discords* published by Badger.

Claude McKay's *Spring in New Hampshire* published by Grant Richards.

Robert Russa Moton's *Finding a Way Out* published by Doubleday and Page.

Alice Dunbar Nelson's *The Dunbar Speaker and Entertainer* published by Nichols.

Emmett Jay Scott's *Negro Migration During the War* published by Oxford Univ. Press.

James Weldon Johnson appointed the first black officer (secretary) of NAACP and campaigns for the withdrawal of U.S. troops occupying Haiti.

Friends of Negro Freedom founded.

Harlem Stock Exchange founded.

Theatrical Owners and Bookers Association (TOBA) founded.

National Negro Theatre Corporation founded.

1921

UNIA's first mission sails to Liberia with goal to begin the repatriation of African Americans.

Representative L. C. Dyer of Missouri sponsors an anti-lynching bill in Congress.

At the age of 15, Josephine Baker runs away from home, becomes Bessie Smith's maid, and soon proves her own singing ability.

Shuffle Along, the first musical revue written and performed by blacks, opens in New York on May 22. With music by Eubie Blake and lyrics by Noble Sissle, the revue launches the careers of Josephine Baker and Florence Mills.

By Right of Birth, a movie about black American life, produced by the Lincoln Motion Picture Company.

Charles S. Gilpin receives the Spingarn Medal for his performance in the title role of O'Neill's *Emperor Jones*, June 30.

Countee Cullen's first published poem, "I Have a Rendezvous with Life," appears in the De Witt Clinton High School (New York) literary magazine, *The Magpie*.

Langston Hughes' first published poem, "The Negro Speaks of Rivers," appears in *The Crisis*, the NAACP's journal.

Marcus Garvey inaugurated provisional president of the "Republic of Africa," August 31.

The Light, a weekly newspaper for blacks which also publishes fiction, appears in New York. It is renamed *Heebie Jeebies* in 1925, and the *The Light and Heebie Jeebies* in 1927.

Harry Pace founds Black Swan Records in Harlem.

Black artist May Howard Jackson creates a sculpture of black writer Jean Toomer.

Exhibition of work by black American artists (including Henry Tanner, Laura Wheeler Waring, W. E. Scott, Meta Fuller, W. E. Braxton) held at the 135th Street branch of The New York Public Library.

Benjamin Brawley's *Social History of the American Negro* published by Macmillan.

Twenty-one blacks and ten whites killed in a riot in Tulsa, Oklahoma.

Leslie Pickney Hill's *The Wings of Oppression* published by Stratford.

Joshua Jones's *Poems of the Four Seas* published by Cornhill.

Robert T. Kerlin's anthology *Contemporary Poetry of the Negro* published by Hampton Normal and Agricultural Institution.

Penman Lovingood's *Famous Modern Negro Musicians* published by Press Forum.

Marcus Garvey founds African Orthodox Church, September.

Second Pan African Congress, September.

Colored Players Guild of New York founded.

The doctor of philosophy degree is awarded for the first time to black women: Evan B. Dykes, English at Radcliffe; Sadie T. Mossell, Economics at the University of Pennsylvania; Georgiana R. Simpson, German at the University of Chicago.

1922

Colonel Charles Young dies in Liberia, January 7.

UNIA marches with the NAACP and YMCA in support of Congressman Dyer's federal anti-lynching bill. On January 26, the Dyer Anti-Lynching Bill becomes the first anti-lynching legislation to pass the House of Representatives.

Claude McKay's *Harlem Shadows* published by Harcourt, Brace.

Bert Williams dies, March 15.

James Weldon Johnson's *The Book of American Negro Poetry*, an anthology of contemporary black American verse, published by Harcourt, Brace; revised, 1931.

Black singer Marian Anderson begins her concert career with a debut at the Town Hall in New York.

King Oliver's Creole Jazz Band takes up residence at the Lincoln Gardens dance hall in Chicago.

Strut Miss Lizzie, a black musical revue, opens in New York.

Goat Alley, a tragedy about black American life written by the white dramatist Ernest Culbertson, opens on Broadway.

In Washington, D.C., the Howard Players perform *Genefrede*, a play about the life of Toussaint L'Ouverture, the Haitian revolutionary, and *The Danse Calinda*, a Creole pantomime by Ridgely Torrence.

Meta Fuller's sculpture *Ethiopia Awakening* exhibited at New York's Making of America Exposition.

The Tanner League of Washington, D.C., holds exhibition of works by black American artists (including Meta Fuller) at Dunbar High School.

Mary B. Talbert, former president of the NAACP, awarded the Spingarn Medal for service to the women of her race and the restoration of the Frederick Douglass home, June 20.

F. G. Detweiler's *The Negro Press in the United States* published by the Univ. of Chicago Press.

Charles S. Johnson and Graham R. Taylor's *The Negro in Chicago: A Study of Race Relations and a Race Riot* published by the Univ. of Chicago Press.

Georgia Douglas Johnson's *Bronze* published by Brimmer.

René Maran's *Batouala* published by Seltzer.

Frederick Douglass Memorial Home in Washington, D.C., dedicated as a museum, August 12.
William Pickens' *The Vengeance of the Gods and Three Other Stories* published by A.M.E. Book Concern.
Thomas S. Stribling's *Birthright* published by Century.
Clement Wood's *Nigger* published by Dutton.
Carter G. Woodson's *The Negro in Our History* published by Associated Publishers.

1923

Eric Walrond becomes assistant editor of *The Negro World*.
Economic recovery begins six years of unprecedented growth in corporate profits, consumer products, and stock market prices.
Spingarn Medal awarded to George Washington Carver, head of the Department of Research, and director of the Experiment Station at Tuskegee Institute, Alabama, for distinguished research in agricultural chemistry, September 4.
First Catholic seminary for education of black priests dedicated in Bay St. Louis, Mississippi, September 16.
United States Department of Labor states that almost 500,000 blacks left the South during the previous twelve months, October 24.
Garvey arrested for mail fraud and sentenced to five years in prison. He charges that most of his troubles stem "from my opponents of the colored race . . . ." He serves three months before President Harding orders his release.
The Urban League, founded in 1910 to assist blacks who migrated to the cities, publishes the first issue of *Opportunity* magazine, a literary forum for artists and authors of the Harlem Renaissance, edited by Charles S. Johnson.
Jean Toomer's *Cane* published by Boni and Liveright.
Runnin' Wild, a musical revue by Blake and Sissle, opens on Broadway and introduces the 1920s to its most famous dance, the Charleston.
Claude McKay speaks at the Fourth Congress of the Third International in Moscow, June.
Bessie Smith makes her first recordings of "Downhearted Blues" and "Gulf Coast Blues," which catapult her to stardom.
King Oliver's Creole Jazz Band makes thirty-seven recordings with Louis Armstrong that usher in jazz's great classical period; and Duke Ellington arrives in New York City.
The *Chip Woman's Fortune* by the playwright Willis Richardson opens in May on Broadway, staged by the National Ethiopian Players. It is the first serious Broadway play by a black American.
Eugene O'Neill's *All God's Chillun Got Wings* performed by the Ethiopian Art Players at Fazi Theatre, Washington, D.C.
Paul Green's *In Abraham's Bosom* performed by Cleveland's black theatrical group, the Gilpin Players, at the Karamu Theater, Cleveland.
Henry O. Tanner awarded France's Legion of Honor.
Freeman H. M. Murray lectures at the Washington meeting of the American Negro Academy on "Black folk as they have been portrayed in representative American art, sculpture, and painting."
Waldo Frank's *Holiday* published by Boni and Liveright.
Philosophy and Opinions of Marcus Garvey (2 vols.) published by Universal Publishing.
Robert T. Kerlin's anthology *Negro Poets and Their Poems* published by Associated Publishers; reprinted, 1925.
William Pickens' *Burst Bonds* published by Jordan and More Press; revision of 1911 ed.
Dorothy Scarborough's *The Land of Cotton* published by Macmillan.
The Cotton Club opens, Fall.

Lafayette Players Stock Company ceases production after seven years of serious drama in Harlem.

Third Pan African Congress.

1924

The National Origins Act (or Immigration Restriction Act) is passed, excluding Asian immigration and limiting European immigration by nationality to 2 percent of each country's immigrant population in the United States as of 1890. Passage reflects the political influence of the Ku Klux Klan and the prevalence of Nativism.

Marcus Garvey's *Aims and Objects for a Solution of the Negro Problem Outlined* published by Universal Negro Improvement Association.

Civic Club Dinner, March 21, brings together black writers and white publishers.

The Emperor Jones opens in London with Paul Robeson in the title role of Brutus Jones.

Joshua Jones' *By Sanction of Law* published by Brimmer.

New York Representative Emanuel Cellar introduces legislation to provide for the formation of a blue-ribbon panel to study the racial question.

Paul Robeson stars in *All God's Chillun Got Wings*, May 15.

Jessie Fauset's first novel, and the first by a woman of the Harlem Renaissance, *There is Confusion*, published by Albert and Charles Boni.

Arnold and Clarence MacDonald Maloney's *Some Essentials of Race Leadership* published by Aldine House.

Opportunity magazine hosts dinner at the Civic Club in New York to honor Fauset's novel and to herald the new school of writing by younger blacks. The magazine sponsors the first annual literary contest to discover new black talent. *The Crisis* also announces literary prizes this year.

Louis Armstrong comes to New York to join the Fletcher Henderson Orchestra at the Roseland Ballroom.

Kelly Miller's *The Everlasting Stain* published by Associated Publishers.

Chocolate Dandies, a musical revue starring Josephine Baker, opens on Broadway.

Roland Hayes, a black singer, receives the Spingarn Medal for his great artistry through which he "so finely interpreted the beauty and charm of the Negro folk song" and won a place as soloist with the Boston Symphony Orchestra, July 1.

Roland Hayes gives a concert in Carnegie Hall with William Lawrence as accompanist.

Paul Whiteman gives first concert of classical jazz in New York.

Henry O. Tanner's religious paintings are exhibited at Grand Central Art Galleries in New York City.

W.E.B. Du Bois' *The Gift of Black Folk* published by Stratford.

Julia Peterkin's *Green Thursday* published by Knopf.

Newman Ivey White and Walter Clinton Jackson's *Anthology of Verse by American Negroes* published by Trinity College (Durham, N.C.).

Fletcher Henderson, first musician to make a name with a jazz band, opens at Roseland Ballroom on Broadway, October 3.

Walter White's *The Fire in the Flint* published by Knopf.

Countee Cullen wins first prize in the Witter Bynner Poetry Competition.

Immigration Act excludes immigrants of African descent from the United States.

Negro Art Institute (formerly American Negro Academy) founded.

1925

Eric Walrond publishes an essay "On Being Black" in *The New Republic*, bringing him a measure of attention from the literary world.

Black physicians admitted to practice in Harlem Hospital.

Sherwood Anderson's *Dark Laughter* published by Grosset and Dunlap.

Charles Drew of Washington, D.C., wins Amherst College Ashley Grid Trophy for being most valuable member of the 1924 squad, January 1.

Hallie Quinn Brown's *Our Women: Past, Present, and Future* published by Aldine House.

Adelbert H. Roberts elected to Illinois state legislature, the first black since reconstruction days, January 10.

Hallie Quinn Brown's *Tales My Father Taught Me* published by Homewood Cottage.

Garvey convicted of mail fraud and jailed in the Atlanta Penitentiary.

Du Bose Heyward's novel *Porgy* published by Doubleday.

Greenwood, Mississippi, ministers and prominent businessmen lead mob which lynches two blacks, March 14.

James Weldon and J. Rosamond Johnson's *Book of American Negro Spirituals* published by Viking Press.

Black playwright Garland Anderson's *Appearances* opens on Broadway.

Henry E. Krehbiel's *Afro-American Folksongs* published by Schirmer; reprint of 1914 ed.

Countee Cullen, New York University poet, awarded honorary Phi Beta Kappa key, March 28.

Haldane McFall's *The Wooings of Jezebel Pettyfer* published by Knopf; reprint of 1897 ed.

Marian Anderson wins the New York Philharmonic singing competition.

Howard Odum and Guy B. Johnson's *The Negro and His Songs* published by the Univ. of North Carolina Press.

Mob at Oscella, Louisiana, flogs and shoots a minister for "preaching equality," April 18.

Zora Neale Hurston becomes editor of *The Spokesman* and directs the journal toward literature based on black folklore.

Dorothy Scarborough's *On the Trail of Negro Folksongs* published by Harvard Univ. Press.

Brotherhood of Sleeping Car Porters founded, May 8, organized by A. Philip Randolph.

Countee Cullen's first book of poems, *Color*, published by Harper and Brothers.

Harry T. Burleigh honored by Temple Emmanuel Congregation of New York City at end of 25th year as soloist, May 16.

Survey Graphic publishes a special March issue devoted entirely to black arts and letters, "Harlem: Mecca of the New Negro," introducing the poetry, fiction, and social essays of the Harlem Renaissance to the magazine's white literary audience. Illustrated throughout with Winold Reiss's striking black-and-white pastels of black Americans.

James Weldon Johnson, former U.S. consul in Venezuela and Nicaragua, former editor, secretary of NAACP, and poet, receives the Spingarn Medal for distinguished achievements as author, diplomat and public servant, June 30.

The New Negro, Alain Locke's expanded book version of the *Survey Graphic* Harlem issue, published by Albert and Charles Boni.

Recent Portraits of Representative Negroes, an exhibition of Winold Reiss, held at the 135th Street branch of The New York Public Library.

Sargent Johnson, a leading Renaissance artist, exhibits his work at the San Francisco Art Association.

Archibald Motley, a leading Renaissance artist, wins the Francis Logan Medal from the Art Institute of Chicago for his painting *A Mulatress*.

Carter G. Woodson's *Negro Orators and Their Orations* published by Associated Press.

American Negro Labor Congress held in Chicago, October.

Louis Armstrong records first of "Hot Five and Hot Seven" recordings which influenced jazz, November 11.

1926

President Coolidge tells Congress the country must provide "for the amelioration of race prejudice and the extension to all elements of equal opportunity and equal protection under the laws, which are guaranteed by the Constitution."

Roland Hayes gives a recital at Symphony Hall, Boston.

Carl Van Vechten's novel of Harlem life, *Nigger Heaven*, published by Alfred A. Knopf.

Negro History Week founded by Carter G. Woodson and the Association for the Study of Negro Life and History, February.

The Weary Blues, Langston Hughes' first book of verse, published by Knopf.

Savoy Ballroom opens in Harlem, March.

Hallie Quinn Brown's *Homespun Heroines and Women of Distinction* published by Aldine House.

Langston Hughes, writing in *The Nation* magazine, urges black artists to write from their experience and to stop imitating white writers.

Wallace Thurman, Langston Hughes, Zora Neale Hurston, Aaron Douglas, and Richard Bruce Nugent launch *Fire!!*, a magazine of the literary and artistic rebels of the Harlem Renaissance, in November; illustrated by Aaron Douglas and Rich Bruce Nugent.

William Arms Fisher's *Seventy Negro Spirituals* published by Oliver Ditson.

Carter G. Woodson, historian and founder of the Association for the Study of Negro Life and History, receives the Spingarn Medal for ten years' devoted service in collecting and publishing the records of the Black in America, June 29.

W. C. Handy and Abbe Niles's *Blues: An Anthology* published by A. and C. Boni.

Krigwa Players founded by *The Crisis*, July.

James Weldon and J. Rosamond Johnson's *The Second Book of Spirituals* published by Viking Press.

Dr. William S. Scarborough, scholar and educator, dies, August 9.

Robert Emmett Kennedy's *Black Cameos* published by A. and C. Boni.

Blackbirds, starring Florence Mills, opens in New York to great acclaim.

Robert Emmett Kennedy's *Mellows: A Chronicle of Unknown Singers* published by A. and C. Boni.

The Shadows, a black American "Little Theatre," opens in Chicago.

John H. Nelson's *The Negro Character in American Literature* published by the Univ. of Kansas Press.

Paul Green's *In Abraham's Bosom* opens at the Provincetown (Massachusetts) Playhouse; wins a Pulitzer Prize.

Howard Odum and Guy B. Johnson's *Negro Workaday Songs* published by the Univ. of North Carolina Press.

The Harmon Foundation holds the first of its annual art exhibitions of painting and sculpture by black artists. First juried show is held at the 135th Street branch of The New York Public Library and is later shown in Chicago; Palmer Hayden wins the William E. Harmon First Award and Gold Medal in Fine Arts for his painting entitled *The Schooner*. The Second Award is given to Hale Woodruff.

Newell Niles Puckett *Folk Beliefs of the Southern Negro* published by the Univ. of North Carolina Press.

Aaron Douglas completes a series of interpretative illustrations for *The Emperor Jones*. Two of his illustrations published with a *Theater Arts Monthly* article, "The Negro and the American Stage."

Walter White's *Flight* published by Knopf.

Florence Mills dies, November 1.

Carnegie Corporation purchases Arthur Schomburg's collection of Afro-Americana for the New York Public Library for $10,000.

Eric Walrond's collection of short stories *Tropic Death*, his only book, published by Boni and
     Liveright.
Twenty-three blacks are reported lynched during the year.

1927

In assorted legislation and judicial verdicts, Colorado, Illinois, and New Jersey lessen segrega-
     tion in schools, but segregation statutes are firmed in Southern states.
In Chicago, the Urban League organizes a boycott of stores that do not hire blacks. In 1929
     boycotts are started in several other Midwest cities.
President Coolidge commutes Garvey's sentence and deports him from the United States to
     the British West Indies as an undesirable alien.
Bill "Bojangles" Robinson and Ethel Waters star on Broadway in *Blackbirds*.
In Pennsylvania and West Virginia, nonunion black labor brought from the South to the coal
     fields, weakening the position of the United Mine Workers. Racial strife ensues as hysteri-
     cal rumors of rape and miscegenation spread through white mining communities.
United States Supreme Court strikes down Texas law barring blacks from voting "white
     primary," March 7. Texas then enacts a law allowing local committees to determine
     voter qualifications.
In Abraham's Bosom by Paul Green, with an all-black cast, wins the Pulitzer Prize, May.
Porgy by Dorothy and Du Bose Heyward opens at the Theatre Guild on Broadway.
Anthony Overton, businessman, receives the Spingarn Medal his successful business career
     climaxed by the admission of his company as the first black organization permitted to
     do insurance business under the requirements of the State of New York, June 28.
Duke Ellington brings his band to the Cotton Club.
Ethel Waters first appears on Broadway, July.
Plays of Negro Life, edited by Alain Locke and Montgomery Gregory and illustrated by
     Aaron Douglas, published by Harper and Brothers.
The Blondiau Theatre Arts Collection of African Art exhibited at the New York Circle in
     New York.
Paul Robeson and Lawrence Brown give a benefit recital for the Harlem Museum of African
     Art at the Town Hall in New York.
An exhibition of black artist W. E. Braxton's paintings, pastels, and drawings held at the
     opening of the Department of Negro Literature and History in the 135th Street branch
     of The New York Public Library.
Henry O. Tanner receives the National Bronze Medal at an exhibition held at the National
     Arts Club galleries in New York City.
James Weldon Johnson's book of poetry *God's Trombones: Seven Negro Sermons in Verse*
     published by Viking, with illustrations by Aaron Douglas. Douglas executes his first
     mural, *Fire!*, for Club Ebony at 129th Street and Lenox Avenue in Harlem.
The Negro in Art Week, an exhibition of African sculpture, modern paintings and sculpture,
     and books, drawings, and applied art, along with "A Night of Music," sponsored by the
     Chicago Woman's Club and the Art Institute of Chicago.
Miguel Covarrubias' *Negro Drawings* published by Knopf.
Countee Cullen's *Ballad of the Brown Girl, Copper Sun*, and *Caroling Dusk* published by
     Harper and Brothers. The third book, an anthology of poetry by black Americans,
     includes illustrations by Aaron Douglas.
Robert Nathaniel Dett's *Religious Folksongs of the Negro* published by Hampton Institute.
Arthur Huff Fauset's *For Freedom: A Biographical Story of the American Negro* published
     by Franklin Publishing and Supply.
Thomas Jefferson Flanagan's *The Road to Mount Keithan* published by Independent Publishers.
Four Negro Poets published by Simon and Schuster.

Langston Hughes' *Fine Clothes to the Jew* published by Knopf.

Charles S. Johnson's *Ebony and Topaz: A Collection* published by Opportunity.

James Weldon Johnson's *The Autobiography of an Ex-Coloured Man* (1912) reprinted by Knopf.

Robert Emmett Kennedy's *Gritny People* published by Dodd, Mead.

Alain Locke and Montgomery T. Gregory's anthology *Plays of Negro Life* published by Harper and Brothers.

Mary White Ovington's *Portraits in Color* published by Viking.

Julia Peterkin's *Black April* published by Bobbs-Merrill.

John Charles Wesley's *Negro Labor in the United States* published by Vanguard.

Walter White awarded a Guggenheim Foundation grant.

Louis Armstrong in Chicago and Duke Ellington in New York begin their careers with bands of renown.

Opportunity suspends literary contests because of weak material.

Floyd Calvin's News Service founded.

Harlem Globetrotters basketball team established.

Harlem Businessmen's Club founded.

Chicago Urban League boycotts white stores for discrimination.

Fifth Pan African Congress, in New York, fails.

1928

Claude McKay's first novel, *Home to Harlem*, published by Harper and Brothers; jacket is illustrated by Aaron Douglas.

W.E.B. Du Bois' *The Dark Princess* published by Harcourt Brace.

Countee Cullen marries Nina Yolande Du Bois, daughter of W.E.B. Du Bois, April 9.

Rudolph Fisher's first novel, *The Walls of Jericho*, published by Knopf.

Nella Larsen's novel *Quicksand* published by Knopf.

Julia Peterkin's *Scarlet Sister Mary* published by Bobbs-Merrill.

Walter Adolphe Roberts' *Pan and Peacocks* published by Four Seas.

Wallace Thurman's *Negro Life in New York's Harlem* published by Haldemann-Julius.

Newman Ivey White's *Negro American Folksongs* published by Harvard Univ. Press.

Carter G. Woodson's *Negro Makers of History* published by Associated Publishers.

Charles W. Chestnutt receives the Spingarn Medal for his "pioneer work as a literary artist depicting the life and struggle of Americans of Negro descent, and for his long and useful career as scholar, worker and freeman in one of America's greatest cities," July 3.

T. J. Woofter's *Negro Problems in the Cities* published by Doubleday Doran.

Monroe Nathan Work's *Bibliography of the Negro in Africa and America* published by Wilson.

The Dark Tower in A'Lelia Walker's townhouse opens.

The *Saturday Evening Quill* appears in Boston, published by a group of black American writers who constitute the Quill Club, founded in 1925.

The Harlem Experimental Theatre opens with a run of *Goat Alley*.

The Exhibition of Fine Arts Productions of American Negro Artists held under the auspices of The Harmon Foundation at International House in New York. May Howard Jackson wins the Second Award for her sculpture.

Archibald Motley has a one-man exhibition at the Ainslee Galleries in New York.

Oscar DePriest, the first black from a non-Southern state to be elected to Congress, November 6.

The Exhibition of African Sculpture and Handicraft from the Traveling Collection of Harlem Museum of African Art of New York City held at Howard University, Washington, D.C.

Palmer Hayden has a one-man exhibition of his works at the Bernheim-Jeune Gallery in Paris.

Winold Reiss's portraits of black Americans on St. Helena Island, South Carolina, published in *Survey Graphic*.

In November, Wallace Thurman founds *Harlem: A Forum of Negro Life*, a literary magazine to succeed *Fire!!* It includes illustrations by Aaron Douglas and Richard Bruce Nugent. White vogue for Harlem slumming at its height.

1929

Martin Luther King, Jr., born, January 15.

Alain Locke begins publishing annual reviews of black literature in *Opportunity* magazine, along with announcements of art exhibitions and book illustrations.

Negro Experimental Theatre founded, February.

Brotherhood of Sleeping Car Porters receives charter from AFL, February 23.

Wallace Thurman's first novel, *The Blacker the Berry*, published by Macaulay. Thurman's play *Harlem* opens on Broadway and draws negative criticism from black American commentators.

Claude McKay's second novel, *Banjo*, published by Harper and Brothers; jacket illustrated by Aaron Douglas. It receives poor reviews but sells well.

The Black Christ by Countee Cullen published by Harper and Brothers, but receives poor reviews.

Oscar DePriest tells an audience of 2500 gathered at a rally at Harlem's Abyssinian Baptist Church that blacks will never make substantial progress until they elect political leaders whose fortunes are dependent on their ability to fight for black interests.

Benjamin Brawley's *The Negro in Literature and Art in the United States* published by Dodd, Mead.

V. F. Calverton's *Anthology of American Negro Literature* published by Modern Library.

Jessie Fauset's novel *Plum Bun* published by Stokes.

Taylor Gordon's *Born to Be* published by Covici-Friede.

J. H. Harmon's *The Negro as a Businessman* published by Associated Press.

Robert Emmett Kennedy's *Red Bean Row* published by Dodd, Mead.

Nella Larsen's novel *Passing* published by Knopf.

Paul Morand's *Black Magic* and *New York* published by Viking Press.

Robert Russa Moton's *What the Negro Thinks* (1920) reprinted by Doubleday Doran.

Walter White's *Rope and Faggot: The Biography of Judge Lynch* published by Knopf.

Connie's Hot Chocolates opens *Ain't Misbehavin'* on Broadway, with music by Fats Waller and with Louis Armstrong in the orchestra.

Richmond Barthe, a leading Harlem Renaissance sculptor, executes an oil portrait of Harold Jackman. Barthe wins a Rosenwald grant and continues his studies of sculpture in New York.

Negro Art Theatre founded, June.

Mordecai Wyatt Johnson, president of Howard University, receives the Spingarn Medal "for his successful administration as first black president of the leading black university in America," July 2.

W. T. Francis, appointed American consul to Liberia by President Coolidge, dies in Africa, July 15.

National Colored Players founded, September.

Aaron Douglas commissioned to paint decorations and mural designs for Fisk University's Erasto Milo Cravath Library in Nashville, Tennessee.

The Harmon Foundation sponsors the exhibition *Paintings and Sculpture by American Negro Artists*, held at the National Gallery in Washington, D.C. Archibald Motley wins the painting award for *The Octoroon*.

The stock market crash on October 24, Black Thursday, brings to an end the Jazz Age and marks the beginning of the Great Depression.

Francis E. Rivers, the first black lawyer admitted to the New York Bar Association.

There are ten known lynchings in the United States during the year; Florida leads with four.

1930

The Green Pastures, with an all-black cast, opens on Broadway, February 26, featuring Richard B. Harrison as "De Lawd."

Randolph Edmonds' *Shades and Shadows* published by Meador.

An NAACP campaign helps prevent confirmation of U.S. Supreme Court nominee John H. Parker, one-time self-admitted opponent of the franchise for blacks. The NAACP also helps unseat three of the senators who voted for him in later elections.

Four Lincoln Poets published by Lincoln University.

Charles S. Johnson's *The Negro in American Civilization: A Study of Negro Life and Race Relations* published by Holt.

James Weldon Johnson's *Black Manhattan* published by Knopf.

Henry A. Hunt, principal for Fort Valley High and Industrial School, receives the Spingarn Medal "for twenty-five years of modest, faithful, unselfish and devoted service in the education of colored people of rural Georgia and the teaching profession in that state," May 3.

Jack Thompson becomes welterweight champion of the world when he defeats Jackie Fields, May 9.

Louise Venable Kennedy's *The Negro Peasant Turns Cityward* published by Columbia Univ. Press.

The New York *Times* announces that the "n" in "Negro" will hereafter be capitalized, June 7.

Mrs. Mary McLeod Bethune selected as one of the fifty leading women of America compiled by contemporary social historian Ida Tarbell, June 22.

Gilmore Millen's *Sweet Man* published by Viking Press.

Joel E. Spingarn elected President of NAACP.

Carl Whitke's *Tambourine and Bones* published by Duke Univ. Press.

Charles Gilpin, noted actor, dies.

Colored Merchant's Association founded.

Universal Holy Temple of Tranquility founded.

Temple of Islam, later to become the "Black Muslims," founded by Fard Mohammed in Detroit.

1931

Richard B. Harrison receives the Spingarn Medal for his "fine and reverent characterization of the Lord" in Marc Connelly's play, *The Green Pastures,* March 22.

Scottsboro trial, in Alabama, runs from April through July, resulting in a battle between the NAACP and the International Labor Defense, a Communist-controlled group, for the right to represent the young defendants who are charged with rape.

Arna Bontemps' *God Sends Sunday* published by Harcourt Brace.

Benjamin Brawley's *A Short History of the American Negro* published by Macmillan.

E. R. Embree's *Brown American* published by Viking Press.

Jessie Fauset's *The Chinaberry Tree* published by Stokes.

Langston Hughes' *Dear Lovely Death* published by Troutbeck, *The Negro Mother* and *Scottsboro Limited* by Golden Stair Press, and *Not Without Laughter* by Knopf.

Robert Emmett Kennedy's *More Mellows* published by Dodd, Mead.

Vernon Loggins' *The Negro Author: His Development in America to 1900* published by
     Columbia Univ. Press.
George S. Schuyler's novel *Black No More* published by Macaulay.
Sterling Denhard Spero and Abram L. Harris's *The Black Work* published by Columbia Univ.
     Press.
Jean Toomer's *Essentials* published by Lakeside Press.
Dr. Daniel Hale Williams, founder of Chicago's Provident Hospital, dies, August 4.
A'Lelia Walker dies, August 16.
Houseowner's League founded.

1932

The Spingarn Medal goes to Robert Russa Moton, principal of Tuskegee Institute, "for his
     thoughtful leadership of conservative opinion and action on the Negro in the United
     States, as shown in the U.S. Veterans' Hospital controversy at Tuskegee; by his stand on
     education in Haiti; by his support of equal opportunity for the Negro in the American
     public school system; and by his expression of the best ideals of the Negro in his book,
     What the Negro Thinks," May 20.
Twenty young black intellectuals embark for Russia to make a movie, *Black and White,* June.
Arna Bontemps and Langston Hughes' *Popo and Fifina* published by Macmillan.
Sterling Brown's *Southern Road* published by Harcourt Brace.
Countee Cullen's novel *One Way to Heaven* published by Harper and Brothers.
Rudolph Fisher's *The Conjure Man Dies* published by Covici-Friede.
E. Franklin Frazier's *The Negro Family in Chicago* published by the Univ. of Chicago Press;
     revised 1934.
Langston Hughes' *The Dream Keeper* published by Knopf.
Welbourne Kelly's *Inchin' Along* published by Morrow.
Claude McKay's *Gingertown* published by Harper and Brothers.
Scott Nearing's *Freeborn: An Unpublishable Novel* published by Urquart Press.
Julia Peterkin's *Bright Skin* published by Bobbs-Merrill.
George S. Schuyler's *Slaves Today* published by Harcourt Brace.
Wallace Thurman's *Infants of the Spring* published by Macaulay. *The Interne* by Thurman
     and Abraham L. Furman also published by Macaulay.
James Ford runs for national office as vice-presidential candidate for the Communist party,
     November.
Mass defection from the Republican party begins.
Franklin Roosevelt elected President, but with little support from blacks who observe omis-
     sion of their objectives from the Democratic Platform.
Alhambra Theatre closed.
Lincoln Theatre closes to reopen as Mount Moriah Baptist Church.

1933

Jessie Fauset's *Comedy, American Style* published by Stokes.
NAACP makes its first attack on segregation and discrimination in education and files suit
     against the University of North Carolina on behalf of Thomas Hocutt; case lost on a
     technicality, March 15.
Fannie Hurst's *Imitation of Life* published by Collier.
The Spingarn Medal goes to Max Yergan, Y.M.C.A. secretary among the native students of
     South Africa for ten years, for being "a missionary of intelligence, tact and self-

sacrifice, representing the gift of cooperation and culture which American Negroes may send back to their Motherland . . . ," July 1.

James Weldon Johnson's *Along This Way* published by Viking Press.

More than one-fourth of urban blacks are on relief. New Deal programs aid housing and education of blacks, but traditional segregation policies are generally followed. One exception is the Civilian Conservation Corps camps in New England and the Pacific states, which are integrated.

Claude McKay's *Banana Bottom* published by Harper and Brothers.

Julia Peterkin and Doris Ullman's *Roll, Jordan, Roll* published by Ballou.

National Negro Business League ceases operations after 33 years.

1934

Arna Bontemps' *You Can't Pet a Possum* published by Morrow.

In Northern and border states, 52% of blacks, compared with about 12% of whites, are on relief.

Nancy Cunard's *Negro* published by Wisart.

The American Federation of Labor's organization committee rejects a resolution introduced by A. Philip Randolph to end discrimination, stating that no discrimination exists in the labor organization.

Randolph Edmonds' *Six Plays for the Negro Theater* published by Baker.

Mississippi Senate passes a law permitting a private citizen, one C. W. Collins, to spring the trap to hang three blacks accused of raping Collins' daughter, March 10.

Langston Hughes' *The Ways of White Folks* published by Knopf.

Zora Neale Hurston's *Jonah's Gourd Vine* published by Lippincott.

William Taylor Buwell Williams, dean of Tuskegee Institute, wins the Spingarn Medal "for his long service as field agent of the Slater and Jeanes Funds and the General Education Board, his comprehensive knowledge of the field of Negro education and educational equipment, and his sincere efforts for their betterment," June 29.

Charles S. Johnson's *The Shadow of the Plantation* published by Univ. of Chicago Press.

The Black Muslim Headquarters established in Chicago. Elijah Muhammed is the leader.

James Weldon Johnson's *Negro Americans: What Now?* published by Viking Press.

Arthur Mitchell defeats Oscar de Priest for the Illinois Congressional seat held by the latter, November 7, thereby becoming the first black Democrat to be elected to Congress in the twentieth century.

George Lee's *Beale Street Where the Blues Began* published by Ballou.

Anti-lynch bill fails, as Roosevelt does not support it.

American troops are withdrawn from Haiti.

Rudolph Fisher and Wallace Thurman die within four days of each other, December 22 and 26.

W.E.B. Du Bois resigns from *The Crisis* and NAACP.

Lafayette Theatre closes.

Bishop W. Sampson Brooks, founder of Monrovia College in Liberia, dies in San Antonio, Texas.

Apollo Theatre opens.

Harlem Economic Association founded.

1935

Richard B. Harrison dies in New York City, March 18.

Harlem Race Riot, March 19.

Countee Cullen's *The Medea and Other Poems* published by Harper and Brothers.

Zora Neale Hurston's *Mules and Men* published by Lippincott.
Joe Louis defeats Primo Carnera at Yankee Stadium, June 25.
Mrs. Mary McLeod Bethune, founder and president of Bethune Cookman College, Daytona
    Beach, Florida, receives the Spingarn Medal, June 28: "In the face of almost insuperable
    difficulties she has, almost single-handedly, established and built up Bethune-Cookman
    College . . . ."
James Weldon Johnson's *St. Peter Relates an Incident* published by Viking Press.
Willis Richardson and May Miller Sullivan's *Negro History in Thirteen Plays* published by
    Associated Publishers.
Porgy and Bess, with an all-black cast, opens on Broadway, October 10.
Mulatto by Langston Hughes, the first full-length play by a black writer, opens on Broadway,
    October 25.
Maryland Court of Appeals orders University of Maryland to admit Donald Mung, Novem-
    ber 5.
National Council of Negro Women founded in New York City with Mrs. Mary McLeod
    Bethune as president, December 5.
U.S. Supreme Court Justice Roberts upholds the Texas law that prevents blacks from voting
    in the Texas Democratic primary. The decision is a setback to the NAACP, which has
    waged several effective legal battles to equalize the ballot potential of the black voter.
The NAACP bitterly criticizes Roosevelt for failure to present or support civil right legisla-
    tion.
Percy Julian, a black chemist, develops physostigmine, a drug for treatment of glaucoma.
50 percent of Harlem's families unemployed.

1936

John Hope, president of Atlanta University, receives the Spingarn Medal, July 3: "a distin-
    guished leader of his race, one of the foremost college presidents in the United States,
    widely and favorably known throughout the educational world."
Jesse Owens wins four gold medals at the Berlin Olympics, but is snubbed by the Chancellor
    of Germany, Adolph Hitler, August 9.
Roosevelt gains increasing support from blacks who feel he would like to achieve more for
    them than Congress allows and wins an overwhelming reelection victory.
NAACP files first suits in campaign to equalize teachers' salaries and educational facilities,
    December 8.
The U.S. Supreme Court requires Maryland University to admit a black student, Donald
    Murray, to its graduate law school.

1937

Claude McKay's autobiography *A Long Way From Home* published by Lee and Furman.
Blacks continue to benefit from New Deal programs, but not to the same degree as whites. In
    the South, black tenants leave farms as government policies encourage the use of wage
    labor.
U.S. Supreme Court rules picketing a legal means for blacks to seek redress of grievances.
William H. Hastie confirmed as judge of the Federal District Court in the Virgin Islands,
    thereby becoming the first black federal judge, March 26.
In Pennsylvania, a new law denies many state services to unions discriminating against blacks.
Joe Louis defeats James J. Braddock in Chicago for the heavyweight boxing championship of
    the world, June 22.

Richard Wright becomes editor of *Challenge Magazine,* changes the title to *New Challenge,* and urges blacks to write with greater "social realism."

Walter White, executive secretary of the NAACP, receives the Spingarn Medal for his personal investigation of 41 lynchings and 8 race riots and for his "remarkable tact, skill and persuasiveness" in lobbying for a federal anti-lynching bill, July 2.

In Spain, between 60 to 80 of the 3200 Americans who fight for the Republican side in the Civil War are black. Oliver Law, a black from Chicago, commands the Lincoln Battalion.

Bishop Isaac Lane, a bishop of the Colored Methodist Episcopal Church and founder of Lane College, dies, July 2, at the age of 103.

Bessie Smith dies, September 26.

1938

James Weldon Johnson dies, June 24.

Adam Clayton Powell, Jr., and other black leaders convince white merchants in Harlem to hire at least one third blacks and to promise equal promotion opportunities.

Billie Holiday appears with Artie Shaw's band. Boogie Woogie popularized at a Carnegie Hall concern given by three blacks.

Boxer Henry Armstrong defeats Barney Ross for the welterweight championship and Lou Ambers for the lightweight championship. Armstrong is also featherweight champion and thus holds three championships concurrently.

First woman black legislator, Crystal Bird Fauset of Philadelphia, elected to the Pennsylvania House of Representatives, November 8.

United States Supreme Court rules that states must provide equal educational facilities within its boundaries, December 12.

No Spingarn Medal awarded this year.

1939

Broadway opening of *Mamba's Daughter* gives Ethel Waters her greatest stage triumph, January 14.

D. E. Howard receives a patent for his invention of "an optical apparatus for indicating the position of a tool," January 24.

The University of Wisconsin refuses a gift whose donor limits use of funds to white students only, February 18.

Mrs. Franklin D. Roosevelt resigns from the Daughters of the American Revolution when Marian Anderson is barred from singing in Constitution Hall in Washington, D.C., in March. Anderson gives her Easter Sunday open air recital before 75,000 people assembled at the Lincoln Memorial.

NAACP launches drive to obtain one million signatures on anti-lynching petition, April 22.

Mississippi Senator Theodore C. Bilbo introduces "Back to Africa Bill" in the United States Senate, April 23.

Joe Louis knocks out Tony Galento in the 4th round, June 28.

The Spingarn Medal given to Marian Anderson, contralto, July 2.

J. Matilda Bolin appointed the first black woman judge in the United States; she is made judge of the Court of Domestic Relations in New York City by Mayor Fiorello La Guardia, July 22.

NAACP Legal Defense and Educational Fund organized as a separate organization, October 11.

Intimidation and cross-burning by the Ku Klux Klan in the black ghetto of Miami fail to discourage over 1,000 of the city's registered blacks from appearing at the polls. The Klan parades with effigies of blacks, who will alledgedly be slain for daring to vote.

1940

The census places black life expectancy at 50 years, and white at 62.

Nearly one-fourth of blacks live in the North and West.

The U.S. Supreme Court rules that black teachers cannot be denied wage parity with white teachers.

Richard Wright's *Native Son* published in February and becomes one of the best-sellers of the year.

Virginia legislature chooses "Carry Me Back to Ole Virginia" by black composer James A. Bland as the state song in April.

Marcus Garvey dies in London, June 10.

Louis T. Wright, surgeon, receives the Spingarn Medal "for his contributions to the healing of mankind and for his courageous, uncompromising position held often in the face of bitter attack," July 19.

Benjamin Oliver Davis, Sr., is appointed Brigadier General, the first black general in the history of the American armed forces, October 16. Responding to NAACP pressure, Franklin Delano Roosevelt announces that black strength in the Armed Forces will be proportionate to black population totals.

Langston Hughes' *The Big Sea* published by Knopf.

In a mass meeting, West Indians in New York oppose the transfer of West Indian islands to the United States.

Claude McKay's *Harlem: Negro Metropolis* published by Dutton.

Eighty thousand blacks vote in eight Southern States.

Part One:
Theory and Questions

W.E.B. DU BOIS AND THE THEORY
OF A BLACK AESTHETIC

DARWIN T. TURNER

During the past twenty years many black artists and critics began to insist that work by Afro-Americans must be created and evaluated according to a Black Aesthetic. That is, the work must be appropriate to Afro-American culture and people, and its excellence must be defined according to black people's concepts of beauty. In *The Crisis of the Negro Intellectual* (1967), Harold Cruse pointed to the need for a Black Aesthetic when he castigated Negro critics for failing to establish an appropriate perspective of the relationship of Negro art to Negro culture. Cruse accused critics of rejecting their own folk culture in order to adopt models and ideas devised and approved by whites. Thus, Cruse charged, most Negro critics ignored what should have been their major responsibility: to encourage and to determine standards for original ideas, methods, materials and styles derived from the unique character of black American culture. In even sharper tones, such critics as Imamu Amiri Baraka, Larry Neal, Don L. Lee, Hoyt Fuller, and Addison Gayle, Jr.—to name only a few of the most prominent—insist that black artists must seek subjects, themes and styles within the culture of black folk, that they must use these materials for the benefit of black Americans, and that the resulting art must be evaluated according to criteria determined by black people.

Of course it is not new for a nation, race, or ethnic group to devise an individual aesthetic. To the contrary, a cursory view of the history of European, English, and American literature reveals such a kaleidoscope that one wonders how anyone could argue that only one aesthetic can exist or could deny that any group has a right to define its own aesthetic. An aesthetic, after all, is merely a judgment of what is beautiful according to the tastes of the judge. After determining what kinds of drama were preferred by cultivated Greeks, Aristotle propounded a standard for drama. If William Shakespeare had followed that aesthetic, he might have written excellent imitations of Greek drama, but he would not have created the melodramatic shatterings of unity that dismayed Augustan critics and delighted the Romantics. Dante and Chaucer taught readers to respect the beauty of their native languages. With scant regard for the beliefs of the subjects in question, Rudyard Kipling and James Fenimore Cooper prescribed criteria for determining the beauty in the character of a "good" native. Many people have found beauty in the political theories of Machiavelli or of John Locke, but few would argue that both theories derive from the same aesthetic. When Emerson, Melville and Whitman pronounced the need for an American literature, they were arguing for an American aesthetic for literature. Equally diversified standards of beauty could be revealed in a history of painting, music, philosophy, or any of the humanistic pursuits. The fact is, any group of people which feels its identity as a group shapes and defines its own aesthetic, which it is free to change in a subsequent generation or century.

It should not be surprising, therefore, that black Americans should insist upon a need of a Black Aesthetic; for, if their African ancestry has not always bound them together, they have nevertheless found identity as a group in their exclusion from certain prerogatives of American citizenship. What is surprising then is not the concept of a Black Aesthetic in literature but that, even before the Harlem "Renaissance," it was articulated distinctly by W.E.B. Du Bois, who has been identified disparagingly with the conservative literary practices of The Genteel Tradition and with the efforts of Negroes to become assimilated by separating themselves from the folk culture. Nevertheless, before the New Negro movement had been labeled, years before Langston Hughes insisted upon the right of new artists to express their individual dark-skinned selves without caring whether they pleased white or black audiences, W.E.B. Du Bois proposed a Black Aesthetic or—as I prefer to designate it in relation to Du Bois—a theory of art from the perspective of black Americans.

Du Bois did not clearly define or delimit his theory. Despite his sustained interest in art, Du Bois was a social scientist and a political leader who considered art—especially literature—to be a vehicle for enunciating and effecting social, political, and economic ideas. Therefore, he sketched literary theory rather than constructing it with the total concentration characteristic of one whose major concern is the art itself. Moreover, like other theorists, Du Bois sometimes experienced difficulty with the practical applications of his theories. For instance, although he first urged black writers to present life exactly as they saw it, he later feared that the writers were over-emphasizing lurid aspects. Consequently, to correct what he considered an imbalance, he began to urge more conservative pictures of Negro life. One must admit also that Du Bois, unlike Wordsworth or T. S. Eliot, never created in his fiction, drama, and poetry the great work which would both illustrate and justify his literary theory.

Despite whatever weaknesses he may have revealed in definition or application, there is value in examining Du Bois's theory of black art—not only because it was of extreme importance to his efforts to create a strong and respected black population, but also because he was able to pronounce it from a prominent public platform during the Harlem "Renaissance," a significant moment in the development of literature by Afro-Americans. A more complete study should examine the relationships between Du Bois's theories and his own writing. And certainly a further study should analyze the relationships between his theories and the work of black writers of the Renaissance. This essay, however, is restricted to an examination of Du Bois's theory of black art as he shaped it and applied it as editor of *The Crisis* through the height of the Renaissance to the mid-Depression moment at which his insistence on the importance of independent black institutions became one of the wedges to separate him from the National Association for the Advancement of Colored People.

In 1921, the dawning of a literary Renaissance might have been viewed in the historical research of Carter G. Woodson and the cultural history of Benjamin Brawley. Its rays may have been glimpsed in the popularity of the musical *Shuffle Along*, written by Miller, Lyles, Sissle and Blake, or in the interest in black people displayed by such white writers as Ridgely Torrence and Eugene O'Neill.

By 1921, however, W.E.B. Du Bois had been working for many years as editor of *The Crisis* to promote literary activity and to foster racial pride through literature. As early as 1912, he had solicited manuscripts from and had published work by such previously unknown writers as Georgia Johnson, Fenton Johnson, and Jessie Fauset. In an editorial in 1920, he had recited his pride in the accomplishments of *The Crisis* and the need for a "renaissance of American Negro literature":

> Since its founding, THE CRISIS has been eager to discover ability among Negroes, especially in literature and art. It remembers with no little pride its covers by Richard Brown, William Scott, William Farrow, and Laura Wheeler; and its cartoons by Lorenzo Harris and Albert Smith; it helped to discover the poetry of Roscoe Jamison, Georgia Johnson, Fenton Johnson, Lucian Watkins, and Otto Bohanan; and the prose of Jessie Fauset and Mary Effie Lee. Indeed, THE CRISIS has always preferred the strong matter of unknown names, to the platitudes of well-known writers; and by its Education and Children numbers, it has shown faith in the young.
>
> One colored writer, Claude McKay, asserts that we rejected one of his poems and then quoted it from Pearson's; and intimates that colored editors, in general, defer to white editors' opinions. This is, of course, arrogant nonsense. But it does call our attention to the need of encouraging Negro writers. We have today all too few, for the reason that there is small market for their ideas among whites, and their energies are being called to other and more lucrative ways of earning a living. Nevertheless, we have literary ability and the race needs it. A renaissance of American Negro literature is due; the material about us in the strange, heartrending race tangle is rich beyond dream and only we can tell the tale and sing the song from the heart.[1]

By 1921, Du Bois was inculcating pride in Afro-American children through his publication of *The Brownies' Book*, in which—writing as "The Crow"—he taught respect for the blackness of the crow.[2]

In a more characteristic manner, writing with the confidence which Alain Locke later identified with the "New Negro," Du Bois admonished Negroes to accept artistic presentations of the truth of Negro life. In "Criteria for Negro Art," he wrote:

> We are so used to seeing the truth distorted to our despite, that whenever we are portrayed on canvas, in story or on the stage, as simple humans with human frailties, we rebel. We want everything said about us to tell of the best and highest and noblest in us. We insist that our Art and Propaganda be one.
>
> This is wrong and the end is harmful. We have a right, in our effort to get just treatment, to insist that we produce something of the best in human character and that it is unfair to judge us by our criminals and prostitutes. This is justifiable propaganda.
>
> On the other hand we face the truth of Art. We have criminals and prostitutes, ignorant and debased elements, just as all folks have. When the artist paints us he has a right to paint us whole and not ignore everything which is not as perfect as we would wish it to be. The black Shakespeare must portray his black Iago as well as his white Othello.
>
> We shrink from this. We fear that evil in us will be called racial, while in others it is viewed as individual. We fear that our shortcomings are not merely human but foreshadowing and threatenings of disaster and failure. The more highly trained we become the less we can laugh at Negro comedy—we will have it all tragedy and the triumph of dark Right over pale Villainy.
>
> The results are not merely negative—they are positively bad. With a vast wealth of human material about us, our own writers and artists fear to paint the truth lest they criticize their own and be in turn criticized for it. They fail to see the Eternal Beauty that shines through all Truth, and try to portray a world of stilted artificial black folk such as never were on land or sea.
>
> Thus, the white artist, looking in on the colored world, if he be wise and discerning, may often see the beauty, tragedy and comedy more truly than we dare.[3]

Admitting that some white writers, such as Thomas Dixon, might see only exaggerated evil in Negroes, Du Bois nevertheless insisted that blacks would survive any honest treatment of Afro-American life:

> We stand today secure enough in our accomplishment and self-confidence to lend the whole stern human truth about ourselves to the transforming hand and seeing eye of the Artist, white and black, and Sheldon, Torrence and O'Neill are our great benefactors—forerunners of artists who will yet arise in Ethiopia of the Outstretched Arm.[4]

Within the next two years the Renaissance of the New Negro produced its first literary works: *Shuffle Along* (1921) was enthusiastically received by a Broadway audience; Claude McKay and Jean Toomer created *Harlem Shadows* (1922) and *Cane* (1923); Willis Richardson's *The Chip Woman's Fortune* (1923) became the first serious play by an Afro-American to be staged on Broadway. Even during these early triumphs, however, Du Bois worried about a barrier which might obstruct the creation of honest black art—the prejudice of American audiences, who expected blacks to be "*bizarre* and unusual and funny for whites."[5]

In the same essay, written for a predominantly white audience rather than the more mixed audience of *The Crisis*, Du Bois's exploration of the possibilities for Negroes in the contemporary theater led him to more optimistic conclusions. If they could escape from the prejudiced expectations of white audiences, they could create strong Negro drama by emphasizing their blackness.

As evidence, Du Bois cited The Ethiopian Art Theatre's successful performances of *Salome*, *The Chip Woman's Fortune*, and *The Comedy of Errors a la Jazz*. Published statements by the company explained that Director Raymond O'Neill restrained the black performers from attempting to imitate the more inhibited white actors. Instead, he encouraged them "to develop their peculiar racial characteristics—the freshness and vigor of their emotional responses, their spontaneity and intensity of mood, their freedom from intellectual and artistic obsession."

Du Bois was even more pleased by the Ethiopian Players' selection of black subjects. Unintentionally paraphrasing William Dean Howells' earliest praise of Paul Laurence Dunbar, Du Bois insisted that blacks could make a distinctive contribution to American drama by interpreting black subjects. He did not oppose black actors who wished to demonstrate their ability to perform "white" roles for white audiences. Nor did he deny the usefulness of expanding the cultural awareness of black audiences by staging "white" plays for them. Of greatest importance, however, was the opportunity for black actors and writers to examine "their own terrible history of experience."

Black writers, he admitted, would develop slowly. The race needed to gain "something of that leisure and detachment for artistic work which every artist must have." As evidence that serious black dramatists were emerging despite their lack of leisure, he called attention to his own *The Star of Ethiopia*, a pageant commemorating blackness.

Wise men believe, Du Bois concluded, "that the great gift of the Negro to the world is going to be a gift to Art." The Ethiopian Players were significantly promoting awareness of this talent by beginning to peel from drama critics "the scales that blinded them for years to the beauty of Negro folk songs, that make them still deaf to the song of Negro singers and but half-alive to the growing Negro drama and the ringing Negro actor."

Even in less laudatory reviews, Du Bois thrilled to Negro writers who truthfully and seriously probed into problems of Afro-American life. Although he complained that Jean Toomer weakened *Cane* by too little knowledge of Georgia, excessive striving for artistic effect, dearth of feeling, and "much that is difficult or even impossible to understand," Du Bois boasted,

> The world of black folk will some day arise and point to Jean Toomer as a writer who first dared to emancipate the colored world from the conventions of sex. It is quite impossible for most Americans to realize how straight-laced and conventional thought is within the Negro World, despite the very unconventional acts of the group. Yet this contradiction is true. And Jean Toomer is the first of our writers to hurl his pen across the very face of our sex conventionality. . . . [His women are] painted with a frankness that is going to make his black readers shrink and criticize; and yet they are done with a certain splendid, careless truth.[6]

In 1925, writing for a predominantly white audience, Du Bois became the first significant critic to probe issues which remain not fully resolved today, even though they are fundamental to the establishment of a Black Aesthetic: what is the difference between art by a Negro and Negro art? Or, what are the unique characteristics of Negro art?

Although he praised Henry O. Tanner, Charles W. Chesnutt, and William Stanley Braithwaite as artists, Du Bois denied that they had contributed significantly to American Negro art. American Negro art, he explained, was a group expression consisting of biographies written by slaves and by free blacks who had achieved

> . . . poetry portraying Negro life and aspirations, and activities, of essays on the "Negro Problem" and novels about the "Color Line" . . . pictures and sculptures meant to portray Negro features and characteristics, plays to dramatize the tremendous situation of the Negro in America, and, of course, . . . music[7]

American Negro art "was built on the sorrow and strain inherent in American slavery, on the difficulties that sprang from Emancipation, on the feelings of revenge, despair, aspirations, and hatred which arose as the Negro struggled and fought his way upward" (pp. 53–54).

Whenever a mass of millions having such common memories and experiences are granted intellectual freedom and economic wealth, Du Bois explained, they will establish a school of art which, whether using new methods of art, will inevitably bring new content—a truth which is different from anything else in the world: "If this truth . . . is beautifully expressed and transformed from sordid fact into art it becomes, from its very origin, new, unusual, splendid" (p. 54).

The uniqueness of Afro-American artistic expression had been revealed and discovered in "new music, new rhythm, new melody and poignant, even terrible, expressions of joy, sorrow, and despair." This new music, Du Bois argued, was earning respect. Next to win recognition would be Negro literature, which presented "new phrases, new uses of words, experiences unthought of and unknown to the average white person." Creating "a distinct norm and a new set of human problems" (p. 55), the new writers were impeded only by white readers' inability to understand the work and by black readers' stubborn demands for favorable propaganda. As the new artists matured, they would improve in thought and style. In the process of maturing, they would move from the wild music, laughter, and dancing of slavery into a more deliberate, purposeful, restrained, but true artistic expression.

The conclusion of Du Bois's magnificent effort to define Afro-American art betrays a weakness which gives a curious ambivalence to his criticism. He could identify the substance of that art but not the spirit. Whenever the spirit manifested itself in an exuberance which offended his temperament—his personal preference for decorum—Du Bois, wincing, felt compelled to excuse or denounce the work. Because he did not believe such wildness to be a characteristic inherent in the Afro-American psyche, he identified it, if genuine, as evidence of the manner in which slavery had distorted or repressed the psychological development of blacks. Just as often, he feared that the wildness was not a sincere expression of the artist but an effort to attract popularity from white critics by repeating the clichés about the character of black people. Unable to resolve this dilemma, which he failed to perceive as a dilemma, Du Bois at times seems a genteel anachronism as a critic during an era characterized by wildness of whites, as well as blacks. This was the gay Jazz Age of sheiks and flappers, raccoon coats and skirts that bared the knees, bootleg gin and speakeasies where one Charlestoned in shooting distance of well-known racketeers, "new" morality and trial marriages, free love and lurid front page headlines about the latest love-nest scandal. It was an era of youth, in which many whites, Freuding themselves from their Puritan inhibitions, enviously projected upon blacks the image of the primitive untroubled by the inhibitions of society. In such an era, it is not surprising that even a relatively sedate but young Countee Cullen atavistically boasted that his heart was "pagan-mad" and that the blood of blacks was hotter than that of whites. Not so for New-England-born, Harvard-trained W.E.B. Du Bois, who was fifty-seven-years old before Cullen published his first volume of poems. Quite simply, Du Bois knew that he was not pagan-mad; but he was Negro. Therefore, Negroes were not inherently pagan-mad. Therefore such wildness was not essential to, or desirable in, Negro life and art.

Instead one sought Beauty and Truth. In *The Crisis* of May 1925, Du Bois proclaimed a new editorial policy:

> We shall stress Beauty—all Beauty, but especially the beauty of Negro life and character; its music, its dancing, its drawing and painting and the new birth of its literature. This growth which *The Crisis* long since predicted is sprouting and coming to flower. We shall encourage it in every way . . . keeping the while a high standard of merit and never stooping to cheap flattery and misspent kindliness.

At the same time, Du Bois continued his demands that black readers accept realistic portraits:

> We are seriously crippling Negro art and literature by refusing to contemplate any but handsome heroes, unblemished heroines and flawless defenders; we insist on being always and everywhere all right and often we ruin our cause by claiming too much and admitting no faults.[8]

As early as 1926, however, Du Bois's statements reveal the ambivalent sentiments or the inherent contradictions which have deceived critics who unsuspectingly have fixed Du Bois at one or another of his positions. In a complimentary review of *The New Negro* (1925), Du Bois wrote:

> With one point alone do I differ. . . . Mr. Locke has newly been seized with the idea that Beauty rather than Propaganda should be the object of Negro literature and art. His book proves the falseness of this thesis. This is a book filled and bursting with propaganda, but it is a propaganda for the most part beautiful and painstakingly done. . . .
> . . . If Mr. Locke's thesis is insisted upon too much it is going to turn the Negro Renaissance into decadence. It is the fight for Life and Liberty that is giving birth to Negro literature and art today and when, turning from this fight or ignoring it, the young Negro tries to do pretty things or things that catch the passing fancy of the really unimportant critics and publishers about him he will find that he has killed the soul of Beauty in art.[9]

In the same issue of *The Crisis*, Du Bois, announcing the second annual Krigwa awards competition in literature and art, emphasized both his belief that Negro art must act as propaganda and his willingness to accept reflections of all avenues of Afro-American life:

> We want especially to stress the fact that while we believe in Negro art we do not believe in any art simply for art's sake. . . . We want Negro writers to produce beautiful things but we stress the things rather than the beauty. It is Life and Truth that are important and Beauty comes to make their importance visible and tolerable. . . .
> Write then about things as you know them. . . . In *The Crisis*, at least, you do not have to confine your writings to portrayal of beggars, scoundrels and prostitutes; you can write about ordinary decent colored people if you want. On the other hand do not fear the Truth. . . . If you want to paint Crime and Destitution and Evil paint it. . . . Use propaganda if you want. Discard it and laugh if you will. But be true, be sincere, be thorough, and do a beautiful job. (p. 115)

Undoubtedly, Du Bois remembered the dictum of John Keats that Beauty is Truth and Truth is Beauty. With whatever license is granted to a poet, however,

Keats ignored any responsibility for explaining his meaning. More lucidity is generally required of a literary critic.

If one extracts the essence of Du Bois's instruction to black readers, his rebuttal of Locke's doctrine, and his exhortation to prospective contestants, one recognizes a general pronouncement that literature by blacks must be unflinchingly true to Afro-American life even in its pictures of the ugly and the unheroic. It also must be didactic and beautiful. Even viewed superficially, the proposition seems difficult to use as a touchstone for any single work of art.

The critical process is further complicated by Du Bois's failure to clarify his abstractions. Although he occasionally perceived the need, he never successfully defined Beauty in relation to material, thought, or method—perhaps because he presumed his taste to be characteristic of all people. In "Criteria of Negro Art," a speech prepared for the 1926 Chicago Conference of the NAACP, Du Bois made his most detailed effort to resolve the question of the relation of beauty to Afro-American art; yet, in his initial premise, he reflected his assumption that his standards were the standards for all blacks—at least for all cultivated blacks. "Pushed aside as we have been in America," he wrote, "there has come to us not only a certain distaste for the tawdry and flamboyant but a vision of what the world could be if it were really a beautiful world." Du Bois continued:

> After all, who shall describe Beauty? What is it? I remember tonight four beautiful things: The Cathedral at Cologne, a forest in stone, set in light and changing shadow, echoing with sunlight and solemn song; a village of the Veys in West Africa, a little thing of mauve and purple, quiet, lying content and shining in the sun; a black and velvet room where on a throne rests, in old and yellowing marble, the broken curves of the Venus of Milo; a single phrase of music in the Southern South—utter melody, haunting and appealing, suddenly arising out of night and eternity, beneath the moon.[10]

Du Bois's rhetoric is persuasive. His emphasis is upon apparent catholicity of taste. Yet a question obtrudes. Does the beauty of the scene at Cologne depend upon the viewer's reaction to a particular style of architecture and a particular quality of song? Would Du Bois's sense of ultimate beauty in the scene have been marred if the music had not been "solemn song" but jazz?

Even if Du Bois had resolved questions about Beauty, he still would have failed to appreciate the complexity of Pilate's question. Du Bois perceived a difference between a black man's and a white man's awareness of the Truth of Negro life. But he failed to comprehend that black men themselves may differ in their visions of the Truth of Afro-American life. In consequence, whereas he rejected obviously idealized portraits as untrue, he often admitted bewilderment that young authors never wrote about the decent, hard-working Negroes in their own families. Moreover, although he graciously urged young writers to describe the sordid if they wished, he soon suspected them of rejecting authentic pictures of low black life in favor of derogatory stereotypes.

I do not intend to demean Du Bois by suggesting that his definitions, criteria, and perceptions are inferior to those of other artists and critics still esteemed by many literary scholars. To the contrary, compared with others of his century—or any century—he fares well. His concept of Beauty certainly is as valid and as meaningful as Edgar Allan Poe's definition of poetry. Du Bois's assumption that his visions of Beauty and Truth were universally accepted is no more arrogant than Matthew Arnold's presumption that, from his preferences in poetry, he had acquired touchstones with which to measure the excellence of the poetry of any country. Instead of wishing to demean Du Bois, I merely suggest that, because he based his critical judgment on abstractions which were concrete to him but not necessarily to all other black contemporaries, the application of his theory to particular works of black writers sometimes resulted in appraisals significantly different from those of younger black artists, who shared their own perceptions of Beauty and Truth.

Significantly, although his interest in Beauty and Truth suggests a concern for "universal" values—a concept too often used to minimize the work of a black writer on a theme of black life, Du Bois's discussions of Beauty and Truth in literature always led him to a position strikingly comparable in spirit, if not always in detail, to that adopted by many current exponents of Black Arts: literature must serve a function for the good of black people, and its worth must be judged by black people.

He concluded his discussion of Beauty in "Criteria of Negro Art":

> Thus it is the bounden duty of black America to begin this great work of the creation of Beauty, of the preservation of Beauty, of the realization of Beauty, and we must use in this work all the methods that men have used before. And what have been the tools of the artist in times gone by? First of all, he has used the Truth—not for the sake of truth, not as a scientist seeking truth, but as one upon whom Truth eternally thrusts itself as the highest handmaid of imagination, as the one great vehicle of universal understanding. Again artists have used Goodness—goodness in all its aspects of justice, honor and right—not for sake of an ethical sanction but as the one true method of gaining sympathy and human interest.
>
> The apostle of Beauty thus becomes the apostle of Truth and Right not by choice but by inner and outer compulsion. Free he is but his freedom is ever bounded by Truth and Justice; and slavery only dogs him when he is denied the right to tell the Truth or recognize an ideal of Justice.
>
> Thus all Art is propaganda and ever must be, despite the wailing of the purists. I stand in utter shamelessness and say that whatever art I have for writing has been used always for propaganda for gaining the right of black folk to love and enjoy. I do not care a damn for any art that is not used for propaganda.

And in rhetoric prophetic of a Black Aesthetic, he surged to a climax:

. . . the young and slowly growing black public still wants its prophets almost equally unfree. We are bound by all sorts of customs that have come down as second-hand soul clothes of white patrons. We are ashamed of sex and we lower our eyes when people will talk of it. Our religion holds us in superstition. Our worst side has been so shamelessly emphasized that we are denying we have or ever had a worst side. In all sorts of ways we are hemmed in and our new young artists have got to fight their way to freedom.

The ultimate judge has got to be you and you have got to build yourselves up into that wide judgment, that catholicity of temper which is going to enable the artist to have his widest chance for freedom. We can afford the Truth. White folk today cannot. As it is now we are handing everything over to a white jury. If a colored man wants to publish a book, he has got to get a white publisher and a white newspaper to say it is great; and then you and I say so. We must come to a place where the work of art when it appears is reviewed and acclaimed by our own free and unfettered judgment.[11]

Du Bois argued that young black writers were being diverted from their artistic responsibilities especially by the popularity of Carl Van Vechten's *Nigger Heaven*, which he denounced as "an affront to the hospitality of black folk (who admitted Van Vechten to their circles) and to the intelligence of white." In Du Bois's opinion the book was pernicious, not only because its commercial success persuaded blacks to pander to white stereotypes of their life but also because it destroyed both Beauty and Truth:

It is a caricature. It is worse than untruth because it is a mass of halftruths. . . . [To Van Vechten] the black cabaret is Harlem; around it all his characters gravitate. . . . Such a theory of Harlem is nonsense. The overwhelming majority of black folk there never go to cabarets. . . .

Something they have which is racial, something distinctly Negroid can be found; but it is expressed by subtle, almost delicate nuance, and not by the wildly, [sic] barbaric drunken orgy in whose details Van Vechten revels. . . .

Van Vechten is not the great artist who with remorseless scalpel probes the awful depths of life. To him there are no depths. It is the surface mud he slops in. . . . Life to him is just one damned orgy after another, with hate, hurt, gin and sadism.

Both Langston Hughes and Carl Van Vechten know Harlem cabarets; but it is Hughes who whispers,

> "One said he heard the jazz band sob
> When the little dawn was grey."

Van Vechten never heard a sob in a cabaret. All he hears is noise and brawling.[12]

Earlier Du Bois had lamented the limitations of DuBose Heyward's *Porgy* because, by excluding educated Afro-American Charlestonians, it implied that the waterfront world was a total picture of black life in that city. Nevertheless, Du Bois now insisted that Porgy himself had a human and interesting quality absent from Van Vechten's characters.

How does one determine that a writer has created characters who are human as well as interesting? Can any reader truly determine whether an author has delineated degraded characters with compassion or has exploited them?

Du Bois could not find answers to these questions. Perhaps his orientation to scientific research persuaded him that sincerity can be measured. Or perhaps, more concerned with other matters, he did not even consider the questions fully; the theory was clear to him at least. A black should write honestly about the Afro-Americans he knew. So created, a work would sparkle with Truth and Beauty. It would be useful black literature. If, however, the writer seemed excessively absorbed with cabaret life, Du Bois was prepared to impale him with the pen reserved for those who dished up black humanity piping hot to a slobbering white public.

Even if he did not fully examine questions needed to clarify his own criteria of art, Du Bois nevertheless quickly sensed a possible weakness in his efforts to propagandize for the race by encouraging young blacks to write about themselves. What if, for the sake of publication, they all began to imitate Van Vechten?

Earlier in 1926, Du Bois had initiated a symposium on "The Negro in Art." He asked various authors and publishers to consider several questions:

> Are writers under obligations or limitations as to the kinds of characters they portray? Should authors be criticized for painting the best or the worst characters of a group? Can publishers be criticized for failing to publish works about educated Negroes? What can Negroes do if they are continually painted at their worst? Should Negroes be portrayed sincerely and sympathetically? Isn't the literary emphasis upon sordid, foolish and criminal Negroes persuading readers that this is the truth and preventing authors from writing otherwise? Is there danger that young colored writers will follow the popular trend?[13]

The overlapping questions reveal Du Bois's basic concern: is the literary world conspiring to typify Negroes by sordid, foolish, and criminal characters? And if so, what can be done to prevent that?

Some of the responses by whites must have confirmed Du Bois's worst fears. Carl Van Vechten bluntly stated that the squalor and vice of Negro life *would* be overdone "for a very excellent reason." Such squalor and vice offer "a wealth of novel, exotic, picturesque material." He discounted pictures of wealthy, cultured Negroes as uninteresting because they were virtually identical with those of whites, a pronouncement which validates Du Bois's convictions about Van Vechten's superficiality. The only thing for the black writer to do, Van Vechten concluded, was to exploit the vice and squalor before the white authors did.[14]

Henry Mencken chided blacks for failing to see the humor in the derogatory caricatures created by Octavus Cohen. Instead of applying scientific criteria to art, he added, blacks should write works ridiculing whites.[15] Mencken did not explain who would publish the caricatures of whites.

Another white author, John Farrar, shrugged off the stories of Octavus Cohen with the admission that they amused him immensely and seemed not to libel Negroes. In contrast, although he confessed scant knowledge of the South, he thought Walter White's novel *The Fire in the Flint* "a trifle onesided."[16] William Lyons Phelps mildly admonished Negroes to correct false impressions by setting good examples in their lives.[17] Having no answers but more questions, Sinclair Lewis proposed a conference to consider the issues. He also suggested establishing a club for blacks—at a small hotel in Paris.[18]

Sherwood Anderson reminded *The Crisis* that he had lived among Negro laborers, whom he had found to be "about the sweetest people I know," as he had said sometimes in his books. In short, he wrote, Negroes were worrying too much and being too sensitive; they had no more reason to complain about their portraits in literature than whites would have.[19] Julia Peterkin asserted that Irish and Jewish people were not offended by caricatures, so Negroes should not be. She used the occasion to praise the "Black Negro Mammy" and to chastise Negroes for protesting against a proposal in Congress to erect a monument to the Mammy.[20]

Such responses probably did not surprise Du Bois, but they strengthened his conviction that black writers must fight for their race. Even the sympathetic white writers revealed flaws. For example, Paul Green's Pulitzer Prize winning play *In Abraham's Bosom* impressed Du Bois as an example of "the defeatist genre of Negro art which is so common. . . . The more honestly and sincerely a white artist looks at the situation of the Negro in America the less is he able to consider it in any way bearable and therefore his stories and plays must end in lynching, suicide or degeneracy."[21] Du Bois added that, even if such a writer learned differently by observing black people's refusal to accept failure, the publisher or producer would prohibit a portrayal of triumphant blacks. Pathetic, inevitable defeat or exotic degeneracy—these would be the dominant images of black life unless black writers corrected the images.

In April, 1927, while announcing the annual competition in literature and art, Du Bois reminded his readers of the impressive black heritage revealed in the fine arts of Ethiopia, Egypt, and the rest of Africa. In contemporary America, he insisted, that heritage must be continued in the art of spoken and written word. It must not be restrained by the white person's desire for silly and lewd entertainment; it must not be blocked by the black person's revulsion from unfavorable images. "The Negro artist must have freedom to wander where he will, portray what he will, interpret whatever he may see according to the great canons of beauty which the world through long experience has laid down."[22] Du Bois was beginning to sound like his future son-in-law Countee Cullen. He would now accept anything black writers wanted to do if only they did it beautifully, but he was no more specific about his concept of Beauty.

When James Weldon Johnson published *God's Trombones* (1927), Du Bois rejoiced at Johnson's preservation of the Negro idiom in art, Johnson's beautiful poetry, and Aaron Douglass's wild, beautiful, unconventional, daring drawings, which were stylized to emphasize Negroid rather than Caucasian features of the black figures.[23]

But works by whites continued to disappoint him even when they were sufficiently good to be recommended to readers. His praise of *Congaree Sketches* by E. C. L. Adams was dampened by what he felt to be a significant omission:

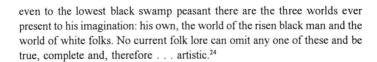

> even to the lowest black swamp peasant there are the three worlds ever present to his imagination: his own, the world of the risen black man and the world of white folks. No current folk lore can omit any one of these and be true, complete and, therefore . . . artistic.[24]

In the entire collection, Du Bois complained, he found not one allusion to the rising black man characterized by ambition, education, and aspiration to better earthly things.

In 1928, black writers provided Du Bois with examples which he used to illustrate his concept of the difference between praiseworthy black literature and atrocious black literature. He hailed Nella Larsen's *Quicksand* as a "fine, thoughtful and courageous novel," the best by any black writer since Chesnutt.[25] Subtly comprehending the curious cross currents swirling about black Americans, the author, he felt, created an interesting character, fitted her into a close plot, and rejected both an improbable happy ending and the defeatist theme: "Helga Crane sinks at last still master of her whimsical, unsatisfied soul. In the end she will be beaten down even to death but she never will utterly surrender to hypocrisy [sic] and convention."

In contrast, Du Bois stated that Claude McKay's *Home to Harlem* was a shameful novel, redeemed only by the fact that the author was "too great a poet to make any complete failure in writing." Du Bois noted virtues in the work: the beautiful, fascinating changes on themes of the beauty of colored skins; McKay's emphasis upon the fact that Negroes are physically and emotionally attracted to other Negroes rather than to whites; and the creation of Jake and Ray, interesting and appealing characters. Despite these commendably perceptive insights into black life, Du Bois argued, *Home to Harlem* pandered to white people's enjoyment of Negroes portrayed in

> that utter licentiousness which conventional civilization holds white folk back from enjoying—if enjoyment it can be called. That which a certain decadent section of the white American world, centered particularly in New York, longs for with fierce and unrestrained passions, it wants to see written out in black and white and saddled on black Harlem. . . . [McKay] has used every art and emphasis to paint drunkenness, fighting, lascivious sexual promiscuity and utter absence of restraint in as bold and as bright colors as he can. . . . Whole chapters . . . are inserted with no connection to the main plot, except that they are on the same dirty subject. As a picture of Harlem life or

of Negro life anywhere, it is, of course, nonsense. Untrue, not so much on account of its facts but on account of its emphasis and glaring colors.

Between the levels of *Quicksand* and *Home to Harlem*, Du Bois placed Rudolph Fisher's *The Walls of Jericho*. Fearful that casual readers would draw from it only echoes of Van Vechten and McKay, Du Bois stressed the psychological validity of the two working-class black people who are the focus of the major plot. The book's weaknesses were the excessive sophistication and unreality of the background and such minor characters as Jinx and Bubber, who speak authentically but do not seem as human as the major figures. But, Du Bois continued in bewilderment, Fisher "has not depicted Negroes like his mother, his sister, his wife, his real Harlem friends. He has not even depicted his own soul. The glimpses of better class Negroes are ineffective make-believes."[26] Why? Du Bois asked. Hearing no answer, he concluded with the hope that Fisher's novel was an indication of black novelists' movement upward from Van Vechten and McKay.

Despite his frequent attacks upon white authors' distortions of black life and black people, Du Bois did not contend that white Americans could never portray blacks successfully. Exceptions occurred: Paul Green wrote sincerely even though he belabored the defeatist theme; the E. C. L. Adams book *Nigger to Nigger* was a sincere attempt to collect and present the philosophy of black peasants. Nevertheless, such exceptions did not relieve his skepticism:

> I assume that the white stranger cannot write about black people. In nine cases out of ten I am right. In the tenth case, and DuBose Heywood [sic] is the tenth case, the stranger can write about the colored people whom he knows; but those very people whom he knows are sometimes so strange to me, that I cannot for the life of me make them authentic.[27]

In the waning moments of the Renaissance, Du Bois seemed increasingly reluctant to castigate an Afro-American writer except when that writer rejected his blackness. For example, although he had previously objected to Wallace Thurman for glib, superficial comments on black life and culture, Du Bois, when reviewing *The Blacker the Berry*, merely remonstrated with Thurman for not believing his thesis:

> The story of Emma Lou calls for genius to develop it. It needs deep psychological knowledge and pulsing sympathy. And above all, the author must believe in black folk, and in the beauty of black as a color of human skin. I may be wrong, but it does not seem to me that this is true of Wallace Thurman. He seems to me himself to deride blackness. . . .
>   It seems that this inner self-despising of the very thing he is defending makes the author's defense less complete and sincere.[28]

Du Bois's review of Marc Connelly's *Green Pastures* (1930) was a peroration of what he had tried to teach to readers, writers, and critics during the decade:

All art is propaganda, and without propaganda there is no true art. But, on the other hand, all propaganda is not art. . . . . If a person portrays ideal Negro life, the sole judgment of its success is whether the picture is a beautiful thing. . . . If he caricatures Negro life, and makes it sordid and despicable, the critic's criterion is . . . solely, is the idea well presented?
　　. . . . The difficulty with the Negro on the American stage, is that the white audience . . . demands caricatures, and the Negro, on the other hand, either cringes to the demand because he needs the pay, or bitterly condemns every Negro book or show that does not paint colored folk at their best. Their criticisms should be aimed at the incompleteness of art expression— at the embargo which white wealth lays on full Negro expression—and a full picturing of the Negro soul.[29]

In the early years of the 1930s, while America floundered in an economic depression, it was clear that night had fallen on the heyday of the Harlem Renaissance. If Afro-Americans—intelligentsia, artists, and workers alike—were not cast out, they were at least ignored by a huge republic trying to pull itself erect. As Du Bois re-examined the position of blacks in America during those troubled times, he re-evaluated his own ideas about the appropriate course for his people. For a decade, from a platform within an integrated and pro-integrationist NAACP, he had argued that black writers must do things for black people and must be judged by black people. Now he extended that concept of black independence and black control to the entire spectrum of black existence in America: black people must develop and control strong black institutions for the good of black people. Coming as it did from the pages of the voice of the NAACP, and from a man whom white supremacists had vilified as the chief advocate of integration, the idea probably was even more startling when Du Bois expressed it in the 1930s than when, a quarter of a century later, Stokely Carmichael re-introduced it tersely as "Black Power."

Although Du Bois seemed unable to convert those who immediately attacked his position, he tried repeatedly to explain the logic which guided him to a seemingly inescapable conclusion. Personally, he still believed the best society to be an integrated one—a fact which should be obvious to anyone who remembered that, for more than twenty-five years, he had dedicated himself to effecting the full integration of blacks into American society. Despite his private desires, however, he was compelled to admit a bitter truth:

　　. . . that we are segregated, apart, hammered into a separate unity by spiritual intolerance and legal sanction backed by mob law, . . . that this separation is growing in strength and fixation; that it is worse today than a half-century ago and that no character, address, culture, or desert is going to change it in one day or for centuries to come.[30]

In such a deplorable circumstance, it is futile to pretend that one is simply an American: one must recognize that he is a Negro. It is pointless to argue that there is no such creature as an American Negro when twelve million human beings are identified and treated as Negroes. It is senseless to continue to debate whether or not segregation is desirable; segregation is a fact. In such a circumstance, the only matter for American Negroes to debate is what they can do to prevent their genocide. The solution, he explained, was to "carefully plan and guide our segregated life, organize in industry and politics to protect it and expand it and above all to give it unhampered spiritual expression in art and literature" (p. 177).

A step which blacks could take immediately was to make their institutions more serviceable by concentrating on their true purpose. That is, as one could no longer deny the fact of being Negro, so it was absurd to pretend that a Negro college was just another American college. It must be recognized as a Negro institution:

> A Negro university in the United States of America begins with Negroes. It uses that variety of English idiom which they understand; and above all, it is founded on a knowledge of the history of their people in Africa and in the United States, and their present condition . . . then it asks how shall these young men and women be trained to earn a living and live a life under the circumstances in which they find themselves. (p. 175)

Beginning with such a premise, he explained, the Negro university would expand from the examination of black life, history, social development, science, and humanities into a study of all life and matter in the universe. The study must begin with a focus on black people, and it must continue from the perspective of black people. This is not merely the best route; it is the only route to universality.

In the antithesis of this theory, Du Bois found reasons for his failure to bring about the kind of literary Renaissance of which he had dreamed—one in which honest, artistic literary works about blacks by blacks would be bought and read by blacks. Such a Renaissance never took root, he now argued; the so-called "Renaissance" failed

> because it was a transplanted and exotic thing. It was a literature written for the benefit of white people and at the behest of white readers, and starting out privately from the white point of view. It never had a real Negro constituency and it did not grow out of the inmost heart and frank experience of Negroes; on such an artificial basis no real literature can grow. (p. 176)

By the time he published *Dusk of Dawn* seven years later, Du Bois had practiced his theory. After severing connections with the NAACP, Du Bois had returned to Atlanta University to help develop a strong black institution. Although he was less interested in explaining artistic theory than he had been earlier, his brief summation in *Dusk of Dawn* roots him firmly in a Black Aesthetic and identifies him, more clearly than any previous statement, as a progenitor of a Black Arts movement. Creative art, he stated, was essential to the development and transmission of new ideas among blacks:

The communalism of the African clan can be transferred to the Negro American group. . . . The emotional wealth of the American Negro, the nascent art in song, dance and drama can all be applied, not to amuse the white audience, but to inspire and direct the acting Negro group itself. I can conceive no more magnificent or promising crusade in modern times.[31]

To achieve this end, black people must be re-educated in educational institutions oriented to black people:

There has been a larger movement on the part of the Negro intelligentsia toward racial grouping for the advancement of art and literature. There has been a distinct plan for reviving ancient African art through an American Negro art movement, and more specially a thought to use the extremely rich and colorful life of the Negro in America and elsewhere as a basis for painting, sculpture, and literature. This has been partly nullified by the fact that if these new artists expect support for their art from the Negro group itself, that group must be deliberately trained and schooled in art appreciation and in willingness to accept new canons of art and in refusal to follow the herd instinct of the nation. (p. 202)

In two decades of conscious and unconscious questing for a Black Aesthetic, W.E.B. Du Bois experienced many difficulties in shaping and applying an idea which, he sensed, was sound. Some of the difficulties resulted from his personal limitations: his failure to clarify criteria, his dependence upon undefined abstractions, his inability to harmonize his awareness of the utilitarian value of literature for a specific group with his concern for the creation of Truth and Beauty, his fallacious assumption that his aesthetic was necessarily the aesthetic of most black people. Perhaps the major reason for his lack of success, however, is that, with this idea as with many others, Du Bois was twenty-five to fifty years ahead of those twelve million blacks he wanted to lead from self-respect to pride to achievement.

Today, a Black Arts movement exists; and, many black writers and educators are seriously defining the dimensions of a Black Aesthetic. Even today, however, when one considers the work of some self-identified Black Arts dramatists and poets who picture only the vice, squalor, contemptibility, and failure of black communities, one imagines Du Bois, in some afterworld he could not envision, muttering unhappily, "No. No. No! Will they never understand? To be black is to be beautiful and strong and proud."

NOTES

1. Du Bois, "Negro Writers," *Crisis* 19 (1920): 298–99.
2. Elinor D. Sinette, "The Brownies' Book," *Freedomways* 5 (Winter 1965): 138–39.
3. Du Bois, "Negro Art," *Crisis* 21 (1921): 55–56.
4. "Negro Art," p. 56.

5. Du Bois, "Can the Negro Serve the Drama?" *Theatre* (July 1923): 16–22.

6. Du Bois, "The Younger Literary Movement," *Crisis* 27 (1924): 161–62. Du Bois probably did not know that Toomer had spent less than a month in Georgia.

7. "The Social Origins of American Negro Art," *Modern Quarterly* 3 (Autumn 1925): 53ff. Subsequent references will appear parenthetically in the text. It is easy to understand Du Bois's exclusion of Tanner, who did not always paint Negro subjects, and Braithwaite, who consciously avoided poetic themes which would identify him as Negro. It is more difficult to explain Du Bois's rejection of Chesnutt. In *The Marrow of Tradition* (1901), at least, Chesnutt wrote about discrimination with a violence which provoked screams of anguish from Southern white reviewers. Perhaps Du Bois's judgment was influenced by the fact that for many years Chesnutt's racial identity was concealed by the editors of *The Atlantic*, in which his stories were printed. The matter seems especially ironic when one recalls that Chesnutt's daughter, in a biography, stated that her father began writing fiction because he believed that there was a need for Negroes to interpret the lives and problems of Negroes.

8. *Crisis* 30 (1925): 9.

9. *Crisis* 31 (1926): 141.

10. "Criteria of Negro Art," *Crisis* 32 (1926): 292.

11. "Criteria of Negro Art:" 296–97.

12. "Books," *Crisis* 32 (1926): 81–82.

13. *Crisis* 31 (1926): 165.

14. "The Negro in Art," *Crisis* 31 (1926): 219.

15. "The Negro in Art:" 219–20.

16. *Crisis* 32 (1926): 280.

17. *Crisis* 32 (1926): 280.

18. *Crisis* 32 (1926): 36.

19. *Crisis* 32 (1926): 36.

20. *Crisis* 32 (1926): 238–39.

21. *Crisis* 34 (1927): 12.

22. *Crisis* 34 (1927): 70.

23. *Crisis* 34 (1927): 159.

24. *Crisis* 34 (1927): 227.

25. *Crisis* 35 (1928): 202.

26. *Crisis* 35 (1938): 374.

27. *Crisis* 36 (1929): 125.

28. *Crisis* 36 (1929): 249–50.

29. *Crisis* 37 (1930): 162.

30. "The Negro College," *Crisis* 40 (1933): 177. Subsequent references will appear parenthetically.

31. *The Dusk of Dawn, an essay toward an autobiography of a race concept* (New York: Harcourt, 1940), p. 219. Subsequent references will appear parenthetically.

BLACK–WHITE SYMBIOSIS:
ANOTHER LOOK AT THE LITERARY
HISTORY OF THE 1920S

AMRITJIT SINGH

In *Harlem Renaissance* (1971), Nathan Irvin Huggins describes the white–black relationship in America as symbiotic: "Blacks have been essential to white identity (and whites to black)." Huggins's use of this biological concept bears heavily on the main thesis of his book which argues that the black American's confusions over identity are uniquely American: "White Americans and white American culture have no more claim to self-confidence than black." Huggins's approach is valuable because in focusing on the role of black–white interdependence (conscious and unconscious) in shaping American character and culture, it allows us to gain perspective on the overrated issues surrounding assimilationism versus nationalism in black American life.[1] However, what makes Huggins's thesis controversial is the absoluteness with which he views the black American's dilemmas in self-definition on equal terms with the white American's. The term "symbiosis" in its original sense is more to the point here; symbiosis is defined as "the relationship of two or more different organisms in a close association that may be but *is not necessarily of benefit to each*"[2] (Italics added). Time and again in American history, the one-sided and unequal relationship between blacks and whites has obliged blacks to serve as eternal footmen holding the identity coats for whites.

On the literary scene of the twenties, this symbiosis is measured best by the nature of white writing on black life and by the quality of exchanges, real and potential, between black and white writers and intellectuals. In retrospect, it seems that these literary efforts failed, with one or two partial exceptions, to rise above the major stereotype—the Negro as a primitive—that so strongly dominated the public mind in those years. Although the image of the Negro as primitive was not entirely new on the American scene, it caught the American imagination in a big way for the first time in the twenties. A number of factors combined to turn the Negro, as Langston Hughes would put it later, into a vogue. Historically, commercialism and standardization that followed industrialism led to increasing nostalgia for the simple, forceful and unmechanized existence that the Negro came, for various reasons, to represent. In the Jazz Age it had become fashionable to defy prohibition and to find joy and abandon in exotic music and dance. In such an atmosphere, "the Negro had obvious uses: he represented the unspoiled child of nature, the noble savage—carefree, spontaneous and sexually uninhibited."[3] European artists Pablo Picasso and George Braque found insight and inspiration in African sculpture to develop their interest in cubism. The exotic curiosity of a few in African art forms was matched by the romantic interest of many in primitive life and culture, an interest that made little distinction between Africans and Afro-Americans. A popular misinterpretation of Freudian theory contributed to the promotion of primitivism in Europe and North America. Freud was seen as the champion of instinct over intellect in a revolt against the Puritan spirit. In his *Civilization and its Discontents*, Freud had contended that civilization was based upon the renunciation of "powerful instinctual urgencies," and that the privation of instinctual gratification demanded by the cultural ideal was a major source of neurosis. No wonder, then, that popularized Freudianism became "the rationalization of sex primitivism," and gave the "cult of the primitive . . . an extraordinary foothold on this continent."[4]

On the plus side, this Negro fad of the twenties in the United States led to an unprecedented artistic activity that focused on the depiction of the Negro in fiction, drama, poetry, painting and sculpture. More white writers in the South as well as the North wrote about the Negro, and in sheer quantity the record remains unmatched to this day. One group of writers and intellectuals, centered at the University of North Carolina, Chapel Hill, devoted their careers almost entirely to Negro-related writing.[5] Known generally as writers of the Southern Renaissance, the group included Paul Green, Julia Peterkin, DuBose Heyward, T. S. Stribling, Elizabeth Lay Green, and Edward Sheldon. Friederich Koch, the director of the University's little theater group, the Carolina Playmakers, and former student of George Pierce Baker, particularly encouraged plays that made artistic use of Negro themes. Under the leadership of Harry Woodburn Chase, the Massachusetts-born president of the University, liberal Southern social scientists such as Frank Graham and Howard Odum published many important studies of the Negro, and in 1927, 1928 and 1929, the *Carolina Magazine* devoted one number entirely to work by Negro contributors. In the North, many white writers, such as Eugene O'Neill, Sherwood Anderson, and e. e. cummings, followed the trend already set by Gertrude Stein's "Melanctha" (1909) and Vachel Lindsay's *The Congo* (1914) in presenting the alleged primitivism of the Negro as a bulwark against increasing standardization. Besides, anthropologists like Franz Boas and Melville Herskovits published many pioneering studies of the Negro.

The most significant result of the Negro vogue was the encouragement that black musicians, writers, and other artists received from white audiences and important white individuals. Jazz and blues thrived and defined the mood of the period. Black musicians—Roland Hayes, Duke Ellington, Louis Armstrong, Bessie Smith, among others—came to public attention. In 1921, *Shuffle Along,* produced by Flourney Miller and Aubrey Lyles, ran for so long at the 63rd Street Theatre that it came to symbolize black New York. It was followed on Broadway by the moderate success of many other revues of the same variety. Black actors and actresses like Josephine Baker, Charles Gilpin, Paul Robeson, and Florence Mills gave spectacular performances in plays by black and white dramatists. In painting and sculpture, black artists such as Aaron Douglas, Hale Woodruff, Richard Barthe, and others moved away from the academic realism of Henry O. Tanner to experiment in a variety of styles and to attempt a more objective and effective self-portrayal.

But it is in literature that we see the most impressive results of this new and open mood. There were more books published by blacks in the twenties than ever before, and it would not be until the sixties that Afro-American literary activity would again exhibit equal or greater vitality. The collective literary product of the period is indicated today by the term "Harlem Renaissance" or "Negro Renaissance." The young writers of the period were guided and encouraged not only by their black seniors, such as Alain Locke, James Weldon Johnson, Charles S. Johnson, Walter White, W.E.B. Du Bois and Jessie Fauset, but also by many sympathetic whites, including Waldo Frank, Carl Van Vechten, Victor F. Calverton, and others.

It is not my purpose here to attempt a detailed history of the Harlem Renaissance as a movement. It has been done elsewhere.[6] It is agreed that the phenomenon identified generally as the Harlem Renaissance appeared on the American scene during the closing years of World War I, was publicly recognized by men such as Alain Locke and Charles S. Johnson in 1924 or 1925, and had begun declining about the time of the stock market crash in 1929. While the Afro-American creative writing of this brief period of ten years or so is duly credited for its abundance and variety, it is felt that the black writers of the period failed to achieve their potential as writers and did not fully grapple with the implications of Alain Locke's elaborate effort to develop a conscious "local color" movement of Afro-American arts. The stock market crash had no doubt severely hampered white America's ability to sustain and enjoy the Negro fad. Perhaps, as Ralph Ellison has pointed out, the black writer of the twenties "had wanted to be fashionable and this insured, even more effectively than the approaching Depression, the failure of the 'New Negro' movement."[7] Black writers had "climbed aboard the bandwagon" of exoticism and decadence signalled by Carl Van Vechten's *Nigger Heaven* and enjoyed the era when the Negro was in vogue. By the mid-thirties, exotic and genteel novels were no longer popular with the publishers and were attacked by a new breed of black writers and critics. In 1934, Eugene Saxton, who had handled Claude McKay's work at Harper and Brothers, bluntly informed him that his popularity had been part of a passing fad.[8] In 1940, Langston Hughes spoke for many when he said, "I had a swell time while it [the Negro Renaissance] lasted. But I thought it wouldn't last long. . . . For how could a large number of people be crazy about Negroes forever?"[9]

Although Carl Van Vechten's *Nigger Heaven* (1926) was not the first or the only work by a white writer to exploit the exotic-primitive stereotype in relation to the Negro, it was certainly the most influential novel in establishing this image in the minds of the reading public in the twenties. The book ran into several editions and sold over 100,000 copies; it fanned an unprecedented nationwide interest in the Negro and clearly demonstrated the commercial value of books written in the primitivistic framework. A few months before the publication of this book, as a participant in the symposium on "The Negro in Art—How Shall He be Portrayed?" initiated by Du Bois in the pages of *The Crisis*, Carl Van Vechten had made a statement most revealing of his attitude to the subject. He had said:

> The squalor of Negro life, the vice of Negro life, offer a wealth of novel, exotic, picturesque material to the artist. On the other hand, there is very little difference if any between the life of a wealthy or cultured Negro and that of a white man of the same class. The question is: are Negro writers going to write about this exotic material while it is still fresh or will they continue to make a free gift of it to white authors who will exploit it until not a drop of vitality remains?[10]

Nigger Heaven thus represented a real threat of preemption to young black writers if the latter refused to heed Van Vechten's advice and exploit a market ripe and eager for exotic versions of black life.

Described by a contemporary as an "archeologist of the exotic," Carl Van Vechten was interested in the Negro long before he published *Nigger Heaven*. Born and brought up in Cedar Rapids, Iowa, he came to New York in 1906 after studying at the University of Chicago and working a short stint as journalist for the *Chicago American*. He was among the first to take jazz seriously as an art form and had become interested in the Negro by way of jazz and Gertrude Stein. In 1913 he saw a Negro vaudeville show, *Darktown Follies*. "How the darkies danced, sang, and cavorted," Van Vechten recalled later in his *In The Garret*. "Real nigger stuff this, done with spontaneity and joy in the doing." By this time, he was promoting interracial gatherings by entertaining blacks at his home. During the early twenties, he came to know many black writers and leaders, such as Walter White, James Weldon Johnson, Countee Cullen, Langston Hughes, Zora Neale Hurston, Rudolph Fisher, and Eric Walrond. Soon he was a regular visitor in Harlem and, according to Ethel Waters, came to know more about New York's black belt than any other white person with the exception of the captain of Harlem's police station.[11]

Even before publishing his own book, Van Vechten was influential as a friend and adviser to black writers. He was in fact their major contact with white journals and white publishers. He was also responsible for many contacts between white and black artists. Through his interracial parties and gatherings in Harlem and in the Village, he made it smart to be interracial. Ethel Waters recalled meeting Eugene O'Neill, Sinclair Lewis, Dorothy Thompson, Alfred Knopf, George Jean Nathan, Alexander Woolcott, Heywood Broun, Cole Porter, Noel Coward, and Somerset Maugham at the Van Vechten apartment.[12] Paul Robeson's singing at an interracial gathering at Van Vechten's place led directly to his first New York concert. Van Vechten was instrumental in getting Langston Hughes's first two volumes of poetry, *The Weary Blues* (1926) and *Fine Clothes to a Jew* (1927), accepted for publication by Alfred Knopf. Through Van Vechten again, Hughes found his way to the pages of *Vanity Fair*. He also persuaded Alfred Knopf to publish James Weldon Johnson, Nella Larsen, Rudolph Fisher, and Chester Himes.

Although a detailed analysis of *Nigger Heaven* may not be pertinent here, it is necessary to indicate the influence Van Vechten and his book had on the milieu and literary careers of the Harlem Renaissance writers. *Nigger Heaven* is the story of Mary Love, a prim and pretty Harlem librarian, who falls in love with Byron Karson, a struggling young writer. Byron, a recent graduate of the University of Pennsylvania, has been told that he has promise, which he interprets to mean: "pretty good for a colored man." Mary Love cannot take sex and love lightly. Randolph Pettijohn, the numbers king, desires her and offers her marriage. "Ah ain't got no education lak you, but Ah got money, plenty of et, an' Ah got love," he tells her. Byron meanwhile fails to find a job compatible with his level of education and refuses to accept a menial job. The exotic and primitive aspects of Harlem life surround Byron's orgiastic affair with Lasca Sartoris, "a gorgeous brown Messalina of Seventh Avenue." Lasca, however, deserts Byron for Pettijohn. Byron avenges himself by impulsively firing two bullets into the prostrate body of Pettijohn, who has already been killed by Scarlet Creeper. At the end, Byron surrenders helplessly to the police.

The spectre of *Nigger Heaven* lurks behind most book reviews written after 1926. Benjamin Brawley, Allison Davis, and W.E.B. Du Bois asserted that some younger black writers and many white writers were misguided by *Nigger Heaven*, and they argued that the emphasis on the exotic and the primitive, the sensual and the bawdy in the depiction of the Negro was detrimental to the blacks' political future in the United States.

If the fad of primitivism cannot be blamed entirely on Van Vechten or on the group of whites who wrote about the Negro in the twenties, it is reasonable to conclude that the book seems to have had a crippling effect on the self-expression of many black writers by either making it easier to gain success riding the bandwagon of primitivism or by making it difficult to publish novels that did not fit the profile of the commercial success formula adopted by most publishers for black writers. The unusual success of *Nigger Heaven* and later of McKay's *Home to Harlem* clearly indicated an eagerness for works exalting the exotic, the sensual, and the primitive. This interest had "no minor effect on the certain members of the Harlem *literati* whose work was just what the Jazz Age ordered." Thus, black writers who were willing to describe the exotic scene "had no trouble finding sponsors, publishers and immediate popularity."[13] In his autobiography *The Big Sea* (1940), Langston Hughes recalled the pessimistic judgment of Wallace Thurman, who thought that the Negro vogue had made the Harlem Renaissance writers "too conscious of ourselves, had flattered and spoiled us, and had provided too many easy opportunities for some of us to drink gin and more gin. . . ."[14]

So the decade of the twenties was replete with black literary activity which for the most part took its cue from and satisfied the deep psychological needs of the white majority. Out of weakness or necessity, many black writers felt obliged not to offend the white readers' (and whose else were there in the twenties?) preconceptions of the Negro. A consideration of literary works by black authors highlights two dominant trends that form a revealing pattern of near-obsessive concern with the major white stereotype of Afro-American existence. The first trend is defined by such black writing which, like much writing on the subject by white contemporaries (although with significant minor variations), presents black life as exotic and primitivistic. One thinks, for example, of novels such as Arna Bontemps's *God Sends Sunday* (1931), Claude McKay's *Home to Harlem* (1928) and *Banjo* (1929), and poems such as Countee Cullen's "Heritage" and Waring Cuney's "No Images." On the other hand were works by writers who with equal force and terror attempted to show that the black American was different from his white counterpart only in the shade of his skin. These writers found it expedient to plead their case by presenting black middle-class characters and situations in their fictional works in order to demolish the prevailing stereotype. Among such works one may mention the novels by Jessie Fauset, Walter White, Nella Larsen and W.E.B. Du Bois. However, the primitivistic mode had such wide and deep appeal among their readership that white publishers often hesitated to publish their works. Zora Gale, for example, had to come to Jessie Fauset's rescue with a preface to *The Chinaberry Tree* (1931) because the publisher said "White readers just don't expect Negroes to be like this."[15] But it was important for these black writers to be published by major publishers and to reach the white audiences at whom their works were primarily aimed. When H. L. Mencken suggested that Walter White seek a Negro publisher for his unrelentingly propagandistic novel *Fire in the Flint* (1924), White replied: "It is not the colored reader at whom I am shooting but the white man and woman . . . who believes that every lynching is for rape, who believes that ex-confederates are right when they use every means, fair or foul, to keep the nigger in his place."[16]

This evidence is corroborated even by statements by such writers who had, consciously or unconsciously, dispensed the white stereotypes in their own works, or else had striven to remain independent in their views on race and art. When, in 1930, Arna Bontemps submitted for publication his first novel "with autobiographical overtones about a sensitive black boy in a nostalgic setting," many editors suggested that he rewrite the novel into a sensual-primitivistic story centered around a minor character.[17] The result was published the following year as *God Sends Sunday*. Even Claude McKay, whose *Home to Harlem* had successfully tapped the market fed a few years before by *Nigger Heaven*, resented and rejected the suggestion from some quarters that he should "make a trip to Africa and write about Negro life in pure state." He complained that white critics approached his work "as if he were primitive and altogether [a] stranger to civilization. *Perhaps I myself unconsciously gave that impression*"[18] (Italics added). Jean Toomer, the mystical poet-observer of *Cane* (1923), complained to Waldo Frank that his friendship with Sherwood Anderson could not develop because the latter "limits me to Negro." "As an approach," Toomer added, "as a constant element (part of the larger whole) of interest, Negro is good. But to try to tie me to one of my parts is surely to lose me. My own letters have taken Negro as a point, and from there have circled out. Sherwood, for the most part, ignores the circles."[19]

Some of the writers, especially Hughes, experienced white patronage of a different kind. Langston Hughes, Zora Neale Hurston, Louise Thompson, and some other young black artists had a rich white patron who wanted them to express their "primitive" instincts in their work for the generous support offered. Later in his career, Hughes was never able to recall his experience with this patron without getting sick in the stomach, but in the early thirties he found courage to leave the relationship because, to quote Hughes, "I did not feel the rhythms of the primitive surging through me, and so I could not live and write as though I did. I was only an American Negro—who had loved the surface of Africa and the rhythms of Africa—but I was not Africa. I was Chicago and Kansas City and Broadway and Harlem."[20] Hughes, in fact, asserted his artistic independence by promising to steer clear as much of the white readers' stereotypes as those of the black middle-class readers' taboos. He expressed his views strongly in a *Nation* article entitled "The Negro Artist and The Racial Mountain" (1926), which remains the clearest statement on the subject to come from the period. Late in the thirties, Hughes also summed up the Negro writer's difficulties with white publishers. First of all, he complained, Negro books are considered by editors and publishers as exotic and placed in a special category like Chinese or East Indian material. His more serious charge was that books by black writers cannot sell unless they "make our black ghetto in the big cities seem very happy places indeed, and our plantations in the deep south idyllic in their pastoral loveliness. . . . When we cease to be exotic, we cease to sell."[21]

If among black writers Hughes was one of the few exceptions to the bandwagon influence of the white stereotype, there were some exceptions on the other side too. The most significant man among the whites, who supported and encouraged black writing in the twenties without capitulating to the primitivistic view of black life, was an intellectual rather than a creative writer. V. F. Calverton, who edited the first *Anthology of American Negro Literature* (1929) for the Modern Library, encouraged black writers, intellectuals, and journalists in the pages of his journal, *The Modern Quarterly*. Born George Goetz (1900–1940), Calverton was a literary radical whose interests were as diverse as literature, anthropology, sociology, Marxism and hypnosis.[22] As an independent-minded Marxist, he tried to look at American life and literature and Afro-American contributions to them in socio-economic terms. His sharp sense of the Negro's economic status in American life would allow little scope in his vision for the exotic-primitive type. In grappling with the socio-economic and literary issues of his time, Calverton became fully sensitive to the rigidity of the American color caste. In an essay on the Negro, written for Harold E. Stern's *America Now* (1938), he said:

> Being a Negro in the U.S. today is like being a prisoner in a jail which has several corridors and squares, in which it is possible occasionally to see the sun and walk amid the flowers and fields that belong to the unimprisoned elements of humanity. Beyond the contours of that circumscribed world there is little territory, economic or physical, in which he can have that freedom necessary for individual advance and social progress.[23]

Calverton's deep understanding of the Negro's status in a segregated, limiting world did not make him blind—as it did many latter-day white sociologists—to other elements in the life of black Americans. He traced the origin of blues, spirituals and labor songs to the peculiar socio-economic conditions of slavery and extolled these art forms as "America's chief claim to originality in cultural history."[24]

Although close to the Communist Party in the twenties, Calverton broke away from it in 1933 and remained an unorthodox Marxist, to the end expressing independent views as a social and cultural critic. He urged the Party to see the futility of attempting to transplant the Russian experiment in the United States where unique conditions existed because of widespread industrialization. Calverton also tried unsuccessfully to interest black Marxists and intellectuals in his thesis called "Cultural Compulsive." According to him, the compulsive nature of social thought explained the limited character of a people's point of view. It assumed that it was impossible for any mind to achieve objectivity in its evaluation of social phenomena. The awareness of this inescapable subjectivity, he thought, would allow for more care and flexibility in criticism "within the radius of the cultural compulsive itself." Black Americans could, thus, use this "cultural compulsive" thesis as a basis for functional social theory in their struggle for social and cultural rights. Regardless of whether one agrees or not with Calverton's views, one cannot but marvel at his ability to have remained untouched by the pervasive stereotype of his time, especially when one considers the depth and sincerity of his interest in black American life. Looking back, Calverton's independent commitment to the racial situation in the United States seems all the more impressive in view of the facile involvement of many blacks in the thirties and forties with the rhetoric of the American Communist Party.

However, the exceptional independence of white stereotypes that Calverton showed underscores only the general failure of black and white authors to escape the influence of the commercial success formula represented by certain works about blacks by white writers. Also, while a certain combination of factors dramatized the white–black symbiosis on the literary scene of the twenties, its relevance to other periods of American history is well expressed in the following words of Saunders Redding:

> The Negro, and especially later, the Negro writer, has always known who he is. . . . Certainly he has not had to seek it. Quite the contrary, he has tried to lose it; . . . The Negro's identity was locked into the white man's fantasy construct of the slave, and Emancipation did not free him. The fantasy construct (perpetuated as an historical fiction), as Alain Locke pointed out forty years ago, was the image of the Negro that none but the negro himself wanted to reject. And in order to do this, he had first to suppress the knowledge and deprive himself of the redemptive use of his true identity. . . . The [slave] identity was still useful to the [white] conscience, for it justified the social abuses practised against their freedom, and since the identity of the Negro was locked into this, he could not rid himself of the one without ridding himself of the other. And this, strange and aberrant though it may be, is what he did, or tried to [do]—in fact, in fiction, and in verse.[25]

Too long have black writers either succumbed to white stereotypes or else been obliged simply to try to fight these stereotypes to an early death. The burden has been heavy and generally debilitating, as evidenced in many Afro-American literary works. The exceptions are so few that they only prove the rule. Not until very recently have blacks been able to publish works that are not partially or wholly determined by the peculiar preconceptions of white audiences, white editors, and white publishers at any given time. One is beginning to observe the impact of growing black audiences, the presence of black publishers and the traumatic changes that America experienced in the sixties. The true meeting of the minds between black and white artists is symbolized best by the meetings that never took place between Jean Toomer and Allen Tate, both from the South and both proponents of new ideas and experiments in literature. They corresponded and planned twice to meet at a small Louisiana railroad station. They never met. One can only hope that genuine attempts at the portrayal of the Negro may come from both black and white writers with the conviction, to borrow Ellison's words, that "it is important to explore the full range of American Negro humanity and to affirm those qualities which are of value beyond any question of segregation, economics or previous condition of servitude. The obligation was always there and there is much to affirm."[26]

NOTES

1. Huggins, *Harlem Renaissance* (New York: Oxford Univ. Press, 1971), pp. 12, 84, 305.
2. *The American Heritage Dictionary* (1969).

3. Robert Bone, *The Negro Novel in America*, rev. ed. (New Haven: Yale Univ. Press, 1965), p. 59.

4. Oscar Cargill, *Intellectual America* (New York: Macmillan, 1941), p. 608.

5. This brief résumé of this group of writers is based on Trudie Engel, "The Harlem Renaissance" (Master's thesis, Univ. of Wisconsin, Madison, 1959), pp. 72–81.

6. See relevant sections in Huggins, *Harlem Renaissance*; Arna Bontemps, *Harlem Renaissance Remembered* (New York: Dodd Mead, 1972); Amritjit Singh, *The Novels of the Harlem Renaissance: Twelve Black Writers, 1923–1933* (State College: Pennsylvania State Univ. Press, 1976).

7. James Thompson, Lennox Raphael, and Steven Canyon, "A Very Stern Discipline: An Interview with Ralph Ellison," *Harper's* (Mar. 1967): 79.

8. *The Passion of Claude McKay: Selected Poetry and Prose, 1912–1948*, ed.Wayne Cooper (New York: Schocken, 1973), p. 36.

9. Langston Hughes, *The Big Sea* (New York: Hill and Wang, 1940), p. 228.

10. *Crisis* 31 (1926): 219.

11. Ethel Waters, *His Eye Is on the Sparrow* (New York: Doubleday, 1951), p. 195.

12. Waters, *His Eye Is on the Sparrow*, p. 196.

13. Faith Berry, "Voice for the Jazz Age, Great Migration or Black Bourgeoisie," *Black World* 20 (Nov. 1970): 12.

14. Hughes, *The Big Sea*, p. 238.

15. Based on Marion L. Starkey, "Jessie Fauset," *Southern Workman* 62 (May 1932): 217–20.

16. Letter from Walter White to H. L. Mencken, 17 October 1923, NAACP papers, Manuscripts Division, Library of Congress, Washington DC. Quoted in Charles F. Cooney, "Walter White and the Harlem Renaissance," *Journal of Negro History* 57 (July 1972): 232.

17. Bontemps, "The Awakening: A Memoir," in *Harlem Renaissance Remembered*, pp. 25–26.

18. "A Negro to His Critics," *New York Herald Tribune Books* 6 (Mar. 1932).

19. Jean Toomer to Waldo Frank (c. 1922–3). Quoted in Mark Helbling, "Sherwood Anderson and Jean Toomer," *Negro American Literature Forum* 9 (Summer 1975): 36.

20. *The Big Sea*, p. 325.

21. Quoted in Donald Ogden Stewart, *Fighting Words* (New York: Harcourt, Brace & World, 1940), pp. 58–59.

22. For a detailed analysis of Calverton's interest and involvement with Black Americans, see Haim Genizi, "V. F. Calverton: a Racial Magazinist for Black Intellectuals, 1920–1940," *Journal of Negro History* 57 (July 1972): 241–53.

23. "The Negro" in Stearns, *America Now* (New York: Literary Guild, 1938), p. 485.

24. Calverton, "The Growth of Negro Literature," *Anthology of American Negro Literature* (New York: Modern Library, 1929), p. 3.

25. Saunders Redding, "The Problems of the Negro Writer," *Massachusetts Review* 6 (1964–5): 58–59. See also the two seminal essays on white portrayal of Negro characters by Sterling Brown: "Negro Character as Seen by White Authors," *Journal of Negro Education* 2 (Jan. 1933): 180–201; "A Century of Negro Portraiture in American Literature," *Massachusetts Review* 7 (1966): 73–96; and Edward Margolies, "The Image of Primitive in Black Letters," *Midcontinent American Studies Journal* (Fall 1970): 70–76.

26. Ellison, *Shadow and Act* (New York: Random House, 1964), p. 17.

This article is a revised version of an article which appeared in a book printed in India and permission has been granted by The Oxford Univ. Press-India to reprint.

THE OUTER REACHES:
THE WHITE WRITER AND BLACKS IN THE TWENTIES

RICHARD A. LONG

Langston Hughes's often-made remark that the Harlem Renaissance was the time when Negroes were in style immediately raises the question, with whom? In *Only Yesterday* by Frederick Lewis Allen, which lives up to its subtitle "An Informal History of the Nineteen-Twenties," Negroes are mentioned only as the objects of intolerance, along with Jews and, in some instances, Roman Catholics. No black writer or spokesman is referred to, and the only white writer Allen mentions who dealt with blacks in his work is Eugene O'Neill. Nevertheless scores of writers, journalists and editors are referred to in Allen's book. Of course Allen's concern is social history and not literary history. Thus it is necessary to see Hughes's remark in its true context, that of literary fashion, which occupies only a limited portion of the total matrix of any society, but which, at least to students of literature, wears well and longest, so that in retrospect we see a period primarily through its literary history.

Black folk entered the larger American consciousness in artistic form, dubiously, only at the end of the twenties in the nightly radio series, *Amos and Andy*, performed by two white vaudevillians who prospered so mightily that in the twilight of their years they were golf companions of President Eisenhower. An analogue to the burlesque of Amos and Andy, which was heir to black-faced minstrelry—always a source of laughter to the aryan out for a laugh—were the writings of Charleston-born Octavus Roy Cohen, who published short stories—mainly vignettes of black bumptiousness[1]—regularly in the *Saturday Evening Post* from 1918 until well after the twenties.

More formal literary and dramatic treatments of the Negro were, however, a part of the scene in the twenties, and in the thought of serious critics, black and white, did form part of the mosaic of the Harlem Renaissance. With the exception of Carl Van Vechten and of Paul Green,[2] however, the white writers in question had little or no contact with the black intelligentsia.

An image of the black man which was to have a great impact on the Harlem Renaissance was that projected in Eugene O'Neill's *The Emperor Jones* (1920), first produced by the Provincetown Players, with the black actor Charles Gilpin in the title role. In later productions of the play, Jules Bledsoe and Paul Robeson appeared in the title role. The play was thought to mark a new step in the treatment of the black man on the American stage. First of all, the black is clearly the protagonist; the role is virtually a monologue. The performance requires a *tour de force* of the actor, serving to indicate the high caliber of black dramatic talent. Secondly, Brutus Jones is a highly complex character capable of considerable introspection, and this seemed to be an improvement on the stereotype black-as-buffoon. Finally, though he sustains a morally appropriate defeat, it is at the hands of other blacks whom he has attempted to subjugate in a colonialist manner. The scenario was suggested by the life of Henri Cristophe of Haiti, a country then being "self-determined by United States Marines."[3]

The Emperor Jones has remained in the minds of most critics a major American play. It is not without its limitations, however, from a black perspective. Brutus Jones is reduced from a swaggering bravo to a simpering hulk in twenty-four hours by atavistic superstition induced by the beating of drums in the forest. The implication is clear. Nevertheless, the positive features, particularly the central role it gave a black actor, was emphasized by most black commentators.

In 1923, Eugene O'Neill's play about intermarriage, *All God's Chillun Got Wings* was produced. The delicacy of the theme alone would seem to have sharply limited its success, and while it was generally approved for its seriousness, it was not often referred to except that it had been a good vehicle for Paul Robeson. Actually the play is more typical of O'Neill's work than *The Emperor Jones*. Its theme of unrequited love and veiled hate, of madness and failure, mindless sacrifice and frustration, bind it to the O'Neillean cosmos. With very mild editing, the fact that the protagonist is black could be expunged without materially affecting the drama.

Paul Green entered the scene in 1926 with the production of *Abraham's Bosom*, which won a Pulitzer Prize in 1927. Green's play is set forty years earlier and deals with the frustration experienced by a black leader in establishing a school not approved by the whites and only weakly wanted by the blacks. It ends in the inevitable tragedy, following the protagonist's killing of the antagonist, his white half-brother.

At least three other dramas by white authors, all based on prose fiction, should be mentioned for the period. The novel *Porgy* was dramatized with great success by its author DuBose Heyward and his wife Dorothy. Its subsequent metamorphosis into the opera *Porgy and Bess* makes it one of the monuments of the American stage. An unsuccessful dramatization of Julia Peterkin's *Scarlet Sister Mary*, with Ethel Barrymore in blackface as the heroine, was justifiably a failure. The biblical paraphrase *Ol' Man Adam and His Chillun* was dramatized with great success by Marc Connelly in *The Green Pastures*, whose stage success derived chiefly from the mastery of the black actors and the music of the Hall Johnson singers.[4]

In 1922 T. S. Stribling published a novel, *Birthright*, dealing with the return home to the South of a Harvard-educated Negro bent on racial uplift. Against the harsh realities of Southern life he is, of course, doomed to disillusion and defeat. While purportedly a "realistic" novel, its hero is in fact quite unrealistic, certainly not resembling in any way a statistically important type and perhaps no highly schooled black at all. The rigors of his schooling would have ordinarily honed him for the magnolia circuit. While white critics were generally kind, both William Stanley Braithwaite and Benjamin Brawley forcefully condemned the novel.[5] Writing years later, Sterling Brown is a bit kinder. After rating stereotypes and weaknesses, he says:

> But Stribling does protest against the Southern belief that all Negroes are carefree and happy. His description of Negro lodges, funerals, and workaday life are authentic. Most important of all, *Birthright* places the Negro at the center of the picture, attempts to show the influence of environment upon character, is ironic at the vaunted Southern understanding of Negroes, and attacks injustice.[6]

Sterling Brown's opinion might be taken as typical of that of informed black readers at the time of the book's appearance, for it was indeed an attempt to treat black folk seriously in a work of fiction.

A second novel of 1922, *Nigger* by Clement Wood, was not esteemed more highly. It was a realistic novel tracing a black family from slavery to the present. Wood, whose later non-fiction piece on Alabama met Du Bois's exacting requirements,[7] was well acquainted with Southern life and the Negro and unsentimental about both. Its title might well have affected its reception, though it was a serious work of fiction.

Neither Stribling nor Wood devoted further attention in this period to fiction of Negro life. The former's next two novels were set in Venezuela. Clement Wood achieved some distinction as a critic and practitioner of verse.

1925, the year of Alain Locke's *New Negro*, was also the year of publication of DuBose Heyward's *Porgy*. Heyward, a minor poet, was a native of Charleston, South Carolina, and well acquainted with the life of the humble black people who lived in the waterfront area. In *Porgy*, he describes a cycle in the life of the residents of a tenement, Catfish Row, focusing on a professional beggar, Porgy, whose legs are atrophied and useless. The people of Catfish Row are treated with humor and compassion and emerge as dignified victims of human tragedy. The tone of the book is, not surprisingly, paternalistic, and the blacks are in the long run perceived not as exotics, but as primitives.

In a sense Heyward merely confirmed the racist preconceptions of his readers, eschewing the tasks undertaken by Stribling and Wood. In another, he may be seen as the heir of the dialect writers who, in a sense, collected people for their intrinsic interest. The theme of atavism held considerable fascination for Heyward. Two examples should suffice. One describes the fatal brawl of Crown with Robbins:

> Like a thrown spear, he hurled his lithe body forward under the terrifying hook, and clinched. Down, down, down the centuries they slid. Clothes could not hold them. Miraculously the tawny, ridged bodies tore through the thin coverings. Bronze ropes and bars slid and wove over great shoulders. Bright, ruddy planes leaped out on backs in the fire flare, then were gulped by sliding shadows. A heady, bestial stench absorbed all other odors. A fringe of shadowy watchers crept from cavernous doorways, sensed it, and commenced to wail eerily. Backward and forward, in a space no larger than a small room, the heaving, inseparable mass rocked and swayed. Breath labored like steam. At times the fused single body would thrust out a rigid arm, or the light would point out, for one hideous second, a tortured, mad face. Again the mass would rise as though propelled a short distance from the earth, topple, and crash down upon the pavement with a jarring impact.[8]

This passage also could be suspected of providing titillations best analyzed by a Freudian critic.

A more secular example occurs in the description of the parade of "The Sons and Daughters of Repent ye Saith the Lord":

> For its one brief moment out of the year the pageant had lasted. Out of its fetters of civilization this people had risen, suddenly, amazingly. Exotic as the Congo, and still able to abandon themselves utterly to the wild joy of fantastic play, they had taken the reticent, old Anglo-Saxon town and stamped their mood swiftly and indelibly into its heart. Then they passed, leaving behind them a wistful envy among those who had watched them go,—those whom the ages had rendered old and wise.[9]

It was not the novel *Porgy* that black audiences took to their hearts, but its embodiment as a stage piece in which black actors truly realized the creatures of Heyward's imagination.

Heyward's later novel *Mamba's Daughters* (1929), dramatized a decade later, may be said to be a product of the information generated by the Harlem Renaissance. While Mamba, a folk matriarch, is a resident of the familiar Charleston waterfront, the upward mobility of her granddaughter brings us into the presence of black folk who have Hepplewhite and Chippendale in their parlors and who talk about Harry T. Burleigh and Henry Ossawa Tanner. In the last pages of the novel, in which themes of race and color predominate, the heroine sings the "Negro National Anthem" which is quoted in full. Its authors, James Weldon Johnson and his brother J. Rosamond Johnson, are identified.[10]

The South Carolina Low Country of which Charleston is the metropolis produced another fictionalist concerned exclusively with rural and primitive black folk, Julia Peterkin, who wrote three novels during this period: *Black Thursday* (1924),[11] *Black April* (1927), and *Scarlet Sister Mary* (1928), which won a Pulitzer Prize in 1929. The most profound commentary on the meaning of Julia Peterkin's work was, quite unwittingly, made by the author herself in the commentary to a book of photographs of the folk who made her fortune, *Roll Jordan Roll* (1933).[12] There she reveals herself as a hidebound heir of the planter class, full of affection for the blacks who know their place. The two latter novels have rather more black sexual intrigue in them than one would expect a nice Southern white lady of the time to be interested in, but it is this element, rather than fortitude in the face of poverty, which accounts for the popularity of the work; though blacks were not conspicuous among Julia Peterkin's admirers, she had a definite impact on the compounding of the notion that they were somehow "in style."

The novel by a white author which had the greatest impact on the Harlem Renaissance was Carl Van Vechten's *Nigger Heaven* (1926), which took the Harlem of the Renaissance for its subject. The best-selling novel repelled many blacks with its title alone. Many of those who got beyond the title found its allusions to Harlem lowlife unsavory. For the white literary public, however, Van Vechten had done it again. What he had done was reveal to his readers another part of the diversity of his own experience. For Van Vechten was a very personal novelist stringing weak fiction on his own notebook observations of people and places. His essentially impressionistic manner had lifted him to fortune with *The Tattooed Countess* (1924), and he thus had a ready-made audience avid for more thrills. Van Vechten actually wrote quite consciously in the tradition of the "Decadent Novel," and a major influence on him was Ronald Firbank.[13]

In 1924 Van Vechten had written an introduction to an American edition of Firbank's magnificently decadent *Prancing Nigger*. Set on an imaginary Caribbean island, this novel of primitive, exotic blacks may be easily perceived as fantasy. Van Vechten had hoped, doubtless, to achieve some of the same deftness of touch with *Nigger Heaven*, but his theme, his intentions, and finally the nature of his talent conspired against it. Harlem was not the stuff of fantasy.

The major emphasis of *Nigger Heaven* is not at all on the element that respectable black opinion, led by Du Bois, deplored. The two chief characters, Mary Love and Byron Kasson, are certainly as cultivated and refined as any products of American education could be in the nineteen-twenties. Byron, of course, has a tragic flaw, and is the victim of his own undisciplined personality and disordered ambition, but that is clearly set forth. The sensationalism and "low-life" of the novel is incidental and decorative. Like many of Van Vechten's works the novel is a *roman à clef.*[14] However, it was the sensationalism and not the salon chatter which gave the book its brief renown.

Among many uses of black characters for subsidiary purposes, two important examples should be noted. Sherwood Anderson in *Dark Laughter* (1926) uses blacks and their healthy but mindless laughter as an inchoate Greek chorus. Edna Ferber in *Show Boat* (1926), which was to become even more popular as a stage work, depicts blacks on the Mississippi as background for a tale which includes the tragic mulatto theme in its foreground.[15]

The white writer who wrote about black folk in the twenties, whether they were central to his fiction or merely ancillary, was writing for a white audience, both publishers and public. He was himself a part of that public. The social position of the black and the mythic ideology which supported it would tend to inhibit such writers from leaving the well-established terrain on which the black played his simple and simple-minded destiny, an endless cycle of dancing and laughing, of joy and sorrow, of frenzied loving, of shooting and knifing, and occasionally of spectacular, back-breaking toil. The most artful portrayal of this pure tradition was probably Roark Bradford's *Ol' Man Adam and His Chillun* (1928), which announces itself as fantasy, but a fantasy more believed by white Americans than any realistic work could ever be.

As we have seen, Van Vechten's willingness to depict blacks in Harlem who are intellectual and avant-garde was vitiated by a need to depict a variety of sensationalism that he himself had probably not observed and which was unknown to Dr. Du Bois and the readers of *Crisis.*

The most significant thing about the black as subject in the fiction and drama of white writers in the twenties is the apparent increase in incidence of treatment, which, combined with the Harlem Renaissance itself and the triumph of jazz, seemed to herald a new acceptance of the black presence in the nation at large. This impression was widely held. It was more deceptive than not.

NOTES

1. Collections of his short stories in the period under discussion were the following: *Polished Ebony* (1919), *Highly Colored* (1921), *Assorted Chocolates* (1922), *Epic Peters* (1930).

2. Green taught at the University of North Carolina in his native state, but was known to some black intellectuals. His wife, Elizabeth Lay Green, prepared the study outline, *The Negro in Contemporary American Literature*, highly commended by Du Bois in "The Browsing Reader" section of *Crisis* 36.

3. The phrase is O'Neill's, who describes the island where his play is set as not yet having received that blessing. The American occupation began in 1915 and was concluded only in 1933.

4. The dates for the theater pieces are: *Porgy*, 1925; *Scarlet Sister Mary, The Green Pastures*, 1929. The latter won a Pulitzer Prize in 1930.

5. WSB in the *Boston Evening Transcript*, 19 April 1922; BB in the *Springfield Republican*, 23 April 1922.

6. *The Negro in American Fiction* (Washington, 1937), p. 115. I have used the Atheneum reprint of 1969 which is bound together with *Negro Poetry and Drama*.

7. Review of *These United States*, ed. Ernest Gruening, in *Crisis* 30 (1925): 25.

8. *Porgy* (New York: Grosset & Dunlap, 1925), pp. 19–20.

9. *Porgy*, pp. 114–15.

10. For a discussion which places the lyrics in the perspective of Johnson's work see Richard A. Long, "A Weapon of My Song: The Poetry of James Weldon Johnson," *Phylon* 32 (1970): 374–82.

11. *Black Thursday* is actually a collection of short stories in which the same characters recur.

12. The photographs are by Doris Ullman.

13. For this tradition see Richard A. Long and Iva G. Jones, "Towards A Definition of the 'Decadent Novel,'" *College English* 22 (1961): 245–59.

14. The heroine could have been suggested by many serious young women in the Harlem of the twenties. The hero is modeled, physically, on Harold Jackman. Van Vechten appears in the novel himself as his *alter ego* Gareth Johns. Adora Boniface, the Harlem hostess, is modeled on Alelia Walker (and, I have been told, an Atlantic City hostess, Rhetta Braswell). Lasca Sartoris is modeled on the singer Nora Holt, who years later became the dowager of New York music critics as the critic for the *Amsterdam News*.

15. For a discussion of this theme in novels about blacks, see Sterling Brown, *The Negro in American Fiction* (1937; reprint, New York: Atheneum, 1968), *passim*.

IN PURSUIT OF THE PRIMITIVE:
BLACK PORTRAITS BY EUGENE O'NEILL
AND OTHER VILLAGE BOHEMIANS

JOHN COOLEY

Many literary and cultural histories of the nineteen twenties fail to make sufficient connection between two simultaneous artistic movements in New York City: the Village Bohemians and the Harlem Renaissance.[1] Since these movements have been described in detail elsewhere, this examination will focus on some of the relationships between them and, in particular, on the ways in which white writers of the period, especially O'Neill, Waldo Frank, and Vachel Lindsay drew from black life and culture.

Clearly, a new kind of black portraiture began to emerge after the First World War. Blacks were less often seen in connection with the plantation society of the South, and far less often were they relegated to servile roles; whites began to look to urban black culture with new interest. Rather consistently, they found in black life certain values and strengths which seemed to have been lost by their own culture. As one observer put it, "by 1920 the Negro had become a white New Yorker's pastime."[2] This was, after all, the Jazz Age, and jazz seemed the perfect broom with which to sweep out the last cobwebs of "Victorian" culture. During this period blacks found, and not always to their pleasure, that they had become for white bohemian and avant-garde artists a symbol of freedom from restraint, a source of energy and sensuality. In fact, there is no single idea or theme that unifies the writing of the Village Bohemians any more coherently and strikingly than their interest in primitivism.

The black portraits in Eugene O'Neill's plays serve as an illustration of the ways in which white writers of the twenties worked with black life. Most white writers in New York during this period were close observers of Harlem life and readers of the emerging literature of the Harlem Renaissance. O'Neill's *The Emperor Jones*, his most significant black portrait, deserves close scrutiny as an illustration of white fascination with black life, of the search by white writers for fresh images and material, and of persistent stereotypes that lingered in white thinking.

The opening of *The Emperor Jones*, on November 1, 1920, may be viewed as a monumental event in American theater. As O'Neill's biographer, Travis Bogard, expressed it, that night catapulted O'Neill and the Provincetown Players "beyond any horizon they had envisioned."[3] The opening was greeted with wildly favorable reviews. Alexander Woollcott, writing in the *Times*, described the play as "an extraordinarily striking and dramatic study of panic fever."[4] Heywood Broun observed that it seemed "just about the most interesting play that has yet come from the most promising playwright in America."[5] Broun went on to praise Charles Gilpin, the black actor who played Brutus Jones: "Gilpin was great. It is a performance of heroic stature." The play was literally an overnight success. The next morning a long line of theatergoers waited to buy tickets, and a thousand subscriptions were sold during the first week.[6] Originally scheduled for a two-week engagement, *The Emperor Jones* ran for 490 performances in New York before going on the road.

Not only was the play popular with white theatergoers, the hit of the season, but it was regarded as a "breakthrough" play in American theater. In addition to being boldly innovative in its staging techniques, *The Emperor Jones* was the first American play to employ black actors and develop a major black portrait. O'Neill's black portraits in *Thirst* (1914, a collection of five one-act plays), *The Moon of the Caribbees* (1918), *The Dreamy Kid* (1919), and *All God's Chillun Got Wings* (1924) stand as evidence of a growing white interest in portraying black life concurrent with the emergence of the Negro Renaissance of black self-awareness and artistic expression. Despite this new interest in dramatizing black life, hardly any black actors were cast in black parts. Even O'Neill's earlier productions, *Thirst* and *Caribbees*, employed white actors in blackface. Thus, *The Emperor Jones* holds a very special place in Black American Theater. In her study of Negro playwrights, Doris Abramson comments that O'Neill's plays and Paul Green's *In Abraham's Bosom* deserve credit for thrusting dramatizations of black life beyond the level of the minstrel show.[7] In his O'Neill biography, Travis Bogard comments that the play proved a black figure and "an ordinary American could become a subject of pathetic concern and on occasion could rise to the height of a tragic figure." He expresses the judgment of a fair number of critics in saying ". . . American theater came of age with this play."[8] Although there is some truth to such statements, O'Neill's play deserves re-evaluation in the context of the Harlem Renaissance and the "New Negro" movement. In this context O'Neill's portrait of Brutus Jones will be seen as a combination of several white stereotypes of black character, each of them well established in earlier white literature.

By the time *The Emperor Jones* opened at the Provincetown Playhouse, Harlem was the largest black community in the world. It had already grown its own sizeable class of artists and well-educated people. At the heart of the Harlem Renaissance was a serious effort on the part of black artists to interpret black life on its own terms. To be sure, works like *The Emperor Jones* and Waldo Frank's *Holiday* (1923), Sherwood Anderson's *Dark Laughter* (1925), and Carl Van Vechten's *Nigger Heaven* (1926) provided encouragement to black writers and, as Robert Bone puts it, "created a sympathetic audience for the serious treatment of Negro subjects."[9] This interest among white writers in a literature of black experience also led to frequent patronage and sponsorship of black writers.[10] What has been largely overlooked is that this was a two-way process. White writers drew their materials and inspiration from the Renaissance, including a great burst of interest in Africana, and often at great expense to black life. The "New Negro" movement was both a celebration of black achievement and a declaration of freedom from the white myths, melodramas, and stereotypes that characterized the "Old Negro." In the introduction to his celebrated anthology of a decade of black writing, *The New Negro* (1925), Alain Locke declared: "The popular melodrama has about played itself out, and it is time to scrap the fictions, garret the bogeys and settle down to a realistic facing of facts. The day of 'aunties' and 'uncles' and 'mammies' is equally gone. Uncle Tom and Sambo have passed on. . . ."[11] Regrettably, Locke's assessment was too optimistic. *The Emperor Jones* itself is an example of the way in which old racial clichés and myths were perpetuated, even in highly regarded literature.

Despite the new consciousness that was growing in and around Harlem and the call for greater sensitivity and realism in portraits of black life, O'Neill drew his black material from exotic settings and "Old Negro" sources. In 1909 he traveled to the rain forest of Honduras on a prospecting adventure. According to Travis Bogard, he was haunted by the presence of the jungle, and "he claimed that the pulse of blood in his eardrums during a bout with malaria on the trip gave him the idea of the drumbeat used throughout the play."[12] O'Neill and Vachel Lindsay, author of "The Congo" (1917), were influenced by Africana such as Stanley's *In Darkest Africa*, and Charles Sheeler's *African Negro Sculpture*.[13] It seems likely that both had also read Conrad's *Heart of Darkness*, with its depiction of the primordial darkness. Yet neither Lindsay nor O'Neill lifts his work to the level of Conrad's conclusion that savagery can reside in the hearts of all men. A more detailed account of the drumbeat idea for the play comes from another of O'Neill's biographers, Croswell Bowen. She quotes O'Neill as saying: "One day I was reading about one of the religious feasts in the Congo and the uses to which the drum was put there—how it starts at a normal pulse and is slowly accelerated until the heartbeat of everyone present corresponds to the frenzied beat of the drum. Here was the idea of an experiment. How could this sort of thing work on an audience in a theater?"[14] The idea of the magic silver bullet came to O'Neill from a black circus employee. He told O'Neill the story of

Vilbrun Guillaume Sam, who became dictator of Haiti and held onto his position for about six months. President Sam boasted, according to the version O'Neill heard, "They'll never get me with a lead bullet. I'll kill myself with a silver bullet first. Only a silver bullet can kill me."[15] From these sources and perhaps others O'Neill hit upon the two staggering effects of his play: the terrifying presence of the jungle and the increasing tempo of the tribal drumbeat.

It is generally well known that O'Neill waged and finally won an energetic campaign to get Charles Gilpin, who played Brutus Jones superbly, reinvited to the annual New York Drama League dinner of 1920. The original invitation had been withdrawn when members of the League protested at being asked to dine with a Negro. O'Neill was furious and exerted such pressure on the League that they reinvited the black actor. Yet the O'Neill who championed Gilpin on that occasion showed a very different attitude on another. Gilpin, obviously unhappy with certain aspects of his role, made several changes in the script, including a substitution of "black baby" for O'Neill's "nigger." When O'Neill discovered this, he told Gilpin, "If I ever catch you rewriting my lines again, you black bastard, I'm going to beat you up."[16] These two incidents seem to be characteristic of O'Neill's racial ambivalence. He could both defend Gilpin against segregation and call him a "black bastard." He created a role that helped to establish the careers of Charles Gilpin and Paul Robeson, yet approached his black portraits with insensitivity and maladroitness, perpetuating pejorative images of black life, as I shall point out.

As the play opens, Brutus Jones, after fleeing from the United States, has established himself within two years as emperor of a small island in the West Indies. Life has become so pleasant that he has almost forgotten the possibility of white intervention or a native revolt. In rising to his position of wealth and power, Jones has exhibited those qualities of free-enterprise leadership he has assimilated from successful whites during his ten years as a pullman car porter: shrewdness, aggressiveness, self-reliance, strength of will.

Yet this reasonably attractive and heroic portrait of a black adventurer quickly turns to stereotype. Consider the playwright's opening description of the protagonist:

> Jones enters from the right. He is a tall, powerfully-built, full-blooded Negro of middle age. His features are typically Negroid, yet there is something decidedly distinctive about his face—an underlying strength of will, a hardy, self-reliant confidence in himself that inspires respect. His eyes are alive with a keen, cunning intelligence. In manner he is shrewd, suspicious, evasive. He wears a light-blue uniform coat, sprayed with brass buttons, heavy gold chevrons on his shoulders, gold braid on his collar, cuffs, etc. His pants are bright red, with a light-blue stripe down the side. Patent leather laced boots with brass spurs, and a belt with a long-barreled, pearl-handled revolver in a holster, complete his makeup. Yet there is something

not altogether ridiculous about his grandeur. He has a way of carrying it off.[17]

The words "yet" and "not altogether ridiculous" reveal O'Neill's essential attitude toward Jones. The emperor has certain "distinctive" qualities despite his "typically Negroid" features. His dress is perhaps "not altogether" but mostly "ridiculous."

O'Neill's portrait of Jones might be compared with Roi Ottley's description of Marcus Garvey's parade through Harlem in August 1920:

> His Excellency, Marcus Garvey, Provisional President of Africa, led the demonstration bedecked in a dazzling uniform of purple, green, and black, with gold braid, and a thrilling hat with white plumes "as long as leaves of Guinea grass."[18]

The occasion was the first national convention of the four-million-member United Negro Improvement Association, of which Garvey was the much heralded president. Given the attention paid Garvey in the New York newspapers, it is likely that O'Neill would have been aware of this "Black Moses" and of his plans for the recolonization of Africa. O'Neill's portrait of Jones and Ottley's description of Garvey are strikingly similar. When O'Neill finished work on *The Emperor Jones*, in September 1920, Garvey was still at the apex of his power. Ironically, the fate of Brutus Jones seems to anticipate the eventual corruption that later riddled Garvey's U.N.I.A., and his disgrace and eventual deportation. Despite these parallels and possible influences, O'Neill's treatment of Emperor Brutus Jones creates quite a different effect, as we shall soon see.

Even though O'Neill establishes Jones as an individual with a particular past and a distinct personality, the tone of his portrait is pejorative. The Emperor Jones is more clown than hero, ultimately a laughable pretender to be pitied and dismissed. O'Neill's bias reveals itself as the play progresses, presenting the defeat not of white colonialism and free enterprise, as some critics would have it, but of an "uppity" black man who presumed to model himself after successful white exploiters. The revenge of the play is complete as Jones reverts to a savage and is defeated, then killed by his own people.

When he discovers a rebellion is in the making, Jones leaves his palace swiftly and reaches the margin of the primitive landscape, the great forest, with ease. Having studied the methods of white colonialists, he has made elaborate plans for just such an emergency, stashing away a supply of food and memorizing the trails through the forest. He also knows where to meet a French gunboat that will take him to Martinique and to the fortune in taxes he has extracted from his subjects.

It quickly becomes clear that Jones is his own worst enemy, virtually defeating himself in the jungle with his own irrationality even before the natives begin to hunt him. Although prepared to penetrate the jungle before his pursuers mobilize, he is ill-equipped to venture the jungle of his mind. O'Neill has allowed his hero to succeed temporarily by imitating what he has learned from white colonialism and capitalism. Once under the pressure of pursuit, however, this modern black hero quickly disintegrates to his former tribal identity. Like the black people in Vachel Lindsay's "The Congo," he is terrified he will encounter "skullfaced, lean witch-doctors" and "tattooed cannibals" with "voo-doo rattles."

For a time the forces opposing him are kept at bay. In Scene Two Brutus can find neither his cache of food nor the trail he has marked, and this begins to unnerve him. It is the "formless fears"—manifestations of his own growing fear and guilt—that he cannot tolerate. In reaction he fires the first of his six bullets.

Scenes Three and Four reinforce the feeling that we are being conducted through the jungle of a man's mind in storm. In these hallucinatory episodes Brutus imagines he meets first Jeff, the black man who died of razor wounds he inflicted, then the prison gang and the white guard he killed. If a man is plagued and tormented by his own past and his unconscious, how can he expect to cope with his conscious mind and external reality?

In the first four scenes O'Neill has employed techniques which appear in many of his plays. The first of these is the retrograde movement of Jones away from crisis and from life itself. As Eugene Waith comments, "The backward movement of [O'Neill's] characters is always flight from the problems posed by existence; forward movement is the heroic, sometimes ecstatic, acceptance of them."[19] The second technique, as John Gassner puts it, is O'Neill's "response to the vogue of depth psychology" through which he attempts to dramatize "subconscious tensions."[20] With Scene Five he adds to these a third dimension, based on the general concept known as atavism. Atavism stems from two general postulates: that some individuals exhibit traits and characteristics of ancestors, absent in intervening generations, and that individuals occasionally revert to the features and lifestyles of their ancestors.

This fifth scene is crucial to our understanding of the play. In the three previous incidents Brutus Jones has faced images from his own past. It has been possible, so far, to believe that O'Neill is presenting an *Inferno*-like trip through Jones's personal past. The hallucinations can even be explained as resulting from Jones's extreme hunger. "Sho'! Dat was all in yo' own head an' yo' eyes. Wasn't nothin' there! Wasn't no Jeff! Know what? Yo' jus' get seein' dem things 'cause yo' belly's empty and you's sick wid hunger inside. Hunger 'fects yo' head an' yo' eyes. Any fool know dat" (p. 38). With Scene Five, however, we move from Jones's personal to his racial past. He has long since lost his emperor's costume; he is barefooted now and clad in a loin cloth, his body scratched and bruised. He has already cast off the trappings of royalty; the light-blue jacket with its gold chevrons and braid, the patent leather boots, the brass spurs. Terrified by the last encounter, Brutus collapses beside a stump, overcome by feelings of guilt over the deaths of Jeff and the prison guard. "Lawd! I done wrong! . . . Forgive me, Lawd! Forgive dis po' sinner! *(Then beseeching terrifiedly)* An' keep dem away, Lawd! Keep dem away from me! And stop dat drum soundin' in my ears! Dat begin to sound ha'nted, too" (p. 42).

He rises from this prayer imagining he is in the midst of a slave auction; a group of white Southern ladies and gentlemen are looking at him admiringly, prepared to bid handsomely. Brutus watches the pantomime before him, the auctioneer's silent spiel, the planters raising their fingers in bidding. ". . . *Convulsed with raging hatred and fear,*" Brutus shouts, "Is dis a auction? Is yo' sellin' me like dey uster befo' de war? . . . I shows you I'se a free nigger, damn yo' souls!" (pp. 44–45). He fires at the auctioneer and the planter. With the shots, the walls of the forest close in on the auction, and Jones, crying out, rushes headlong into the forest.

In Scene Six Jones find himself inside the hold of a slave ship. He has receded further back in racial time and—as with the slave auction—beyond the experimental level of his own existence. He is moving back through the history of slavery. Shackled with other slaves to the walls of the vessel, Jones is at first terrified by his new circumstance, throwing himself to the deck to "shut out the sight." But he soon resigns himself and joins them in their wail of despair: " . . . his voice, as if under some uncanny compulsion, starts with the others, swaying back and forth. His voice reaches the highest pitch of sorrow, of desolation" (p. 47).

The last of the hallucinatory scenes finds Jones, by now a stone-faced shell of a man, before his ancestral and racial birthplace, and presumably on the shores of the Congo. There is nothing overtly terrifying about the setting: it is quiet; he is alone. Jones sinks before the stone altar, kneeling in devotion to its unknown deity, "as if in obedience to some obscure impulse. . . . " Then Brutus catches hold of himself, shocked by his own obeisance before a pagan altar, and cries for help from his Christian God. He tries to resist the pagan cult but is so thoroughly hypnotized by its ritual dance and the gestures of the witch-doctor that even his resistance becomes feigned, a pantomime expressing flight and pursuit: "Jones has become completely hypnotized. His voice joins in the incantation, in the cries; he beats time with his hands and sways his body to and fro from the waist. The whole spirit and meaning of the dance has entered into him, has become his spirit" (p. 49). O'Neill has been preparing us for this culminating scene from the moment Jones entered the jungle—and before. From momentary harmony with his racial past, he realizes—in horror—the intent of the frenzied dancing: "The forces of evil demand sacrifice. They must be appeased. . . . Jones seems to sense the meaning of this. It is he who must offer himself for sacrifice" (pp. 49–50). Despite his fervent prayers, he receives no help from the Christian God. Although Jones survives the scene, it is a pyrrhic victory, for he has had to fire his silver bullet at the crocodile god. He emerges from the depths of the forest a defeated ruin of a man, and is shot by his pursuers with a silver bullet.

Edwin Engle sees *The Hairy Ape*, rather than *The Emperor Jones*, as O'Neill's fullest exploration of primitivism and atavism. O'Neill himself characterized Yank as "a symbol of a man, who has lost that old harmony with nature, the harmony which he used to have as an animal and has not acquired in a spiritual way."[21] In fact, none of O'Neill's heroes finds easy sanctuary or salvation; if not terrified by emanations from their own past, they are brutalized by the economic and industrial forces of the present. Characteristically, O'Neill's heroes live in a perilous state, either enslaved or suffering a loss of vitality. Engle indicates O'Neill's debt to Jack London and Frank Norris in the use of the ancestral past. Both explored in their novels the "theme of the persistence in modern man of the brutish cave man" in which a dissociation of personality results from the conflict between the hero and his primordial ancestry.[22]

The particular thrust of *The Emperor Jones*, however, is in the direction of a black atavism. It exploits those stereotypes in the white imagination which associate blacks with the savage and a jungle landscape. It is as if O'Neill were saying that the argument for *black* atavism is more plausible because of the black man's more recent jungle past. Jones's thin surface of reason crumbles before the great, seething maelstrom of his fears, "ha'nts," apparitions, and the call of his "pagan" religion. It surges through his blood; the beat of the tom-tom is the beat of his savage heart, the drumbeat stopping at the instant of his death. The modern black man is a walking savage thinly disguised by western culture and religion; he is his own greatest enemy—or so the play would have it.

It is not particularly surprising that O'Neill was inclined to depict Jones as a savage who had taken on the veneer of white culture. Sterling Brown documents a sizeable body of antebellum white literature which emphasizes the alleged savage and beastly qualities of black people.[23] Among these works are Charles Carroll's *The Negro a Beast* (1900) and Thomas Dixon's infamous *The Leopard's Spots* and *The Clansman* (1903). Dixon's images of savage black men ravaging precious white women were too blatantly racist to influence many other writers. Yet in more subtle ways, writing in what I call the savage mode reinforces the assumption that blacks are innately primitive people. Such writing may be seen as appealing to what Roy Harvey Pearce calls a "gentle, civilized terror in the presence of the savage."[24] *The Emperor Jones* appealed emotionally to many who probably would have rejected the same ideas, if considered rationally.

Brutus Jones embodies some of the oldest white stereotypes of black character. We recall from the opening scene the gaudy, somewhat absurd, although "not *altogether* ridiculous" [italics are mine] costume Jones wears. His name has about it a comic suggestiveness as well: Brutus the Brute. It is not unlike the name suggestion of Babo (baboon) in *Benito Cereno*. By invoking that vein of white humor regarding elaboration and pretense in black names (Emperor Brutus Jones), O'Neill establishes a mock-serious tone from the start, and puts Jones's position as emperor in comic jeopardy.[25] The gaudy facade of the palace, pillars, and throne, and the absence of subjects, only add to this atmosphere. In the jungle he becomes a Sambo figure; his "eyes pop out," and he is too scared to run. The defeat of Jones is the defeat of a black pretender, not of the white entrepreneurs and exploiters he copied, for O'Neill made him a mock-emperor in a gaudy costume.

In his autobiography *The Big Sea*, Langston Hughes describes the disastrous and abbreviated run of *The Emperor Jones* in Harlem:

> Somewhat later, I recall a sincere but unfortunate attempt on Jules Bledsoe's part to bring "Art" to Harlem. He appeared in Eugene O'Neill's *The Emperor Jones* at the old Lincoln Theater on 135th Street, a theater that had, for all its noble name, been devoted largely to ribald, but highly entertaining, vaudeville of the "Butterbeans and Susie" type. The audience didn't know what to make of *The Emperor Jones* on a stage where "Shake That Thing" was formerly the rage. And when the Emperor started running naked through the forest, hearing the Little Frightened Fears, naturally they howled with laughter.
>
> "Them ain't no ghosts, fool!" the spectators cried from the orchestra. "Why don't you come on out o' that jungle—back to Harlem where you belong?"
>
> In the manner of Stokowski hearing a cough at the Academy of Music, Jules Bledsoe stopped dead in his tracks, advanced to the footlights, and proceeded to lecture his audience on manners in the theater. But the audience wanted none of *The Emperor Jones*. And their manners had been all right at the other shows at the Lincoln, where they took part in the performances at will. So when Brutus continued his flight, the audience again howled with laughter. And that was the end of *The Emperor Jones* on 135th Street.[26]

Although O'Neill's Harlem audience probably knew little, intellectually, of psychic journeys and the racial unconscious, they knew that the jungle had no connection with their lives, and they recognized the stereotypes O'Neill was using.

Ironically, the play continued to succeed outside of Harlem. The excellent performances of the black actors Gilpin and Robeson and the theatrical effects O'Neill gleaned from his superficial contacts with black life combined to produce a play that, along with a few others by O'Neill, "shaped the course of American Drama in its most significant developmental period, from 1915 to about 1930."[27] Nor did *The Emperor Jones* die in the succeeding decades as an antiquated and pejorative portrait of a black man. DuBose Heyward, author of *Porgy*, wrote the scenario for the film version of *The Emperor Jones*, which also starred Paul Robeson. Louis Gruenberg's operatic version of the play opened at the Metropolitan Opera in January 1933, with Lawrence Tibbett as Jones.

How are we to account for this popularity, even into our own time? To be sure, the play incorporated stunning effects, and was strengthened by excellent black acting. Yet black critics and audiences were able to see the stereotypes and the "put-down" that white audiences took delight in: the "civilized terror in the presence of the savage," as Pearce so aptly phrased it. Had O'Neill been less interested in dramatic effects, less swayed by racial stereotypes, he might have written authentic tragedy in which Brutus Jones came to the recognition that he had exploited and underestimated the skill of his own people. Instead, O'Neill gives the last lines to the Cockney Smithers, establishing beyond all doubt the play's racial bias. Smithers dismisses Jones *and* his assassins with contemptuous scorn. "Stupid as 'ogs, the lot of 'em! Blarstered niggers!"

The writing of two other Village Bohemians, Waldo Frank and Carl Van Vechten, also needs to be considered. Frank founded the influential journal *Seven Arts* in 1917, and became close friends with black writer Jean Toomer. Throughout Frank's writing runs one common strand: a depiction of America as a nation dominated by puritanism and oppressed by intellectual sterility. In his exasperation he termed White American Culture "a vast and juiceless California fruit." Like many other writers of his generation, Frank felt that America and Europe were spiritually wounded.

As a source of salvation for the terrible sickness he saw plaguing American life, Frank turned to the soil and to the lives of blacks living in the rural south. He once observed that most whites would probably regard the "Alabama Negro as an illiterate, often drunk, rather vulgar creature," but to Frank this same black farmer "drew from the soil, and the sky a grace which is refined like the grace of a flower."[28] Quite understandably, the black characters in Frank's novel *Holiday* (1922) are bursting with a wholesome earthiness even as they live in fear of the pathetic white society that dominates them.

Waldo Frank went to greater lengths than any other white writer of this period to research black life. For example, he travelled with Jean Toomer through the South and lived in black communities during the fall of 1921 and the winter of 1922. The remarkable thing about these trips is that Frank passed as a black man so he could experience black life as an insider. Toomer coached him in the nuances of black speech; they rode the Jim Crow coaches together and lived with Toomer's friends in Alabama, Mississippi, and Louisiana. Here was a unique sharing of common materials by a black and a white writer, each filling his notebooks—Toomer, for what emerged as his justly famous novel, *Cane*, and Frank, for his own mediocre novel, *Holiday*.[29] For all the insight he gained into black life and racial conflict, *Holiday* is flawed by a melodramatic plot, cumbersome symbolism, and a ponderous style.

More important to the Harlem Renaissance was the influence and writing of Carl Van Vechten. "Carlo," as he was called by Langston Hughes, had his own literary salon, from which he conducted a "know the Negro" campaign. He brought writers of both races together, striving to overcome prejudice and misunderstanding. He also helped a number of black writers find publishers for their work. His novel *Nigger Heaven* (1926) explored the seamy and primitive side of Harlem life, much to the shock of some Harlem writers, but it was perfectly packaged for that insatiable white appetite in the 1920s—for anything black and primitive.

By contrast, the Harlem Renaissance represented a serious effort by black artists and critics to interpret black life on their own terms. To be sure, works like *The Emperor Jones, Holiday,* and *Nigger Heaven* provided encouragement, if not challenge, to black writers. As Robert Bone put it, they "created a sympathetic audience for the serious treatment of Negro subjects."[30] It was surely a two-way street, for white writers encouraged and occasionally sponsored the works of their black counterparts; but they also drew their materials and inspiration from black life, and often at its expense.

Black writers in Harlem during the Renaissance expressed a growing objection to "counterfeit" portraits of black life. Black critics writing in journals such as *Dial, Opportunity, Crisis, Outlook,* and *Independent* assessed portraits of black life produced by white and black writers alike. Benjamin Brawley commented that well-intentioned white writers such as O'Neill, Ridgley Torrence (*Granny Maumee*), and Ernest Culbertson (*Goat Alley*) apparently portrayed blacks as primitives because their cultural blinders limited them to a conception of blacks as "inferior, superstitious, half-ignorant." Such writers, he continued, could not begin to render the "immense paradox of racial life."[31] Toward the end of the decade further resistance to white images of black life began to be heard. *Crisis,* for example, ran a five-issue symposium on how black people ought to be depicted in American literature.[32] George C. Morse summarizes much of the objection to primitive portraits and voodooism in fiction in his comment, "They are legion who believe that if a native band from the jungles of Africa should parade the streets beating their tom-toms, all the black inhabitants of our city would lose their acquired dignity and dance to its rhythm by virtue of inheritance alone."[33]

Despite the new consciousness that was growing in Harlem, we have seen that some of the old stereotypes of blacks persisted in white literature, and that certain new ones were created. Quite consistently, whites continued throughout the twenties, and even more recently, to look to black life as a source of primitivism.[34] No matter how complementary the intention, the result is a quality of racial predisposition that impedes realistic depiction of black lives. In *The Big Sea,* Langston Hughes comments aptly on this point. He was for a time sustained by a white patroness who was willing to support his work so long as he shaped it to her conception of black culture. Eventually he had to sever the relationship, as he realized that her demands were a threat both to his art and his self-identity:

> She wanted me to be primitive and know and feel the intuitions of the primitive. But, unfortunately, I did not feel the rhythms of the primitive surging through me, and I could not live and write as though I did. I was only an American Negro—who had loved the surface of Africa and the rhythms of Africa—but I was not Africa. I was Chicago and Kansas City and Broadway and Harlem.[35]

NOTES

1. Frederick Hoffman, *The Twenties: American Writing in the Postwar Decade* (New York: Viking, 1949) and Robert Bone, *The Negro Novel in America* (New Haven: Yale Univ. Press, 1965). Far more thorough is Nathan Huggins' *Harlem Renaissance* (New York: Oxford Univ. Press, 1971).

2. See Doris Abramson, *Negro Playwrights in The American Theatre* (New York: Columbia Univ. Press, 1969).

3. Travis Bogard, *Contour in Time: The Plays of Eugene O'Neill* (New York: Oxford Univ. Press, 1972), p. 134.

4. Cited in Croswell Bowen, *The Curse of the Misbegotten: A Tale of the House of O'Neill* (New York: McGraw-Hill, 1959), p. 132.

5. "'Emperor Jones' By O'Neill Gives Chance for Cheers," *New York Tribune*, 4 Nov. 1920: 8.

6. Bogard, *Contour in Time*, p. 134.

7. Abramson, *Negro Playwrights in The American Theatre*, p. 27.

8. Bogard, *Contour in Time*, p. 134.

9. *The Negro Novel in America* (New Haven: Yale Univ. Press, 1958), p. 60.

10. Bone, *Negro Novel in America*, p. 60.

11. *The New Negro* (New York: Albert & Charles Boni, 1925), p. 5.

12. Bogard, *Contour in Time*, p. 135.

13. Bogard, *Contour in Time*, p. 135.

14. Bowen, *Curse of the Misbegotten*, p. 132.

15. Bowen, *Curse of the Misbegotten*, p. 131.

16. Arthur and Barbara Gelb, *O'Neill* (New York: Harper & Bros., 1960), p. 449.

17. Eugene O'Neill, *The Emperor Jones* (New York: Appleton, 1921), pp. 10–11. Subsequent references to this edition appear parenthetically within the text.

18. Roi Ottley, *New World A-Coming* (New York: Arno Press and The New York *Times*, 1968), p. 76.

19. "Eugene O'Neill: An Exercise in Unmasking," *O'Neill*, ed. John Gasner, (Englewood Cliffs, N.J.: Prentice Hall, 1964), p. 33.

20. "The Nature of O'Neill's Achievement: A Summary and Appraisal," *O'Neill*, p. 166.

21. *The Haunted Heroes of Eugene O'Neill* (Cambridge, Mass.: Harvard Univ. Press, 1953), p. 54.

22. Engle, *Haunted Heroes*, p. 54.

23. "Negro Characters as Seen by White Authors," *Journal of Negro Education* 2 (1933): 179–203.

24. *The Savages of America: A Study of the Indian and the Idea of Civilization* (Baltimore: Johns Hopkins Univ. Press, 1965), p. 243.

25. In this context of established white stereotypes of black people, comments such as those of Emil Roy [see *Comparative Drama* 2 (Spring 1968): 22ff.] that "Jones's red pants and gaudy throne link him with suffering heroes like Prometheus," and "disguised gods like Apollo" seem ludicrous.

26. *The Big Sea* (New York: Hill & Wang, 1940), pp. 258–59.

27. Bogard, *Contour in Time*, p. xiii.

28. Waldo Frank, *In the American Jungle* (New York: Farrar & Rinehart, 1936).

29. Waldo Frank, *Holiday* (New York: Boni & Liveright, 1923).

30. Bone, *Negro Novel in America*, p. 60.

31. "The Negro in American Fiction," *Dial* 60 (1916): 445.

32. For detailed discussion on this topic see Seymour L. Gross, "Stereotype to Archetype: The Negro in American Literary Criticism," in *Images of the Negro in American Litera-*

ture, ed. Seymour Gross and John Edward Hardy (Chicago: Univ. of Chicago Press, 1966), pp. 1–26.

33. "The Fictitious Negro," *Outlook and Independent* 152 (1929): 578–79.

34. See John Cooley, *Savages and Naturals: Black Portraits by White Writers in Modern American Literature* (Newark: Univ. of Delaware Press, 1982).

35. Hughes, *The Big Sea*, p. 325.

GOING TO SCHOOL TO DU BOSE HEYWARD

WILLIAM H. SLAVICK

DuBose Heyward's brief ascendancy among Southern regionalists in the middle 1920s—as poet, novelist, and playwright—was quickly eclipsed by the emergence of the Fugitive poets, Elizabeth Madox Roberts, Thomas Wolfe, and William Faulkner by the end of the decade. Today he is little more than mentioned in discussion of important figures in the Southern Renaissance, but his social realism, which juxtaposes the sterility of the white Charleston aristocracy and the possibility of life in the Negro community, deserves recognition.

It is within the framework of the Harlem Renaissance—black writers from Kansas to the Indies and from New Orleans to New York as well as Eugene O'Neill, Sherwood Anderson, Carl Van Vechten, and Waldo Frank—that Heyward remains significant. His novel *Porgy*, with its human treatment of Catfish Row; the 1927 Broadway staging of the DuBose and Dorothy Heyward version; and *Mamba's Daughters*, a second Charleston novel concerned with the relationship of black primitivism and folk culture to high art and changing times, all qualify Heyward for such consideration. Heyward has been mistakenly introduced as a "member of Harlem's intellectual colony" and "a Southern Negro of the old tradition," but he was of the Charleston white aristocracy (an ancestor signed the Declaration of Independence) and apparently did not meet any members of the Harlem "intellectual colony" until late 1926.[1] His identification with the Harlem Renaissance has continued in second-hand booksellers' catalogs and occasional identification of him as a black writer. But in assessments of the Harlem Renaissance, Heyward is given a relatively small place. This is mistaken.

Heyward's keenness of observation of the black man in Charleston and its surrounding environs—in his own community—is marked by an authority and freedom from the exotic and fake often lacking in Anderson, Van Vechten, O'Neill, and the less gifted of the black writers. His largely successful escape from stereotypes was recognized by Donald Davidson, who approved of the way Heyward's "Negro was allowed to stand forth as a human being in his own right" and by Countee Cullen, who called *Porgy* the "best novel by a white about Negroes he had read" and suggested that it "gives one the uncanny feeling that Negroes are human beings and that white and black southerners are brothers under the skin."[2] Cullen's remarks properly extend the measure of Heyward's realism to an understanding of white Southerners as well.

At a time when much of the interest in Harlem focused on the black man's primitive innocence and freedom from inhibitions, Heyward was painfully aware that the black man was being forced to change in Charleston and Harlem, a change that endangered those very qualities whites had come to admire. Heyward emphasized this awareness in the poem-prayer prelude to *Porgy:*

> Porgy, Maria, and Bess,
> Robbins, and Peter, and Crown;
> Life was a three-stringed harp
> Brought from the woods to town.
>
> Marvelous tunes you rang
> From passion, and death, and birth,
> You who had laughed and wept
> On the warm, brown lap of the earth.
>
> Now in your untried hands
> An instrument, terrible, new,
> Is thrust by a master who frowns,
> Demanding strange songs of you.
>
> God of the White and Black,
> Grant us great hearts on the way
> That we may understand
> Until you have learned to play.[3]

Such a burden of change marks all of Heyward's fiction as well as his three plays.

Heyward's most intense interest in the black world of Charleston also parallels the post-World War I disillusionment with civilization and turn from Puritan restraint to the primitive qualities found in African art and the uninhibited night world of Harlem. Also, on his own and apart from the literary world's turn toward primitivism, Heyward's sense of the deadness of white Southern culture and study of Catfish Row led him to see in simple folk not an escape into primitive exoticism but into the possibility of life. For Heyward, the primitive life he admired and envied is observed and realized rather than thinly imagined. That life is rooted in the earth, the past, and ordinary daily experience. The result is a responsibility and restraint in treatment notably missing from "The Congo," *Nigger Heaven, Dark Laughter*, and O'Neill's plays.

Finally, Heyward came to recognize, as others did not, what the essential rhythm of Negro life was. He appreciated the strength of the black man's faith, the reality of his community, and the essentiality of his race's suffering and long history of suffering. In 1959, a long-time leading Harlem writer summed up Heyward's accomplishment. Langston Hughes suggested that Negro writers could go to school to Heyward, the writer, who saw, "with his white eyes, wonderful, poetic human qualities in the inhabitants of Catfish Row that makes them come alive in his book."[4]

I

Heyward was slow to find his proper subject in the black man. In 1918, he had clipped a story of a crippled goat-cart beggar shooting at a woman and noted the beggar's display of manhood. Later he explained that, before seeing the article, he "had concluded that such a life could never lift above the dead level of the commonplace," while in the brief account "one could read passion, hate, despair."[5] Nevertheless the 1918 clipping went unused for several years.

Only two poems collected in his first two volumes had dealt with the black man and none of his seven apprentice stories. Those two poems look sharply into the black man's plight in a white man's world. "Gamesters All" is a brief drama of a fatalistic crapshooter's instinctive gamble for freedom through flight and a policeman's single "sporting"—albeit fatal—shot. The ironic tone is clear. (Heyward had witnessed such a shooting; it was this experience that made him decide to write about blacks.) "Modern Philosopher" balances images of black servants who lack Puritan morals but work faithfully in the white world, "undaunted by a century of strife," and a black world of carefree music and simple faith. Another poem, "Jasbo Brown," published in 1925, is a flawed imitation of Vachel Lindsay and recounts the lonely life of a blues pianist. Heyward did not pursue this interest in black experience further, however, until after he had traveled north to the MacDowell Colony in 1922 and 1923 where he met his wife, a budding Ohio playwright; had spent some time in New York City; and, in 1924, had sold his insurance business to give himself entirely to writing. Upon returning to the MacDowell Colony in 1925, he settled down to writing *Porgy*.

The *Porgy* story is simple and familiar, a story of a summer in a Negro quarter in Charleston at the turn of the century. It is novella length and seemingly little more than a series of vignettes in structure. But *Porgy* is generally considered Heyward's most accomplished work and it is, with Jean Toomer's *Cane*, the most successful piece of fiction associated with the Negro Renaissance of the 1920s.[6] It was also the first longer work of fiction with predominantly Negro characters to appeal to the whole country.

That appeal results from Porgy's heroic but doomed effort to find human dignity and happiness. The achievement is in Heyward's realization of the conflict that leads to Porgy's defeat. In Bess, Porgy finds contentment. Surviving the hurricane, Porgy experiences a sense of worth: "'You an' me, Bess,' he said with conviction. 'We sho' is a little somet'ing attuh all'" (p. 148). But in the end, when Bess is gone, the Row leaves "Porgy and the goat alone in an irony of morning sunlight" (p. 196). His superstitious fear of Crown's corpse, the white world's interference, and Bess's weakness for men and drugs in Porgy's absence bring defeat.

The weaknesses of Porgy and Bess are representative of Catfish Row. The Negroes of the Row are unready for the world in which they must live. Porgy is more intelligent than most, but—like Crown, Clara, and Jake, Bess and Sportin' Life—his hopes and self-discipline are insufficient. Primitive instincts, innocence, and lack of self-discipline; the forces of the white world surrounding them; and fate are formidable antagonists and their undoing. The movement of the summer toward Porgy's defeat is really a choral movement in which all move from life and hope and love toward death, resignation, and loneliness.

The one notable power the protagonists bring to the struggle is a spirit of community. Catfish Row has its own inner rhythm and style; its own code, especially in dealing with the white world; and its rituals of joy and defeat. Thus, the single enveloping conflict is the almost, but not even, struggle of Catfish Row with the snares of life. Heyward's genius is his ability to explore the operation of this complexity of forces in the modest space of *Porgy.*

The initial scene, the crap game that ends in Crown's murder of Robbins, begins the orchestration of these forces. The murder is enacted before "shadowy watchers" who "wailed eerily" (p. 20). Porgy, who "shivered violently, whimpered in the gloom, then threw himself across his threshold," is a focal witness (p. 21). Heyward's imagery turns the scene into an atavistic ritual: Crown exhibits "gleaming teeth," "thrusting jaw," "sloping brow," and the "prehensile claw" of a cotton hook, and he emits a "low snarl." "Down, down, down the centuries they slid," the narrator tells us, until "a heady, bestial stench absorbed all other odors" (pp. 19–20). Since Robbins most aspires to white ways, Crown's conquest is a victory for the jungle.

The following saucer burial is a community ritual of identification with Robbins, of resignation, of common cause in financing the burial, and, finally, of triumphant song in consignment of Robbins to heaven. The burial spirituals, one providing a catharsis of grief and the other an act of faith, are followed by the panic of superstition as all flee the graveyard—the second hymn has not quieted primitive fears of death.

The episode begins with a growling thunderhead that left "the air hot, vitiated, and moist" and the Row irritable, as Crown's "moody silence" illustrates (p. 16). It ends with the police taking Peter away as a material witness and a creditor repossessing his things.

In Part I, the setting becomes characters, the characters a community, and the community an action, with the Row as protagonist and nature, primitivism, and the white police as antagonists. It is a recurrent pattern, as the other tragedies of love in the book demonstrate. In another powerful Row scene, the conjure-beset Clara abandons herself in the storm in a futile effort to save Jake. The separation of Porgy and Bess involves Crown's bestiality, Bess's wildness, and Porgy's "aboriginal" laugh; the jailing of Bess and then Porgy; and Porgy's superstitious fears (p. 172). The Porgy–Bess relationship is emphasized by the space given it and by its centrality. It is also marked by strong suggestions of a mythic–moral dimension: a snake-like Sportin' Life tempts the repentant Bess, and Bess, who passes a rattler in search of a fan-shaped leaf in the Kittiwar wilderness, meets a seducer, Crown, whose "small wicked eyes burned" (p. 119). But whether agents or principals, the antagonists remain the same.

The structure of the novella is itself an illustration of Heyward's subtle shifts of attention between Porgy and the Row and among the forces—the primitive, the white world, and fate—opposed to the Row's good fortune. After the wild fight and emotional outpouring of Part I, the second part is a quiet interlude between encounters with primitive and white power. Part III involves both Porgy's conquest of Archdale with his odorous goat cart and Bess's conquest by life in the white man's jail. Apart from Bess's encounter with Crown and the consequent apprehension regarding his return, the primitive parade and picnic in Part IV show the Row in command of its fate. But then, in Part V, the storm confronts the Row with Destiny personified. In Part VI, the Row saves Porgy from discovery, after his murder of Crown, but then a solitary buzzard settling on the roof of his room sends him in flight from a primitive sense of doom toward the woods of his origin and into the casual hands of white justice.

Each of the major characters in the novel is, the action suggests, a distinctive battlefield for these forces. Porgy is shrewd, sensitive, hopeful, and patient. But his shriveled legs and primitive laugh upon killing Crown and his fear of Crown's corpse indicate that he remains divided. Bess recognizes Porgy's humanity and love, but her honesty and sense of values reside in a primitive mind challenged in ways it has not been disciplined to withstand. Serena's straitlaced Puritan religion leads her to reject the life of the Row and her husband to his death, just as Crown's violence exiles him from society. As an emancipated Harlem black, Sportin' Life is an example of the tragedy Heyward sees awaiting Negroes divorced from their roots and values and cast loose in the modern world. Maria, who presides over the island of humanity that is the Catfish Row chorus—as surrogate mother, moral arbiter and symbol of order, is herself caught between her dependence on conjuring and her grudging respect for Christianity while authoritatively upholding the Row's basic law of survival. The characters of Catfish Row tell us that the Negro's effort to "learn to play" is beset with major difficulties.

How does Heyward view these powerful antagonistic forces and assess their effects on Catfish Row?

The initial characterization of the primitive influence operating in Heyward's world is in the poem prelude reference to the journey of Row inhabitants from "woods to town." The primitive traits and acts of the Row are traceable less to atavistic memory than to the isolated, elemental, largely undisciplined life—the free natural life (a real or fancied antecedent of the Golden Age)—of Negro cabins hidden away from plantation houses and the demands of white society. In that world, Heyward posits, the black man had his own relaxed code and way of life, which help explain Crown's conduct, Porgy's violent defense of Bess, and the characters' sundry superstitions. The separation from that natural state and its simple gratifications of emotional need, rather than some African susceptibility to drugs, better explains Bess's lapses. Heyward's characters are, first of all, Americans, and their conduct is rooted in their American experience.

Heyward is not altogether unambiguous in defining the primitivism encountered in Catfish Row. The African note is struck in the initial description of Porgy's "unadulterated Congo blood" and his "pleasant atavistic calm" (pp. 13–14). The lapses into wildness are frequent. Crown turns into a beast in the fight with Robbins. Under the influence of dope, Bess "whirled like a dervish and called horribly upon her God, striking and clawing wildly" (p. 86). The parade strikes a "wild, barbaric chord" (p. 113). Animal imagery extends from the atavism of the crap game fight to Maria's characterization of Sportin' Life as a "yellow snake" (p. 127). However, Heyward also associates certain traits he admires—Porgy's "infinite patience" and "unrealized, but terrific, energy" and the marchers' abandon in the parade—with the Row's primitive character (p. 13). Yet, the repeated falls, which Eric Bentley sees as unrelieved, and the often violent note in the past suggest as well Heyward's somewhat condescending participation in the common Southern belief of the time that it might take centuries to civilize the Negro and that perhaps he is, after all, somehow less than a man.[7] In any case, the handicap of the primitive past is so great that none surmount it.

These ambiguities remain unresolved in *Porgy*, but Heyward's attitude is sufficiently clear. The lapses of Porgy, Bess, Crown, even those of Clara and Jake, are, first of all, lapses in a learning process such as might be found following from the frustrations of virtually any simple rural folk thrust into a modern industrial society. But their frequency and seriousness indicate a level of difficulty that contributes greatly to the effect of pathos. At the same time, in such major scenes as the saucer burial, the parade and picnic, the hurricane, and the choral exchange of silences with Porgy in his loss of Bess, Heyward recognizes a primitive dimension, a culture, that he clearly admires and would not see disappear in the adjustment to "town."

The lack of atavistic motivation, the narrator's civilized view of the Row's failings, the restraint and the understatement indicate a notable movement toward genuine realism in the treatment of primitivism. Thus, Heyward's primitivism must be clearly distinguished from the pseudo-realism that Alain Locke called the "last serious majority cliché, that of blood atavism and inherited Negro primitivism."[8] Where an inhibited Van Vechten character wallows in self-pity at her lack of the primitive passions she sees in other blacks, Heyward evokes a largely indefinite sense of atavistic influences but focuses on the lack of discipline and on the depth and quality of human feeling in the Row's and Porgy's expressions. While Heyward identified such primitive traits as savagery and strange rhythms as relics of a heritage quite unlike white Anglo-Saxon Protestantism, he also saw them as expressions of the elemental life Southern blacks experienced. And he knew very well that the song and dance of Catfish Row was the simple black man's ritual response to his frustrations and suffering in a white world and in no significant sense was it atavistic in origin or the continuance of African tradition. Heyward's restraint in the handling of primitivism is further evidenced by contrasting it with the strongly lyrical and mystical qualities in Toomer's Georgia scenes and in the haunting world of Julia Peterkin's superstitious and passionate rural folk. But the important distinction here is its distance from Van Vechten. When Van Vechten says, "She watched Lasca and Byron glide softly, dangerously, like panthers," it is something else than Heyward's big stevedore crossing the court, "his body moving easily with the panther-like flow of enormous muscular power under absolute control" (p. 44).[9] Heyward's simile is only a simile, fitting for the muscular stevedore. Van Vechten's is coupled with "dangerously" and follows the insistence that Lasca and Byron are more animal than she is or whites are in general. Heyward's blacks never forget, as does Vachel Lindsay in "The Congo," the 200 years between the jungle of his imagination and 1900. Nor does he ever, as Countee Cullen in "Heritage," have his contemporary characters hear great African drums beating.

Thus Porgy comes much closer to honesty about Negroes, closer to squaring with reality than does what Ralph Ellison calls the "Paul Robeson and silver bullet in the jungle bill of goods" of *Emperor Jones* and many other works of the Negro Renaissance.[10] As Harlan Hatcher observed long ago, Heyward succeeds in "giving to the primitive life the illusion of complete realism without losing the sense of awe and wonder and pathos which belong to romance."[11] It might be added that Heyward does so without sacrificing or ignoring what Alain Locke calls the disciplined, sophisticated, laconic, and fatalistic qualities of African expression.[12] Porgy manifests all of these qualities in an environment of exuberance and emotional upheaval, among a people whose art is equally emotional.

When primitive forces and nature do not bring trouble to the Row, the white man does. On the other hand, whites make no positive contribution to the Row beyond an occasional partial amelioration of the suffering other whites have caused. In this sense, the story becomes Heyward's ironic response to his prayer in the prelude poem: it is a story of the non-understanding of the Negro until he has "learned to play," for the understanding the Row receives from the white community is invariably a parody of understanding. The whites laugh as Robbins' funeral passes. The "vile-mouthed bearded Teuton" merchant leaves Peter only a chrome of "the Great Emancipator," which makes the reference to Porgy's "new emancipation" ironic (p. 33, p. 48). Peter well understands the white man's readiness to start him again on his weekly furniture installments: "'De buckra sho got nigger figgered out tuh a cent'" (p. 62).

Archdale's assistance to Peter and Frasier, who sells divorces outside the law, is pure paternalism. And the whites go on laughing—at the colorful parade as well as at Porgy's futile goat-cart flight from the police. Beyond this pervasive irony, Heyward's comments on race relations are largely concentrated in a few pages where Bess appears before the magistrate and the jail and jailers' attitudes are described. The scene begins with a description of the judge:

> Behind a high desk sat a man well past middle age. His florid complexion caused his long grey mustache to appear very white. His eyes were far apart and suggested a kindness that was born of indolence, rather than of wide compassion. His hands were slender and beautifully made, and he sat with elbows on desk, and fingertips touching. When he spoke it was in a drawl that suggested weariness. (p. 87)

Turning to the jail, Heyward notices that "When life reaches a certain level of misery, it envelopes [sic] itself in a protective anesthesia which deadens the senses to extremes" (p. 92).

Frank Durham notes that there is no "conscious cruelty, no sadistic malignancy on the part of the judges or the jailers" but "merely apathy, indifference, and an occasional flash of the affection one might display while punishing a wayward child."[13] But the irony in the jailers' indifference and the judge's hands, mustache, and impatience with crime's inconvenience to him is evident: the jailers' indifference is inhumanity, and the judge's indifference is insensitivity to the consequences of his casual use of unlimited power.

This account also reveals another side of Heyward's handling of this antagonist, however: Heyward's comment about the Negro being anesthetized against further suffering, though the further suffering may be fatal, appears to be only accidentally ironic. It is also Heyward's commonplace excuse for white indolence. As Frances Newman, a contemporary Southern novelist, noted, Heyward should "leave the souls of black folks to black folks."[14]

Archdale is a white bridge to the Row, but less so than the police are an instrument and symbol of the Row's isolation from the white community. This isolation of the Row from the white world is further emphasized by the narrator's lack of omniscience. While Heyward's narrator stations himself inside the Row, no inner thoughts of the Row's inhabitants serve to contradict the white narrator's perspective.

The Row's isolation is an element in Heyward's realism and allows him to focus narrowly on the Row—more closely on an urban Negro community than had any previous white American writer. But it is also part of a narrative strategy by which Heyward finds the white community inadequate in meeting its responsibility to the Row while stopping well short of a full exploration of the realities of racism in South Carolina in the "Golden Age." There are no black–white confrontations, as Samuel Allen has noted; the crippled hero is no threat to the white community, and the one Negro of stature is kept altogether away from whites.[15] Except for that one revealing moment of attention to the courtroom and jail, the Row's difficulties are attributed not to a faulty social order but to a few unscrupulous merchants and insensitive police officers. The Row's inhabitants are themselves largely uncomplaining and resigned to incarceration, exploitation, and the harshness of the elements. The very brevity of the quickly shifting vignette scenes cloaks the lack of interiority and allows great freedom in choice of moments to treat or ignore. Finally, the white aristocratic narrator condescends: while he respects primitive virtues and the Row's community spirit, his emphasis is on primitive failings, social immaturity, resignation, and, always, defeat. As James Southall Wilson observed, "Heyward's darkies have the distilled honey of the Old South's sweetness in their mouths."[16]

This limited perspective means that Heyward's dedication to realism is incomplete. But in a deeper sense *Porgy* is more authentically realistic than such omissions might suggest. For Heyward is historically quite accurate—and, therefore, implicitly critical—in placing the Row squarely in that Southern order which recognizes for the Negro no past or future or real place in the present. The Row is a place apart, an enigma, and no real white communication with it is possible despite the relaxed view of life and other qualities its citizens share with the other Charleston.

Life in the Row has a timeless quality; only Porgy seems to sense that life is passing unfulfilled. But the Row is repeatedly forced—in such experiences of terror and death as the Robbins–Crown fight, the saucer burial, the resort to conjurers, and the unnatural power of the hurricane—to contemplate the primacy of the future. After death in the Row, life reasserts itself, as in the adoption of Clara's baby. But the working of Destiny is not only another adversary; it effects a resignation and humility before life shared by all.

The storm is the central experience of fate in the novel. Porgy responds in fear and wonder and soon all turn to the "Sabior" who offers a "home in de rock" (p. 152). In such scenes, Heyward employs the spiritual, a choral folk expression, to provide a powerful articulation of the inner life of the Row. As Heyward observed in 1931: "The spiritual said everything for him that he could not say in the new language that he found here—awe in the presence of death—his racial terror of being left alone—his escape from bondage into the new heaven—everything."[17]

The events of *Porgy* call forth the Negro's profound response—primitive, human, Christian—to the workings of fate. Also, Heyward skillfully employs sun imagery to indicate the movement of fate, a sun casual, indifferent, benevolent, comforting, concealing, and, finally, mockingly benevolent. Fate overwhelms all, and its ways are as whimsical, as merciless and harsh, as the weather. Nature, sun, time, and the cosmos are beyond man's power; nor has Christianity, Heyward implies, reduced their awesomeness to human size for the Row. Humbled, the Row does not challenge fate.

Heyward's exploration of the array of forces confronting Catfish Row authenticates the Row's reality. The reader sees Porgy, crippled and alone, and Bess, alone and desperate, as representatives of that back-alley community, seeking to reconcile past, present, and future, at least to accept their meeting, and to survive in the face of the obstacles they afford. In accounting for so much, Heyward largely compensates for the sentimentality found in the simplifications of white supremacy, the cosmic, and primitivism.

Porgy has faults. One of its largest is a point of view that remains on the outside while conspicuously surmising what is inside. Heyward's unwillingness to quarrel with that complacent society mutes the irony the story demands and causes him to miss the fullness of the black man's suffering. Clearly, Heyward strikes a gentleman's bargain with Charleston.

Far overbalancing any failings are those "wonderful, poetic human qualities." Heyward's characters are sometimes dismissed as stereotypes, but they are not. None of his characters fits James Weldon Johnson's 1928 characterization:

> What is the Negro in the artistic conception of white America? In the brighter light, he is a simple, indolent, docile, improvident peasant; a sing-ing, dancing, laughing, weeping child, picturesque beside his log cabin and in the snowy fields of cotton; naively charming with his banjo and his songs in the moonlight and along the lazy Southern rivers; a faithful, ever-smiling and genuflecting old servitor to the white folks of quality; a pathetic and pitiable figure. In a darker light, he is an impulsive, irrational, passionate savage, reluctantly wearing a thin coat of culture, sullenly hating the white man, but holding an innate and inescapable belief in the white man's super-iority; an everlasting alien and irredeemable element in the nation; a menace to Southern civilization; a threat to Nordic race purity; a figure casting a sinister shadow across the future of the country.[18]

And while all of the adjectives John Hope Franklin sees characterizing the maga-zine and press depictions of the Negro during Heyward's formative years—ignorant, lazy, improvident, clownish, irresponsible, childish, criminal—are in some ways applicable to Catfish Row, the Row is not a composite reflection of these images.[19] These elements are played down. Sportin' Life clowns, but not for white audiences. Porgy's clowning is deliberate frustration of white power. Porgy also plays Uncle Tom, but he is never servile and lives for no white master. Heyward's erotic primitive, Crown, is quickly exiled to the nearest facsimile of Africa.

Porgy represents, instead, Heyward's view of the Negro at his best. He is sensitive to rhythm and color, better attuned than whites to the elemental rhythms and mysteries of life, committed to justice, and desirous of a human life of love and peace. His weaknesses are a primitive legacy of fear he has yet to overcome, his loneliness, and the ability to kill to secure himself from that loneliness. He is, finally, only human; he would survive and escape loneliness in love. Porgy is not the complex Negro character Ellison calls for in his essay on "Twentieth Century Fiction and the Black Mask of Humanity" and offers in *Invisible Man*. But Porgy is, in his time and setting and role as central representative, the first among several representatives of a society complex and human enough to transcend the stereotypes.

Moreover, although it shackles him to fear, Porgy's primitivism provides him many good qualities. As Heywood Broun's review observed, Heyward grants Porgy's, the Negro's, superiority over the white man, at least in sensitivity, rhythm, and emotion.[20]

The book's worth is in Heyward's revelation of Porgy's humanity. In *Porgy,* the "instrument" of freedom requires "strange songs" from the Row, songs which the past, the white community, and an uncertainty about the future make it difficult to play. Yet, despite the irony that accompanies this freedom—for such freedom requires conformity—there is a poignancy and pathos about the Row's affirmation of life in the face of great odds.

Affirmation is made possible by the book's substantial realism. The search in *Porgy* is not so obtrusive, perhaps because it is less consciously pursued by the characters than observed as a way of life lived in the Row. What Heyward envies in the Row is that it confronts the elemental forces of life without the inhibitions and repressed feelings of the mannered white aristocracy and that it is a living community of mutual interests, affections, and cares. What Heyward sees in Porgy is a sensitive man who finds identity and dignity in a summer of love and accepts his loss as summer ends. The failure of any of Heyward's white characters to achieve as much makes *Porgy's* affirmation all the more notable.

II

Porgy is doubly important in the Harlem Renaissance. The novel offers a fully-realized black world and a fully-realized black hero of unmistakable humanity. The play, which Heyward adapted from the novel with his wife Dorothy, added to that small number of plays that gave black actors their first access, in the Twenties, to the serious Broadway stage. Moreover, the changes for the stage result in a fuller appreciation of the role of Negro folk expression and a richer understanding of the inner spirit—the rhythm—of the black community. For by 1927 Heyward felt that he had identified the "unique characteristic" in Negro life that made the blacks take delight in the white man's envy.[21] It was the "secret law" of "rhythm," which he defined as "a sort of race personality that dominated and swayed the mass, making of it a sum vastly greater than the total of its individual entities." So the dramatization of *Porgy* became a challenge to "give the flow of life . . . its proper place in the canvas":

> That it was bigger than the individual who moved upon it was evident, for it had driven its dark stream on under our civilization, while generations came, were swept forward by it, and vanished. As with singing, where the Negro seldom excels as a soloist and yet with three or four friends picked up almost at random creates a successful chorus, so in their work and play it is the mass rhythms, the concerted movements, the crowd laughter, the

communal interrelationships of the Negro quarter that differentiate it most sharply from its white slum neighbour. We felt that the play in order to possess any degree of verisimilitude must show its people moving in response to the deep undertow of this tide. . . . (pp. xiii–xiv)

Heyward attributed their success in expressing what Stark Young called the "glow" and "rhythm of life" to the cast's involvement in the unconscious rhythms of the primitive Negro in becoming "a living representation" of Catfish Row (iv).[22] And to the play's techniques:

We used the spirituals as they actually occur to express emotional stress when the limited spoken vocabulary becomes inadequate. We employed the rhythmic, spontaneous prayer with which the primitive Negro makes his supplications; the unfaltering rhythm of time, expressed in the ebb and flow of day and night, and the chiming of St. Michael's bells; and the crowd movements, with their shifting pattern of colour and sound. (pp. xvii–xviii)

But the Heywards also place more emphasis in the play upon the community, where rhythm is generated, than does the novella. There is more song and group movement. And, as Frank Durham points out, the scene structure is usually a mass effect, then a dramatic dialogue, followed by a mass effect.[23]

While the heightened dramatic effects make the play a lively folk drama, the proportion and harmony between community and main characters is sacrificed. Primitivism fades as theme but balloons as atmosphere in the pervasive Negro rhythms. The moral theme becomes central, so the race conflict is soft-pedalled, lest it now have to be faced directly in moral terms. To accomplish this obscuration, Heyward makes the Row a minstrel world and shifts the primary focus to the next world—a shift to which Heyward's use of spirituals contributes largely.

Disjointed, too, is Heyward's pursuit of life in the play. While individual characters move toward racial stereotypes of the 1920s—clown, loose woman, brute and bad (Harlem) nigger—Heyward is identifying life as the ability to experience rhythm, secular and Christian.

Judged as a play, the characters remain too simple and Porgy is too unchanging. In him there is no radical incongruity with ordinary life, no defiance of the universe. He is essentially a good fellow who corresponds to our ideals; too little of his inner life is exposed for us to identify with him. In the end, he blindly refuses the awareness the sunlight offers. The conflict is too slight and unconcentrated. Characters seldom confront one another. Important scenes cease to be functional.

Still, the play overcomes most of the major failings of the novella. The excessive primitive weakness, white patronizing, and stoic acceptance of fate largely disappear. The narrator with his pretentious and fancy words is absent, an immediate consequence of which is stronger dramatic scenes.

The most notable addition is the secret "rhythm" Heyward had discovered and expressed in music and group expression. It saves—and makes—the play and sweeps almost all objections before it. As Oliver M. Sayler observed: "No one can sit through 'Porgy' in the theatre and deny that his eyes, ears, and mind have been played on like so many instruments by the various hands of rhythm. No one can read 'Porgy,' the novel or the play, and report half so vivid an experience."[24] The price Heyward pays in the adaptation is considerable, though, especially the sacrifice of the novel's subtle unity and some of the elements comprising it.

Ironically—and perhaps most importantly—it was the courtly and reserved white aristocrat, Heyward, along with O'Neill and Ridgely Torrence, who forced Harlem to recognize and appreciate the American black folk culture and experience what it was so studiously ignoring.

Heyward also did the libretto and many of the lyrics for *Porgy and Bess.* The primary virtue of America's first folk opera is its transformation of the Row into an effective chorus and the agency of song to reveal theme and character more effectively than does the play. Spirituals, songs, refrains, and chants powerfully convey the Row's contentment with this world and faith in the next, and give voice to the community's heart. But song also becomes interior monologue for the characters, from Porgy to Sportin' Life, and becomes an excellent vehicle for their expression of feeling. Although the admixture of the Gershwins' music and New York City style led to some criticism of the opera's Charleston authenticity, Heyward clearly manages, once more, to convey that rhythm and community life he so admired.

In 1926, between the *Porgy* novella and the play, Heyward published a novella, *Angel*, and a story, "The Half Pint Flask." The first is the somewhat strained story of a young girl who moves from an Eden-like union with life through the Calvinist judgment of her father into exile in the barren and harsh life of the mountains, finally to turn hopefully to a future in town when her old lover arrives to take her away. *Angel* is the first of several Heyward novels in which whites futilely seek the inner harmony with life he recognizes in Catfish Row.

"The Half Pint Flask" is the story of the encounter of an obsessed scientist who is studying "Negroid Primates" on Ediwander Island with the evil voodoo spirit Plat-eye. Here Heyward reaches behind *Porgy* to a *cul de sac* in the world of progress, the first of three excursions he made into the primitive life of the "woods." The others were his 1933 movie scenario for Eugene O'Neill's *The Emperor Jones*, and a late play, "Set My People Free," later entitled "Charleston, 1820," completed by his wife.[25] The movie scenario opens with an African ceremonial dance fading into an equally rhythmic church scene. The dramatization of Denmark Vesey's 1820 uprising includes a lonely island night scene which moves, as the drums beat, from primitive ecstasy and voodoo to Old Testament messianism; throughout, the drums call the conspirators back to the gods of their fathers.

"The Half Pint Flask" is seriously flawed by Heyward's narrative strategy. Still, even at a distance, Courtney, the courtier-narrator, recognizes the double world of the Ediwander Negro community, placid by day and possessed by primitive rhythms and powers at night and more than a match for the scientist's rationalism. Courtney is open to the clear evidence of Plat-eye's existence, a judge of Barksdale's arrogance and racial prejudice, and sensitive to the rhythmic flow of island life from night to day and sun to moon. The sense of setting, primitive beliefs, and the rhythm and color of *Porgy* are all here. The distinctive difference is Heyward's respect for the harmonious half-pagan life of the Ediwander blacks, a balance of order and mystery, resistant to any change or violation—however anachronistic its inscrutable ways might appear to Barksdale.

In each of these works, Heyward's handling of the primitive scene has a Poe-like, Gothic quality. What is interesting, though, is that the African note is not struck in an educated poet's atavistic moment in Harlem, but on an offshore Carolina island geographically and culturally as near as one could get to Africa in the United States. The blacks of "The Half Pint Flask" are nearest the "woods" and are the least involved with whites. Without individualized black characters, "The Half Pint Flask" remains a general commentary on Heyward's search for life: Barksdale lacks what the Ediwanders have.

III

By 1928, when *Mamba's Daughters* was serialized in the *Women's Home Companion*, Heyward was ready to look directly at the Negro's effort, in the 1920s, to "learn to play." Catfish Row is the point of departure, unchanged from *Porgy* except in its blatant amorality. One major difference, though, is that Mamba leaves the community of freedom and common cause in which she finds her being: "Nigger gots tuh git diff'ent kind ob sense now tuh git long. Ah gots daughtuh, an' she gots daughtuh, an' all-two dem female is born fuh trouble. Ah gots tuh be ready when de time come.'"[26] Mamba's anxiety sets the story in motion. The near-static process of *Porgy* becomes dynamic and the clash between tradition and change inevitable. A second difference is that the white world is not peripheral. The story of Saint Julien de Chatigny Wentworth, the white narrator and observer who is also in search of life, only to have to admit his relative failure in celebrating Lissa's success, provides a second plot. As Mamba, Hagar, and Lissa negotiate the obstacles, they not only involve Saint's world but comment upon his life.

Generally, the struggle is again with the alien forces met in *Porgy*. But the concern here is not survival; it is what of the primitive past can be taken into the future, in how the black man can change without losing his identity. And in *Mamba's Daughters*, a greater force than the Row's united front appears to make victory possible: love.

Primitivism shows itself here as animality and a native sense of rhythm. There is the animality of the physical scene where, after leaving Gilly's corpse in the swamp, Hagar broke "savagely" through the tangle until she found high ground: "Crouched over almost on all fours, with prehensile hands tearing her way through the undergrowth, the great woman emerged like a prehistoric creature quitting its primal slime, and climbed out upon the knoll" (p. 274). Hagar is a sort of driven animal from the start, massive and powerful but lacking the intelligence to avoid trouble or to control her simple instincts. The difference with *Porgy* here is that the wilderness of Mamba's daughters is an unpremeditated burst of feeling, not deliberate violence, as with Porgy, or a brutal way of life, as Crown's. Moreover, strong racial feeling is important as a critical element Lissa must not lose in her transformation into a Metropolitan opera star. On the other hand, Lissa's mother, Hagar, is too simple—and good-hearted—to survive in white society: her expressions of feeling too often lead to jail.

The name of the game is accommodation. But Lissa finds such accommodation as the leading forces in the cultured Negroes' Monday Night Music Club make—aping white manners, tastes, and styles—impossibly sterile and alien. She can discipline her art, can meet the Music Club's technical standards, but no more than her mother or grandmother can Lissa abandon for their Victorian mode the "gaiety of life" or the other strong feelings of life that she recognizes as part of her racial identity and which seek expression in her song (p. 68). Hagar must accommodate her feelings for Lissa by living in exile from her daughter.

In an "Introduction on the American Negro in Art," published with the play version of *Porgy*, Heyward had tried to identify what he called "the secret law of rhythm." He had recognized it as a "sort of race personality that dominated and swayed the mass, making of it a scene vastly greater than the total of its individual activities" (p. x). This evasive definition and the example of Sam Smalls that follows are less helpful than Heyward's indication in *Mamba's Daughters* of what lies behind that faculty Lissa shares with other Negroes of "giving her whole being to an emotion" (p. 208). Passing the jail with North, who has just dismissed a revival service as "'a lot of dirty Negroes,'" Lissa finds the "night suddenly dark with the suffering of the thousands who had lain there in the cages—slaves, freemen, her own people" (p. 218). And the following Sunday, she "let herself go into the music" (p. 219). This quality is again reflected in the preference of the congregation for Rev. Whaley's God "who wanted them to pour their sorrow out in a flood of song. . ." (p. 188). As Heyward defines and illustrates it, rhythm would seem to be the Negro's unique expression, with his whole being, of the strong experience of suffering and longing and joy common to the race, an expression that communicates truth and infects those of the race who join the expression.

In *Mamba's Daughters*, the vehicle of expression, which may also be a vehicle of persuasion, is music—spirituals, shouts, or jazz. For Mamba and her daughters, it is primarily song, and it would appear that racial rhythm or feeling reaches its most subtle, profound expression in this verbal and physical form. So we meet song, from the doorway harmony of Maum Netta and Mamba's "longing throb" to Lissa's New York triumph (p. 12). Mamba even seals Saint's and Valerie's love by taking them on an adventure that speaks tongues of wildness and rhythm:

> Over them, like the crash of breakers, swept the terrific, cumulative intensity of the worship, now throbbing with an old terror of jungle gods, again lifting suddenly into rapt adoration of the new Christ. This, and the pounding rhythms of the spirituals, the amazing emotional release wrought by the

music, so fascinated and yet frightened the white girl that she sat huddled against Saint, clinging to his hand with tense fingers, her head pressed against his shoulder. (p. 164)

Mamba and her daughters all express themselves in song, culminating in Lissa's disciplined Met performance: "The song lifted and hovered above the shadowed figures in a repressed agony of yearning and supplication" (301).

The rhythm of the Row and race seen at the beginning extends from the swaying bodies singing spirituals at the mining camp to the church near the Charleston jail where the "air rocked to a deep solid chorus . . . shaving harmonies with fractional notes so fine and so spontaneous that no written page could ever capture and prison the sound" (p. 217).

As the authentic vehicle by which the essence of racial integrity is expressed and transmitted to the future, Lissa must somehow honor and reconcile rhythm with her musical training. This reconciliation is, moreover, her avenue to social and economic success in a white world. The story of Mamba and her daughters is, then, the story of three women, each a story of struggle and sacrifice toward Lissa's achievement of this goal, the consistent vehicle of which is song. Mamba leaves the Row and sings. The lonely, inarticulate, slaving Hagar finds voice only in song. Lissa's voice is to be trained.

Lissa is tempted to emulate her friend Gardinia who manages to satisfy the Monday night snobs with only the slightest sacrifice of her "sheer animal spirits," and, in New York, to give way to the "alien syncopation of laughter and song" in the lazy rhythms of Harlem (p. 228, p. 300). Lissa resolves her conflict—the conflict between racial spirit and art—only when she fully appreciates the sacrifices that have brought her to New York, a resolution her final Met song reflects:

> The music caught the mood of the sky. The arresting dissonances, the sharp syncopations of the early acts, were no longer individually evident but seemed to merge into a broader irresistible current of sound. The rhythm, too, was no longer a thing separate. It became a force as indistinguishable and pervasive as the life current. It was a fundamental law that moved light, music, the sway of the crowd, the passage of time, in a concerted and inevitable progression. The artificial declamations of operatic convention were gone. The cast was reduced to two elemental forces. The crowd with its heavy mass rhythms and reiterated choruses was the body, and the single transendent [sic] mezzo-soprano that soared above it was the spirit, aspiring, daring, despairing, lifting again. (p. 306)

When Lissa sings the "National Anthem of the American Negro" for an encore, Wentworth feels something reaching back to claim "its heritage of beauty from the past" (p. 308).

Lissa's accomplishment represents the kind of victory over change—perhaps of Heyward's wishful thinking—that Heyward hoped for but had appeared to despair could come. In his first essay "And Once Again—the Negro," published in 1923, he wonders if the Negro is "an aeon behind, or an aeon ahead of us."[27] However, his main concern in this essay is that the old Negro ways that led to happiness will succumb, with urbanization, to a "stiffling moral straitjacket," because the Negro is blindly submissive. "He is about to be saved," Heyward observes with sorrow and fear. Such salvation meant the disappearance of the Negro's soul, his racial integrity, and what Heyward described in 1931 as "his spontaneous abandonment to emotion, his faith in his simple destiny."[28]

Lissa's success constitutes Heyward's response to those black voices of the Harlem Renaissance who recognized only high art as created by whites as the proper objective for black expression. But Heyward's sense of the fullness of Negro humanity directs his attention as well, perhaps more credibly, to the still stronger force that stands against an excessive and self-destructive primitivism and that conquers changes: Mamba's and Hagar's love, which becomes a testament for all their kind.

Hagar, like Mamba, is seen sketchily, but she emerges clearly as a combination of great physical strength, great simplicity, and great virtue—and as doomed in town as Billy Budd in the world. She has risked jail to save the worthless Bluton from bleeding to death so that when her efforts for Lissa are completed and her suicide is necessary to assure Lissa her chance, she deliberately ends her long loneliness. Her violence, then, is a matter of simplicity and strength, moral outrage, and maternal concern. And it is always balanced by humility. When she is gone, Lissa "imagined her as vast inarticulate power—encompassing love, possessing her all the more now because of her silence" (p. 294).

Heyward has a problem in aesthetic distance with Saint Wentworth, the pattern of whose early life largely reflects Heyward's own. The narrator is divided, until the last page, between sentimental attachment to the remnant of Charleston aristocratic tradition, including approval of Saint's success story, and criticism of the weakness and sterility, compromises and inadequacies, of that world. In short, Saint's pursuit of identity and freedom parallels Lissa's maturation. But where his intellectual curiosity, artistic sensibility, and social awareness suggest a great potentiality for freedom and a fullness of life, he succumbs to the pressures of class and meets only the challenge of a business career. Freedom, fulfillment, become participation in the rituals of the Charleston aristocracy with the means to do so. But then he recognizes that Lissa had pursued the beautiful and lonely ecstasy of her dream while he had been guided out of that delight in dreamy loneliness into social responsibility, pursued within more or less acceptable limits: economic responsibility, paternalism in race relations, marriage and family, and, perhaps, later, leisurely dabbling in art. Mamba and her daughters have transcended economics. The same quest for freedom occupies Heyward in *Peter Ashley* and *Lost Morning*. Are economic success, social conformity, and the role of gentleman compatible with life? Is Saint dead and only the creative Lissa alive? Now, almost desperately, Saint vows, "Life would still be an adventure" (p. 266).

But the narrator looks at Saint's sensitive mouth and realizes that he is no hero. He lacks the faith of Mamba and her daughters. Likewise, in his relationships with Mamba, Hagar, and Lissa, we find less than courage. He meets the demands of *noblesse oblige* but he is passive toward the black masses and accepts the white power structure at the mine.

But Heyward does not stop with parallel stories. In *Porgy,* black and white worlds largely avoid one another and the burden of responsibility is only once recognized. Here, as the black man's claim to dignity clashes with the white man's fear of change, Heyward's realism cannot ignore the facts. Atkinson notes how the impersonality of the race problem dies when one confronts an individual "battling with destiny, needing a leg up most terribly" (pp. 71–72). White supremacy, in its more callous forms, rules supreme at the phosphate mine where Hagar works, and Saint's silence appears to defend the status quo. Also, while Heyward scrupulously avoids not only overt criticism of the aristocracy and white supremacy, the aristocracy emerges pale, wan, dull, racist, and perhaps irrelevant, but the inadequacy and evils of white supremacy become apparent as well. If there is no future for the black man in *Porgy,* neither is there here. He can be an Uncle Tom, like Whaley, a corrupt lackey, like Gilly, a slum landlord, a sterile parody of white culture, or he can gamble, like Mamba, sacrifice and die, like Hagar, or flee, like Lissa.

Notably, *Mamba's Daughters* is Heyward's last work treating of the Charleston Negro. But his accomplishment in that novel, if more diffuse, is as many-sided as in *Porgy.* The climate of change that overlays the balancing of plots produces, finally, an ironic effect. The Wentworths laugh at Mamba and Saint achieves economic success among the miners, but the last laugh is Mamba's and the miraculous economic success is Hagar's. Aristocracy leans on racism and decadence results; out of subjugation comes the Negro's strength. Out of the Negro's primitive rhythm comes art; in the white aristocracy the "essential spark" never appears. Apparently, Heyward's last word in *Mamba's Daughters* is this contrapuntal statement, this overarching irony. Heyward might be called a memorialist of Low Country society in this novel, but the implications of the changes in fortune in the course of the story go beyond the memorialist's fidelity. Again, as were those elsewhere who turned to the Negro in the Twenties, Heyward is looking for life. He does not find it in Charleston manners or business success but among those who are living. And, better than in *Porgy,* he understands what that life is.

IV

Mamba's Daughters was Heyward's last work before the Depression hit and Harlem's hopes plunged. But Heyward's pursuit of the key to life did not end when he turned away from Catfish Row in the Thirties. It is largely subdued in *Brass Ankle*, a play, where a too passive Ruth Leamer's participation in the beauty and rhythm of life is crushed by Race and Progress. In *Peter Ashley,*

Peter turns from his own judgment about Secession and slavery and his own talent in the realization that he would sacrifice anything for his past, his place, and his people. In *Lost Morning* and *Star Spangled Virgin*, however, Heyward again probes the spirit's escape from the deadness of contemporary life.

In *Lost Morning*, Felix Hollister's compromise of his artistic talent for the security of home, marriage, and money comes unstuck under the pressures of his increasingly cold and calculating wife and the commercial-industrial values of Exeter she has adopted, and the urging of an assistant. To recover the lost morning of his art and life he must free himself from a world without heart or inner life and assert his independence. Alone in New York, he sees that good work is done by "a man who has given himself to life and let it eat him."[29]

Star Spangled Virgin, published in 1939, is located in the Virgin Islands, far from the Harlem Renaissance in time and place. But in his last work, Heyward returns to a theme that appears variously in each of his first three longer works of fiction: those who remain in harmony with the rhythms of nature in the corrupted atmosphere of civilization and progress are purer, wiser, and happier—and to be envied. In *Lost Morning* the civilized white man's one hope to experience the mysterious depths of life appears to be in art. Felix can recover the pulse of life—the rhythm of nature—only by an uncompromising dedication to art.

In *Star Spangled Virgin* this theme receives its strongest, yet least obtrusive, expression in that there is a general black victory over the evils accompanying white change. Adam Work, who has abandoned his earthy common-law Crucian wife and children, returns from Tortola and his church-wed wife, Victoria. From his boat, he smells the earth of St. Croix and would be reunited with Rhoda and the land. But that is not possible until Rhoda has led her crusade to success in saving the native matriarchy from bureaucratic meddling; a season of public relief and the consequent dissipations and white seductions ("Noodeal") passes. The novel ends with a ritual under the open sky, on Adam's and Rhoda's own land:

> He felt the old irresistible pull and sweep of her in the dark beside him. It communicated itself to the earth upon which he lay, and set it rocking. It poured into his body, and for a moment he choked with the beat of it in his throat. Then the separate elements yielded themselves to the march of a universal rhythm, and he could not have said which was the woman, which the man, and which the earth that bore their weight upon its sustaining hand.[30]

V

With the publication of *Porgy*, Heyward began to recognize that life eluded him and his kind, and so he pursued it into Catfish Row, Hagar's heart, and the artist's lonely garret. Initially, his work is a series of personal struggles of lonely characters to find life—in rhythm, love, art, community, freedom, or integrity—in a changing traditional society which denies life. As a Southern writer, Heyward is a transitional figure between Mencken's "Sahara of the Bozarts" and the younger Wolfe and Faulkner. His role is to memorialize the past and to criticize the present, to tell the truth—not all of it, but enough to be called courageous for his time. When Heyward is done, the illusion of the white aristocracy's superiority is dispelled. Certain primitive Negro strengths and qualities, particularly rhythm, and a *joie de vivre* are seen, along with the reality and uniqueness of the Negro community, the Negro's dissembling for the white audience, and that pathetic self-hatred of Hagar and those inhabitants of the Row who deprecate themselves as "just niggers." Also, the relentless inroads of the modern industrialism and progress are seen everywhere so that the truth of his vision is primarily social: the struggles of his characters are chiefly with society or representatives of it. Southern society and social institutions invariably fail Heyward's characters, black and white. They exclude the possibility of black dignity. They require that whites conform to class and community mores. The demand for conformity frustrates the harmony with nature, community, love, spirit of sacrifice, and dedication Heyward's blacks know as life.

Catfish Row, on the other hand, has made the necessary accommodations to the urban white world. And with common values and faith that weather death and defeat, it lives, uninhibited, a real community. Only here is there the necessary freedom to pursue and realize a meaningful personal life. Perhaps Heyward's first poem, "Gamesters All," should be read primarily in this context: the black gambler seeks freedom at any cost; the policeman who shoots him is actually enslaved by his racist role.

Life in Heyward's South, then, is found only in the black community where man's tie to nature has not been broken, where dead social codes do not frustrate freedom, and where rhythm and religion give meaning to the struggle for survival and dignity in the white man's world. Consequently, Porgy, Mamba, Hagar, Lissa, Adam, and Rhoda all have the energy, courage, and endurance to reach out for life until they achieve it, if only vicariously.

Heyward's additional contributions to the image of the black man in the Harlem Renaissance may be more precisely defined. The Harlem Renaissance occurs against a background of demeaning stereotypes and exaggerated primitivism that deny the black man's dignity. These distortions and others—fancied primitivism, exoticism, and indulgence in varying forms—continue through the Thirties. But in the early Twenties Southerners Heyward, T. S. Stribling, and Julia Peterkin, as well as Jean Toomer and, to a lesser degree, others, begin to examine the human qualities of the black man with a truth that changes that image significantly. Heyward's special place in this group is that his Southern Negroes are relatively contemporary, urban, involved in the white man's world, and seen through the double perspective of a paternalistic white Southern aristocrat and an honest observer who satisfies even Negro critics in his fidelity to the truth. If Heyward's paternalism is condescending, so is it sympathetic and understanding. And while he filters out the harsher truths, the reader does not escape complacent and guiltless.

More important is that honesty and understanding as Heyward moves inside the Negro community to see its passions, hopes, fears, suffering, code, community order, ties with the past, and capacity to prevail. In his close observation and awareness of the full complexity of what he sees, he rescues Negro primitive qualities from ersatz distortions to reveal the elements that make the Negro more responsive to life and nature than his mannered white Charleston neighbors. Specifically, the rhythm Heyward sees is neither primitive exuberance, the echo of atavistic drums, or both, but the essential element in the cultural expression of a folk close to the earth and their God and joined in suffering and misery, joy and hope. In the Harlem Renaissance, Nathan Huggins tells us, "The Negro was in the process of telling himself and the world that he was worthy, had a rich culture, and could make contributions of value."[31] Heyward was showing the Negro and the world.

Most important of all, he simply shows us Porgy and Hagar performing in the intimacy of a black world, an opportunity seldom given Faulkner's Negroes. Thus, Heyward won an audience for fiction that treated the Negro seriously and sympathetically as a human being that no American writer since Twain and Joel Chandler Harris had reached. The strength, the determination, the faith that the nation recognized in the Civil Rights movement in the South in the Sixties, Heyward had recognized in the Catfish Row community scenes forty years before.

Heyward's importance to the Harlem Renaissance, then, is his success in showing the black man's humanity and culture in the world of nature, his own society, primitive influences, change, white racism, and fate, as illustrated in the concluding lines of *Porgy*:

> The keen autumn sun flooded boldly through the entrance and bathed the drooping form of the goat, the ridiculous wagon, and the bent figure of the man in hard, satirical radiance. In the revealing light, Maria saw that Porgy was an old man. The early tension that had characterized him, the mellow mood that he had known for one eventful summer, both had gone; and in their place she saw a face that sagged wearily, and the eyes of age lit only by a faint reminiscent glow from suns and moons that had looked into them and had already dropped down the west.
>
> She looked until she could bear the sight no longer; then she stumbled into her shop and closed the door, leaving Porgy and the goat alone in an irony of morning sunlight. (p. 196)

In the spring of 1965, I had occasion to mention Heyward to the young black fiction writer William Melvin Kelley whose first novel *A Different Drummer* and collection of stories were attracting considerable interest. His response was to quote much of this passage. Apparently, we can still go to school to DuBose Heyward.

Sixty years after the appearance of *Porgy* and fifty after the 1935 premier of *Porgy and Bess*, these claims for Heyward appear more firmly established than when they were first made. *Porgy and Bess* reappears regularly, on stage and in recordings, recalling its fictional origin. A film of "The Half Pint Flask" improves upon the story. At the 1985 Heyward Centennial Conference in Charleston, that story and the fiction and theater versions of *Porgy* and *Mamba's Daughters* provided the focus of attention in papers by Theodore Rosengarten, Harlan Greene, John Crum, James Meriwether, Susan W. Walker, and Frederic Roffman, demonstrating the integrity of Heyward's work in several art forms, his kinship with the black writers of Harlem, his contributions to black advances on the American stage, his delineations of black classes and subtle changes in race relations, and the humanity of his black characters. A concurrent Gibbes Art Gallery exhibition was appropriately titled "Charleston and the Age of Porgy and Bess."

NOTES

1. Herschel Brickell, "Creator and Catfish Row," *New York Herald Tribune Books*, 10 Mar. 1929.

2. "Critic's Almanac," *Nashville Tennessean*, 3 Feb. 1929; Cullen, "Book Shelf," *Opportunity* 3 (Dec. 1925): 379.

3. DuBose Heyward, *Porgy* (New York: George H. Doran, 1925). Subsequent references are to this edition.

4. "Writers: Black and White," in *The American Negro Writer and His Roots: Selected Papers from the First Conference of Negro Writers, March, 1959*, ed. John O. Killens (New York: American Society of African Culture, 1960), p. 43.

5. DuBose Heyward, "Introduction on the American Negro in Art," in *Porgy: A Play in Four Acts*, by Dorothy Heyward and DuBose Heyward. Theatre Guild Acting Version (Garden City, NY: Doubleday, 1928), p. ix.

6. On one occasion Heyward's and Toomer's careers lightly touched. John Bennett, an editor of the South Carolina Poetry Society's *Yearbook*, anxiously wrote Heyward, the society's executive secretary, when he discovered that Toomer had become an associate member of the society. A crisis in the Charleston blueblood organization was averted by quietly listing Toomer as a member in the next *Yearbook* but omitting the usual courtesy reference to his new book, *Cane*. See John Bennett to DuBose Heyward (19 Aug. 1923), Bennett Papers, South Carolina Historical Society, Charleston, S.C.

7. "A Major Musical," *New Republic* (6 April 1953): 31.

8. "The Negro in American Literature," *New World Writing* 1 (April 1952): 28. According to Charles Glicksberg, this pseudo-realism was a form of psychological regression to nature, the spontaneous, and the decadent. Add condescension, he argues, and you have "white slumming": writers cast Negroes in the roles of child-like, emotional, and irrational creatures engaged in atavistic dances and tribal crimes without ever questioning whether blood is a creative principle or whether Negroes are truly so anti-intellectual. See "The Negro Cult of the Primitive," *Antioch Review* 4 (Mar. 1944): 49.

9. *Nigger Heaven* (New York: Knopf, 1926), p. 165. Subsequent references are to this edition.

10. Ralph Ellison, telephone interview with the author, Milwaukee, Wis., 22 Oct. 1967.

11. *Creating the Modern American Novel* (London: Williams & Norgate, 1936), p. 145.

12. "The Legacy of the Ancestral Arts," in *The New Negro: An Interpretation*, ed. Locke (New York: Albert & Charles Boni, 1925), p. 153.

13. *DuBose Heyward: The Man Who Wrote Porgy* (Columbia: Univ. of South Carolina Press, 1954), p. 70.

14. "Orchestrated," *New York Herald Tribune Books*, 18 Oct. 1925.

15. "Negritude and Its Relevance to the American Negro Writer," in *The American Negro Writer and His Roots*, p. 15.

16. "Back-Country Novels," *Virginia Quarterly Review* 8 (July 1932): 467.

17. DuBose Heyward to Kathryn Bourne, 21 Dec. 1931. Cited from Frank Durham, "DuBose Heyward's Use of Folklore in His Negro Fiction," *The Citadel: Monograph Series* no. 2 (Charleston: The Citadel, 1961), pp. 18–19.

18. "The Dilemma of the Negro Author," *American Mercury* 15 (Dec. 1928): 478.

19. "Introduction," *Three Negro Classics*, ed. Franklin (New York: Avon, 1965), p. viii.

20. "It Seems To Me," *New York World*, 14 Oct. 1925.

21. Heyward and Heyward, *Porgy: A Play in Four Acts*, p. xiii. Subsequent references are to this edition.

22. Stark Young, "Races," *New Republic* (26 Oct. 1927): 261.

23. *DuBose Heyward: Southerner as Literary Artist* (Ph.D. diss.: Columbia Univ., 1953), p. 342.

24. "The Play of the Week," *Saturday Review of Literature* 4 (29 Oct. 1927).

25. Eugene O'Neill, *The Emperor Jones with a Study Guide for the Screen Version of the Play*, by William Lewin and Max J. Herzberg (New York: Appleton, 1949), p. 60. Lewin and Herzberg do not identify the source for Heyward's statement.

26. DuBose Heyward, *Mamba's Daughters* (New York: Doubleday, 1929), p. 36. Subsequent references are to this edition.

27. *The Reviewer* 4 (Oct. 1923), cited from Emily Clark, "DuBose Heyward," *Virginia Quarterly Review* 6 (Oct. 1930): 551.

28. DuBose Heyward, "The Negro in the Low Country," in *The Carolina Low-Country*, ed. Augustine T. Smythe et al. (New York: Macmillan, 1932), pp. 186–87.

29. *Lost Morning* (New York: Farrar & Rinehart, 1936), pp. 268–69.

30. *Star Spangled Virgin* (New York: Farrar & Rinehart, 1939), p. 230.

31. *Harlem Renaissance* (New York: Oxford Univ. Press, 1971), p. 59.

"REFINED RACISM": WHITE
PATRONAGE IN THE HARLEM RENAISSANCE

BRUCE KELLNER

Despite their good intentions, white intellectuals and philanthropists bestowed mixed blessings in support of black artists and writers during the Harlem Renaissance. Their involvement contributed indirectly to the Black Arts Movement of the 1960s, yet the cost to the 1920s is undeniable. The black writer both thrived and suffered, torn between well-meant encouragement from the white race to preserve his racial identity (usually described as "primitivism") and a misguided encouragement from his own race to emulate the white one. Madame C. J. Walker's products, designed to straighten hair, and surely those of her competitors, designed to lighten skin, as well as the regular practice of black comedians wearing blackface makeup, are extreme examples at opposite ends of this appalling scale. Nevertheless, at the time of the Harlem Renaissance, that "renaissance" would never have progressed beyond Harlem without the intervention and support of white patrons. Inevitably, such support manifested itself in action which in retrospect seems patronizing, but to deny its positive aspects is intellectually indefensible. White patronage, for good as well as ill, was merely an unavoidable element in getting from the past to the present, and the roles of people like Albert C. Barnes, for example, Charlotte Mason, all the Spingarns—Joel and Amy and Arthur—and Carl Van Vechten, make a strong supporting cast. Some were bad actors; some were better.

Alphabetical order is a reasonable approach to such a list; coincidentally, it is an order leading from the weakest to the strongest involvement with the Harlem Renaissance, although quantity and quality are rarely equal.

I

Albert C. Barnes—"the terrible tempered Barnes" as Carl McCardle called him[1]—might begin either list. This brash and opinionated Philadelphia millionaire began to collect impressionist and post-impressionist art around 1907, and fifteen years later he founded the Barnes Foundation in Merion, Pennsylvania, with what was then the most important collection of work by Henri Matisse in America, along with substantial representations of Renoir, Dégas, Picasso, Cézanne, and dozens of other celebrated painters. During the years Barnes was amassing these holdings, he rescued African art from ethnology, "stripping [art] of the emotional bunk," he declared, "[with] which the long-haired phonies and that fading class of egoists, the art patrons, have encumbered it."[2] He extolled the aesthetics of African art, even though he could define it only in abstract terms, unable to get far beyond vague references to color and line and space. But he saw himself with the "emotional intensity of a moral reformer. . . . as one of the few true friends of black Americans, . . . beleaguered by misinformed and even racist others," as historian Mark Helbling put it.[3] In 1923, when Barnes was trying to write an essay called "Contribution to the Study of Negro Art in America," he called on the influential black educator Alain Locke for assistance. Locke, in turn, sensing possibilities for financial as well as emotional support for young black artists, encouraged a friendship by introducing Barnes to several figures who would shortly become active in the Harlem Renaissance, among them Walter White, already a powerful gadfly in the NAACP. White himself was trying to do an article about black art in America just then and sought help from Barnes; but White had cited several of those "long-haired phonies" as his authorities, and not surprisingly Barnes damned it. Then, when white editor H. L. Mencken turned down Barnes's article to consider White's for publication in *The American Mercury*, the "terrible tempered Barnes" began to court the Urban League's Charles S. Johnson, hoping that an issue of the organization's magazine *Opportunity* might be devoted to African art, featuring his own article, of course, and offering his Foundation as bait since it exhibited black and classical Greek and Egyptian sculpture side by side. Like Locke, Johnson welcomed Barnes's knowledge, his own decorum able to hold in check his reactions to the paranoid outbursts that emanated regularly from Merion, Pennsylvania. *Opportunity* did run a special issue on African art, with Barnes's essay, but his impact was not felt fully until the following year when the white periodical *Survey Graphic* gave over its March 1925 issue to "The New Negro." That title was used for Locke's impressive anthology eight months later, with Barnes's article expanded, and reproductions of various works of African art in the Barnes Foundation.

Albert C. Barnes was an important voice in attempting to give to both races a sense of what negligence had lost, but he tried to focus the reconciliation of a primitive African art and a new cultural spirit among the emerging black intellectuals of the Harlem Renaissance, and Alain Locke was dissatisfied with his questionable analysis. Actually, Locke had hoped to engage Carl Van Vechten to write an article about black American art, but at that time Van Vechten was contributing almost monthly essays on various black subjects to the posh white magazine *Vanity Fair* and begged off, leaving Locke with Barnes's "kindly but vague assertions" that white Americans were devitalized because of their comfortable culture.[4] Of the white American, Barnes wrote in *The New Negro*: "Many centuries of civilization have attenuated his original gifts and have made his mind dominate his spirit. He has wandered too far from the elementary human needs and their easy means of natural satisfaction. The deep and satisfying harmony which the soul requires no longer arises from the incidents of daily life." The imagination of the black American, on the other hand, he contended, had been intensified by the existence of racism. The "daily habit of thought, speech, and movements of Afro-Americans," he continued, "are flavored with the picturesque, the rhythmic, the euphonious." As for African art, Barnes was only able to say that the "renascence of Negro art" was as "characteristically Negro as are the primitive African sculptures."[5] What that "characteristic" was, however, Barnes could never make clear, so it is not surprising that Alain Locke wrote an essay of his own on the subject for *The New Negro*, even though his argument was similar—that African art was at the root of Afro-American artistic expression. Fifty years later, Nathan Irvin Huggins, in his pioneering study of the Harlem Renaissance, suggested that such a conviction was a measure of our distance from our true identity: "America and Americans were provincials. That was the problem. Black men as well as white men were forced through condition and education to look elsewhere for the springs of civilization and culture.... So black men yearned as American provincials, to find meaning and identity in Africa; their frustration was a measure of their Americanization."[6]

By 1925, Albert C. Barnes's emphasis on form and abstract content in African art and his innocent physical descriptions of what he had squirrelled away in Merion, Pennsylvania, do not really come to terms with the influence of primitivism at all. His concern with the cultural identity of black Americans, however, the African collection in the Barnes Foundation, and certainly his money, speak to that cultural awakening during the twenties.

II

Money seems to be the only contribution made to the movement by Mrs. Rufus Osgood Mason, born Charlotte Louise Vandevere Quick, and called "godmother" by her protégés when she could get her way. She got it most of the time, because the purse strings she controlled were like tentacles. They gave rein to young black writers; they could strangle. As Agatha Cramp in Rudolph Fisher's *The Walls of Jericho*, as Dora Ellsworth in Langston Hughes's *The Ways of White Folks*, and, indeed, as Godmother in Zora Neale Hurston's *Dust Tracks on a Road*, Charlotte Mason has been immortalized, but with marked ambivalence.

Widowed at fifty-one when her physician husband died at seventy-three, Mrs. Mason first used her vast wealth in some preliminary anthropological studies of American Indians, even making some field trips at the turn of the century. She was interested as well in psychology and psychic phenomena, through her husband's influence, but by the twenties her interests had shifted to the primitive and therefore innocent elements (or so she judged them) in Afro-American arts and letters.

From her regal penthouse on Park Avenue, surrounded by Indian and African artifacts, minor though respectable European paintings, eighteenth-century French furniture, a staff of servants, and a retinue of white toadies, this old dowager ruled over a stable of young Afro-American artists and writers. At one time or another during the Harlem Renaissance, she considered as her personal property both Hughes and Hurston, as well as Aaron Douglas, Richmond Barthé, Hall Johnson, Claude McKay, Louise Thompson, and especially Alain Locke. None of them was permitted to divulge her identity as the source of their good fortune, even though one or another of them served as escort on several occasions. Langston Hughes remembered her white chauffeur driving him home to Harlem after these outings to the theater, and Louise Thompson remembered similar discomfort. When God-mother wished to communicate with her godchildren by mail, she employed the services—without pay presumably—of white sometime poet Katherine Garrison Chapin and her sister, sometime sculptor Cornelia, members of an artistic circle that included muralist George Biddle and his wife Helene Sardeau. To young and inexperienced black writers, the power of that white world, not to speak of its glamour, must have been somewhat intimidating, but they were privy to it so long as they fulfilled Charlotte Mason's expectations. They were to live in Harlem; they were to emphasize in their work what she identified as folk culture or primitivism, and they were to eschew subjects she judged as didactic or smacking of social reform. Plenty of those letters the Chapin sisters were obliged to write for her to Alain Locke, after all, expressed her open hostility toward organizations designed to improve relations between the races.

She paid Langston Hughes's living expenses while he was writing his first novel, *Not Without Laughter*. She underwrote the single performance on Broadway of Zora Neale Hurston's musical drama *The Great Day*. She picked up the monthly rental for Richmond Barthé's Greenwich Village studio so he could devote all his time to sculpture. She financed research trips, college tuition, rehearsal time in concert halls; she doled out pocket money for shoes, winter coats, bus fares; and she called each of her protégés "my child." She invested today's equivalent of about half a million dollars in young black artists and writers, but she broke off the alliances when her charges proved disloyal by abandoning what she considered the purity in their work, its "primitivism." Because she believed in "primitivism" with cult fervor and disapproved of social protest, the breaks were frequent and the value of the support, as Nathan Irvin Huggins suggested, was questionable: "Whatever other burdens Negro artists carried, this arrangement stigmatized Negro poetry and prose of the 1920s as being an artistic effort that was trying to be like something other than itself."[7]

Langston Hughes was still a Lincoln University student when Alain Locke took him to Mrs. Mason's apartment. As was her wont, she sat on a dais at one end of the drawing room *in* rather than *on* a chair best described as a throne, and before Hughes left she slipped him a fifty dollar bill. To Zora Neale Hurston, Mrs. Mason delivered a monthly $200 stipend for two years. At today's rate of exchange that pushes $30,000. Both rewarded her in their autobiographies: Hurston claimed that she and her godmother were mystically tied together, pagans spiritually joined; Hughes wrote in awe of her power that he didn't "know why or how she still found time" for him, since she moved in circles far removed from his own.[8] Both broke with her when their work was less than what she considered "beautiful," which is to say "primitive." By that time, however, the stock market had fallen, and Harlem's plight replaced its popularity. Hughes's poems began to reflect a world in which Mrs. Mason had no interest, and he asked to be released, to remain a friend but without the onus of financial obligation. In turn, in venom apparently, she berated his talent and his character. It was not a reaction that surprised Hughes's friend Louise Thompson, a young teacher who had been brought to the Mason apartment by black painter Aaron Douglas, and who escaped from it when she realized its power to corrupt.

One of the most fascinating figures of the Harlem Renaissance, Louise Thompson deserves a biography of her own, and it is not untoward to include its outlines here, since the role of the white patron is perhaps more clearly defined through her than through the better known Hughes and Hurston. Louise Thompson brought to the movement an awareness of racism in its various disguises that strongly influenced her later life as well as the lives of many of the young black artists and writers with whom she came in contact.

Reared in several states as her stepfather moved from job to job, Louise Thompson was often the only black child in town, so that first exposure to racism was an awareness of isolation. Then at Berkeley she encountered it in the form of indifference from her fellow students—white, of course, until, awakened to her own potential when W.E.B. Du Bois lectured there, she took a teaching job in Arkansas. Her students were barely able to read, in a community where isolation and indifference were too easily replaced by racial violence, and her memories of its terrors were still clear sixty years later. In the mid-twenties, she went on to the Hampton Institute to teach business administration and there encountered another form of racism, somehow more invidious. A "refined racism," as she later called it, hid comfortably behind the mask of white patronage.

At the height of the Harlem Renaissance, she was denied the right to any social exchange with her students; black and white faculty members could neither publicly nor privately fraternize; and the predominately white administration demanded strict enforcement of social rules from another age. At a time when on white campuses F. Scott Fitzgerald coeds rouged their knees and their male counterparts carried hip flasks, Hampton's black students were not allowed to date. Even weekend movies in the college chapel required a faculty member as chaperone for every four students. At that juncture, Louise Thompson accepted a National Urban League scholarship in New York and began to come in contact with many young black intellectuals, among them Wallace Thurman, editor of the notorious *Fire!!*, spokesman for the movement, and scandalous *bon vivant*. They married after a brief courtship and separated six months later. It was at that time that she came under the influence of Charlotte Mason who employed her as secretary to Hughes and Hurston. Long afterward, Louise Thompson said she might have known on her first visit what lay ahead when, nervous and trying to please, she exclaimed at the extravagant bouquet of flowers on the dining table. "Which color do you prefer, my child?" she remembered Mrs. Mason asking. When she said she thought the red ones were especially pretty, Mrs. Mason withered her with a smile: "Yes, of course, you *would* prefer red...."[9] Godmother, who tried to disguise her suffocating hold on young black writers with largesse, only convinced Thompson to break her ties, and, she later declared, she convinced Langston Hughes to do the same. But Hughes was a long time in recovering his emotional equilibrium while Thompson was not. To complete this capsule biography of an extraordinary woman, she went on to conduct seminars all over the South for the Congregational Education Society; she organized that group of young black intellectuals who went to Russia to make a movie in Moscow about life in America (which never got made, incidentally); she was deeply involved in the Scottsboro Case and the National Committee for Political Prisoners; and she served for fifteen years in the International Workers Order. Wallace Thurman died in 1934, and in 1940 she married William Patterson, who had been the lawyer for the Scottsboro boys. But Charlotte Mason had left permanent scars, as she had on many of her protégés, and Louise Thompson's bitterness over the disturbing contradiction in patronage that could so subtly transform itself into patronizing behavior left her with some disturbing suspicions about the role of the white supporter. The weight of evidence was strong.

As for the eccentric Charlotte Mason, with her strong biases about what Negro art was supposed to be, she remains a shadowy figure, denied by accident or intention an obituary in *The New York Times* when she finally died, at the age of ninety-two, and, in the work of her own protégés given only cautious attention. Without her support, would we have had Richmond Barthé's *Feral Benga*? Langston Hughes's *Not Without Laughter*? Zora Neale Hurston's anthropological studies? Perhaps.

III

The most selfless of these white philanthropists were surely the Spingarn brothers, Arthur and Joel. They devoted their lives to racial equality as the leading twentieth-century abolitionists and constant supporters of the National Association for the Advancement of Colored People and its interests, motivated by the indifference of the white race, the despair of the black race, and the driving need they felt for integration. Both were involved in the founding of the NAACP, and as early as 1914 both were touring at their own expense to picket in the South against Jim Crow laws. Arthur was the NAACP's lawyer from its beginnings, its vice-president from 1911, and its president from 1940 until his retirement in 1966, as well as its unpaid legal counsel until his death in 1971. His first of several legal successes for the race came in 1927, when the Supreme Court upheld his challenge to the all-white Democratic primary election in Texas, and that one was succeeded by many others. At the beginning of his career, Arthur Spingarn's law practice suffered because of his racial sympathies, but he believed in later years that his racial sympathies actually increased it. Like his brother, he believed unquestioningly in the theory of the "talented tenth," sharing with W.E.B. Du Bois and many others the idea that within any group there would be ten percent capable of extraordinary achievement, gifted by the gods or by circumstances to speak for the rest. If white America could be awakened to that "talented tenth" in black America, they reasoned, segregation would diminish, conditions would improve, and in time prejudice would disappear. Hindsight tells us that the theory was too firmly grounded in idealism ever to survive the dream. The advocates of art as well as its practitioners do not, alas, populate the "untalented ninetieth" in either race.

Arthur Spingarn's brother Joel, three years his elder, began his career as a professor of comparative literature at Columbia University with a formidable reputation as a scholar—he was an authority on the Italian philosopher and art critic Benedetto Croce—but that lasted less than a decade. A colleague had been dismissed because of a breach-of-promise suit against him; when Joel Spingarn rose in defense of academics being allowed their private lives, he was fired too, although he seems not to have mourned long. Twenty-five years later he celebrated the anniversary with a cocktail party for his friends, many of them, perhaps most, Afro-Americans.

Long before he left Columbia, Joel Spingarn had been deeply involved with the race. Already, he had dismissed politics, failing in a bid for a congressional seat in 1908 and resigning from the Republican party in 1912 because it had no black delegates. By that time, from his family home, Troutbeck, New York, he was editing his suffragist newspaper *The Amenia Times* and was deeply committed to the NAACP. He served as its chairman of the board until 1919, its treasurer until 1930, and its president until his death. His wife, Amy, completed his final term of office. Joel Spingarn's long tenure was not entirely smooth. Black newspapers like the *New York Age* regularly complained because of too many whites in influential positions in the NAACP, and W.E.B. Du Bois, who respected Spingarn's commitment as well as his intellect, inevitably and understandably resented what was at that time a practical necessity. At the same time, he recognized Joel Spingarn's contributions and paid them strong tribute. In 1914, as I observed earlier, the Spingarn brothers barnstormed to protest segregation practices. In 1915, Joel Spingarn attempted to stop showings of D. W. Griffith's racist film epic *The Birth of a Nation*. In 1916, he organized the first Amenia Conference, with many influential blacks in attendance, to formulate official policy combatting racial inequities. In 1917, he drafted the first deferral anti-lynching legislation. In 1918, as a major in the army, he laid aside his anti-separatist stand long enough to force the establishment of a black officers' training school. Independently wealthy after 1919, he devoted the majority of his time to the NAACP, and he was in part responsible for its 300 branches by 1921. Both Joel Spingarn and his wife, Amy, regularly contributed funds to the NAACP throughout their lives and spent a good deal of time soliciting funds from others for its various causes. In 1925, when the literary contests in *The Crisis* and *Opportunity* were at their height, Amy Spingarn established financial awards of her own, voted by a committee to Rudolph Fisher for fiction, Marita Bonner for drama, and Countee Cullen for poetry (Frank Horne and Langston Hughes placing second and third in the latter category). Joel Spingarn himself had long before established the most prestigious award for the race, the Spingarn Medal, and he insured its continuance by setting up a trust fund in his will. The gold medal was to be awarded annually for "the highest and noblest achievement of an American Negro during the preceding year or years." The cover of the June 1914 issue of *The Crisis* carried a drawing of the medal's design.

For the record, it went first, in 1915, to Ernest E. Just, a professor of physiology at Howard University, and next to Lieutenant Colonel Charles Young of the United States Army. In subsequent years, through the period of the Harlem Renaissance, the Spingarn Medal was awarded to critic/poet William Stanley Braithwaite; lawyer Archibald Grimké; W.E.B. Du Bois; actor Charles Gilpin; sociologist Mary Burnett Talbert; educator George Washington Carver; James Weldon Johnson; singer Roland Hayes; historian Carter G. Woodson, who founded the *Journal of Negro History*; Anthony Overton, who was president of the Victory Life Insurance Company; novelist Charles W. Chesnutt; Howard University president Mordecai Johnson; Fort Valley, Georgia, Industrial School president H. A. Hunt; Tuskeegee's Robert Russa Moton; Max Yergan, who directed the YMCA in Africa; Tuskeegee's William T. B. Williams; educator Mary McLeod Bethune. Later recipients also active during the Harlem Renaissance included Walter White; labor leader A. Philip Randolph; Paul Robeson; and Langston Hughes. Now that list has little to do with white patronage, but it is certainly an impressive one, and it speaks well for Joel Spingarn, a ruthless and single-minded integrationist whose belief in the "talented tenth" never seemed to waver. We may know that the roots of such a theory can never be more than an ideal in purely practical terms, but the names of the recipients of the Spingarn Medal must surely give pause for hope.

IV

The last white patron in this brief catalog, Carl Van Vechten, is probably the most controversial, the one about whom white as well as black scholars feel strong prejudice. Nathan Irvin Huggins's conclusions in his book on the period of the Harlem Renaissance do not underestimate Van Vechten's contributions, but, he contends, "it is open to question how well, or in what way, Van Vechten served Harlem and the Negro" and equally important to question how well they "served him."[10] In *When Harlem Was in Vogue*, David Levering Lewis allows that Van Vechten "praised everything artistically good or promising with enthusiastic good sense, balanced by sympathetic dismissal of whatever Harlem produced that was clearly mediocre,"[11] but he allows for the possibility "that Van Vechten was a literary voyeur, exploiting his Harlem connections in order to make himself even richer."[12] On the other hand, James Weldon Johnson said Van Vechten was "one of the most vital forces in bringing about the artistic emergence of the Negro in America,"[13] and the assessments of Van Vechten's contemporary biographers reinforce that judgment.

By the time Carl Van Vechten had become addicted to black arts and letters during the twenties, he was already well established as a music critic of considerable perception and, on the strength of four highly popular novels, a successful writer hardly in need of being "served," at least not financially. But he certainly seems to have discovered the potential for artistic excellence in the race before the race had fully realized that for itself, and he announced it with the same enthusiasm he had brought to any number of other matters labeled *avant-garde* in their own time. It is not difficult, however, to understand why others—white as well as black—might misinterpret Van Vechten's motives, assuming, on the basis of his reputation as a dandy and a dilettante, that he was not only self-serving but slumming.

His interest was of long standing, however. At the turn of the century, Van Vechten had fallen under the spell of ragtime and, before the first world war, of jazz, about which he wrote in *Red* (from the mid-twenties), it "may not be the last hope of American music, nor yet the best hope, but at present, I am convinced, it is its only hope."[14] Even before he had praised the music of Igor Stravinsky, Erik Satie and George Gershwin, the operas of Richard Strauss, the dancing of Isadora Duncan and Anna Pavlova, the writings of Gertrude Stein—all in advance of anybody else in America—he had begun his campaign. In 1914, he was advocating in print the formation of a Negro theater organization, with black actors and black playwrights.

In the mid-twenties he met Walter White through their mutual publisher and, through him, he came to know the entire set of Harlem literati, including his greatest friend, James Weldon Johnson. If Van Vechten needed a catalyst for his growing enthusiasm for black arts and letters, he found it in that remarkable figure. He met the young poets Langston Hughes and Countee Cullen, and eventually Eric Walrond, Wallace Thurman, and Zora Neale Hurston—the latter responsible for having coined the term "niggerati" to describe the young black intellectuals of the period, and for having dubbed Carl Van Vechten the first "Negrotarian." Shortly, he had arranged for the work of Cullen and Hughes to appear in the pages of the prestigious *Vanity Fair*, and through his instigation Alfred Knopf published Hughes's first collection of poems *The Weary Blues* as well as novels by Nella Larsen and Rudolph Fisher. For *Vanity Fair*—as popular and influential in the twenties, apparently, as any magazine in recent history—

Van Vechten wrote several articles himself: about the spirituals, about the blues, about blues singers Bessie Smith and Ethel Waters, about black theater. He wrote dozens of reviews of books by black writers; he financed Paul Robeson's first recitals of spirituals in New York; and he became, in Nathan Irvin Huggins's apt phrase, "the undisputed downtown authority on uptown life."[15] Although he devoted an inordinate amount of time to shabby pursuits—getting drunk regularly in speakeasies, collecting handsome Harlem sycophants about him, unconsciously propagating stereotypes through his own delight in Harlem's exotic elements—there is nothing in any of his work to suggest that his respect and admiration were not genuine, and it is clear that his desire to share his discoveries resulted in a cultural interchange unique at the time. In their glamorous apartment, Van Vechten and his wife, the Russian actress Fania Marinoff, entertained frequently and lavishly, always with fully integrated guest lists. The parties were eventually reported as a matter of course in some of the black newspapers of the city, and Walter White called their West 55th Street address "the mid-town office of the NAACP."[16]

And then Carl Van Vechten wrote *Nigger Heaven*. The title alone guaranteed controversy, but readers were violently split in their reactions to the content, and despite the support of several influential black writers, there was widespread feeling that he had used his Harlem acquaintances badly. *Nigger Heaven* is no great novel, but it certainly created a large white readership for black literature, and it popularized Harlem and brought plenty of money into the cabarets north of 125th Street. Whether those two influences are close enough in value to be mentioned in the same sentence is open to question. *Nigger Heaven* is usually criticized because of its preoccupation with Harlem's seamy side, although only about a third of the action takes place in speakeasies and bedrooms. Those passages surely are rough and erotic, and blacks espousing the theory of a "talented tenth," eager to put a best foot forward in Harlem, did not enjoy seeing it depicted as frequently engaged in the Charleston, or otherwise tangled up in the bedsheets of pimps and courtesans. The other two-thirds of the novel is about Harlem's black intelligentsia, with a pedantic heroine and a feeble hero locked in a pathetic little romance that ends in melodramatic violence more appropriate for the silent movies of the period. W.E.B. Du Bois wanted to burn the book, but Wallace Thurman suggested that a statue of the ofay author be erected in Harlem. The real problem with *Nigger Heaven* is not a question of either its sincerity or its scandal-mongering, but the fact that it is consciously didactic, a deliberate attempt to educate Van Vechten's already large white reading public by presenting Harlem as a complex society fractured and united by individual and social groups of diverse interests, talents, and values. The scandalous drinking and sleeping around in *Nigger Heaven* goes on in all of Van Vechten's novels; such vagaries are hardly limited to the white race. In his afterword to a subsequent paperback edition of *Nigger Heaven*, Van Vechten declared, "Negroes are treated by me exactly as if I were depicting white characters, for the very excellent reason that I do not believe there is much psychological difference between the races."[17] As a consequence—though it is probably true that this only proves itself to somebody willing to read Van Vechten's other novels—*Nigger Heaven* is best understood as the one of his books which has characters who happen to be black. But who could have known that, or have even cared to, faced with a title like *Nigger Heaven*?

Whatever its limitations, the novel strengthened Van Vechten's ties with the race—certainly he lost no friends because of it—and increased his loyalty. Through the rest of his long career, he devoted his time and substantial funds from his million-plus inheritance beginning in 1927, to a wider recognition of black achievement, first, by making documentary photographs of virtually every celebrated black person. The list is staggering, in quality as well as quantity, and especially in the number of people photographed before their talents were generally recognized; but Van Vechten's eye and ear had been fairly unerring since the turn of the century, so it is not surprising to discover Shirley Verett at 24, Leontyne Price at 23, Lena Horne at 22, Diahann Carroll at 18, and about thirty years ago such subjects as James Baldwin, Alvin Ailey, Harry Belafonte, James Earle Jones, Chester Himes, LeRoi Jones, and Arthur Mitchell. Second, Van Vechten established the James Weldon Johnson Memorial Collection of Negro Arts and Letters at Yale University, surely one of the greatest repositories for black studies, and he specified in his will that any money ever realized from reprints of his own books and photographs be donated to the collection's endowment fund. It is difficult to conceive of the books written since Van Vechten's death, on various black figures and subjects, without the materials he amassed and collected and supported.

None of the preceding discussion addresses itself to the subtle distinction between patronage and patronizing. From the vantage point of the 1990s, it is difficult to embrace without strong reservation the naiveté and paternalism of the twenties as faultless when sincere, or forgivable when devious. It is doubtless easy for the one to become the other, but it may be almost as easy for the one to *seem* to become the other—blanket judgments are always dangerous—because of black dismay over the circumstances that led to white patronage in the first place.

NOTES

1. Carl McCardle, "The Terrible Tempered Barnes," *Saturday Evening Post* (21 Mar. 1942): 93.
2. Quoted in McCardle, "The Terrible Tempered Barnes": 93.
3. See Mark Helbling, "African Art: Albert C. Barnes and Alain Locke," *Phylon* 43 (1982): 61.
4. Alain Locke, "The Legacy of the Ancestral Arts," *The New Negro* (1925; reprint, New York: Atheneum, 1969), p. 254.
5. Albert C. Barnes, "Negro Art in America," *The New Negro* (1925; reprint, New York: Atheneum, 1969), p. 20.
6. Nathan Irvin Huggins, *Harlem Renaissance* (New York: Oxford Univ. Press, 1971), pp. 82–83.

7. Huggins, *Harlem Renaissance*, p. 129.

8. Langston Hughes, *The Big Sea* (New York: Knopf, 1940), p. 324.

9. Louise Thompson Patterson, interview with the author, Nov. 1983.

10. Huggins, *Harlem Renaissance*, p. 93.

11. David Levering Lewis, *When Harlem Was in Vogue* (New York: Knopf, 1981), pp. 182–83.

12. Lewis, *When Harlem Was in Vogue*, p. 181.

13. Quoted in Bruce Kellner, *Carl Van Vechten and the Irreverent Decades* (Norman: Univ. of Oklahoma Press, 1968), p. 233.

14. Carl Van Vechten, *Red* (New York: Knopf, 1925), p. xv.

15. Huggins, *Harlem Renaissance*, p. 100.

16. Quoted in Bruce Kellner, *"Keep A-Inchin' Along": Selected Writings of Carl Van Vechten About Black Arts and Letters* (Westport, CT: Greenwood, 1979), p. 8.

17. Carl Van Vechten, *Nigger Heaven* (1926; reprint, New York: Avon, 1951), p. 189.

CARL VAN VECHTEN PRESENTS THE NEW NEGRO

LEON COLEMAN

The Negro Renaissance of the 1920s was a reflection in literature and art of the cultural changes experienced by the American Negro as he left the rural South for the economic and social advantages found in northern cities. The crowded, bustling life of the northern ghettoes accelerated the breakdown of older patterns of Negro life and thought, and gave rise to the concept of the "New Negro." Although the meaning of the term was somewhat vague, it contained the implication of the Negro's psychological break with past racial attitudes of subservience, humility, and self-apology. Negro writers, musicians, and painters of the Twenties attempted to give artistic expression to the more positive attitudes of self-acceptance and self-respect which the image of the New Negro seemed to connote. Rejecting past depictions of Negro life by Negro artists as being either too polemical or too apologetic, many of the young artists of the Negro Renaissance sought to portray Negro life objectively.

During the early years of the decade, writers of the Negro intelligentsia who aspired to portray the image of the New Negro were faced with two major difficulties: the absence of an audience for their work and the lack of a means of publication. In addition, there was disagreement among the artists of the Negro Renaissance as to how the Negro should be portrayed. Some felt that the lower-class stratum of Negro life should be ignored; others believed that the vital elements of the Negro's cultural heritage were to be found primarily in lower-class Negro folk-life. These problems were further complicated by the struggle of most of the Negro artists to overcome the cultural dualism inherent in being both black and American.

The publicity which attended the announcement of the New Negro concept was instrumental in bringing the problems confronting Negro Renaissance artists to the attention of white sympathizers. Of all the white well-wishers who became interested in the advancement of Negro expression in the arts, it was Carl Van Vechten who figured most prominently in assisting the members of the Negro Renaissance in their search for solutions to these problems.

In the latter years of the Twenties, as a result of the success of his novel *Nigger Heaven*, Carl Van Vechten received extensive publicity, both in America and abroad, associating him with Harlem and with the Negro Renaissance. Unfortunately the vehement controversy which was aroused by the book among Negro critics and the Negro press, who attacked it, and the Negro authors and friends of Van Vechten, who defended it, had the effect of obscuring the true nature and extent of Van Vechten's role in the Negro Renaissance. Many of the later Negro scholars and critics have not escaped a partisan view of Van Vechten's contribution, while others have virtually ignored him.

Professor Sterling Brown of Howard University has dismissed Van Vechten as "one of the pioneers of the hegira from downtown to Harlem; he was one of the early discoverers of the cabaret, and his novel, *Nigger Heaven*, is to the exotic pattern what *Swallow Barn* was to the contented slave."[1] Hugh Gloster, writing in 1948, characterized Van Vechten as "merely a literary faddist capitalizing upon a current vogue and a popular demand."[2]

In discussing the significance of the Negro Renaissance at a forum concerned with a retrospective view of the New Negro, Charles S. Johnson, then President of Fisk University, mentioned Van Vechten only as one of a number of white judges of *Opportunity* magazine's literary contests, although five years earlier he had publicly acknowledged that Van Vechten was the first white American writer to portray the New Negro objectively.[3] Benjamin Brawley, on the other hand, condemned Van Vechten for debasing the writing of Negro authors through the influence of *Nigger Heaven*.[4] In John Hope Franklin's history of American Negroes, a chapter is devoted to the Harlem Renaissance in which Van Vechten is referred to as one of a group, including Victor F. Calverton, H. L. Mencken, and Joel Spingarn, who lent "their pens to the encouragement of Negroes and the use of Negro materials."[5] Another Negro scholar, J. Saunders Redding, merely lists Van Vechten among other active white liberals of the period who were invited to parties given by the Negro elite.[6]

The importance given to Van Vechten's role in the Negro Renaissance by his adherents contrasts markedly with these minimizing estimates. George Schuyler, a member of the Harlem group, has stated that:

> His [Van Vechten's] great legacy to future generations is the honor of having boldly entered where lesser men feared to tread having wrought a real revolution in the white man's thinking about the Negro.[7]

In a letter to Van Vechten concerning his approval of the article cited above, Schuyler further credits him with securing for the Negro artist the psychological satisfaction of "recognition and acceptance from the top."[8] James Weldon

Johnson, the closest friend to Van Vechten among the Negro writers, felt that his importance in aiding Negro artists should not be underestimated.[9] At least one Negro author, Zora Neale Hurston, feared that the magnitude of Van Vechten's contribution to Negro arts and letters might suffer diminution with the passing of time. She wrote to him in July 1947, requesting permission to do his biography because, as she stated:

> You have had such a tremendous influence on the arts of the last twenty-five years, that I think it ought to be precipitated out of the mass of lies that are now growing up. People are now brazenly claiming credit for the many things that you were responsible for.[10]

Among white scholars who have called attention to Carl Van Vechten's role as mentor for the New Negro, Cedric Dover in *American Negro Art* (1960), Robert Bone in *The Negro Novel in America* (1958), Klaus Jonas in *Carl Van Vechten: A Bibliography* (1955), Edward Leuders in *Carl Van Vechten and the Twenties* (1955) and *Carl Van Vechten* (1964), and Bruce Kellner in *Carl Van Vechten and the Irreverent Decades* (1968) unanimously agree that Van Vechten fulfilled a unique role in furthering the Negro Renaissance, but none of these authors has considered the extent of Van Vechten's contribution in sufficient detail to provide a definitive evaluation. Without this kind of evaluation it is impossible to judge the validity of statements about Van Vechten such as that made by Lincoln Kirstein in 1964 regarding the influence of Carl Van Vechten upon the freedom marchers in Mississippi:

> Carl was too old to march to Mississippi last summer, but many who did go, even if they never suspected it, may have been reinforced by his long labors in the preservation and vitalization of everything that is best in the American Negro tradition; . . .[11]

or to judge the accuracy of an aphorism current during the latter half of the Twenties which states "If Carl Van Vechten was not responsible for the birth of the Negro Renaissance, he was certainly its midwife."[12] The following survey of Van Vechten's activities in behalf of the newly-born movement may serve as a basis for evaluating the importance of his contribution.

I. VAN VECHTEN'S GENERAL WRITING ON NEGRO TOPICS

The aid and encouragement that Carl Van Vechten rendered to the artists of the Negro Renaissance took three forms: first, general writing upon Negro arts and artists; second, assistance in securing publication for the works of individuals and encouraging their efforts through bringing them to the attention of the public; and third, attempts to promote social contacts between Negro artists and their white counterparts, thus disseminating information about Negroes to the wider community.

During a twelve-month period beginning in June 1926, Carl Van Vechten published ten articles and five book reviews concerning Negro music, theater, and literature. Eight of the articles appeared in *Vanity Fair*; one in *Theatre Magazine*; and one in the *Crisis*. All of the book reviews, with one exception, were published in the book section of the *New York Herald Tribune*.

In his writing upon Negro topics, Van Vechten sought to share his enthusiasm for his discoveries with the public; and by publicizing Negro artists' works, he attempted to create an audience for them. To achieve this goal, he turned to the news media, the newspapers and magazines, whose value as vehicles for publicity he knew well from his own experience as a critic for the *New York Times*. The articles and book reviews that he wrote concerned aspects of Negro life that were new, timely, even controversial. These articles became newsworthy in themselves because they were written by a literary celebrity at a time when, as Van Vechten's biographer Bruce Kellner comments, literary figures occupied a position just vacated by opera stars and not yet usurped by movie stars.[13] Van Vechten's method of publicity was a refined form of ballyhoo, applied with skill, in an era that adored the term. However, there is an additional element discernible in the articles. In some of them Van Vechten, in his capacity as a critic of the arts, attempted to guide Negro creative efforts by proffering advice, which often touched upon some of the problems of the Negro Renaissance.

The appearance of the major portion of Van Vechten's Negro articles in *Vanity Fair* was far from accidental. *Vanity Fair* was very much the *dernier cri* in the mid-Twenties. Under the editorship of Frank Crowninshield, it was a slick, sophisticated magazine concerned with the theater, the fine arts, and the world of ideas. Its list of contributors is a veritable *Who's Who* of famous names in music, literature, criticism, and art. Crowninshield was a good friend of Van Vechten, and had published Van Vechten's contributions since 1917. According to Van Vechten, Crowninshield published everything that he wrote about Negroes and "thus did a lot towards establishing them with other editors because at that time it was very rare to have a story about a Negro even in the newspapers and the magazines."[14]

Although Van Vechten frequently disclaimed publicly that he was a propagandist for the Negro cause, privately he sometimes admitted that this was true. In connection with the *Vanity Fair* articles, he stated that they did contain implied propaganda.[15] He took every opportunity in his writing to include names of Negro novelists, poets, dancers, singers, and artists in a manner calculated to whet the public's curiosity. In one article, "Prescription for a Nigger Theater," he mentions with praise the names of twelve Negro performers who could be heard and seen only in Harlem cabarets.[16] In a review of Walter White's novel *Flight*, Van Vechten eulogizes the writing of Paul Laurence Dunbar, Charles Chesnutt, and James Weldon Johnson. After extolling Chesnutt's *House Behind the Cedars* and calling Johnson's *Autobiography of an Ex-Colored Man* "an invaluable source-book" for the study of Negro life, he remarks that both books are out of print.[17] In a review of *The New Negro* he includes the names of six singers and dancers who were all successful on the stage or concert platform but who actually were only remotely connected with the book.[18] By these and other means he attempted to arouse public awareness to the existence of talented Negroes in the arts.

"The first time I heard Spirituals sung by a Southern Chorus . . . ," Van Vechten recollects, "I was bowled over."[19] While visiting Ellen Glasgow in Richmond, Virginia, in 1923, Van Vechten heard the spiritual singing of the Sabbath Glee Club, which so impressed him that he wrote an article about them in Miss Glasgow's magazine *The Reviewer.*[20] His lasting enchantment with the spirituals is revealed in his *Vanity Fair* article[21] "The Folksongs of the American Negro: The Importance of the Negro Spirituals in the Music of America";[22] and his *New York Herald Tribune* reviews of seven published collections of Negro songs and spirituals.[23]

In writing about the spirituals, Van Vechten admires them for the "unpretentious sincerity" that makes them equal or superior to any folk music in the world, and he esteems them as the "simple, spontaneous outpouring from the heart of an oppressed race."[24] It was their simplicity and artlessness, which he felt made the spirituals unique, that caused him to decry efforts made by both white and Negro singers to "concertize" them. He thought that Negro singers, particularly, destroyed the authenticity of the spirituals by refusing to sing them in dialect. Recognizing that many Negroes were ashamed of the spirituals because of their association with slavery, he states that this attitude is changing: "The intelligent members of the race are doing more to perpetuate these melodies, the most important contribution America has yet made to the literature of music, than anyone else."[25]

Van Vechten's reviews of collected spirituals and folk songs were, as might have been expected, highly laudatory. It was his contention that no time should be wasted in searching out and preserving these specimens of indigenous folk art before they were lost forever. He was ahead of his time in suggesting that these songs should be recorded by phonograph before they disappeared.[26]

It was Van Vechten's enthusiasm for the spirituals that was partly responsible for his launching the concert career of Paul Robeson. After appearing in Eugene O'Neill's plays *The Emperor Jones* and *All God's Chillun Got Wings*, which O'Neill wrote with him in mind, Paul Robeson found his acting career limited because of a lack of Negro plays with suitable parts. He had been moderately successful as a ballad singer in cabarets, but he had an ambition to sing spirituals. He would often entertain at parties by singing spirituals without accompaniment. On one occasion, he sang at the home of Van Vechten accompanied for the first time on the piano by Laurence Brown, the accompanist of Roland Hayes. Van Vechten's immediate enthusiasm sparked the arrangement by a small group of friends for a concert by the two men, which was held at the Greenwich Village Theatre in April 1925. This concert was so successful that it was followed by two others within a few months. At each concert, according to a report, "scores of people were turned away and . . . the enthusiasm of the audience knew no bounds."[27]

For the second concert, Van Vechten wrote panegyrical program notes in which he remarks that he would rather hear Robeson and Brown sing *Little David Play on Your Harp* "than hear anyone else sing anything." But he modestly declined to mention his role in arranging the first concert. He attributes the success of the concerts to the variety of moods expressed by the Negro songs, which surprised the audience, and to the evangelical rendering of the spirituals sung in dialect by Robeson, who was not ashamed to indulge in the vocal characteristics of Negro inflection.[28] The following year, on January 5, 1926, Robeson and Brown presented a song recital at Town Hall which received laudatory notices in the major newspapers of New York and Boston.

Van Vechten's acquaintance with the blues as a Negro art form came somewhat later than his discovery of the spirituals. In 1925, he wrote to Langston Hughes that he had just heard Bessie Smith and Ethel Waters for the first time. Also, in May 1925, Van Vechten requested Hughes to supply him with information about the blues for an article that he was preparing for *Vanity Fair*. Hughes replied, describing his own reaction to the blues, which Van Vechten used in his article, acknowledging his obligation to the young poet.

Two *Vanity Fair* articles, "The Black Blues" and "Negro 'Blues' Singers," and one book review in the *New York Tribune*, "Mean Ole Miss Blues Becomes Respectable," attest to Van Vechten's zeal in promoting public awareness to the artistry inherent in the blues and in blues singing. In the first article in *Vanity Fair*, Van Vechten again points out that Negroes look down upon their own music, refusing to appreciate the artistic value of the blues because the blues are humble in origin and occasionally too frank in expression. He credits W. C. Handy with introducing him to the technical aspect of performing the blues, and he praises the blues for their poetic and imaginative use of "rich idioms, metaphoric phrases and striking word combination." He feels that "they deserve the same serious attention that has tardily been awarded to spirituals."[29]

Van Vechten's next *Vanity Fair* writing on the subject of the blues appeared in March 1926. It is a paean of praise for the blues singing of Bessie Smith, whose records he had begun to collect by the boxful. The article presents, once again, his exhortation for Negro artists to make use of their folk heritage without self-consciousness. He begins by recounting his experience on Thanksgiving Day in 1925, when he and some friends had journeyed to Newark, New Jersey, to a theater where Bessie Smith was appearing. They were the only whites present in the audience. Van Vechten comments that Bessie Smith may be crude and primitive, but "she represents the true folk-spirit of the race. She sings the blues as they are understood and admired by the coloured masses."[30] After the performance, Van Vechten, accompanied by his wife Fania, went backstage for his first meeting with Bessie Smith. Langston Hughes wrote to Van Vechten the following January that he had met Bessie backstage in Baltimore and had informed her about Van Vechten's forthcoming article:

> She remembered you and your wife but didn't seem at all concerned as to whether articles were written about her or not. And her only comment on the art of the Blues was that they had put her 'in de money.'[31]

In succeeding months, Bessie Smith became better acquainted with Van Vechten. She sang at his parties and, during the Thirties, posed for a photograph by him. A review of *"Blues,"* edited by W. C. Handy, enabled Van Vechten to again direct attention to James Weldon Johnson, whom he credits as the first person to point out the serious merits of the blues. Prior to the publication of Handy's book, Van Vechten asserts, there were only two other serious advocates of the blues besides Mr. Johnson—Dorothy Scarborough and himself. He expresses the hope that other Negro musicians will be encouraged to preserve on paper the original form of the blues.[32] Van Vechten's championship of Negro music as a native American art form provided artistic and critical sanction for a part of the Negro's cultural heritage that had been largely unknown to whites and deplored by some Negroes. He warned Johnson that "There is going to be a riot of interest in Negro music. . . . You now have the upper hand; don't let anybody else get it."[33]

Viewing the state of the Negro theater, Van Vechten found that white producers had already skimmed off the cream. In the article "Prescription for a Nigger Theater," he took a hard look at the shortcomings of the Negro musical revue, which had declined in popularity since the initial success of *Shuffle Along* in 1921. He charged that each successive revue was an imitation of the one which proceeded it, repeating the same formula of the "over-reddened lips," "the chorus of girls so light and powdered that they seem white," and the same tiresome repetition of the haunted cemetery scene and the "inevitable levee or plantation scenes."[34] In Van Vechten's opinion, the white producer had stolen the best features from the Negro stage, leaving the Negro producer with the stale features of the white stage.

His advice for improvement echoed that offered by Max Rheinhardt in an interview given during the previous year. Rheinhardt, who had thought that Negro musicals were original and artistic, advised Negro actors and dramatists to be original, to sense the folk spirit, to develop the folk-idiom, and above all to beware of allowing the original Negro technique of expression to become smothered in an imitation of white acting.[35] Van Vechten, too, suggested that the Negro should be original and portray Negro life as only Negroes could, by presenting scenes of Negro life with imagination and style. His conclusion is that "if the Negro will stick to his own . . . he will be able to evolve . . . a type of entertainment which will be world famous, instead," he adds prophetically, "of the fad of a few people for a few moments."[36]

With the writing of "'Moanin' Wid a Sword in Ma Han,'" Carl Van Vechten addressed himself directly to the artistic problems of the Negro Renaissance and summed up his opinions regarding the emergence of the Negro artist as an objective portrayer of Negro life.[37] In this article he made explicit the implications of his earlier articles. He states, categorically, that Negro artists have not exploited their own resources; instead it is the white artist who has done so. He cites, as evidence, the fact that the Charleston, which originated in Harlem, has as its most famous performer not a Negro but two white dancers, Fred Astaire and Ann Pennington. Similarly, in music the Negro has failed to make use of his heritage. The spirituals are heard, with few exceptions, only in tepid concert versions; and the blues, which are never sung by Negro performers in white theaters, are never presented in Negro revues for white audiences.

Van Vechten felt that the same situation prevailed in literature. In his view, there exists a "wealth of exotic and novel material" in the picturesque elements of Negro society, but Negro writers shun it because of an understandable sensitivity which is "based on the fact that white writers about the Negro have chosen to depict the squalor and vice of Negro life rather than its intellectual and cultural aspects." Although the new school of Negro writers has seen the advantage of using this material, he sees little hope for them, since they lack encouragement from the Negro public which cannot look objectively upon the portrayal of the Negro in fiction. Carl Van Vechten concludes by stating that "the Negro, though justifiably sensitive about his past, must use the material with which he is most familiar and which is his heritage, if he hopes to succeed." The alternative, which he had mentioned in an earlier piece, was to let this wealth of material be exploited by white writers. The article in *Vanity Fair* contains the last public advice that Van Vechten offered to Negro writers; at the time of its publication, he was working on the second draft of *Nigger Heaven*.

II. VAN VECHTEN'S AID AND ENCOURAGEMENT TO INDIVIDUALS

The first *Opportunity* literary contest for black writers, as well as the contests of 1925 and 1926, were sponsored by Casper Holstein, who was ostensibly a real estate dealer and a night club operator, but who actually derived most of his income from the numbers game in Harlem. He was well known for his philanthropy, although he did not seek publicity. The only exception was his donation of the literary prizes to *Opportunity* which were known as the "Holstein Literary and Art Prizes," and which totaled a thousand dollars.

In December 1926, Van Vechten wrote to Charles S. Johnson, the editor of *Opportunity*, that he wished to show his appreciation for the magazine and to encourage young writers to give their best efforts to it. He offered to contribute a $200 cash award for the best signed contribution to appear during 1927. The judges for the Van Vechten award were his former professor, Robert Morse Lovett, who was then an editor of the *New Republic*, James Weldon Johnson, and Charles S. Johnson. They awarded the prize to Dantes Bellegarde for an article, "Haiti under the United States." Claude McKay and Langston Hughes were among six who received honorable mention. *Opportunity* lost its principal award donor in 1928, when Holstein was kidnapped and held for $50,000 ransom. This made Van Vechten's contribution to the 1928 contest doubly welcome. Van Vechten changed the name of the award to "The Award in Memory of Florence Mills Offered by Carl Van Vechten," and it was won by E. Franklin Frazier for an article titled "The Mind of the Negro." It was awarded in the fateful year of 1929.

Aside from his general assistance to the artists of the Negro Renaissance, Van Vechten was instrumental in furthering the careers of many Negro artists through personal help. Often this took the form of writing prefaces for their books, blurbs for the dust jackets, and favorable quotations for book advertisements. In other instances, Van Vechten took direct action in finding an outlet for their work.

Carl Van Vechten was wholly responsible for the reappearance in print of Johnson's *Autobiography of an Ex-Coloured Man*. The novel, published in 1912, had been long out of print; in fact, when Van Vechten wanted to read it in 1925, he had to wait until Adele Astair finished reading a copy which she had borrowed from a friend. When he received the book, he read it in one sitting and pronounced it a "remarkable book." He found occasions in his articles to mention both the book and its author whenever possible. In March 1925, Van Vechten wrote Johnson that he had found an opportunity to mention him in a review of a book by Alexander Woolcott. By May 1926 he had arranged for the republication by Alfred Knopf of Johnson's *Autobiography*, which came out in 1927 with an introduction by Van Vechten. Van Vechten's own copy bears an inscription by James Weldon Johnson: "To my best of friends, Carl Van Vechten, who rediscovered and rescued this book."

The friendship shared by Johnson and Van Vechten was a deep and abiding one. They dined at each other's home so frequently that Van Vechten, in 1930, expressed an interest in acquiring a house across the street from the one owned by Johnson. In one letter, written in 1926, Van Vechten states that his happiest days were spent with Johnson and his wife Grace. After Johnson's death in an automobile accident in 1938, Van Vechten wrote:

> During his lifetime, I always had the feeling that James Weldon Johnson was a great man, perhaps the greatest it has ever been my good fortune to know personally. I have frequently remarked that, had he been a white man, at least . . . he would have been Ambassador to the Court of St. James; at the most, he might have been President of the United States.[38]

One of Carl Van Vechten's favorite writers among the Harlem literati was Langston Hughes. Hughes, like Van Vechten, believed that Negro art was necessarily racial art, since the Negro artist, if he used the material that he knew best, was bound to reflect his background and his racial environment. Hughes was first introduced to Van Vechten by Walter White in the middle of the dance floor at Happy Rhone's cabaret in Harlem on November 10, 1924, the night that Hughes returned to America from his European wanderings. They did not meet again until the occasion of the *Opportunity* awards dinner nearly a year later. At that time Van Vechten requested that Hughes send him his poems to read.

After reading the poems, Van Vechten praised them for their beauty and sensitivity and returned them to Hughes in Washington, D.C., suggesting that he rearrange them for publication and perhaps use the title of the prize-winning poem, "The Weary Blues," as the title for the book. He added: "I shall do my best to get it published because it is a beautiful book." A few days later, when Hughes returned the poems, Van Vechten, in a letter dated Wednesday, informed him that "Knopf is lunching with me today and I shall ask him to publish them and if he doesn't some one else will." In the same letter, Van Vechten asked Hughes for permission to write an introduction to the book. The following day, Thursday, he wrote Hughes that he had given the poems to Knopf, and on Sunday Van Vechten was able to send Hughes the good news that Knopf had accepted *The Weary Blues* for publication and that the book would probably appear in January, 1926. In addition, he told Hughes that he had spoken to *Vanity Fair* about him and that the editors were anxious to see his work, and he requested some more poems. Langston Hughes responded in a letter dated May 18, 1925, and expressed his gratitude, saying, "... I imagined I'd be all summer looking for a publisher, if I ever found one. You're my good angel! How shall I thank you." A week later, Van Vechten received another note of appreciation, this time from Alain Locke, who thanked him for his interest in Hughes, which "is much appreciated by his friends, and by all of us interested in this promising movement."

The September 1925 issue of *Vanity Fair* contained the first poems by Langston Hughes to appear in a major white periodical. Four poems by Hughes were included in a boxed center column surrounded by an article by Virgil Thompson on "The Future of American Music." Van Vechten provided an introduction which consisted of a brief sketch of the career of the poet, a mention of the forthcoming publication of his *Weary Blues*, and an evaluation of the poems. Van Vechten lauds them for their sensitivity, racial reflection, beauty, color and warmth.[39] A similar note, bringing *Vanity Fair* readers up to date on Hughes's career, was published in the May 1926 issue. Van Vechten remarks upon the publicity which followed Vachel Lindsay's reading of Hughes's poems at the Washington hotel where Hughes was working as a busboy. *Vanity Fair* readers, he states, would not have been amazed, having been introduced to Hughes's poetry some months earlier. He includes two of Hughes's latest poems, which he regards as representing "an attempt that almost no other Negro poet has made," that of capturing the spirit of the Negro folksong.[40] The poems, "A Lament Over Love" and "Fortune Teller Blues," are in dialect, and are strongly reminiscent of the rhythm and form of blues lyrics.

Van Vechten continued to assist Langston Hughes in every way possible. He gave a party for him to which he invited people who would help to promote his book, and he encouraged Hughes to write a book about his travel experiences. Van Vechten felt that such a book would be very timely, since "now is the psychological moment when everything chic is Negro." He also acted as Hughes's unofficial literary agent. When Ridgely Torrence refused to publish one of Hughes's poems in the *New Republic*, Van Vechten remarked, in a letter to Hughes, "We'll get it in somewhere else. I'll try the *Nation* next."

Before the first Hughes article appeared in *Vanity Fair*, Van Vechten had rushed into print with a note in that magazine about Countee Cullen, whom he had met at the same time that he met Hughes. "Countee Cullen: A Note About the Young Negro Poet" was published in June 1925, and offered Van Vechten the opportunity to catalogue the names of fifteen Negro Renaissance artists who were, he said, examples of the talent that was pouring out of Harlem. He characterized Cullen as one of the best of the Negro writers and praised his poetry as suave, brittle, lyrical and possessing intellectual elegance.[41] Van Vechten offered Cullen a chance to publish with Knopf, but Cullen, who was better known than Hughes, had accepted another offer. However, a letter from Walter White informed Van Vechten that Cullen was "highly elated" over the publication of his poems in *Vanity Fair* and was "especially grateful" for Van Vechten's aid.

Walter White was another recipient of Van Vechten's aid. In 1924, shortly after their first meeting, he acknowledged Van Vechten's efforts to promote *Fire in the Flint* by saying that if the novel achieved success it would be largely due to Van Vechten's generosity. He was so impressed by Van Vechten that in 1927 he named his son Carl, for which he was criticized in an editorial by a Chicago Negro news magazine.[42]

Walter White constantly sent promising Negro writers and painters to the Van Vechten apartment in New York. Among these was Rudolph Fisher, whose story "City of Refuge" White had read in the *Atlantic Monthly*. In August, 1925, Fisher visited Van Vechten, who liked him "immensely" and was very sorry to see him leave. When Fisher completed his novel *The Walls of Jericho*, Van Vechten arranged its publication with Knopf in 1928. Another visitor was Aaron Douglas, who arrived at Van Vechten's door a few weeks after Fisher's visit. Douglas brought with him a portfolio of his paintings, whose subject matter (Charleston dancers and jungle scenes), as well as his skill in rendering them, caused Van Vechten to remark to Hughes that one day Douglas would be famous. Later he wrote Hughes that he had been able to get Douglas "several book jackets to do at Knopf's."

The list of Negro writers, singers, and painters who received personal encouragement from Van Vechten is long, and was so actively promoted by Van Vechten that it was a matter of gossip column comment. One columnist, observing Van Vechten's behavior at the premiere performance of the Negro revue *Africana*, states wryly:

> There was the passion of possession in Mr. Van Vechten's claps and cheers. Did not Mr. Van Vechten discover Miss Waters? Did not Mr. Van Vechten make Miss Waters what she is today? Is not Mr. Van Vechten satisfied? As we peasantry put it, I'll say![43]

One of the reasons for Van Vechten's enthusiasm for Ethel Waters, apart from her acknowledged ability in singing and dancing, was that her performances were rooted in the Negro folk tradition. She sang with more refinement than Bessie Smith or Clara Smith, as she interpreted the blues to sophisticated Negro and white audiences, but she did not lose the true Negro characteristic of voice and gesture. Ethel Waters, agreeing in principle with Langston Hughes, once stated in an interview that Negro artists could stand on their own heritage.[44]

Another singer, Taylor Gordon, owed the beginning of his career to the good offices of Carl Van Vechten. Gordon auditioned for Van Vechten at their first meeting in Van Vechten's apartment. This led to the arrangement of Gordon's first concert of spirituals by the Theater Guild in 1925, with Van Vechten supplying a program note of praise. A few years later Gordon wrote a letter to Van Vechten telling of his experience in Paris which Van Vechten found so amusing that he showed it to his friends. When Taylor Gordon returned, Van Vechten encouraged him to write about his life, and in 1929 Gordon's autobiography was published with the title *Born To Be*.

By 1927, Van Vechten had become so well known for his aid to Negro artists that the *Pittsburgh Courier* regarded anyone approved by him to be assured of success. The paper reported that James Allen, a self-taught photographer, had been made a staff member of a photography firm where he had begun as an errand boy. The paper commented that "Langston Hughes introduced him to Carl Van Vechten and the young man is now on his way to prominence." In the case of Allen, the statement was true. Van Vechten arranged for Allen to meet and photograph important subjects, in accordance with the plan Van Vechten had suggested to Hughes. The initial contacts later resulted in James Allen's opening his own studio.

Not so well known, perhaps, were such facts as these: Van Vechten made an annual contribution to the Harlem Y.M.C.A. He repeatedly worked to secure famous performers for NAACP benefits. He gave financial assistance to Negro Renaissance artists. These facts must have been unknown to one lady novelist of the Negro Renaissance group, who stated that she did not like Van Vechten much and questioned his motives "for attending and making possible these mixed parties." The "mixed parties," however, were an important aspect of Carl Van Vechten's attempt to break down racial barriers and were a practical application of his concept for promoting better race relations.

III. VAN VECHTEN'S PARTIES: SOCIAL MEANS TO A RACIAL END

At the time, in 1924, when Van Vechten first began to get "violently interested" in Negroes, personal contacts on an equal basis between Negroes and whites were exceptional rather than customary. White persons came into contact with Negroes in the course of their daily affairs without really noticing them as individuals, deriving their general conception of Negroes from the stereotypes presented in magazines, in films, and on the stage. One reporter for *The New York Times* confessed, in 1935, that he had entirely accepted the stage presentation of the Negro as a simple and naive person because those that he met in real life seemed at least superficially similar to their stage brethren.[45] Viewing Negroes as an undifferentiated mass often caused whites to react with surprise when they met Negroes of intelligence and ability.[46] Van Vechten himself did not escape the commonly held white conception of Negro homogeneity. He states that he was quite happy one night in 1924 to discover a Negro whom he hated as a person, because until that time he had considered them all as one. Significantly, it was after this episode that he began to invite Negroes to his home. Thereafter, he never thought of people as Negroes, but as friends who happened to be Negro.

It was Van Vechten's theory that prejudice against Negroes was based upon a complete ignorance on the part of the American public about Negro life, and that this was the great trouble in race relations. He wife Fania echoed his belief in an interview in England, stating that "color prejudice and racial strife are due to ignorance and thoughtlessness. They will disappear as knowledge and culture advance."[47] The Van Vechtens were not alone in their optimistic outlook. This theory about the betterment of race relations, and their own efforts to implement it, seemed to be the only approaches to the problem possible at the time.

The almost complete isolation of the Negro masses from any meaningful contact with the white community during the early Twenties left open only those areas of common interests in the arts, in education, in sociology, and in the entertainment world as points of contact between the races. Those who were active in these interests on both sides of the racial barrier saw the possibility that by extending their participation in these activities the barrier itself might be breached. This concept of improving race relations was somewhat similar to the idea, held by the Talented Tenth during the nineteenth century, of breaching caste with class. It differed from the older concept in that art, talent, and intellectual ability were to be substituted for class on both sides. In theory, once the wider community became aware of the existence of the Negro intelligentsia and of Negro creative artists, ignorance concerning the character and ability of Negroes would diminish, and prejudice, based on ignorance, would wane.

This concept was voiced in an early issue of *Opportunity* in a report on the performance of *Salome*, presented by a Negro and white theater association. The reporter noted that the common interest in the play shared by a mixed audience caused speculation as to whether "such a movement would not tend to break down race prejudice."[48] In *The New Negro*, there were also expressions of the opinion that art would be a means of transcending the barrier of race. Paul Kellogg, the editor of *Survey Graphic*, felt that the response by both races to the Negro's cultural gifts could lead to a new approach to the race problem, and could provide swifter progress than a "multitude of heavy treatises," and Alain Locke agreed wholeheartedly. "Art is slowly but surely knitting a close kinship between white and colored Americans," announced the *New York World*, and it cited the activities of Roland Hayes, Harry Burleigh, Paul Robeson, and Negro revues as doing their share to soften race prejudice.[49] Given the virulence of race prejudice in America in the Twenties, it was easy to see small signs as great portents. Even the *Nation* looked hopefully at the organization of a Negro–Caucasian club, which sought to promote sympathy and friendship through formal and social contacts at the University of Michigan.[50] But Langston Hughes found that not all white college students were amenable to such interracial activities. Speaking at a college in Pennsylvania, he asked the students what they could do along interracial lines to combat prejudice, and one student replied that "he joined the Ku Klux Klan on account of niggers like me!"

There were other dissidents to the cultural education theory. One of these suggested that the Negro intellectuals leave the "cabarets of the jaded dilettantes and help the mass of their brothers in the economic fight."[51] Another critic thought that those people who were interested in Negro artists should extend their interest to include all Negroes and work to secure political reforms. But for the most part, even those Negro and white officials of the NAACP and the Urban League, who were working at the grass roots level of racial betterment, agreed that racial understanding could best be achieved by the racial intermingling of those who were intellectually and artistically equals.

Carl Van Vechten's application of the theory of "mixing" was put into practice at a time when, as Langston Hughes relates, "white people seemed to feel themselves very brave if they let themselves be seen with a colored person."[52] As a part of Van Vechten's efforts to promote social contacts between the Negro writers, singers, and artists and his white friends of similar talents and interests, he began to invite them to his apartment without inquiring among either group as to whether such arrangements were acceptable. He carefully concealed from both that there was any ulterior motive underlying his frequent gatherings. Instead of a frontal assault by propaganda upon the racial wall, he preferred to wear it down by habitually traversing it. Only occasionally during this period did he admit to close friends what he was attempting to do. His wife, in an interview for the *London Sunday Herald*, did reveal their commitment by saying:

> My husband and I . . . have learned so much about the drawbacks cultured colored people in America suffer . . . that we are engaged in a crusade to break down the colour bar.[53]

In letters to James Weldon Johnson, Langston Hughes, and Charles Chesnutt, Van Vechten confided his aims to further the Negro cause. Chesnutt's reply, in 1926, indicates the reliance that he placed upon the efforts of influential whites in the improving of race relations; he states:

> It is up to you and men like you, to say what can be done, and to do it if you feel so disposed, as to what you have written to me . . . seems to make it plain that you do.

The Twenties were famous for parties, at which there was always food and, especially, drink in abundance. During the latter half of the decade, the white intelligentsia gave a great many parties to which Negroes were invited, but only Van Vechten's parties were "so Negro," as Langston Hughes recalls, that they were reported in the Negro newspapers. For Van Vechten, party-giving was, at least in part, a social means to a racial end. In his *Oral History*, he admits that by giving parties with Negroes present he had "a great deal of success in proselytizing, because other people began to take this up," and although it was just a fad for many people which did not continue, "for me," he adds, "it was something that meant something." He reiterates that he never resorted to "pure propaganda," because he was able to do more good with another method of procedure. One facet of his "other" method of procedure consisted of bringing people of like interests together, and just letting them interact personally, without intervention. Of his own role in the method he states simply: "I'm a catalyst, mainly."

At Van Vechten's parties, which often lasted until dawn, George Gershwin might be found playing the piano, and Paul Robeson or Bessie Smith might be heard singing to a group which might include such frequent guests as Helena Rubenstein, Salvador Dali, James Weldon Johnson, H. L. Mencken, Louis Untermeyer, Fannie Hurst, Miguel Covarrubias, Witter Bynner, Walter White, Langston Hughes, Theodore Dreiser, as well as many other celebrities of various kinds and colors from various parts of the world. In his capacity as catalyst, Van Vechten would move unobstrusively among the guests filling their glasses. A Negro society note, typical of the coverage given to Van Vechten's parties, reports a party for the French writer Paul Morand, at which the Van Vechtens entertained in their "characteristically informal manner," and lists the names of Negroes who represented Harlem at the affair.[54]

Parties often offered opportunities for Negro artists to make contacts with influential white people. As the custom of interracial parties spread, the areas of contact increased. At one party, given by Alma Wertheim, James Weldon Johnson met Louis Bruenberg, who had set Johnson's poem "The Creation" to music. Mrs. Wertheim became interested in the work, and through their efforts it was presented at Carnegie Hall with a portion of the Boston Symphony Orchestra directed by Sergei Koussevitzky, and with Jules Bledsoe as soloist. At Van Vechten parties, William Rose Benet first heard spirituals sung by Paul Robeson, Laurence Brown, and Jules Bledsoe, and he reported in the *Saturday Review* that the more spirituals he heard, the more moving and beautiful he felt them to be.[55] DuBose Heyward, whose novel *Porgy* inspired Gershwin's opera *Porgy and Bess*, attended a Van Vechten party and met Negroes socially for the first time. He was so moved by this experience that during the same night he inscribed Van Vechten's copy of *Porgy:*

> To Carl Van Vechten
> 12:30 A.M. November 4th, 1926
> In memory of this night and new friends.

The Van Vechten apartment also served as a place for the Negro intellectuals and artists to meet each other. Zora Neale Hurston wanted very badly to meet Ethel Waters and had written letters to her that remained unanswered. She informed Van Vechten of the fact and he responded by giving a dinner for Zora. Guests included Sinclair Lewis, Dwight Fiske, Anna May Wong, and Ethel Waters. This was the beginning of a warm friendship between Zora and Ethel. In May 1925, Langston Hughes had asked Van Vechten to introduce him to Zora

Neale Hurston, and to give Bessie Smith, whom Hughes had not then met, some blues he had written for her.

The extensive "mixed" party-giving and party-going did not escape the notice and criticism of the press, both Negro and white. One such notice commented that Van Vechten and his actress wife had taken to meeting "various colored persons socially."[56] Percy Hammond of the *New York Herald Tribune* noted that "a band of prominent N.Y. white folks . . . led by Carl Van Vechten and other intrepid abolitionists" had clasped the flower of Ethiopia by the hand to "help them even the rough places" and mingled with them in "soirees."[57] Some of the Negro newspapers, reflecting a middle-class attitude toward "mixing," also denounced them. The Chicago *Whip* judged, from a distance, that the understanding achieved by the "literary and artistic cults of [the] white and black races of New York" was an "unholy alliance of thrill seekers and revellers."[58] Van Vechten, as usual, was unperturbed.

Prior to the publication of *Nigger Heaven* in August 1926, many people of both races discounted or misunderstood Van Vechten's attempts to aid and encourage members of the Negro Renaissance. The publication of the novel strengthened their belief in the correctness of their assessment. A month before the novel was published, however, an article which appeared in a British newspaper, *The Yorkshire Press*, gave Van Vechten's efforts a far more accurate evaluation than any which had been expressed in America. The article begins by summarizing the race situation:

> Americans and not only Americans—derive a great deal of their amusement from the work of the coloured peoples. They dance to their music, they read their books and their poetry, they watch them act in their plays, and yet the prejudice against 'the confounded niggers' remains as strong as ever.

The article points out that a small number of Negroes in America had recently emerged into literary prominence, and singles out Van Vechten as being most important in fostering this improvement in the Negro's status. It states that Van Vechten used

> . . . direct methods to open up the way for the Negro artist to find a channel through which he might express his ideas. At the expense of a great deal of time, energy and money[,] Mr. Van Veckten [sic] survived the sneers from more narrow minded white people and succeeded in his great campaign against the American taboo.[59]

In 1927, when the Negro Renaissance had flowered into a vogue, a copy of *The New Negro* was presented to Carl Van Vechten. It was signed by James Weldon Johnson, Jessie Fauset, Jean Toomer, W.E.B. Du Bois, Zora Neale Hurston, Rudolph Fisher, Walter White, Alain Locke, and many others. The presentation of the book symbolized the importance of Van Vechten's efforts in aiding the artists of the Negro Renaissance.

NOTES

1. Sterling Brown, "Negro Character as Seen by White Authors," *The Journal of Negro Education* 2 (Jan. 1933): 182.

2. Hugh M. Gloster, *Negro Voices in American Fiction* (Chapel Hill: Univ. of North Carolina Press, 1984), p. 162.

3. Charles S. Johnson, "The Negro Renaissance and Its Significance," in *The New Negro Thirty Years Afterward* (Cambridge: Harvard Univ. Press, 1955), p. 85.

4. Benjamin Brawley, *The Negro Genius: A New Appraisal of the Achievement of the American Negro in Literature and the Fine Arts* (New York: Dodd, 1937), pp. 235–38 *passim.*

5. John Hope Franklin, *From Slavery to Freedom: A History of American Negroes.* 3d ed. (New York: Knopf, 1967), p. 499.

6. J. Saunders Redding, *The Lonesome Road: The Story of the Negro's Part In America* (Garden City, NY: Doubleday, 1958), p. 277.

7. George S. Schuyler, "The Van Vechten Revolution," *Phylon* 2 (Dec. 1950): 368.

8. George S. Schuyler to Carl Van Vechten, letter dated 4 Nov. 1950.

9. The following inscription, signed by James Weldon Johnson and dated 28 Sept. 1929, appears on the back cover of a compilation of gifts of Carl Van Vechten to the Yale University Library:

Dear Carl—Has anyone ever written it down—in black and white—that you have been one of the most vital factors in bringing about the artistic emergence of the Negro in America?

10. Zora Neale Hurston to Carl Van Vechten, letter dated July 1947, in the James Weldon Johnson Collection, The Beinecke Rare Book and Manuscript Library, Yale University (hereafter cited as the Johnson Collection).

11. Lincoln Kirstein from an unpublished eulogy for Carl Van Vechten (23 Dec. 1964), Johnson Collection.

12. Reprint (corrected and amended by Van Vechten) of George S. Schuyler's article, "The Van Vechten Revolution," *Phylon* 2 (Dec. 1950): 362–68. In the Johnson Collection.

13. Bruce Kellner, *Carl Van Vechten and the Irreverent Decades,* (Norman: Univ. of Oklahoma Press, 1968), p. 151.

14. Carl Van Vechten, *Oral History,* p. 216.

15. Carl Van Vechten, *Oral History,* p. 216.

16. Carl Van Vechten, "Prescription for a Nigger Theater," *Vanity Fair* (Oct. 1925): 46, 92, 98.

17. Carl Van Vechten, "A Triumphant Negro Heroine," *New York Herald Tribune Books,* 11 April 1928: 3.

18. Carl Van Vechten, "Uncle Tom's Mansion," *New York Herald Tribune Books,* 20 Dec. 1925: 5.

19. Carl Van Vechten, Catalogue note, Johnson Collection, p. 244.

20. Carl Van Vechten, "Pastiches at Pistaches. The Sabbath Glee Club of Richmond," *The Reviewer* 4 (Jan. 1924): 98–103.

21. Carl Van Vechten, *Vanity Fair* (Mar. 1925): 40, 78, 84.

22. Carl Van Vechten, "The Folksongs of the American Negro: The Importance of the Negro Spirituals in the Music of America," *Theatre Magazine* 42 (Aug. 1925): 24, 63.

23. Carl Van Vechten, *New York Herald Tribune,* 25 Oct. 1925, 20 Dec. 1925, 31 Oct. 1926.

24. Carl Van Vechten, *Theatre Magazine* 42 (Aug. 1925): 65.

25. Carl Van Vechten, *Vanity Fair* (July 1925): 25.

26. Carl Van Vechten, "Songs of the Negro," *New York Herald Tribune Books,* 25 Oct. 1925: 2. Also, "Don't Let Dis Harves' Pass," *New York Herald Tribune Books,* 31 Oct. 1926: 5.

27. Rita Romilly, "Concerning a Singer and an Actress," *The New Age* (10 Sept. 1925): 229.

28. Carl Van Vechten, Program in the Johnson Collection.

29. Carl Van Vechten, "The Black Blues," *Vanity Fair* (Aug. 1925): 57, 92.

30. Carl Van Vechten, "Negro 'Blues' Singers," *Vanity Fair* (Mar. 1926): 106.

31. Langston Hughes to Carl Van Vechten, letter dated Jan. 1926 in the Johnson Collection.

32. Carl Van Vechten, "Mean Ole Miss Blues Becomes Respectable." *New York Herald Tribune Books*, 6 June 1926: 1.

33. Carl Van Vechten to James Weldon Johnson, letter in the Johnson Collection.

34. Carl Van Vechten, "Prescription for a Nigger Theater," *Vanity Fair* (Oct. 1925): 46, 92, 98, passim.

35. "Max Rheinhardt Reads the Negro's Dramatic Horoscope," an interview by Alain Locke, *Opportunity* 2 (May 1924): 146.

36. Carl Van Vechten, *Vanity Fair* (Oct. 1925): 98.

37. Carl Van Vechten, "Moanin' Wid a Sword in Ma Han'," *Vanity Fair* (Feb. 1926): 61, 100, 102.

38. Carl Van Vechten, note in the Catalog of the Johnson Collection at The Beineke Rare Book and Manuscript Library, Yale University, p. 384.

39. Carl Van Vechten, "Langston Hughes: A Biographical Note," *Vanity Fair* (Sept. 1925): 62.

40. Carl Van Vechten, "Langston Hughes," *Vanity Fair* (May 1926): 70.

41. Carl Van Vechten, "Countee Cullen: A Note About the Young Negro Poet," *Vanity Fair* (July 1925): 62.

42. Editorial in *Heebie Jeebies*, 2 July 1927: 2.

43. Robert Garland, "Well What of It?" *New York Telegram*, 14 July 1927.

44. Mary Rennels, "Mary Rennels Says," Cleveland, Ohio *Press*, 6 Feb. 1928.

45. Bernard Sobel, "Finds Most Characters Incomplete," *New York Times*, 17 May 1935.

46. George S. Schuyler, "Our White Folks," *American Mercury* 20 (Dec. 1927): 390.

47. Arnold Dawson, "Tolerance or Death," *London Daily Herald*, 9 June 1927.

48. Esther Scott, "Negroes Actors in Serious Plays," *Opportunity* 1 (April 1923): 21.

49. Lester A. Walton, "Art Is Helping in Obliterating the Color Line," *New York World*, 17 May 1925.

50. William Pickens, "Youth Attacks the 'Color Line,'" *Nation* 122 (2 June 1926): 637–38.

51. Michael Gold, "Where the Battle is Fought," *Nation* 123 (14 July 1926): 37.

52. Langston Hughes to Carl Van Vechten, letter, 22 May 1927, Johnson Collection.

53. *London Sunday Herald*, 22 May 1927.

54. Geraldyn Desmond, Pittsburgh *Courier*, 9 April 1927.

55. William Rose Benet, "Cursive and Discursive," *Saturday Review* 2 (23 Jan. 1926): 505–7.

56. "Town Topics," 22 April 1926, (an unsigned newspaper clipping in the Johnson Collection).

57. Percy Hammond, "Oddments and Remainders," *New York Herald Tribune*, 21 Feb. 1926.

58. "Renaissance," Chicago *Whip*, 23 April 1927.

59. *The Yorkshire* (U. K.), 22 July 1926.

"WHAT WERE THEY SAYING?":
BLACK WOMEN PLAYWRIGHTS OF
THE HARLEM RENAISSANCE

NELLIE Y. MCKAY

The history of the Harlem Renaissance continues to engage both the scholars of Afro-American cultural and intellectual history and those of literary and aesthetic criticism even now, more than fifty years after that period came to an end. The impact of this brief, exciting interlude in the development of black arts and culture was sufficiently powerful to have influenced every succeeding generation of black writers and critics. In the field of literary studies, a great deal has been said and written about the period, and many of the writers who produced the works have, and rightly so, been heralded, applauded, and given the critical treatment that brings public recognition of their achievements. In our times, the names of Jean Toomer, Countee Cullen, Langston Hughes, and Claude McKay have become synonymous with the Harlem Renaissance and the development of Afro-American literature in the early twentieth century. Yet our ability to name these writers with authority is only the beginning of our knowledge of the Afro-American literary terrain of the 1920s. More work remains to be done to bring others, no less worthy than those with whom we are familiar, into full public view.

The excitement of the Harlem Renaissance was recaptured by the scholarship that emerged in the 1960s and early 1970s. This work, consciously aggressive in its affirmation of black culture, opened up new avenues of awareness of the importance of the early period, and the self-assurance it engendered has led to dynamic re-visionings of the meaning of the Afro-American experience and its relationship to the larger American society. In this new awareness, the contributions of some of the women who were prominent in the cultural and intellectual life of black America, from Phyllis Wheatley in the eighteenth century to writers and thinkers up until the middle of the twentieth century, have even more recently begun to gain a measure of the merits they deserve. In terms of black women and drama, the retrospective view reveals some interesting information, and provides another valuable position from which to observe literary creativity at the intersection of race and gender.

In the overall picture, studies in the history of the evolution of Afro-American drama inform us that current developments in the field come out of a well-grounded tradition with deep roots in the twin concerns for the role and function of art and the search for racial dignity in an oppressive society. As the scholarship of James V. Hatch and others demonstrates, black writers, including women, have always taken drama and playwriting seriously.[1] In addition, the unquestionable brilliance of several modern contemporary black playwrights adds an exciting dimension to the research in this genre.

The Harlem Renaissance was a special time in the evolution of black women playwrights in America. The first black woman to publish a play did so in 1918, sixty-three years after William Wells Brown's *Miralda, or the Beautiful Quadroon* became, in 1855, the first dramatic work by a black person to find its way into print in America. In contrast, Lucy Terry's "Bars Fight" of 1746, written 109 years earlier than Brown's play, earns her the place of the earliest black American poet of whom we have a record in this country. Harriet Wilson's *Our Nig: Or Sketches from the Life of a Free Black* (1859) makes her, along with Martin Delaney, one of the two people who hold third place in time for the U.S. publication of a novel by a black American. While the first black minstrel troupe (the Georgia Minstrels) was organized in 1865, and black women performers were admitted to the stage as early as 1891 in Boston, for black writers, especially for the women, the development of a body of written work in drama lagged behind those of fiction and poetry. This began to change toward the end of the second decade of this century.

Between 1918 and 1930, eleven black women published a total of twenty-one plays. Most were only one act in length, but all contributed to making women full participants in an overall effort to develop a black dramatic tradition in letters. It should be noted, however, that the art and the industry of the black theatre of that time did not particularly complement each other. Writers concerned with the former insisted on developing realistic portrayals of black life in their work, with the result that most of their plays were unacceptable for the commercial theater of the period. On the stage, minstrelsy, in its original form, was no longer the vogue, the cork-blackened faces having disappeared and the chorus of beautiful young black women having become a part of the new Negro musicals. Now too, trained musicians were on the stage, but the predominant image was that of the "exotic" Negro in gay song and dance routines. Montgomery Gregory, black critic of the Harlem Renaissance and beyond, observed that while these shows represented "notable advances" over what preceded them, they "fundamentally" carried on the old minstrel tradition. He thought they were "an imitation from the Negro's point of view of a caricature of himself," and had no artistic value.[2] The peak of that tradition came with *Shuffle Along*, which reached the New York stage by way of the Howard Theatre and Philadelphia in 1921, starring the famous Bert Williams and Florence Mills. This show was one of the most successful of its kind, and is credited by some as having launched that aspect of the Harlem Renaissance. "It represented the kind of theatre that [one group of] Negro performers, musicians, and writers had moved to from minstrelry with great success."[3]

It was enormously acclaimed at New York's 63rd Street Theatre, and matched the mood of the "flaming twenties" when the Negro was in vogue. Gregory and others like him conceded that this kind of theatre offered work and some opportunities to many black entertainers who developed "stage ability" in this way and succeeded in elevating what they did to the level of art, but it was of no benefit to a great many others. Specifically, it did not reflect the mood or the artistic talents of numbers of thoughtful black writers, or expose and nurture the abilities of serious black character actors.

In the serious literary and artistic categories, women and men suffered. Jean Toomer's *Balo* (1924) and *Natalie Mann* (completed in the mid-1920s) and John Matheus's *Cruiter* (1926) were among those by black men which did not achieve success in that time. *Balo*, a folk play, examines some of the strengths of black folk culture; *Natalie Mann*, an expressionist drama, for which Toomer has been applauded as having been "ahead of his time" in American theatrical history, explores the emptiness of pretensions to upper-class status and cultural "passing" by some black people; while *Cruiter* addresses the theme of the dehumanization of poor blacks that follows in the wake of northern industrial white recruitment of cheap black labor in the South. *Balo* had a short run at the Howard Theatre during its 1923–24 season; *Natalie Mann* has never been produced and was not published until 1980; and although *Cruiter* won the *Opportunity* magazine prize in 1926, it too was never performed. Garland Anderson was more fortunate than many of his black playwright compeers of the time. His *Appearances* (1925) made him the first Afro-American to have a dramatic work on Broadway. The story of a black bellhop who is falsely accused of raping a white woman (who turns out not to be white) and who uses his own will to goodness to overturn the charges against him, it had twenty-three performances in New York in 1925, then toured in Los Angeles, Seattle, Chicago, and San Francisco between 1927 and 1929. In 1930 it made a brief appearance on the London stage. Ironically, *Appearances*, which critic Clinton Oliver calls "a highly didactic dramatization of Christian Science doctrines," received poor responses from the black community.[4]

Meanwhile, white dramatists including Eugene O'Neill with *The Emperor Jones* (1920) and *All God's Chillun Got Wings* (1924); Paul Green with *In Abraham's Bosom*, a Pulitzer Prize winner (1926); and DuBose and Dorothy Heyward with *Porgy* (1926) were using Negro themes to help make names for themselves on the American stage. Between 1917 and 1930, by some estimates, no less than fifteen white playwrights "with various degrees of merits" had works with "Negro" themes produced on Broadway.[5] While I realize this is a generalization, the work of many white playwrights did not address the experiences of blacks in any serious way, and in their present historical context, they illuminate how wide a gap then existed between popular theatrical representations and the reality of Afro-American life. Further, as playwright Loften Mitchell reminds us, while the "Negro" as subject was introduced into the American theatre in 1769, from the beginning, in the hands of white playwrights, the characterizations were marked for stereotyping, ridicule, and the denial of individual human status. The pre-eminent American playwrights of the early decades of the twentieth century did little to alter or improve that situation.

Against this background of the popular black musical revue and the white dramatists with their unrealistic presentations of black life, although they tried, serious black writers of the era had few illusions about making careers writing for the stage. However, as with Toomer's *Balo*, some of the plays by these men and women were performed on non-commercial stages in Harlem, Washington, D.C., and in other urban centers with concentrations of black life. Some were included in anthologies such as *Plays of Negro Life* (1926), *The Yearbook of Short Plays* (1931), *Fifty More Contemporary Plays* (1928), and *Carolina Magazine* (1929); while *Crisis* and *Opportunity* magazines provided consistent invaluable publication outlets for many of these writers.

The heralds of black women's published dramatic writings in the 1920s were *Rachael* and *Mine Eyes Have Seen*, the first written by Angelina Weld Grimké, the second by Alice Dunbar-Nelson. Although *Mine Eyes Have Seen* appeared in print in 1918 in Boston, while *Rachael* did not appear until 1920, Grimké's play was originally presented by the NAACP in 1916 at the Myrtill School in Washington, D.C. This work claims fame as possibly the oldest extant play by a black woman, and is unusual because it is one of the few full-length ones to come out of the group at the time. It broke other important ground as well. For one, it was the NAACP's first attempt to use drama as one way to focus national attention on racial oppression, and as such it lent itself to the storm of controversy surrounding contemporary discussions of the role of art in society. For another, theatre experts believe it to be the second serious play written by a black person to be publicly performed by black actors.[6] *Rachael* was also performed at the Neighborhood Playhouse in New York, and in Cambridge, Massachusetts.[7]

Rachael is an angry play, revealing Grimké's enormous outrage at the impact of racism on the individual and collective group lives of black people. The action focuses on Rachael, a young black woman who sacrifices her chances for domestic happiness by turning her back on marriage and the joys of motherhood because she is convinced that the destructive effects of racism on the lives of black children are too high a price to pay for whatever personal satisfactions she might derive from them. Rachael has dreams of her unborn children coming to her and pleading that they not be brought into a world in which their unnecessary suffering is so inevitable. This consciousness of a would-be mother's dilemma comes to her from her observations of how young children whom she comes into contact with react to their first encounters with overt racism. It is impossible, even with the greatest outpouring of parental love, for any black child to escape its withering blight. All are diminished by it.

Bitter and satirical in its commentary, the play responds to events of an era when the lynchings of black people were commonplace and frequent occurrences, and when rampant segregation, racial discrimination, and a denial of humanity assaulted black people at every turn. Rachael's solution to the problem is dramatically drastic and a symbol of her feelings of psychological defeat in the face of awesome odds. For the black people who read or saw this play in performance, it emphasized the seriousness of their situation in America; for white liberals and others sympathetic to the plight of black people, it brought into sharp focus the extent to which white racism eroded humanity and threatened the social fabric of a nation that had been established on the premises of justice and equality for all people.

Rachael also embodies a strong feminist consciousness and draws our attention to the fact that Grimké's concerns for issues of autonomy, responsibility, and self-determination are not confined to race relationships, but extend to gender as well. Her condemnation of paternalism and condescension is no less acrid toward one form of oppression than toward the other. The heroine's response to her suitor, who believes that her decision not to marry comes from a too-serious response to the problems of race along with his own wish to determine the course of her life, makes this abundantly clear. "I wonder if you know how—maddening you are?" she asks him. "Why, you talk as though my will counts for nothing," she continues, then follows that with a definitive statement: "It's as if you're trying to master me. I think a domineering man is detestable."[8] She is an independent person who assumes full responsibility for the choices she makes. She is also a woman who claims authority over her body and her actions and accepts the consequences of her decisions. In the context of the play, she is a political individual who helps to establish the right of black women to take their place in the forefront of the struggle which addressed itself to the most important and difficult issues that were facing black people in America.

Rachael met with mixed reviews from those who saw it in 1916. There were a number of people who objected to the propaganda aspects of the plot because they held firmly to the belief that black drama, as well as other forms of Afro-American creative writing, should focus strictly on artistic concerns and not become involved in political issues. Within this artistic/intellectual community, ideological differences over the definition of the role of art eventually led to the organization of the Howard Players, a group that chose to perform only noncontroversial, apolitical plays. While black artists and critics have continued to debate the issues surrounding this quandary for many years, there seemed to be a consensus on the part of black women playwrights in the years immediately following the debut of Grimké's play to follow in her footsteps and to take the relationship between art and identity seriously. As a result, they wrote a number of plays that presented images of black life opposed to the exotic ones that appeared in the commercial theatre of the time. In these they made no attempt to disguise their political motives and they spoke directly to the realistic problems that black people, especially black women, faced in their daily lives.

Rachael also makes us aware that educated, middle-class, and to a certain extent privileged black women in the early part of this century were conscious of and deeply troubled by the social implications of race, not only for themselves as individuals, or for their group, but for all black people. Angelina Weld Grimké was a light-skinned, mixed-blood woman who grew up in "the liberal, aristocratic atmosphere of Boston," and who later spent most of her life as a teacher in Washington, D.C.[9] Many of the women who were involved in literature at this time came from similar backgrounds and shared other qualities with her. They were educated and in some cases well travelled; they kept abreast of current literary trends and were involved in civic activities. They had strong opinions on political and other issues that affected black life, and they spoke passionately on these in private and public forums inside and outside the black community. They were professional women (most were school teachers) who asserted their independence through the ways in which they chose to conduct their lives. They had few children of their own, although they were generous in giving their time and financial resources to help raise the children of other members of their families. Some, like Grimké, never married; others, like Dunbar-Nelson, had more than one marriage. Grimké's play was a good representative of the manner in which they integrated their major concerns with other areas of their lives, and a forerunner to much of the kind of writing women of her social group would do during the 1920s.

Much of Grimké's writings remain in manuscript, and we eagerly await the work of critic Gloria Hull to discover the full extent of her contributions to the literary life of her age. Hull claims that the poetry (for which Grimké is best known) is "delicate, musical, romantic, and pensive," and the critic speaks of the whole corpus as "predominantly sad and hushed," with "muted" sounds and colors.[10] While it may be true that there was "buried" sadness in Grimké's personal life, there is no question that she was deeply concerned with the world outside her private sphere. She wrote other plays, fiction, and expository prose. One work of hers we know of which has a close relationship to *Rachael* is her short story "The Closing Door." This appeared in Margaret Sanger's *Birth Control Review* in 1919 and reinforces our sense of the extent of her political commitment to causes affecting the lives of black women in particular. It is also interesting that Grimké, who never married and never had children, should find in the issues surrounding the lives of young mothers and children important materials from which to mount her own protest against racial and gender oppression.

Of the twenty plays that followed *Rachael*, and which were written by black women in the period under scrutiny, nine have central concerns connected to the conflicts of race and gender issues, six take in a wide variety of non-racial, non-gender conflict themes, two are comic in their portrayal of black folk life, one is a folk tragedy resulting from long-held superstitions, one an African dance drama, and one the story of a black warrior-poet of the sixth century. While it is clear that the topic these women chose to dramatize most often was that of the conflicts of race and gender, the variety of their other subjects, and the differences in the techniques they employed, serve to illustrate their collective intent to follow their own courses and set their own agenda as they struggled to find a place for themselves within a newly developing tradition.

Several of these playwrights have multiple works to their credit, and it is also interesting to note that several women wrote different kinds of plays. A good example of this can be seen in the three plays by Thelma Duncan: *The Death Dance* (1927), a ritual drama set in Africa; *Sacrifice* (1930), a non-racial play on the theme of friendship; and *Black Magic* (1931), a comic situation, based on old superstitions, that takes place in a Southern black rural community. This kind of versatility is also to be found in the works of Marita Bonner and Georgia Johnson (to be discussed later), and in May Miller's two plays, *Scratches* (1929), a drama with no racial content, and *Graven Images* (1930), which makes use of the myth of racial confrontation between Moses and Miriam during the long journey from Egypt to the Promised Land, and places American racial problems in a universal context. Along with these note must be made of Maud Cuney-Hare's *Antar of Arby* (1929), which is based on the legends of the romantic heroism of Antar, one of the cornerstones of Arab literature. The plays that are set outside of the United States reveal an awareness of a Pan-African consciousness among the women and serve the function of linking Afro-Americans to people of color in other parts of the world, thus expanding the knowledge of a larger cultural history. As a group, the works of these writers manifest how well they understood the implications of their creativity in relationship to the world outside of their own, as well as the questions of identity and individuality. They are historically important because they indicate the breadth of interests the women encompassed. These women authors took all aspects of the black experience and beyond as their territory, and thus asserted their connectedness to all parts of the human heritage.

Alice Dunbar-Nelson's *Mine Eyes Have Seen*, a one-act play, was published in the *Crisis* in April 1918. It addresses the question of the responsibility that black men may or may not have to participate in American-supported wars abroad. The timing was propitious. As World War I drew to a close, the black community became more aware of and incensed by the many indignities that black servicemen suffered in Europe at the hands of their American commanding officers, even as they were willingly making the ultimate sacrifice. In addition, the atrocities that they and all other black people suffered at home were not abating. Black anger was not always contained, and violence, connected to the treatment of black soldiers, erupted in several parts of the country in these years. For most Afro-Americans, the large issue in this dilemma went beyond their responses to the immediate situation, and compelled the need for a moral imperative to challenge the magnitude of their oppression. The question was one of whether black men should ever accept responsibility for military loyalty to a country that was not willing to treat black citizens as human beings. On one hand, Dunbar-Nelson explores issues surrounding the abusive use of power by white people against black people, and on the other, ways in which black people can search for autonomy and human dignity in the face of such oppression. As in Grimké's play, the themes are those of autonomy, human dignity, and the abuse of power as they affect Afro-Americans individually and collectively. The action of this play occurs at the intersection of race, class, and economic oppression. There are vivid portraits of human squalor and reports of the physical and psychological abuse that the black characters suffer at the hands of both Southern and Northern white people. It seems logical that the young man who is called to military duty will resist and refuse to comply with the order. He has been deprived of a home and parents because "niggers had no business having such a decent home," especially in the South, and he has seen his older brother become crippled in a "factory hell" because of the management's disregard for human life. He has no reason for willingly serving in the military. However, Dunbar-Nelson's protagonist chooses the path of "blind" patriotism, and he responds positively to the call.

In this work the playwright is concerned with how Afro-Americans respond to the racism that overtly intrudes on their lives when they make certain kinds of crucial decisions. A judgment for or against military service was rife for this debate. Alice Dunbar-Nelson, a journalist, poet, short-story writer, dramatist, and English teacher, was also an anti-war activist and a member of the American Friends Peace Committee who made "militant" political speeches across the country on behalf of this organization.[11] She well understood the interconnections between the sacrifices the underclasses were asked to make in wartime, and the power of those who profited in many ways from wars. Her play, with its ironic twist on the "Battle Hymn of the Republic," is biting satire on the political blindness that keeps people from seeing how they participate in and help to perpetuate their own oppression, and on the power that supports that blindness. *Mine Eyes Have Seen* emphasizes the need for a perceptive personal analysis of the ways in which moral and political choices are made.

But if Dunbar-Nelson gained little contemporary recognition for her moral stand, history has proved that her vision was clear. Stripped of the niceties of literary conventions, the themes in this play were to surface again, and with a good deal of violence, fifty years after she raised them. When, in the 1970s, significant numbers of black and white young men, many from the underclass, refused to participate in another American foreign war, their protest was against the sacrifice of their lives in a conflict which for them seemed predicated on the tenets of racism at home and abroad.

In the discussion of issues directly affecting the lives of women, that of the right of poor black women to have access to birth control was one that concerned women playwrights of the 1920s. Noted above was Angelina Grimké's short story on the subject in 1919. In that same year Mary Burrill published a play on it, also in the *Birth Control Review*. This is a unique work in black drama because it is completely centered in the dilemma of poor, rural, uneducated black women—the most powerless of social groups. Burrill's plot develops around a woman with many children who dies in childbirth on the day that her eldest daughter is preparing to leave for Tuskegee Institute in search of a better way of life for herself and an opportunity to help her younger siblings. Mother and daughter perceived the latter's leaving home as their only hope of breaking the vicious chain of poverty and ignorance that had been the lot of the women in the family, perhaps for many generations. The mother's death denies them both the dream, for the daughter becomes responsible for the care of the younger children, and will no doubt, herself, repeat the cycle of her mother's life. Burrill's play points out that one group of women, caught in the vice of race, poverty, and sexuality, experiences unnecessary despair and entrapment.

The controversy over access to birth control information has had devastating effects on the lives of all poor, uneducated, lower class women in America. As this play demonstrates, the issue is not one of a family's having more children than they can afford to raise comfortably, but of what the inaccessibility to certain kinds of information means for social mobility, education, self-determination, health, infant and female mortality, and economic viability. The victimization of ignorance and poverty is in part the heritage of poor women's inability to control the sizes of their families in any practical way. It is one that passes down from one generation to the next. The blame is not on the individual, Burrill shows us, but on a system that withholds vital information and access from special groups of people because they belong to those groups that are voiceless in the world where such decisions are made.

Also, contrary to some beliefs commonly held by some people in the rest of the society, Burrill's play points out that the women caught in this situation are neither oblivious nor passive in their attitudes to it. They are anxious to change it. Mrs. Jasper, the mother in the play, wants her daughter to attend school because she is the hope of the future, but she also pleads with the visiting nurse to let her (the mother) have birth control measures so that she can take her own steps to begin to control the size of her family and, by extension, her life. It is against her wishes and better judgment that she should continue to produce babies in her present condition. She understands that she "sits in [the] darkness of ignorance," and she realizes that the light of knowledge is being withheld from her. This light will enable her to reorder her life on her own terms. The irony is that the nurse withholds life-saving information because the law forbids it.

Race, gender, and class oppression intersect in this play. While white women are also caught in this predicament, there is little contention over the idea that race is one predominant factor in the economic condition of large numbers of black women. Thus women like Mrs. Jasper are confined to their class standing because of their race, while their gender is an added liability in the sphere of their social and personal vulnerability. On the other hand, women of the upper and middle classes, who have always had ready access to health and welfare means and information that the poor can have only through government tax-supported agencies, have done little to alleviate the political pressure that deprives poor women of similar access. The play draws attention to a particular plight of women and raises the question of the responsibility that the rest of the society bears toward those whom its legal apparatus has condemned as unworthy of certain rights and privileges because of the class and race accidents of their birth.

Georgia Douglass Johnson, whose name is often mentioned in concert with those of Angelina Weld Grimké and Alice Dunbar-Nelson, because the three women knew each other and were friends during many years of their lives, is, like her two friends, better known for poetry than for drama. As poets, these three women were older, had written, and had published before the years accorded to the Harlem Renaissance. While they were supportive of the efforts of the younger writers of the era, they seemed not to have had any direct involvement with the literary movement of the 1920s. Johnson wrote five plays, three of which fit into the years of the '20s, while two, *Frederick Douglass* and *William and Ellen Craft*, based on the escape episodes in the slave narratives, seem to have been done later. They appeared in *Negro History in Thirteen Plays* (1935), edited by Willis Richardson and May Miller.

Of Johnson's three plays of the 1920s, two, *A Sunday Morning in the South* (1925) and *Blue Blood* (1928), embody themes of race, and one, *Plumes* (1929), is a folk play with a tragic ending. In the last of these, the mother of a sick child is unable to let go of old superstitions and vacillates in her decision to secure medical attention for her offspring. While she tries to make up her mind, the worst happens, and her greater distress comes from never knowing whether this outcome might have been avoided. A play of this kind demonstrates that the women who were writing were not only critical of social problems connected with race and gender issues originating in the society external to the black community, but were also concerned about the internal problems that perpetuated ignorance and self-destruction within the group.

Blue Blood is a combination of the sentimental novel and slave narrative traditions, but Johnson uses the paradigms to describe the psychological violence that white male power often exercises over the lives of black women. On the eve of their wedding day, a young black couple discovers that they are sister and brother, children of the same white father, a revelation that saves them from an incestuous relationship. The mothers of the couple, black women, had been sworn to secrecy regarding the paternity of their offspring by the perpetrator of this act, and only through a wish to claim "blue blood" for each of their children just before the wedding takes place do they discover their common bond. Central to the violence implied by the playwright is the withholding of information— the secret that each woman felt forced to hold for many years. From the days of slavery, black women, for a number of reasons, were often forced to collude with white men who induced them to sexual activity, especially when children were the outcome of that activity. Slave narratives are replete with fugitive slaves' claims that while they are unsure of who their fathers were, it had been whispered about that they were the sons and daughters of their masters. In keeping these secrets of white men, black women were double victims while the men escaped the repercussions of their actions. In this play the mothers suffer, but so do the children. The price of their "blue blood" is the violence of shame, secrecy, and pain.

A Sunday Morning in the South deals directly with the physical violence of lynching, with the irrationality of the act, and the inability of the black community to protect its men from that terror. The threat of lynching was a form of intimidation that held the black community hostage for many decades between Reconstruction and the 1940s.[12] In Johnson's play, on a Sunday morning in the South, an innocent young man is taken from his home and put to death by a white mob after he is accused by a young white woman of having sexually molested her the evening before. Not even the honorable record that his aged grandmother has among the town's most prestigious white citizenry is able to save him from this bloody death. There is an accusation and a murder, no opportunity for the victim to refute the charge, and no evidence to prove that he is guilty of the crime. On the contrary, he is a hard-working, law-abiding citizen who believes that American democracy will eventually win the day, and in fact he was at home asleep at the time of the alleged crime. The irony is largely in the fact that the murder takes place on a Sunday morning in a religious community, and as the young man is hauled to his death the church bells ring to summon the murderers to worship. No doubt they will do so immediately after they have completed their act of "justice." The hypocrisy of Southern religion has been a topic for black commentary since the days of the slave narratives, as writers have called into question the contradiction between doctrine and actions on the part of many professed Christians in the South. Johnson's work belongs to a well-established tradition in the literature.

Lynching was one of the most heinous atrocities that white America has ever perpetuated against black America. In its commission, it was a crime intended to strip black America of power, autonomy, and humanity. Perhaps no other outrage against blacks, except slavery, has ever elicited as uniform a consensus in its condemnation by black people from all walks of life. It is not surprising that dramatists joined poets and fiction writers in attempting to delineate the horrors of this exercise of violence. Although lynching was not practiced only on black men, they belonged to the group that was most vulnerable to its ravages, and black women writers were vocal in their expressions of outrage against it. Johnson's play was one of the many outcries that penetrated the oratory of speech and writing in the 1920s.

Myrtle Livingston's *For Unborn Children* (1926) goes to the heart of the motivation for lynching black men and locates it in racism rather than in the often stated justification given by white men, that of protecting white women's virtue. In this play, a young black man is lynched because of his honest intentions toward a young white woman. However, he also understands that even if they had had a chance to marry, there would have been no opportunity for a life together, or to raise children. Before he dies he concludes that interracial relationships are inevitably doomed because of racism, and are best served by their non-existence. In a similar way as Grimké's *Rachael, For Unborn Children* makes its point through overstatement rather than faithful representation of real-life situations. However, the point itself is well taken. Livingston was concerned, as were the other writers of her time, to drive home her message, and has to be counted among those who forcefully and honestly registered protest on issues of this magnitude.

Perhaps the most interesting black woman dramatist during the years of the Harlem Renaissance was Marita Bonner, who at that time taught English in Washington, D.C. Bonner was born in Massachusetts and had attended Radcliffe College, where one year she was selected as one of the sixteen best writers among graduate and undergraduate students at Harvard, and admitted to the class of the famous professor Charles Townsend Copeland. During the 1920s, her works, three plays and a prize-winning essay, were published in *Crisis* and *Opportunity*. Had she written nothing else, her drama *The Purple Flower*, which, like Jean Toomer's *Natalie Mann*, uses expressionist techniques, would have earned her a place of recognition among all American playwrights who were experimenting with this form in the 1920s.

The Purple Flower is set in the Middle-of-Things-as-They-Are, which the playwright also describes as the End-of-Things for some, and the Beginning-of-Things for others, in a place that Might-be-here, there, or anywhere—or even nowhere. The characters are Sundry White Devils, whose main feature is their artfulness, especially in their abilities to assume different forms, and the Us's, a group which consists of characters of different and opposite colors, and who look like something or nothing. The action occurs on an open plain which faces a hill called Somewhere, and which has an opposite distant boundary called Nowhere. The White Devils live on the side of the hill in Somewhere, and spend their time trying to prevent the Us's, who live in the valley between Somewhere and Nowhere, from climbing up to the top of the hill. The Us's, on the other hand, are determined to climb the hill to reach the Purple Flower that grows at its peak. If they can achieve their goal, they too will be Somewhere, just like the White Devils.

Among themselves, the Us's determine strategy designed to outwit the wiles of the White Devils, and which will give them a chance to climb the hill and reach the Purple Flower. There had been a number of earlier attempts to achieve this, but all had met with failure. They believe they have found the solution to their problem when they agree to bring together all of their resources, including the freewill offering of their blood, and to use them to make a collective assault on their enemies. They realize that this is an effort that requires the ultimate sacrifice: blood.

The Purple Flower is an allegory in which Bonner describes one view of the seriousness of the situation between white and non-white peoples in the world. The purple flower, also described as the Flower-of-Life-at-Its-Fullest, is the symbol of universal humanity, and holds the power to change the life conditions of the oppressed Us's. They will each be Somebody and Somewhere when they reach it. In the course of their discussion on how to achieve their goal, the Us's realize that it is impossible for individual action to achieve success in this under-taking, and so they must act in concert. It is important for us to be aware of the diversity that comprises the group of Us's and thus acknowledge Bonner's move to see the Afro-American predicament in a global context, and cutting across lines of age and class. Peoples of all colors, ages, and stations in life are represented among them, and all share equally in the burden to seek their collec-tive freedom. Like others of her contemporaries, Bonner understood very clearly that black people in America were only one group that suffered as a result of racial oppression, and in this play she takes an active stand and notes the necessity for black Americans to join with other oppressed peoples in their struggle for freedom. What is also interesting about this play is its conclusion. Bonner is not satisfied to advance the idea of the possibilities of a bloody revolution between the white and non-white peoples of the world; she seems convinced that it is inevitable. The play ends with two questions: "When?" and "Is it time?"

If Jean Toomer was ahead of his time in experimenting with expressionist forms in the early part of the 1920s, then Marita Bonner also made an important breakthrough in the boldness of her statement and the form in which she ex-pressed it. Many playwrights expressed their frustration with social conditions of black life at the time, but Bonner belonged to a small minority who went beyond that to place black American oppression within the framework of world oppression based on the hierarchy of race. Perhaps only the well-known W.E.B. Du Bois, among black Americans at the time, was as articulate in pointing out the political and economic connections between the almost world-wide white domi-nation of colored peoples across the globe and the situation of Afro-Americans in this country.[13]

And while Jean Toomer had experimented with expressionism earlier in the decade, it is unlikely that Bonner was aware of *Natalie Mann*. Besides, this was not a form that gained popularity among black writers during the 1920s, nor did other black women playwrights attempt to use it. In light of these facts, her technical achievements must be seen as even more outstanding. Like Toomer, she probably felt that the weight of her message could not be adequately borne by any of the more familiar dramaturgical techniques. Here she shows her ability to use symbol and allegory to transform political necessity into artistic adven-ture. For Bonner's play was revolutionary in its time. On the one hand, it re-sembles more the confrontational drama of the 1960s and 1970s that came out of the black community than the literature of the 1920s.[14] On the other, the drama and literature of the 1960s and 1970s did not speak to a revolution that was global in nature. Her political horizon went further than that of many of the militants who followed her forty years and more later. Bonner deserves to be recognized as a writer who made a considerable contribution to the history of black drama.

Bonner's other plays, *The Pot Maker* (1927) and *Exit an Illusion* (1929), are less engaging than *The Purple Flower*, but they are noteworthy because in each she attempts to experiment beyond the confines of realistic drama. The first appeared in *Opportunity* and the second in the *Crisis*. *The Pot Maker* is a folk play. A newly-called black country preacher sets a trap to destroy his wife and her lover but falls victim to a similar fate himself. The play compares human actions to the story of a pot maker who carefully mends his broken wares, then tests each piece for its ability to withstand the pressures of its surroundings. The moral of the piece is that the flaws in humanity will be healed when people behave toward each other without jealousy and anger. This is the only one of Bonner's plays in which the characters speak in dialect. It uses a realistic setting but employs analogy as the vehicle for its action. In this way Bonner extends the conventional boundaries of the black folk play of her day. In *Exit an Illusion*, once again she departs from realistic portrayal to experiment with symbolic action and staging. The plot revolves around a young man who kills his girl-friend because he is jealous of her relationship with a man whom he thinks is white. Exit, the supposed rival, however, is an illusion, a fact which the dis-gruntled lover discovers only after he has destroyed the woman whom he loves.

Bonner's work stands out because she was a gifted writer who dared to risk extending her vision beyond the traditional limits of the writings going on around her. Today we might well wonder what she might have achieved had she re-ceived the necessary encouragement for her work in the 1920s.

Although Marita Bonner did not focus on issues connected specifically with women's lives, as we have seen, many other black women playwrights of the Harlem Renaissance did so. This is not surprising. At the same time, it is also evident that these women were intimately concerned with racial matters, and that they saw the black community as a unit, and they expected men and women to work together on all areas of the problems they faced. There is woman-centeredness in their writings, but no diminution of the need for positive rela-tionships with men. In characterization, the women in the plays are neither exotic nor passive, regardless of their economic or educational status. They respond and react to life around them with full awareness of the conditions against which they struggle. Their anger and pain are never muffled, and they are never want-ing in courage. The middle-class professional women who wrote these plays were not trying to create genteel worlds for black women in their art. They were interested in producing images that represented the lives of black people as honestly as they could. While they did not achieve fame or receive adequate recognition for their efforts, they left their mark on the literature of their day.

NOTES

1. See James V. Hatch, ed., *Black Theatre U.S.A.: Forty-Five Plays by Black Americans* (New York: Free Press, 1974); Doris Abrahamson, *Negro Playwrights in the American Theatre 1925–59* (New York: Columbia Univ. Press, 1967); Sterling Brown, *Negro Poetry and Drama* (1937; reprint, New York: Atheneum, 1969); and Loften Mitchell, *Black Drama: The Story of the American Negro in the Theatre* (New York: Hawthorne Books, 1967).

2. Montgomery Gregory, "The Drama of Negro Life," in *The New Negro*, ed. Alain Locke (New York: Albert & Charles Boni, 1925), p. 156.

3. Abrahamson, *Negro Playwrights*, p. 26.

4. Clinton F. Oliver and Stephanie Sills, eds., *Contemporary Black Drama From A Raisin in the Sun to No Place to be Somebody* (New York: Scribner's Sons, 1971), p. 15.

5. Oliver and Sills, *Contemporary Black Drama*, p. 15.

6. Hatch, *Black Theatre U.S.A.*, p. 1. In the African Grove Theatre (1820–1822), the first professional black theatre in this country, *King Shotaway*, a play based on a slave insurrection on the island of St. Vincent in the British West Indies, was performed. This was perhaps the first work of its kind—a serious play by a black writer—to reach the stage by way of black actors. Also see Hatch, "Introduction," *Rachael*, by Angelina Weld Grimké, p. 137.

7. Oliver and Sills, *Contemporary Black Drama*, p. 14.

8. Angelina Weld Grimké, *Rachael, Black Theatre U.S.A.*, p. 157.

9. Gloria Hull, "Under the Days: The Buried Life and Poetry of Angelina Weld Grimké," *Conditions: five—the black women's issue* 2:2 (Autumn 1979): 18.

10. Hull, "Under the Days," 18.

11. Hatch, *Black Theatre U.S.A.*, p. 173.

12. In 1924, the year before this play was written, sixteen blacks were lynched across the country. In 1925 the number was eighteen, and in 1926, there were twenty-nine. In the decade of the 1920s the highest number, fifty-eight, were lynched in 1921, and the lowest number, sixteen, were lynched in 1924 and 1927. See Walter White, *Rope and Faggot* (New York: Arno, 1969) for lynching statistics 1882–1927. One of the early crusaders against this heinous crime was Ida B. Wells (1862–1931), the first black woman journalist. See Wells, *Crusade For Justice* (Chicago: Univ. of Chicago Press, 1970) for her personal account of this struggle to put an end to lynching.

13. See W.E.B. Du Bois, "The White World," in *Dusk of Dawn, An Essay Toward an Autobiography of a Race Concept* (New York: Schocken, 1940). This is an especially poignant essay on the topic, but Du Bois had been speaking out on issues of white imperialism, capitalism and world racial politics for most of the 1920s.

14. There was anger and protest in the literature of the 1920s, and one has only to look at the writings of Claude McKay and Langston Hughes to realize that. However, there were many writers who were more concerned with the celebration of the black identity, and who wrote optimistically of the future for blacks in America. Some were willing to observe the possibilities of drastic confrontations, initiated by blacks, if conditions did not change. But few ventured to express a sense of an inevitable bloody confrontation.

SELECTED BIBLIOGRAPHY

Bonner, Marita. *Exit an Illusion*. *Crisis* 36 (1929): 335–36, 352.

_____. *The Pot Maker*. *Opportunity* 5 (Feb. 1927): 43–46.

_____. *The Purple Flower*. *Crisis* 35 (1928): 9–11, 28, 30.

Burrill, Mary. *Aftermath*. *The Liberator* 2.4 (April 1919): 10–14.

_____. *They That Sit in Darkness*. *Birth Control Review* 3.9 (Sept. 1919): 5–8.

Cuney-Hare, Maud. *Antar of Araby*. In *Plays and Pageants from the Life of the Negro*. Ed. Willis Richardson. Washington, DC: Associated Publishers, 1930. 27–73.

Duncan, Thelma. *Black Magic*. In *The Yearbook of Short Plays*. Ed. Claude Merton Wise and Lee Owen Snook. Chicago: Row, Peterson & Company, 1931. 217–32.

_____. *The Death Dance*. In *Plays of Negro Life*. Ed. Alain Locke and Montgomery Gregory. New York: Harper & Brothers, 1927. 321–32.

_____. *Sacrifice*. In *Plays and Pageants from the Life of the Negro*. Ed. Willis Richardson. Washington, DC: Associated Publishers, 1930. 3–24.

Gaines-Shelton, Ruth. *The Church Fight*. *Crisis* 31–33 (1926): 17–21.

Grimké, Angelina. *Rachael*. Boston: Cornhill, 1920.

Johnson, Georgia Douglass. *Blue Blood*. In *Fifty More Contemporary One-Act Plays*. Ed. Frank Shay. New York: Appleton, 1928. 299–304.

_____. *Plumes*. In *Plays of Negro Life*. Ed. Alain Locke and Montgomery Gregory. New York: Harper & Brothers, 1927. 287–99.

_____. *A Sunday Morning in the South* (1925). In *Black Theatre U.S.A.–Forty-Five Plays by Black Americans*. Ed. James V. Hatch. New York: Free Press, 1974. 211–17.

Livingston, Myrtle. *For Unborn Children. Crisis* 31–33 (1926): 122–25.

Miller, May. *Graven Images*. In *Plays and Pageants from the Life of the Negro*. Ed. Willis Richardson. Washington, DC: Associated Publishers, 1930. 109–37.

_____. *Scratches. Carolina Magazine,* "Negro Play Number" 61 (April 1929): 36–44.

Nelson, Alice Dunbar. *Mine Eyes Have Seen. Crisis* 15 (1918): 271–75.

Spence, Eulalee. *The Fool's Errand*. New York: Samuel French, 1927.

_____. *The Starter*. In *Plays of Negro Life*. Ed. Alain Locke and Montgomery Gregory. New York: Harper & Brothers, 1927. 206–14.

_____. *Undertow. Carolina Magazine.* "Negro Play Number" 61 (April 1929): 5–15.

CRAB ANTICS AND JACOB'S LADDER:
AARON DOUGLAS'S TWO VIEWS OF *NIGGER HEAVEN*

CHARLES SCRUGGS

As those of us interested in the Harlem Renaissance know, Carl Van Vechten's best-selling *Nigger Heaven* (1926) caused a furor of controversy in its own time.[1] Today the furor has died down but not the controversy; the charges against *Nigger Heaven* are still alive. The novel is sensational; it extols "primitivism";[2] and its influence was pernicious, turning an authentic literary movement into a sideshow for rich, irresponsible white folk.[3] Van Vechten has his modern defenders,[4] but no one has answered Nathan Huggins's indictment of the novel: "What is missing . . . is a clear moral or intellectual perspective that might engage the reader in the dramatic issues of Negro life."[5] In my opinion, "primitivism" has been the red herring that has prevented Huggins and others[6] from seeing that at the center of *Nigger Heaven* is "a clear moral [and] intellectual perspective" that engages "the reader in the dramatic issues of Negro life."

I want to argue that the best critic of Van Vechten's novel is not a literary critic but a black artist who was commissioned by Alfred Knopf (Van Vechten's publisher) to illustrate the advertisements for *Nigger Heaven*. Aaron Douglas did two drawings (now housed in the Beinecke Library at Yale University); one was to appear in journals read mainly by whites, the other in journals read almost exclusively by blacks. Although each illustration makes its appeal to a different audience, neither one deals with "primitivism" as a theme in the novel,[7] and yet each presents a distinct view of *Nigger Heaven*. As Douglas himself would write to Van Vechten immediately after the novel's publication, "you have . . . pointed the way very clearly and definitely to young writers of color."[8] I would also add that Douglas's drawings point "very clearly and definitely" to the craftsmanship and thematic complexity of *Nigger Heaven*, and that the "young writers of color" who were influenced by the novel recognized the same themes in the novel that Douglas revealed in his two drawings. In this paper, I offer two interpretations of *Nigger Heaven* that are based upon Douglas's acute perceptions.

The ostensible purpose of the first drawing (Plate 1) was to illustrate a blurb that Knopf used to puff the novel in popular (white) periodicals: "In *Nigger Heaven*, he [Van Vechten] analyzes the fascinating and inscrutable drama that takes place in the gallery of the vast theatre of New York—from which the white world below can be seen, but which it cannot see."[9] Knopf said that the term "nigger heaven" was not a special coinage of Van Vechten's. Rather, it was black slang for the balcony in a theater, slang that could be used in another metaphorical sense to describe "the geographical position of Harlem." Harlem is, after all, uptown.

At first glance, Douglas's drawing seems to present a visual transcription of the verbal message: the figures in the gallery are framed by a border as though they were on stage (rather than being part of the audience). The drawing appears simply to illustrate the advertising pitch that white readers of this novel will be given a privileged view of a "fascinating" milieu. Notice, however, that the drawing deviates from Knopf's blurb in one important particular—none of the figures look down upon the white world, but rather look at and talk to one another. Moreover, they are angry—not with the white world but with each other. There are several passages from *Nigger Heaven* that may have inspired Douglas to conceive his drawing in the manner he did. Here is *Nigger Heaven*'s Lasca Sartoris venting her spleen against "respectable" Negroes:

> These uplifters! They all make me sick. The black motto is: Drag down the topmost, no matter how much his influence might help you to rise. Put the rollers under him! Get rid of him. He's a menace. . . . These Niggers! she cried. Well, I learned life from them. They taught me to kick my rivals. They taught me to hate everybody who got more than I did. And I'll say this: they gave me the strength with their dirty tricks to lift myself out of the muck and mire they call Negro society.[10]

A pattern emerges from Lasca's tirade: envy drags people down, but Lasca has been strong enough to lift herself out. For "Negro society" is like a barrel of crabs—those at the bottom envy those at the top, and try to pull them down; and those at the top learn to hate in self-defense, some even climbing out of the barrel if given the opportunity.

Recently, anthropologist Peter J. Wilson has used this metaphor (society as a barrel of crabs) to explain the social mechanics of an island (Providencia) in the Caribbean, and his theory is a useful tool for analyzing the social mechanics of Harlem life in *Nigger Heaven*. (Curiously, Van Vechten's two favorite novels on black life were set in the Caribbean.)[11] Wilson's theory is that "crab antics" on Providencia result from the conflict between two different value systems: one imposed from without, the other from within. According to Wilson, both systems operate dialectically within the culture, neither one ever completely separate from the other.

The influence of colonizer upon colonized creates the value system from without, a system run by the inflexible laws of *respectability.* Such a system shapes a class structure that is both undemocratic and arbitrary. For the Gods seem to bestow respectability by chance; yet chance is fate: a light skin, a fortunate marriage, a lucky birthright. These things bring a person closer to being accepted by the white world or by that part of the black world in which the white man's values are primary.

Running counter to the system based on respectability is the one created by *reputation.* This value system arises from within the indigenous culture and is the true expression of *"communitas."*[12] Although the idea of reputation is based upon differentiation (different kinds of reputation), it is also located in the idea of equality—anyone can achieve it. Hence on Providencia, a person can be a singer, a lover, a schoolteacher, a carpenter, etc. and so achieve status through his or her own efforts. Nonetheless, as Wilson notes, no matter how secure a person's reputation, it can always be compromised by the world of respectability.

Wilson's last insight brings us back to Lasca Sartoris. On the surface, she seems like a pillar of strength; indeed, Nathan Huggins calls her the one "truly strong character" in the novel.[13] But we miss the point if we fail to see the ironic link between Lasca's contempt for "These uplifters" and her claim that "they gave me the strength with their dirty tricks to *lift* myself out of the muck . . ." For Lasca is condemned to defining herself against the very people that she loathes. Trapped within their matrix, she plays out the role of pariah she has been given. Her rebellion is itself a recognition of the power that "Negro society" has over her. For its members will not permit her to have her reputation. By definition, her "reputation" as erotic woman is bad. Hence Lasca deliberately flaunts "Negro society," making her pleasures even more extreme and herself even more unrespectable.[14]

Thus Douglas had another idea in mind besides Knopf's advertisement when he put his angry black figures within a frame. Visually he was saying this: no matter how different black people are from each other, they are all caught in the same social system. He saw that Van Vechten was functioning as a cultural anthropologist in *Nigger Heaven,* and so he attempted to illustrate Van Vechten's theme that Harlem represented a unique sociological situation: it was both an ethnocentric culture (note the two black caryatids in Douglas's drawing holding up the gallery) and a colonized culture. And as a colonized culture, it was influenced by white values from without, and these values often created tensions within the total social fabric. Here is Dick Sill (who will soon climb out of the barrel by "passing" for white) talking to a naive Byron Kasson on the subject of surviving in Harlem: "you'll have to fight your own race harder than you do the other . . . every step of the way. They're full of envy for every Negro that makes a success. They hate it. It makes 'em wild. Why, more of us get on through the ofays than through the shines" (pp. 119–20).

Van Vechten is not being a racist here. He was "struggling" in *Nigger Heaven*, as he told H. L. Mencken, to understand "Ethiopian psychology,"[15] and he is pointing out a psychological truth: oppressed people often turn their anger on those nearest them (transferred aggression). For in the eyes of white people (like the couple who insult Byron and Mary in Central Park) a crude sort of democracy prevails in the black world: *all* blacks are alike. Yet in actual fact black culture in Harlem has its own intricate codes of social behavior, its own class structure. Those who live secure in the world of reputation like Aaron Sumner don't play the game of crab antics, but those who live solely in the world of respectability are always insecure. Hence among the aristocracy in *Nigger Heaven*, the Brooklyn set scorns Hester Albright and her mother, who belong to the Washington set, but mother and daughter in turn take their revenge by scorning the Harlem set. Those who claim respectability claim it as an exclusive right, for respectability is an assertion that all blacks are not alike. Those outside the pale, like the black lower classes, delight in putting the "rollers" under those higher up, for this too is an assertion: "you up there are black and no better than we are." In short, the white man's "democracy" accelerates the natural human tendency toward envy and malice.

And crab antics are made even more complicated by the unpredictable element in human interaction. For instance, Byron Kasson sympathizes with the New Negroes whose writings go unappreciated by the "uncultured mob," and his loyalty leads to this angry reflection: " . . . he thought how the uneducated Negroes delighted in keeping the upper level as low as possible, pulling them down, maliciously, even with glee, when they were able to do so" (p. 179). Yet Byron's perception of "uneducated Negroes" is only half true, as the loss of his job as an elevator operator shows. By not stooping to conform to his social milieu, Byron alienates the working class, for his indifference is read as arrogance. Hence Byron has unconsciously added fuel to an already explosive situation.

What happens to Byron is a variation on a theme that Van Vechten has discussed elsewhere as the "firecrackers" phenomenon. In a novel by that name— *Firecrackers*, published the year before *Nigger Heaven*—Gareth Johns explains how it works. Most people live isolated lives, says Johns, but every once in a while a person will make contact with another that will start a chain reaction. The energy of this chemical process can be compared to what happens when you light a firecracker "in a packet of firecrackers":

> . . . the flash [of the first] fires the fuse of the second, and so on, until, after a series of crackling detonations, the whole bunch is exploded, and nothing survives but a few torn and scattered bits of paper, blackened with powder. On the other hand, if you fail to apply the match, the bunch remains a collection of separate entities, having no connection one with any other.[16]

No doubt Van Vechten wanted to write *Nigger Heaven* after *Firecrackers* because it must have seemed to him that the tension between respectability and reputation in Harlem creates "a packet of firecrackers" ready to explode. Both Lasca and Pettijohn threaten the world of respectability in different ways— Lasca with her sexual candor (and power), Pettijohn with his tainted money. Appropriately, after failing to break into high society, Pettijohn ends up with the outcast Lasca right before his death.

Moreover, although caste lines exist in Harlem, people live within close proximity to one another, and hence (as George Schuyler noted in a perceptive review of the novel) "rub shoulders"[17] and create friction. To quote Van Vechten in *The Blind Bow-Boy*, Pettijohn is "the catalyst . . . which effects a chemical reaction while appearing to take no part in it."[18] Both the Creeper and Byron blow up because of him, and he is oblivious to the fact that he is the cause of their anger. The novel's ending could serve as a paradigm for the failed social connections in Harlem: low (Creeper), middle (Pettijohn) and high (Byron) all meet at the Black Venus and explode, without any of them really knowing one another. The ending could also serve as a paradigm for the failed personal connections in the novel: Lasca becomes Byron's "firecracker," as Byron becomes Mary's, as Pettijohn becomes the Creeper's.

On the surface, the novel is a love story, or rather, a series of abortive love stories: Byron Kasson/Mary Love; Byron Kasson/Lasca Sartoris; Randolph Pettijohn/Mary Love; the Creeper/Ruby Silver. Yet this theme serves only to illustrate how the characters, though often belonging to different social classes, are interconnected through the twin poles of respectability and reputation. In the Prologue of *Nigger Heaven*, Van Vechten shows how two value systems threaten to clash, how in black society they exist in a kind of sustained tension. The novel begins with a portrait of Anatole Longfellow (alias the Scarlet Creeper) strolling Seventh Avenue. Pimp, lover, fashion-king—he is the cock-of-the-walk among the denizens of Harlem's lowlife. His reputation in this society is defined by his sexual prowess, and his reputation is his life. His personal style is regal. Indeed, the first time we see him he is extending his *noblesse oblige* to his friend "Duke." Moreover, his reputation is confirmed later in the Prologue when a beautiful woman (Ruby Silver) offers to pay him for his services as a lover. Even the self-made Randolph Pettijohn pays deference to the Creeper's status: "Nobody like duh Creeper fo' close an' women, nobody a-tall" (pp. 7–8).

Yet all is not perfection in Zion. The thought of Pettijohn does not make the Creeper happy, and he does not know why. Van Vechten's skill is to slowly unfold the reason to his readers while keeping it hidden from the Creeper. For though the Creeper believes that Pettijohn's reputation is of a distinctly lower order, Pettijohn is not content to live in the Creeper's world and be judged by the Creeper's values. Beginning as a lowly hot-dog vendor, he has already moved into the numbers racket and has become known as the "Bolito King." And to crown his achievements, he has built a successful cabaret called "The Winter Palace." As Book One begins, not only has the "Bolito King" created an empire to rival the Creeper's, but he hopes that this empire will catapult him into the world of respectability.

Van Vechten obliquely hints at this potentially explosive situation in the Prologue, and through the Creeper's narrative point of view. By the end of novel, this happy "primitive" (as he has been called) will no longer be happy. He will suffer his first anxious moment when he loses his girl, Ruby Silver, to Pettijohn, and he will kill Pettijohn in impotent rage, this violent act being a striking contrast to his cool composure in the novel's first scene. Why is his rage impotent? He senses that there is a value system that conflicts with his own, that he is no part of and cannot compete with. That Ruby leaves his magnificent, studly self for the overweight Pettijohn is something his own limited point of view cannot understand, and so in his confusion and fear he simply lashes out. Ironically, Pettijohn takes up with Ruby because he fails to get the woman that he wants.

Van Vechten uses the presence of Randolph Pettijohn to connect the Prologue to the first scene of Book One. This device is a clever strategy, because Van Vechten invites us to see what it is that Pettijohn wants. Moreover, the setting he is placed in is worlds away from the Creeper's Seventh Avenue, and yet, as the ending of the novel shows, what happens at Adora Boniface's lavish country home will eventually reconnect Pettijohn to Seventh Avenue.

A wealthy woman from a questionable background (a stage career), Adora throws Gatsby-like parties in which old money and new money mix but do not mingle. At this party is Mary Love, a librarian who has neither old or new money, but she does have respectability (both her father and mother have college educations). Adora throws her parties to attract people like Mary, and Pettijohn attends them to meet people like her. For Pettijohn now wants the outward and visible sign of his newly acquired prosperity; he wants, as he tells Mary in his clumsy, straightforward way, "a nice, 'spectable 'ooman for a wife" (p. 38).

Van Vechten's brilliant stroke is to let us see Pettijohn's proposal through Mary's eyes—hers is the narrative point of view throughout Book One. Van Vechten moves his readers from the lowest to the highest segment of Negro society through a change of scenes and a shift in point of view, and yet he lets us see how they are connected. For like the Creeper, Mary too is made uneasy by the presence of Pettijohn, and she too feels superior to him. Yet there is a difference between the Creeper's reaction to Pettijohn and Mary's. Mary feels threatened by Pettijohn's vulgarity, for in Mary's world Pettijohn *is* vulgar. Those qualities that made him great in the world of reputation—street-wisdom and stamina— serve him ill in the world of respectability.

Thus Mary rejects Pettijohn's offer, for she wants something more than ostentatious wealth, the only image of Pettijohn that she will permit herself to see. And yet Mary wants something else besides mere respectability, and at Adora's party she catches a glimpse of a young man diving into a swimming pool who seems to represent it. She is taken by his grace, his perfect sense of control, "the symmetrical proportions of his body" (p. 24). The young man turns out to be Byron Kasson, fresh out of college and burning to be a writer. That Mary's initial response to him is aesthetic reveals her character, for she too lives in the world of art. However, her response also reveals her blind spot, for she expects Byron to be as graceful a man as he is a diver. She assumes that he has style in terms of reputation (intrinsic merit) and not just respectability. Like Isabel Archer in *A Portrait of a Lady*, she mistakes aesthetic surface for moral substance.

Lacking Pettijohn's solidarity, Byron has only the temperament implied by his name. Self-indulgent and self-pitying, he wants to be a writer but lacks the discipline to be either an artist or a man. Moreover, he has an ambiguous relationship to both black and white worlds. Unable to escape the influence of his caucasian education at college, he is nevertheless too proud to pass for white. And although he says he wants to write about black life, he finds Harlem lowlife too repugnant and Harlem highlife too artificial. When the ubiquitous Gareth Johns suggests that he write about the world of Aaron Sumner's dinner party, he dismisses it as imitative—"too much like Edith Wharton's set" (p. 107). Yet his indictment is not only unjust (to Wharton as well as to Sumner) but ironic. Not only does Byron end by writing a story that sounds like "Madam Butterfly" (as Mary Love notes), but his remark about Sumner is based on envy. For Sumner has what Byron wants: true culture based on reputation, not respectability. Byron, however, tries to diminish Sumner by reducing him to the world of respectability—"Edith Wharton's set"—and hides his envy by implying his moral superiority to Sumner.

Van Vechten subtly exposes Byron's hypocrisy by having him apply a story to Sumner that in fact applies to himself. That story is Charles Chesnutt's "A Matter of Principle," whose satirical theme is akin to Dr. Johnson's famous remark about Mrs. Macaulay: "Sir, your levellers wish to level *down* as far as themselves, but they cannot bear levelling *up* to themselves." A member of Cleveland's blue-veined society, Cicero Clayton speaks eloquently of "a higher conception of the brotherhood of man," [19] but his actions bespeak the low motives behind this moral principle. In his desire to level everything down to himself, he attempts to marry his daughter to a visiting Negro congressman, who reportedly has exceedingly pale skin. Such an alliance, Clayton thinks, will strengthen his ties to the white world and will cause him and his family to rise in respectability in black society. However, the possibility that the black congressman may be coal black instead of near white throws Clayton into a panic; to receive this kind of man into his house would be a violation of "principle." The story's comic denouement leaves Clayton a sadder but not a wiser man, yet Chesnutt's satire has stripped him clean for us to see. Clayton's "higher" idealism was only a base desire for social prestige. And like a crab, he was not above stepping upon others to get out of the barrel.

In conjuring up Chesnutt's story, Byron projects Clayton's character upon Sumner. Now Byron can think of a reason why he didn't go to Sumner for help when he arrived in Harlem, and of course that reason is a matter of principle:

> These successful persons [Clayton and, by implication, Sumner] liked to
> be seen with whites or with light coloured or more famous members of their
> own race. Well, until he was famous he refused to be patronized. (p. 178)

As with Lasca's portrait, the repetition of words ("famous" . . . "famous") reveals
the irony. Byron's animus towards Sumner is no moral principle. Becoming a
writer means being "famous" as a New Negro; means having "successful" people
as friends; means, indeed, having those things white people have—"a chance
to earn money, to be respectable," as Byron tells Mary (p. 148). Although Byron
has the same dreams as Sumner (or his image of Sumner), he pretends that they
are somehow of a higher order. For, in truth, Byron is a snob—he believes
himself superior to Sumner and his "Edith Wharton's set." After all, Sumner is
only a businessman pretending to culture; whereas Byron is an artist.

In reality, Byron is a hollow man caught between two worlds. Unable to
succeed as a writer, he has no status based upon reputation; though scornful of
the world of respectability, respectability (light skin, college education) is all he
has. That he drowns in Lasca's arms is Van Vechten's comment on respectability
when it becomes a person's sole support system. It is not by accident that both
the Creeper and Byron fire their guns in rage into Randolph Pettijohn, for in the
end both men have been reduced to style without substance. Nor is it by accident that Byron becomes the novel's third and last narrative point of view, for
Van Vechten links the Creeper and Byron by the novel's beginning and ending.
The sense of this ending is that both the Creeper and Byron are brought low
(made to creep) through the agency of Randolph Pettijohn.[20]

Yet Van Vechten also wants us to see the differences between the two men.
The Creeper shoots Pettijohn because Pettijohn has injured his reputation by
taking Ruby; whereas Byron fires into the dead body of Pettijohn because by
taking Lasca, Pettijohn has painfully revealed to Byron the vacuity of a life
based on respectability. Or we might look at the contrast in another way. The
Creeper had achieved reputation within his world, and he is afraid of losing it;
whereas Byron has only respectability to cling to, and this life buoy cannot save
him from the flood of his own emotions.

The novel's ending, then, explains the meaning of the novel's epigraph. Van
Vechten chose a passage from Countee Cullen's *Heritage;* what it does not refer
to is as important as what it does:

> All day long and all night through,
> One thing only must I do:
> Quench my pride and cool my blood,
> Lest I perish in the flood.

The blood that needs to be cooled is not the blood that desires to return to a
more primitive ancestral past—Cullen's "dark blood damned within."[21] Van Vechten
chose this epigraph for its stoical implications: in Harlem, a person lives in a

world without maps (or in a world of conflicting maps), and if he is to survive the "flood" of his own rage and bewilderment, he had better learn to find a non-self-destructive means of expressing his emotions.

Elsewhere, in his last novel (*Parties*, 1930), Van Vechten uses the image of the dance as a metaphor for grace under fire. The white characters in this novel figuratively dance the dance of death. Caught in a web of modern ennui, they move from party to party, love affair to love affair. One night they visit a Harlem cabaret and watch black people dance. Van Vechten's description of the dancers is comparable to Jake's description of Romero in *The Sun Also Rises*:

> For here every individual effort was devoted towards the expression of electricity and living movement. Each dancer gave as serious attention to his beautiful vocation *as if he were in training for some great good game. . . . [The Dancers] became that perfect expression of self so often denied human beings.*[22] (italics added)

The attitude behind this statement is hardly that of happy-go-lucky hedonism. Rather, Van Vechten's use of the two metaphors (life as dance, dance as game) echoes the stoic philosophers, who often compared a person's preparation for life to an athlete's training for the Olympic games.[23] For Van Vechten, energy ("electricity") must be expressed within the controlled movement of the dance, and it is the image of the dance that serves as a judgment upon the desperate lives of the white characters in the novel whose energies are continually dissipating into meaningless acts.[24]

Van Vechten was a student of dance, admiring not only its grace but the strength that was necessary to it: "Great strength is the basis of all great dancing, for a dancer must be tireless in face of any difficulty."[25] The metaphorical implications of this statement are obvious for *Nigger Heaven*: the Creeper dances down Seventh Avenue, but fittingly declines to dance in "The Winter Palace"; Mary dances out of control at the Charity Ball, as Lasca dances magnificently, yet Lasca has not the "strength" to escape her own metaphor—her dance becomes one of excess, of everything pushed to the limit (e.g., her dance with Byron at the Black Mass). Mary expects Byron to "dance" in real life as well as he literally dances and dives, but he lacks the "strength" to do so. Mary rejects the clumsy Pettijohn because he can't dance, but as Adora reminds her, Pettijohn in his own way is a dancer—he has danced all the way from his hot-dog stand to "The Winter Palace," appropriately a dance hall.

Van Vechten wrote as much about music, especially black music, as he did about dance;[26] blues lyrics are not merely decorative elements in *Nigger Heaven*. They serve to function as the "stopper" in the "old song" that Mary sings to her father:

> Got the world in a jug,
> Stopper's in my hand. (p. 111)

The stopper keeps the world in the jug, because the world is always threatening to run out and overwhelm a person, even when he thinks he has it bottled up. By definition, the blues distrust happiness, because happiness is tenuous; sorrow, on the other hand, is real, and more or less permanent. It seems built into the scheme of things, whether it be unrequited love, the white man, or bad crops. And yet the blues make poetry out of suffering, control the "flood" by expressing it. Van Vechten gives us a good example of this when he contrasts a song a black woman is singing in the Black Venus with the emotions of a distraught Byron as he rushes into this noisy cabaret. The sense of the woman's lyric applies to Byron—I'm miserable since "you" (read Lasca) went away—and because of his misery, he is quick to realize the connection. But he misses the whole *modus operandi* of the song's total expression—its verbal irony, her ambiguous delivery. Because you have jilted me, the song says, that's the reason "ah run aroun," (p. 277). And this fact, the singer adds, is "all over town." In other words, the singer is not just bemoaning her fate; she is hinting that she is not through running around. Indeed, that she has been jilted is just the excuse she needs *to* run around! Byron, of course, can't see the humor—he is too lost in his own misery and confusion. The "flood" of the cabaret overwhelms him and he furiously empties his pistol into a dead body. The singer, however, has used her song to ride the "flood" to safety.

Music and dance sometimes create a momentary sense of *communitas* in the novel. Even a prig like Hester Albright can be moved by the spirituals, and Clara Smith's blues simply but adequately express in feeling what cannot be resolved in argument when the young intellectuals—Dick Sill, Mary Love, Howard Allison, Olive Hamilton—all attack the race problem from their separate points of view. Moreover, dance serves to break down caste lines at the Charity Ball. Because Van Vechten took black music seriously as a sophisticated mode of expression, he is contemptuous of a simple-minded attitude toward it, as evinced by his portrait of white novelist Roy McKain (probably Jim Tully) who visits a Harlem cabaret one time and is convinced by what he sees that all of Harlem is filled with singing, dancing, happy darkies.

Clearly the people Van Vechten admires are those who dance upon the "flood" of life, who have "great strength" to keep from drowning, who turn adversity into beauty. Howard Allison, Aaron Sumner, Mary's father, Byron's father, Welcome Fox—these people live in the world of reputation, not respectability. To quote Walt Whitman: "they do not . . . whine about their condition." Nor do they whimper in front of the white race—witness Mr. Love's impulse "to kill the first white man he encountered" after reading an account of a lynching in Georgia (p. 92). Some may be cultured (Aaron Sumner), some not (Welcome Fox), but each has an inner toughness.[27] Even Adora Boniface exhibits this quality until her mind is turned by the laws of respectability. We see the comic side of Adora's character when at the Charity Ball(!) she tells Mary Love that she will not permit Pettijohn's newly acquired "tart" (Ruby Silver) to appear in her house—this from a former "tart" who now aspires to higher things. As Campaspe Lorillard says in *The Blind Bow-Boy,* "only those are vulgar who make pretensions to be what they are not" (p. 156).

Perhaps Mary Love's flaw lies in her failure to realize that Randolph Pettijohn, despite his lack of education, has more in common with her father than does Byron. She can only see the surface of this diamond in the rough, just as she can't see through Byron. But whatever her flaw, she does not illustrate, as critics have argued, Van Vechten's penchant for "primitivism."[28] Falling in love, this sheltered librarian projects her liberated emotions upon her race, and we miss the point if we miss the comedy of the situation: "We are all savages, she repeated to herself, all, apparently, but me!" (p. 90). This woman who now laments her lost "primitive birthright" is the same woman, we remember, who found Randolph Pettijohn's amorous intentions too direct. Moreover, all of Book One reflects Mary's point of view, and in projecting her views upon Van Vechten, critics have simply overlooked the novelist's narrative strategy. Finally, if Mary's loosening of the stays seems extreme, she ought to be compared to two other Van Vechten characters who find themselves locked in the embraces of Eros: Ella Nattatorrini in *The Tattooed Countess* (1924) and Gunnar O'Grady in *Firecrackers* (1925). Whatever the racial nature of Mary's fall, it also partakes of the slippery nature of being human.

II

Classical themes were no strangers to Van Vechten. Indeed, he insisted to Mabel Dodge Luhan that all his novels were "modern variations around [them]": *Peter Whiffle* is Electra or Hamlet; *The Blind Bow-Boy* is my version of the Pilgrims Progress and *The Tattooed Countess* is Phaedra. . . . My intention in writing is to create moods to awaken unconscious echoes of the past, to render to shadows their real importance."[29] Van Vechten made this statement in 1925, two years before *Nigger Heaven*, but years later he would pinpoint the classical theme in that novel: "The plot of *Nigger Heaven* is one of the oldest in the world, the story of the Prodigal Son, without the happy ending of that Biblical story. In my book a boy from a small town is bewitched, bothered and bewildered by a big time Lady of Pleasure and is unable to meet the demands made upon his character by life in a big city."[30] Nor would Van Vechten try to duck his indebtedness to two black novelists who had treated this theme before him: Paul Lawrence Dunbar in *The Sport of the Gods* (1902) and James Weldon Johnson in *The Autobiography of An Ex-Colored Man* (1912). Indeed, Van Vechten was instrumental in getting Knopf to reissue Johnson's novel in 1927, to which Van Vechten wrote a new introduction. In that introduction, he acknowledged that for his own novel *The Autobiography of An Ex-Colored Man* had proved an "invaluable source-book for the study of Negro psychology." Again, he was thinking of "psychology" that was not innate but created—"born in the USA." He made this clear later on in the same introduction when he discussed his indebtedness to Dunbar's novel, which had

described the plight of a young outsider who comes to the larger New York
Negro world to make his fortune, but who falls a victim to the sordid snares
of that world, a theme which I elaborated on in 1926 to fit a newer and much
more intricate social system.[31]

What Van Vechten was saying of course is that when Dunbar and Johnson
wrote their novels, Harlem had not yet become identifiable as a Negro city.[32]
Indeed, Van Vechten was making a perceptive observation, for not only were
Dunbar and Johnson concerned with other settings besides that of the city (for
Dunbar, the anti-pastoral world of the South;[33] for Johnson, the whole varied
American scene), but when they did focus on the city in their novels, they
treated the black community within the larger context of New York. Moreover,
this black community did not exist uptown, but downtown—specifically in the
area known as the Tenderloin.

Van Vechten prided himself on being the first novelist (white or black) to treat
Harlem as a separate entity: a city within a city with an "intricate social system."
As we have seen, he wanted to be both a sociologist and social satirist. Yet he
also saw himself as a myth-maker, as Aaron Douglas was to perceive. For
Douglas's two drawings call attention to two possible meanings of "Heaven" in
the novel's title. In the first drawing (Plate 1), Douglas attempted to make the title
understandable to white readers by using a visual metaphor. Because black
readers knew too well the grim irony of the metaphor ("nigger heaven" / balcony), Douglas changed the meaning of "Heaven" in the first drawing by placing it in a new context in the second (see Plate 2), that of myth instead of
metaphor. It was this second drawing that Knopf commissioned for an advertisement that would appear (though not exclusively) in the black periodicals.
Thus in September, 1926, Knopf placed an advertisement in *Opportunity* along
with Douglas's second drawing.[34] This drawing (Plate 2) depicts a theme in Van
Vechten's novel that again transcends Knopf's verbal advertisement: Harlem as
a potential Heavenly City ("nigger *heaven*").

The figure in the foreground and to the right is a black Jacob who looks
longingly up a ladder that reaches to heaven. In the background is the earthly
city, complete with skyscraper, church, and factory. The significant feature of
this drawing is the sense of open space, as opposed to the sense of entrapment
depicted in the first drawing. Moreover, instead of the artificial stage lights of
the first drawing, the sun in the second drawing seems to herald a new day. In
addition, the ladder that leads up to heaven, though slightly to the left of the
city, is firmly planted in it, as though Douglas were making a connection between the earthly city of Harlem and the Heavenly City of the Bible.

There is, however, a disquieting note: looking closely at the objects that make
up the image of the city, one perceives a second black face that seems to be
formed by the smoke coming out of one of the buildings. This face looks angry,
and it stares back at the city, as if it is determined to wring its destiny out of the
city through battle. Was Douglas thinking of Claude McKay's *Harlem Shadows*

(1922) when he created this aspect of his drawing? The aggressive face almost seems to echo a line from McKay's poem "The White City" in which McKay's hatred makes his "heaven in the white world's Hell."[35]

Obviously Knopf did not want to emphasize this aspect of Harlem's shadows in *Opportunity*. He wanted to sell the novel as a love story, so the following lines accompanied Douglas's drawing: "*Nigger Heaven* is a story of two lovers, climbing Jacob's ladder under the shadows of Harlem." Here the shadows are softened, as though they create the perfect ambience for romance. Douglas, however, knew better, as the subtle implications of his drawing show. Although there is a love affair in the novel between Byron and Mary, there is also a love-hate affair between man (and woman) and city. The character in the foreground (looking up the ladder) and the face in the background point to a tension between the individual and his environment, and again a line from Claude McKay best expresses Douglas's (and Van Vechten's) theme: "I love this cultured Hell that *tests* my youth!" (italics added).[36] In *Nigger Heaven*, the city (both New York and Harlem) will test the mettle of black people, and as Douglas correctly saw, this battle could only be depicted in mythical terms.

Van Vechten had two mythical figures in mind when he wrote *Nigger Heaven*: Jacob and the Prodigal Son. One climbs the ladder to the Heavenly City; the other descends it into the Hell of the Black Venus. The Jacob myth of course is never fulfilled in the novel, but it is there by implication because *Nigger Heaven* seems in part to be an answer to Alain Locke's mythical Harlem in *The New Negro* (1925). Published a year after Locke's famous anthology, *Nigger Heaven* serves as a gloss upon Locke's assumptions about Harlem: the idea of the organic community, of the artist who stands at its center, of the audience who supports him. Indeed, as treated by Locke, Harlem appears to be a secular version of the Heavenly city, with the black artist replacing St. Augustine's deity.[37] Hence the curious overlap between the publication of *The New Negro* and the writing of *Nigger Heaven* should not be overlooked. Van Vechten began a first draft of *Nigger Heaven* (November 3, 1925),[38] just as *The New Negro* was being published (October, 1925), and he was writing a review of *The New Negro* for *The New York Herald Tribune* (published on December 20, 1925)[39] at the same time that he was finishing up a first draft of the novel (December 21, 1925).[40]

His review of *The New Negro* is laudatory, but one remark he makes about Locke's preface to the anthology points to his own thematic preoccupations in *Nigger Heaven*. Although Locke paints "a brilliant picture of the general intellectual attitude of the new literary figures," the truth is, added Van Vechten, "the New Negro does very little group thinking."[41]

"Group thinking," of course, had been at the core of Locke's myth about Harlem, not in the sense of conformity but of shared experience. Having studied under Josiah Royce at Harvard, Locke took his mentor's notion of a "province"—a rooted culture in a specific locale—and applied it to Harlem. A healthy "provincialism" gave a person a feeling of belonging, paradoxically allowing him to develop his own unique personality within the protective shade of a common ethos.[42] Locke argued that Harlem was not a ghetto but a community. Rich and poor, urban and rural, foreign (West Indian, African) and domestic—all have come to Harlem for various reasons, yet all end by discovering "one another."[43] The locale of the city has created a "great race welding" and a "common consciousness" (p. 7). And using Royce's paradox, Locke argued that it has also created a "New Negro," one who, having sloughed off his old inauthentic self, now finds his true identity by seeing himself in others.

The idea of a New Negro, then, suggested a transformation from Old to New, and Locke in *The New Negro* had borrowed Frederick Jackson Turner's thesis of the "frontier" as an influence upon American life and changed its location from west to north: "In the very process of being transplanted, the Negro is becoming transformed" (p. 6).[44] As a "frontier," Harlem had stirred the democratic impulse within the race. For Locke argued that in fleeing to the city, the masses had forced "the professional man" to follow, and the result of the two groups living cheek by jowl in Harlem has led to a new civic awareness on the part of those higher up. The artist—by definition, one of the elite—also lives close to the source of his art by living close to the masses; and as he celebrates their lives in song and story, they will respond to the accuracy of his vision by giving him their support. Thus "the Negro artist," said Locke, "out of the depths of his group and personal experiences, has to his hand the conditions of a classical art." (p. 47).

In the Harlem of *Nigger Heaven*, things will not be so cozy for the New Negro (artist or otherwise), as Robert Kasson warns his son Byron: "Harlem is a great Negro city, the greatest Negro city in the world, and it is surely as full of pitfalls for young men as all great cities are" (p. 171). Here Van Vechten deflates Locke's argument by noting that Harlem is *like* all "great cities." Moreover, even this is not Van Vechten's last word on the subject of the city as myth. Even though he debunks the reality of community in *Nigger Heaven*, he does not discount the possibility that Harlem will become the Heavenly City of Locke's imagination. Indeed, he recognizes that Locke's ideal of a civilized community has validity if only because the city has been its most expressive symbol within the history of Western Civilization:[45]

> A Negro city almost as large as Rome! We couldn't have counted on that a few years ago. You have everything here: shops and theatres and churches and libraries . . .
>   And cabarets, added Mary. You should have mentioned them first. (p. 102)

At Aaron Sumner's dinner party, Dr. Lancaster makes an analogy between a classical symbol of civilization (Rome) and Harlem; whereas Mary short-circuits the visiting Doctor's enthusiasm by reminding him of the negative side of the city, the dives that link Harlem with St. Augustine's earthly city (also Rome). The analogy with Rome is heady stuff but not necessarily false. The first half of

Nigger Heaven reflects Van Vechten's admiration for the energy of Harlem that touches all black lives within the radius of its spinning wheel:

> Ezekiel saw the wheel
> 'Way in the middle of the air;
> and the little wheel run by faith,
> And the big wheel run by the grace of God;
> 'Tis a wheel in a wheel.
> 'Way up in the middle of the air. (p. 76)

The spiritual that Webb Leverett sings is based on the Old Testament prophet's apocalyptic vision, one that encompasses two cities: the fallen Jerusalem of the sinful, the renewed Jerusalem of the righteous. The big wheel in the song reflects the primal energy in God's universe, energy that can either empower the earthly city or rain fire upon it. As positive energy, the city manifests itself as Aaron Sumner's home, as Mary Love's library, as the blues in the cabarets that Mary ridicules, as the Creeper's graceful tread down Seventh Avenue, as Randolph Pettijohn's hot-dog stand, as Howard Allison's stubborn persistence. As negative energy, the city can cause havoc within the little wheel of men. "Wheels within wheels," thinks a confused Byron about his relationship to black life, "A vicious circle" (p. 176).

Like Alain Locke, Van Vechten admired Harlem because its whirling wheel produced the kind of energy that made Rome the home of the muses. He gives voice to this ideal through Russett Durwood, a thinly disguised portrait of H. L. Mencken. As editor of the *American Mars* (*Mercury*), Durwood rejects Byron's story but gives some good advice: ". . . learn something about your own people," seek out the "facets" of Harlem's diamond, wrestle with the angel like Jacob by immersing yourself in the destructive element (pp. 223, 225). And, indeed, on one occasion Harlem does move Byron to a moment of transcendence. Going to work as an elevator boy, he has a vision of the black masses as the Chosen People, "all leaving the walled, black city temporarily to labour in an alien world" (p. 187). Yet such is his repugnance to Harlem's masses that he is unable to write about them. Failing to immerse himself in the destructive element, the destructive element comes to him in the form of Lasca Sartoris, the black widow at Harlem's heart that awaits the Prodigal Son who has neither Jacob's craftiness nor his endurance.[46]

Perhaps as he was conceiving his drawing, Douglas was thinking of Plato's ladder of love (Eros) in *The Symposium* as well as the Biblical story of Jacob, for as Blanche Gelfant has noted, ". . . desire has always been the great energizing theme of the American city novel since the startling appearance in 1900 of Dreiser's *Sister Carrie*."[47] The hunger that the city creates can elevate or destroy, can either move one to see beauty, or to mistake acts of self-destruction for beauty.[48] On the lowest level of Eros, Harlem symbolizes sensual desire, as expressed by Ruby Silver to the Creeper: "Dis place where Ah met you—Harlem

. . . Ah calls et Nigger Heaven!" (p. 15). On a higher level, however, Eros makes possible a potentially symbiotic partnership between Byron and Mary, itself having symbolic implications for Harlem as a city of art. Byron as writer, Mary as sensitive critic—together they point to the idea of a mutually nourishing community of artist and audience. Van Vechten underscores the sheltering aspect of Mary's love by associating her with a garden (Central Park), casting the two lovers as Adam and Eve: "I think of it as *my* Park, and now I've led you into it" (p. 143). But brutal white people remind them of the illusory nature of their happiness, how defenseless they are in their imaginary heaven. Hence when Byron and Mary cross over the line back into Harlem, Byron can only think of the metaphor of "nigger heaven" in negative terms: isolated and crammed together, black people in Harlem look down in longing at the whites in the "orchestra seats," but the whites only look up "to laugh or sneer" (p. 149). For Byron, "nigger heaven" is nigger hell, and in his self pity, Byron forsakes Mary and descends into the nightmare of his imagination: the Black Venus. Not hearing the blues singer, he hears only a din of noise. The Black Venus has become Harlem in microcosm for him—pandemonium, a city of demons.

Both Mary and Byron are more than realistic characters; in mythical terms, they reflect the perils of being a New Negro. Mary of course is the more sympathetic of the two. She is a genuinely cultured woman, cosmopolitan in the best sense of the word; her love of African art complements her wide knowledge of French and American literature. Her tragedy, like that of Lily Bart in *The House of Mirth*, is that her worth goes unrecognized by the man she loves. Byron merely wants her as a cheerleader for himself, and he mistakenly puts her in his notion of "Edith Wharton's set." And yet there *is* something precious about Mary. Like Lily Bart, she seems several degrees removed from experience, filtering it always through the lens of literature (e.g. Gertrude Stein).[49] Just as Lily cannot perceive the solidarity of Mr. Rosedale, so Mary can only see Pettijohn as pushy ambition.

It is not that Mary and Byron are too "educated" or too "civilized," as some critics have said.[50] This argument is the flip side of "primitivism." Byron's problem is that his father's efforts have propelled him into a world where it is easy to forget his father's virtues. And Mary's problem is that her education must be enlarged to include the world of the cabaret as well as the world of the library. For it is the cabaret that produces the blues that Mary emotionally responds to but won't recognize as great art. Specifically, Mary needs ballast in the form of what Hortense J. Spillers has called the "resources" of the female blues singer, resources that will allow her both to celebrate and subdue the demonic powers of sex.[51] That these resources are present in black life Van Vechten shows on almost every page; his many and varied references to black music stand side by side his many and varied references to black (and white) literature. Perhaps one reason why he asked Langston Hughes to write new poems to replace the blues lyrics of the first six editions of the novel[52] is that Van Vechten believed that Hughes had successfully integrated high and low art through his poetry.

Although the resources do exist to unite the disparate elements in black life—culture/experience; high/low art; class divisions—Van Vechten's final assessment is that unity in Harlem is still waiting to be born. The separate points of view of the novel's narrative reflect Harlem's fractured universe, just as the novel's denouement illustrates Van Vechten's grim theme: the only time that people from different classes connect in Harlem is to do each other ill.

III

Nigger Heaven's influence upon black writers after 1926 has always been acknowledged, has often been deplored, but has never been clearly defined. David Levering Lewis presents us with the broad (and traditional) view:

> With the sales of *Nigger Heaven* soaring, younger writers like Langston Hughes, Zora Hurston, and Wallace Thurman saw that the old genteel literary traditions would no longer do. They were not going to deny themselves Van Vechten's privilege of exploring the underside of Afro-American life.[53]

And conversely, novelists like Jessie Fauset and W.E.B. Du Bois took it upon themselves to uphold "genteel" standards in the face of this onslaught of vulgarity and decadence.

This view isn't wrong—indeed, one would have trouble trying to refute it. The problem is, it doesn't tell us very much, and it tends to shut down further investigation. If my discussion of the novel is correct, Van Vechten did not limit himself to the "underside of Afro-American life." As a novelist, he functioned as a sociologist, a myth-maker, and a satirist. "My extreme tribute to the novel," said black sociologist Charles S. Johnson in 1926, "is that I wish a Negro had written it."[54] I want to suggest that many black novelists did try to rewrite it after 1926, not in the sense of imitating it but in the sense of reshaping it in terms of their own vision of black life. Yet whether they agreed with Van Vechten or hated him, they in their novels were spinning off themes that he made popular in *Nigger Heaven*: the motif of the Prodigal Son, crab antics in the city, the myth of the city (heavenly/demonic; community/crab antics).

Not surprisingly, both Jessie Fauset in *Plum Bun* (1929) and Du Bois in *Dark Princess* (1928) used the motif of the Prodigal Son (in Fauset's case, "Daughter") to answer *Nigger Heaven*. In *Plum Bun* Angela Murray revolts from provincial Philadelphia to pass for white in exciting, open-ended New York. Like Byron Kasson, she discovers that the city is full of pitfalls. At its center is an *homme fatal*, false friends, delusive hopes. What she discovers is that Philadelphia has the sense of community that she longed for all along. And yet in answering Van Vechten, Fauset makes Harlem into a mirror image of Philadelphia, only more cosmopolitan and without Philadelphia's class snobbery. Like Van Vechten's Harlem, Fauset's is an artistic center, but the Byrons of the world are transferred to Greenwich Village. In *Dark Princess*, Matthew Towns is the Prodigal Son as Negro politician, ensnared in the crab antics of Chicago's black political system. Wasting his substance in Plato's cave, he has lost the fine ideals of his youth, as symbolized by the dark Indian princess Kautilya. One day she reappears in his life, and leaving behind a possible career as a congressman, he reunites himself to the values he had betrayed. For Du Bois, the symbol of the earthly city is the subway that Matthew Towns helps build before he leaves with the princess for India. It symbolizes the tunnel-vision of the declining West, too blinded by its materialism to see the future. The future that will replace the present belongs to the darker peoples of the world and its form is expressed at the end of the novel by Matthew's mother: "I am seekin' for a City—for a City in de Kingdom."[55] Du Bois solves the problem of crab antics in the real city—which he describes in great detail—by ignoring their ultimate reality.

Wallace Thurman placed Van Vechten's Prodigal Son in a comic light.[56] In *Infants of Spring* (1932), Thurman depicted a whole houseful of Prodigal Sons. Of course, they were not supposed to be Prodigal Sons; they were supposed to be Negro intellectuals—artists and writers—who lived in an updated version of Ezekiel's temple ("Niggerati Manor") in the restored Jerusalem. In truth, however, they had all flocked to Harlem to take advantage of the vogue of the Negro renaissance, and instead of creating art, they threw parties and drank gin. Moreover, the house itself becomes a parody of community, degenerating into the city of Babel when no one at the salon held by Dr. Parkes (Alain Locke) can agree upon the first principles of Negro art. Thurman's title comes from Shakespeare but his inspiration comes from Van Vechten. Like Byron, the intellectuals of "Niggerati Manor" have uprooted themselves to come to Harlem but have planted themselves in cloud-cuckoo land. Niggerati Manor is in Harlem but not of it, and as such the artists (even the good ones) live an isolated, hothouse existence.

In *Not Without Laughter* (1930), Langston Hughes treated the prodigality of the Prodigal Daughter as her most heroic feature. Growing up in a small town in Kansas, Harriett Williams learns blues lyrics from her roustabout uncle, Jimboy Rodgers, who learns them in turn from the "big dirty cities of the South."[57] Jimboy and the rebellious Harriett stand in opposition to Aunt Hager, Harriett's mother, who symbolizes the ways of the small town. Yet Aunt Hager's Christian fortitude is as necessary to Harriett's future as is Jimboy's pagan joy—together the twin legacies of uncle and mother help to transform Harriett into a substantial woman. At the novel's end, she becomes a blues singer in Chicago, and for Hughes she symbolizes the best of both worlds—past/present; urban/rural. Unlike her sister Tempy, who remains static in her respectability, Harriett is fluid like her music, transforming adversity into the living Protean energy of her song.[58] Because she has the "resources" of the blueswoman, she with her young nephew will become "dancers of the spirit" (p. 313) in the iron heart of the city.

To borrow a phrase from Charles S. Johnson, perhaps the popularity of *Nigger Heaven* made it possible for black novelists to tell "family secrets."[59] In *Quicksand* (1928), *Passing* (1929), *The Blacker the Berry* (1929), *The Walls of Jericho*

(1928), and *One Way to Heaven* (1932), they examined the various reasons why different levels of black society failed to make connections.

Countee Cullen's *One Way to Heaven* presents the counterpart to Wallace Thurman's house of artists. At Constancia Brandon's elegant home, the rich and famous meet twice a week to discuss books written by the New Negro, but books soon take second place to drink and gossip. Supposedly Constancia's "temple" (as she calls it)[60] is to provide a haven of appreciation for the rising stars in Harlem's firmament, yet the real artist in the novel is not a New Negro but a confidence man named Sam. That his existence goes unnoticed by the rich and famous is Cullen's icy comment upon the perceptions of the members of the Negro aristocracy, who bicker among themselves but cannot see beyond the prejudices of their class. In Cullen's novel, there is more than one way to get to Heaven, and Cullen created an aesthetic structure to match his theme: rich and poor live in such separate worlds (as do the Creeper and Mary) that they split the plot in two.

In *Passing*, Nella Larsen focused on the vicious implications of crab antics, noting that when threatened, someone like the "respectable" Irene Redfield became D. H. Lawrence's quintessential American: "hard, isolate, . . . and a killer."[61] In *The Blacker the Berry*, Wallace Thurman carried the intricacies of crab antics even further than had Van Vechten. The white author had touched upon the color line within the race, but the elite in *Nigger Heaven* took more pride in their education than they did their light skin. Thurman set out to educate Van Vechten.

In analyzing the source of Emma Lou Morgan's inferiority complex, Thurman did not simply want to show that there is color prejudice within the race. He tried to communicate the mechanics of the total societal situation, how various factors combine (such as color, class, and wealth) to create a society that is as complicated in its codes of behavior as those in a Jane Austen novel. Emma is not simply pushed to the bottom of the barrel because she is black; she is also poor *and* "a snob."[62] Caught up in a bewildering world whose signs she continually misreads, she actually shares the prejudices of the people who condemn her. She finally learns through a character in the novel modeled on Van Vechten (Campbell Kitchen—Thurman's joke on Van Vechten's penchant for unusual names)[63] to accept "herself by herself" (p. 227). The advice Kitchen gives her is the same philosophy advocated by Campaspe Lolliard in *The Blind Bow-Boy*: ". . . doors yielded more easily to the casual, self-centered individual than to the ranting, praying pilgrim" (p. 227). Yet "pilgrim" is what Emma becomes by taking Kitchen's advice, and appropriately she can discover that she should "find— not seek" (p. 227). Despite its pitfalls, Harlem has an openness denied Boise, Idaho, and thus has enabled this Prodigal Daughter to flee the chains of her own self-hatred.

Perhaps the most striking example of crab antics is Rudolph Fisher's novel, *The Walls of Jericho*. The title contains the novel's central metaphor: the "walls" that separate people from one another and from themselves. From the very beginning, barriers divide white and black, men and women, self and mask, "rat" and "dickty." Fisher even suggests that the world of reputation based on manliness is a mask, one created by the presence of "dickties." What the "dickties" don't prize, i.e., virility, Bubber and Jinx claim as their essence. Hence segments of black society influence one another, but the points of connection go unnoticed. Fisher borrows Van Vechten's metaphor of The Charity Ball to define the caste lines within black society and to suggest the means by which they might be overcome. Again, the crucial symbol is that of the dance: "Out on the dance floor, everyone, dickty and rat, rubbed joyous elbows, laughing, mingling, forgetting differences. But whenever the music stopped everyone immediately sought his own level."[64]

By the novel's end, not all the walls are destroyed, but Fisher hints that one wall that came a-tumbling down may be the most significant demolition of all. The economic partnership between Joshua Jones and Fred Merrit, rat and dickty, respectively, seems to imply the birth of a new Harlem, one that will replace the divisive earthly city of Jericho. That Jones is an artist among piano movers adds another dimension to the optimism of the novel's conclusion. Harlem will now have the economic self-sufficiency it needs to become the Heavenly City of Alain Locke's imagination.

Not surprisingly, almost everyone during the Harlem Renaissance thought of Claude McKay's *Home to Harlem* (1928) as the most glaring example of Van Vechten's influence; and yet if my analysis of *Nigger Heaven* is correct, *Home to Harlem* seems the least indebted novel of those I've discussed. For one thing, Jake and Ray (despite their differences) are not Prodigal Sons but picaros; for another, McKay leaves the black middle class out of his novel—the "chef" on the Pullman train is only a lowlifer putting on airs—and by so doing, he leaves out the dimension of crab antics that is so conspicuously present in *Nigger Heaven*. The picture McKay presents of Harlem is that of black peasant life given an added electric charge by the city.[65] This life has a rhythm all its own—half madness, half ecstasy, all Dionysus. Yet McKay never romanticizes Harlem, and perhaps his closest resemblance to Van Vechten lies in his perception that Harlem's vitality and its savagery are two sides of the same coin. If unprepared, a person can be overwhelmed by the "flood." Even Jake, McKay's image of healthy, natural man, catches the clap, and is nearly killed by the love-mad Zeddie. Ray expresses the difficulty of trying to live in Harlem, for it is "too savage about some things,"[66] and such savagery seems to preclude the possibility of an intellectual life.

Thus *Nigger Heaven* and *Home to Harlem* address an issue that is central to Alain Locke's *The New Negro* and to the fiction of the black novelists that follow Van Vechten: to what extent is the city "home"? Both Jake and Ray flee Harlem, and it destroys Byron. For some, the city enthralls but threatens to engulf (Helga Crane in *Quicksand*);[67] for others, it becomes the setting for an unforeseen salvation (Emma Lou Morgan). And for still others, it justifies Locke's optimism about the city as community (*The Walls of Jericho*). But whatever the perspectives, it is to Aaron Douglas's credit that he saw they were all implied in Van Vechten's novel. He agreed with Eric Waldrond that *Nigger Heaven* was a "frontier work of enduring order,"[68] for it helped to define for the black novelist the lines of investigation that could be applied to the city. And those lines, I insist, were not circumscribed by the limited perspective of "primitivism." Van Vechten's acute eye for social analysis (crab antics) and his use of myth helped make possible an urban tradition in American fiction that has not yet been fully appreciated.

NOTES

1. For the reaction of readers in the 1920s, see Jervis Anderson, *This Was Harlem: A Cultural Portrait, 1900–1950* (New York: Farrar, Straus, Giroux, 1982), pp. 217–20; Nathan Irvin Huggins, *Harlem Renaissance* (New York: Oxford Univ. Press, 1971), pp. 113–16; Chidi Ikonné, *From Du Bois to Van Vechten: The Early New Negro Literature* (Westport, CT: Greenwood, 1981), pp. 26–27; Bruce Kellner, *Carl Van Vechten and the Irreverent Decades* (Norman: Univ. of Oklahoma Press, 1968), pp. 209–33; *"Keep A-Inchin' Along": Selected Writings of Carl Van Vechten about Black Art and Letters*, ed. Bruce Kellner (Westport, CT: Greenwood, 1979), pp. 73–78; David Levering Lewis, *When Harlem Was in Vogue* (1981; rpt. New York: Random House, Vintage, 1982), pp. 181–90. These accounts are fascinating, but they only touch the tip of the iceberg. The hostility of the black press to the novel is a story in itself, at times making Du Bois' savage review of *Nigger Heaven* in the *Crisis* (Dec. 1926) sound positively urbane. Nor was the reaction of the black press always uniform. Within the *Pittsburgh Courier* a battle raged for almost a year over the virtues and vices of the novel. As early as June 19, 1926, Walter White puffed the novel in his column before it had appeared in bookstores. In the same newspaper, George Schuyler defended it twice (with reservations)—6 Nov. 1926, 4 June 1927. Editor Floyd Calvin ruthlessly attacked it (6 Nov. 1926) and those "who backed the volume from the start; who lent it their moral support, and who attempted to justify its appearance when published." On March 12, 1927, Hubert Harrison attacked the Negro renaissance through Van Vechten, and on April 16, 1927, Langston Hughes despaired: "I admit I am still at a loss to understand the yelps of the colored critics and the reason for their ill-mannered onslaught against Mr. Van Vechten."

2. See Addison Gayle, Jr., *The Way of the New World: The Black Novel in America* (Garden City: Doubleday, 1975), pp. 86–90; also, see Lewis *When Harlem Was in Vogue*, pp.188–89; Huggins, *Harlem Renaissance*, pp. 102–13. While not the originator of the charge, Sterling Brown has done the most to perpetuate it. See Sterling Brown, "Negro Character As Seen By White Authors," *The Journal of Negro Education* 2 (Jan. 1933): 182: ". . . his novel, *Nigger Heaven*, is to the exotic pattern what *Swallow Brown* was to the contented slave." In *The Negro in American Fiction*, Brown makes Van Vechten's novel responsible for a whole school of "urban primitives." See *Negro Poetry and Drama and The Negro in American Fiction* (1937; rpt. New York: Atheneum, 1968), p. 132. As used by the novel's critics, "primitivism" has never been clearly defined. For instance, no one has thought to apply to *Nigger Heaven* Arthur O. Lovejoy's distinction between different kinds of primitivisms. See Arthur O. Lovejoy et al., eds., *A Documentary History of Primitivism and Related Ideas* (Baltimore: Johns Hopkins Univ. Press, 1935), pp. 9–11. Not rooted in definition, the word is used for its negative connotations and attracts adjectives ("exotic," "atavistic," "hedonistic," "escapist," "decadent") that suggest a pernicious flight from restraint, civilization, and/or reality. Since it is easy to play fast and loose with "primitivism," characters as different as Anatole Longfellow (the Scarlet Creeper), Lasca Sartoris, Byron Kasson, and Mary Love have all been seen as examples of it. One example suffices to show that "primitivism"

confuses more than it clarifies. Recently David Levering Lewis has stated that the Creeper in the novel's prologue exists merely to titillate white readers (*When Harlem Was in Vogue*, p. 185), and yet it was Du Bois himself—Van Vechten's *bête noir*—who had said that the white author "began a good tale with the promising figure of Anatole. . . ." (*Crisis*, Dec. 1926). Curiously, when the novel first appeared, "primitivism" was not the central issue among both black and white critics. The question most often raised was whether Van Vechten had depicted Harlem accurately and the Negro sympathetically. Those who liked the novel said that Van Vechten had dropped his usual mode of social satire for "realism" and objective reporting. Those who disliked it claimed, with Du Bois, that Van Vechten had not presented "a true picture" of Harlem life, but had focused on the sordid to the exclusion of everything else. Yet even here there was disagreement; some claimed that Van Vechten had focused almost exclusively on the upper classes, and that at times his book sounded like propaganda for the NAACP.

While not absent from the early criticism, "primitivism" as a charge against the novel picked up steam as *Nigger Heaven* became a best-seller and an influence on black novelists. Du Bois, for instance, compared the truthful expression of black life in Jessie Fauset's *Plum Bun* to the emphasis upon the "bizarre, the unusual, and the exotic" in *Nigger Heaven* and Claude McKay's *Home to Harlem* (see *Crisis*, April 1929). Conversely, Alain Locke praised the "vital rhythms of Negro life" in *Home to Harlem* over the "decadent muck of the city gutter" in *Nigger Heaven* (see *Opportunity*, Jan. 1929). Ironically, two years earlier, Locke had written Van Vechten personally to congratulate him for writing a "novel of manners." Alain Locke to Carl Van Vechten, 2 Sept. 1926, Carl Van Vechten papers, Rare Books and Manuscripts, The New York Public Library, Astor, Lenox and Tilden Foundations—hereafter referred to as NYP.

Van Vechten himself must bear some of the responsibility for having his novel placed in the camp of "primitivism." In the *Crisis* symposium for 1926 ("The Negro in Art"), he said, "The squalor of Negro life, the vice of Negro life, offer a wealth of novel, exotic, picturesque material to the artist" (*Crisis*, Mar. 1926). Those who wish to be charitable might argue that Van Vechten was saying the same, but with a different emphasis, as what Richard Wright would say fifteen years later at the end of his essay, "How 'Bigger' Was Born": namely, that if the American artist complains of the vacuity of American culture, he might do well to look at Afro-American life, for all the ingredients of a great literature are there. Of course, Wright dwells upon the tragic implications of "the squalor of Negro life." Yet even so, could not synonyms for Van Vechten's words be applied to *Native Son* ("exotic"=unusual; "novel"=of a different kind; "picturesque"=graphic)? Nevertheless, those who wish to be uncharitable to Van Vechten have argued that by using words like "exotic" and "picturesque," Van Vechten was revealing the kind of attitude he would take toward "the squalor of Negro life." He would simply exploit this material, as he did in *Negro Heaven*, to amuse white folk. Yet even here we might do well to remember D. H. Lawrence's dictum: observe what novelists do—not what they say.

Another reason that *Nigger Heaven* came to be seen as an example of "primitivism" is that Alfred Knopf often advertised it that way. Here is an example from *The New York World* (27 Aug. 1926): "Why go to cabarets when you can read *Nigger Heaven*!" My point is that "primitivism" stuck to *Nigger Heaven* like Brer Rabbit to Tar Baby for a variety of extra-aesthetic reasons, ranging from Van Vechten's own flamboyant life (his interracial parties, his visits to Harlem's cabarets) to the American cultural scene, to the complicated world of politics within the Harlem Renaissance itself. All these things prevented the novel from getting a fair hearing in the 1920s, and in the 1930s when the Harlem Renaissance was no longer in vogue, both "primitivism" and *Nigger Heaven* were linked together as two diseases that helped kill the literary movement.

3. See Sterling A. Brown, "A Century of Negro Portraiture in American Literature," in *Black Voices*, ed. Abraham Chapman (New York: New American Library, 1968), p. 575.

Also, see Harold Cruse, *The Crisis of the Negro Intellectual* (New York: William Morrow, 1967), p. 35. Brown's attack is directed at *Nigger Heaven* as pernicious influence; Cruse's, upon Van Vechten as cultural patron.

4. Notably Bruce Kellner in *Carl Van Vechten*, pp. 209–23. Kellner calls *Nigger Heaven* "if not his best novel . . . certainly his most polished one" (p. 220). Also, see Chidi Ikonné, who rightly complains that almost everyone talks about what the novel says but "not 'how it says it.'" Unfortunately, Ikonné ends his discussion of *Nigger Heaven* with a statement that should begin it: ". . . *Nigger Heaven* deserves a better treatment than it has received so far" (p. 36). Ikonné drops his study of the novel's craft at a point when its relationship to theme is becoming interesting: the Creeper as Byron's *döppelganger.* For another sympathetic analysis of the novel, see Edward Lueders, *Carl Van Vechten* (New York: Twayne, 1965), pp. 95–106.

Van Vechten's relationship to the Harlem Renaissance also has its eloquent defenders. See Kellner, *"A-Inchin',"* pp. 3–15; Leon Coleman's "Carl Van Vechten Presents the New Negro," in this volume; Edward Lueders, *Carl Van Vechten and the Twenties* (Albuquerque: Univ. of New Mexico Press, 1955), pp. 123–26.

5. Huggins, *Harlem Renaissance*, p. 107.

6. Mark Helbling argues that two contradictory views toward "primitivism" exist in *Nigger Heaven*, and that they reflect an ambivalence within Van Vechten himself. See his "Carl Van Vechten and the Harlem Renaissance," *Negro Literary Forum* 10 (Summer 1976): 42. I insist that the ambivalence exists only because Helbling has inherited a critical tradition ("primitivism" in *Nigger Heaven*) and cannot see beyond the terms of that tradition.

7. It is worth noting by way of contrast that when Douglas came to do the cover for the book jacket to Claude McKay's *Home to Harlem* (1928), he did focus upon the Dionysian aspects of black urban life. In the foreground stands a black figure, a black Orpheus perhaps, who has just spent the night singing and dancing in a cabaret and who now, still singing and dancing, ushers in the dawn of a new day in the city. This book jacket is preserved in the Beinecke Library at Yale University.

8. Aaron Douglas to Carl Van Vechten, 6 Aug. 1926, NYP.

9. Borzoi Broadside, August 1926, 8 (New York: Knopf, 1926). Curiously, this blurb appeared in *The American Mercury* (Aug. 1926) and in *The New York Herald Tribune* (29 Aug. 1926) but with Douglas's second drawing (Plate 2). Evidently Knopf felt that both drawings were appropriate for periodicals read primarily by whites, but that Douglas's second drawing would be reserved exclusively for periodicals read by blacks. In my research, I have never found Douglas's first drawing (Plate 1) used in black newspapers or black magazines.

10. Carl Van Vechten, *Nigger Heaven* (New York: Knopf, 1926), pp. 257–58—hereafter citations in my text are to this edition.

11. On the book jacket of Knopf's reprinting (1925) of Haldane MacFall's *The Wooings of Jezebel Pettyfer* (1896), Van Vechten called it "the best novel yet written about the Negro. It is certainly the best one I have ever read." Van Vechten also admired (and gave the American title to) Ronald Firbank's *Prancing Nigger* (1924). Aesthetically, Van Vechten enjoyed MacFall's ribald humor and Firbank's delicate irony—see his introduction to the American edition of *Prancing Nigger*. However, Van Vechten was also fascinated by the sociological perspectives of both novelists, their perceptions of the complex social dynamics of black Caribbean society: the tensions between pastoral and urban, colonized and colonizer, and the dramatic conflicts within black culture that these tensions created. These two novels may have influenced Van Vechten in *Nigger Heaven* in yet another way. Everyone knows that the novel is a *roman à clef*, yet according to Bruce Kellner "no one in particular served as a model for Anatole Longfellow, the Scarlet Creeper." See Kellner, *"A-Inchin',"* p. 74. I would suggest that the Creeper has a fictional antecedent in Charlie Mouth (*Prancing Nigger*, see especially the opening of Chapter 11) and Masheen Dyle (*The Wooings of Jezebel Pettyfer*).

12. Peter J. Wilson, *Crab Antics: The Social Anthropology of English-Speaking Negro Societies of the Caribbean* (New Haven: Yale Univ. Press, 1973), p. 153.

13. Huggins, *Harlem Renaissance*, p. 109.

14. Both Lewis and Huggins use Lasca to prove, in Huggins's words, that "Try as he might to illustrate that Negroes were much like other people, Van Vechten's belief in their essential primitivism makes him prove something else" (*Harlem Renaissance*, p. 111). That is, Lasca's sexual excesses (like the Creeper's criminality) have Van Vechten's tacit approval, because they symbolize the essential nature of the race. Yet both critics fail to perceive the irony lurking in the history of the character who commits these sexual excesses. As a young girl who wished to escape her poverty, Lasca married for money, thinking that cash would help her rise above her lot. Yet like a character in Dante's *Inferno*, she continues to re-enact the one thing she betrayed, which was love. Her sexual excesses do not symbolize an unrestrained libido, only entrapment—within herself and within Negro society. She seems to have no purpose in life but hedonism and hatred, both dead ends. Unlike Byron, she is strong, but she dissipates her strength seeking atonement for the past and revenge upon the present. Both Lewis and Huggins treat *Nigger Heaven* as though it were merely an occasion for Van Vechten to parade his opinions upon black life; they fail to see that his characters have an aesthetic integrity as characters, that they function within a fictional universe whose laws are as intricate as the culture he analyzes.

15. Carl Van Vechten to H. L. Mencken, 30 Nov. 1925, NYP, quoted in Lewis, *When Harlem Was in Vogue*, p. 184.

16. Carl Van Vechten, *Firecrackers* (New York: Knopf, 1925), pp. 167, 168.

17. George Schuyler, "Views and Reviews," *Pittsburgh Courier*, 6 Nov. 1926. "Physicians, bootleggers, lawyers, pimps, gamblers, dentists, prostitutes, hairdressers, schoolteachers, and vendors of stolen goods, all rub shoulders. It is often difficult to tell which is which."

18. Carl Van Vechten, *The Blind Bow-Boy* (New York: Knopf, 1923), p. 132—hereafter citations in my text are to this edition.

19. Charles Chesnutt, *The Wife of His Youth and Other Stories* (1899; rpt. Ann Arbor: Univ. of Michigan Press, 1968), p. 131. Van Vechten had tremendous respect for Chesnutt as a writer of fiction, no doubt due in part to Chesnutt's ability to delineate the world of manners within black life.

20. Ikonné perceptively notes that both men are sexual "creepers." See Ikonné, *From Du Bois to Van Vechten*, p. 35.

21. Countee Cullen, *Color* (New York: Harper, 1925), p. 37.

22. Carl Van Vechten, *Parties: Scenes from Contemporary New York Life* (New York: Knopf, 1930), pp. 186–187.

23. See Epictetus, *The Enchiridion*, trans. Thomas W. Higginson (New York: Bobbs-Merrill, 1948), pp. 27–28.

24. Recently, Francis Ford Coppola's movie *The Cotton Club* (1984) made use of the same metaphor in a similar context. Blacks use the dance as an expression of self and an expression of community (youth and age, brother and brother, lover and lover); whereas whites use their guns to destroy themselves. In *The Romantic Image* (New York: Macmillan, 1957), Frank Kermode discusses the image of the dance as an important symbol in modern art—see chapter four ("The Dancer").

25. Carl Van Vechten, "Eloquent Alvin Ailey," in *The Dance Writings of Carl Van Vechten*, ed. Paul Padgette (New York: Dance Horizons, 1974), p. 25.

26. See Kellner, *"A-Inchin',"* pp. 29–58.

27. These people illustrate Campaspe Lorillard's philosophy in *The Blind Bow-Boy*: "I have no respect for martyrs. Any one who is strong enough shapes the world to his own purposes, but he doesn't do it roughly; he accomplishes his object . . . by appearing to be in sympathy with those who oppose him. Conform externally with the world's demands and you will get anything you desire in life" (p. 71). One may not approve of this philosophy, but one can hardly call it "primitivism."

28. See Lewis, *When Harlem Was in Vogue*, p. 189; Huggins, *Harlem Renaissance*, p. 108; Helbling, "Carl Van Vechten and the Harlem Renaissance," p. 46.

29. Carl Van Vechten to Mabel Dodge Luhan, 8 Oct. 1924, Carl Van Vechten Collection, Beinecke Rare Book and Manuscript Library, Yale University, cited in Helbling, "Carl Van Vechten and the Harlem Renaissance," p. 42.

30. Carl Van Vechten, "A Note by the Author," *Nigger Heaven* (1926; rpt. New York: Avon, 1951).

31. James Weldon Johnson, *The Autobiography of an Ex-Colored Man* (1912; reprint, New York: Knopf, 1927), p. vii.

32. See Anderson, *This Was Harlem*, pp. 49–71; also, see Gilbert Osofsky, *Harlem: The Making of a Ghetto* (New York: Harper & Row, 1965), chapters 2, 8, 9, 10.

33. In *Blues, Ideology, and Afro-American Literature* (Chicago: Univ. of Chicago Press, 1984), Houston A. Baker has a brilliant essay on the novel as an attempt to subvert the Plantation Myth by presenting a revisionist "fiction" of its own (pp. 114–38).

34. See Advertisement for *Nigger Heaven* in *Opportunity* 4 (Sept. 1926): unnumbered page. The same advertisement ran in *The Chicago Defender* on 28 Aug. 1926. Douglas's drawing was also used as the logo for James Weldon Johnson's review of *Nigger Heaven*: "Romance and Tragedy in Harlem: A Review," *Opportunity* 4 (Oct. 1926): 316.

35. Claude McKay, *Harlem Shadows* (New York: Harcourt, Brace, 1922), p. 23.

36. McKay, "America," *Harlem Shadows*, p. 6

37. Locke gave special emphasis to this theme in *The New Negro* by replacing an article entitled "The Church and the Negro Spirit" in the *Survey Graphic* with one (written by himself) called "The Legacy of the Ancestral Arts."

38. See Kellner, *"A-Inchin',"* p. 82.

39. "Uncle Tom's Mansion," *New York Herald Tribune Books*, 20 Dec. 1925; reprinted in Kellner, *"A-Inchin',"* pp. 58–64.

40. Carl Van Vechten to H. L. Mencken, 21 Dec. 1925, Mencken Papers, NYP. "Today I finished the first draft of my new novel 'Nigger Heaven.'"

41. Kellner, *"A-Inchin',"* pp. 63.

42. Josiah Royce, "Provincialism," in *The Social Philosophy of Josiah Royce*, ed. Stuart Gerry Brown (Syracuse: Syracuse Univ. Press, 1950), pp. 49–69.

43. Alain Locke, *The New Negro* (1925; rpt. New York: Atheneum, 1968), p. 6—hereafter citations in my text are to this edition.

44. The idea of "transformation" is crucial to Turner's thesis that the frontier made democracy a reality in America. See "The Significance of the Frontier in American History," in *The Turner Thesis*, ed. George Rogers Taylor (Lexington, MA: D. C. Heath, 1972), p. 22. Locke made the comparison of Harlem to the "western frontier" more explicit in the *Survey Graphic* (Mar. 1925), the Special Negro Number (edited by him) that was to become the basis of *The New Negro*. See Vol. 6, p. 629. This idea was further developed in Paul Kellogg's article in *The New Negro* called "Negro Pioneers."

45. See Monroe K. Spears, *Dionysus and the City: Modernism in Twentieth-Century Poetry* (New York: Oxford Univ. Press, 1970), p. 70: "The word *city* derives from *civitas*, city-state, which is properly an aggregation of *cives*, citizens; *civilization* has the same derivation." See also Werner Jaeger, *Paideia: The Ideals of Greek Culture*, 2nd ed. (New York: Oxford Univ. Press, 1945), I: xxii.

46. Both Dunbar and Johnson had associated the city with a temptress. In *The Autobiography of an Ex-Colored Man*, New York is like a "great witch . . . enticing" people with her seductive charms, a metaphor that Johnson was later to develop in his poem "The White Witch" (*Fifty Years and Other Poems*, 1917). In Johnson's novel, a white woman known as the "widow" sits in the "Club," trying to ensnare black men (including the narrator) in her web. In Johnson's poem "The Prodigal Son" in *God's Trombones* (1928), the young man goes to Babylon, again associated with "sweet-sinning women." In *The Sport of the Gods*, Dunbar describes New York as "insidious wine" that intoxicates a man when he is there and makes him "hunger for the place when he is away from it." Again the city is feminine, identified specifically in Joe Hamilton's mind with Hattie Sterling, his "Heart's Desire."

47. Blanche Gelfant, "Sister to Faust: the City's 'Hungry Woman' as Heroine," *Novel* 15 (Fall 1981): 38.

48. See Blanche Gelfant, *The American City Novel* (Norman: Univ. of Oklahoma Press, 1954), pp. 70, 71.

49. But surely her memorized passage from *Melanctha* has an ironic appropriateness. Like the cautious Jeff Cambell, this cautious librarian will become "excited" by Eros. Instead of complaining of Van Vechten's quotations from famous authors (white and black) in *Nigger Heaven*, critics might do well to discuss them as analogues to the dramatic action.

50. See Donald Pizer, "Carl Van Vechten and The Spirit of the Age," in *Towards a New American Literary History: Essays in Honor of Arlin Turner*, eds. Louis J. Budd, Edwin H. Cady, and Carl L. Anderson (Durham: Duke Univ. Press, 1980), pp. 217–18. Also, see Huggins, *Harlem Renaissance*, p. 108; Gayle, *Way of the New World*, p. 89. Aaron Sumner, Robert Kasson, Mr. Love, and Howard Allison all have college degrees, and their education has not made them unfit to live in the world. However, Byron has been educated at a white college, this in part explaining why he has difficulty engaging himself with black life. If we are tempted to interpret this fact as an example of Van Vechten's anti-educational bias, we should remember that Toni Morrison has described a similar situation in *Song of Solomon*: First Corinthians was educated at Bryn Mawr.

51. Hortense J. Spillers, "Interstices: A Small Drama of Words," in *Pleasure and Danger: Exploring Female Sexuality*, ed. Carole S. Vance (Boston: Routledge, Kegan, Paul, 1984), p. 86. The passage is worth quoting in full (italics added): "The Burkean pentad of fiction—act, agency, scene, agent, and purpose as the principal elements in the human drama—is compressed in the singer into a living body, insinuating itself through a material scene, and *in that dance of motives*, in which the motor behavior, the changes in countenance, the vocal dynamics, the calibration of gesture and nuance in relationship to a formal object—the song itself—is a precise demonstration of the subject turning in fully conscious knowledge of her own resources toward her object." Spillers's point is that no matter how self-destructive the singer's life may be in actuality, in the song the singer *dances* because she has the "resources" to keep chaos under control.

52. Van Vechten had failed to get permission to use "Shake That Thing" in the novel, an omission that proved expensive for Knopf. Van Vechten then asked Langston Hughes to write new lyrics for the song, and Hughes subsequently came to write new poems for all the blues lyrics in *Nigger Heaven*. For a more detailed discussion of Knopf's legal difficulties, see Kellner, *Carl Van Vechten*, pp. 212–13.

53. Lewis, *When Harlem Was in Vogue*, pp. 190, 191.

54. Charles S. Johnson to Carl Van Vechten, 10 Aug. 1926, NYP.

55. W.E.B. Du Bois, *Dark Princess* (New York: Harcourt, Brace, 1928), p. 310.

56. Zora Neale Hurston wrote a very funny burlesque of the Prodigal Son story called "Book of Harlem." Never published, it can be found in the James Weldon Johnson Collection, The Beinecke Rare Book and Manuscript Library, Yale University. Also, see Robert Hemenway, *Zora Neale Hurston* (Urbana: Univ. of Illinois Press, 1977), p. 31. Hurston sends her Prodigal Son (Mandolin) "to great Babylon," where there resides not only beautiful brown-skin "Shebas" but "the chief of the Niggerati, who is called Carl Van Vechten." (It is worth noting that in the original biblical story the Prodigal Son goes not to a city but to a "far country." See Luke 15:13).

57. Langston Hughes, *Not Without Laughter* (1929; rpt. New York: Knopf, 1968), p. 54—hereafter citations in my text are to this edition.

58. Compare Baker, *Blues, Ideology, Afro-American Literature*, p. 9: "As driving force, the blues matrix thus avoids simple dualities. It perpetually achieves its effects as a fluid and multivalent network."

59. Charles S. Johnson to Carl Van Vechten, 10 Aug. 1926, NYP, quoted in Kellner, *Carl Van Vechten*, p. 217.

60. Countee Cullen, *One Way to Heaven* (1932; rpt. New York: AMS Press, 1975), p. 165.

61. D. H. Lawrence, *Studies in Classic American Literature* (1922; rpt. New York: Doubleday, 1951), p. 73.

62. Wallace Thurman, *The Blacker the Berry* (1929; rpt. New York: Macmillan, Collier, 1970), p. 35—hereafter all citations in my text are to this edition.

63. Characters modeled on Carl Van Vechten also appear in other novels by black writers: he is Conrad White in *The Walls of Jericho*, Walter Derwent in *One Way to Heaven*, Hugh Wentworth in *Passing* and *Quicksand,* and Hinckle Von Vampton in Ishmael Reed's *Mumbo Jumbo* (1972). He is also called Paul Vanderin in Maxwell Bodenheim's *Ninth Avenue* (1926), a novel that attempted in part to answer *Nigger Heaven.*

64. Rudolph Fisher, *The Walls of Jericho* (1928; rpt. New York: Arno, 1969), p. 74.

65. I am indebted to Alain Locke for this insight—see his "Retrospective Review," *Opportunity* 7 (Jan. 1929): 9.

66. Claude McKay, *Home to Harlem* (New York: Harper & Brothers, 1928), p. 129.

67. Of course the irony here is that Helga is eventually swallowed up by that marvelous parody of pastoral man, the Reverend Mr. Pleasant Green.

68. Eric Waldrond, "Nigger Heaven," *Saturday Review of Literature* 3 (2 Oct. 1926): 153—quoted in Kellner, *Carl Van Vechten,* p. 213.

BLACK NO MORE:
GEORGE SCHUYLER AND THE POLITICS OF "RACIAL CULTURE"

JANE KUENZ

This essay is part of a larger work that examines the cultural production of the "New Negro" within certain African-American expressive forms of the period now commonly known as the Harlem Renaissance. Though used to describe newly-freed African Americans after the Civil War, the term "New Negro" was subsequently adopted and modified in the post-reconstruction era by African American writers and intellectuals who sought to intervene in the ideological organization of "race" by reimagining and re-presenting in art, literature, music, and political and everyday cultural practices what it means to be black and American. In general, I am interested in interrogating the intersection of national, racial, and cultural identities within one period in the U.S. in which articulating new forms for that relation was a central political and aesthetic project. More covertly, my concern is twofold: 1) to focus on the 1920s in part to provide a context and history for current debates about the source and nature of racial identity, particularly in relation to claims to national belonging or exclusion; and 2) to critique certain recurring moves in American racial discourse among both racist and anti-racist groups.

This is academic language for issues with which most people are familiar, some intimately. They are also ones which increasingly frame public discussion of African-American life. For example, the cover of a recent *Village Voice* asks "Who's Winning the Black Studies War?" For those of its readers unaware that there is a "war" for Black Studies, or of what that might mean, the *Voice*'s editors illustrate its battlelines with the iconographic images of, on the one hand, Henry Louis Gates, Jr., currently at the Du Bois Institute at Harvard, shown with his books and stuffy white shirt, and, on the other, Molefi Asante, the Godfather of

Afrocentricity, expansive in a striped dashiki, welcoming us home to Mother Africa or perhaps only the African-American Studies Department at Temple, which he chairs. The dichotomy referenced by these differing images is an old if largely false one. As author Greg Thomas acknowledges but cannot quite believe (Asante's picture on the cover is the sign of who's "winning"), the binary that would locate Gates's post-structuralist multiculturalism independent of Asante's African nationalism is one that has insufficiently attended to the ways in which these categories help define each other.[1]

What is interesting to me about the *Voice* article is the way it recapitulates a recurring debate within African American political and aesthetic thought whose terms have been variously defined: Thomas calls it, rather crudely I think, the battle of the Multiculturalists or Acculturationists vs. the Liberationists. The fact that Thomas can't decide if Gates is a "multiculturalist" or an "acculturationist" is one sign that the multiplicity of positions within African American thought has been collapsed in the service of a familiar form of dualistic thinking which prefers to figure its debates as "wars" of two opposing and preferably antagonistic sides. Briefly, what we know as "multiculturalism" respects the integrity of cultural difference and seeks to preserve it in distinct units. What Thomas calls "acculturation" asserts and finds strength in the fluidity and hybridity of all cultures, while the "liberationists" claim the liberatory potential of single-minded attention to one's own.

The question of what "one's own" culture might be is the central issue here as it has been for the African diaspora since its inception. It turns up in the Harlem Renaissance in debates about whether or how black experiences in the U.S. affect the cultural inheritance of Africa presumably available to African Americans through the exigencies of race. This question of whether or not there is such a thing as an essential "racial culture" or "racial art" shapes George Schuyler's famous debate with Langston Hughes in two 1926 issues of *The Nation* and undergirds his 1931 satiric novel *Black No More*.[2] The novel has only recently reappeared in print, but the essays have always been used, in much the way Gates and Asante are being used in the *Voice*, as a framework to represent the period and in the process oversimplify a complex debate about the relation of race to culture and the claims either can make on nationality.

Appearing at the height of the Harlem Renaissance, Schuyler's "The Negro-Art Hokum" is a full-frontal attack on some of the movement's basic tenets: At a time when New Negroes were calling on artists to discover an essential core—variously defined as racial or cultural—and give it form in music, poetry, and fiction, Schuyler attacks the notion that any such thing exists, calling the belief in an essential racial quality to art so much "hokum" and arguing that because African Americans are "merely . . . lampblacked Anglo-Saxons," they should—and in fact do—create art in the European and American traditions in which their consciousnesses are shaped (p. 662). A week later in "The Negro Artist and the Racial Mountain," Langston Hughes differs by inviting his readers to be "Negro enough to be different," to recognize and use "racial culture"—"the eternal tom-

tom beating in the Negro soul"—in order to give to their creations what he calls "racial individuality"—their "heritage of rhythm and warmth" (p. 526).

Like Jessie Fauset and Nella Larsen, these essays always appear together in anthologies and critical discussions in such a way that the former suffers from proximity to the latter: while the complexities of Hughes's conception of racial culture in relation to economic circumstances have been ironed out in the service of a gung-ho rhetoric of racial pride, the subtleties of Schuyler's arguments have been rendered ludicrous by their abstraction from his immediate context and by the superimposition of what became his later conservative beliefs. These included supporting Goldwater in 1964, protesting King's Nobel prize in terms so extreme his home paper refused to publish it, blaming the 1967 uprisings on civil rights leaders, joining the John Birch Society, and allowing himself to be carted out on occasion as its resident enlightened black person. It is not true that African Americans are "merely lampblacked Anglo-Saxons," nor is it fair to say, as Schuyler does, that "the literature, painting, and sculpture of Aframericans . . . is identical in kind with the literature, painting, and sculpture of white Americans" or that "any group under similar circumstances would have produced something" akin to the spirituals of the black South (p. 662).

Although Schuyler attempts to historicize African American folk culture, he makes the typical conservative mistake of going only half-way: he emphasizes the primacy of environment and history over "the 'peculiar' psychology of the Negro" in the creation and elaboration of aesthetic traditions, but his conception of history does not allow for the possibility that some of those traditions found in the cultures of Africa not only continued in the New World among free and enslaved peoples, but that they actively influenced and transformed the cultures they encountered here (p. 662).

Though he overstates his case, Schuyler's concerns are real: rhetoric like Hughes's that speaks of "urges toward whiteness" and their implied denials of certain kinds of blackness not only misses his point, but elides the categories of race and culture he will put into play in *Black No More*. He is skeptical of those patrons and do-gooders in Greenwich Village and Harlem "whose hobby is taking races, nations, peoples, and movements under their wing" and who, in doing so, are prepared to insist that African Americans are "living in a different world," that there are, in the words of "sainted Harding," "'fundamental, eternal, and inescapable differences' between white and black America" (pp. 662, 663). Taking Hughes to task for assuming the progressive quality of the working-class and folk culture he valorizes in his poetry and in "The Negro Artist," Schuyler points out that by and large "it is the Aframerican masses who consume hair-straightener and skin-whitener." He concludes archly that "your American Negro," on Seventh Street or anywhere else, "is just plain American" (p. 662).

This is a familiar debate now as it was at the time, and like many of his contemporaries in the twenties, probably the majority, Schuyler worries as Du Bois did that Hughes's thinking is naive and politically dangerous. He is particularly disinclined to indulge in racial romanticism of any kind. *Black No More* is a monument to this refusal, a satiric dystopia so brutal in its depiction of the absurdities to which we carry our obsession with race that it has typically found fans only among earnest graduate students and science fiction nerds. The novel follows the ups and downs of picaro-cum-trickster Max Disher in profiting from the work of Dr. Junius Crookman, lately of Germany. Crookman's research has resulted in a treatment which lightens dark skin permanently, effectively transforming "Negro" into "Caucasian" and creating, as it were, the assimilated American population simultaneously feared and anxiously awaited by commentators on the national scene. As might be expected, however, the happy amalgamation of the country's different peoples never happens. To a black public wild to have it, Crookman's "Black-No-More" makes them not just white, but whiter than white, too white apparently for regular white folks determined to be distinguished as such. As Crookman later naively reports, Black-No-More makes one a shade paler than garden-variety whites who reason with consequent enlightenment that "if it were true that extreme whiteness was evidence of the possession of Negro blood, . . . then surely it were well not to be so white" (p. 219). Even though a secret research project reveals against the hopes of its sponsors that over 50% of the "white" American population has "tainted blood,"—leading one "Nordic" to admit that "we're all niggers now" (p. 193)—a subsequent reversal and redrawing of racial boundaries ensues, made complete and authoritative with the help of churches, courts, schools, labor unions, newspapers and magazines, social and biological sciences, political and cultural organs, and all the other ideological state apparatuses integral in the erection and maintenance of a really good oppressive system.

To be fair, when Schuyler's novel appeared early in 1931, it entered a culture primed for its reception by more than three decades of apprehensive and contradictory public fulmination, posing as and often passing for reasoned debate, on the subject of racial essences and their relation to national character. Richard Hofstadter describes this period as "surprisingly nervous and defensive" over the prospect that "Anglo-Saxondom," of which the U.S. was the last, best hope, was losing ground to other races.[3] Coping with this fear took a variety of forms—anti-immigration policies, Jim Crow laws, eugenics, and lynching—as did the fear itself: while some worried about the "race suicide" caused by what was called "the dread incubus of miscegenation" and "the lawless policies of hyphenation" and evident in decreasing birthrates among the "American race"—Theodore Roosevelt's term for white people who vote—others debated the risks and benefits of racial mixing as though it were something about to be launched into for the first time.[4] Sterility was the chief threat for the children of such matches in spite of the fact that non-whites were routinely described as more vital and vigorous than their white counterparts, whose very effeteness became the sign of both their incapacity for manual labor in factories and their singular ability to meet the demands of democratic life.

This last requires special attention: the belief that the blood of the "Anglo-Saxon"—or the more sweeping "Nordic," later just "white"—augurs a peculiar orientation toward democratic principles and the talent for implementing them in public life. Proposals to halt immigration and at least one serious suggestion to relegate African Americans to reservations attempted to systematically exclude people who were deemed unassimilable not because of race *per se*, but because cultural differences, which conveniently happened often to coincide with race, made them incapable of understanding and appreciating "freedom" and the democratic institutions that give it form. African Americans, it was argued, lacked the love of "freedom" that distinguished "Anglo-Saxons," proof of which lay in the fact that blacks had once had the bad form to be enslaved.[5]

What I want you to see here is how the rhetorical elision of race and culture allows racist writers to continue spouting the same beliefs under the less egregious heading of "cultural difference." In this way, their argument that black cultural traditions prevent African Americans from being full Americans seems to overlap with and actually agree with the reverse arguments of Harlem Renaissance artists that a growing body of art by African Americans, based on those same distinctively black traditions, in fact evidences just the opposite: that African Americans are fully American and thus deserving of equal rights and treatment. James Weldon Johnson puts this very directly in his important "Preface" to the 1922 *Book of American Negro Poetry*: "Nothing," he says, "will do more to change the mental attitude [of white Americans] and raise [the] status [of African Americans] than a demonstration of intellectual parity by the Negro through the production of literature and art."[6] In this setting, the rhetorical disappearance of race behind culture that shows up first in the alignment of whiteness with democracy and freedom and then in the disavowal of blackness in conjunction with the same makes up the heart of a national ideology dependent on the continued ability of its majority group to think of itself and its interests as "white" and "American" and then not recognize that this connection has been made. In other words, a political or critical emphasis on culture allows concepts of race and nation to merge, with the net result that some people will be forever excluded from the latter. As H. H. Bancroft wrote in 1919, it is one thing for the Negro to labor among us, but "as an American citizen, he is a monstrosity."[7]

It should not be surprising, then, that if they would be taken as monstrously incompatible with American citizenship, George Schuyler might be wary of the peculiar, the racial, and the different in African American life and art. Nor should it come as a surprise that his criticism of Hughes's emphasis on "racial art" was less popular among the majority white population than were Hughes's pronouncements, which could be and often were simply ignored or taken as further evidence of the essential differences among the races and black acceptance of that fact. Schuyler's too-casual "lampblacked Anglo-Saxons" would have gotten him attacked from all sides. In *Democracy and Race Friction* (1914), John Mecklin fretted about "the impatient, all but militant and antisocial attitude of an influential section of the Negro press" whose language "implies that the Negro is only an Anglo-Saxon who is so unfortunate as to have black skin."[8] Most agreed with Madison Grant that school, church, good English, new clothes, and the experience of fifty years do not "transform a Negro into a white man."[9]

That Schuyler is well aware of this background for his debate with Hughes is clear at the end of his essay when he argues that it is "'scientists' like Madison Grant and Lothrop Stoddard," along with the "scions of slaveholders," and "the patriots who flood the treasury of the Ku Klux Klan," who "broadcast all over the world . . . the baseless premise, so flattering to the white mob, that the blackamoor is inferior and fundamentally different." And it is on this premise, Schuyler continues, that is "erected the postulate that [the Negro] must needs be peculiar, and when he attempts to portray life through the medium of art, it must of necessity be peculiar" as well (p. 663). Schuyler knows that though such declarations of difference were the dogma of a good portion of Harlem Renaissance aesthetics, they were also frequently forthcoming from white speakers, where they were often prefaced by concerns for preserving the racial integrity of white America, by which is meant its economic and social privilege. Lothrop Stoddard, author of the bestselling *The Rising Tide of Color*, had argued explicitly along these lines only two years before the publication of *Black No More*. Advocating to a predominantly black audience the pursuit of "cultural recognition" rather than "social equality," Stoddard declared in his 1929 Chicago Forum debate with Du Bois that "Keeping white America unimpaired . . . is not fundamentally a matter of superiority or inferiority *per se*; it is a matter of racial difference." Stoddard argues to the amusement of his audience that "bi-racialism," including Jim Crow laws, is not a "caste" system because it "does not imply relative questions of superiority or inferiority, but is based upon the self-evident fact of difference."[10] Self-consciously playing on rhetoric like Hughes's in "The Negro Artist" and even like Du Bois's in the same debate, Stoddard attempts to keep the discussion focused on questions of distinctive racial traits rather than on what Du Bois had posed as a focus in his opening statement: the fact that "the whole system of exploitation" of black labor the world over is "the kernel of the organization of modern life" and "modern white civilization" in particular.[11]

The "whole system of exploitation" is the focus of much of *Black No More* as well. It should be noted that Schuyler's attack on "Negro Art" was consistent with his socialist beliefs, and, true to form, a large part of the novel is devoted to critiquing the kinds of economic motivations and prerogatives fueling "race ecstasy" of all stripes in the U.S. Crookman's name is instructive, but the novel as a whole suggests repeatedly that what makes American racism peculiarly virulent and absurd is its relationship to the brand of capitalism developing here. While the entire economic and social structure of the white South reels in confusion as newly-minted whites attain leadership roles in the Knights of Nordica and black babies are born to what appear to be white parents, in Northern urban centers the initial consequence of the marketing of Black-No-More is the collapse of the race industry in the U.S.: black-only banks and real estate agencies fold; Harlem stores and beauty parlors go bankrupt; and all those "race men" for whom the fight against white discrimination has been a steady source of income and publicity are left with literally nothing to do. While this is biting satire, Schuyler saves most of his venom for those who most deserve it. He repeatedly demonstrates the arbitrary character of racial categories in an analysis of the construction of whiteness against blackness within the context of labor. As con man turned union buster, Max does not merely manipulate white working class racism; instead, as Du Bois predicted in *Black Reconstruction* and David Roediger has confirmed at length in *The Wages of Whiteness*, Max teaches workers to think of themselves and their interests as white even when many of them are actually "black." That is, he teaches them to identify whiteness with the company's interests and themselves with both. Blackness is thus constructed, paradoxically, as both a threat to labor and as labor's fondest memory of its prealienated joys.[12]

The absent middle of Du Bois's thesis that whiteness and the privileges attendant to it make up a kind of "wage" paid to workers for their complicity is the unspoken knowledge that that same "whiteness" is essentially an empty thing, that whatever distinctive value it has is rendered meaningless by the erasure necessary to secure it. Crookman's machine is an electric chair; his "process" turns people white in a manner depicted in the novel as the violent interpellation of subjects into a brutal and faceless economic system, the effects of which actually precede the changes. If Zora Neale Hurston's verbal pyrotechnics about what it means to "become colored" (in "How It Feels to Be Colored Me")[13] progressively deconstruct a series of received truths about the location of identity in race, then the entire plot of *Black No More* enacts this argument, thwarting, in the process, the easy alliance between race and culture undergirding a lot of Harlem Renaissance arguments. Here, for example, is Schuyler's description of the heady days of scrimping and saving the money necessary for a Crookman makeover:

> Gone was the almost European atmosphere of every Negro ghetto: the music, laughter, gaiety, jesting and abandon. . . . The happy-go-lucky Negro of song and story was gone forever and in his stead was a nervous, money-grubbing black, stuffing away coins in socks, impatiently awaiting a sufficient sum to pay Dr. Crookman's fee. (p. 87)

"The almost European atmosphere of every Negro ghetto," is the first clue here, the aside that reverses the polarity of "white" and "black" and thus confirms the suspicion that they are interchangeable: as goes the "Negro of song and story," so goes the "European atmosphere" of their community. With this, Schuyler aligns "European" with "black" and sets both off from "American," presumably "white" and clearly capitalist or, at least, "money-grubbing." It is a subtle move, one that plays on Europe's status as a kind of floating signifier in American racial taxonomies. Though it certainly had its share of non-white people in 1931, in the great morass of national discourse— including that of a lot of African Americans—"Europe" clearly signified "whiteness," particularly as it was manifested as "culture," "civilization," or their idiot cousin, "our heritage." Europe was also, ten years after the war, as it had been before, openly regarded and publicly described as a positive alternative for African Americans to Jim Crow America.[14] Schuyler's play on Europe accounts for both significations, for "European atmosphere" specifically denotes something other than a racial or national connection to black communities in the U.S.: in both there is the kind of freedom from self-consciousness, discrimination, and prejudice one enjoys among like-minded folks—the thing that encourages one to be "happy-go-lucky" and which here is implicitly equated with European "civilization" and presumably the unacknowledged "heritage" of all those white Americans still gloating in the post-*Plessy* days of "separate but equal." Schuyler's elision of European and Negro is made doubly potent by the modification of the latter. In 1931, the "happy-go-lucky Negro of song and story" is an intentionally open-ended description: Is this Negro disappearing as a consequence of Crookman's Black-No-More the ubiquitous "happy darky" of racist caricature or the authentic folk creator of African American music and literature described by Hughes five years earlier in *The Nation*? Finally, though he mocks the end-product, Schuyler's joke is that it is the becoming rather than the being that really renders one "white," that "whiteness" is not a physical attribute at all; for finally it is not Dr. Crookman's process, but their own efforts and desire to be white that account for the changes in Schuyler's characters. At no time are the novel's "blacks" as "white" as they are before their actual physical transformation: secreting away nickels and dimes, they become "nervous," "money-grubbing," and "impatient"—people rather like the "hard, materialistic, grasping, inbred society of the whites" Max later encounters in Atlanta. In short, before they have even availed themselves of Crookman's "Black-No-More," they are already the overcivilized, uptight white people of popular imagination, and their premature transformation suggests what Schuyler may have discerned in 1926: that wanting to be white is a really white thing to do.

Certainly it was for a lot of white people and not just in 1926. As I've already noted, the first quarter of this century was marked by a racial panic more vicious even than our current one. It has been frequently noted that Murray and Hernstein's 1994 *The Bell Curve* revisits many of the same anti-immigrant and anti-black arguments of our earlier "race theorists" and that they do so in much the same language and categories of unchanging difference.[15] It has not, however, been generally remarked that the terms and categories of these arguments mirror, as they did in the past, those put forth by a range of anti-racist groups on the left and, in particular, those of the supposedly opposing sides of the *Voice*'s "Black Studies War": the proponents of Afrocentricity and of what is called, rather too loosely, multiculturalism.

It has been relatively easy—too easy, actually, in light of our continued hostility to nationalist ventures in general and black nationalisms in particular—to ferret out the essentialism in Asante's version of racial culture. It has proven much more difficult to critically apprehend and analyze these moves when they turn up in different venues. But, as Stoddard's debate with Du Bois suggests, a politics that asks us to know and appreciate different "cultures" or claims that each should be valued in its own right or for the simple fact of its "distinctiveness" is one not significantly different from that which asks us to ignore the political and economic character of the crises motivating our group identifications by claiming that cultural difference, understood as a form of racial difference renders ineffective any attempt to alter them. Like racial nationalisms grounded in romanticized versions of difference, or current "scholarship" like Murray and Hernstein's that uses it as an excuse for oppressive social policies, multiculturalist formulations assume an unbroken sequence of cultural transmissions, qualified by specific circumstances, but loyal finally to the integrity and continuation of an originary conception of racial identity and a form for its expression. Each grounds its claims in a theory of race as identical to "culture" unaffected in any great way by what's outside of it and, in the argument of Murray and Hernstein, thus impervious to "help" from it.

As I've said, one irony of the trope of diversity, of the praise for difference between groups, is the frequent if not logically necessary disavowal of difference within them. While this sense of group coherence may be comforting to an African diaspora increasingly unable to cover over differences in class, gender, sexuality, and political consciousness, it offers its own discomforts to those who refuse it. For example, in his opening salvo in "the Black Studies War" as it is described by Thomas, Asante says, "I am clear that the aping of whites is the road to neither intellectual respect nor ethical decency. Africans who exhibit confusion about their personal identities cannot hope to be clear about cultural identity."[16] Though Gates is certainly no stranger to these kinds of remarks, anyone who has had their identity called into question on the grounds of authenticity knows how coercive these disavowals can be. That they are disciplinary should not be surprising since, as I've tried to show, Schuyler's fall from critical grace demonstrates as much.

This is not to argue against recognizing the very real differences among people in our country, only that we rethink how we respond to that fact. Moreover, it is important to historicize African-American racialist rhetoric if only to show how and why, in spite of their similarities, they nevertheless differ from the white racist rhetoric or offer a specific, strategic response to it. Regardless of the post-structuralist moves done in its name, the elimination of "race" as an essential category does not alleviate the need for its preservation as a practical political one. Much of the resentment of Schuyler in the 1960s springs from this very argument—his refusal to recognize racial categories as significant even though these same categories were both the locus of discrimination in the daily life of African Americans as well as the point of identification in the Civil Rights Movement that fought against it. Besides these pragmatic political appropriations, there are other personal needs addressed, if not entirely satisfied, by essentialist notions of "blackness," prominent among which is the psychological space they afford in which to enjoy the relative freedom and joy of feeling, as Angela Davis remembers it, "nurtured and caressed" by an "empowering, but abstract community of Black people" who "have no particular [and, thus, possibly conflicting] identity other than that they [are] Black."[17]

While the brute fact of living in post-Reconstruction United States, not to mention having to read the daily pronouncements of people like Stoddard and Burr, impressed upon many the advantages of eschewing "race" as a social category of any necessary importance, many also felt the desire and probably the need to retain cultural traditions not just as an affirmation of their value and beauty, but also as a form of resistance to white racist discourse seeming always to be closing in and threatening to shut them out. In other words, the need to answer racist diagnoses and prescriptions for "the Negro" is qualified by the Harlem Renaissance desire to spotlight distinctive African American cultural accomplishments. In a 1915 syllabus for a course on "Race Contacts," Alain Locke tries to reconcile these goals by arguing that race is a "practice," that it "operates as a tradition, as preferred traits and values." Attempting to preserve the possibility of distinctive cultural traits among a given people, Locke does so by making them a matter of choice.[18]

Locke's is a complex argument, grounded in the need for concrete political change and sensitive to the risk of mystifying racial bonds in pursuit of it. His is a kind of intellectual subtlety we will have to cultivate if we are to think through what have become intractable problems. If, like a little formalism, a little history is a dangerous thing, then one way out of the problem I have tried to delineate is to historicize more, perhaps first by recognizing whiteness as a similarly enacted set of choices. Most white people have not had to do this, of course, and the ubiquitous presence of our whiteness makes it only more difficult. It is important to try, however, because doing so forces the necessary move from valorizing difference and, thus, keeping it in place and at a distance,[19] to understanding how, in Stuart Hall's words, "race is a modality in which class"—and we might add gender, sexuality, and nationality—are "lived."[20] As Schuyler and others tried to show, making whiteness visible exposes and undercuts much of its authority as the unstated referent in culture, in national identity, and in interpretations of both.

Unfortunately, it's not that easy to do, although some have tried. In the British video *Being White* (Albany Video, London), white interviewees are assembled individually and in groups. When asked to discourse freely on what it is like to be a white person, they are visibly perplexed. The question doesn't make sense to them because they don't understand what they are being asked to describe. When they do speak, they take one of two tacks: they talk about black people (or Pakistani or Indian) or they carve out some kind of ethnic identity within whiteness— Irishness, for example—which, like the recourse to blackness, appears to bring whiteness to the surface but actually only displaces it.[21] Ruth Frankenberg encounters a similar problem in her interviews with 30-odd white women. She recounts the story of one woman who, like most of the others, either cannot describe her own racial identity or simply denies its existence. After warmly reciting the virtues of family life for her friend and incorrectly locating those virtues in the friend's Hispanic traditions rather than the cramped quarters and minimal wages which together produce "familial closeness" and "health"—they eat beans because they cannot afford meat—one woman dismisses the possibility of any such distinctive culture in her own family by saying they are only "Wonder Bread" people. Thus, in the very process of insisting on the absence of whiteness, she actually locates its presence with such specificity in the mass produced commodity items of modern capitalism.[22]

That what we know and live as whiteness is in some way related to the development of commodity capitalism hardly seems a point worth stressing. That such might be said about the lived experience of contemporary forms of blackness perhaps does. As bell hooks has argued, black cultural nationalisms like those appearing in the Harlem Renaissance and Asante's work often emerge in response to appropriations of African American expressive culture by those who would decontextualize and possibly erase the specific historical and social context of black experience and particularly when that experience is then reissued in the culture at large in the form of style: "blackness" as consumable cultural product.[23] Certainly this fear would have been a major concern during the 1920s when "Negro material" was being snatched up and used by white writers with little or no appreciation for the conditions of its production.

It is in part to reassert those conditions that Harlem Renaissance artists like Aaron Douglas reference the motifs of African art in their own work. Yet such tactics are not without their own problems. For example, though Douglas uses Africa as an alternate conceptual site on which to ground the rearticulation of African American identity and history—to represent it as something that predates the experience of slavery in the United States—his own methods call attention not to the inevitability of that tradition, but to its constructedness. While good information was increasingly available, it would have been difficult to know much about Africa or African art in the 1920s in any terms other than those provided by social sciences only recently emerging from a history of complicity with colonialist endeavors. Douglas studied African art as it came to him within the delimiting contours of anthropological discourse. He and others learned about it from viewing the ethnographic exhibits at the American Museum of Natural History. "In those days, they were just curios," says Douglas of the "artefacts" he observed in storage at the Brooklyn Museum.[24] In language reminiscent of colonialist archeology, Howard University artist and art historian James Porter suggests this method of introduction has had its effects in Douglas's early style where one can see the "dismemberment of a traditional art for the sake of rearranging the motifs thus plundered. Their representational value is negligible."[25]

That Douglas was not naively attempting to reproduce what he found in the basement of the Natural History Museum should go without saying. His willingness, however, to "dismember" his sources and reshape them suggests the representational instability of a metaphor that took its power largely from claims to an authentic relation to Africa and its history, yet could ground them only in versions of itself. One irony of this predicament is that above and beyond what it may or may not have enabled in this country, the "glorification of African models in both art and literature," including, if not especially, those with little or no actual knowledge of Africa "contributed to the emergence of a black African consciousness" on that continent.[26] In other words, that very American pastiche of African motifs, scenes, and themes that appears in Harlem Renaissance art made available to Africans a new idea of themselves and their future and did so by packaging for consumption an identity articulated through another place and history, i.e., by producing racial authenticity as a commodity. Similarly, Langston Hughes may fear the effects of "American standardization" on the "racial individuality" of African Americans, but his argument for preserving a presumably stable and knowable form of black identity treats it as just the kind of commodity he otherwise argues it is peculiarly enabled to resist.

Can a commodified identity be authentic?[27] Does this question matter anymore? What can it mean to say there is no authentic "racial culture" linking black people or anyone else except that which can be made available only as already hyped? These are not questions that are going to go away any time soon. Right now there are millions of young people in the United States and elsewhere whose various identifications, including racial identifications, are managed primarily if not entirely through the buying and playing of rap music. Though its critics argue that rap's "authenticity" in terms of African-American musical and cultural traditions has been compromised by its progressive accommodation to the commodity form (moving from turntables to CDs) and to capitalist systems for the production, distribution, and consumption of music, it is these same systems that make the music available to listeners and, this is the important part, that make its listeners available to each other. If, for Hughes, African-Americans know themselves as a collective identity by resisting commodification, for the rapper, as R.A.T. Judy has recently argued, authenticity is understood to be already an effect of commodification—something one gets by playing a CD— and any identity so referenced is already indeterminate and unstable.

That many people find the prospect of unstable histories and indeterminate identities threatening goes without saying. Clearly what Hughes fears is the loss of a sense of community seen necessary for both psychic survival and political action. Such traditional formulations of community, however, are increasingly difficult to sustain in a world where one experiences "authentic identity" as a function of capitalist exchange. Moreover, instability may be the necessary condition for seeing whiteness as only tenuously connected to the power and privilege it otherwise appears to embody. As Schuyler no doubt understood and consequently feared, in the U.S. more than anywhere, "wanting to be white" was all about wanting to obscure that insight, and its corollary, being "Negro enough to be different," did not contradict that formulation so much as rephrase it. His knack in *Black No More* for occupying both sides of his argument with Hughes—on the one hand representing race as a cultural construction while on the other showing the progressive loss of something looking very much like "black authenticity"—is enabled by just this elision of whiteness in the United States with the United States itself. While this is the same conclusion reached by much white racist discourse and an ironic one for the writer whose work consistently assumes "the Negro's essential American-ness," Schuyler reproduces it in *Black No More* only to empty it of any necessary racial meaning. The only New Negroes being produced in this Harlem are the whitened blacks gradually abandoning it and finding, on the other side, a parallel system of color prejudice working against them there too. Here, "blackness" can always reemerge but only within class in the form of the threat of alienated labor or as the comforts unavailable in an alienated world. It is here that "Negro ghetto" can be mistaken for "Europe": in both, "laughter" and "abandon" are found in quantities directly proportional to their distance from Black-No-More, Inc., which, as we finally discern, is synonymous with the United States itself. It is not race, then, but the particular politics developing in the U.S.—"hard, materialist, grasping, [and] in-bred"—that highlights the material similarities between "European" and "Negro," makes "whiteness" visible, and in the process renders "blackness" and "Americanness" mutually exclusive.

NOTES

1. Greg Thomas, "Who's Winning the Black Studies War? *Village Voice* 40, no. 3 (1995): 23–29.

2. Langston Hughes, "The Negro Artist and the Racial Mountain," *Nation* 122 (23 June 1926), pp. 692–94; reprint in *The Documentary History of The Negro People in the United States, 1910–1932*, ed. Herbert Aptheker (Secaucus, NJ: Citadel, 1973), pp. 525–30. George Schuyler, "The Negro-Art Hokum," *Nation* 122 (16 June 1926): pp. 662–63, and *Black No More: Being an Account of the Strange and Wonderful Workings of Science in the Land of the Free, A.D. 1933–1940* (1931; rpt. Boston: Northeastern Univ. Press, 1989). Subsequent references to the essays and the novel will be noted in the text.

3. *Social Darwinism in American Thought* (1944; rev. ed. Boston: Beacon, 1955).

4. Clinton Stoddard Burr, *America's Race Heritage* (New York: National Historical Society, 1922), pp. 155, 10; Theodore Roosevelt, "Race Decadence," *New Outlook* 97 (8 April 1911), 763. Roosevelt calls "willful sterility" in marriage—by which he means anyone with fewer than four children—"the cardinal sin against the race" (763).

5. See Reginald Horsman, *Race and Manifest Destiny: The Origins of American Racial Anglo-Saxonism* (Cambridge: Harvard Univ. Press, 1981) for a history of what he calls "the secular myth of the free nature of Anglo-Saxon political institutions."

Besides Burr, other significant "race theorists from the earlier era include Charles Conant Josey, *Race and National Solidarity* (New York: Charles Scribner's Sons, 1923); Albert Wiggam, *The Fruit of the Family Tree* (Indianapolis: Bobbs-Merrill, 1924); Lothrop Stoddard, *The Rising Tide of Color Against White Supremacy* (New York: Charles Scribner's Sons, 1920); John Moffatt Mecklin, *Democracy and Race Friction: A Study in Social Ethics* (New York: Macmillan, 1914, 1921); and Madison Grant, *The Passing of the Great Race* (1916; rev. ed. New York: Charles Scribner's, 1918).

6. Johnson, ed., *The Book of American Negro Poetry* (New York: Harcourt, 1922; rev. ed. 1931), p. 9.

7. *Retrospection*, qtd. in Mecklin, *Democracy and Race Friction*, p. 75.

8. Mecklin, *Democracy and Race Friction*, p. 46. Mecklin references the *New York Age* and an editorial in *The Crisis* conveniently titled "Anarchism."

9. Grant, *Passing of the Great Race*, p. 16.

10. "Shall the Negro be Encouraged to Seek Cultural Equality?" Report of Debate Conducted by the Chicago Forum. Affirmative: W.E.B. Du Bois; Negative: Lothrop Stoddard. March 17, 1929 (Chicago: Chicago Forum Council, 1929), pp. 13, 15.

11. "Shall the Negro Be Encouraged to Seek Equality?" pp. 8–9.

12. David Roediger, *The Wages of Whiteness: Race and the Making of the American Working Class* (London: Verso, 1991), p. 12. In "Sambos and Minstrels" (*Social Text* 1 [1979]: 149–56), Sylvia Wynter provides a Deleuzian analysis of a similar phenomenon: "Thus the value of white being needs to be constantly realized, recognized, attained by the social act of exchange with the relative non-value of black being, a non-value represented by the Symbolic Negro/Sambo. It is this social act of exchange that communicates to the white about his own autonomy, an autonomy which as in the case of white workers . . . the white does not experience in other aspects of his life" (153).

13. Zora Neale Hurston, "How It Feels To Be Colored Me," in *I Love Myself When I'm Laughing . . . & Then Again When I'm Looking Mean and Impressive: A Zora Neale Hurston Reader*, ed. Alice Walker (Old Westbury, NY: Feminist Press, 1979), pp. 152–55.

14. At least until white Americans complained. Though many people assume that it was only artists and performers who spent time in Europe, this was not the case. Lewis says that 1928 was a record year for African American travel to the continent, though it is also—a year before the stock market crash—the beginning of the end of the relative freedom enjoyed there. See David Levering Lewis's account of discrimination against African Americans in what had been open establishments, including Paul and Essie Robeson's disillusionment at the Grill Room of the Savoy House. *When Harlem Was in Vogue* (New York: Knopf, 1981), pp. 254–55.

15. Charles Murray and Richard J. Hernstein, *The Bell Curve: Intelligence and Class Structure in America* (New York: Free Press, 1994).

16. Qtd. in Thomas, "Who's Winning the Black Studies War?", p. 23.

17. Angela Y. Davis, "Black Nationalism: The Sixties and the Nineties," in *Black Popular Culture*, ed. Gina Dent (Seattle: Bay Press, 1992), pp. 317, 319.

18. Alain Locke, "The Concept of Race as Applied to Social Culture," *Howard Review* 1 (1924): 290–99; reprinted in *The Critical Temper of Alain Locke: A Selection of His Essays on Art and Culture*, Jeffrey C. Stewart (New York: Garland, 1983), p. 428.

19. See Trin T. Minh-ha's discussion of "bounded" cultures that are set off in special physical or psychic "reservations" in the name of "preservation" with the result of reasserting rather than undermining the centrality of dominant culture and its notions of the normative. "Difference: A Special Third World Women Issue?" *Discourse* 8 (1986–1987), pp. 11–37.

20. Stuart Hall, "Race, Articulation and Societies Structured in Dominance," in *Sociological Theories: Race and Colonialism* (Paris: UNESCO, 1980), pp. 304–45.

21. See Richard Dyer's discussion of this video in "White," *Screen* 29 (1987), pp. 45–46.

22. Ruth Frankenberg, *White Women, Race Matters: The Social Construction of Whiteness* (Minneapolis: Univ. of Minnesota Press, 1993).

23. bell hooks, *Black Looks: Race and Representation* (Boston: South End, 1992), p. 30.

24. Quoted in Alvia J. Wardlaw, "A Spiritual Libation: Promoting an African Heritage in the Black College," in *Black Art Ancestral Legacy: The African Impulse in African-American Art* (New York: Harry N. Abrams and the Dallas Museum of Art, 1989), p. 59.

25. James A. Porter, *Modern Negro Art* (New York: Dryden, 1943), p. 115.

26. Valentin Mudimbe, *The Invention of Africa: Gnosis, Philosophy and the Order of Knowledge* (Bloomington: Indiana Univ. Press, 1988), pp. 77, 90.

27. This question organizes many of the concerns of R.A.T. Judy's "On the Question of Nigga Authenticity," *boundary 2* 21.3 (1994): 211–30, to which this discussion is indebted. He poses it on page 214.

Part Two:
Art and Answers

JEAN TOOMER AND THE SOUTH: REGION AND RACE AS ELEMENTS WITHIN A LITERARY IMAGINATION

CHARLES T. DAVIS

If we are to take the word and trust the memories of those who participated in the Negro Renaissance in the 1920s, the most exciting single work produced by the movement was *Cane*, by Jean Toomer.[1] *Cane* appeared in 1923,[2] the work of an author not entirely unknown. Portions of *Cane* had appeared in *The Crisis* and in an impressive number of little magazines known for their commitment to revolutionary ideas and experimental writing. The list reads like the index of the study by Hoffman, Allen, and Ulrich, *The Little Magazine: Broom, Double Dealer, Liberator, Little Review, Nomad, Prairie and S4N*. It suggests that Toomer was a part of a lively intellectual world that considered with great seriousness the cultural situation of America at the time.[3] And it suggests too that the publication of *Cane* was an event of national consequence, not a local or provincial phenomenon or simply a racial one, the case, indeed, if Toomer's achievement were simply the satisfaction of being another Negro who had managed to publish a book. After all, just a year before, T. S. Eliot had published *The Waste Land* in another of these little magazines, *The Dial*, and we have just barely recovered from that event. Toomer arrived with a bang, and with a set of qualifications that could hardly be more impressive.

Though Toomer's achievement is not limited, finally, by reference to either region or race, it exploits in an unusual way both of these elements. Technically, Toomer was not a Southerner. Or to put it better, his connection with the South was not direct; it resembles Frost's association with New England. Robert Lee Frost was born in San Francisco, of parents originally from New England; Nathan Eugene Toomer, later called Jean, whose parents were originally from the South, with family ties to the state of Georgia, was born in Washington, D.C., in 1894. For both writers the connection with the region was a form of recovery of a lost heritage. Gorham Munson, who wrote a book about Frost, as well as participating vigorously in the organization and the direction of little magazines concerned with the future of modern machine culture, put the point plainly when he said in a review of *Cane* that Toomer "desired to make contact with his hereditary roots in the Southland."[4] For both writers, then, the return was a passionate involvement with counter-cultural implications; that is to say, Frost and Toomer deliberately turned their backs upon contemporary urban culture to seek a more satisfying reality in rural surroundings. In a loose sense their attitudes can be called pastoral. Munson sketches the typical background for the pastoral quest, probably without an intimate knowledge of Toomer's early life: ". . . one infers a preceding period of shifting and drifting without settled harborage. Weary of homeless waters he turns back to ancestral soil. . . ."[5]

"Shifting" does accurately describe much of what we know of Toomer's early career, which displays an excessive movement from place to place and a rapid change from one intellectual commitment to another. After graduation from Dunbar High School in Washington, D.C., Toomer enrolled in 1914 at the University of Wisconsin, moved to the Massachusetts College of Agriculture in 1915, and stopped for a while in Chicago in 1916. Later there were brief sojourns in Milwaukee and New York. Always in between there was a return to Washington. Not until 1920 does his movement about the country stop, when Toomer settled in Washington, convinced then that he should devote his time and energy fully to reading and writing.

The outline of Jean Toomer's autobiography,[6] a work projected but never apparently completed, reveals an active and wide-ranging mind. The attraction to agriculture and physical culture seemed to be uppermost at Madison, Wisconsin; the exposure to socialist and materialist thought occurred in Chicago, and to the writings of Bernard Shaw in Milwaukee. Working as a clerk in New York City and later as a general manager for Acker and Company in 1919 in Ossining made possible the cultivation of a whole range of new interests, music among them. But meeting new people was just as important to him as the authors he read, Goethe, Whitman, Ibsen, and again Shaw, or the lectures he attended. Though Toomer met at this time Lola Ridge, the American editor of *Broom*, E. A. Robinson, Witter Bynner, Scofield Thayer, and other literary figures prominent in the New York scene, no one had a greater impact upon him than did Waldo Frank, whose *Our America* he had read with care. It is the New York adventure that seemed to be decisive in turning Toomer's attention to art. When the inevitable return to Washington came in 1920, Toomer was prepared to commit himself to more systematic reading, addressing not only all the works of Waldo Frank, but books by Tolstoy, Flaubert, Baudelaire, Dostoyevsky, Sinclair Lewis, Dreiser, Sherwood Anderson, Frost, and Freud. He read the little magazines too, absorbing from Frank and others a critical attitude toward an American society which had become warped by the demands of modern technology and unchecked urbanization. Toomer was ripe for a sweeping commitment of some kind in 1920, one that would affirm man's basic emotional life rather than intellectual achievement, one, as Frank put it graphically later, that would protect him from the stink of the marketplace and keep him "warm underneath, in the soil, where the throb is."[7]

The specific form of Toomer's commitment was determined by a factor beyond his control, by his ancestry, which involved intimately both region and race, both the recognition of the South as home and the affirmation of an allegiance to the black race. Jean was the grandson of P. B. S. Pinchback, who was at one time during Reconstruction days Lieutenant-Governor, then Acting Governor, of the state of Louisiana. He was the son of Pinchback's daughter Nina, who had married briefly Nathan Toomer, a union that actually terminated in 1895, after a year of marriage, and was formally dissolved in 1899. Jean was especially close to his grandparents, with whom he lived after Nina's death in 1909. The strong emotions that swept through Toomer's consciousness while he was writing *Cane* were deeply intertwined with his concern for his grandfather's declining health. Indeed, Toomer recalled in the notes for an autobiography that Pinchback died the day after he had finished the first draft of "Kabnis." The suggestion of the end of an era, so strong in *Cane*, may owe something to the feelings and the sympathies of the young artist as he observed the last moments of a man, once so powerful and vigorous, reduced to a broken and pathetic figure.[8] The journey to New Orleans to place Pinchback's body in the vault already occupied by Toomer's mother must have reinforced the intimation of an imminent conclusion, aroused the echoes in his ears of a "swan-song"[9] that was personal as well as cultural.

The event that provoked Toomer's emergence as an artist had preceded Pinchback's death; it had, no doubt, psychic reverberations of great consequence. This was the period of three months in 1921 that Toomer spent in Georgia. He had accepted an offer to replace a principal of a school in Sparta who had gone North to raise funds for the school, a necessity familiar to the administrators of many Southern black educational institutions at the time. For Toomer, going to Georgia was a return. Both Grandfather Pinchback and father Nathan Toomer had come from Georgia. Jean recalls the impression that the new Georgia scene made upon him: "The setting was crude in a way, but strangely rich and beautiful. . . . There was a valley, the valley of *Cane*, with smoke-wreaths during the day and mist at night. . . ."[10]

The discovery of the physical characteristics of the region was only a part of Toomer's total response. Another part had more to do with what was heard rather than what was seen. The artist was moved by the spirituals sung by the blacks in Georgia. He was touched not merely by their beauty but by the sense that they represented a dying folk-spirit, a creative impulse doomed to be destroyed by the small town and then the city, by the inevitable encroachment of industry, commerce, and the machine. What occurred, of course, was the coalescence of two quite divergent drives in Toomer. One, certainly, as Munson suspected, was the desire to stop the drift in his life, to find a home, even though a temporary one. The second was the expected reaction of a talented but disciplined student well trained in the curriculum promoted by Waldo Frank and Sherwood Anderson. In discovering his heritage, Toomer rejected contemporary culture, with its emphasis upon urbanization and a machine technology.

The touchy point about Toomer's return is race or, rather, allegiance to a race. The problem is more complicated than it appears to be. In Georgia Toomer identified with the life of blacks, and he acquired in this way a deep appreciation for the richness and strength that came from the intimate connection existing there between man and soil. Arna Bontemps, in his "Introduction" to a reissue of *Cane*, quotes from a letter written by Toomer to the editors of the *Liberator* magazine in the summer of 1922 which offers matter that has a direct bearing on this point. In it Toomer describes his racial background: ". . . I seem to have (who knows for sure) seven blood mixtures: French, Dutch, Welsh, Negro, German, Jewish, and Indian." Then he adds, in which must have seemed at the time an amazing piece of heresy: "Because of these, my position in America has been a curious one. I have lived equally amid the two race groups. Now white, now colored." American society in 1920, perhaps less so now, was pathologically sensitive to racial attachments. It was bad enough for Faulkner, early in the next decade, to create a character in *Light in August* who was a Negro by sociological definition alone,[11] but here from young Toomer, in life, not in art, we have the assertion that he could choose his racial identity. He adds in the letter to the *Liberator*: "Within the last two or three years, however, my growing need for artistic expression has pulled me deeper and deeper into the Negro group. And as my powers of receptivity increased, I found myself loving it in a way that I could never love the other. It has stimulated and fertilized whatever creative talent I may contain within me. A visit to Georgia last fall was the starting point of almost everything of worth that I have done."[12]

Toomer chose to be black. His stance was artistically useful because he allowed himself maximum freedom in defining his heritage. It was not something that he had to accept because he was trapped, as many Americans were, by history or family or caste or race. It was something that he discovered, or, since the discovery was essentially a matter of consciousness, something that he made. Toomer brought rare objectivity and sensitivity to his task, and in his time perhaps only he was equipped to create his form of the South, preeminently a black South, one just as strongly projected as the old forms, but more beautiful in the description of the land, more complicated in revealing the tangled, half-articulated emotions of its people, and more deeply human.

Making something new demands a rejection of what is at hand. As a black American in 1920, Toomer had available to him at least three forms of the South, none of which he accepted.

There was the world created by the plantation tradition, especially by the dialect poems of Paul Laurence Dunbar, which had appeared originally in the late nineteenth and early twentieth centuries and had been reprinted, subsequently, in special editions, sometimes lavishly illustrated.[13] This was a black South full of memories of good times on the old plantation, demonstrations of the efficacy of Christian piety, and antics of collapsible, indestructible comedians in blackface. What is referred to here is the popular impression of Dunbar's verse, reinforced by faithful and frequent recitation by blacks and whites all over America. A study of the whole Dunbar canon reveals a troubled poet deeply sensitive especially to the materialist and mechanistic thought at the turn of the century. But Dunbar's South, for most Americans, was not to be distinguished from that projected by the minstrel stage and created nostalgically in sentimental fiction. By 1920 blacks had ceased to take it seriously, if they ever had, except for those enterprising artists who sought to extract from it profitable theatrical or musical formulas.

A second South was linked to the name of Booker Washington, who offered it to the world on the pages of *Up From Slavery*.[14] These presented a picture of improving relations involving blacks and whites and an improving economic status for blacks. Patience, Christian virtue, and hard work would result in prosperity soon; but civil rights, the vote, and full citizenship would take longer. Survival demanded the compromise of manhood, perhaps, but Washington had the Social Darwinist's faith that all good things would come in time to those best equipped to have them. Washington's South was real enough, but by 1920 it had lost credibility with most black intellectuals. His reality seemed to be restricted to those oases in the South that tended to justify his convictions. Meanwhile, the masses of blacks in the South lived poor, desperate lives unleavened by the force of Booker's rhetoric.

The design of the South that inspired greatest conviction among intellectual blacks was that sketched by W.E.B. Du Bois in *The Souls of Black Folk, The Crisis* magazine, *Darkwater*, and elsewhere.[15] Certain salient features stand out. Du Bois claimed that a condition of naked oppression existed in the South, which was not improving as a place for blacks to live and to work. The people who seemed to be most oppressed lived in rural areas where law and sharp business practices combined to exploit them. Du Bois asserted that Washington's optimistic predictions about economic progress for blacks in the South was empty, if not absent, when blacks lacked the basic rights of citizenship to protect their property. The hope for an improved life rested with the leadership of the Talented Tenth, the educated members of the black middle class to be found largely in the towns and the black schools. At issue for Du Bois always was manhood, which could not be sustained by anything other than a broad and liberal education (rather than industrial training) and could not survive the daily humiliations imposed by a segregated society.

The South that Toomer made succeeded in reversing nearly all of Du Bois' conclusions, without echoing Dunbar's pious sentiments or referring to the necessity for a pragmatic accommodation with whites in Southern communities. What supported the new view was not facts, as Du Bois would define them, not statistical surveys coming out of Atlanta University, but an emotional response, a young man's impression of the black heritage he had returned to discover.

Toomer saw a beautiful land of pine trees, mist, and red soil (not the red clay that Du Bois despised so thoroughly that he refused to bury his infant son in it),[16] a land in which fertility was finally stronger than terror, though moved by a threat of violence that seemed all-pervasive. He admired the black "peasants," the strong people who lived close to the soil and reflected in their preoccupation with sex and mystical religious experience the fertility of the land. "Peasants"[17] is Toomer's term, with a meaning far removed from the "peasants" of Faulkner's *The Hamlet*, descriptive there of farmers who had been exploited and humiliated by ruthless predators. The weak people in Toomer's South (Esther is one of them) were the shopkeepers, the light-skinned Negroes of the middle class, the potential members of the group that Du Bois had labelled the Talented Tenth. They lived in the towns, and they were both attracted and repelled by the crude black energy they saw in the peasants. Life was the issue here, and middle class conventions and aspirations denied life and, incidentally, love. Black manhood survived in the South as a response, in part, to a more powerful force. But only in part. Fred Halsey, a pillar of strength in the dramatic narrative "Kabnis," has other sources of power: pride in his profession as a master craftsman and an owner of a wagon-shop, and delight in using his mind in debating with the professors, Lewis and Kabnis. The signs of degeneration are present everywhere—in the lack of coordination of body and spirit, in sexual excess and in mystical hysteria. They are external as well as internal, with the menace of physical violence, with death by lynching always close. The forces of degradation may kill the body but not destroy the integrity and the spirit of the truly strong: Barlo, the black preacher; Tom Burwell, Louisa's black lover in "Blood Burning Moon"; Fred Halsey. Toomer's Southern exposure produced a wholly new way of looking at Southern life, one that is related clearly to the position of the Nashville Fugitives, as Bontemps notes in his "Introduction,"[18] but one quite different, finally, because the controlling point of view is black, not white.

The invaluable documentation of Toomer's approach to the South found in his letters and in his notes toward an autobiography throws light upon the poem "Song of the Son," which functions really as a form of preface to the whole of *Cane*. We are introduced to the consciousness of a poet-speaker who imposes unity upon the verses, sketches, narratives, and symbolic signs that make up the body of the work.

"Song of the Son" describes a return to a scene from which the poet has been long separated. The initial lines suggest an amount of detachment. In much the way that Whitman often did, in "Crossing Brooklyn Ferry," for example, the poet requests the landscape to arrange itself for his pleasure:

> Pour O pour that parting soul in song,
> O pour it in the sawdust glow of night,
> Into the velvet pine-smoke air to-night,
> And let the valley carry it along,
> And let the valley carry it along. (p. 21)

What is at stake is not merely the desire for physical delight, though this is strong; the poet realizes that he is responding to "that parting soul," the spirit in the land. The reference to "parting" introduces the problem of time. The poet has returned "just before an epoch's sun declines," at that moment when the land is losing a value that it has long possessed. This is one that the speaker was either not aware of or not appreciative of when he was present at this scene before. The value itself is the culture of "A song-lit race of slaves," a culture that was unique and rich. For one thing, it was intimately tied to the land, so deeply intertwined that the slaves can be referred to as organized growths—"dark purple ripened plums." For another, the culture is sad, "plaintive," because the slaves were under pressure, suffering, indeed, from oppression and because, further, it is disappearing, dying. The two characteristics form the basis for song, for the spirituals sung by the slaves and other forms of artistic expression that flowed naturally from a unified existence. What is being lost, as the poet looks and ruminates, is song, along with other vestiges of the slave culture, not simply the music itself but the ability to make music. We are not told what the hostile forces are that oppose song, though we are led inevitably to speculate about them—perhaps, freedom from suffering, or the city, or education, or modern society. The poet has returned in time to secure possession of one vestige of the old culture, one "plum" providing the seed that would enable him to reconstruct the earlier civilization. This is important to do because of the ancient beauty that becomes now available to him and because the new awareness forms a basis for new songs, to be created, no doubt by the poet. The double emphasis cannot be missed: "What they [souls of slavery] were, and what they are to me" (p. 21). The conclusion of the poem resembles the dramatic end of "Out of the Cradle Endlessly Rocking," when Whitman says, after at least a partial reconciliation with death, symbolized by the sea: "The sea whisper'd me."[19]

"Song of the Son" presents the consciousness that stands behind the varied verbal structures in *Cane*. In the poem it is a sophisticated intelligence yearning for completion and adequate expression and finding the means for achieving these ends in contact with the South and with a newly discovered black culture. It plays multiple roles elsewhere in *Cane*. It is responsible for the sympathy and understanding expressed by the narrator of "Karintha" and "Carma," for that need to explain the actions of the characters in the stories, to place their behavior within an appropriate intellectual context. On occasion the consciousness becomes embodied in characters, in the curious "I" figures in "Becky" and "Fern" who seek to penetrate the deeper mysteries and contradictions of Southern life. Always one of the important functions of the brooding intelligence which invests *Cane* is projection, as significant characters, despite difference in race and station in society, share the desire for a fuller life, one in which their half-understood and half-articulated impulses may have a place.

The preoccupation with the problems of consciousness is responsible for the design in *Cane*. Toomer is not content simply to explore the situations in which an alien Northern intelligence confronts Southern realities; he is as much concerned with analyzing the factors that have shaped the Northern mind. He sees the necessity for regional connection, for the Northern black to acquire the emotional strengths that black Southerners still possess, though they may be rapidly losing them. What haunts Toomer's mind is a circle based upon regional relationships, or, more accurately, a broken circle, since the author does not reach the point in *Cane* of successful prefiguration, the anticipation of the full existence for man, what would be called later the "all around development of man," involving the "constructive functioning" of body, emotions, and mind.[20]

Toomer's own comments on the structure of *Cane* are invaluable and offer a beginning for any discussion of the organization of the whole work. In December 1922, Waldo Frank received a letter from Toomer announcing the completion of *Cane* and defining the principles which were intended to give unity to his achievement:

> From three angles, *Cane*'s design is a circle. Aesthetically, from simple forms to complex ones, and back to simple forms. Regionally, from the South up to the North, and back into the South again. Or, from the North down into the South, and then a return North. From the point of view of the spiritual entity behind the work, the curve really starts with Bona and Paul (awakening), plunges into Kabnis, emerges in Karintha, etc., swings upward into Theater and Box Seat, and ends (pauses) in Harvest Song.[21]

Toomer's first comment on form is plain enough and requires little explanation. The Georgia tales and "Kabnis" are reasonably straightforward narratives, with intensities that are either lyric or dramatic. They are without the symbolic complexity of the middle section of *Cane*, the one devoted to the North. We find here the experimental sketches "Seventh Street," "Rhobert," and "Calling Jesus," presenting a level of abstraction not discovered elsewhere. Moreover, in the narratives "Theater" and "Box Seat" symbolic devices and distortion are employed with subtlety and effectiveness. The dance in "Theater" represents the ideal of a fulfilled relationship between Dorris and John, who come from different classes in the highly stratified black society of Washington, D. C. In "Box Seat" the seats in the Lincoln Theater are "slots," "bolted houses" (p. 117), cutting Muriel off from rewarding connection with anyone else, especially from her desperate would-be lover Dan. In both stories the emphasis is placed upon what the characters think rather than upon what they do. "Box Seat" relies more heavily upon distortion than does "Theater," a fact particularly evident with the use of the dwarf to stand for the revulsion which the conventional Muriel feels toward any life existing outside of her cherished middle-class patterns. There is a deliberate correspondence between the complexity of Toomer's literary technique and the complexity of Northern urban environment. What is magnified, thereby, is struggle of the human spirit, bound by dehumanizing conventions and mechanical restrictions, to achieve freedom and satisfaction.

The more puzzling part of Toomer's statement of intention involves the reference to regions. We have an apparent contradiction: we begin *Cane* either in the South or in the North, and we conclude the work either in the South or in the North. What seems to be apparent nonsense becomes rewardingly clear only when the element of consciousness is considered, what Toomer calls "the spiritual entity behind the work."[22] The external order for *Cane*, recorded simply as it appears, establishes the first background in Georgia, the second in Washington and Chicago, and the third again in Georgia. It is South, North, South.

But if the action is viewed organically, we take our cue from the form of the consciousness as defined by "Song of the Son." Toomer suggests that we begin with "Bona and Paul," a story in which Paul discovers that he is not like Bona. The racial difference, felt deeply first in the Crimson Gardena, a night club in Chicago, is the basis for Paul's rejection by Bona; at the same time Paul experiences something less painful and equally important, the need to explain his attraction for Bona to the huge black man who opens and shuts the door of the night club. Frustration, then, is accompanied by the intimation of a new connection, "awakening,"[23] Toomer called it. "Kabnis," looked at this way, is the direct confrontation with what it means to be black in the South. The trial for the Northern Kabnis is disturbing, humiliating and apparently futile, with only infrequent suggestions of black strength. The affirmation of difference and the tribute to black emotional power are to be found in the Georgia stories, especially in the portraits of sensual black women. The progress of consciousness moves next to the North where city realities are weighed against Southern black strength. Dorris's dance and Dan's plea to the prim Muriel grow from the same impulse that moves Karintha and Carma. This is stated most explicitly in "Box Seat," when Dan sits beside a portly black lady in the Lincoln Theater. Her fragrance arouses racial memories in Dan: "Her strong roots sink down and spread under the river and disappear in blood lines that waver South. Her roots shoot down. Dan's hands follow them. Roots throb. Dan's heart beats violently. He places his palms upon the earth to cool them. Earth throbs" (p. 119). The center of the resistance to the frigid and mechanical North is located in racial memories that linger, shards and vestiges of an old black culture.

"Harvest Song" in this context is the conclusion of *Cane*. It is a poem that denies its title, since it is not the celebration of work done well and the grain collected. What is missing is enjoyment, the ability of the poet to taste and to receive nourishment from the product that has demanded so much sweat and toil:

> I am a reaper whose muscles set at sundown. All my oats are cradled.
> But I am too chilled, and too fatigued to bind them. And I hunger. (p. 132)

Nourishment and enjoyment demand friendship with others, a sense of brotherhood and community. The poet, though he is reluctant and too timid to attempt the unexpected, moves to a point that he cries out to his fellow laborers:

> O my brothers, I beat my palms, still soft against the stubble of my har-
> vesting. (You beat your soft palms, too.) My pain is sweet. Sweeter
> than the oats or wheat or corn. It will not bring me knowledge of my
> hunger. (p. 132)

There is no sign that the cry is responded to, as it is, say, in another harvest poem, Frost's "The Tuft of Flowers."[24] And without response there is not satisfaction for hunger, nor even the knowledge of what hunger is. "Harvest Song" offers a strong plea for human values, for the virtues of emotional connection, one that relates immediately to Toomer's description of Northern society, in which mind, work, and propriety have crushed soul.

The central movement of *Cane*, interpreted in terms of a developing consciousness, is then North, South, North. The curve ends, Toomer writes, in "Harvest Song," but the term that he uses as a substitute for "ends," that is to say, "pauses," is a better one.[25] The poet stands poised at the end of "Harvest Song," waiting for the responding cry that does not come. The progress of the curve stops, short of completion, the fulfillment of a design that might be viewed as a rounded circle. Toomer is not prepared to explore completion or to celebrate a triumphant ending—nor was this his intention—because completion would mean nothing less than the promise of a redeemed America, a fusion of North and South, a region that for him is emotional and black.

Curveship has another meaning for the structure of *Cane*. In the same letter to Frank in which he suggested various ways of reading his newly completed work, Toomer wrote: "Between each of the three sections, a curve. These, to vaguely indicate the design."[26] It is useful to consider what this means when we look at the relationship between the sections. What may be promised is a substantial connection in materials and problems. We discover with close examination that that kind of correspondence does exist in fact, with significant differences separating the sections resting, rather, in the way the familiar questions are resolved.

The first two sections, one devoted to the Georgia scenes and the other to urban episodes, connect in this fashion, and, indeed, seem to balance each other. The same problems thread their way through both divisions of the book. Karintha and Avey suffer from excessive, indirected, almost unconscious sexuality. But there is a difference: men are still awed by Karintha's mysterious beauty, but some cynics, not the narrator, consider Avey to be a common whore. "Fern" and "Calling Jesus" are comments on the attempted invasion of the body by the soul, with vastly different consequences. Fern welcomes the descent of the spirit that startles her more worldly city-admirer. On the other hand, the unnamed girl of "Calling Jesus" rejects the possibility of a larger and more deeply mystical experience because she is content with her "large house" and absorbed in shallow dreams. Only Jesus can bring a change. Esther in the story given her name and Dan in "Box Seat" share a common urge for freedom and love and are reduced to near madness by the insensitivity and lack of understanding in their love objects. Esther's pathetic proposal to Barlo seems ridiculous and absurd to those who frequent Nat Bowle's place because the pattern of her sterile existence is far removed from that of ordinary black people. Dan's cry causes disruption in the Lincoln Theater partly because he sees accurately, as others do, that Muriel's impulse to reject the gift of the dwarf performer is based upon a conventional distaste for what is considered in life crude, deformed, and black. "Blood-Burning Moon" and "Bona and Paul" present interracial affairs that end in failure, but with a difference. White Bob Stone, despite his family tradition and his inherited contempt for blacks, makes a total commitment to his love for the black Louisa to the point of willing his own death. The black Paul loses the white Bona as a consequence of a moment of distraction. The fine words which state Paul's passion reveal also a lack of integration in his personality and his inability to give himself wholly to love in the way that Stone or his black rival, Tom Burwell, do. In Toomer's world the pulse of life beats more slowly in Chicago.

"Kabnis," in one sense, is a fitting conclusion for *Cane* because it gives expression to nearly all of the themes developed in the two earlier sections. We find the intense resentment of middle class restraints, the undirected sexuality, the attempt to achieve a mystical knowledge of some kind, and the awesome gap between the races. "Kabnis" is also an effective demonstration of the disjunction between mind and emotion that has haunted the black characters of the urban section. But *Kabnis*, as Toomer suggested, falls earlier within the development of the central consciousness informing the whole book, at some point before the discovery of the energy of black folk to be found in "Karintha" and "Carma." There are suggestions of that power in Kabnis's futile effort to extract wisdom from Father John, the old black man who is a vestige of the slave civilization. Viewed within the perspective of the organic cycle, "Harvest Song" offers a more appropriate termination. Frustration is not localized. There the long lines of free verse and the repetitive elements recall Whitman's poems of celebration, but the American harvest is sterile. Unhappiness, pain, fear, and hunger are incongruously present with the sources of the good life immediately at hand. And all paths in *Cane*, whether in the North or in South or whether pursued by blacks or whites, lead to this disturbing end.

Cane owes everything to the symbolic representation of region and race. Toomer discovered his blackness in Georgia, and armed with this revelation he was able to construct a pattern of life which contrasted with what he had seen about him in the cities of the North. Neither pattern was to be satisfying finally. The writing of *Cane* occurred at a very special moment in Toomer's life. This time came when his awareness of his own heritage was heightened by the impending death of grandfather Pinchback, when his sense of the corruption of modern urban society was keen as a result of a close intellectual association with Waldo Frank and Sherwood Anderson, and when the exposure to black rural life in Georgia resolved momentarily his own ambivalent and uncertain feelings about racial identity. This moment was enough to link him to other writers of The Harlem Renaissance, who were at the same time struggling to conquer feelings of uncertainty and inadequacy of a different kind in an effort to achieve an expression of that which was most authentic in their lives.

Toomer was correct when he commented in retrospect that *Cane* was a "swansong."[27] It was the end not only of a way of Southern black life, as he saw it, but of his own commitment to place that life within art. Even during the year of *Cane*'s publication, 1923, Toomer's attention turned to problems that he considered to be more fundamental than the challenge of producing another work modeled on *Cane*. When he looked at his friends and acquaintances, many of whom were committed in some way to the world of art, he was compelled to say:

> Most of the men and women were growing into lopsided specialists of one kind or another; or, they were almost hopelessly entangled in emotional snarls and conflicts. And neither literature nor art did anything for them. In short, my attention had been turned from the books and paintings to the people who produced them; and I saw that these people were in a sorry state. What did it really matter that they were able by talent to turn out things that got reviews?[28]

Toomer continued to write, but he was not destined to produce anything that matched *Cane*'s power. His primary concern became experimentation in life rather than in art, an endeavor to be heavily influenced by contact with Gurdjieff's ideas, occurring for the first time in 1923. Before we deplore the loss to art as a consequence of this decision, we should recall that it was the aftermath of another experiment in life, Toomer's brief period of existence as a black in Georgia, that brought us *Cane*.

NOTES

1. For example, Countee Cullen wrote: "I bought the first copy of *Cane* which was sold, and I've read every word of it. . . . It's a real race contribution, a classical portrayal of things as they are." Letter to Jean Toomer, 29 Sept. 1923, Jean Toomer Collection, Fisk Univ. Archives, Nashville, Tenn., Box 1, Folder 12, No. 386. Charles S. Johnson, editor in 1923 of *Opportunity: A Journal of Negro Life*, recalled in later years his reaction to the emergence of Jean Toomer: "Here was triumphantly the Negro artist, detached from propaganda, sensitive only to beauty." Arna Bontemps, "The Awakening: A Memoir," in *The Harlem Renaissance Remembered*, ed. A. Bontemps (New York: Dodd, Mead, 1972), p. 9.

2. Published by Boni & Liveright, Inc. The edition cited throughout this study is a Perennial Classic paperback edition published by Harper & Row (New York, 1969). Subsequent references to *Cane* will appear parenthetically in the text.

3. Sherwood Anderson's interest in *Cane* is to be measured by this generous offer: "I hope to write something about Cane for Freeman but it had been given to some one else. If your publisher knows of any place I can write of it I'll be mighty glad to do it. My admiration for it holds." Letter to Jean Toomer, 14 Jan. 1924, Toomer Collection, Box 1, Folder 1, No. 51.

4. "The Significance of Jean Toomer," *Opportunity* 3 (Sept. 1925): 262.

5. "The Significance of Jean Toomer," 262.

6. Toomer Collection, Box 14, Folder 1.

7. Letter to Jean Toomer, 25 April 1922, Toomer Collection.

8. Toomer Collection, Box 14, Folder 1, No. 59.

9. Toomer Collection, Box 14, Folder 1, No. 59.

10. Toomer Collection, Box 14, Folder 1, No. 59.

11. Joe Christmas in *Light in August* (New York: Random House, 1932).

12. Letter to the *Liberator*, 1922, quoted by Arna Bontemps in his Introduction to *Cane*, pp. viii–ix.

13. Dunbar's poems appeared originally in six volumes during his lifetime: *Oak and Ivy* (1893), *Majors and Minors* (1895), *Lyrics of Love and Laughter* (1903), *Lyrics of Sunshine and Shadow* (1905). In addition there were special editions like *Poems of Cabin and Field* (New York: Dodd, Mead, 1899), with photographs by the Hampton Institute Camera Club and Decorations by Alice Morse.

14. Doubleday, 1901.

15. *The Souls of Black Folk* (Chicago: A. C. McClurg, 1903); *Darkwater: Voices from Within the Veil* (New York: Harcourt, 1920).

16. In "Of the Passing of the First-Born," *The Souls of Black Folk* (New York: Fawcett, 1961), p. 155.

17. Letter to the *Liberator*, Introduction, *Cane*, p. ix.

18. Bontemps, Introduction, *Cane*, p. xvi.

19. *Leaves of Grass*, ed. H. W. Blodgett and Sculley Bradley (New York: Norton, 1968), p. 253.

20. Outline for an autobiography, Toomer Collection, Box 14, Folder 1, pp. 63–64.

21. Letter to Waldo Frank, 12 Dec. 1922, Toomer Collection, Box 3, Folder 6, No. 800. Toomer supplies no punctuation for the titles.

22. Letter to Frank, 12 Dec.1922.

23. Letter to Frank, 12 Dec. 1922.

24. Robert Frost, *Complete Poems* (New York: Holt, Rinehart & Winston, 1949), pp. 31–32. The terminal lines are: "'Men work together,' I told him from the heart, / 'Whether they work together or apart.'"

25. Letter to Frank, 12 Dec. 1922.

26. 12 Dec. 1922.

27. Outline for an autobiography, Toomer Collection, Box 14, Folder 1, p. 59.

28. Outline for an autobiography, Toomer Collection, Box 14, Folder 1, p. 63.

"THE CANKER GALLS...," OR, THE SHORT PROMISING LIFE OF WALLACE THURMAN

DANIEL WALDEN

Although New York City in the 1920s was for most whites a joyous, expanding metropolis, for many blacks, Wallace Thurman among them, it was a city of refuse, not a city of refuge. Growing up at a time when many Americans—after World War I—were eager to get back to what Warren Harding would call "normalcy," Thurman reached Harlem at the moment when white Americans looked to black America, north of 110th Street and along Lexington and Convent Avenues, as the bastion of primitivism and earthiness. Some whites came to gape, some to laugh, but many came to seek exuberant escape in the so-called exotic primitivism of Negro cabaret life. As Langston Hughes exclaimed in *The Big Sea*, "thousands of whites came to Harlem night after night, thinking the Negroes loved to have them there, and firmly believing that all Harlemites left their houses at sundown to sing and dance in cabarets, because most of the whites saw nothing but the cabarets, not the houses."[1]

During these years, nearly all the black writers and artists drifted to New York. As might be expected, most were drawn by the promise of New York City as a center where art and literature would flourish. In Hughes' contemporary opinion, what was important was that black writers spoke their own words, their own truths, no matter whether blacks, or whites, were pleased or offended. For in this decade, publishers opened their doors to black authors and poets and artists. What was significant was that in New York City the NAACP, *The Crisis*, *Opportunity*, and several black newspapers flourished. As early as 1920, W.E.B. Du Bois pointed out, Claude McKay, Langston Hughes, Jean Toomer, Countee Cullen, Anne Spencer, Abram Harris and Jessie Fauset had already been published in *The Crisis*.

Of the whites drawn to Harlem and to black life, only a minority were inter-ested in the discovery and development of black talent. For black writers and artists the 1920s represented an era of opportunities and hopes. It was the decade in which the writers replaced apologetics and militancy and racial propa-ganda with their own voices as their *raison d'être*. True, Walter White's *Fire in the Flint* (1924), W.E.B. Du Bois' *Dark Princess* (1928), and George Schuyler's *Slaves Today* (1931) maintained an offensive, anti-racist posture. But most writ-ers tried to be writers; following the advice of Henry James (whether they had read him or not), they let their stories unfold and their characters evolve out of their stories. In some cases, the psychology of caste and the racial experience, echoing Charles Chesnutt's early models, became dominant aspects; for Rudolph Fisher, the everyday life of blacks in Harlem, linked to the trauma of Southern exposure to Northern urbanism, was played out much as everyday life was depicted by other authors. And, in Carl Van Vechten's *Nigger Heaven* (1926), a white novelist so successfully portrayed blacks in urban New York that he called up the most violent pros and cons of the period, and to a certain extent set out the parameters within which all black novelists would be judged. A "blow in the face" to Du Bois, *Nigger Heaven* was "an absorbing story" to James Weldon Johnson; Gwendolyn Bennett coined "Van Vechtenizing around," to describe the ways in which tourists saw Harlem. As Hugh Gloster put it, no matter the negative criticism, the pull of the exotic exerted an influence hard to deny. It is in the grip of all these forces that Wallace Thurman, with William Jordan Rapp, produced *Harlem* (1929), a play dealing with life in the ghetto; *The Blacker the Berry* (1929), and *Infants of the Spring* (1932).

Wallace Thurman, "the most symbolic figure of the Literary Renaissance in Harlem," brilliant, consumptive, desperate, was the focal point for black Bohemia in the late 1920s.[2] The inner circle included Rudolph Fisher, M.D., writer, Langston Hughes, poet, and Zora Neale Hurston, novelist. They knew the great ones, W. E. B. Du Bois, James Weldon Johnson, Carl Van Vechten, and they knew the other Renaissance writers and critics, George Schuyler, Countee Cullen, Jean Toomer, Arna Bontemps, Alain Locke, Benjamin Brawley, and Charles S. Johnson. It was Du Bois, Locke and Brawley who contended that a true renaissance in black literature was in the making.[3] The inner circle wished it were true but had their doubts. Of them all, Thurman's desire to become "a very great writer like Gorki or Thomas Mann," said Langston Hughes, stuck out like a sore thumb. Unfortunately, the strong feeling that he was "merely a journalistic writer" made him melancholy, suicide-prone, and disillusioned;[4] his self-hatred engendered by his dark complexion, and his reliance on bad gin, were by-products of the despair which marked his decline and early death after a brilliant and promising career.[5]

Wallace Thurman was born in Salt Lake City, Utah, in 1902. His very dark skin defined him as a black though he had an Indian grandmother who married a Jewish peddler. His friends describe him as his pictures present him—a dark-skinned man. After high school he attended the University of Utah for two terms

(1919 to 1920) as a pre-medical student, and then the University of Southern California. After his years in California he arrived in New York City in 1925, at the inception of what Locke called "The New Negro" Movement. During his years in Los Angeles in the early 1920s he apparently read about Harlem, and even promoted it in his own magazine, *The Outlet.* In New York Thurman worked briefly for *The Looking-Glass* and then in 1926 became managing editor of *The Messenger,* a radical monthly, the voice of A. Philip Randolph and black socialism. Also in 1926 he helped found the short-lived little magazine *Fire.*[6] In 1929 his first novel, *The Blacker the Berry,* came out; in 1929 he co-authored the play *Harlem,* with William Rapp, editor of *True Story* magazine, and he also took on a job as a reader at Macauley's. Thurman also began publishing fiction and ghostwriting stories for *True Story.* In 1932 he became editor-in-chief at Macauley's, published his second novel, *Infants in the Spring,* and co-authored his third and last novel, *The Interns,* with Abraham L. Furman. He wrote articles for the *Independent, Bookman* and *The New Republic.* On December 11, 1934, he died of tuberculosis in a hospital ward, in Bellevue Hospital, according to one account, on Welfare Island, according to another.[7]

There is general consensus that it was Thurman's ability to read exceptionally fast as well as his perceptive critical abilities that led to his being hired at *The Messenger* in 1926 (and subsequently by Macauley's in 1929). That summer, with Hughes, Hurston, John P. Davis, Gwendolyn Bennett and the painter Aaron Douglas, he founded *Fire,* "a new experimental quarterly devoted to and published by younger Negro artists."[8] The magazine's overpowering drive, Hughes wrote in *The Big Sea,* was "to burn up a lot of the old, dead conventional Negrowhite ideas of the past, *épater le bourgeois* into a realization of the existence of the younger Negro writers and artists, and provide us with an outlet for publication not available in the limited pages of the small Negro magazines then existing."[9]

Fire was a one-issue publication, however. In it appeared Cullen's "From the Dark Tower," a story by Bruce Nugent that Hughes called "a green and purple story," and Thurman's "Cordelia the Crude," a story of a young woman who "had not yet realized the moral import of her wanton promiscuity nor become mercenary," a girl of sixteen who by the end of the story was working, dancing, and drinking in a well-known whorehouse on 134th Street near Lenox Avenue. Benjamin Brawley said that *Fire*'s "flame was so intense that it burnt itself up immediately"; after Du Bois and other writers in the black press castigated the journal, it expired.[10] Unfortunately, Thurman, who had advanced most of the money for its publication, had to spend the next few years paying off the debt. Another short-lived journal that he founded two years later, *Harlem, a Forum of Negro Life,* also folded, after only two issues.[11]

These were turbulent years in Harlem. Locke's *The New Negro* brought together the talents of many of the writers. But Carl Van Vechten's *Nigger Heaven* reflected the context in which almost all these writers worked. In her column in *Opportunity,* Gwendolyn Bennett noted that by October, two months after publication, white sightseers, visitors and other strangers were said to be "Van Vechtenizing" in Harlem. "Intrigued by the primitivistic portrayal of the Negro in the book, whites from downtown and elsewhere temporarily neglected Greenwich Village to explore Harlem and enjoy the Negro." In fact, among the good reviews were those by Thurman, in the *Messenger*, September, 1926; Charles S. Johnson, in the *Pittsburgh Courier*, September 4, 1926; James Weldon Johnson, in *Opportunity*, October, 1926; and George Schuyler, also in the *Pittsburgh Courier*, November 6, 1926. Among the many dissenting views, Du Bois's argument is persuasive, according to which *Nigger Heaven* is "a blow in the face . . . an affront to the hospitality of black folk and to the intelligence of white," a caricature, a mass of half-truths, and "a hodgepodge of laboriously stated facts, quotations and expressions, illuminated here and there with something that comes near to being nothing but cheap melodrama."[12]

Although Van Vechten's emphasis on jazz, sex, atavism and primitivism was rejected in many quarters, his influence was profound. It is in this context that Wallace Thurman in 1929 published *The Blacker the Berry*, a study of interracial color prejudice operating upon Emma Lou Morgan, black daughter of a light-skinned mother whose family motto was "whiter and whiter every generation" until their grandchildren would be able to pass and race would no longer be a problem. Feeling the burden of blackness, as Wallace Thurman did, his character Emma Lou is further depressed when she learns that it was her color that forced the estrangement of her mother from her second husband. Leaving Boise, Idaho, as close as Thurman apparently could get in urban tone to Salt Lake City, Emma Lou attends the University of Southern California (also paralleling Thurman's career), and tries to get a job in Harlem. Denied employment because she is so dark, she falls in love with a mulatto-Filipino, Alva, but her obsession with color drives him off. After finishing college at the City College of New York she tries again to help Alva, who is now an alcoholic and burdened by an idiot child, and is again rejected. Emma Lou, seemingly an ordinary, normal person in every way, is apparently the victim of color prejudice, in both white *and* black America.[13]

Thurman, probably influenced by *Nigger Heaven* or by the prevailing disposition to portray Harlem in its most vivid colors, describes Harlem's cabaret life, the rent parties, speakeasies (this was during Prohibition), vaudeville shows and ballroom dances as they were. But his emphasis on sex, alcohol, dancing, and gambling makes the balance disappear. Even serious fictionalized discussions with Langston Hughes (Tony Crews) and Zora Neale Hurston (Cora Thurston) turn into reinforcements of the author's already apparently set opinions. During a discussion with Campbell Kitchen (clearly modeled on Carl Van Vechten), we read that it was Van Vechten who "first began the agitation in the higher places of journalism which gave impetus to the spiritual craze. . . . It was he who sponsored most of the younger Negro writers, personally carrying their work to publishers and editors." In spite of Thurman's disinclination to give Du Bois, Locke, and Johnson credit for *their* pioneering work, it is true that Van Vechten can be credited with earnest spadework. Significantly, in his novel

Thurman was most angry at those blacks who perpetuated discrimination against blacks, especially black women. The doggerel verse he quotes is eloquent testimony to that: "Yaller gal rides in a limousine; /Brownskin gal rides the train. / Black gal rides in an ol' oxcart, /But she gits there jes' the same."[14]

Thurman, contrary to the emerging literary style, made a dark-skinned girl his protagonist. Black, except for the followers of Marcus Garvey, did not become fashionable or popular until the 1960s. On the other hand, in all fairness, it has to be said that Thurman's point was that prejudice and racism existed within the black community, not that there was an inherent advantage in blackness. Given the growing belief that "white was right," as Mrs. Morgan put it, it was not surprising that Emma Lou's color led to her mother's rejection; in turn, following the practice of many dark-skinned women (and some men), Emma Lou used skin whiteners and hair straighteners and preferred light-skinned men. At the end, if one accepts the proviso that experience is the best teacher, Emma Lou has come to terms with her identity and her color.

Unfortunately, the title, taken from an old Negro folk saying, "The blacker the berry, the sweeter the juice," has to be taken ironically, bitterly. For the point has to be made, Emma Lou was too black, too conscious of her blackness; it had to dawn on her, as it did on Thurman eventually, that the fault lay only partially in her color. As Thurman put it, "what she needed to do now was to accept her black skin as being real and unchangeable, to realize that certain things were, and would be, and with this in mind, begin life anew, always fighting, not so much for acceptance by other people but for acceptance of herself." But this also seems to mean that *The Blacker the Berry*, while inspired by a man's talent and commitment, failed because it lacked subtlety and complexity.[15]

In his second novel, *Infants in the Spring*, the focus is on Niggeratti ("Nigger" plus "literati") Manor, a huge residence cut up into studios for black artists and writers. Actually both blacks and whites live there, most of them unproductive, along with their retinues. Raymond Taylor, a talented writer hampered by his excessive race consciousness, Samuel Carter, a white militant desiring martyrdom, Eustace Savoy, a black singer hesitant about singing Negro spirituals, Pelham Gaylord, a painter and poet of little talent, Paul Arbian, a black, dissipated, homosexual painter, and Stephen Jorgenson, a white obsessed with, then repelled by, black women and primitivistic Harlem, make up the cast. Unfortunately, as Thurman's Taylor puts it, except for Jean Toomer, "the average Negro intellectual and artist has no goal, no standards, no elasticity, no pregnant germ plasm."[16] On the other hand, when the avowed brains and talent of the Negro Renaissance are brought together, their substantive essence is lost in the heat of a socio-political debate over Pan-Africanism, activism or personal self-expression. In common with Langston Hughes's words in "The Negro Artist and the Racial Mountain," whose views he would surely have known, Thurman opted for individuality. "Let each seek his own salvation." Similarly, in accord with Shakespeare's *Hamlet*, that "The canker galls the infants of the spring/ Too oft before their buttons be disclosed," Thurman castigated Renaissance artists' and writers' exploitation of the whites from downtown who supported the Renaissance so long as it could remain Niggeratti Manor. In the most sarcastic tones, one of his black characters says, "Being a Negro writer in these days is a racket and I'm going to make the most of it while it lasts."[17]

Thurman was one of the fledgling writers of the Renaissance. As a character like Raymond Taylor he could imaginatively interact with, and comment on, the personalities integral to the times. Knowing that "The American Negro . . . was entering a new phase in his development," that he "was about to become an important factor in the artistic life of the United States," Raymond still clung to the belief that unless he, or Paul, or others "began to do something worth while, there would be little chance of their being permanently established." The point is that among the emotional arguments, in the midst of the calls for a turn or return to "pagan inheritance," or "Marxism," it is Thurman's balanced view that we admire today. Answering Dr. Parkes (who reflects Alain Locke), the noted college professor who calls for a return to Africa to resurrect "our pagan heritage," as well as Fenderson, who complains about everything, and Madison, who uses Lenin as his role-model, Cedric (Eric Walrond), backed up by Raymond (Thurman), heatedly comments: "Well . . . why not let each young hopeful choose his own path? Only in that way will anything at all be achieved?"[18]

Thurman, brooding and magnetic, to a significant degree ridiculed the Renaissance of which he was part. While he was at the center of this movement, he denounced the quality of the literature because it laid at best a shaky foundation for the future. He looked for reasons within himself and the race. "That ninety-nine and ninety-nine hundredths per cent of the Negro race is patently possessed and motivated by an inferiority complex," he wrote, is a central cause. That he had the talent but not the greatness of theme and expression so needed was another. Given such rationales, not trying was an escape. Yet, as he expressed it in *The Blacker the Berry*, he also wrote it in *Infants in the Spring*, and this must be accepted as vintage Thurman: "Individuality is what we strive for. Let each seek his own salvation."[19]

In Thurman's vision the Renaissance was doomed to fail. "At first glance," it is affirmed at the end of *Infants*, "it could be ascertained that the skyscraper [Niggeratti Manor] would soon crumble and fall, leaving the dominating white lights in full possession of the sky." Given this assumption, Thurman felt that black writers should not be propagandists but writers, that they should not be race writers. It is not surprising that his persona, Raymond, is told that "race to you means nothing. You stand on a peak. . . . Propaganda you despise. Illusions about Negroes you have none." Nor is it surprising that shortly after *Infants* was published, Thurman, emancipated from everything but himself, liquor, T.B., and despair, died.[20]

Thurman's inclinations were correct. It was important to foster good writing, to reward excellence and talent. His major fault flowed from his intense self-hatred, self-doubt, and a penchant for criticism above fiction. He knew that, in the 1920s, to be successful he would have to patronize the white audience that bought the books and trekked uptown; he also knew that he wanted to write honestly, as Rudolph Fisher had done, of black Harlem as a black man, because he was black, and for blacks. In "Cordelia the Crude" he drew a character who represented an honest portrayal of Negro life; at the same time, he undoubtedly recognized the difficulties he faced in hanging the dirty wash out to dry, for all to see. "It makes no difference if this element of their life is of incontestable value to the sincere artist. It is also available and of incontestable value to the insincere artists and prejudiced white critics."[21]

Thurman, Robert Bone has written, was the aspiring undertaker of the Negro Renaissance. Consistent with Countee Cullen's advice that the job of the Negro writer was "to create types that are truly representative of us as a people," he tried to remain true to himself; but he misused satire, he paraded his pet hates, and he was, finally, too heavy-handed in his writing. On the other side, driven by his anger, his sense of rejection, his consciousness of color, and the realization that there was no resolution in sight, he ended *Infants* on a positive note. Although Paul slashed his wrists with a Chinese dirk, Thurman's forced ending concluded that art would be produced by individuals of talent who were willing to work hard with the self-consciousness that defied crippling doubt.[22]

Thurman undeniably was a writer of power and talent. An insider in the Harlem literary circles, he was even referred to as one of the central pivots of the Harlem Renaissance. Yet when Thurman is weighed as a writer, it is certain that he will be found wanting. Unable to control the rich literary material with which he worked, he consistently imposed a morbid look on his characters and developed stories and novels so atomized that he ultimately wound up at cross purposes with himself. His irony was well placed, whether in "Cordelia the Crude" in *Fire*, 1 (November 1926), or in *Harlem* (1929). In the latter work, a simple Southern mother seeing her family torn apart by the vagaries of Harlem, by the "sweetback" of the "hot-stuff man," by lotteries and vice, by the necessity of having rent parties, is helpless to intervene; religion and family are her refuge of last resort. Cordelia, caught up in the wild life of the city, is almost destroyed by poverty and the city. It was a startlingly realistic drama. It was also a very successful, overly melodramatic play about the harshness of life and black disillusionment. In Edith Isaacs's opinion, "Violent and undisciplined as the play was, it left a sense of photographic reality."[23]

In the same way, Thurman's talent burst out in *The Blacker the Berry* and *Infants of the Spring*. In debunking the "Negro Renaissance," in parading his pessimism, Thurman exemplified how strongly he felt about the enduring quality of the literature of the Harlem writers. He believed, as one of his characters phrased it in *Infants of the Spring*, "Being a Negro writer in these days is a racket, and I'm going to make the most of it while it lasts." No wonder Langston Hughes described him as having a prodigious capacity for gin, though he detested it; no wonder Hughes wrote that Thurman liked being a Negro but thought it a great handicap.[24] Most significantly, as a very dark-skinned black man who met discrimination everywhere, he set out to record honestly and realistically black life in Harlem, but wound up compromising his principles. As Margaret Perry says, "he usually settled for capitalizing on its exotic-erotic elements in order to succeed." Unhappy when forced to be with blacks, rejected so often when with whites, he wrote, "I was fighting hard to refrain from regarding myself as martyr and an outcast." Yet it was both the martyr and outcast that dominated the content and the style of his writing. In the end he exhausted himself trying to please the public while at the same time trying to write with a New Negro honesty. It is entirely appropriate that *Infants*, a neurotic novel in which he brooded introspectively on the "failure" of the Harlem Renaissance, derives its title and theme from Laertes' advice to Ophelia:

> The canker galls the infants of the spring
> Too oft before their buttons be disclosed,
> And in the morn and liquid dew of youth
> Contagious blastments are most imminent.

Thurman's pessimism dominates his satire. The cancer that gnawed at his vitals, the cancer of Bohemianism, was a combination of color, caste and dilettantism. If he had the talent, his heavy-handedness, mixed with equal parts of disillusion and despair, of himself and the alleged achievements of the 1920s, overcame his native ability. "The most self-conscious of the New Negroes," writes Robert Bone, "he ultimately turned his critical insight against himself and the wider movement with which he identified."[25] Wanting to be a very great writer, he seems to have known he was merely a journalist. Melancholy, suicide-prone, he tried to say but ended up shouting that phoniness in the Harlem Renaissance was rampant even as he insisted, with Emersonian firmness, that capitulation to badges and names, to large societies, and dead institutions must give way to the free and individual spirit. Where he meant to write fiction, he wrote criticism; he wrote didactically. He failed, but he failed magnificently.

In December 1934, both Rudolph Fisher and Wallace Thurman died. In Dorothy West's eyes, years after the event, Thurman's death "was the first break in the ranks of the New Negro." Ironically, Thurman, who liked to drink gin, but *didn't* like to drink gin, died of T.B. in the charity ward of City Hospital, Welfare Island, New York. He would have liked to have believed, as he put it in *The Blacker the Berry*, that everyone must find salvation within one's self, that no one in life need be a total misfit, but he could not totally break with his sense of gloom and despair and rejection and self-abnegation. In terms of his literary contributions, he was one of the significant but less than major figures of the Renaissance. However, to quote Mae Gwendolyn Henderson, "His significance . . . far exceeds the work he left behind. Not only was he tremendously influential upon the younger and perhaps more successful writers of the period, but his life itself became a symbol of the New Negro Movement."[26]

NOTES

1. *The Big Sea* ([1940]; rpt. New York: Hill & Wang, 1964), p. 225.
2. Dorothy West, "Elephant's Dance," *Black World* 20 (Dec. 1970): 85.
3. S. P. Fullinwider, *The Mind and Mood of Black America* (Homewood, IL: Dorsey, 1969), 132–33.
4. Arthur P. Davis, *From the Dark Tower* (Washington, DC: Howard Univ. Press, 1974), p. 109; also see Fullinwider, pp. 154–55, and letters from Thurman to Jordan Rapp, 1929, in James Weldon Johnson Collection, The Beinecke Rare Book and Manuscript Library, Yale University.
5. Robert Bone, *The Negro Novel in America* (New Haven: Yale Univ. Press, 1958), pp. 92–93.
6. Ernest Boynton, Jr., "Wallace Thurman," in *Dictionary of American Negro Biography*, ed. Rayford Logan (New York: Norton, 1982), pp. 590–92.
7. Boynton, "Wallace Thurman;" also see Davis, *From the Dark Tower*, p. 109.
8. Wallace Thurman, "Negro Artists and the Negro," *New Republic* (31 Aug. 1927): 37–39.
9. Quoted in Hugh M. Gloster, *Negro Voices in American Fiction* (New York: Russell & Russell, 1965), p. 114.
10. *Fire* 1 (Dec. 1926); Benjamin Brawley, *The Negro Genius* (New York: Dodd, Mead, 1937), p. 135.
11. Boynton, "Wallace Thurman," p. 591.
12. Gloster, *Negro Voices*, p. 160; W.E.B. Du Bois, "Criteria of Negro Art," *Crisis* 33 (1926): 290–97.
13. *The Blacker the Berry* (1929; rpt. New York: Collier, 1970), pp. 12, 21; Gloster, *Negro Voices*, pp. 168–69.
14. *Blacker the Berry*, pp. 192, 179.
15. Fullinwider, *Mind and Mood in Black America*, p. 156; *Blacker the Berry*, pp. 256–57, 221, 226.
16. *Infants of the Spring* (New York: Macaulay, 1932), pp. 221, 144; Gloster, *Negro Voices*, p. 170.
17. Gloster, *Negro Voices*, p. 171; *Infants*, pp. 240, 230.
18. *Infants*, pp. 61–62, 236–40.
19. *Infants*, pp. 140, 240; Thurman to Jordan Rapp, 1 Aug. 1929, Johnson Papers.
20. *Infants*, pp. 284, 143.
21. Doris Abramson, *Negro Playwrights in the American Theatre 1925–1959* (New York: Colombia Univ. Press, 1969), p. 41.
22. Bone, *Negro Novel in America*, p. 93; Countee Cullen, "The Negro in Art," *Crisis* 32 (1926): 193; Margaret Perry, *Silence to the Drums* (Westport, CT: Greenwood, 1976), pp. 92–93; Nathan Huggins, *Harlem Renaissance* (New York: Oxford Univ. Press, 1973), p. 243.
23. Edith Isaacs, *The Negro in the American Theatre* (New York: Theatre Arts, 1947), p. 86.
24. Thurman, *Infants*, p. 230; also see Langston Hughes, *The Big Sea*, pp. 235–39.
25. Bone, *The Negro Novel*, p. 94
26. West, "Elephant's Dance," 85.

COUNTEE CULLEN: A KEY TO THE PUZZLE

MICHAEL L. LOMAX

The early poems are as good as one remembers them, the later ones
inferior. The puzzle is why Cullen did not merely stop growing but
was thrown back.

Helen Wolfert, PM, March 16, 1947

"Ladies and gentlemen!" black critic Alain Locke announced in 1926, a peak
year of the Harlem Renaissance, "A genius! Posterity will laugh at us if we do
not proclaim him now."[1] Much of Locke's time and energy, guidance and concern had been focused on the New Negro artists of the era, and now his efforts
in their behalf were being rewarded amply with what he considered the unques-
tionably high literary standard achieved in *Color*, a first volume by the young
black poet Countee Cullen. With this volume, the New Negro had taken a significant step forward, according to Locke, and, as if to prove that point, his hosan-
nas were picked up only a little less enthusiastically by other critics not so
personally involved in Cullen's career.

White reviewers were impressed and willingly admitted that Cullen's volume
heralded a new and higher epoch in black American literature. "With Countee
Cullen's *Color*," wrote Clement Wood in the *Yale Review*, "we have the first
volume of the most promising of the younger Negro poets. There is no point in
measuring him merely beside Dunbar . . . and other Negro poets of the past and
present: he must stand or fail beside Shakespeare and Keats and Masefield,
Whitman and Poe and Robinson."[2] Most other white reviewers were not quite
so unqualified as Wood and did not presume to place Cullen among such an
auspicious group of English and American poets. While they did invoke Cullen's
obvious and admitted literary influences, they still compared the young black

poet favorably. "Much of his work is reminiscent of Miss Edna St. Vincent Millay and of A. E. Houseman," wrote one reviewer in *The Independent*, "but always it is informed with something personal to him, some quality of his own. It is never purely imitative."[3]

The reviewers noted that the volume betrayed certain youthful weaknesses, but they were quick to point out that *Color* suggested a potentially powerful literary talent—a fact which they felt far overshadowed any incidental weaknesses. "There are numerous things which Mr. Cullen as a poet has not yet begun to do . . ., but in this first volume he makes it clear that he has mastered a tune," wrote poet Mark Van Doren. "Few recent books have been so tuneful— at least so tuneful in the execution of significant themes."[4]

Color and Cullen did not entirely escape negative criticism, though, and significantly it was white reviewers who pointed to Cullen's arch-traditionalism and lack of stylistic originality as major flaws in his work. Locke's review had mentioned Cullen's rhyming, but glossed over it by invoking Pope as the model for what he euphemistically termed "this strange modern skill of sparkling couplets."[5] The white reviewers were not, however, so quick to justify Cullen's old-fashioned style. "Perhaps the only protest to Mr. Cullen that one cares to insist on is against his frequent use of rhetorical style which is surely neither instinctive in origin nor agreeable in effect," wrote *Poetry's* reviewer. "Lofty diction in poetry when it is unwarranted by feeling . . . is liable to seem only stilted and prosy."[6] The general silence of black reviewers on this point seems to suggest their own agreement with Cullen. The majority black critical view was that New Negro artists should express themselves in time-honored forms and thus give stature to their racial themes. By performing well, within the confines of established literary traditions, black artists would demonstrate their capabilities in a way that could not be disputed.

White reviews of *Color* included one uniform and rather predictable response. They all stated that Cullen's real importance was not merely as a black poet writing of his people's experiences but as a poet expressing the universal human experience. "But though one may recognize that certain of Mr. Cullen's verses owe their being to the fact that he shares the tragedy of his people," wrote Babette Deutsch in *The Nation*, "it must be owned that the real virtue of his work lies in his personal response to an experience which, however conditioned by his race, is not so much racial as profoundly human. The color of his mind is more important than the color of his skin."[7]

Ironically, though, it was this specifically racial element in his work which most forcefully appealed to black reviewers. "His race and its sufferings," wrote Walter White, "give him depth and an understanding of pain and sorrow."[8] White's emphasis was echoed in other black reviews which praised Cullen as the first real spokesman for sensitive and educated blacks who daily suffered through the pressures and hardships of the American racial experience. "The poems which arise out of the consciousness of being a 'Negro in a day like this' in America," wrote Jessie Fauset in *The Crisis*, " . . . are not only the most beautifully done but they are by far the most significant in the book. . . . Here I am convinced is Mr. Cullen's forte; he has the feelings and the gift to express colored-ness in a world of whiteness. I hope he will not be deflected from continuing to do that of which he has made such a brave and beautiful beginning."[9]

Certainly the "colored-ness" which Jessie Fauset praised as an essential feature of Cullen's first volume was a quality which she sensed rather than a sentiment which she found expressed in clear and forthright statements. There were too many non-racial poems for that; and too many poems in which, as she herself pointed out, "the adjectives 'black' or 'brown' or 'ebony' are deliberately introduced to show that the type which the author had in mind was not white."[10] At least in part, though, this inclusion of non-racial and peripherally black poems did suggest Cullen's own particular brand of "colored-ness." For within the context of *Color* as a whole, they implied the tentativeness of Cullen's assertions of a strong sense of his own black identity. These poems, appearing along side verse dealing with specifically racial themes, point to the Du Boisean "double-consciousness" as the central contradiction in Cullen's appraisal of his own racial identity. Neither black nor white, Cullen saw himself somewhere in between, an undefined individual consciousness for whom "colored" became as good a label as any. Thus, the volume as a whole and several poems in particular are haunted by the unresolved conflict in Cullen's perception of himself as simultaneously a black man and a culturally assimilated though, admittedly, socially ostracized Westerner. This central tension became the source of dramatic conflict in Cullen's and *Color*'s best known poem, "Heritage." In it, Cullen confronted the contradictions within his own identity and, though finally incapable of resolving them, he articulated his emotional and intellectual struggle with honesty and a rarely-achieved eloquence.

The opening lines of "Heritage" introduce Cullen's conflict in terms of tensions between past and present, Africa and America:

> What is Africa to me:
> Copper sun or scarlet sea,
> Jungle star or jungle track,
> Strong bronzed men, or regal black
> Woman from whose loins I sprang
> When the birds of Eden sang?
> *One three centuries removed*
> *From the scenes his fathers loved,*
> *Spicy grove, cinnamon tree*
> *What is Africa to me?*[11]

Africa was a frequent symbol in New Negro poetry for a pristine black identity which had not been confused by the values, "progress" and materialism of Western society. Ironically, this pastoral image bore little actual relation to contemporary colonial Africa or even to Africa three centuries before, but was instead the product of a long tradition of popular literary stereotypes. Cullen's Africa, peopled with wild animals and "young forest lovers . . . / Plighting troth beneath the sky," was just another literary conception—part Edgar Rice Burroughs, part courtly romance. Yet, in spite of Cullen's historical naiveté, the essential personal problem still emerges, the conflict between a conscious and intellectualized Western self and a self which intuitively senses a bond with a lost past as well as elements of a degraded present:

> So I lie, who always hear,
> Though I cram against my ear
> Both my thumbs, and keep them there,
> Great drums throbbing through the air.
> So I lie, whose fount of pride,
> Dear distress, and joy allied,
> Is my somber flesh and skin,
> With the dark blood damned within
> Like great pulsing tides of wine
> That, I fear, must burst the fine
> Channels of the chafing net
> Where they surge and foam and fret.[12]

Elsewhere in *Color* Cullen had attempted to establish bonds with elements of the racial present, elements which he usually excluded from the limited range of his sensitive and, admittedly, bourgeois outlook. In "Black Magdalens" and "Atlantic City Waiter" he tried to capture the meaning of experiences toward which he responded ambivalently, feeling simultaneously a sense of separation and a kind of bond as well. The results were forced and shallow, without the compassion achieved, for example, by McKay in "Harlem Shadows" and "Harlem Dancer"—poems in which the Jamaican poet establishes himself as an observer of those within the race who have been degraded, but in which he also affirms the essential humanity of those who have been thus debased. Cullen, on the other hand, though he may have chosen to observe such elements in black life, could not resolve his own tensions of disassociation and thus could not really affirm what he saw. He remained uncomfortable in the face of such elements and thus could only ineptly describe them. The Cullen who was later to chafe under the title "Negro poet" and who saw validity only in established European modes of expression could not accept as valuable the totality of black experience, as did Langston Hughes in "The Negro Speaks of Rivers." Still, at least the conclusion of "Heritage" suggests that in 1925 Cullen was not quite ready to accept a totally Western identity:

> *All day long and all night through,*
> *One thing only must I do:*
> *Quench my pride and cool my blood,*

Lest I perish in the flood.
Lest a hidden ember set
Timber that I thought was wet
Burning like the dryest flax,
Melting like the merest wax,
Lest the grave restore its dead.
Not yet has my heart or head
In the least way realized
They and I are civilized.[13]

"Heritage" leans towards bonds of racial unity. So does *Color* as a whole, and so do Cullen's works of the early twenties. In light of Cullen's later shift to the opposite pole of assimilation, and his easier acceptance of a more catholic and eclectic Western identity, one wonders why his first volume bore this black stamp. The answer lies in the *milieu* of the 1920s. *Color* is the product of personal struggle in an atmosphere which reinforced all that was racially distinctive. Sophisticated whites were Negrophiles who wanted to see blacks as essentially different from their own boringly Western selves. Cullen, in spite of strong misgivings, was willing to do as many other New Negroes did, and thus he bowed to white desires. So, much of his later writing became a retraction of the position taken during the twenties. But whatever Cullen did and said later, *Color* remains an impressive and landmark volume, one which quickly established its author as the New Negro poet *par excellence*. To many critics, it also suggested a promise and future which Cullen did not fulfill.

Countee Cullen's sudden and premature death in 1946 at the age of forty-two shocked those who remembered him as he had been at the time of *Color*'s publication, just two brief decades before, then a youthful poet with an auspicious future. At the time of his death, he was still a relatively young man and certainly, in terms of sheer talent, a gifted one as well. And in spite of what had appeared to be a too lengthy hiatus, there were those close to him who felt that his future might have been more productive. "Creative writers sometimes have long periods of silence," mused Langston Hughes. "Had he lived he might have written brilliantly and beautifully again."[14] But Cullen's untimely death certainly put an end to such speculations. Neither his youthful promise nor his more matured talent were to be fulfilled. And when Cullen's career is viewed in a more dispassionate and, perhaps, somewhat less generous light than Hughes affords, such sanguine prognostications of what might have been had Cullen only lived hardly seem realistic. In fact, there is a real sense in which Cullen's death, rather than cutting short a still potentially productive career, instead marked a final coda to the poet's bitter period of decline. At forty-two, Cullen had not been a progressively maturing artist confidently expressing his own vision of life—in this case, his vision of black life in America. Rather, with his original gifts atrophying from disuse, Cullen remained a forced-black man who never adjusted comfortably to his racial identity.

During the bleak years which followed the Harlem Renaissance, Cullen continued to publish but without his earlier success. The Depression cut short white interest in black art, and Cullen barely survived the loss of his white audience. Without their interest he rejected entirely the racial themes of the 1920s, limiting himself to the more conventional poetic concerns of love and death. By the 1940s, he had exhausted these and, except for occasional forays into children's literature, wrote practically nothing at all.

Fittingly enough, Cullen made plans before his death to take a final bow in the role of poet. In 1945, he compiled a collection of his published poems and appropriately titled it *On These I Stand*. The volume was to be "an anthology of the best poems of Countee Cullen."[15] He clearly intended the collection to be a final monument to his poetic career and thus, whatever else he might do in the future, it could serve as a basis for evaluating that favored part of his literary life. The volume appeared in 1947, almost exactly one year after his death, and, as he had anticipated, critics used *On These I Stand* as a scale for measuring his entire career. Unfortunately, the final evaluations were not so impressive as Cullen had apparently anticipated.

John Ciardi pointed out that the keyword for Cullen's early career had been "promise." But with his death, "this edition of his selected poems is total. And . . . the total disappoints the large claims that have been made for him."[16] Looking through the volume, Ciardi and other critics reviewed Cullen's chronologically arranged poems and discerned a pattern of slow but unquestionable decline. His career was a "descending curve," wrote *Poetry*'s reviewer, as he traced the lines of deterioration from Cullen's best serious verse of the 1920s through the mediocre and poorer products of later years.[17] Everyone seemed to agree that at the time of his death Cullen had reached a literary low point. Still the question remained: Why? The answers were not so uniform.

Some critics answered that the problem lay in Cullen's conservative response to literary traditions:

> Cullen was singularly unaware of what was going on in the world of poetry. In the age of Pound and Eliot, he tortured syntax and used such words as "aught" and "albeit." He nowhere shows any evidence of studying the styles of any modern poets other than Millay, Wylie, and Housman, although, according to Robert Hillyer, he wrote imitations of most of the older poets in the days at Harvard that preceded the publication of *Color*. Perhaps because of his failure to absorb the technical discoveries of his contemporaries, he was singularly unself-critical and could allow such monstrosities . . . to be printed. Certainly his failure to study carefully what other poets did is in part responsible for his never developing a style peculiarly his own. Even the good poems in *On These I Stand* could have been written by any other craftsman, they bear no stylistic signature.[18]

Yet, while one of Cullen's deficiencies was obviously a problem of technique, such stylistic considerations do not satisfactorily resolve the issue. For Cullen could at times, through content, overcome his largely self-imposed limitations. "When the observation contained in the poem is directed and personal, dealing immediately with people seen and events that really occurred," Ciardi pointed out, "the poem emerges movingly."[19] That, however, occurred only rarely. Generally, Cullen substituted literary sentiments for sense and feeling and real, intimate response. In later poems, he seemed to have lost whatever original ability he had had to discern between artificial feelings and personal perceptions. He lost the ability to capture essential experiences, as he had done in "Heritage." The result for his later poetry was a bland mixture; trite sentimentality expressed in the most outmoded style.

Most white critics thought that Cullen had lapsed into clichés because the demands of race had driven him away from the sincere, personal introspection which was his true concern. According to them, Cullen's natural impulse led toward intimate expression in such pristine forms as the sonnet and "the neat, sensitive, and immediate lyric."[20] Yet, "Increasingly, Cullen's poetry . . . evidences a triumph of conscience over his particular gift, as if he told himself, 'don't you play now. Just do your work.'"[21] To work, according to this view, was to write of racial matters—a necessary subject because he was black, an unfortunate one since he was a poet. In this view, the moral and the aesthetic responsibilities were incompatible, irreconcilable. In spite of personal inclinations to do otherwise, Cullen tragically chose race above art. "Somehow or other . . . ," Cullen had admitted, as if to substantiate this argument, "I find my poetry of itself treating of the Negro, of his joys and sorrows—mostly of the latter, and of the heights and depths of emotion which I feel as a Negro."[22] The result of such a decision was that Cullen lost his personal roots and in the process his basis for an individual vision. Without the direction he might have achieved as an integrated individual, this argument went, Cullen's only refuge was in the expression of worn and meaningless sentiments.

Race does indeed appear to be at the root of Cullen's problem, but not for those reasons suggested by white critics. Cullen had once said that he viewed poetry ideally as "a lofty thought beautifully expressed."[23] The issues of race in America constrained this ideal and trespassed upon Cullen's separate pristine world of poetry and art. For race meant harshness, violence and ugliness, all directly opposite to the delicate beauties which he envisioned as the true concerns of poetry. During the 1920s, when whites were enthusiastic Negrophiles, Cullen joined with other New Negroes in, to quote Langston Hughes, expressing their "individual dark-skinned selves without fear or shame."[24] The result for Cullen was a vital and often electric poetry, full of the tensions produced by an unresolved sense of his own racial identity in direct conflict with his desire to gain recognition from an enthusiastic white audience which demanded that blacks be different. With the waning white enthusiasm of the Depression, however, Cullen reasserted his intention to be a poet, not a black poet, and accordingly moved away from racial themes. His rejection of race as a thematic priority is nowhere more strongly expressed than in his short poem, "To Certain Critics," in which Cullen defiantly asserted: "I'll bear your censure as your praise, / For never shall the clan / Confine my singing to its ways / Beyond the ways of man."[25] With his rejection of race, Cullen concentrated on the essentially fatuous literary artificialities which were, according to him, the poet's true concern.

Du Bois recognized this shift, labelled it a shortcoming, and pointed to it as the reason why Cullen's career "did not culminate":

> His career was never completed. In a sense it was halted in mid-flight and becomes at once inspiration and warning to the American Negro group. First inspiration: the group needs expression. Its development toward self-revelation may become one of the greatest gifts of any group of people to modern civilization. The burning experience through which it has come is unique and precious. No one else can give voice and body to it but Negroes.
>
> It is sheer nonsense to put before Negro writers the ideal of being just writers and not Negroes. There is no such possibility. Englishmen are English from birth to death and in that fact lies most of the value of their contribution. The ideal of pure art divorced from actual life is nothing but an ideal and of questionable value in any day or time. Least of all is it of value today when the whirling tragedy, bitterness, blood and sweat of our intricate and puzzling life on this earth calls and even shrieks for that knowledge of each other's soul which only the soul itself in its own individual experience can furnish.
>
> The opportunity then for literary expression upon which American Negroes have so often turned their backs is their opportunity and not their handicap. That Countee Cullen was born with the Twentieth Century as a black boy to live in Harlem was a priceless experience. . . .
>
> Yet, as I have said, Cullen's career was not finished. It did not culminate. It laid [a] fine, beautiful foundation, but the shape of the building never emerged. . . . [26]

Du Bois's evaluation does indeed strike home. Cullen's refusal to accept race as a basic and valuable segment of his total identity was an evasion which prevented him from further straightforward and clear development. Race did not have to be a circumscribing point of view. Nor was Cullen compelled to do as Langston Hughes did and make it the conscious subject of all he wrote. Race was, however, an inescapable aspect of his identity which, in spite of all he said to the contrary, did affect him. What Du Bois failed to point out was that Cullen's racial equivocations were rooted deeply in the Harlem Renaissance itself. For the decade of the 1920s was a period of racial confusion and contradiction. Blacks were in vogue, but the values many New Negroes lived by, and the goals they sought, were white. Blacks were forced to play racial roles they did not find comfortable in order to achieve recognition from whites. Few New Negroes overcame the limitations of the period and were able to assert and maintain their own more solid racial and personal integrity. Langston Hughes was one of those few. Countee Cullen was not.

NOTES

1. *Opportunity* 4.1 (Jan. 1926): 14.
2. "The Negro Sings," *The Yale Review* 15 (1926): 824.
3. *The Independent* 15 (7 Nov. 1925): 539.
4. *New York Herald Tribune*, 10 Jan. 1926.
5. *Opportunity* 4.1 (Jan. 1926): 14.
6. George H. Dillon, *Poetry* 28 (April 1926): 51.
7. "Let It Be Allowed," *Nation* 121 (30 Dec. 1925): 763.
8. "A Negro Poet," *Saturday Review of Literature* 2 (13 Feb. 1926): 556.
9. "Our Book Shelf," *Crisis* 31 (1926): 238.
10. "Our Book Shelf," p. 238.
11. Countee Cullen, "Heritage," in *Color* (New York: Harper & Brothers, 1925), p. 36.
12. "Heritage," pp. 36–37.
13. "Heritage," pp. 40–41.
14. "Here to Yonder," *Chicago Defender*, 2 Feb. 1946.
15. *On These I Stand* (New York: Harper & Row, 1947), p. iii.
16. John Ciardi, Review of *On These I Stand*, *Atlantic Monthly* (Mar. 1947): 144.
17. Harvey Curtis Webster, "A Difficult Career," *Poetry* 70 (July 1947): 234.
18. "A Difficult Career," 224–25. Webster was, of course, wrong in saying that Cullen's work at Harvard preceded *Color*. *Color* was already off the press when Cullen arrived in Cambridge in September of 1925. The poems written at Harvard are found in *Copper Sun*.
19. Ciardi, Review of *On These I Stand*, p. 145.
20. Ciardi, Review of *On These I Stand*, p. 145.
21. Helen Wolfert, *PM*, 16 Mar. 1947: 7.
22. Interview, *The Chicago Bee*, 29 Dec. 1927.
23. Winifred Rothermel, "Countee Cullen Sees Future for the Race," *St. Louis Argus*, 3 Feb. 1928.
24. Langston Hughes, "The Negro Artist and the Racial Mountain," *Nation* 122 (23 June 1926): 694.
25. *The Black Christ* (New York: Harper, 1929), p. 63.
26. W.E.B. Du Bois, "The Winds of Time," *Chicago Defender*, Jan. 1946.

"A LACK SOMEWHERE":
NELLA LARSEN'S *QUICKSAND* AND THE HARLEM RENAISSANCE

LILLIE P. HOWARD

> All of us know that the gay and sparkling life of the so-called Negro Renaissance of the '20's was not so gay and sparkling beneath the surface as it looked.
>
> (Langston Hughes, *The Big Sea*)

That the Harlem Renaissance represents the most phenomenal outpouring of art in all of its forms—music, drama, poetry, fiction, dance, sculpture, painting—by Black Americans since Africans reached these shores in the 1600s, there is no doubt. Much of the art from that period still remains and much of what we find in contemporary Afro-American literature, art, or music is not new but a re-creation of themes, variations of dreams, first posited by black artists during the 1920s. The Harlem Renaissance, then, like no other period before or after it, represents the pinnacle of artistic achievement for Black Americans. It was "the period when the Negro was in vogue."[1]

During the 1920s, masses of people, but Black people in particular, were taking the picaresque journey toward the self, toward freedom, possibility, opportunity. It was a journey that had hitherto been thwarted by slavery, share-cropping, injustices of momentous proportions, not all of these the makings of whites. When the thousands of Black picaros arrived in New York and began to express themselves, Black America was in its heyday. Or so we are told. Few Blacks believed this, however, even back then.

For one thing, says Langston Hughes, the famous Cotton Club was "a Jim Crow Club for gangsters and monied whites" and the "cabarets and bars where formerly only colored people laughed and sang" were frequented by whites who were given "the best ringside tables to sit and stare at the Negro customers—like amusing animals in a zoo" (pp. 224–25). For another thing, continues Hughes, "The ordinary Negroes hadn't heard of the Negro Renaissance, and if they had, it hadn't raised their wages any. As for all those white folks in the speakeasies and nightclubs of Harlem—well, maybe a colored man could find *some* place to have a drink that the tourists hadn't yet discovered" (p. 228).

The all-consuming dilemma was as W.E.B. Du Bois had described it near the turn of the century—the problem of the color line, the problem of being Black in a country that favored white.[2] How to get past the knowledge of that fact, how to get past the practices that governed that fact, how to be both Black and American? How to accept one's Blackness and still be, still dream, feel secure, still achieve? It was not easy. That does not mean, however, that Blacks were not striving to reconcile themselves, or that they were not succeeding. Some were.

A great many of the "stars" of the Renaissance, however, were most unhappy. Their lives and their literature reflect this fact. Langston Hughes, who knew many of the writers of the period, admits in his autobiography, *The Big Sea*, that he wrote poetry only when he felt bad. That his output was prodigious we all know. In the same volume, Hughes describes Wallace Thurman as a "strangely brilliant black boy, who had read everything, and whose critical mind could find something wrong with everything he read." Thurman "wanted to be a great writer, but none of his works ever made him happy." Though his works were "important" and "compelling, . . . none of these things pleased Wallace Thurman. . . . So he contented himself by writing a great deal for money, laughing bitterly at his fabulously concocted 'true stories,' creating two bad motion pictures of the 'Adults Only' type for Hollywood, drinking more and more gin, and then threatening to jump out of the windows at people's parties and kill himself" (pp. 234–35). What Thurman himself thought about the Renaissance and about life in general we can glean, then, from the amount of gin he consumed and from his own ironic parody of the period, *Infants of the Spring*.

That Zora Hurston was not exactly laughing all the time, in spite of the humorous stories she often told, we can see from her letters to her white patron, Charlotte Osgood Mason, to Carl Van Vechten, whom she considered a friend, and to various others. Hurston's real success as a writer did not come until the 1930s, after the stock market crash had dimmed the lights in glittering Harlem. Like Thurman, however, Zora was never satisfied with her work, feeling after each publication that "my goal still eludes me. I am in despair because it keeps ever ahead of me."[3] Jean Toomer's unhappiness is so painful that, save Nellie McKay and Darwin Turner, both Toomer scholars, we would rather not see, preferring instead to read *Cane* and wonder what might have been had *Cane*'s swan song not been for Toomer as well as for Georgia.[4]

The point is that the many "happenings" in Harlem were happening for whites rather than for Blacks. And that just as thousands of Southern Blacks had packed up their suitcases and come to Northern cities to look for themselves, so whites were flocking to Harlem, to Greenwich Village, and to Europe, to search for themselves too. In Harlem, the black performers and the white lookers-on were both searching for identity, yet both were mostly unhappy. The jagged irony. Beneath the laughter, then, beneath the loud glitter of the Harlem nightclubs, beneath the heady achievements of the Harlem Renaissance, was an undercurrent of sadness of tragic proportions.

Part of the difficulty for Blacks was the burden of double consciousness as Du Bois describes it in *The Souls of Black Folk*: "The Negro ever feels his twoness; an American, a Negro; two souls, two thoughts, two irreconciled strivings, two warring ideals in one dark body, whose dogged strength alone keeps it from being torn asunder" (p. 45). Part of the problem came from aping whites, no matter what the compelling attractions, to the extent that all identity or the possibility for identity was erased. Nella Larsen's *Passing* is a case in point. The other part of the problem is more elusive, inexplicable, "a lack somewhere"—something missing inside the person who is searching for identity.[5] This is Jean Toomer's story, and this also is the compelling drama of Nella Larsen's *Quicksand* (1929), a novel which, because it explores many of the problems Blacks encountered in their search for identity, may be seen as the Black world distilled, the other side of the Harlem Renaissance—a look beneath the surface at a character who is unable to reconcile the disparate strivings within herself and is thus "torn asunder."

Quicksand depicts a young black woman with all the possibilities for success—which in this case means coming to a knowledge of and acceptance of self in spite of the constraints of the larger world. For reasons she is never able to name, however, Helga Crane is driven to efface herself. What happens to Helga is a fitting comment on the inability of Harlem, New York, or any other city to be more than a gilded six-bits (like Hurston's short story of the same name) to doubly-conscious people who were hankering after whiteness while simultaneously lacking the basic capacity for knowledge of self, and thus for real identity—what the Harlem Renaissance was all about.

Larsen's *Quicksand* records the picaresque movements of Helga Crane as she seeks a clearer understanding of self and sustained happiness. The novel records this journey toward self which, in spite of her physical movements—from Naxos (in the South) to Chicago to New York to Copenhagen, back to New York, then to the Deep South—spins Helga round and round in the same spot until she is virtually bogged down inside of herself. As William Bedford Clark points out, Helga "flees from the imperative of self-knowledge, seeking to allay the dissatisfactions which arise from within her with a change of scene and society. Her refusal to face the reality about herself in turn distorts her perception of the reality around her, finally breeding tragic consequences."[6] By the end of the novel, not even physical movement is possible. The pain the reader is made to feel is for the death of Helga's search and thus the death of Helga. Crane, who always seemed on the verge of meaningful discovery but who lacked the necessary mettle for real insight and for change, has, by the end of the novel, taken her last feeble stand against herself—

> For in some way she was determined to get herself out of this bog into which she had strayed. Or—she would have to die. (p. 219)

—and she has lost:

> And hardly had she left her bed and become able to walk again without pain, hardly had the children returned from the homes of the neighbors, when she began to have her fifth child. (p. 222)

Helga, whose dilemma is so acute because she cannot reconcile herself to the reality of her race, or her sexuality, is driven toward a materialism which masks the essence of herself, and lacks the basic capacity to accept herself as she is and to move forward from this knowledge. At key points in Helga's life as she quests for happiness, she replaces one obsession with another until, having explored and exhausted all obsessions she can name, nothing remains except the nameless. As Mary M. Lay has discovered, each turning point is accompanied by a contemplation scene which rivals that of Isabel Archer in Henry James's *Portrait of a Lady*.[7] For Helga, however, each contemplation is a new exploration of the same question. Family is replaced with materialism, with sexuality, with race. The same question, at least in terms Helga can accept, remains answerless.

When the novel opens, Helga Crane is, by most standards, a success. Young, intelligent, attractive, she is a schoolteacher in a Southern educational institution, "the finest school for Negroes anywhere in the country" (pp. 25–26). She has achieved a certain stature, and though she has no family to speak of, she is nevertheless engaged to a fellow-schoolteacher whose family is of some consequence. Recognizing the need for proper social connections in order to be accepted by the assimilated Black middle class, Helga, who is the offspring of a black father and a Scandinavian mother, has sought legitimacy through her fiancé James Vayle. She feels that having the proper family connections will still the discontent within her, and give her the necessary entrée to happiness:

> No family. That was the crux of the whole matter. For Helga, it accounted for everything, her failure here in Naxos, her former loneliness in Nashville. It even accounted for her engagement to James. Negro society, she had learned, was as complicated and as rigid in its ramifications as the highest strata of white society. If you couldn't prove your ancestry and connections, you were tolerated, but you didn't "belong." You could be queer, or even attractive, or bad, or brilliant or even love beauty and such nonsense if you were a Rankin, or a Leslie, or a Scoville; in other words, if you had a family. But if you were just plain Helga Crane, of whom nobody had ever heard, it was presumptuous of you to be anything but inconspicuous and comfortable. (pp. 34–35)

Even without the proper family connections, however, Helga Crane *has* been anything but "inconspicuous and conformable," and stands apart from her peers for reasons that, at least on the surface, have nothing to do with family. Even her closest friend was "a little afraid of Helga. Nearly everyone was" (p. 41), partly because of "her longing for nice things" (ibid.), partly for what her detractors called "pride" and "vanity"—the beginnings of the trappings of materialism. Seeing the teachings of the school as hypocritical, Helga "had never quite achieved the unmistakable Naxos meld, would never achieve it, in spite of much trying. She could neither conform, nor be happy in her nonconformity . . . a lack somewhere" (pp. 32–33).

Helga's quest for materialism is inseparable from her quest for the proper family. Both would bring status and security: "Always she had wanted, not money, but the things which money could give, leisure, attention, beautiful surroundings. Things. Things. Things" (p. 119). Most of her teacher salary had gone "into clothes, into books, into the furnishings of the room which held her. All her life Crane had loved and longed for nice things. Indeed it was this craving, this urge for beauty which had helped to bring her into disfavor in Naxos . . ." (p. 31).

Ironically, though Helga needs money, wants security, she is unable to take the necessary steps to attain either. Marriage to either her colleague at Naxos, James Vayle, or to the artist Axel Olsen in Copenhagen would have given her what she desired. Unlike the characters in Larsen's *Passing*, however, Irene Redfield, who marries a successful black doctor, and Clare Kendry, who marries a successful white businessman—neither for love—Helga marries neither. She admits that "To relinquish James Vayle would most certainly be social suicide, for she had wanted social background" (p. 35); and when she rejects Olsen's proposal, she feels that "in some way, she would pay for this hour. A quick brief fear ran through her, leaving in its wake a sense of impending calamity. She wondered if for this she would pay all that she'd had" (p. 150).

Helga might even have been able to marry the man she really loves, Dr. Robert Anderson, head of the school in Naxos, later "welfare worker of some big manufacturing concern" in New York. When she might have responded favorably to Anderson's overtures, however, she does so with sarcasm and aloofness, only offering herself to him after he has married her best friend. It is ironic, too, that Helga would love the man who, though attracted to her because of it, refuses to acknowledge her sexuality or his own: ". . . no matter what the intensity of his feelings or desires might be, he was not the sort of man who would for any reason give up one particle of his own good opinion of himself. Not even for her" (p. 181). Sexuality and "good family" were, after all, contradictory terms. Society said so. And neither Anderson nor Helga was a social rebel, at least not yet, though for Helga, there was the impending "hardiness of insistent desire" (p. 179). And, of course, soon there would be the Reverend Mr. Pleasant Green, "proffering his escort" (p. 191).

That Helga with her aspirations would actually marry the Reverend Green is perhaps the surprise of the novel. But no, she had had enough of simply things. She had had things in Naxos and not been satisfied; things in New York and yet she had fled to Copenhagen; in Copenhagen she had had so many things that she had become one herself, a mannequin dressed by others, a mere exotic decoration that "didn't at all count" (p. 1 24). "Helga herself felt like nothing so much as some new and strange species of pet dog being proudly exhibited. . . . And in spite of the mental strain, she had enjoyed her prominence" (p. 123). But as in Naxos, in New York, in Copenhagen, Helga had grown helplessly discontent:

> She desired ardently to combat this wearing down of her satisfaction with her life, with herself. But she didn't know how. . . . Frankly the question came to this: what was the matter with her? Was there, without her knowing it, some peculiar lack in her? Absurd. . . . Why couldn't she be happy, content, somewhere? Other people managed, somehow, to be. To put it plainly, didn't she know how? Was she incapable of it? (p. 140)

What Helga has unconsciously resolved, it seems, is to unleash her sexuality, and as Axel accuses her of being capable of doing, selling herself to the highest bidder. Perhaps in that direction she will find the satisfaction, the happiness she seeks. When Anderson will not buy, Helga is so devastated that she becomes ill: "For days, for weeks, voluptuous visions had haunted her. Desire had burned in her flesh with uncontrollable violence. The wish to give herself had been so intense that Dr. Anderson's surprising, trivial apology loomed as a direct refusal of the offering" (p. 182). But then there was the Reverend Mr. Pleasant Green, discovered in a storefront church where the gutterworn, disheveled Helga, taken for a "scarlet 'oman," a "Jezebel," has managed to shelter herself and find religion, a temporary opiate to still her discontent. "And in that moment," says the narrator, Helga "was lost—or saved" (p. 189).

In the "tiny Alabama town" where Green is the "pastor to a scattered and primitive flock," Helga achieves some "relative importance" (p. 196). As with grade school, Naxos, Chicago, New York, and Copenhagen, Helga is at first fascinated by the novelty of the experience. As with each of her prior experiences, she feels that now she would be happy, "compensated for all previous humiliations and disappointments" (p. 197), certain that the feeling of satisfaction would last forever. In each of her prior experiences, she had never been happier longer than a year. In Alabama, however, with the Reverend Green, she was certain that she had found "the intangible thing for which, indefinitely, always she had craved. It had received embodiment" (p. 200). That "the intangible thing" was connected with her sexuality is indisputable:

> And night came at the end of every day. Emotional, palpitating, amorous, all that was living in her, sprang like rank weeds at the tingling thought of night, with a vitality so strong that it devoured all shoots of reason. (p. 202)

Because she has an acceptable outlet for her sexuality, because she is preoccupied with work, her own house, garden, chickens, pig, husband, three children, and God, Helga is able to blot out successfully the reality of her life with Green for twenty months and, with her faith in God, longer: "Secretly, she was glad that she had not to worry about herself or anything. It was a relief to be able to put the entire responsibility on someone else" (p. 208).

At the beginning of the novel, Helga rejects Naxos because it tried to change the students into what they were not: "Teachers as well as students were subjected to the paring process, for it tolerated no innovations, no individualisms. . . . Enthusiasm, spontaneity, if not actually suppressed, were at least openly regretted as unladylike or ungentlemanly qualities. The place was smug and fat with self-satisfaction" (p. 29). When she returns to the South several years later, however, Helga approaches her neighbors from the Naxos' advantage:

> Her young joy and zest for the uplifting of her fellow men came back to her. She meant to subdue the cleanly scrubbed ugliness of her own surroundings to soft inoffensive beauty, and to help the other women to do likewise. Too, she would help them with their clothes, tactfully point out that sunbonnets, no matter how gay, and aprons, no matter how frilly, were not quite the proper things for Sunday church wear. There would be a sewing circle. She visualized herself instructing the children . . . in ways of gentler deportment. (p. 197)

For reasons the reader finds difficult to understand, Helga now feels smug and self-satisfied. Perhaps having relinquished the responsibility of her own life to another, she now feels free to mold the lives of others.

The pain involved in giving birth to her fourth child, however, proves to be too much for Helga, even with her faith, even with her life in the hands of another. In fact, the pain is so powerful that it becomes a kind of secondary reality,[8] displacing the first reality she has manufactured these many months. By the time she emerges from the clearer darkness of this pain, Helga is ready to admit her love for Anderson, her hatred for Green, the superficiality of her religion. And, of course, as with all contemplation scenes in the past, she has decided to flee: " . . . for she had no talent for quarrelling—when possible she preferred to flee. That was all" (p. 34). This time, however, she will flee later, after she has regained her strength: "It was so difficult. It was terribly difficult. It was almost hopeless. So for a while—for the immediate present, she told herself— she put aside the making of any plan for her going. I'm still, she reasoned, too weak, too sick. By and by, when I'm really strong—" (p. 221).

Just as Helga's blind quests for materialism, for the proper family, and for an acceptable outlet for her sexuality show fragmentation of self, so her ambiguity about her race shows why she can never be whole, why there will always be a void within her, happiness forever looming. "The end result of the journey from land, from one's roots, from one's ancestral past," says Addison Gayle in a discussion of Toomer's *Cane*, "means to sever all relationships with the race, to become one with the men and women of the novels of Johnson, Fauset, and

Nella Larsen. It means, too, this journey from race, and thus from self, to surrender one's identity, which once lost, is impossible to regain again."[9]

As Gayle describes it, Helga, who comes from mixed parentage, "cannot accept the definition of herself as Black in the terminology of whites or affluent Blacks" (p. 133). She is not comfortable with the middle-of-the-road stance of her middle-class black friend Anne Grey who "hated white people with a deep and burning hatred . . . but aped their clothes, their manners, and their gracious ways of living. While proclaiming loudly the undiluted good of all things Negro, she yet disliked the songs, the dances, and the softly blurred speech of the race" (p. 92). Nor is Helga willing to be "yoked to these despised black folk . . . self-loathing came upon her. They're my own people, my own people, she kept repeating over and over to herself. It was no good. The feeling would not be routed" (p. 101).

Perhaps to prepare herself for her impending visit to her aunt in Copenhagen, Helga feels it necessary to divorce herself totally from Blacks: "She didn't, in spite of her racial markings, belong to those dark segregated people. She was different. She felt it. It wasn't merely a matter of color. It was something broader, deeper, that made folk kin" (p. 102). On the liner, en route to Denmark, Helga revels "like a released bird in her returned feeling of happiness and freedom, that blessed sense of belonging to herself alone and not to a race" (p. 114). With Helga determined to disavow her Blackness, it is ironic that it is her color or race that the Danes wish to highlight and do. It is consistent, though again ironic, that Helga would blossom under this accent of her race, see it as right, actually revel in her Blackness, particularly in a country where she is a mere oddity that "did not at all count" (p. 124). Her thinking is decidedly middle class, closer to that of Anne Grey, though Helga never admits that fact.

Helga feels that it is the "acceptable" side of Blackness the Danes are highlighting in her, nothing dark or primitive. When she attends a circus where Black American dancers shamelessly perform, she is "filled with a fierce hatred. She felt ashamed, betrayed, as if these pale pink and white people among whom she lived had suddenly been invited to look upon something in her which she had hidden away and wanted to forget" (p. 143). Later she realizes that what the dancers possess, what the Danes see in her is "a precious thing, a thing to be enhanced, preserved" (ibid.). The portrait Axel Olsen has painted of Helga emphasizes this fact, though Helga disclaims the portrait, contending that it was of "some disgusting sensual creature with her features" (p. 152). When she returns to America, however, her "disgusting" sensuality is in the foreground of her life, central to her relationships with others.

From the beginning of the novel to the end, Helga moves from the black middle class in Naxos to the Black middle class in New York to the upper-class whites in Copenhagen to poor, "primitive" Blacks in Alabama. At one time or another, she shares allegiances with each group, but never squarely shares an allegiance with herself. While she constantly seeks the approval of others, she is incapable of approving herself, of approving her Blackness. Because she can thus never realize an identity which ignores this irrefutable fact of race, Helga Crane is fated to never know who she is.

That society, the world, the irreconcilable fact of being Negro and American are not to blame for Helga's quagmire here, the novel makes clear. The arguments of Hortense Thornton to the contrary, there are alternatives all along the way for Helga and the reader to see.[10] James Vayle, who at first is as mortified as Helga at the hypocrisies of Naxos, becomes "naturalized" nevertheless and is able to function well in that environment. When Helga complains to Robert Anderson about the suffocating Naxos environment, he responds with an insight and a prescription for living which Helga might have appropriated for her own use: "Some day you'll learn that lies, injustice, and hypocrisy are a part of every ordinary community. Most people achieve a sort of protective immunity, a kind of callousness, toward them. If they didn't, they couldn't endure" (pp. 50–51). Anne Grey, in spite of her own ambiguities about race, has found a happiness she enjoys; the Danes show Helga the essence of herself, that there is something precious, to be valued, about her Blackness; Robert Anderson shows her that uncontrolled or undisciplined sexuality may hurt more than it helps, may cost more than one can ever pay. Helga admires Miss Denney, a member of the Black middle class, who is frequently seen with whites, because Denney "had the assurance, the courage, so placidly to ignore racial barriers and give her attention to people" (p. 112). That her world is filled with alternative ways of being, Helga seems unaware. If she is aware, she is not cognizant of the implications of those lives for her own. Search as one might, one may not find an identity in America or abroad. But characters in the novel point out that one might fashion an identity for one's self, "out of material bequeathed by both the white and the black worlds."[11] A mulatto, then, need not necessarily be tragic. And, in spite of the epigraph to the novel from Langston Hughes's poem "Cross," one's racial heritage need not automatically be a burden.

That Helga Crane is unable to take advantage of what she has inherited from her black-white past suggests a lack somewhere in her character. That her life, her thwarted dreams, her inability to be reflect realities of the Harlem Renaissance period suggests the impotence of the period for many, while not detracting one whit from the many accomplishments of those who, in spite of or because of their strivings, stood "on top of the mountain free within themselves."[12]

NOTES

1. Langston Hughes, "Harlem Literati," in *The Big Sea* (New York: Hill & Wang, 1940) p. 228. Other references are noted parenthetically.

2. W.E.B. Du Bois, *The Souls of Black Folk* (1903; reprint, New York: New American Library, 1969), p. 45.

3. Zora Neale Hurston to Marjorie Kinnan Rawlings, n.d., Special Collections, Univ. of Florida, Gainesville.

4. See Nellie Y. McKay's *Jean Toomer, Artist: A Study of His Literary Life and Work, 1894–1936* (Chapel Hill: Univ. of North Carolina Press, 1984) and Darwin Turner's "Jean Toomer:

Exile," in *In a Minor Chord: Three Afro-American Writers and Their Search for Identity* (Carbondale: Southern Illinois Univ. Press, 1971), pp. 1–59.

5. Nella Larsen, *Quicksand* (New York: Collier, 1928), p. 33. Other references are noted parenthetically.

6. William Bedford Clark, "The Heroine of Mixed Blood in Nella Larsen's *Quicksand*," in *Identity and Awareness in the Minority Experience, Selected Proceedings of the First and Second Annual Conferences in Minority Studies, March 1973 and April 1974* (LaCrosse: Univ. of Wisconsin Press, 1975), p. 234.

7. Mary M. Lay "Parallels: Henry James's *The Portrait of a Lady* and Nella Larsen's *Quicksand*," *CLAJ* 20 (1977): 475–86.

8. The phrase "secondary reality" was suggested to me by Professor James Gleason, a colleague at Wright State who is currently writing a book with the working title "Secondary Reality and the Fiction of Southern Writers." While I am not using the term as Gleason defines it, I am not certain I would be using it at all had I not heard Professor Gleason read a paper on "Fitzgerald's Fiction and the Secondary Reality."

9. Addison Gayle, Jr., "The Confusion of Identity," in *The Way of the New World: The Black Novel in America* (New York: Anchor, 1975), p. 120.

10. Hortense Thornton, "Sexism as Quagmire: Nella Larsen's *Quicksand*," *CLAJ* 16 (1973): 285–301.

11. Addison Gayle, *Way of the New World*, p. 139.

12. Langston Hughes, "The Negro Artist and the Racial Mountain," *Nation* 122 (23 June 1926): 692, 694.

LANGSTON HUGHES: EVOLUTION OF THE POETIC PERSONA

RAYMOND SMITH

Langston Hughes's career as a poet began with the publication of "The Ne-gro Speaks of Rivers" in the June 1921, issue of *The Crisis*. By 1926, before the poet had reached the age of twenty-five, he had published his first volume of poems, *The Weary Blues*. Of this volume Alain Locke, the leading exponent of "The New Negro," announced that the black masses had found their voice: "A true people's poet has their balladry in his veins; and to me many of these poems seem based on rhythms as seasoned as folksongs and on moods as deep-seated as folk-ballads. Dunbar is supposed to have expressed the peasant heart of the people. But Dunbar was the showman of the Negro masses; here is their spokes-man."[1] With the publication of his second volume of poems, *Fine Clothes to the Jew* (1927), Hughes was being referred to as the "Poet Laureate of the American Negro." During a visit to Haiti in 1932, he was introduced to the noted Haitian poet Jacques Roumain, who referred to Hughes as "the greatest Negro poet who had ever come to honor Haitian soil."[2] When the noted Senegalese poet and exponent of African negritude, Léopold Senghor, was asked in a 1967 interview "In which poems of our, American, literature [do] you find evidence of Négritude?" his reply was "Ah, in Langston Hughes; Langston Hughes is the most spontaneous as a poet and the blackest in expression!"[3] Before his death in 1967, Hughes had published more than a dozen volumes of poetry, in addition to a great number of anthologies, translations, short stories, essays, novels, plays, and histories dealing with the spectrum of Afro-American life.

Of the major black writers who first made their appearance during the exciting period of the 1920s commonly referred to as "the Harlem Renaissance," Langston Hughes was the most prolific and the most successful. As the Harlem Renais-sance gave way to the Depression, Hughes determined to sustain his career as a poet by bringing his poetry to the people. At the suggestion of Mary McLeod Bethune, he launched his career as a public speaker by embarking on an extensive lecture tour of the South. As he wrote in his autobiography: "Propelled by the backwash of the 'Harlem Renaissance' of the early 'twenties, I had been drifting along pleasantly on the delightful rewards of my poems which seemed to please the fancy of kindhearted New York ladies with money to help young writers. . . . There was one other dilemma—how to make a living from *the kind of writing I wanted to do*. . . . I wanted to write seriously and as well as I knew how about the Negro people, and make *that* kind of writing earn me a *living*."[4] The Depression forced Hughes to reconsider the relation between his poetry and his people: "I wanted to continue to be a poet. Yet sometimes I wondered if I was barking up the wrong tree. I determined to find out by taking poetry, my poetry, to my people. After all, I wrote about Negroes, and primarily *for* Negroes. Would they have me? Did they want me?"[5]

Though much of the poetry Hughes was to write in the thirties and afterward was to differ markedly in terms of social content from the poetry he was producing in the twenties, a careful examination of his early work will reveal, in germinal form, the basic themes which were to preoccupy him throughout his career. These themes, pertaining to certain attitudes towards American and vis-à-vis his own blackness, had in fact been in the process of formulation since childhood. Hughes's evolution as a poet cannot be seen apart from the circumstances of his life which thrust him into the role of poet. Indeed, it was Hughes's awareness of what he personally regarded as a rather unique childhood which determined him in his drive to express, through poetry, the feelings of the black masses. Hughes's decision to embark on the lecture tour of Southern colleges in the 1930s is not to be taken as a rejection of his earlier work; it was merely a redirection of energies towards the purpose of reaching his audience. Hughes regarded his poetry written during the height of the Harlem Renaissance as a valid statement on Negro life in America. The heavily marked volumes of *The Weary Blues*, *Fine Clothes to the Jew*, and *The Dream Keeper* (published in 1932 but consisting largely of selections from the two earlier volumes) used by Hughes for poetry readings during the thirties and forties and now in the James Weldon Johnson Collection at Yale University, indicate that Hughes relied heavily on this early work and in no way rejected it as socially irrelevant.

Hughes's efforts to create a poetry that truly evoked the spirit of Black America involved a resolution of conflicts centering around the problem of identity. For Hughes, like W.E.B. Du Bois, saw the black man's situation in America as a question of dual consciousness. As Du Bois wrote in his *Souls of Black Folk* (1903): "It is a peculiar sensation, this double-consciousness, this sense of always looking at oneself through the eyes of others, of measuring one's soul by the tape of a world that looks on in amused contempt and pity. One ever feels his twoness,—an American, a Negro; two souls, two thoughts, two unreconciled strivings; two warring ideals in one body, whose dogged strength alone keeps it from being torn asunder."[6] Hughes was to speak of this same dilemma in his famous essay, published in 1927, concerning the problems of the black writer in America, "The Negro Artist and the Racial Mountain": "But this is the mountain standing in the way of any true Negro art in America—this urge within the race toward whiteness, the desire to pour racial individuality into the mold of American standardization, and to be as little Negro and as much American as possible."[7] In *The Weary Blues* (New York: Alfred Knopf, 1926), Hughes presented the problem of dual consciousness quite cleverly by placing two parenthetical statements of identity as the opening and closing poems, and titling them "Proem" and "Epilogue." Their opening lines suggest the polarities of consciousness between which the poet located his own persona: "I Am a Negro" and "I, Too, Sing America." Within each of these poems, Hughes suggests the interrelatedness of the two identities: the line "I am a Negro" is echoed as "I am the darker brother" in the closing poem. Between the American and the Negro, a third identity is suggested: that of the poet or "singer." It is this latter persona which Hughes had assumed for himself in his attempt to resolve the dilemma of divided consciousness. Thus, within the confines of these two poems revolving around identity, Hughes is presenting his poetry as a kind of salvation. If one looks more closely at Hughes's organization of poems in the book, one finds that his true opening and closing poems are concerned not with identity but with patterns of cyclical time. "The Weary Blues" (the first poem) is about a black piano man who plays deep into the night until at last he falls into sleep "like a rock or a man that's dead." The last poem, on the other hand, suggests a rebirth, an awakening, after the long night of weary blues: "We have tomorrow/ Bright before us/ Like a flame."[8] This pattern of cyclical time was adopted in the opening and closing poems of *Fine Clothes to the Jew*, which begins in sunset and ends in sunrise. Again, it is the blues singer (or poet) who recites the song: "Sun's a risin', / This is gonna be ma song."[9] The poet's song, then, is Hughes's resolution to the problem of double consciousness, of being an American and being black.

Hughes viewed the poet's role as one of responsibility: the poet must strive to maintain his objectivity and artistic distance, while at the same time speaking with passion through the medium he has selected for himself. In a speech given before the American Society of African Culture in 1960, Hughes urged his fellow black writers to cultivate objectivity in dealing with blackness: "Advice to Negro writers: Step *outside yourself,* then look back—and you will see how human, yet how beautiful and black you are. How very black—even when you're integrated."[10] In another part of the speech, Hughes stressed art over race: "In the great sense of the word, anytime, any place, good art transcends land, race, or nationality, and color drops away. If you are a good writer, in the end neither blackness nor whiteness makes a difference to readers." This philosophy of artistic distance was integral to Hughes's argument in the much earlier essay "The Negro Artist and the Racial Mountain," which became a rallying call to young black writers of the twenties concerned with reconciling artistic freedom with racial expression: "It is the duty of the younger Negro artist if he accepts any duties at all from outsiders, to change through the force of his art that old whispering 'I want to be white' hidden in the aspirations of his people, to 'Why should I want to be white? I am a Negro—and beautiful!'"[11] Hughes urged other black writers to express freely, without regard to the displeasure of whites *or* blacks, their "individual dark-skinned selves." "If white people are glad, we are glad. If they are not, it doesn't matter. We know we are beautiful. And ugly too. If colored people are pleased we are glad. If they are not, their displeasure doesn't matter either. We build temples for tomorrow, strong as we know how, and we stand on top of the mountain, free within ourselves" (p. 694). In this carefully thought-out manifesto, Hughes attempted to integrate the two facets of double consciousness (the American and the Negro) into a single vision—that of the poet. His poetry had reflected this idea from the beginning, when he published "The Negro Speaks of Rivers" at the age of nineteen. Arna Bontemps, in a retrospective glance at the Harlem Renaissance from the distance of almost fifty years, was referring to "The Negro Speaks of Rivers" when he commented: "And almost the first utterance of the revival struck a note that *disturbed* poetic tradition."[12] (Italics mine)

In Hughes's poetry, the central element of importance is the affirmation of blackness. Everything that distinguished Hughes's poetry from the white avant-garde poets of the twenties revolved around this important affirmation. Musical idioms, jazz rhythms, Hughes's special brand of "black-white" irony, and dialect were all dependent on the priority of black selfhood:

> I am a Negro
> Black as the night is black
> Black like the depths of my Africa.[13]

Like Walt Whitman, Hughes began his career as a poet confident of his power. Unlike Whitman, however, who celebrated particular self ("Walt Whitman, the Cosmos"), Hughes celebrated racial, rather than individual, self. Hughes tended to suppress the personal element in his poetry, appropriating the first person singular as the fitting epitome of universal human tendencies embodied in race. "The Negro Speaks of Rivers" seems almost mystical in comparison to Whitman's physicality:

> I've known rivers:
> Ancient, dusky rivers.
> My soul has grown deep like the rivers.[14]

One could venture too far in this comparison; of course, Whitman declared himself the poet of the soul as well as the body. Few would deny he had mystical tendencies.

In Hughes, however, there is little hint of the egotism in which Whitman so frequently indulged. Indeed, Hughes was hesitant to introduce the element of the personal into his poetry. In an essay published in the journal *Phylon* in 1947 on his "adventures" as a social poet, Hughes remarked that his "earliest poems were social poems in that they were about people's problems—whole groups of people's problems—rather than my own personal difficulties."[15] Hughes's autobiographical account of the writing of "The Negro Speaks of Rivers" confirms this point, and sheds light on the process by which Hughes transformed personal experiences into archetypal racial memories. The poem had evolved out of personal difficulties with his father, who had emigrated to Mexico when Langston was a child, and had not seen his son in over a decade. Hughes had been summoned unexpectedly by his father to join him in the summer of 1919, hoping to persuade the son to enter into the business world. The elder Hughes felt nothing but contempt for the country and the race he had left behind. The following conversation, recorded in Hughes's autobiography *The Big Sea*, suggests the irreconcilable differences between the two:

"What do you want to be?"
"I don't know. But I think a writer."
"A writer?" my father said. "A writer? Do you think they make money?"
. . . .
". . . Learn something you can make a living from anywhere in the world, in Europe or South America, and don't stay in the States, where you have to live like a nigger with niggers."
"But I like Negroes," I said.[16]

The following summer, on a train trip to Mexico, Hughes's dread of the eventual confrontation with his father over his future vocation led to the writing of the poem: "All day on the train I had been thinking about my father, and his strange dislike of his own people. I didn't understand it, because I was Negro, and I liked Negroes very much." Despite Hughes's severe emotional state, the poem itself displays little hint of the personal anxiety that led to its creation.

Perhaps the closest Hughes ever came to incorporating his personal anxiety into a poem was his "As I Grew Older," published initially in 1925, and later included in *The Weary Blues*. The poem is almost reduced to abstractions; it is a landscape of nightmare, a bleak and existential examination of blackness. The poet begins by recalling his "dream," once "bright like a sun," but now only a memory. A wall which separates the poet from his dream suddenly appears, causing him severe anxiety. It is at this point that the poet is thrust back upon himself and forced to seek an explanation for his dilemma:

Shadow.
I am black.

These two lines appearing at the center of the poem provide the key to his despair and to his salvation. As he begins to realize that his blackness is the cause of his being separated from his dream, he simultaneously realizes that blackness is central to his ontology. It is as much a physical reality as it is a metaphysical state of mind. In order for the dream to be restored, the spiritual and the physical blackness must be reintegrated. As the poet examines his hands, which are black, he discovers the source of his regeneration as a full person:

> My hands!
> My dark hands!
> Break through the wall!
> Find my dream!
> Help me to shatter this darkness,
> To smash this night,
> To break this shadow
> Into a thousand lights of sun,
> Into a thousand whirling dreams
> Of sun![18]

In order for the poet to transcend his temporal despair, he must accept the condition of his blackness completely and unequivocally. The poem thus ends, not in despair, but rather in a quest for self-liberation, dependent on the affirmation "I am black!"

The words had been used much earlier by another poet, W.E.B. Du Bois, far better known as the founder of the NAACP, editor of *The Crisis*, and lifelong champion of black pride. His poem "The Song of the Smoke," published in the magazine *Horizon* in 1899, opened with the words:

> I am the smoke king,
> I am black.

Later in the poem, Du Bois wrote these ringing lines:

> I will be black as blackness can,
> The blacker the mantle the mightier the man,
> My purpl'ing midnights no day may ban.
>
> I am carving God in night,
> I am painting hell in white.
> I am the smoke king.
> I am black.[19]

The poem, published when Hughes was five years old, prefigures the point in time, fifteen years later, when the careers of the two—Du Bois and Hughes—would converge, with the publication of Hughes's poem "The Negro Speaks of Rivers," in Du Bois's journal *The Crisis*, with the poem's dedication also going to Du Bois.

This early connection between Hughes and Du Bois is important, for it was Du Bois who was calling for a renaissance of black culture as early as 1913, in an essay on "The Negro in Literature and Art": "Never in the world has a richer mass of material been accumulated by a people than that which the Negroes possess today and are becoming conscious of. Slowly but surely they are developing artists of technic who will be able to use this material."[20] By 1920, Du Bois was actually using the word "renaissance" in referring to the new awakening of black creativity in the arts: "A renaissance of Negro literature is due; the material about us in the strange, heartrending race tangle is rich beyond dream and only we can tell the tale and sing the song from the heart."[21] This editorial in *The Crisis*, almost certainly read by Hughes, must have encouraged him to submit the poem for publication. In his autobiography, Hughes credited Du Bois and *The Crisis* for publishing his first poems and thus giving his literary career its first official boost: "For the next few years my poems appeared often (and solely) in *The Crisis*. And to that magazine, certainly, I owe my literary beginnings, insofar as publication is concerned."[22]

While Hughes certainly owed Du Bois a debt of gratitude for his official entrance upon the literary scene, it seems that Hughes's very special sensitivity as a budding young poet developed organically from his experiences as child. Though he did credit Dunbar and Sandburg among his influences, these literary mentors pale in light of what Hughes had to say about his method of poem-writing: "Generally, the first two or three lines come to me from something I'm thinking about, or looking at, or doing, and the rest of the poem (if there is to be a poem) flows from those first few lines, usually right away" (p. 56). This spontaneity of approach worked both for and against Hughes. Many of his poems, written in hasty response to some event reported in yesterday's newspaper, for example, have badly dated. The spontaneity that resulted in his best poetry came from the depths of his own experiences as a black man in America, though these personal experiences often were disguised as archetypal ones.

The tension between his awareness of growing up black and his acceptance of the "dream" of America, however tenuously defined, provided the dynamic for his poetry. From an early age, Hughes developed the distinction between the social versus the physical implications of black identity in America: "You see, unfortunately, I am not black. There are lots of different kinds of blood in our family. But here in the United States, the word 'Negro' is used to mean anyone who has *any* Negro blood at all in his veins. In Africa, the word is more pure. It means *all* Negro, therefore *black*" (p. 11). During a trip to Africa as a merchant seaman in 1922, he discovered that the Africans who "looked at me . . . would not believe I was a Negro" (p. 11). The semantic confusion was of American origin. Whatever the semantic distinctions, Hughes desired to be accepted as Negro by the Africans, and was disappointed with their reaction to him.

Hughes's middle-American background (he grew up in Lawrence, Kansas) sheltered him from some of the more blatant forms of racial prejudice toward Negroes in other regions of the country. When he lived in Topeka, he attended a white school, his mother having successfully challenged the school board to have him admitted. Most of his teachers were pleasant, but there was one "who sometimes used to make remarks about my being colored. And after such remarks, occasionally the kids would grab stones and tin cans out of the alley and chase me home" (p. 14). For a while he lived with his maternal grandmother, from whom he heard "beautiful stories about people who wanted to make the Negroes free, and how her father had had apprenticed to him many slaves . . . so that they could work out their freedom. . . . Through my grandmother's stories always life moved, moved heroically toward an end. . . . Something about my grandmother's stories . . . taught me the uselessness of crying about anything" (p. 17). Hughes's poem "Aunt Sue's Stories," published in *The Crisis* in July of 1921, furnishes an example of how Hughes transformed such memories into poetry. His childhood was not a happy one in Lawrence, as he related in his autobiography, and he turned to books for solace (p. 16). Parallels between his childhood experiences and later poems abound. Many of his poems focused on unhappy or wrongly treated children, for whom the American dream had no relevance. This empathy with wronged children had its origins in Hughes's own unhappiness as a child.

Many of his poems about black laborers originated out of his difficulties in finding work while in school. A job he had in a hotel, cleaning toilets and spitoons, while only in the seventh grade, was to result in one of his more well-known poems, "Brass Spitoons," included in his second volume of poetry, *Fine Clothes to the Jew* (1927). Four decades after a local theatre owner put up a sign "NO COLORED ADMITTED" in Lawrence, Kansas, Hughes would recall the event in *ASK YOUR MAMA*:

> IN THE QUARTER OF THE NEGROES
> WHERE THE RAILROAD AND THE RIVER
> HAVE DOORS THAT FACE EACH WAY
> AND THE ENTRANCE TO THE MOVIE'S
> UP AN ALLEY UP THE SIDE[23]

A beating administered by a group of white toughs in Chicago the summer before the Chicago riots would be transformed into "The White Ones" seven years later:

> I do not hate you,
> For your faces are beautiful, too.
> I do not hate you,
> Your faces are whirling lights of loveliness
>   and splendor, too.
> Yet why do you torture me,
> O, white strong ones.
> Why do you torture me?[24]

These parallels between Hughes's early life and his later poetry indicate that he had formulated certain attitudes towards his race and towards white America before he had ever considered the idea of becoming a poet.

It was only by accident that he became a poet. He was elected to the position of class poet at Cleveland's Central High because, as he humorously recalled, he was a Negro, and Negroes were supposed to have "rhythm." "In America most white people think, of course, that *all* Negroes can sing and dance, and have a sense of rhythm. So my classmates, knowing that a poem had to have rhythm, elected me unanimously—thinking, no doubt, that I had some, being a Negro. . . . It had never occurred to me to be a poet before, or indeed a writer of any kind."[25] Thus the role of poet was thrust upon Hughes by accident, or perhaps, by design, because he was Negro in a white society. It was the social implications of his blackness, however, that fitted him for the role. The incidents of his childhood and youth had marked Langston Hughes as a black man, and his poetry would affirm his acceptance of the mission, to be a spokesman for the black masses.

At the same time, Hughes could not deny the double nature, the dual-consciousness of being an American as well as a black. The very fact that he had been chosen by his classmates as class poet *because* he was Negro only accentuated his separateness from them. By the same token, he had never been completely exposed to the full brunt of prejudice, American-style, during his youth. Up until the time of his Southern lecture tour of 1931, his acquaintance with Southern mores had been merely peripheral. Indeed, he often began these programs by explaining how truly "American" his upbringing had been: "I began my programs by telling where I was born in Missouri, that I grew up in Kansas in the geographical heart of the country, and was, therefore very American."[26] His audiences, which consisted largely of Southern Negroes, must have found his initial declaration of Americanism rather disorienting. As Hughes himself explained in his autobiography, this firsthand encounter with racial prejudice in the South provided an introduction to an important aspect of racial heritage to which he had never been fully exposed: "I found a great social and cultural gulf between the races in the South, astonishing to one who, like myself, from the North, had never known such uncompromising prejudices."[27]

In a poem published in *The Crisis* in 1922, Hughes outlined his ambivalence towards the region in rather chilling imagery:

> The child-minded South
> Scratching in the dead fire's ashes
> For a Negro's bones.

He indicated in the poem's conclusion that the South had a strong attraction, but that he was more comfortable in resisting its allure:

> And I, who am black, would love her
> But she spits in my face
> And I, who am black,
> Would give her many rare gifts
> But she turns her back upon me.[28]

In the same year that Hughes published "The South," Jean Toomer published *Cane*. One of the poems in *Cane*, "Georgia Dusk," evoked similar imagery:

> A feast of moon and men and barking hounds,
> An orgy for some genius of the South
> With blood-hot eyes and cane-lipped scented mouth,
> Surprised in making folk-songs from soul sounds.[29]

Where Toomer's *Cane* was the product of direct experience (a six-month sojourn in Georgia as a rural schoolteacher), Hughes's South was an imaginatively evoked nightmare. The last lines of Hughes's poem suggest that he was not yet ready to embrace the Southern experience as Toomer had done. Hughes's Gothic South was a far cry from Toomer's seductive lines in "Carma":

> Wind is in the cane. Come along.
> Cane leaves swaying, rusty with talk,
> Scratching choruses above the guinea's squawk,
> Wind is in the cane. Come along.[30]

If Hughes feared the direct Southern confrontation during the twenties, he found much to admire in those Southern blacks who came to settle in the teeming cities of the North, and from them he derived material for his poetry. In seeking communal identity through them, Hughes overemphasized the exotic, as this passage from *The Big Sea* indicates: "1 never tired of hearing them talk, listening to the thunderclaps of their laughter, to their troubles, to their discussions of the war and the men who had gone to Europe from the Jim Crow South. . . . They seemed to me like the gayest and the bravest people possible—these Negroes from the Southern ghettoes—facing tremendous odds, working and laughing and trying to get somewhere in the world" (pp. 54–55). The passage suggests the attitude of a sympathetic observer rather than that of an engaged participant. In some ways, Hughes's attitude towards Southern Negroes was directly counter to his father's. According to Langston, the elder Hughes "hated Negroes. I think he hated himself, too, for being a Negro. He disliked all of his family because they were Negroes and remained in the United States" (p. 40). Hughes, on the other hand, proudly affirmed his racial heritage. Where his father rejected both race and country, Hughes could reject neither.

At the end of his lecture programs in the South, Hughes would recite his poem "I, Too, Sing America." As often as he invoked this poem, he would be reaffirming his faith in the American dream. Some of Hughes's earliest poems reveal an almost childlike faith in the American ideal, as in the opening lines of "America," first published in 1925:

> America is seeking the stars,
> America is seeking tomorrow.
> You are America.
> I am America
> America—the dream,
> America—the vision.
> America—the star-seeking I.

The same poem affirmed the unity of black and white America:

> You of the blue eyes
> And the blond hair,
> I of the dark eyes
> And the crinkly hair,
> You and I
> Offering hands . . . [31]

This affirmation of racial unity had a direct relation to Hughes's experience with racial integration at Cleveland's Central High, where he was often elected to important class positions because of his acceptability to various white ethnic factions: "Since it was during the war, and Americanism was being stressed, many of our students, including myself, were then called down to the principal's office and questioned about our belief in Americanism. . . . After that, the principal organized an Americanism Club in our school, and . . . I was elected President" (*The Big Sea*, p. 31). While this experience might serve to strengthen his faith in an ideal America, it also, paradoxically, reinforced his sense of separateness as a Negro. His race was clearly an advantage in terms of popularity among his peers; still, it was his color which marked him as different.

At the same time, Hughes's experience in racial integration set him apart from the experience of those Negroes from the South whose lifestyle he so admired. Hughes must have realized that his experience vis-à-vis that of most black Americans was rather unique. Though he claimed at times to have had a typical Negro upbringing, it was nevertheless different, as he pointed out in this passage from *The Big Sea*: "Mine was not a typical Negro family. My grandmother never took in washing or worked in service or went to church. She had lived in Oberlin and spoke perfect English, without a trace of dialect. She looked like an Indian. My mother was a newspaper woman and a stenographer then. My father lived in Mexico City. My grandfather had been a congressman" (p. 303). In addition, Hughes harbored no grudges against white society: "I learned early in life not to hate *all* white people. And ever since, it has seemed to me that *most* people are generally good, in every race and in every country where I have been" (p. 14).

Hughes often sought to dispel the distinction between American and Negro by affirming his nationality in no uncertain terms. The following incident from his autobiography illustrates this point. He had been teaching English to Mexicans during his final summer in Mexico with his father. The teacher who was to replace him was a white American woman who found it incredible that a Negro could be capable of teaching anything:

> When she was introduced to me, her mouth fell open, and she said: "Why, Ah-Ah thought you was an American."
> I said: "I am American!"
> She said: "Oh, Ah mean a white American." Her voice had a Southern drawl.
> I grinned. (p. 78)

Another incident from his autobiography concerns his refusal to deny his race. On the return trip to the United States from Mexico after his first summer there, Hughes attempted to purchase an ice cream soda in St. Louis. The following exchange took place:

> The clerk said: "Are you a Mexican or a Negro?"
> I said: "Why?"
> "Because if you're a Mexican, I'll serve you," he said. "If you're colored, I won't."
> "I'm colored," I replied. The clerk turned to wait on someone else. I knew I was home in the U. S. A. (p. 51).

These incidents were to have their counterparts in his poetry, where he could affirm with equal assurance his two credos of identity: "I am a Negro" and "I, Too, Sing America." But while affirming these polar commitments, Hughes was alienated from both of them. As a black man, he was aware that his race had never been granted full participation in the American dream. His exposure to the possibilities of that dream, however, through his experience with racial integration, and his relative innocence (this was to disappear, of course) in matters of Southern mores, would distinguish his circumstances from the lot of the black masses, with whom he sought to identify to the extent of becoming their spokesman. This peculiar set of conditions allowed Hughes to assume a degree of sophistication in racial matters quite unusual among his contemporaries, white or black. This sophistication, coupled with his insistence on maintaining the necessary aesthetic distance of the artist, provided the stimulus for his poetry and endowed the poet with a sense of mission. He was absolutely confident of his self-imposed mission as a poet of the black masses. His familiarity with white Bohemian intellectual circles in New York during the twenties provided him with the additional stimulus of communicating his message across racial lines. Thus two kinds of poetry emerged in the twenties: the black vernacular poetry, utilizing dialect, jazz talk, and everyday subject matter; and "message" poetry, which concentrated on the position of the black man in white America. *The Weary Blues*, Hughes's first book, contained much of this message poetry, besides some experiments in jazz poetry ("The Cat and The Saxophone," "Blues Fantasy," "Negro Dancers"), and additional non-racial lyrics. The second book, *Fine Clothes to the Jew*, concentrated almost entirely on the vernacular subject matter, and contained many poems written in blues dialect. These two tendencies in Hughes's early work were to predominate throughout his career.

Shakespeare in Harlem (1942), for example, may be considered a sequel to *Fine Clothes*, while *Montage of a Dream Deferred* (1951) integrated the vernacular subject matter with the thematic concerns introduced in *The Weary Blues*. *Montage*, along with *ASK YOUR MAMA* (1961), will probably remain Hughes's most important achievements in poetry since his work of the twenties. *ASK YOUR MAMA*, permeated with humor, irony, and exciting imagery, contains echoes of "The Negro Speaks of Rivers," "As I Grew Older," and "The Cat and the Saxophone." As in these earlier poems, Hughes transforms personal experiences and observations into distillations of the Black American condition.

Hughes wrote in his autobiography: "My best poems were all written when I felt the worst. When I was happy, I didn't write anything" (p. 54). When he first began writing poetry, he felt his lyrics were too personal to reveal to others: "Poems came to me now spontaneously, from somewhere inside. . . . I put the poems down quickly on anything I had a hand when they came into my head, and later I copied them into a notebook. But I began to be afraid to show my poems to anybody, because they had become very serious and very much a part of me. And I was afraid other people might not like them or understand them" (p. 34). These two statements regarding his poetry suggest deep underlying emotional tensions as being the source of his creativity. And yet the personal element in Hughes's poetry is almost entirely submerged beneath the persona of the "Negro Poet Laureate." If, as Hughes suggested, personal unhappiness was the cornerstone of his best work, it then follows that, in order to maintain the singleness of purpose and devotion to his art, he would be required to sacrifice some degree of emotional stability. Thus poetry became a kind of therapy, masking deeper emotional tensions. We know from his autobiography that Hughes experienced two severe emotional breakdowns. The first one had to do with a break with his father over the course of his vocation; the second followed upon a break with his wealthy white patroness in the late twenties over the kind of poetry he was writing. Both of these emotional traumas were directly related to his decision to become a poet of his people.

The persona of the poet was the role Hughes adopted in his very first published poem, as *the Negro* in "The Negro Speaks of Rivers." It was a persona to which he would remain faithful throughout his lengthy career. The link between his personal experiences and his poetry has been suggested in this paper. It cannot be defined because it seems clear that Hughes suppressed the more frightening excursions into his own personal void. Poetry was an outlet as well as a salvation. Only occasionally, as in the poem "As I Grow Older," does Hughes provide a window upon his inner anxieties, and even in this poem the real root of these anxieties is hidden, and the poem becomes an allegory of the black man's alienation in white America. Hughes's early attempts in the twenties to fill the role of Poet Laureate of the Negro led him to create a body of work that was organic in nature. The traditional literary sources of inspiration were for the most part bypassed. The source of his poetry was to be found in the anonymous, unheard black masses: their rhythms, their dialect, their life styles. Hughes sought to incorporate this untapped resource of black folk language into a new kind of poetry. His personal experiences, as related in his autobiography, combined with this folk material to provide thematic dimension to his work. The basic themes regarding the American dream and its possibilities for the black man were always present in his poetry. The tension between the unrealized dream and the realities of the black experience in America provided the dynamic. This tension between material and theme laid the groundwork for the irony which characterized Hughes's work at its best.

NOTES

1. Review of "The Weary Blues," *Palms* 4.1 (Oct. 1926): 25.

2. Langston Hughes, *I Wonder As I Wander* (1956; rpt. New York: Hill & Wang, 1964), p. 31.

3. Quoted in Arthur P. Davis, "Langston Hughes: Cool Poet," in *Langston Hughes: Black Genius: A Critical Evaluation*, ed. Therman B. O'Daniel (New York: William Morrow, 1971), p. 25.

4. *I Wonder As I Wander*, pp. 4–5.

5. *I Wonder As I Wander*, pp. 41–42.

6. *The Souls of Black Folk* (1903; rpt. Greenwich, CT: Fawcett, 1961), pp. 16–17.

7. *Nation* 122 (23 June 1926): 692.

8. *The Weary Blues*, p. 109.

9. Langston Hughes, *Fine Clothes to the Jew* (New York: Knopf, 1927), pp. 17–89.

10. "Writers: Black and White," in *The American Negro Writer and his Roots* (New York: American Society of African Culture, 1960), p. 44.

11. "Negro Artist and Racial Mountain," p. 694.

12. "Negro Poets, Then and Now," in *Black Expression: Essays by and About Black Americans in the Creative Arts*, ed. Addison Gayle, Jr. (New York: Weybright & Talley, 1969), p. 83.

13. *The Weary Blues*, p. 108.

14. *The Weary Blues*, p. 22.

15. "My Adventures as a Social Poet," *Phylon* 8 (Fall 1947): 205.

16. *The Big Sea* (1940; reprint, New York: Hill & Wang, 1963), pp. 61–62.

17. *The Big Sea*, p. 54.

18. *The Weary Blues*, pp. 55–56.

19. W.E.B. Du Bois, "The Song of the Smoke," (1899; rpt. in *Dark Symphony: Negro Literature In America*, ed. James A. Emanuel and Theodore L. Gross [New York: Free Press, 1968]), p. 44.

20. *The Seventh Son: The Thought and Writings of W.E.B. Du Bois*, ed. Julius Lester (New York: Random House, 1971), 1:451.

21. *The Emerging Thought of W.E.B. Du Bois: Essays and Editorials from The Crisis*, ed. Henry Lee Moon (New York: Simon & Schuster, 1972), p. 354.

22. *The Big Sea*, p. 72. Subsequent references to *The Big Sea* will appear parenthetically in the text.

23. Langston Hughes, *ASK YOUR MAMA: 12 MOODS FOR JAZZ* (New York: Knopf, 1961), p. 5.

24. *The Weary Blues*, p. 106.

25. *The Big Sea*, p. 24.

26. *I Wonder As I Wander*, p. 57.

27. *I Wonder As I Wander*, p. 52.

28. *The Weary Blues*, p. 54

29. *Cane* (1923; rpt. New York: University Place Press, 1967), p. 22.

30. *Cane*, p. 16.

31. "America," *Opportunity* 3 (June 1925): 175.

A FISHER OF BLACK LIFE:
SHORT STORIES BY RUDOLPH FISHER

MARGARET PERRY

It is not surprising that little of the work done in the short story form by Rudolph Fisher (1897–1934) is known; there has never been a collection of all his short stories,[1] and this hampers the scholar in pursuit of a unified view of Fisher's themes and style. In the early part of our century, short stories written by black authors had little appeal to the primary reading public, which was white; Fisher seems to have been the exception to this, however. Although his stories were published frequently in Negro publications, he also appeared in non-Negro publications such as *Atlantic Monthly* and *McClure's*, and thus was able to reach a wider audience of short-story readers. Despite this, little space is devoted to Fisher in critical histories of the American short story. Indeed, the central metaphor of Black Invisibility can be said to have been operating among critics of the short story in America. In an effort to rectify this neglect, the present article explores the stories of Rudolph Fisher, both published and unpublished, and places them within the context of the times in which he lived. The precise time in history, as well as the place—Harlem, its spirit—were significant elements in Fisher's fiction; indeed, they were perhaps the reasons he felt impelled to capture his world within the strictures of the short-story form. Full of wit, irony, humor, and some acerbity, Fisher has enriched the world of literature in a medium Frank O'Connor has called our "national art form."[2]

Rudolph Fisher, born in Washington, D.C., on 9 May 1897, was brought up mainly in Providence, Rhode Island, where he completed his studies at Classical High School in 1915 with high honors. In 1915 Fisher matriculated at Brown University, majoring in English and biology. Following graduation, Fisher remained at Brown through the next academic year in order to get his M.A., then attended Howard University Medical School, where he graduated with highest honors in 1924. Beginning private medical practice in 1927, he later specialized in roentgenology and opened an X-ray laboratory. Fisher died on 26 December 1934, after his third operation for an intestinal ailment.

Fisher's first published story, "City of Refuge," was written while he was still in medical school, and appeared in *Atlantic Monthly* during February 1925. In addition to unpublished stories, Fisher wrote two plays, "The Vici Kid" and "Golden Slippers," neither of which was ever published or produced. According to his sister, the late Pearl M. Fisher: "like most writers, Dr. Fisher's ambition was to write the great Negro novel."[3] Though Fisher did publish two novels—his second one, *The Conjure Man Dies*, was the first detective novel by a Black American—it is through his short stories that he presented the widest view of Black American life in Harlem. In a radio interview, Fisher stated the following: "Harlem is the epitome of American Negro life . . . I intend to write whatever interests me. But if I should be fortunate enough to become known as Harlem's interpreter, I should be very happy."[4]

Harlem's interpreter—this was his expressed desire, and this was the goal he achieved through all of his fiction, as well as in his articles. The reading public responded to Fisher's role as a reflector of the life in the nation's Black capital during the 1920s, for one newspaperman wrote: "De Maupassant used Paris for his chess-board, while Fisher moves his dusky pawns over the field of Negro Harlem, a location quite as interesting as 'dear Paree.'"[5] At last the reading public would be entertained with literature that reflected the informing spirit of the Afro-American race, the cultural *temenos* sustaining the unique character of Black life from country to town to city, in particular, Harlem. The model of life, the white life, was to be just another version of real life rather than the version that would overpower the Black reality of living. Sometimes, of course, the evil or injustice evolving from what whites *could impose* upon blacks is treated with satiric strokes by Fisher, such as in "High Yaller." Still, Fisher seems, in his portraits of life in Harlem, to have realized what Octavio Paz observed when writing about the majority and minority in Mexico: "Without otherness there is no oneness."[6] So Fisher was, indeed, "Harlem's interpreter."

Fisher's fascination with Harlem came with the times, and his only regrets seemed to be the effects of white incursion into Harlem's places of entertainment. He hoped that the whites would also venture to explore more than this obvious part of Harlem and learn to understand Black life in general: "Maybe," he wrote, "they are at least learning to speak our language."[7] Not really—but as long as the writings of Rudolph Fisher exist, everyone, Black and white, can learn to enjoy the sights and sounds of Negro Harlem during the 1920s, the city that King Solomon Gillis first viewed with wide-eyed joy and fascination by saying: "Done died an' woke up in Heaven." It was a little of everything, and Fisher's canvases faithfully paint the people and places in its mosaic of dark and light hues.

The short stories of Rudolph Fisher have a sense of literary history behind them, for he ploughed the same fields as the masters of this art, such as Poe, Gogol, and James. There are times, indeed, when Fisher gives the impression that he went from studying the nineteenth-century writers directly to his desk to write, ignoring practitioners of the art who were his own contemporaries. In an earlier review of Fisher's work I noted that "Both stories ['City of Refuge' and 'Miss Cynthie'] illustrate Fisher's ability to transform life into art through control of characterization, plot, and diction, and insistence on a single effect at the story's conclusion."[8] Fisher was a traditionalist in form, then; but he was also one in point of view, in his themes, and in the values he stressed through the major characters he created. One might also venture to say that Fisher often wrote in the mode of dramatic comedies, eschewing tragedy in any case, even in the stories that end unhappily.

Fisher writes comedy in the classical sense, as Gilbert Murray states in *The Classical Tradition in Poetry*, comedy that has at its core "a union of lovers." This re-creation of acts and emotions, mimesis, moves from conflict to resolution within the very special milieu of Black Harlem. The overall impression one gets of Fisher's use of the short story form is that he engages the reader in a positive, comic view of life which arises from the lyric impulse to sing mainly about triumph, about the possibility of being saved or renewed. Once again, to quote Murray: "Tragedies end in death. Comedies end in marriage."[9] Murray is not referring to marriage as a legal procedure, but is alluding to the joy that issues from a harmonious end to the strife and conflict within the imaginative work. It seems he is seeking not only the melody but also the harmony, as Shelley wrote in his famous *Defence of Poetry*. One is always conscious of an ordered universe in Fisher's world; he writes about the ruptures that are brought on by disharmony, the disjointedness that must be replaced at the denouement by order.

There are important non-literary elements in Fisher's stories that should also be noted, because he emphasizes them consistently. He was a satirist and social historian through the medium of the short story; thus, we have an accurate portrait of Harlem during the 1920s, whether or not one believes this is the proper function of imaginative literature. Fisher portrays the life of the "rats" and the "dickties" as well as the criminal element and the ordinary wage-earner. We see how life is played out in the cabaret, at rent parties, and we witness the city version of religion as it struggles to recapture the joy and spontaneity of the "down home" mode of expression. As a critic of the city—the city as duper, the city as destroyer of the immigrated Black—Fisher's stories act out the ritual of ruin in which so many men and women were immolated. For some, the family unit is disrupted, as in "The Promised Land" or in "The South Lingers On"; while others, seeking safety and freedom, like King Solomon Gillis in "City of Refuge," find that exploitation, confinement and racism are not limited to the South. In the latter story, Gillis encounters a new sort of racism, explored in several other

Fisher stories—the prejudice of black against black, particularly Afro-American versus British West Indian.

The relationship, or more aptly, the animosity, between the American Black and the West Indian Black is portrayed sharply in several of Fisher's stories; indeed, this topic is the major element of conflict in "Ringtail." Sociologically, there were several reasons for this real and sometimes imagined dislike among the two groups: to many American blacks it seems that the West Indians were arrogant about their "British" background—and many West Indians, like Cyril Sebastian Best in "Ringtail," lorded this so-called advantage over American Blacks. Then, it did appear that West Indians who immigrated to the United States fared better economically and in a shorter length of time. As one character in "Ringtail" says: " . . . they stick too close together an' get ahead too fast. They put it all over us in too many ways. . . . Same as ofays an' Jews."[10]

There was also the movement of "Back to Africa," carried on with parade and pomp, electrifying the masses with a thesis none of them wanted in reality. Going back to Africa and "chasing monkeys" wasn't the dream of American Blacks; so the detractors had a ready-made phrase to coin about Marcus Garvey, leader and symbol of this abortive movement. His fellow-West Indians fell prey to the same expression and it is still used privately to this day by many American blacks (and probably less privately in non-bourgeois society).

There are strains of satire, light in most cases, lurking among Fisher's descriptions of life in Harlem. The picture of Cyril Sebastian Best ("Ringtail") is satirical, particularly at the opening when he is parading in his finery. Fisher mocks the concerns of the "dickties" for the false trappings of bourgeois habits, such as the So-and-So's "supper dansant" described in "Fire by Night." He mocks the fragility of the dickties further in this story when, at the height of a brawl at the "dansant," the women scurry to save their fur coats from invading pool-hall scavengers: "girls who had saved for two years to buy seal wraps; wives who had wheedled for months to get a caracal like Mrs. Jones; women who had undertaken payment for their Persian lambs by installments." There is the hypocrisy of the religious exposed in "The Backslider," and even a hint of satire in the minor appearance of the Goldman brothers in "Miss Cynthie."

Imagery of a world of confinement and darkness—the black world on earth, not Hell (although that is one point, i.e., that Harlem frequently is Hell)— characterizes Fisher's fictional domain. Sometimes there is no value judgment implied in the painting he presents, e.g., "The pavement flashed like a river in the sun" ("Ringtail"); but most often his images and figurative language are undergirded by Fisher principles and points of view. A large proportion of Fisher's imagery derives from his use of similes and metaphors such as "the thoughts that gathered and throbbed like an abscess were suddenly incised" ("High Yaller"); the "roadster . . . snorted impatiently" ("Dust"); "A young bronze giant" ("Guardian"); or, the "ambulance gong was like receding derisive laughter" ("Ringtail"). In a comprehensive sense, the image we have of Harlem is one of "a stage upon which one looked as from an upper box" ("Guardian"). Fisher places Harlem in

an open-air theatre so the reader can view the high and the low, the very fine
Seventh Avenue as well as Lenox Avenue, "the boulevard of the unperfumed."
In painting scenes with colors as well as with sound, Fisher gives the reader
what Mammy, in "The Promised Land," sees from her window: "a screen upon
which flashed a motion picture oddly alive and colorful." Often Fisher invests
inanimate objects with human traits (e.g., the "keyboard grinned evilly"—"Guardian") to indicate a point of view, the author's moral stance. The Blacks, frequently living in "hencoops," the white downtown in "kingly dwellings," the
good and the bad, common and uncommon, the city itself, all enter upon a stage
set up by Fisher and perform their roles in a pageant of contrasts and disharmo-
nies that will eventually end in an orderly resolution. It is difficult to categorize
Fisher's treatment of the rent party phenomenon, whether it is sadness or satire
when he writes (in "The Promised Land"), "You provide music, your friends
provide advertisement, and your guests, by paying admission, provide what
your resources lack." Certainly, Fisher saw that the underlying reason for this
Northeastern version of the "shindig" was in most instances exploitation, because people were having to pay more than a fair price for apartments. In any
case, Fisher was unable to avoid the satiric touch from time to time as a technique for pointing out the meaninglessness of certain habits and concerns in the
Black community.

In highlighting the special qualities that composed life in Harlem at every
stratum, Fisher dramatically portrayed the obsession of blacks with their color.
He turned this self-absorption into an artistic mode with moral as well as social
implications. It has been noted by another critic that Fisher uses color to differentiate between good and bad characters, that "the lighter the skin color the
lower the moral character of the individual." This differentiation is made in several of Fisher's stories, notably "Blades of Steel" and "High Yaller." Fisher offers
readers a gallery of "good" guys and "bad" ones, most often designated by skin
color—dark equaling good and yellow for the low-down cad. Consider for example, the following characters:

"His coarse granular skin was dingy yellow and scarred . . ." ("Fire by
Night");

"Eight-ball . . . was as dark as it is possible for skin to be, smooth and clean
as an infant's . . . " ("Blades of Steel");

"Bus Williams' jolly round brown face beamed down on the crowd . . . "
("Common Meter").

In between the absolute dark and light we have women who are "amber"
("Common Meter"), or "red-brown" ("Guardian of the Law"), or "golden-skinned"
("Miss Cynthie"); the women, in any case, are never black. The darkest woman
of importance in his short stories is Effie Wright in "Blades of Steel," who is

described as having an "almost luminous dark complexion called 'sealskin brown.'" With this obvious attention to color, Fisher reflects the self-consciousness of the decade toward the various shades of 'Blackness.'

It cannot be said that Fisher accomplished every goal he attempted in his short story writing, for there are some structural and linguistic imperfections that do not go undetected. Fisher, with his balanced and sane approach to the difficulties in life, wanted to demonstrate the effects of illusion on individuals. People continually misread the motives of self and other, and thus the seeds for conflict are scattered. Here we have the necessary elements for a good story— action, reaction, and resolution. If the exposition complements these elements, then the production proceeds as it should to a successful completion. This does not always occur, however, in Fisher's stories; there are some weaknesses that are apparent.

One weakness, which appears to derive from Fisher's occasional desire to preach or educate, is that of author intrusion. In "Dust," which is one of his least effective stories, he succumbed to the urge to teach rather than to entertain; he did not move toward the effect he wanted, he commenced with it and rode it to death.

Adopting the role of the totally omniscient author, of course, allowed Fisher to write as he pleased. Still, he was good enough as a short-story writer to understand the necessity of removing unneeded words, the necessity of keeping the movement "tight," yet, more than once, he placed himself as writer into the middle of a story.

Another weakness was a general tendency to write by formula, making a Fisher situation and/or ending predictable, and sometimes too slick or facile. As one critic has written about "Common Meter": "To the cynical modern reader, the outcome is possible only in a fairy tale. The winner is the most noble and upright character, the jazz musician who prizes rhythm above all else and the man whose skin is darkest."[11] Of course, this conforms to Fisher's basic comic style, which anticipates the "happy ending."

Generally, however, Fisher goes swiftly to the heart of his story—moves the reader into the conflict, clearly points to the cast of characters and their features, and concludes the story tidily—leaving no doubt in the mind of the reader concerning the meaning of the tale. A certain stylistic stiffness in Fisher's expository mode sometimes impedes the smooth movement of the story, but this is an authentic feature of his writing. His use of idiomatic Harlem language is another characteristic feature, a strength in terms of authenticity, but also another weakness if taken as it has been by one critic in the following observation: "his use of the Negro idiom, Harlemese, (is) . . . self-conscious."[12]

Despite these weaknesses, Fisher was successful in portraying his fellow black Americans from all strata of Negro life, from the "rats" to the "dickties," and he achieved this goal to a greater degree than any other writer of this period. The last of Fisher's short stories to be published in his lifetime, "Miss Cynthie," leads one to postulate that he was moving closer to the real art of short fiction writing. As Robert Bone has noted, "'Miss Cynthie' constitutes . . . a psychological as well as an artistic triumph. Published in the shadow of impending death, it testifies to Fisher's inner growth and aggravates our loss of his maturing powers."[13]

The importance of "Miss Cynthie" in the canon of Fisher literature does not obscure his lesser tales; but this story is the exemplum of Fisher's overriding concern for the motifs of love and reconciliation, of harmonious union between opposing elements, for that "union of lovers" in the most boundless sense. To say that "Class consciousness is perhaps the single most consistent theme in Fisher's work" is to mistake the means for the goal. Other themes are also found among Fisher's major concerns, such as the futility of prejudice (the irony of it, the waste), or the effects of the lure of the city upon people and the city's power to destroy individuals. Added to his themes is Fisher's employment of language to underscore the characterizations and settings. This wholeness of themes, characterizations, settings, and language exemplifies the concerns of Rudolph Fisher to render the life he witnessed and lived in the transformed manner of mimetic art through the short story.

Fisher is predictable and consistent in his language, in descriptions, exposition, and dialogue. He uses words of confinement frequently, e.g., hencoop, airshaft, underground railroads, suffocation, a religious vocabulary in connection with characters acutely aware of sinfulness, and lastly—Fisher's special forte (or, as has been pointed out, also a weakness)—the language of Black Harlem, "Contemporary Harlemese," to use his own expression.

"City of Refuge" demonstrates Fisher's concern for the tidy progression of a tale from beginning to middle to end; the six sections of the story each lead Gillis closer to his fate. Just as he emerges like Jonah from the whale into Harlem (after being in the "hell" of the subway), he is caught at the end in a cabaret, which is another hell, and truly the place for the lost victims of the city, such as Gillis.

The end of "City of Refuge" reflects the tendency of the modern short story, starting in the 1920s in fact, to place the protagonist in a situation where he receives some illumination as to the truth of his actual plight—a mini-epiphany, as it were—a moment of obvious reversed fortunes but without the insight into his own flawed character as one would have it in Aristotelian tragedy. There is passivity in King Solomon's acceptance of his "mistakes"; that his character has weaknesses does not occur to this protagonist, however. In this fashion, Fisher was certainly part of the mainstream of short story writers during his period of creativity—a time when there was, in short story writing, an underplaying of plot, reversals, total change, or complete insight into the self (or a need to do anything about an internal problem when it was discovered). In part, then, Fisher was writing in the mode of his contemporaries. Also, the fact that "The City of Refuge" has a comic rather than a tragic ending does not lessen the emotional poignancy of Gillis's situation unless, of course, the reader finds untenable Gillis's naiveté and gullibility.

Optimism is integral to the fiction of Fisher, a bourgeois-based belief that an optimistic philosophy of life, a firm Christian faith, and clear comprehension finally of human needs and motives can result in a harmonious conclusion to life's inversions. Because Fisher's aim was to be instructor as well as interpreter, this adoption of a positive and sanguine attitude gave him a limited point of view and made some of his work press too hard upon "a willing suspension of disbelief." Rather than demonstrating alienation from or despair with his group, Fisher—even when satirizing his race—chose to construct his stories around moral principles that served to emphasize the redemptive spirit. As in the case of all writers, of course, the choice was his to make; but the choice vitiated the effectiveness of his avowed wish to be an interpreter of his people.

The intent of his writing, however, cannot be overlooked at any time; and, apparently because he kept his aim clearly in mind, he succeeded. In a sense, he made the leap from individualizing his artistic concerns to informing about a group experience in his literary corpus; he sought to apply universal qualities to a special group and thus tamed "The artist's struggle with his vocation . . . a version of a universal human struggle: of genius with Genius, and of genius with genius loci (spirit of place)."[14] And in demonstrating a manner of bond between his characters and their setting Fisher captures the cultural *témoins* of that Black capital.

What we have in Fisher's stories, then, is a polished portrait of the varied life in Harlem, written in a quick, sometimes witty, sometimes satiric, sometimes acerbic-sounding style. The conflicts between social and moral questions inform many of Fisher's stories—e.g., "The Backslider," "High Yaller," or "The Promised Land"—which highlights his aim to be not only entertaining, but enlightening as well. The social historian works hand-in-hand with the creative artist; the man of conscience stands behind the stories. A descendant of Emerson, Fisher stresses in his stories the notion that the God-loving, God-fearing person can triumph over adversity. If the short story is, as Mark Schorer has said, "an art of moral revelation" (whereas the novel is "an art of moral evolution"),[15] then Fisher accomplished what he wished as an artist practicing this literary genre. His keen observations of life and manners in Harlem, couched in a literary form, demonstrate his very American concern for probing those flaws in our character which he felt could be ameliorated. The personal conflicts of his characters illustrate, once again, a major American concern—the problems stemming from belief versus action; a testing, it seems, of the theory of the American way of life versus the reality of how life is acted out day by day.

Unlike many of the white writers of the 1920s (e.g., Sherwood Anderson, Ernest Hemingway), who frequently chose protagonists who were unattractive and second-rate, Fisher for the most part eschews this sort of character in a principal role and emphasizes the redeeming features of the "good guy." One prominent exception is "Ringtail," although it is not clear to me what attitude Fisher has or the precise point of a story such as this, where the main character certainly succeeds in evil-doing. But in each case where there is a repugnant individual in a Fisher story, a contrasting figure is provided in the balance to represent the author's moral point of view. This, too, is an essential element of his art—to make sure that nothing, then, is left to the reader's inference: characters, setting, theme, point of view, resolution of the plot come together in a conclusion calculated tidily to furnish a panorama of Harlem as painted by a master interpreter of black life in this mecca of multicolored inhabitants.

NOTES

1. This article is an adaptation of the "Introduction" to my edition of Fisher's published stories, *The Short Fiction of Rudolph Fisher* (Westport, CT: Greenwood, 1987).

2. Frank O'Connor, *The Lonely Voice: A Study of the Short Story* (Cleveland: World, 1963), p. 41.

3. Biographical information written by Miss Fisher for the Schomburg Collection, in Rudolph Fisher file (microfiche) at the New York Public Library Schomburg Center for Research in Black Culture.

4. Biographical information, Rudolph Fisher file (microfiche), New York Public Library Schomburg Center for Research in Black Culture.

5. The Cameraman, "Colorful 'Movies,'" *New York Amsterdam News*, 7 Sept. 1927.

6. Octavio Paz, *The Other Mexico: Critique of the Pyramid* (New York: Grove, 1972), p. 75.

7. Rudolph Fisher, "The Caucasian Storms Harlem," *American Mercury* 11 (Aug. 1927): 398.

8. Margaret Perry, *Silence to the Drums; A Survey of the Literature of the Harlem Renaissance* (Westport, Conn.: Greenwood, 1976), p. 112.

9. Gilbert Murray, *The Classical Tradition in Poetry* (New York: Russell & Russell, 1927), p. 38.

10. Pagination will not be given for quotes from individual stories.

11. Thomas Friedmann, "The Good Guys in the Black Hats: Color Coding in Rudolf [sic] Fisher's 'Common Meter,'" *Studies in Black Literature* 7 (Winter 1976): 8.

12. Arthur P. Davis and Saunders Redding, eds., *Cavalcade: Negro American Writing from 1760 to the Present* (Boston: Houghton Mifflin, 1971), p. 337.

13. Robert Bone, *Down Home; A History of Afro-American Short Fiction from its Beginning to the End of the Harlem Renaissance* (New York: Putnam, 1975), p. 159.

14. Geoffrey Hartman, "Toward Literary History," in *Beyond Formalism* (New Haven: Yale Univ. Press, 1970), p. 372. Since I am not a literary historian, I am indebted to Robert Stepto and Henry Louis ("Skip") Gates for introducing me to this concept.

15. Mark Schorer, ed., *The Story, A Critical Anthology* (New York: Prentice-Hall, 1950), p. 433.

CONVERSATIONS WITH DOROTHY WEST[1]

DEBORAH E. MCDOWELL

Dorothy West was born in 1912 to Rachel Pease West and Isaac Christopher West in Boston, Massachusetts, where she attended Girls' Latin School and Boston University. Hers has been a long and varied writing career which spans over sixty years, beginning with a short story she wrote at age seven. When she was barely fifteen, she was selling short stories to Boston newspapers, and before she was eighteen, already living in New York City, she had become a prize-winning author and friend of such luminaries as Countee Cullen, Langston Hughes, Zora Neale Hurston, Claude McKay, and Wallace Thurman.

In what many consider the waning days of the Renaissance, she founded *Challenge*, a literary quarterly, serving as its editor from 1934 to 1937 and co-editor with Marian Minus and Richard Wright after the magazine was re-named *New Challenge* in 1937. In the 1940s she published short stories in the *New York Daily News*, and in 1948, her most well-known work, *The Living Is Easy*.

For the past thirty-eight years she has lived on Martha's Vineyard, contributing since 1968 a generous sampling of occasional pieces and columns to its newspaper, the *Vineyard Gazette*. She is currently at work on a number of projects, including a novel, titled "The Wedding."[2]

McDOWELL: I have put together a set of questions that, taken together, form a rough chronology of your writing career, but we don't have to stick to this. Feel free to let your mind roam over whatever you choose. I thought we could start with the generic interview questions about your beginnings as a writer. When did you start to write? How old were you? What did you write? Who influenced you?

WEST: Well, I think I knew I wanted to be a writer when I was seven. In those days you had to have a "parlor accomplishment," and so I took piano lessons. My teacher, one of my mother's friends, gave me lessons at our home, after which my mother always gave her lunch. While my mother prepared lunch, my teacher would play lovely music on the piano. I don't know if I knew the word "beauty" or used the word "beauty" but I remember loving the beauty of music. During that period, I began to read, and although I don't think I knew the true beauty of words then, I knew that words were more satisfying to me than music. I guess that was because I had a talent for them, but my parents had other ideas for me. I never will forget the day they had a little quarrel about me. I was about five years old. My father said that I was his child and was, therefore, going to be a little businesswoman. (He was a businessman.) My mother said I was not going to be a business woman, but a pianist. I listened to them and I remember turning to my father and saying, "I don't belong to you," and turning to my mother and saying, "I don't belong to you either. I belong to myself." I will never forget the sight of their mouths hanging open.

McD: That was an unusual statement for one so young, but, then, you were no ordinary five-year-old.

WEST: No, I guess I wasn't. I remember that everybody in the family would say in reference to me, "That's no child; that's a little sawed off woman." Evidently, I frequently said things that were "grown-up."

McD: So you knew at age five that you wanted to belong to yourself, which meant, in part, that you wanted to write, but did you ever experience, at any time of your career, any internal conflict about your writing? After all, you were doing something contrary to your family's wishes and expectations.

WEST: Well, I wasn't really. My own parents came to accept and encourage my writing ambitions. I remember my father saying to me one day, "Your little head is for writing books and mine is for buying and selling bananas" (He was known, remember, as the Black Banana King of Boston; no one could ripen bananas the way he could.). He was telling me, in effect, that it was all right for me to write. He supported my writing. I don't remember whether my mother encouraged my writing or not, but she certainly didn't discourage it. She believed in the arts. Remember, she had taken singing lessons herself.

McD: So it wasn't so much your own parents who opposed your writing as other members of the family?

WEST: That's right. I remember a conversation I had with one of my aunts long after I had grown up. She said, "Dorothy, the one thing I will never forgive your mother for, is that she let you become a writer." In those days, you didn't write. You became a doctor or a school teacher. I remember when I first started to write, many people asked me for the name I wrote under, because you didn't disgrace your family by using your own name.

McD: Is that why you used the pseudonym of the *Challenge* pieces?

WEST: That was part of the reason. The other reason is that, since I was editor of the magazine, I didn't want my name to appear on so many of the pieces. Do you want to hear how I chose "Mary Christopher" as a pseudonym?

McD: Yes.

WEST: The story goes that the day I was born, my father touched my hand and said, "Little Mary," the name of his mother. My father's middle name was "Christopher," hence "Mary Christopher," my pseudonym. My mother didn't want me named "Mary." Well, I was born at home, and, in those days, you had two weeks to name any baby that had not been born in the hospital. My mother couldn't decide on a name; she couldn't make up her mind. Well, the census man came to our house shortly before the two-week period was up and asked my mother what she was going to name me. She had just finished reading a novel called *Lady Dorothy of Hadden Hall*. I don't know where the name "Elsie" came from, but she asked the census man, "What name do you like best, 'Dorothy' or 'Elsie'?" Because he didn't care, he just said, arbitrarily, "Dorothy." So that's where I got my name; the census man named me.

McD: What was the first thing you wrote?

WEST: When I was about seven, I wrote a story about a little Chinese girl, though, mind you, I'm sure I had never seen a Chinese girl in my life. My father was very proud of that first story and carried it around in his pocket until he lost it.

McD: What did you write next?

WEST: Another story, when I was fourteen. I wrote it in longhand (I didn't have a typewriter) and submitted it to *Cosmopolitan*. You know Fanny Hurst? Well, I was a great admirer of her style, which I now think atrocious. But being fourteen, I expressed the most sincere form of flattery by imitating her in this story that I wrote about a Jewish girl. It was exactly in her style. I didn't know any better. Well, Ray Long, the editor of the magazine, was very well known and influential in American publishing and maybe even across the world. He wrote me a letter which I am sorry I did not keep, but I was only fourteen. The letter was the most scathing thing I've ever read. He said something like, you are a forty-year-old spinster who knows nothing about love. Plus, he said, they had one Fanny Hurst and so didn't need another. I was totally crushed, then, but in later years, I thought that if he mistook me, a fourteen-year-old, for a forty-year-old woman, the story couldn't have been written too badly.

McD.:   Did you come to your admiration of Hurst independently of Zora [Neale Hurston]?—because, as you know, Hurst is supposed to have introduced Zora to the literary world.

WEST: Yes, I did. I started getting *Cosmopolitan* when I was about thirteen or fourteen and thought that she was the most wonderful writer in the world. That was before I went to New York and met Zora.

McD.:   What other writers beside Fanny Hurst influenced your early work?

WEST: I don't know about influence, but it was around that age [fourteen] that I think I discovered what literary genius was. I was an omnivorous reader, and after school I would go straight to the library. I had worked my way to the D's and checked out Dostoevsky to take home. This particular day, I was at home in my room alone reading *Crime and Punishment*. I think I had read to about page fifty and then, all of a sudden, I got up and began to pace the room. My eyes filled with tears and I remember thinking, "This is genius; this is genius. Now I know what genius is." Dostoevsky became my master, though I knew I would never write like him.

McD.:   Whether you wrote like Dostoevsky or not, you wrote, and you wrote prize-winning stories when you were barely seventeen. Let's talk about your work with the Saturday Evening Quill Club. Would you say you served a kind of apprenticeship in the club?

WEST: Yes, but do you know about the *Boston Post* stories? That's how I joined the Quill Club.

McD.:   No.

WEST: The *Boston Post* was a very good paper in those days. I still don't think I was any more than fourteen or fifteen when the *Post* did a daily short story. At the end of the week, they gave $2, $5, and $10 prizes. Now, in those days, $10 was quite a little money. Eight times out of ten or seven times out of ten, I got the $10 prize and contributed to the family pot. When I got the $2 or the $5 prize, everybody in the family was indignant, because they were so used to my winning the $10 prize. Well, the *Post* stories led to my involvement with the Quill Club. Eugene Gordon, who was the short story editor at the *Post*, invited me to join the

Quill Club. It's interesting, he didn't know I was Black and I didn't know he was Black. Evidently he found out I was Black.

McD.:   Was it a racially mixed club?

WEST: No. It was all Black.

McD.:   Did any of the other group members go on to become published writers?

WEST: No. One, whose name I forget, wrote the society column for one of the Black newspapers in New York. I don't think Eugene Gordon did much writing. The group didn't last very long, but we did get out a magazine. [The magazine, *The Saturday Evening Quill*, was published in June, 1928. It was to have been published annually, but, like so many "little magazines" of the period, it saw only one issue.]

McD.:   What story did you publish in that issue?

WEST: The story was titled "An Unimportant Man."

McD.:   I want to ask you a question about "The Typewriter," the story for which you won the *Opportunity* prize. [West shared the second prize with Zora Neale Hurston.]

WEST: I was about sixteen and a half or seventeen when I wrote it. I have a little notebook in there with the notes for the story: poor man, maybe I said a janitor, rents a typewriter for his daughter who is taking typing lessons. She asks him to dictate a business letter to her one night and then he begins to dictate a letter each night, which gives him some kind of stature in his own mind.

McD.:   So, winning the *Opportunity* prize took you to New York and you decided to stay there and try to make it as a writer?

WEST: Yes.

McD.:   Did you study writing formally?

WEST: Yes, with Dorothy Scarborough and Blanch Colton Williams, both at Columbia.

McD.:   I'm sure you have anticipated questions about the Harlem Renaissance. Now I know you have described yourself as a kind of "little sister" to Langston

Hughes and Countee Cullen, and some of the other male luminaries of the movement. . . [*Interrupted*].

WEST: This is interesting. That is the way I've been described, which surprises me, because that is not how I saw myself. You see, when I went to New York, I was only seventeen-and-a-half or eighteen and, therefore, not a threat to anybody. [Langston Hughes, Claude McKay, and Countee Cullen] were very protective of me. Now some say Claude McKay was my mentor, but I didn't think of him as my mentor, though he did have great influence on me. He would often invite me to his place and scold me. I guess the fact that he invited me indicated that he liked me or he would have left me alone. I think he thought, I hope he thought, I had something to say as a writer.

McD.:   Did he read your work and give you feedback?

WEST: No, I don't remember that he did. Nine times out of ten, when I saw him, he had invited me to his apartment to meet "serious" writers who were almost always white. You see, Claude thought the young Black writers were not serious enough. Therefore, he wanted me to read and meet some serious writers.

McD.:   Who were these "serious" writers?

WEST: I don't remember now. That was many years ago. I do remember that I heard their names bandied about. They were white writers, and well, they had more opportunities.

McD.:   Judging from McKay's letters to you, he saw himself not simply as your mentor; he seemed to be in love with you. Can you talk a bit more about your relationship with him?

WEST: I guess I was his little "handmaiden." He was quite a few years older than I was, and he was very good to me. And, while maybe then, I thought I was being a little sister to him, I guess he liked me in a different way. You see, I'm the oldest living writer from the period now, but then I was the youngest. I was only seventeen-and-a-half when I went to New York, and Zora [Neale Hurston] let me say I was 25. Zora always referred to me as "baby," or something of that sort, in her letters to me. Therefore, when Claude said he loved me (it was always a surprise to me when people said they loved me), I thought he was merely being protective of me.

McD.:   Did you see yourself as a part of the Harlem Renaissance? The bulk of your work actually began to be published long after what most literary historians consider the height of the movement.

WEST: Yes, that's why I started the magazine.

McD.:   You mean, *Challenge?*

WEST: Yes. I started it because I thought the movement was over.

McD.:   How did you get the magazine started? Where did you get the money?

WEST: Well, as you know, I went to Russia in the early thirties. My little joke is that they tried and failed to make a communist out of me. After almost a year there, I was ready to get out of the country. Since it was, by now, obvious to all involved that I was not good communist material, they were perfectly willing to let me go. They gave me $300 in American money. I was the only person of the twenty-two-member delegation to get $300 in spendable dollars. Why I got them, I don't know. Now, $300 doesn't sound like much now, but that was quite a lot of money then. I returned to Boston, where I thought I was going to have to stay (my mother was not well). It was there that I got the idea for the magazine.

McD.:   You know, I have always been puzzled as to why you gave the journal up. After all, you started it with your own money.

WEST: Maybe you don't realize it, but it was very hard for one little woman back then. Women of the present are a little more aggressive than I was back then. I guess you could say I was passive. Plus, I was small and my voice soft. So when the Chicago Group started having meetings about the direction of the magazine, I remember deciding to give it up.

McD.:   Who constituted the Chicago Group and what plans did they have for the magazine?

WEST: It included people from the University of Chicago. They began corresponding with me and they wanted so forth and so on. They planned to take over the magazine.

McD.:   What did they want? Who did the group include beside Richard Wright?

WEST: I don't remember their names, but I think they were all communists. You remember his piece, "Blueprint for Negro Writing"? [Wright's essay was published in the first and only issue of *New Challenge*, Fall 1937. In the January 1936 issue of *Challenge,* West had responded in her editorial to criticisms that the magazine was too "pale pink." One can speculate that Wright's essay, considered by some his *Communist Manifesto,* was an example of the "red" direction in which Wright wanted to move the magazine, a direction with which West was not altogether comfortable.]

McD.:   So they just pulled the magazine out from under you?

WEST: Yes, I got a letter from Richard Wright's lawyer. He didn't ask me himself. He didn't so much as write me a letter. His lawyer sent me a form to sign, giving Wright the rights to something, I can't remember.

McD.:   Well, how did your relationship with Wright change after that? He had been your associate editor for that issue of *New Challenge*.

WEST: I was never crazy about Richard Wright because he was so timid and afraid of white people. I guess it stemmed from his Southern background. And, as you know, that fear translated, as it always does in these cases, into his marrying white.

McD.:   I want to go back to your trip to Russia. You were there nine months, right? What was the purpose of the trip?

WEST: In the thirties, the Russians wanted to do a movie about the poor conditions of Blacks in America, and contacted some American actors. I learned about the trip from Henry Moon [former public relations director of the NAACP], who asked me to go. At first I told Henry something like, "the last thing I'm interested in is Russia and Communism," but he persuaded me to go with him and Langston Hughes and about twenty other people [Their delegation was called the Fellowship of Peace and Reconciliation]. Langston was called in to do something with the script, which had been written by a Russian. Langston thought it was the most awful script he had ever seen. In the meantime, Hugh Cooper, an American engineer, was working on the Dnieper Dam, but he threatened to stop building the dam if the Russians continued the film. The Russians, who were seeking diplomatic recognition by the U.S. (the U.S. had not recognized Russia then; they had no embassy there or anything of that sort), abandoned the film because they feared that it would offend Americans and thereby jeopardize their chances for recognition.

McD.:   Although the film was not finished, did you as a group have any sense of accomplishment from the Russian venture?

WEST: This will seem like a strange answer. That year in Russia was the most carefree year of my life. When I left Moscow and headed for America, I burst into tears. A friend traveling with me wanted to know why. All I could say to her was that I was saying good bye to my youth. I never will forget that. Remember, I was coming back home because my father had died.

McD.: In discussions of the Harlem Renaissance, it is almost a commonplace assumption that the writers of the movement did not fulfill their promise. Even you yourself, in the first editorial of *Challenge* [March 1934], said as much. A popular explanation for that failed promise was that the writers were constrained by a predominantly white audience. What are your thoughts on the relationship between the Black writers and their audience? Is there any validity to this commonplace assumption?

WEST: I was making a harsh judgment, mostly on myself, in that *Challenge* editorial. It's important to remember that we were all young people in New York and it was wonderful and fun. We were excited and too young to settle down. There were the speakeasies, our adventures with the Park Avenue people, as I called them [wealthy white dilettantes]. Besides, you don't know what we had to go through back then, and I'm so glad you don't. In so many ways we were so helpless.

In those days, the women were just like excess baggage or fair game. Remember, I was living in an apartment in New York and Carl Van Vechten used to come and visit and, once in a while, he would try to goose me (I hate to admit this). A'Lelia Walker used to say, "Carlo, let that child alone." [A'Lelia Walker was the daughter and heir of Madame C. J. Walker, wealthy Black entrepreneur, known for her hair straightening products. A'Lelia ran a literary salon that was visited by most of the Harlem Renaissance personalities.]

McD.: So you were propositioned?

WEST: Yes, and let me tell you another side story about my cousin, Helene [Johnson, a prolific poet of the period]. She wrote some poems and Frank Crowley Shields, editor of *Vanity Fair*, gave her a whole page in the magazine. One day he asked to see her and she went to his office where he propositioned her. She came home in tears, and we held hands and got down on our knees to pray. That was the end of her career at *Vanity Fair*. I don't know if that happened in other cases.

McD.: I want to go back to Carl Van Vechten for a minute. As you know he is commonly credited with nursing the "fledging" Black writers along, with introducing them to what you call the Park Avenue crowd that allegedly launched so many of their careers. But a recent book by Charles Scruggs, called *The Sage in Harlem*, argues that H. L. Mencken was a far more powerful influence on the writers of the movement than was Van Vechten. Is there any truth to this claim?

WEST: I certainly heard Mencken's name tossed about at the time, but he was from a different generation. You must understand, when you're in your late teens, early twenties, you always think you know more than a fifty-year-old man. If we were influenced by anyone, it was F. Scott Fitzgerald, at least Wally [Wallace Thurman] was. He wanted to live dangerously and die romantically. Like Fitzgerald, he wanted to drink himself to death. I guess he was young enough to believe that he wasn't really going to die.

McD.:   So are you suggesting that we need to look on that period with a less critical and chastising eye and to see you writers as youthful and carefree?

WEST: Yes. Plus, you must realize, when we came together in New York, we had to make adjustments to each other, adjustments to New York, adjustments to meeting people, to being talked about on radio, etc. We needed time to go off by ourselves. That's one of the reasons I came here (to Martha's Vineyard) to write. We were too taken up with the Park Avenue people. Despite all that, we *were* writing, but not always getting published. I was writing many stories during that time that weren't being accepted. And I wasn't alone.

McD.:   I want to ask you a few more questions about your relationships with other writers of the Harlem Renaissance. You have spoken of your relationships with the prominent males of the movement [Countee Cullen, Claude McKay, Langston Hughes, Wallace Thurman, most notably], but I want to ask you about your relationships with the women writers. Apart from Zora [Neale Hurston], were there other women writers in the movement with whom you interacted? Did you know Jessie Fauset and Nella Larsen, for example? *The Living Is Easy* reminds me so much of Fauset's last novel, *Comedy, American Style* (1933).

WEST: I don't know the novel. Jessie Fauset and Nella Larsen were a different breed from us younger writers. They would feel themselves very much above these up-and-coming young writers. You see, many of them also had real jobs. They didn't live just any old way, as some of us did.

McD.:   So, in other words, when you sat down with a group of writers to talk about your work or whatever, it was likely to be Langston, Wally, Claude, and Countee?

WEST: More than likely, but even Countee was above us, though he didn't act superior. He had a job as a school teacher and Phi Beta Kappa key from Harvard.

McD.:   You are probably best known for *The Living Is Easy*, but you have also written a number of short stories [around sixty], the bulk of which were first published in the *New York Daily News*, right?

WEST: Yes. The first story of mine that they took was "Jack in the Pot," "Jack" being money. For some reason, the editor changed the title to "Jackpot," which is perhaps a better title, since the woman in the story won some money. Maybe forty or fifty years ago, during the Depression, if you went to the movies, you might get a chance to win something. This woman in the story, which I call my statement on poverty, won fifty dollars.

McD.:   How did the story get published in the *Daily News*?

WEST: I wrote the story for the paper's Blue Ribbon Fiction contest, which folded, fortunately for me. I say fortunately, because I then sent it to my agent, George Bye, who liked it very much. I got a telegram from him saying that they would take "Jack in the Pot" if I cut it down to 5,000 words. I'm sure it was the first Black story they ever published. I cut it down and got $400 for it, a good price in that day. George Bye was absolutely the best agent in New York in those days; he worked with all of the best writers and had access to every magazine. He had a great deal of faith in me as a writer.

McD.:   In effect, you had hit the jackpot yourself with "Jackpot."

WEST: Yes. This is a little aside. When I got the check for $400, I cashed it immediately and went straight to Macy's to buy a book. I didn't have a bank account, and so I had this wad. I was never so embarrassed in my life, because when you have $400 rolling out of your handbag onto the floor, it looks like you stole it. The sales people didn't say anything, but I felt exactly like a criminal.

McD.:   You continued to contribute stories to the *Daily News* after "Jack in the Pot"?

WEST: Yes, the owners of the paper let me contribute two stories a month, which kept my writing hand in. They introduced me to Katherine Kelley, the short story editor whom I will always revere. After I wrote "Jack in the Pot," she encouraged me to keep writing, but challenged me to write well. I might have written many more stories, but I spent time trying to write each one well. I think her advice paid off. For example, shortly afterward, I wrote "For Richer, For Poorer," which has been in about eighteen or twenty textbooks and anthologies.

McD.:   Why, then, have you referred to these stories in the *Daily News* as potboilers?

WEST: I guess that was a flippant remark. Maybe it had to do with my proud boast that I could get three stories from one plot. Maybe that's what I meant.

McD.:   In poring through the box of letters, I ran across many rejection letters that editors had written to your agent, George Bye. They all praised the writing [*Interrupted*].

West: Yes, I always said that my rejection letters read like acceptances until the end.

McD.:   Yes, but what these editors all say is that you don't write about Black people, that you're steering away from stories about Black people, which makes for stories that lack vitality, passion. Did you consciously choose to write about whites?

West: Let me tell you why I did, because magazines didn't buy the stories that were about Black people. That's the quickest and easiest answer.

McD.:   So it was for very practical reasons. You must have felt damned if you wrote about Black people and damned if you didn't. On the one hand, they said, in effect, we've had our Black story for the year and so you turned your attention to writing about whites, and, on the other hand, they said, write about your own, because you can't write about what you don't know [*Interrupted*].

West: And the interesting thing is, I was writing about my own. I just didn't always describe my characters as Black. For example, "For Richer, For Poorer" is based on the relationship between my mother and one of her sisters. I just didn't describe them as Black. That's all.

McD.:   That makes me think of *The Living Is Easy*. Wasn't it to have been serialized in *The Ladies Home Journal*, but they changed their minds because of the novel's racial content?

West: Yes. The magazine was very enthusiastic about serializing the novel, but when their board of editors met—Blackwell's; they were powerful people— they decided against it. I have always felt that they feared the loss of advertising revenues by serializing a novel by a Black woman about Black people.

McD.:   I want to ask a few more questions about *The Living Is Easy*. Mary Helen Washington has written that, throughout their literary history, Black women writers have taken a "sacred cow" approach to the treatment of Black female characters. That is, they have maintained a protective, reverential stance toward their characters. Your creation of Cleo Judson in *The Living Is Easy* is a signal departure from that tradition. Cleo is strong, domineering, controlling, willful, somewhat a precursor of Toni Morrison's title character, Sula. What was the genesis of Cleo?

WEST: I think she began with my mother. Though the word had not been invented then, I think it's accurate to say that my mother was a feminist. She was also a Renaissance woman. She could dig cellars, draw, do almost anything. What interested me most about her was her independence and her dominating presence. Whenever my mother came into a room, she was going to dominate everybody. She could just stand in a room and every eye was focused on her. She had *some* personality, a strong personality. She wanted control.

McD.: So you translated these qualities into your creation of Cleo?

WEST: Yes, but I must say that Cleo uses all these traits that make us hate her for a very positive end: to make conditions better for future generations. She wanted the children to have good manners, to speak well, etc. which, she believed, would get them far in life.

McD.: Children figure prominently in your work. Why the fascination with them?

WEST: Well, it's the family that intrigues me most as a writer, particularly the relationships between mothers and children. Maybe it goes back to my childhood and what I observed of my mother. I call her the mother of the world. In any given day in our house, there might be three mothers and their children around. If my mother got up to go outdoors, all the children would follow her. She was like the pied piper.

McD.: What fascinates you most about mothers and children?

WEST: When I was a child, I called grownups the big people. They looked big, and they looked powerful. I didn't want to be exactly like them, but I wanted some of that power. So I'm fascinated by the power that parents have over their children. I guess that's why, when I was a child, the only ambition I had was to be a mother with six children.

McD.: It's interesting to me that Cleo, despite her controlling, domineering, willful nature, lacks passion, sexually speaking. And she isn't the only such character in your work. "Passionless" women crop up repeatedly in your stories—[*Interrupted*].

WEST: Maybe it's because that's all I saw. I didn't know anything about sex, about how babies were born. My mother never told me anything about sex.

McD.: Because you never saw women display passion—[*Interrupted*].

WEST: I never saw my mother kiss my father. You know he was in the fruit business. When he would come home in the evenings, my mother would often say to him, "Take a bath; you stink." But to me, my father smelled of fruit and the earth. That's what he loved. I told you how hard it was for my mother to kiss me. I can't tell you how reserved we Bostonians were.

McD.: What did you write after *The Living Is Easy*?

WEST: I wrote fifty pages of a novel entitled "Where the Wild Grape Grows" and submitted it to Houghton Mifflin. They liked it and said it was "beautifully written," but they rejected it because they didn't think it would sell as a novel.

McD.: Did you finish the novel, despite their rejection?

WEST: No, I didn't, but I did incorporate much of its background into the next novel I started, "The Wedding."

McD.: Why did Houghton Mifflin think "Where the Wild Grape Grows" wouldn't sell?

WEST: Because it was about middle-class Blacks. That rejection bothered me. Writers are always advised to write about what they know best, and the Black middle class is what I know best.

McD.: Speaking of the middle class, much has been made of your background as a "thoroughly bred Bostonian." You're not the only Black woman writer who has worn the label of "thorough breeding." I think, for example, of Jessie Fauset, who is popularly designated a prim and proper "Old Philadelphian." Partisan readers have used her background, which does inform her work, to dismiss her as a writer. Do you feel that your work has been similarly and unfairly criticized?

WEST: Well, it was fear of such criticism that prevented me from continuing work on my novel "The Wedding."

McD.: When was that?

WEST: Maybe sixteen years ago [around 1969]. It coincided with the Black Revolution, when many Blacks believed that middle-class Blacks were Uncle Toms. I feared, then, what the reviewers would say. You see, when I was a young girl and there were Black books published, nine times out of ten, Blacks were asked to review them. I feared that some Black reviewer would give "The Wedding" a bad review because it was a book about Black professional people.

McD.:   So you were intimidated by what the period demanded?

WEST: Well, I wanted the book to be read. I thought it was a good book that should be read, and I felt that if it received a negative review, no one would read it.

McD.:   But books are always getting mixed reviews—a good one here, a bad one there—and are read nevertheless. I agree with you that reviewers certainly help to determine how a book is read or if it is read, but not entirely.

WEST: But you must understand. During that time white publishers were very intimidated by militant Blacks.

McD.:   Did you submit "The Wedding" to a publisher and get a reading that confirmed your fears?

WEST: Yes, I got a Mary Roberts Rinehart grant for the novel and submitted chapters of it to Harper and Row, and they gave me a contract. It was then that the revolution was at its peak, and I cared very deeply about its goals, and, therefore, I couldn't go on writing the novel. Then my personal circumstances began to interfere. I got a nine-to-five job at the *Gazette*, and when you come home after a day's work, you don't always feel like writing. I worked there for two years, and after that, went to work at Harborside [a restaurant on Martha's Vineyard]; I was a cashier. I would go on there at five o'clock in the afternoon, and, very often, I didn't get home until one o'clock in the morning. All of this helps to explain why I didn't finish the novel, but, in the final analysis, I have to take the blame for not finishing it. It was my fault.

McD.:   Although you say that you write best about middle-class Blacks, your stories are frequently about people in impoverished conditions: "The Typewriter," "Jack in the Pot," "For Richer, For Poorer," etc. [Interrupted].

WEST: You know, when I wrote "The Typewriter," I overheard my mother say that she didn't know how I could write the story because I had no firsthand knowledge of poverty. I remember being indignant and saying to her, "I can write about poor people; I can understand how poor people feel."

McD.:   Of course, you can write about poor people; you are a writer, after all. I'm simply curious about your fascination with them.

WEST: Do I think they're more real? (I'm asking myself that question.) Maybe my heart goes out to people in difficult situations. That's why I love children, birds, dogs. I am a defender of the underdog. Do you mind my jumping around?

McD.:   No. Take as much time as you like.

WEST: This is an aside. Nobody knows this; I never even told my mother. As you know, my father was a businessman. Sometimes in the evenings, if he hadn't taken his money to the night drop, he would bring it home, packets of money. This one night he came home. I guess I was around six or seven. I can see my room so vividly. My mother was an immaculate housekeeper, and everything's so clean. I was sleeping in my mother's brass bed, and the moonlight was shining on the bed. My father came into the room and called me. (He called me Dimmie because he couldn't stand the name Dorothy; remember, he wanted me named for his mother, Mary.) Anyway, he placed the packets of money on my bed. My mother always thought money was dirty, so when he put the money on my bed, I thought, "He's putting this dirty money on my bed." He said, "Put your hand on this money, and that will bless it, and I'll double it tomorrow." Reluctantly, I blessed the money, but since this was my father and I loved him, I thought it must have been all right.

McD.:   That's a great story.

WEST: I think that's why, to this day, I don't like money. From that time, I prayed that we would get poor. I don't know why. I guess it's all right to be "rich" if you are surrounded by rich people. I never will forget when I was about seven, mother's youngest brother came into our house on Christmas Eve. He had an armful of presents, and he said, "This is for A; this is for B; this is for C," and so on. They were all for my cousins. My mother asked, "Where's Dorothy's?" He said, "Dorothy has a rich father who can give her everything." My father was the only person to give me presents.

McD.:   What did you do at the *Gazette* when you first went to work there?

WEST: I went to work as a file clerk, but soon after, I began to write various things: the bird column ["The Highland Waterboy"], and first one thing and then another. Then I began "The Cottager's Corner" about the Black people on the island. Then they asked me to do the Oak Bluffs society column, but the column has never been as important to me as some of the other pieces that I did for the paper.

McD.:   You mean, pieces like "No Room For My Niece," "A Black Child's Christmas is Woven," and "Fond Memories of a Black Childhood"?

WEST: Yes. Those pieces. People seem to identify with them a great deal too, especially "No Room For My Niece."

McD.:   Why did you start "The Cottager's Corner"?

WEST: I started it in 1968 because there were many Black people on this island—some, important professionals of quite high intellect. I didn't think anyone knew they were on the island and that, therefore, the only Blacks you could see walking down the streets in Edgartown were servants. If you saw five Black people on the sidewalk, four of them had on white uniforms. I got very tired of walking around Edgartown seeing only servants. Now, I'm very happy to say, there are college kids working over there; there are no more Black people in uniform.

McD.:   Would you say that your career underwent a kind of rebirth when you went to write for the *Gazette*?

WEST: Yes, I would say so, because they let me write what I wanted to. I could write freely about Black people, my family, my childhood.

McD.:   And you had always felt constrained before?

WEST: Yes, as I told you before, when I first started to write, I had trouble getting things published because of the Black content.

McD.:   Can you tell me about "The Highland Waterboy" pieces from the *Gazette*?

WEST: Well the *Gazette* has a bird column that was done regularly by a woman who went on vacation and asked me to take over the column in her absence. Instead of signing my name, I called myself the Waterboy, and people actually believed that this woman, then over sixty, was a young boy. There were about thirty sketches, all about birds.

McD.:   If you started to write when you were seven years old, your writing career has spanned over sixty years. That's a long time. What progression have you seen in your work over this period?

WEST: Simply, I think I write better now than I wrote in the beginning of my career. But, on the other hand, I was recently re-reading some of my stories from the '40s, and was surprised at the writing in some of them, which I think is just as good or better than in some of the more recent things. Stories like "Jack in the Pot" and "For Richer, For Poorer" were written way back then, and they are pretty good. I don't know; I guess, finally, I do believe that I write better now.

McD.:   In what sense?

WEST: Well, simply the quality of the writing; it has improved.

McD.: When you talk about your writing, you refer to your stories, more often than not, though you have published one long novel and undertaken at least three others—[*Interrupted*].

WEST: It's because I think of myself first as a short story writer—[*Interrupted*].

McD.: And yet, your stories have never been collected.

WEST: They haven't been collected, because, as you know, short stories don't sell well. Literary agents try to gamble on using a novel by a writer to sell stories to magazines. I probably would not have written *The Living* or started the other novels had it not been for the fact that stories don't sell. I love short stories; I think they are the most perfect literary form. A novel goes on forever and is a more difficult form to control.

McD.: What would you say has been the highlight of your writing career?

WEST: I'm a funny person to be asked that question, because I say I don't believe in highlights, or, in any case, I don't have highlights. Maybe getting *The Living Is Easy* published was the highlight.

McD.: What are you working on now?

WEST: Well, I'm trying to stay alive and to finish several things. I want to see some of my stories collected; to finish a manuscript called "The White Tribe of Indians"; and to finish my novel "The Wedding."

McD.: You've mentioned "The Wedding" a number of times in our conversations. Can you give me any sneak previews of the novel?

WEST: Well, as I said earlier, it is about middle-class life. I call it living in the oval. This island [Martha's Vineyard] is the background. That's all I'll say.

McD.: What with your writing for the *Gazette*, your social life, your travels to do readings and lectures, etc., I'm surprised that you can find any time to work. How does someone as busy as you find the time?

WEST: Well, you young people give me energy. Your interest in me makes me want to do things. Twenty years ago, I would not have dreamed that I would be invited to these colleges. I've been well received at all of them. Some want me to come back. So, the long and short of it is, you are my inspiration.

McD.: It's mutual because you are ours.

WEST: All right. It gratifies me now at the end of my life that I am not afraid of dying. I'm leaving you my legacy. I'm happy that you're going to live after me.

NOTES

1. This interview was edited from several hours made with Dorothy West at her home on Martha's Vineyard, June 22–26, 1984, and June 26–30, 1985. I would like to thank Nellie McKay for suggesting that I do the interiew and Melinda Griggs, Jane House, and Henrietta Rand for their help with the transcriptions.

2. *The Wedding* (New York: Doubleday, 1995).

HURSTON, HUMOR, AND THE HARLEM RENAISSANCE

JOHN LOWE

> With a few exceptions . . . black fiction has failed to produce the full, self-sustaining humorous hero, primarily because humor is out of place in what is basically a tragic literature.
>
> —Roger Rosenblatt[1]

> I am not tragically colored. There is no great sorrow dammed up in my soul, nor lurking behind my eyes. I do not mind at all. I do not belong to the sobbing school of Negrohood who hold that nature somehow has given them a lowdown dirty deal and whose feelings are all hurt about it . . . No, I do not weep at the world—I am too busy sharpening my oyster knife.
>
> —Zora Neale Hurston[2]

I. ZORA COMES TO HARLEM

The world has finally rediscovered Zora Neale Hurston. Her books are back in print, a new wave of black women writers have claimed her as their literary ancestor, and today's generation is eagerly exploring Eatonville and its citizens in the nation's classrooms. Zora must be somewhere, ridin' high and having the last laugh. Appropriately, when the *New York Times Book Review* recently published a front-page piece on Hurston, they included a great photo: Zora looks out at us, laughing, from the front seat of her Chevy, during one of her folklore collecting trips in the South.[3]

Why did readers turn away from this supremely gifted artist? Although Zora Neale Hurston suffered some outrageous slings and arrows for being born black and female, she also had to be silenced for her outrageous sense of humor. This no longer surprises us when one realizes the extensive role that humor plays in virtually all her works. We now know too, thanks to Cheryl Wall, that Hurston pulled a really fantastic trick on the world by pretending to be ten years younger than she was; census records reveal that she was born in Eatonville, Florida, on January 7, 1891, rather than January 1, 1901. This means, among other things, that she was actually thirty-four when she entered Barnard College, although people around her thought she was in her early twenties.[4]

This element of Hurston's personality and aesthetic did not cause her much real trouble until she arrived in New York in 1925, poised to plunge into the currents of the Harlem Renaissance. Significantly, Robert Hemenway begins his superb biography of Hurston at this critical juncture, picturing her arrival in the city in January with $1.50 in her purse, without a job or friends, "but filled with 'a lot of hope,'" carrying a bag of manuscripts, and with "the map of Florida on her tongue."[5]

Although one would never know it from the various accounts we have of this age of "The New Negro," Hurston was part of the Harlem literati for only a few years; she looms larger in histories of the period because she represents many of the movement's best qualities. Moreover, her rapidly reappearing works now reveal her as one of the most productive, and surely one of the finest writers the group produced. Why, then, have so many scholarly studies, literary biographies by other Renaissance celebrities, and literary histories failed to do her justice? Again, one of the answers lies in how one reacts to her brand of ethnic humor.

Humor is a basic, continuing component in Hurston; to her, laughter was a way to show one's love for life, and a way to bridge the distance between author and reader. But more than this, she was determined to create a new art form based on the Afro-American cultural tradition, something she helped recover and define, as an anthropologist. I shall here analyze Hurston's concept of humor and its importance in her works, using an anthropological and literary perspective. It now seems clear that humor played a crucial role in her initial reception by, and later relations with, the other members of the Harlem Renaissance; in her sense of folklore and its functions; in the anthropological aspect of Hurston's humor, which grew out of her training as a professional folklorist; and in the ever changing and increasing role humor played in her fiction, including her masterworks, *Their Eyes Were Watching God* and *Moses, Man of the Mountain*.

Zora Hurston would quite probably be surprised to hear herself mentioned as one of the more important figures of the Harlem Renaissance; she devotes all of one paragraph to this seminal literary event in her autobiography, *Dust Tracks On a Road* (1942).[6] Others, however, speaking of the period, have frequently noted Hurston's contagious sense of fun, her dramatic appearance, and her store of folktales, anecdotes, and jokes; all this made her a favorite at the fabled Harlem "rent" parties, salons, and gab-fests. Surprisingly, only a few writers in the group were actually from the South. Thus Zora brought a special resonance to the movement, for her "down home" qualities meshed rather well with the new interest in the so-called "primitive," a word that had much more of a cachet in the 1920s. Eventually, however, this at first refreshing quality became embarrassingly close to white stereotypes of blacks.[7]

Unfortunately for Zora Neale Hurston, people have always found stereotypes lurking in folklore as well, and this eventually happened when her colleagues and critics began to scrutinize her fiction, which was so heavily influenced, first, by the Eatonville milieu of her childhood, and then by her anthropological studies and field work. Hurston's critics have failed to understand that stereotypes may also be positive, favorable, even overvalued, as well as negative.[8]

Alain Locke, one of the elder statesmen of the Renaissance and one of Hurston's mentors, touched on these matters in a contribution to *The New Negro* of 1925:

> The elder generation of Negro writers expressed itself in . . . guarded idealization . . . "Be representative": put the better foot foremost, was the underlying mood. But writers like Rudolph Fisher, Zora Hurston . . . take their material objectively with detached artistic vision; they have no thought of their racy folk types as typical of anything but themselves or of their being taken or mistaken as racially representative.[9]

Implicit in Locke's comments is a denial that rural blacks are representative of the race. Gradually, this stance began to affect the literati's view of Hurston herself; at first charmed by her wit and appearance, they began to have reservations about her "seriousness." Sherley Anne Williams offers a sensible explanation of how this concept developed and proliferated in literary history:

> For a long time she was remembered more as a character of the Renaissance than as one of the most serious and gifted artists to emerge during this period. She was a notable tale-teller, mimic, and wit, confident to the point of brashness (some might even say beyond), who refused to conform to conventional notions of ladylike behavior and middle-class decorum. To one of her contemporaries, she was the first black nationalist; to another, a handkerchief-head Uncle Tom. . . . To Alice Walker and others of our generation, Zora was a woman bent on discovering and defining herself, a woman who spoke her own mind.[10]

Williams suggests that Hurston's humor was enjoyed, but found suspect, partially because it was "unladylike." Women very rarely are permitted to take on such a role, in any society. The traditional effort to place normative restrictions on women has sought the model "good girl" who is "Chaste, gentle, gracious, ingenuous, good, clean, kind, virtuous, noncontroversial, and above suspicion and reproach."[11] Virtually all of these communal goals for women are antithetical to the qualities associated with the humorist; it therefore comes as no surprise that women around the world almost never engage in verbal dueling or ritual insult sessions, that no female trickster or clown figure exists in the group narratives of any culture, or that the many trickster figures in world folklore are overwhelmingly male. This prejudice goes so deep that in some cultures women who laugh freely in public are considered loose, even wanton.[12] In American society, moreover, there is a widely held belief that women generally are unable to tell jokes correctly in any case. A female folklorist discovered that even in all-female gatherings, women often "began and ended with apologies: for speaking, for the content of their speech, for speaking too long."[13]

If a woman humorist, per se, is offensive, she can only become more so if she somehow used this stance to obtain money. Much of the long-term damage to Hurston along these lines ultimately came from Wallace Thurman's *roman à clef* of the Harlem Renaissance, *Infants of the Spring* (1932). Thurman, a sharp-tongued, bitter, but brilliant man, almost certainly felt a kind of sibling rivalry towards Hurston. His caricature of her, the figure of Sweetie Mae Carr, a leading light of "Niggerati Manor," severely damaged Hurston's literary image until Hemenway's long-needed biography corrected the picture in 1978:

> Sweetie Mae was a short story writer, more noted for her ribald wit and personal effervescence than for any actual literary work. She was a great favorite among those whites who went in for Negro prodigies. Mainly because she lived up to their conception of what a typical Negro should be. It seldom occurred to any of her patrons that she did this with tongue in cheek. Given a paleface audience, Sweetie Mae would launch into a saga of the little all-colored Mississippi town where she claimed to have been born. Her repertoire of tales was earthy, vulgar and funny. Her darkies always smiled through their tears. . . . Sweetie Mae was a master of southern dialect, and an able raconteur, but she was too indifferent to literary creation to transfer to paper that which she told so well. The intricacies of writing bored her, and her written work was for the most part turgid and unpolished. But Sweetie Mae knew her white folks. . . . "It's like this," she had told Raymond. "I have to eat. I also wish to finish my education. Being a Negro writer these days is a racket and I'm going to make the most of it while it lasts. Sure I cut the fool. But I enjoy it, too. . . . Thank God for this Negro literary renaissance! Long may it flourish!"[14]

Thurman's portrait had an element of truth in it; Hurston *was* interested at this point in finding patrons—but Sweetie's coldly selfish pose is strictly a fiction.

Larry Neal's assessment of Hurston's role during the Renaissance, written a few years before the corrective of Hemenway's biography, shows how lingering the effects of reports like this were. Although he begins by stating that her reputation was perhaps hurt by "the complexity of her personality and the controversy that attended her career," he carries on the tradition by repeating all the old stories, and makes the old charges. "Miss Hurston" is said to be "very bold and outspoken, an attractive woman who had learned how to survive with native wit. . . . " Moreover,

> Zora could often be an inveterate romantic [a traditional male term of derogation for women writers] . . . the historical oppression that we now associate with Southern black life was not a central aspect of her experience . . . she was no political radical. She was, instead, a belligerent individualist who was decidedly unpredictable [another favorite male charge against women] and perhaps a little inconsistent.[15]

Neal also accuses her, as others had before, of being "opportunistic," because she had been Fannie Hurst's secretary and Carl Van Vechten's friend. He then quotes Langston Hughes's oft-cited dig at her, which blithely fails to mention that Hughes himself was the benefactor of the same white patron:

> In her youth, she was always getting scholarships and things from wealthy white people, some of whom simply paid her just to sit around and represent the Negro race for them, she did it in such a racy fashion. She was full of side-splitting anecdotes, humorous tales, and tragicomic stories, remembered out of her life in the South as the daughter of a traveling minister of God. She could make you laugh one moment and cry the next. To many of her white friends, no doubt, she was a perfect "darkie," in the nice meaning they give the term—that is a naive, childlike, sweet, humorous, and highly colored Negro.[16]

Hughes's remarks are revealing; he mentions Hurston's ability to make people laugh, her rural background, and implies a connection between them. He also infers that someone who is funny and from the South therefore comes off as naive, childlike, *humorous*—as if it were a package deal. Hughes, having arrived in Harlem from Cleveland and Washington, here seems to share his contemporaries' stereotypes of the South and Southern Blacks.

Using Hughes and Thurman as his expert "eye-witnesses" to the events of the Renaissance (something many commentators on the period have done), Neal asserts that Hurston commercially popularized Black culture. He is appalled to hear a story about Zora hosting a racially mixed party wearing a red bandana—and he adds, pejoratively, "Aunt Jemima style," obviously forgetting that many other people besides Aunt Jemima wore and wear kerchiefs, especially in the South. Worst of all, she served her guests "something like collard greens and pigs' feet."[17]

Much of the above reveals a sexist, anti-Southern bias among the intelligentsia; fairness, however, demands yet another qualification. A further factor that worked against Hurston was the residual impact of Van Vechten's *Nigger Heaven* (1926). His well-meaning but mistaken emphasis on the exotic and the sensual led him, and many readers and writers, back to old stereotypes, and caused quite a few Black writers and leaders to eschew anything that smacked of the "primitive." It was difficult for many of these people, when confronted with Zora Neale Hurston's comic folk figures, not to see parallel lines of development. Even though she dealt, for the most part, with positive elements of folk culture, they saw only stereotypes; the baby had to go out with the bathwater.

We should also remember that very few Black people of this time really understood the true greatness of Black folk culture—Hurston was one of the first writers or scientists to assess its riches and map its contours.

What led Hurston into her eventual role in Harlem and her subsequent anthropological adventures? Her autobiography, which frequently obscures rather than illuminates her past, does provide clues in this area. *Dust Tracks On a Road* won a race relations award, partly because Hurston quite consciously "accentuated the positive" and avoided bitterness, a quality she scorns in humorous, incongruous terms: "To me, bitterness is the underarm odor of wishful weakness. It is the graceless acknowledgment of defeat" (p. 280). One delights in the absurdity of the combination but also in the unexpected similarities we find in Hurston's equation of bitterness and underarm odor.

This brings us to a central aspect of Hurston's humor, which is virtually identical to her greatest gift as a novelist. She truly "made it new," combining the resources of Afro-American folklore with her own fictional agenda. One of the ways she did this was by using unconventional and unexpected verbal combinations. The juxtaposition of apparently dissimilar objects or concepts is a classic cause of humor.[18]

Similarly, as Hemenway stresses, Zora Hurston was keenly aware of the coexistent cultures of America.[19] Indeed, throughout her text, she functions as a kind of guide and translator, initiating a presumably white reader into the mysteries of Black language and folklore.

Dust Tracks never bores the reader, largely because the book, in celebrating Zora Neale Hurston, also salutes the culture that made her. The text is larded with humor, both as structure and adornment. Hurston uses comic expressions, jokes, and entire collections of humorous effects, to amplify, underline, and sharpen the points she makes. These deceptively delightful words often contain a serious meaning, just as the slave folktales did. Hurston skillfully trims and fits folk sayings into integral parts of her narrative; on the first page, for instance, she describes her home town by saying "Eatonville is what you might call hitting a straight lick with a crooked stick. The town . . . is a by-product of something else" (p. 3). This type of description becomes more pungent when she combines these materials with her own imaginative coinages, as in the following description of her father's family: "Regular hand-to-mouth folks. Didn't own pots to pee in, nor beds to push 'em under. . . . No more to 'em than the stuffings out of a zero" (p. 13). This utterance alone gives proof to Hurston's assertion that the Negro's greatest contributions to the language were (1) the use of metaphor and simile ("hand-to-mouth folks"); (2) the use of the double descriptive ("pots . . . nor beds"); and (3) the use of verbal nouns ("stuffings").[20] It also reveals the way such tools can be used to revitalize language by working simultaneously in the comic mode.

Additionally, this metaphoric and frequently hyperbolic language may be combined with a comically ironic presentation of the discrepancy between appearance and reality in daily bi-racial life, as in this description of what happened when white visitors came to observe at Hurston's Black elementary school:

> We were threatened with a prompt and bloody death if we cut one caper while the visitors were present. We also sang a spiritual, led by Mr. Calhoun himself. Mrs. Calhoun always stood in the back, with a palmetto switch in her hand as a squelcher. We were all little angels for the duration, because we'd better be. She would cut her eyes and give us a glare that meant trouble, then turn her face towards the visitors and beam as much as to say it was a great privilege and pleasure to teach lovely children like us. (pp. 46–47)

The description amuses, partly because of the language and tropes, also partly because (along with the narrator and the black teacher) we know the truth that is hidden from the white visitors. Another aspect of this principle may be seen in comedically sugar-coated scenes that are really put-downs of insipid white culture. When wealthy whites give the young Zora an Episcopal hymnal, she reports "some of them seemed dull and without life, and I pretended they were not there. If white people like trashy singing like that, there must be something funny about them that I had not noticed before. I stuck to the pretty ones where the words marched to a throb I could feel" (p. 52).

The biggest gap, however, for the young Zora to bridge is that between her fictional/imaginary world and her real one:

> My soul was with the gods and my body in the village. People just would not act like gods. Stew beef, fried fat-back and morning grits were no ambrosia from Valhalla. Raking back yards and carrying out chamber-pots, were not the tasks of Thor. (p. 56)

This momentary distaste for the real world is dispelled, however, when Zora becomes initiated into Black adult coded language on the porch of Joe Clarke's store, where the males of Eatonville congregated to swap gossip and have a "lying session," i.e., straining against each other in telling folk tales. "I would hear an occasional scrap of gossip in what to me was adult double talk, but which I understood at times. There would be, for instance, sly references to the physical condition of women, irregular love affairs, brags on male potency. . . . It did not take me long to know what was meant when a girl was spoken of as 'ruint' or 'bigged'" (p. 62). She was also hearing the double talk of animal tales, black interpretations of the Bible,[21] and "tall tales." It wasn't long before she was making up her own "lies" and getting roundly chastised for it by her grandmother (surely a prototype for Nanny in *Their Eyes*), who even utters a malapropism, one of Hurston's favorite devices: "I bet if I lay my hands on her she'll stop it. I vominates a lying tongue" (pp. 71–72). The forced coupling of abominate and vomit creates a delightfully expressive non-word.

Further clashes with authority receive similarly comic treatment: "I just had to talk back at established authority and that established authority hated backtalk worse than barbed-wire pie" (p. 95). It wasn't long, however, until Zora Neale began to see a way to be *rewarded* for her saucy imagination. Leaving home quite early, she became a governess, and soon discovered she could get out of housework by entertaining children with humorous stories; as a lady's maid for a Northern Gilbert and Sullivan company, she found out that she had a gift:

> I was a Southerner, and had the map of Dixie on my tongue. . . . It was not that my grammar was bad, it was the idioms. They did not know of the way an average Southern child, white or black, is raised on simile and invective. They know how to call names. It is an everyday affair to hear somebody called a mullet-headed, mule-eared, wall-eyed, hog-nosed, 'gator-faced, shad-mouthed, screw-necked, goat-bellied, puzzle-gutted, camel-backed, butt-sprung, battle-hammed, knock-kneed, razor-legged, box-ankled, shovel-footed, unmated so-and-so! . . . They can tell you in simile exactly how you walk and smell. They can furnish a picture gallery of your ancestors, and a notion of what your children will be like. What ought to happen to you is full of images and flavor. Since that stratum of the Southern population is not given to book-reading, they take their comparisons right out of the barnyard and the woods. When they get through with you, you and your whole family look like an acre of totem-poles. (pp. 135-36)

This passage provides a deeper understanding of Hurston's comic dimensions and her conception of communal humor. It shows her awareness of the comic possibilities of accent, idiom, dialect, inflection, simile, invective, the tall tale, the boast, and comic anthropomorphism; more importantly, it suggests an awareness of the toast, the dozens, signifying, and marking, all key elements in both Afro-American culture and her fiction.[22]

Hurston, in her anthropological research in the South, found multiple examples of these cultural/verbal genres, which she had always known about; now, however, she was seeing them from the viewpoint of a trained anthropologist. One notes here that Hurston was able to put all this into her fiction only after studying anthropology with Franz Boas and Ruth Benedict at Barnard; there, she found the "spy glass" she needed to re-see her own culture, which had heretofore fit her "like a tight chemise. I couldn't see it for wearing it."[23] Hurston also knew that she would have to find a way to present this material to a white audience that knew little about such verbal conventions. She solved this problem in her autobiography by letting her persona in the book play dumb:

> I heard somebody, a woman's voice "specifying" up this line of houses from where I lived and asked who it was. "Dat's Big Sweet" my landlady

told me. "She got her foot up on somebody. Ain't she specifying?" She was really giving the particulars. She was giving her opponent lurid data and bringing him up to date on his ancestry, his looks, smell, gait, clothes, and his route through Hell in the hereafter. My landlady went outside where nearly everybody else of the four or five hundred people on the "job" were to listen to the reading. Big Sweet broke the news to him, in one of her mildest bulletins that his pa was a double-humpted camel and his ma was a grass-gut cow, but even so, he tore her wide open in the act of getting born, and so on and so forth. He was a bitch's baby out of a buzzard egg. (p. 186)

Hurston, supposedly an innocent, then asks her landlady what it means to "Put your foot up" on a person, and she and we learn that this refers to putting your foot on the victim's porch while you "play in the family," that is, play the dozens (p. 187).

II. THE SHORT FICTION, 1921–1933

The brother in black puts a laugh in every vacant place in his mind. His laugh has a hundred meanings. It may mean amusement, anger, grief, bewilderment, chagrin, curiosity, simple pleasure or any other of the known or undefined emotions.

—*Mules and Men* (pp. 67–68)

Hurston's literary career began in 1921, when Howard University's *Stylus* published her short story, "John Redding Goes to Sea" (reprinted in 1924 by *Opportunity*).[24] The story features an ambitious, yearning central figure in a rural setting, whose wish to go to sea is opposed by tradition-bound women. The tale prefigures Hurston's later work, in that it presents male–female conflicts, a plethora of local-color touches, and references to conjuring and superstition. What's missing is Hurston's fully developed use of dialect, mature mastery of metaphor, and distinctive, humor-laden voice. In some ways the story seems derivative; the wailing, clutching mother is curiously like old Nora in Synge's *Riders to the Sea*. The tale is notable, however, for its depiction of a warm relationship between a black father and son (which Hurston would reprise in *Moses*), and for its aura of irony. The only joker in the story is Nature herself, for John gets his wish to go to sea when a storm knocks him off a bridge, and his dead body sweeps downriver atop a pine tree.

By contrast, "Drenched in Light" (1924) demonstrates all the qualities that were lacking in "John Redding," perhaps because Hurston here begins to use materials from her own experience; the central character, Isie Watts, clearly resembles the young Zora.[25] Considered a "limb of Satan" by her wizened grandmother, Isie spends long hours, as Hurston did (see *Dust Tracks*, p. 36) hanging on the gate-post, looking down the beckoning and shining shell road toward the horizon.

Isie displays her impish and impulsive nature when, egged on by her brother, she attempts to shave the straggling whiskers on her sleeping Granny's chin. The old woman wakes "to behold the business face of Isis and the razor-clutching hand. Her jaw dropped and Grandma, forgetting years and rheumatism, bolted from the chair and fled the house, screaming" (p. 372).

Knowing this alone will bring on a whipping, Isie steals Granny's red tablecloth, drapes it around her shoulders, and runs off to a barbecue, where she amuses everyone with her antics and her dancing. A white woman, travelling through with her obviously bored and boring husband, is entranced; she eventually stops Granny from whipping Isie, pays for the ruined tablecloth, and carries the child off to their hotel to dance for her: "I want brightness and this Isis is joy itself, why she's drenched in light!" (p. 373).

We see a number of new elements in this story, including a more sophisticated use of dialect and metaphor, sharply individualized characters, and most importantly, a buoyant exuberance and energy that emanates from a stronger release of Hurston's comic imagination. The story is also oddly prophetic of the major criticism she would attract in the twenties—posturing for her white patrons and/ or audience—for Isie escapes punishment and in fact wins rewards because of her antics/artistry, whichever you prefer. Hemenway considers the tale evidence of Hurston's considerable thought about her identity as she began to function in the Harlem literary scene.[26]

"Drenched in Light" also begins Hurston's focus upon joking relationships, crucial in pre-literate or largely oral societies, such as those Hurston would later encounter in Jamaica and Haiti, but after her Barnard training, she recognized the importance these structures played in her Eatonville, where folks valued oral ability highly, especially in verbal duelling. Isie and her grandmother amuse us partly because Isie seems impudently intent on establishing a joking relationship, a sentiment the elder figure adamantly refuses to recognize, so much so that her rigidity becomes a source of humor.[27]

"Spunk," Hurston's award-winning 1925 story, deals with a romantic triangle between Spunk, a macho saw-mill worker, the sexy Lena, and her cowardly older husband, Joe.[28] Significantly, the community plays an important role in this story, by using cruel humor to goad Joe into seeking revenge. He attacks Spunk from behind with a razor and is killed. Spunk, convinced that Joe has returned from the dead as a black bob-cat to haunt him, loses his customary aplomb and is killed by the circular-saw. The story shows Hurston's mastery of dialect proceeding, and introduces the concept of communal humor as an instrument of torture. The ending chills with irony: "the women ate heartily of the funeral baked meats and wondered who would be Lena's next. The men whispered coarse conjecture between guzzles of whiskey" (p. 173).

"The Eatonville Anthology," a series of short sketches describing colorful events and characters in Hurston's hometown, is much more amusing and detailed, even though there is no central narrative line in the collection.[29] "The Pleading Woman" pictures a wife who begs merchants for scraps of food, pretending her husband doesn't provide for her: "Hits uh SHAME! Tony don't fe-ee-ee-ed me!" (Hurston reprised the scene for *Their Eyes*, as we shall see.)

Other sketches describe various local eccentrics, but there is also a charming animal tale about the rivalry of Mr. Dog and Mr. Rabbit over Miss Nancy Coon. During the courting ritual, Mr. Dog proposes matrimony by asking "'which would you ruther be—a lark flyin' or a dove a settin'?'"; Hurston would use this particular scene in a more serious way in *Jonah's Gourd Vine*, when John proposes to Lucy.[30]

Despite the obvious differences and relative successes of these early stories, all of them differentiated Zora Neale Hurston from her Harlem Renaissance colleagues. Not only was she from the South; she chose to *write* about the South, from the perspective of a native. Jean Toomer had set his magnificent *Cane* (1923) in Georgia, but it was written from the viewpoint of an outsider. He was never thought of as "down home."

Hurston's one attempt at the time to write about the Harlem scene (the favored subject of her contemporaries), the 1926 "Muttsy," rather sentimentally details the arrival in New York of a timid "down home" greenhorn, Pinkie; she unfortunately finds lodging at the disreputable Ma Turner's place, a combination jook/speakeasy.[31] Pinkie's virginity survives intact until the end of the story, when the title character, a gambler, unable to seduce her, rather improbably marries her. The immigrant-type humor in the story more frequently occurs in Jewish-American fiction, but there was certainly a rich fund of country-type-arrives-on-Lenox-Avenue-from subway's-womb stories around. "Muttsy" is more notable, however, for its Southern materials (one character informs Pinkie and us how properly to eat a fish—straight out of Eatonville lore) than for its Harlem touches. Hurston would later master the latter in "Story in Harlem Slang" (1942),[32] but most of her early successes, unlike "Muttsy," were set in the South.

Appropriately, Hurston really caught fire as a writer with her contributions to *FIRE!!*, the magazine/manifesto issued by Hughes and others in 1926. "Sweat," the more gripping of her two pieces, details the grim story of hard-working Delia Jones and her no-good, philandering husband, a macho devotee of practical jokes.[33] Hurston cleverly transforms this aspect of her villain into a structural device, for the entire story turns on the idea of jokes and joking. She begins with one: Sykes throws his "long, round, limp and black" bull-whip around Delia's shoulders as she is sorting the white folks' clothes she must wash in order to support herself (p. 197). Sykes's prank, based on Delia's abnormal fear of snakes, also adds sexual imagery, and thereby makes the story more complex. Is Delia's phallic fear a sign of her frigidity, which in turn has driven Sykes to the bed of other women?

In any case, Sykes's cruel laughter fills the story; he repeatedly slaps his leg and doubles over with merriment at the expense of the "big fool" he married. Delia too, although grimly serious in her defiance of Sykes, uses comic rhetoric; referring to his mistress, she states "that ole snaggle-toothed black woman you runnin' with aint comin' heah to pile up on *mah* sweat and blood. You aint paid for nothin' on this place, and Ah'm gointer stay right heah till Ah'm toted out foot foremost" (p. 199). Later, alone, Delia takes comfort in folk wisdom: "Oh well, what ever goes over the Devil's back, is got to come under his belly. Sometime or ruther, Sykes, like everybody else, is gointer reap his sowing" (p. 199).

We notice another significant development in this story: the appearance of a communal comic chorus in the personages of the loiterers on the porch of Joe Clarke's store. When Delia passes by with her pony cart delivering clothes, they render the community's sense of pity for her and contempt towards Sykes via a startling collage of everyday objects and actions: "How Sykes kin stommuck dat big black greasy Mogul he's layin' roun' wid, gits me. Ah swear dat eight-rock couldn't kiss a sardine can Ah done throwed out de back do' 'way las' yeah" (p. 200). The men's joint verdict that Sykes "aint fit tuh carry guts tuh a bear" finds confirmation when he brings his mistress Bertha to the store to buy her provisions, and then enjoys it when Delia happens to pass by and witnesses the scene.

After this drama is played out, the men again analyze the ongoing story and its characters, mixing metaphors freely: Bertha is judged to be "a hunk uh liver wid hair on it," who "sho' kin squall. . . . Whyen she gits ready tuh laff, she jes' opens huh mouf an' latches it back tuh de las' notch. No ole grandpa alligator down in Lake Bell ain't got nothin' on huh" (p. 202).

To drive Delia from her house, which he has promised to Bertha, Sykes plays his final joke by keeping a caged rattlesnake on the premises, knowing she is frightened even of earthworms. When she asks him to kill the rattler, he replies with a comically coined word and devastating irony, "Doan ast me tuh do nothin' fuh yuh. Goin' roun' tryin' tuh be so damn asterperious. Naw, Ah aint gonna kill it. Ah think uh damn sight mo' uh him dan you! Dat's a nice snake an' anybody doan lak 'im kin jes' hit de grit" (p. 203).

Normally comic expressions can be used to deadly effect as well. When Delia's fury overflows into courage, she tells Sykes, "Ah hates yuh lak uh suck-egg dog" (p. 204). The imagery is apt, for Sykes, a male (the gender usually associated with dogs) preys on women (egg bearers). When he replies with insults about her looks, she answers in kind, joining a verbal duel that silences him: "Yo' ole black hide don't look lak nothin' tuh me, but uh passle uh wrinkled up rubber [a devastating metaphor of impotence], wid yo' big ole yeahs flappin' on each side lak uh paih uh buzzard wings. Don't think Ah'm gointuh be run' way from mah house either" (p. 204).

The final, terrible Freudian joke also comes at Sykes's expense. He places the rattler in one of Delia's laundry baskets and makes sure there are no matches in the house to light the lamps. Delia discovers the snake, which significantly slithers onto the bed; she flees to the barn, and from there hears a drunken Sykes, confident that his trap has done Delia in, return. Once in the darkened room with the whirring snake, thinking the bed his safest refuge, he leaps onto it and meets his doom. His obsession with male, phallic power finally kills him, in a doubly figurative and dreadfully comic way.

Hurston's short story apprenticeship finally led to her first novel, *Jonah's Gourd Vine*, after the last tale in this early series, "The Gilded Six-Bits," was published in *Story* in 1933; it so intrigued Bertram Lippincott that he wrote her asking if she had a novel in progress.[34] What made this story special? For one thing, it was written after Hurston had been collecting black folklore for several years in the South. Although this material had played a central role in her previous fiction, it now became an even more important element, for she had learned, through scientific observation, how integral and important the *process* of folklore was to black culture, and how pervasive it was in all types of communal functions.

How is this evident in "The Gilded Six-Bits"? The story concerns a young married couple, Missy May and Joe, who create a clean, sunny, happy home out of ordinary ingredients: "Yard raked so that the strokes of the rake would make a pattern. Fresh newspaper cut in fancy edge on the kitchen shelves" (p. 208). Like Janie and Tea Cake in *Their Eyes*, they keep their relationship fresh and lively through elaborate games, jokes, and rituals. Each payday Joe hides and throws money into the door; Missy May pretends to be mad and gives chase, which results in a comic tumble. They speak in hyperbolic but culturally specific terms to express ordinary facts: "Ah could eat up camp meetin', back off 'ssociation, and drink Jurden dry" (p. 210).

When Joe praises the proprietor of the new ice-cream store, Mr. Otis D. Slemmons, who apparently has a lot of gold teeth and money, Missy May expresses her initial contempt through folksy imagery, creating a caricature: "'Aw, he don't look no better in his clothes than you do in yourn. He got a puzzle-gut on 'im and he so chuckle-headed, he got a pone behind his neck. . . . His mouf is cut cross-ways, ain't it? Well, he kin lie jes' lak anybody else. . . . A wouldn't give 'im a wink if de sheriff wuz after 'im'" (p. 211).

Hurston creates a little physical comedy too; while Missy May dresses, Joe, who *admires* a "puzzle-gut" as a sign of prosperity, makes his "stomach punch out like Slemmons' middle. He tried the rolling swagger of the stranger, but found that his tall bone-and-muscle stride fitted ill with it" (p. 212). Later we find that Joe admires Slemmons for his comic/verbal ability as well; he quotes him as saying "who is dat broad wid de forte shake?" (p. 212).

Slemmons succeeds in seducing Missy May one night; Joe unexpectedly comes home and discovers them in the act. His stunned reaction? He laughs, before punching his rival out and grabbing his gold watch-chain. It is a last laugh, in more ways than one; although the marriage continues, its changed state is reflected by the absence of laughter and banter. After a long period of abstinence, Joe returns to Missy May's bed and leaves her the gold watch chain, and its attached coin, which she discovers to be a gilded half dollar. The whole thing has been a joke; Slemmons was an imposter.

When Missy May delivers a son that is "de spittin' image" of Joe, everyone breathes a sigh of relief, especially Joe's formerly suspicious mother, who confesses her previous doubts in a rush of folk-warmed euphemisms: "and you know Ah'm mighty proud, son, cause Ah never thought well of you marryin' Missie May cause her ma used tuh fan her foot round right smart and Ah been mighty skeered dat Missie May wuz gointer git misput on her road" (p. 217). All of this richly metaphorical language lends a great deal of humor and interest to the story, yet is never intrusive as it sometimes is in the more sprawling pages of *Jonah's Gourd Vine*; moreover, although Hurston creates the impression of a natural spontaneity, the metaphors actually work in a system of reference. For example: the rather refined "road" euphemism used by Joe's mother had been employed by Missy May earlier, when she speculated to Joe that they might discover some gold like Slemmons's: "Us might find some gon' long de road some time," for it is indeed in her misbehavior in the "road" with Slemmons that she obtains the gold.

Joe's total forgiveness floods forth after the birth of his son. As he buys a load of candy kisses with Slemmons' gilded six-bits for Missy May, he boasts about the way he outsmarted Slemmons; his story amuses the callous clerk, who remarks to his next customer, a white, "Wisht I could be like these darkies. Laughin' all the time. Nothin' worries 'em" (p. 218), little suspecting the pain that underlies Joe's brave laughter. The story ends when Joe resumes the ritual of throwing money on the porch, accompanied by Missy May's game reply: "Joe Banks, Ah hear you chunkin' money in mah do' way. You wait till Ah got mah strength back and Ah'm gointer fix you for dat" (p. 218). Laughter thus becomes the barometer of success or failure in marriage.

III. THE NOVELS, 1934–1937

Now that we have seen the way Hurston developed her expanding use of humor and folklore in the early short stories, we may discover how this came to fruition in her novels, beginning with *Jonah's Gourd Vine* in 1934.[35]

Here, the novel form permits Hurston to elaborate joking relationships, using kin and non-kin systems and patterns to create a vibrantly textured sense of community and communal wisdom while forming a vehicle both for the narrative and for commentary upon it. We see Hurston working with relatively simple relationships in *Jonah*, and with more complex sets in *Their Eyes*; finally, in *Moses*, she develops a complete system of humorous relationships that combines the features of both networks, for the "chosen" people are simultaneously kin and non-kin with every other member of the "family of God," i.e., the family of Israel.

In a 1934 letter to James Weldon Johnson about her new book, Hurston confided:

I have tried to present a Negro preacher who is neither funny nor an imitation Puritan ram-rod in pants. Just the human being and poet that he must be to succeed in a Negro pulpit. I do not speak of those among us who have been tampered with and consequently have gone Presbyterian or Episcopal, I mean the common run of us who love magnificence, beauty, poetry and color so much that there can never be enough of it.[36]

Thus, while the book itself offers an abundance of laughter, the central character and his profession are never the ultimate butt of Hurston's humor, although his fall from grace within the community is partly measured by the qualitative change in their joking relationship with him.

Jonah tells the story of John Pearson, a rural lad who is called to preach by God; his mission is strengthened and sustained by his wife, Lucy, a saintly but strong figure. She and John resemble Hurston's parents, although there are significant differences, partly because *Jonah* was written after the years of folklore research in the South; Hurston was intent on using this material fictionally. Moreover, she had just written, but had not published, *Mules and Men.* This text had originally been conceived as a straightforward presentation of the research findings, but the publishers wanted a livelier narrative, so Hurston inserted herself into the book, and worked out a whole series of connective conversational tissues for the various components. This makes the book much closer in form to the novel, but it improved Hurston's anthropological technique as well. Both *Mules and Men* and *Tell My Horse*, Hurston's later examination of Caribbean folklore impress us by putting folkloric material into contextual perspective. She lets us know when a joke was told, by whom, and to whom. This practice especially succeeded when she began to incorporate the very same materials into her fiction, for it ensured that the humor found in the novels developed naturally out of the narrative, and indeed, frequently carried the narrative, either overtly or covertly.

The humorous dimensions of *Jonah*, in many ways a great rehearsal for Hurston's masterworks *Their Eyes Were Watching God* and *Moses, Man of the Mountain,* deserve extended analysis.[37] I shall summarize here, however, some of the more important humorous conventions that Hurston employs in the book: verbal duels between the sexes (first with John's parents, Ned and Amy, later between John and Lucy, then John and Hattie); coined expressions; black on black humor; country vs. city humor; courtship riddles and rituals; call and response comic sayings; references to the dozens; a tirade against "book larnin'" *à la* Papp Finn of Twain's masterwork; and many other ingenious modes of humor. Perhaps the two most important comic devices used in the novel are folk proverbs (sometimes piled on rather too thickly, and impeding the narrative) and signifying.

Hurston's purpose in *Jonah* was to show the world the glory of black folklore and language, and their central role in sustaining the community, particularly in the rhetoric of the minister and in the metaphors of everyday games and verbal exchanges. It was meant to demonstrate what Hurston had challenged Blacks in general to do in her December, 1934, article in *The Washington Tribune*: recognize the fact that Afro-American folk expression had an integrity that was every bit as fine as that of Anglo-American culture.[38]

The central battle of the sexes in *Jonah*, which is ultimately tragic, but frequently depicted using a comic technique, includes a declaration by John that becomes a central theme in Janie's story:

> "Jus' 'cause women folks ain't got no big muscled arm and fistes lak jugs, folks claim they's weak vessels, but dass uh lie. Dat piece uh red flannel she got hung 'tween her jaws is equal tuh all de fistes God ever made and man ever seen. Jes' take an ruin a man wid they tongue, and den dey kin hold it still and bruise 'im up jes' ez bad." (pp. 157–58)

This assessment is confirmed in *Their Eyes*, where Janie, the central figure, achieves maturity, identity and independence through the development of a voice, one that ultimately resonates with laughter. She uses this voice, however, in ways that both embrace and transcend the male/female relationships of *Jonah*.

Their Eyes, a book about a quest, ends with the heroine returning to the community for re-integration, whereby she is made whole once again, while enriching society with her newfound wisdom[39] While the various articles and sections of books that deal with Janie's identity have been quite persuasive and illuminating,[40] most critics have entirely neglected the fact that she also excels as a narrator who entertains, indeed, mesmerizes, and much of this comes from her considerable gifts as a humorist. In this respect she is providentially armed, for the community has an arsenal of scorn waiting for her: "Seeing the woman as she was made them remember the envy they had stored up and swallowed with relish. They made burning statements with questions, and killing tools out of laughs" (p. 10), thereby returning us with a vengeance to Freud's concept of laughter as an aggressive force. After Janie wordlessly enters her gate and slams it behind her, "Pearl Stone opened her mouth and laughed real hard because she didn't know what else to do" (p. 11). Like Hester Prynne in the opening scaffold scene of *The Scarlet Letter*, Janie will be the victim of cruel, unthinking humor until she silences it, and unlike Hester, she must "cap" the discussion by having the last laugh herself, as in the finale of the dozens.

Significantly, her friend and initial audience, Pheoby, represents Janie's case to the other women with a scornful humor: "De way you talkin' you'd think de folks in dis town didn't do nothin' in de bed 'cept praise de Lawd" (p. 13). She greets Janie's arrival more positively: "'Gal, you sho looks *good*. You looks like youse yo' own daughter.' They both laughed" (p. 14). The irony and therefore the doubling of the joke lies in the fact that Janie, in a metaphorical sense, *is* her own daughter, in that she has created a new persona out of the woman who left the town some time earlier with Tea Cake. Janie's exuberant appreciation of the dish Pheoby has brought her ("Gal, it's *too* good! you switches a mean fanny round in a kitchen" [p. 15]) inaugurates her in the reader's mind as a woman versed in folk wisdom and humor, and also demonstrates humor's power to quickly initiate intimacy and warmth. (The dish itself, Mulatto rice, is a joke too, since Janie's white blood relates her to the food and causes jealousy within the community.) Hurston extends the food/eating metaphor further; as Janie eats, she comments that:

> " . . . people like dem wastes up too much time puttin' they mouf on things they don't know nothin' about. Now they got to look into me loving Tea Cake and see whether it was done right or not! They don't know if life is a mess of corn-meal dumplings, and if love is a bed-quilt! . . . If they wants to see and know, why they don't come kiss and be kissed? Ah could then sits down and tell 'em things. Ah been a delegate to de big 'ssociation of life. Yessuh! De Grand Lodge, de big convention of livin' is just where Ah been dis year and a half y'all ain't seen me." (pp. 17–18)

The retrospective story of Janie's life begins when she remembers a joke that was played on her as a child. Raised with the white Washburn children, she doesn't know she is Black until all the children view a group photograph. When she exclaims, "Where is me?"—Janie's distinguishing question throughout the book—the assembled group laughs at her. "Miss Nellie . . . said, 'Dat's you, Alphabet [the comic, all-purpose nickname they have bestowed on her], don't you know yo' ownself?' . . . Ah said: 'Aw, aw! Ah'm colored!' Den dey all laughed real hard. But before Ah seen de picture Ah thought ah wuz just like de rest" (p. 29). The frame story of the novel repeats this situation, for once again Janie's identity is at stake for a circle of questioning faces, but this time it is Janie herself who provides the answers, fighting the fire of cruel, aggressive laughter with narrative, uniting, communal laughter. Her voice, multiplied by those of the characters who have shaped and been shaped by her life, does indeed become an alphabet at last, one that spells out the human comedy and condition.

As in Balzac, or Faulkner, Hurston's human comedy is replete with tragedy as well, but virtually everyone in the book has some comic lines. Even Nanny, whose grim revelation of her own history is monumentally tragic, communicates in a dialect-driven metaphor-drenched language. Fearing that Janie has been beaten by Logan Killicks, Nanny erupts with comic invective, signifying, and using a wrong but curiously right word: "Ah know dat grass-gut, liver-lipted nigger ain't done took and beat mah baby already! Ah'll take a stick and salivate 'im!" (p. 40). Logan, however, is notably lacking in humor and quite a few other traits, and Janie falls for the flashy but ambitious Jody Starks, even though he "did not represent sun-up and pollen and blooming trees, but he spoke for horizon. He spoke for change and chance" (p. 5). Moreover, "It has always been his wish and desire to be a big voice" and he intends to develop it in Eatonville, an all-Black town where a man can have a chance. His abundant humor adds an ingredient; he makes Janie laugh: "You behind a plow! You ain't got no mo' business wid uh plow than uh hog is got wid uh holiday! . . . A pretty doll-baby lak you is made to sit on de front porch and rock and fan yo' self . . . " (p. 49). Over the next twenty years, however, this joke pales, for it is grimly prophetic. Jody, now Mayor of Eatonville, soon banishes any sense of fun or joy from their marriage. He, even more than her first husband, wants a proverbial "nice girl" for public view, and "nice" girls don't joke in public.

There is humor aplenty, however, in the salty, gossipy tale-telling, or "lyin'" that goes on on Jody's store porch, which becomes the town center of Eatonville and the new Mayor's bully pulpit as well. But he quickly silences Janie; at the meeting where he is elected Mayor, Janie is called on to make a speech, but Jody intervenes: "Thank yuh fuh yo' compliments, but mah wife don't know nothin' 'bout no speech-makin'. Ah never married her for nothin' lak dat. She's uh woman and her place is in de home" (p. 69). Janie forces herself to laugh in response; apparently this is what a decorative woman does—giggle and be still—but she is inwardly disturbed. Appropriately, these pages of the book are relatively humorless, until the introduction of Matt Bonner's skinny yellow mule, the object of a whole series of jokes played on Bonner:

> "De womenfolks got yo' mule. When Ah come round de lake 'bout noon-time mah wife and some others had 'im flat on the ground usin' his sides fuh uh wash board."
>
> . . . .
>
> Janie loved the conversation and sometimes she thought up good stories on the mule, but Joe had forbidden her to indulge. He didn't want her talking after such trashy people. "You'se Mrs. Mayor Starks, Janie." (pp. 82–85)

Jody does respect Janie's outrage, however, over the physical torture of the old mule; he buys him and pastures the animal just outside the store, as a gesture of largesse. As the mule fattens, new stories are concocted. In one version, he sticks his head in the Pearsons' window (the central family in *Jonah*) while the family is eating; Mrs. Pearson mistakes him for Rev. Pearson and hands him a plate!

When the mule dies, the reader finds out that Jody's combination of a big voice and a sense of humor that originally won Janie is effective with the town as well; at a funeral that mocks "everything human is death," Jody leads off with a great comic eulogy on "our departed citizen, our most distinguished citizen" (p. 95). The result: "It made him more solid than building the schoolhouse had done."

In a daring move, Hurston extends the scene into the realm of the surreal, by adding a parody of the parody: a group of vultures headed by their "Parson" descends on the carcass. "What killed this man?" is the first "call" from the "minister." The response: "'Bare, bare fat.' 'Who'll stand his funeral?' 'We!!!!' 'Well, all right.' So he picked out the eyes in the ceremonial way and the feast went on" (p. 97). When we remember, however, that Janie is telling the book to

Pheoby, this becomes *her* added touch and revenge against Jody, who forbade her to attend the ceremony, much less speak of it.

A revealing passage, central to our consideration of Hurston as humorist, occurs next. Jody, who seemed to relish the mock-funeral, takes on a smug, "dicty" attitude of disapproval after the fact. "Ah had tuh laugh at de people out dere in de woods dis mornin', Janie. You can't help but laugh at de capers they cuts. But all the same, Ah wish mah people would git mo' business in 'em and not spend so much time on foolishness" (p. 98). Janie's response is no doubt Hurston's as well, and we may be sure she is thinking of those critics in the Harlem Renaissance circle who accused her of "cuttin' the monkey" for the white folks. "Everybody can't be lak you, Jody. Somebody is bound tuh want tuh laugh and play," and she is one of them (p. 99).

Jody "has to laugh," too, at the verbal duels of Sam Watson and Lige Moss, regulars on the store porch. Hurston gives them some choice lines from her Eatonville folklore collections, in tales of sheer hyperbole. "The girls and everybody else help laugh." Hurston the anthropologist thereby signals to us the ritualized nature of Eatonville humor and the value it had for the community.

One of the funniest episodes in the book reprises "Mrs. Tony," the begging woman from "The Eatonville Anthology." Once again, she begs the store owner (Jody this time) for some meat—for "Tony don't fee—eed me!" Hurston adds some delicious details too: "The salt pork box was in the back of the store and during the walk Mrs. Tony was so eager she sometimes stepped on Joe's heels, sometimes she was a little before him. Running a little, caressing a little and all the time making little urging-on cries." But when Jody cuts off a smaller piece than she wants, "Mrs. Tony leaped away from the proffered cut of meat as if it were a rattlesnake. 'Ah wouldn't tetch it! Dat lil eyeful uh bacon for me an all mah chillun!'. . . . Starks made as if to throw the meat back in the box. . . . Mrs. Tony swooped like lightning and seized it, and started towards the door. 'Some folks ain't got no heart in dey bosom'. . . . She stepped from the store porch and marched off in high dudgeon!" (pp. 113–15).

Some of the men laugh, but another says that if she were his wife, he'd kill her "cemetery dead," and Coker adds, "Ah could break her if she wuz mine. Ah'd break her or kill her. Makin' uh fool outa me in front of everybody" (p. 116).

Although Mrs. Tony's caricature is meant to be amusing, it has much to do with several levels of the plot, and offers a fine example of the way Hurston uses humor to convey a serious meaning. Mrs. Tony, urging Jody on, telling him he's a "king," exposes Stark's enjoyment in playing the "great man," the man who can afford to be generous in public, as he was earlier when he paid for the mule's "retirement" fund. Futhermore, the scene brings out Jody's falsity (he charges Tony's account anyway) and comically underlines Jody's marital stinginess towards Janie—he doesn't "fee—ed" her spiritually or emotionally. Finally, the men's communal insistence on the propriety of using violence to "break a woman," and the shared assumption that it's Mr. Tony rather than his wife who is the ultimate butt of their humor, lends male communal sanction to Jody's prior slapping of Janie for speaking out of place, and prepares the reader for Janie's final public showdown with Jody.

When Jody's youth and good health begin to wane, he tries to draw attention away from himself by publicly ridiculing Janie. "I God almighty! A woman stay round uh store till she get old as Methusalem and still can't cut a little thing like a plug of tobacco! Don't stand dere rollin' yo' pop eyes at me wid yo' rump hangin' nearly to yo' knees" (p. 121). Such a ritual insult directed at a male would possibly initiate a game of the dozens, or physical violence, but Jody, assuming Janie will know her place and not engage in a forbidden joking relationship, expects her silence. Instead, she accepts his challenge, and powerfully concludes a spirited exchange of charges with him: "'You big-bellies round here and put out a lot of brag, but 'taint nothin' to it but yo' big voice. Humph! Talkin' 'bout *me* lookin' old! When you pull down yo' britches, you look lak de change uh life.' 'Great God from Zion!' Sam Watson gasped. [Sam, we remember, is the chief comedian of the porch] 'Y'all really playin' de dozens tuhnight'" (p. 123).[41] Not only has Janie dared to play a male game, she has "capped" Joe forever with this ultimate insult, and in fact, in the eyes of the community, has effectively emasculated him. "They'd look with envy at the things and pity the man that owned them.... And the cruel deceit of Janie! making all that show of humbleness and scorning him all the time! *Laughing at him!* [my emphasis] and now putting the town up to do the same" (p. 124).

What Jody expresses here is more than a sense of betrayal; he is actually casting Janie in the diabolical role of Trickster, that omnipresent menace of folktales, who, like Brer Rabbit, one of his avatars, strikes down his physical superiors, as David slew Goliath. Significantly, however, Joe can't consciously give her this much credit, and so compares Janie to Saul's scheming daughter.

When Janie later tells this story to Pheoby in the framing device, and thereby, by extension, tells the community, she is doing so from a somewhat privileged position, which she doesn't have earlier in the book. Although multiple restrictions exist against women expressing themselves humorously in public, as we have seen, these are usually relaxed as women age. In many cultures, older women, especially after menopause, are permitted much more verbal freedom, and eventually are allowed to compete with men, if they so choose.[42] In this sense, Janie's challenge of Jody in the male territory of tall tales, verbal dueling, and finally, the doubles and capping, isn't as outrageous to the community as it might be, for she is mature, experienced, and widely recognized as a relatively wealthy, independent woman, who isn't vulnerable to sexual manipulation and appropriation.

At the time of Jody's death, however, some men in the community don't understand this. Janie learns to laugh again after the funeral, partly because of the hypocrisy of her abundant suitors: "Janie found out very soon that her widowhood and property was a great challenge in South Florida ... 'uh woman by herself is uh pitiful thing,' she was told over and again ... " (p. 139). Janie laughs, because the men know plenty of widows, but this one has money.

Her relationship to her eventual third husband, Tea Cake, is central to the book's meaning, and it begins on a note of humor. He walks into the store on a slow day; most of the community is off at a ball game in Winter Park. "'Good evenin', Mis' Starks,' he said with a sly grin as if they had a good joke together. She was in favor of the story that was making him laugh before she even heard it" (p. 144). Their entire first interchange is a series of little jokes, and Janie's thrilled reaction to his invitation to play checkers could just as well apply to his subsequent willingness to admit she is his comic equal: "... she found herself flowing inside. Somebody wanted her to play. Somebody thought it was natural for her to play. That was even nice" (p. 146). Tea Cake wants her to play in every sense of the word, thereby ending the long line of nay-sayers that stretches back to Nanny.

It interests us that Janie doesn't learn his name until they've spent the afternoon together in play; when she learns it is Vergible Woods but he's called Tea Cake, she laughs, and makes it a joke:

> "Tea Cake! So you sweet as all dat?" She laughed and he gave her a little cut-eyelook to get her meaning. "Ah may be guilty. You better try me and see. . . . B'lieve Ah done cut uh hawg, so Ah guess Ah better ketch air." He made an elaborate act of tripping to the door stealthily. Then looked back at her with an irresistible grin on his face. Janie burst out laughing in spite of herself. "You crazy thing!" (p. 149)

But Tea Cake doesn't leave. "They joked and went on till the people began to come in. Then he took a seat and made talk and laughter with the rest until closing time" (p. 150).

It seems important to note here that Tea Cake's courting is done both in private and in public. His second visit again involves a game of checkers, but this time they play in front of an audience. "Everybody was surprised at Janie playing checkers but they liked it. Three or four stood behind her and coached her moves and generally made merry with her in a restrained way" (p. 154).

What Janie and the rest of the community like about Tea Cake is his spontaneity, creativity, and positive attitude toward life. In a moving scene, Hurston pinpoints this, and his teaching quality. Tea Cake combs Janie's hair for her, and says, "Ah betcha you don't never go tuh de lookin' glass and enjoy yo' eyes yo' self. You'se got de world in uh jug and make out you don't know it. But Ah'm glad tuh be de one tuh tell yuh" [see I Corinthians 13:12]. When Janie objects that he must tell this to all the girls, he replies, "Ah'm de Apostle Paul tuh de Gentiles. Ah tells 'em and then again Ah shows 'em" (p. 157-58). Tea Cake's gospel of laughter here becomes the New Testament revision of the Black aesthetic; it is meant to replace the tragic "Old Testament" litany of Nanny and others like her who still labor under the stubborn heritage of slavery. Nanny, we remember, believes that "folks is meant to cry 'bout somethin' or other" (p. 43), and Tea Cake's creed reverses this. His doctrine is profoundly American and hopeful, even though he too has been and will be the victim of white racism—indeed, one could argue that his ultimate death is due to it—but that doesn't blind him to the glories of the world or the possibilities of the self. Like Emerson and Whitman, he believes in living in the "NOW," but his self-love and sheer joy in living come out of a black heritage, and his admonishment to Janie is echoed in a traditional blues lyric: "Baby, Baby, what is the matter with you? / You've got the world in a jug / Ain't a thing that you can't do."

This sense of possibility functions importantly in the world of play. Huizinga has proven play to be a basic human need, which strongly relates to laughter; play, he flatly states, is an instinctual impulse that must be satisfied.[43] Janie, who said as much to Jody, is no exception to this rule, and relishes her third husband's sense of play and laughter. She learns as much as she can from him on this subject during their brief two years together. The verb "to laugh" crops up again and again in the chapters devoted to their marriage. Play is frequently conducted within social parameters (as with the communal game of checkers, card games, the evenings with the people in the Everglades), but it often takes place on the periphery of convention or even outside it (the "widow" Janie and Tea Cake go fishing in the middle of the night). But the games Janie loves most are those that involve Tea Cake's imagination and creativity. Early on in their relationship he pretends to play on an imaginary guitar. Later, arriving in a battered car, he jumps out and makes the gesture of tying it to a post.

The widow Starks's neighbors, however, are not amused; this gets expressed in a litany of play-disapproval: they've seen her "sashayin off to a picnic in pink linen"; "Gone off to Sanford in a car . . . dressed in blue! gone hunting . . . gone fishing . . . to the movies . . . to a dance . . . playing checkers; playing coon-can; playing Florida flip . . . " (pp. 166–67). Janie has flipped the town's expectations; instead of mourning atop the pedestal Jody created for her, she has lost her "class" by gambling on Tea Cake and love. They want her back as an icon of respectability, but that isn't what they say; Pheoby, their emissary, warns Janie, " . . . you'se takin' uh awful chance," to which Janie, twice-married already, replies, "No mo' than Ah took befo' and no mo' than anybody else takes when dey gits married. . . . Dis ain't no business proposition, and no race after property and titles. Dis is uh love game" (p. 171), thereby setting the play element of their relationship out for the community.

Janie's faith is sorely tested in Jacksonville, for during their honeymoon there, Tea Cake vanishes with her hidden two hundred dollars. Janie, learning to trust herself and others, but also to take chances, bears up under the strain of the risk, and is still there, waiting, when Tea Cake comes home to tell her of the party he's given for his friends. Showing her the guitar he's bought and the twelve dollars he has left, he discloses that she's married one of "de best gamblers God ever made. Cards or dice either one" (p. 187). Watching him practice his dice throwing in preparation for an outing is exciting to Janie. He terrifies her when he comes back from his gaming wounded, but as she tends to him, he shows her the three hundred and twenty-two dollars he has made out of her twelve.

Their removal to the Everglades to work on the "muck" with the common people completes Janie's transformation. There, folks "don't do nothin' . . . but make money and fun and foolishness," and Janie grows there, like everything else: "Ground so rich that everything went wild . . . People wild too" (p. 193).

Tea Cake, with his guitar, his songs, his infectious laughter, plays Orpheus for the folk. Janie's growing ability to joke and laugh soon makes her a favorite with the people too, especially after she starts working alongside Tea Cake in the fields. When she and Tea Cake carry on behind the boss's back, "It got the whole field to playing off and on," recalling the role humor played in relieving the drudgery of work in the fields during slave times. Soon, Janie joins Tea Cake in story-telling for the appreciative audience that gathers each night at their shack: "The house was full of people every night. . . . Some were there to hear Tea Cake pick the box; some came to talk and tell stories, but most of them came to get into whatever game was going on or might go on . . . outside of the two jooks, everything on that job went on around those two" (pp. 200–201) Janie learns to "woof," to "boogerboo," to play all the games, and through it all, "No matter how rough it was, people seldom got mad, because everything was done for a laugh" (p. 200).

Even when Janie gets mad over Tea Cake's apparent flirtation, their fight ends with Tea Cake's joking dismissal of the presumed rival: "Whut would Ah do wid dat lil chunk of a woman wid you around? She ain't good for nothin' exceptin' tuh set up in uh corner by de kitchen stove and break wood over her head. You'se something tuh make uh man forget tuh git old and forgit tuh die" (p. 206).

An extremely important passage regarding Hurston's feeling about Black laughter comes in this section, when Janie meets the near-white Mrs. Turner. This racist, who hates her own race, urges Janie to marry a whiter man than Tea Cake. When Janie asks her, point-blank, "How come you so aginst black?" she immediately replies " . . . dey makes me tired. Always laughin'! Dey laughs too much and dey laughs too loud. Always singin' ol' nigger songs! Always cuttin' de monkey for white folks. If it wuzn't for so many black folks it wouldn't be no race problem. De white folks would take us in wid dem. De black ones is holdin' us back" (p. 210). She brags about her almost white brother, who tore Booker T. Washington to pieces in a speech. "All he ever done was cut de monkey for white folks. So dey pomped him up. But you know whut de old folks say, 'de higher de monkey climbs de mo' he show his behind' so dat's de way it wuz wid Booker T." (p. 212). Mrs. Turner thus becomes Hurston's surrogate for all those critics who accused *her* of "cuttin' the monkey for white folks," and it reminds us that although Janie is Hurston's surrogate in the novel, so is Tea Cake, for here he becomes the polar and positive opposite to Mrs. Turner, as an agent of the laughter she hates, and it is he who plots her banishment.

Hurston doesn't stop with Mrs. Turner, either; she exposes the similar racist and sexist view of Black men, whose repository of "black black women" jokes she despised.[44] Sop-de-Bottom compliments Tea Cake on having a light-colored woman, for when the latter slaps Janie for supposedly flirting with Mrs. Turner's brother, "Uh person can see every place you hit her. Ah bet she never raised her hand tuh hit yuh back, neither. Take some uh des ol' rusty black women and dey would fight yuh all night long and next day nobody couldn't tell you ever hit 'em. Dat's de reason Ah done quit beatin' mah woman. You can't make no mark on 'em at all. . . . Mah woman would spread her lungs all over Palm Beach County, let alone knock out mah jaw teeth. . . . She got ninety-nine rows uh jaw teeth and git her good and mad, she'll wade through solid rock up to her hip pockets" (p. 219). Yet after this, Sop-de-Bottom agrees that Mrs. Turner is "color-struck" and helps to run her off the muck! Hurston's clever juxtaposition of these sentiments could harldly be more ironic or more damning.

The wild melee the men start in Mrs. Turner's restaurant is just an excuse to wreck the place; while the destruction is going on, they pay elaborate compliments to their distressed hostess. It's a scene right out of the Marx Brothers. Mrs. Turner is soon on her way to Miami, "where folks is civilized" (p. 226), and presumably, less humorously inclined.

Significantly, when the folk on the muck fear the coming hurricane, they turn to the cheering resources of their culture; they sit in Janie and Tea Cake's house and tell stories about Big John de Conquer and his feats and tricks, listen to Tea Cake's guitar, and then sing a song that comes from the Dozens:

> Yo' mama don't wear no *Draws*
> Ah seen her when she took 'em *Off*
> She soaked 'em in alco*Hol*
> She sold 'em tuh de Santa *Claus*
> He told her 'twas aginst de *Law*
> To wear dem dirty *Draws* (p. 233)

The combination of John de Conquer stories and snippets of dozens lines helps the figures gird up their loins against cosmic forces; John is traditionally a daring figure who frequently gambles with both God and the Devil, and the defiance of the dozens humor is directed against a malevolently approaching Nature. Culture is attempting to ward off the storm.

In the aftermath of the hurricane, whites impress Tea Cake for a burial squad, and several other examples of racial oppression are raised. When Tea Cake comments on the dangers of being "strange niggers wid white folks," Janie adds "Dat sho is de truth. De ones de white man know is nice colored folks. De ones he don't know is bad niggers," which causes Tea Cake to laugh too, helping both of them to bear an unbearable situation (p. 255).

The wrong kind of humor comes into Hurston's range before the book ends. Tea Cake, bitten earlier by a mad dog, lies abed, and a white doctor is called to make a diagnosis. He initially greets his patient with some racist jocularity: "'Tain't a thing wrong that a quart of coon-dick wouldn't cure. You haven't been gettin' yo' right likker lately, eh?' He slapped Tea Cake lustily across his back and Tea Cake tried to smile as he was expected to do but it was hard" (p. 261).

The biggest joker of all, however, seems to be God. Janie ponders, "Did He *mean* to do this thing to Tea Cake and her? . . . Maybe it was some big tease and when He saw it had gone far enough He'd give her a sign" (p. 264).

After Tea Cake dies and Janie, acquitted by a white jury, buries him, she knows she has to return to Eatonville, for there she can sit in her house and live by memories.

Janie knows what to expect from the town, however; "sitters-and-talkers gointuh worry they guts into fiddle strings till dey find out . . . " and Janie's tale, told to Pheoby, is meant to function like Tea Cake's bundle of seeds, which Janie has brought with her; their story is meant for planting in the community, which needs their laughing, loving example. This is implicit in Pheoby's reaction: "Lawd! . . . Ah done growed ten feet higher jus' listenin' tuh you, Janie. An ain't satisfied wid mahself no mo'. Ah mean tuh make Sam take me fishin' wid him after this. Nobody better not criticize yuh in my hearin'" (p. 284).

We readers know this telling is necessary for another reason; earlier, Mrs. Annie Tyler brought out the cruel side of the community's humor. An older woman who is seduced, abandoned, and robbed by a series of young men, she has gone off laughing on her final fling with a younger man named, appropriately, Who Flung. Two weeks later a pitying Eatonville man finds her abandoned and penniless in Tampa; she is the laughingstock of the community upon her return. Similarly, at the beginning of the frame story, when Janie first returns, alone, the neighbors' "burning statements" and killing laughter once again create mass cruelty (p. 10). Janie's transformation, however, gives her words to soothe these sentiments, and to turn them to her favor, since her story, which cheers and illuminates, points the way toward personhood.

Individual achievement finds its ultimate fulfillment in conjunction with others, and as Mary Helen Washington wisely observes, "the deepest and most lasting relationships occur among those black people who are most closely allied with and influenced by their own community."[45] Throughout *Their Eyes Were Watching God*, Hurston indicates that to refuse one's heritage is cultural suicide, and the loss of laughter represents an early symptom. In a unique way, Zora Neale Hurston recognized and harnessed humor's powerful resources; using its magical ability to bring people together, she established the intimacy of democratic communion.

NOTES

1. Roger Rosenblatt, *Black Fiction* (Cambridge: Harvard Univ. Press, 1974), p. 101.

2. Zora Neale Hurston, "How It Feels to Be Colored Me," 1928; rpt. in *I Love Myself When I Am Laughing*, ed. Alice Walker (Old Westbury, NY: Feminist Press, 1979), p. 153; *Dust Tracks On a Road*, ed. Robert Hemenway, 2nd ed. (1942; Urbana: Univ. of Illinois Press, 1984), p. 281. All subsequent citations are to these editions.

3. Henry Louis Gates, Jr., "A Negro Way of Saying," *The New York Times Book Review*, 21 April 1985: 1, 41.

4. Hemenway, Introduction, *Dust Tracks*, pp. x–xi.

5. Robert Hemenway, *Zora Neale Hurston: A Literary Biography* (Urbana: Univ. of Illinois Press, 1978), p. 9.

6. *Dust Tracks*, p. 168.

7. According to Walter Lippmann's classic definition, a stereotype is a set of mental pictures formulated by human beings to describe the world beyond their reach, which are at least in part culturally determined. Lippmann stresses that stereotypes are factually incorrect products of a faulty reasoning process, and that they tend to persist despite new knowledge and education. *Public Opinion* (New York: Harcourt, Brace, 1922).

8. W. E. Vinacke, "Stereotypes as Social Concepts," *Journal of Social Psychology* 46 (1957): 229–43.

9. "Negro Youth Speaks," in *The New Negro*, ed. Alain Locke (1925; rpt. New York: Atheneum, 1970), p. 50.

10. Sherley Anne Williams, Introduction, *Their Eyes Were Watching God*, by Zora Neale Hurston (1937; reprint, Urbana: Univ. of Illinois Press, 1978), pp. ix–x.

11. Greer Litton Fox, "'Nice Girl': Social Control of Women through a Value Construct," *Signs* 2 (1977): 807.

12. For a penetrating analysis of female humor, a subject that only recently has attracted scholarly attention, see chapter 2, "Sexual Inequality in Humor," in Mahadev Apte, *Humor and Laughter: An Anthropological Approach* (Ithaca: Cornell Univ. Press, 1985), pp. 67–81.

13. Robin Lakoff, *Language and Woman's Place* (New York: Harper & Row, 1975), p. 56; Susan Kalčik, "' . . . Like Ann's Gynecologist; or, The Time I Was Almost Raped': Personal Narratives in Women's Rap Groups," *Journal of American Folklore* 88 (1975): 5.

14. *Infants of the Spring* (New York: MacCaulay, 1932), pp. 229–30.

15. Larry Neal, "Eatonville's Zora Neale Hurston: A Profile," *Black Review No. 2*, ed. Mel Watkins (New York: William Morrow, 1972), 11–24.

16. *The Big Sea* (New York: Hill & Wang, 1940), p. 239.

17. Neal, "Eatonville's Zora Neale Hurston: A Profile," p. 23.

18. For Freud's classic statement on the subject, see *Jokes and Their Relation to the Unconscious*, trans. and ed. James Strachey, std. ed. (New York: Norton, 1963), pp. 9–15.

19. Robert Hemenway, Introduction, *Dust Tracks*, p. xvii.

20. Zora Neale Hurston, "Characteristics of Negro Expression," in *Negro: An Anthology*, ed. Nancy Cunard (London: Wishart, 1934), p. 40. Barbara Johnson has recently published a fascinating related study, "Metaphor, Metonymy and Voice in *Their Eyes Were Watching God*," in *Black Literature and Literary Threory*, ed. Henry Louis Gates, Jr. (New York: Methuen, 1984), pp. 205–19.

21. An example, How God Made Blacks: arriving late on the day He handed out color, they crowded in, and thought he said "Git Black" when He said "Git back!" (*Dust Tracks*, pp. 65–69).

22. For discussions of these and related terms in Black humor, see Claudia Mitchell-Kernan, "Signifying, Loud-talking and Marking," in *Rappin' and Stylin' Out: Communication In Urban Black America*, ed. Thomas Kochman (Urbana: Univ. of Illinois Press, 1972), pp. 315–35; Thomas Kochman, "Toward an Ethnography of Black American Speech Behavior," in *Afro-American Anthropology: Contemporary Perspectives*, ed. Norman E. Whitten, Jr., and John F. Szwed (New York: Free Press, 1970), pp. 145–62, and Roger D. Abrahams, "Playing the Dozens," in *Mother Wit from the Laughing Barrel*, ed. Alan Dundes (Englewood Cliffs, N. J.: Prentice-Hall, 1973), pp. 295–309.

23. Zora Neale Hurston, *Mules and Men* (1935; reprint, Bloomington: Indiana Univ. Press, 1978), p. 3.

24. "John Redding Goes to Sea," 1921; rpt. *Opportunity* 4 (Jan. 1926), 16–21.

25. "Drenched in Light," *Opportunity* 2 (Dec. 1924), 371–74.

26. Hemenway, *Zora Neale Hurston*, p. 11.

27. For a cogent summary and discussion of research on this topic, see Apte, *Humor and Laughter*, pp. 29–66. The classic definition comes from A. R. Radcliffe-Brown, who describes a joking relationship as one "between two persons in which one is by custom permitted, and in some instances required, to tease or make fun of the other, who in turn is required to take no offense." "A Further Note on Joking Relationships," 1949; rpt. in *Structure and Function in Primitive Society* (London: Cohen West, 1965), pp. 105–16.

28. "Spunk," *Opportunity* 3 (June 1925), 171–73. This story occupies a central place in Hurston's career, for it was reprinted in the ground-breaking anthology, *The New Negro* (1925).

29. "The Eatonville Anthology," 1926; rpt. in *I Love Myself*, pp. 177–88.

30. See Hemenway's penetrating analysis of this scene, "Are You a Flying Lark or a Setting Dove?" in *Afro-American Literature: The Reconstruction of Instruction*, ed. Dexter Fisher and Robert B. Stepto (New York: MLA, 1979), pp. 122–52.

31. "Muttsy," *Opportunity* 4 (Aug. 1926): 7–15.

32. "Story in Harlem Slang," *American Mercury* 55 (July 1942): 84–96.

33. "Sweat," 1926; rpt. in *I Love Myself*, pp. 197–207.

34. "The Gilded Six-Bits," 1933; rpt. in *I Love Myself*, pp. 208–18.

35. *Jonah's Gourd Vine* (Philadelphia: Lippincott, 1934).

36. Letter from Zora Neale Hurston to Alain Locke, 16 April 1934, cited in Neal, "Eatonville's Zora Neale Hurston: A Profile," p. 16.

37. I shall deal at length with the comic aspects of *Moses* in a future essay.

38. Zora Neale Hurston, "Race Cannot Become Great Until It Recognizes Its Talent," *Washington Tribune*, 29 Dec. 1934.

39. Joseph Campbell's formulation of this principle is enumerated in his *The Hero With a Thousand Faces* (1949; rpt. Princeton: Princeton Univ. Press, 1972).

40. See especially Missy Dehn Kubitschek, "'Tuh De Horizon and Back': The Female Quest in *Their Eyes Were Watching God*," *Black Literature Forum* 17.3 (Fall 1983), 109–14.

41. As Michael G. Cooke notes, however, Janie and Jody are not technically playing the dozens. She *categorizes* him ("big-bellies"); as Cooke states, she "seems to crash through signifying and into denunciation." Michael G. Cooke, *Afro-American Literature in the Twentieth Century: The Achievement of Intimacy* (New Haven: Yale Univ. Press, 1984), p. 77.

42. Apte, *Humor and Laughter*, p. 79.

43. For the full elaboration of his theory, see Johan Huizinga, *Homo Ludens: A Study of the Play Element in Culture* (Boston: Beacon, 1970. Orig. published in Dutch in 1938; trans. from the German ed., 1944).

44. Anyone who doubts this should consult *Dust Tracks*, pp. 225–26.

45. Mary Helen Washington, Introduction, *Black Eyed Susans: Classic Stories By and About Black Women*, ed. Mary Helen Washington (New York: Anchor, 1975), p. xxx.

STERLING A. BROWN
AND THE AFRO-AMERICAN FOLK TRADITION

CHARLES H. ROWELL

One of the concerted efforts of the "New Negro" writers of the Twenties and Thirties was the attempt to reinterpret black life in America and thereby provide a more accurate, more objective, representation of black people than that popularized in the reactionary and sentimental literature of the preceding decades. Alain Locke, a major voice of the New Negro Movement, wrote in the mid-Twenties that "the Negro to-day wishes to be known for what he is, even in his faults and short comings, and scorns a craven and precarious survival at the price of seeming to be what he is not."[1] In their creative works, many New Negro writers subscribed to that position, for they knew that much of the earlier literature about the black experience in the United States was fraught with distorted images of ante- and post-bellum black Americans—their life and culture and their history and traditions. That is, much of the poetry, fiction and drama about black people was based on the sentimental, plantation and minstrel traditions, and, therefore, had little or nothing to do with the lives of black people in America. However numerous their failings might be, New Negro writers, with a high degree of achievement, tried to create a new stage upon which to play out the kaleidoscopic drama of black life in America.

The effort to reinterpret Afro-American life and character went in various directions. Following the "just-like-white-folks philosophy," some writers, for example, created works which emphasized the similarities between blacks and whites. Other writers, subscribing to the decadent white belief in the "exotic Negro," emphasized the so-called "primitivism" of black people. There were, of course, other writers whose aesthetic visions were broader than those of the aforementioned groups. This third group realized that to express the souls of black folk, the artist has to divest himself of preconceived and false notions about black people, and create an art whose foundation is the ethos from which black life, history, culture, and traditions all spring.

It is this third group of New Negro writers—Langston Hughes, Jean Toomer, Zora Neale Hurston, and Sterling Brown among them—who set out to reevaluate "African-American history and folk culture."[2] It is this group of writers who tried to do what James Weldon Johnson said he attempted to do in his later poetry: to rear a superstructure of conscious art upon "the American Negro's cultural background and his creative folk-art."[3] This group of young writers was indeed familiar with the pronouncements that James Weldon Johnson, Alain Locke, and others made on the importance of the Afro-American folk tradition to the development of the black artist.[4] In their efforts to build a self-conscious art upon folk art, these writers, just as their black predecessors (Paul Laurence Dunbar and Charles W. Chesnutt) had done in their more balanced works, brought to Afro-American literature a quality that became one of its main currents: the ethos of black folk. However, of the younger New Negro writers, it was Sterling A. Brown and Zora Neale Hurston, as Larry Neal points out, who made the systematic studies of certain aspects of the Afro-American folk tradition.[5] And much of what Hurston and Brown discovered from their studies found its way into their conscious art. While Langston Hughes concentrated on urban black folk in *The Weary Blues* (1926) and *Fine Clothes to the Jew* (1927), Hurston and Brown, like Jean Toomer in *Cane* (1923), probed deeply into the life and culture of Southern black folk. But, whereas some may argue that Hurston occasionally failed aesthetically in fiction, Brown succeeded in poetry.

Unlike Zora Neale Hurston (1903–1960), whose background was small-town South, Brown was born and reared in Washington, D.C., where his father was a minister of distinction and a professor of religion at Howard University. After he graduated from Washington's Dunbar High School, Brown received the B.A. and M.A. degrees in English literature from Williams College (Massachusetts) and Harvard University, respectively. Such a background was not, however, a liability to him for his preparation as folklorist, critic of Afro-American literature, and poet in the folk manner. Instead his background proved to be an asset, for his New England education and wide reading developed in him a critical sensibility, one which he long used in positive service to the black community. Early in his career as litterateur, he discovered that the representations of black peasants in most books were very different from the black peasants he had known and seen in Washington. Realizing that the images of black people in existing literature were largely false, Brown set out to correct what he saw.

"What motivates a middle-class Black man and a Harvard graduate . . . to devote his life to portraying less well-to-do folks?" queries Genevieve Ekaete. She answers:

> Being Black is the key. . . . According to [Sterling Brown], he was indignant
> at the corrupted folk speech publicized by "white comic writers like Octavus

Roy Cohen." From his experience, Brown says, he knew his people didn't talk that way. It wasn't enough for him to enjoin them to "Stop knowing it all!" He had to bring some semblance of balance by putting his people down on black and white to counter the proliferating distortions from other sources.[6]

Then, too, early in his teaching career Brown "read the new realistic poetry in American life:—that of Frost, Sandburg, Masters, Lindsay and Robinson, for example. In their "democratic approach to the people," Brown saw much that reflected his own thoughts about ordinary people. Brown recalls: "when Carl Sandburg said 'yes' to the American people, I wanted to say 'yes' to my people."[7] Brown's "yes" was to give us carefully wrought poems portraying "common" black folk "in a manner constant with them."[8] His "yes" to black people was also to give us a series of critical works which attempted to counter "the proliferating distortions" of black folk life and character. As early as the Twenties, Brown began writing a series of critical studies and reviews on the portrayal of blacks in American literature. In 1929, he observed that

From Kennedy's "Swallow Barn," about the first treatment of the planta- tion, down to Dixon's rabid Ku Klux Klan propaganda, the Negro has been shown largely as an animal. Kennedy, doing a piece of special pleading, showed the Negro as parasitical, excessively loyal, contented, irrespon- sible, and so forth. Dixon showed his Negro characters, not as faithful dogs, but as mad curs. His brutes are given to rapine, treachery, bestiality, and gluttony.[9]

Like other New Negro writers, Brown knew that such portrayals were neither accurate characterizations nor true expressions of the souls of black folk.

After study at Williams and Harvard, Brown prepared himself to counter dis- torting images of black people perpetuated in American literature. To do so, he read widely and critically into the literature by and about black people, and carefully studied Afro-American history and folk culture. Hence his *Negro Po- etry and Drama, The Negro in American Fiction* (both in 1938), and several important periodical essays and reviews—sources which no serious student of American literature can ignore. But to counter the distorting images as poet, Brown knew he had to go beyond books and his Washington experiences for material: he went directly to black people in the South. That is, as he taught and traveled in the South, he lived among and carefully observed those peasants who created black folk traditions—traditions which sustained them in their daily lives. Writing in 1934 about Brown as "folk poet," Alain Locke asserted that

Sterling Brown has listened long and carefully to the folk in their intimate hours, when they are talking to themselves, not, so to speak, as in Dunbar, but actually as they do when the masks of protective mimicry fall. Not only has he dared to give quiet but bold expression to this private thought and speech, but he has dared to give the Negro peasant credit for thinking.[10]

In a word, when Brown taught and traveled in the South, he became an insider to the multifarious traditions and verbal art forms indigenous to black folk, and through his adaptations of their verbal art forms and spirit he, as poet, became an instrument for their myriad voices. Hence *Southern Road.*

When *Southern Road* appeared in 1932, reviewers, as James Weldon Johnson had observed in his introduction to the collection, were quick to recognize Brown's absorption of the spirit and the verbal art of black folk. Critics realized that Brown had tapped the black folk ethos which later Afro-American poets would draw from, that he had captured the essence of black folk life and culture, without the distortion and sentimentality of earlier American writers. In form and content, most of Brown's poems reflect some aspect of the life and oral traditions of black people. And it is through his folk-oriented poems that he makes his most significant contribution to the corpus of Afro-American poetry.[11]

In the Preface to the 1921 edition of his *Book of American Negro Poetry*, James Weldon Johnson made an influential comment about the direction the black poet in America should take. Inherent in Johnson's seminal statement are the principles embodied in Brown's major poetry. Johnson asserted that what the black American poet

> needs to do is something like what Synge did for the Irish; he needs to find a form that will express the racial spirit by symbols from within rather than by symbols from without, such as the mere mutilation of English spelling and pronunciation. He needs a form that is freer and larger than dialect, but which will still hold the racial flavor; a form expressing the imagery, the idioms, and peculiar turns of thought, and the distinctive humor and pathos, too, of the Negro, but which will also be capable of voicing the deepest and highest emotions and aspirations, and allow of the widest range of subjects and the widest scope of treatment.[12]

To give voice to the common black man in poetry, Brown drew heavily on forms that grew directly out of the black American experience; he made use of Afro-American folksongs—their techniques, idiom and spirit. Brown knew that the ideas and art of the folksongs were expressive of the people who created them; that Afro-American "folk forms and cultural responses," to use the words of George E. Kent, "were themselves definitions of black life created by blacks on the bloody and pine-scented Southern soil and upon the blackboard jungle of urban streets, tenement buildings, store-front churches, and dim-lit bars."[13] What, then, could be more appropriate modes for poetic reinterpretations of black life in America than the worksong, the blues, the spiritual, and the ballad?

In "Southern Road," the title poem of his first collection, Brown draws upon the forms and spirit of the worksong and the blues. To express the tragic voice of despondency of black chain gangs so often seen on Southern roads, Brown fuses adapted techniques of the worksong and the blues. But the aesthetic and ideational result is something more than the blues or the worksong.

Because the worksong as a distinctive form has all but passed away, it is important here to make a brief comment on its nature and function. At one time the worksong was sung by black laborers throughout the Americas and Africa. Like much black music, the worksong is functional; it was composed not for the entertainment of an audience but as an accompaniment to labor. As a functional form of music, the worksong was variously "used to pace work" and "supply a rhythm for work," to give directions, to "help pass the time," and "to offer a partial outlet for . . . tensions and frustrations and angers." Moreover, for convicts, worksongs changed "the nature of the work by putting the work into the worker's framework rather than the guards'."[14] On the worksong accompanying voluntary and involuntary labor, Brown wrote that

> . . . worksongs accompany work in unison. Roustabouts on the levees, steel-drivers, axemen in the woods, the shantymen on the old windjammers, lighten their labor by singing in rhythm with it. A gang driving spikes will sing, punctuating their lines with a grunt as the hammer falls. . . . [T]he verses are somewhat unconnected, the men singing what first comes to their minds, concerned chiefly with the functional rhythm.[15]

Brown's comments are descriptive of the type of worksong which accompanies communal labor and requires group rhythm—what Bruce Jackson calls "timed work," such as cross-cutting, logging, flatweeding, and steel-driving.[16] The grunt ("hunh") Brown mentions is a rhythmical or timing device in some worksongs. In others such as "Here, Rattler, Here," a repeated ejaculatory phrase or line following the song leader's assertion serves the same function. Brown's comments on the worksong, especially his observations on its rhythm and the inconsecutiveness of its stanzas, are essential to our understanding and appreciation of his adaption of its communal form in "Southern Road." The artistic techniques of a worksong like "John Henry Hammer Song" not only bear his comments out but suggest the kind of worksong he drew on for conscious poetry.

A comparison of the first stanzas of "Southern Road" and "John Henry Hammer Song" will show how Brown incorporates the rhythm of the worksong in his poem:

> Swing dat hammer—hunh—
> Steady, bo';
> Swing dat hammer—hunh—
> Steady, bo';
> Ain't no rush, bebby,
> Long ways to go.

> ("Southern Road")

Dis is de Hammer	/hunh/
Killt John Henry	/hunh/
Twon't kill me, baby,	/hunh/
Twon't kill me	

("John Henry Hammer   Song")[17]

Brown punctuates lines one and three with "hunh," the "grunt" he refers to as being uttered "as the hammer falls." Although the transcriber of "John Henry Hammer Song" did not represent the "grunts," the rhythm of the work which the song accompanied probably required that "hunh" be uttered after the song leader's assertions in lines one, two, and three. The "bebby" in Brown's poem and the "baby" in the hammer song serve the same function: they, like the grunt, aid in the rhythm; and they signal the closing of each stanza. Moreover, they suggest the presence of not so much an auditor but a fellow worker, as does the directional "Steady, bo'" in stanza one of Brown's poem. In "Southern Road," Brown, it should be remembered, does not imitate the rhythm of the worksong. Rather, like Johnson in his use of the rhythm of the folk sermon in *God's Trombones*, Brown adapts the rhythm of the communal worksong.

In addition to adapting the rhythm of the communal worksong, Brown takes the worksong to a high level of conscious art. He transforms the worksong into a piece of coherent art by creating stanzas which are connected in content as well as rhythm. Like most worksongs, "Southern Road" is not narrative. Brown's poem does, however, recount a unified and coherent series of situations or conditions of a despondent but stoic convict. That panoramic series produces one effect: sympathy or sorrow for the tragic fate of the speaker who has been sentenced to life imprisonment for murder.

Concentrating on the convict's woes, the poem takes into account the problems of his family in the outside world as well as his own within the confines of the prison. He can do nothing about those problems, for he is powerless. The first stanza is about his own and his fellow convicts' immediate situation. Their work, which has no private goal, is interminable—hence they need not rush. In the following stanzas we discover the cause of his imprisonment, and the mental anguish brought on by it and the condition of his family. In a state of powerlessness, he is tormented psychologically as well as physically, for his daughter has become a street woman; his son, a wanderer; and his wife, a hospitalized mother of a coming child. Moreover, the convict-speaker thinks of his poor mother rocking her misery, and he recalls his father cursing him on his deathbed. The last three stanzas move back to the convict's immediate condition: he is chained ("double-shackled") to dehumanizing labor, with a white guard damning his soul. The final stanza brings his suffering full circle: he is doomed; he is on the chain gang for life—"po' los' boy / Evahmo'." His appears to be an insurmountable despondency, for his powerlessness and that of his lost family, and the social and economic curse of the larger society render him helpless. Unlike the ironic and rebellious speaker in "John Henry Hammer Song" and other worksongs, the speaker in Brown's "Southern Road" assumes a blues attitude. He of necessity resigns himself to his tragic fate.

"No poem more pathetically depicts the despair of the entire race than 'Southern Road,'" writes Jean Wagner.

> Here the entire spirit of revolt is already snuffed out and transcended, since it is seen as useless, and there is a stoic acceptance of destiny. Confronting a hostile universe, the black man knows that he is dolefully alone and has no surviving connection with an outside world that might offer him help or a gleam of hope.[18]

"Southern Road" is a lyrical expression of powerlessness and despondency—one picture of "the tragedy of the southern Negro." It is, then, important to remember that the speaker of the poem is a convict, not a Black Everyman; that his despondency is that of his people, but that other poems in Brown's first collection and elsewhere are needed to round out his picture of the tragic condition of Southern black folk. It is important to remember, too, that in the world of Sterling Brown the black man's response to the inhumanities of his white oppressors is not always acceptance. His response, however futile it may prove to be, is sometimes like that of Joe in "The Ballad of Joe Meek" or that of Sam in "Sam Smiley": revolt in the face of inevitable destruction.

To express the powerlessness and despair of his convict-speaker, Brown also assimilates the stanzaic pattern of the blues. Like the traditional blues stanza, each stanza of "Southern Road" is divided into two parts. Part one constitutes a statement, or presents a situation or problem. Part two gives a response, the speaker's (or more accurately, singer's) reaction to the problem or the effect of the problem upon him. Moreover, as in the blues, the statement of the problem or situation is repeated in "Southern Road" but without the occasional variation. The statement is followed by a concluding response once presented—e.g., "Ball and chain, bebby, / On my min'." A reordering of one of Brown's stanzas reveals how closely it approximates the traditional stanza of the blues:

> Chain gang nevah—hunh—
> Let me go;
> Chain gang nevah—hunh—
> Let me go;
> Po' los' boy, bebby,
> Evahmo'. . . .

Rather than emphasize the speaker's response to the problem as in "John Henry Hammer Song," Brown concentrates on the problem through repetition, thus intensifying the tragic situation of the speaker. In Brown's hands the worksong is transformed into a new blues form, a blues-worksong, permeated with all the resignation and toughness of traditional blues. In the direct and terse idiom characteristic of the Afro-American folksong, Brown, in "Southern Road," captures at once a single and, ultimately, a communal cry of the desponding Southern black voice.

Brown draws more directly on the traditional form, the subjects, and the idiom of the blues in other poems. In some of those, however, he, as self-conscious artist, is less successful than in others in which he fuses various folk and literary techniques. In the former, he, as Alvin Aubert observes of Langston Hughes's direct use of the blues mode,[19] almost replicates those artistic techniques marking the distinctiveness of the blues form. The three poems which comprise "New St. Louis Blues," for instance, adhere too closely to the blues form. In them, Brown uses the two-part three line stanza form of classic blues, each line marked by a caesura. But instead of the common *aab* rhyme scheme, Brown's stanzas are triplets. Aesthetically, these poems are like Hughes's "Morning After" and "Midwinter Blues." They lack what George Kent calls the resources of the blues singer: "the singing voice, instrumental music, facial expression and gesture"— all of which help the singer drive his lyrics "into our spirit."[20]

Brown's poems in the blues mode are more captivating than Hughes's. What interests us most about Brown's poems in "New St. Louis Blues" is the broadness and variety of his subjects and his handling of them. In Hughes's blues mode poems, the central subject is usually love relationships, rendered in the first person and through the associational technique of the blues. Less individualized, Brown's poems in "New St. Louis Blues" cover various subjects. In "Market Street Woman," there is the troubled life of the prostitute, to whom life is "dirty in a hundred onery ways." Written in the first person, "Low Down" describes the down-and-outness of a "bummin' cut plug," who tragically internalizes society's vision of him as a worthless being and who views life and that which follows as a loaded game of dice. "Tornado Blues" recounts the havoc wrought by a storm on a poor black community, which must suffer not only from the storm's destructiveness but from the economic exploitation of the white community also. In "Tornado Blues" and such poems as "Children of the Mississippi," "Foreclosure" and "Cabaret," the Southern black man is a victim of natural disasters as well as racial injustice. These six poems clearly support Jean Wagner's thesis that Brown's poetry "depicts the Negro as the victim not only of the white man, but of all that surrounds him."[21]

Beyond the obvious blues form previously noted, the art of "New St. Louis Blues" is an achievement, for here Brown takes blues techniques to a literary level. In "Tornado Blues" he skillfully uses personification, a figure of speech frequently used in the blues. In some blues such as Leadbelly's "Good Morning Blues," Bessie Smith's "In House Blues" and Leroy Carr's "Midnight Hour Blues," the blues itself is personified. Brown's personification of the merciless tornado and its effects gives irony to the situation in "Tornado Blues." After the heartless wind completes its work and disappears, it leaves in its wake destruction, fear, death and sorrow. The speaker in the poem comments:

> Newcomers dodge de mansions, and knocked on de po' folks' do',
> Dodged most of the mansions, and knocked down de po' folks' do',
> Never know us po' folks so popular befo'—

It is ironic that these poor black people, rather than rich white people, would be visited, for they had little to offer their cruel guests. Brown's extended use of personification gives coherence to "Tornado Blues"—a coherence less directly achieved through the usual associational technique of traditional blues.

In "Ma Rainey," Brown uses the blues in another way, or rather he uses self-conscious poetry to comment on what Larry Neal refers to as the ethos of the blues.[22] Although "Ma Rainey" is a celebration of a single blues singer, Brown's poem is ultimately a description of the general effect and function of all blues singers and their art. The idea of Brown's poem is not unlike some of the views set forth by Larry Neal, Albert Murray and Ralph Ellison on the blues and blues singers. The blues singer, writes Neal, acts "as ritual poet" and "reflects the horrible and beautiful realities of life." "The blues singer," Neal continues, "is not an alienated artist attempting to impose his view on the world of others. His ideas are the reflection of an unstated general point-of-view."[23] Murray sees the blues musician as "fulfilling the same fundamental existential requirement that determines the mission of the poet, the priest, and the medicine man. He is making an affirmative and hence exemplary and heroic response to that which André Malraux describes as *la condition humaine*."[24] For Ellison, Bessie Smith was a "priestess"; she was "a celebrant who affirmed the values of the group and man's ability to deal with chaos."[25] That Brown's Ma Rainey was not "an alienated artist" but a priestess-poet-medicinewoman of the people is voiced throughout the poem. First of all, "as ritual poet" Ma Rainey attracted throngs of people wherever she performed—e.g., in Missouri and

> Fo' miles on down,
> To New Orleans delta
> An' Mobile town. . . .

And when she performed, her first person songs, which expressed the collective experience of her people, moved her auditors, for she could "Git way inside" them: "She jes' catch hold of us somekindaway." Her performance was ritual; and her songs, medicine to "keep us strong." In other words, her effect, though secular, was not unlike that of the black folk preacher in his sermons: it gave her auditors fortitude to confront and endure "de hard luck/Roun'" their "do'" and "de lonesome road" they "mus' go. . . ." Her songs bore witness to their many troubles and, thereby, made meaning of the chaotic world they confronted perpetually. No wonder, then, when Ma Rainey sang "Backwater Blues"—that song of personal and collective suffering from natural disaster—

'. . . de folks, dey natchally bowed dey heads an' cried,
Bowed dey heavy heads, shet dey moufs up tight an' cried,
An' Ma lef' de stage, an' followed some de folks outside.'

Brown's skillful use of the blues mode in part four of "Ma Rainey" is similar to Hughes's in "The Weary Blues." In neither poem is there mere replication. Rather the blues mode is thematically functional in each poem. Brown uses the form to illustrate further the effect of Ma Rainey's blues artist on her auditors. He excerpts and alters lines (one line of the statement and the response) from three stanzas of Bessie Smith's popular "Backwater Blues,"[26] and follows them with a stanza (quoted above) in the blues form. That stanza, a triplet, describes the effect of Ma Rainey's ritualized performance—an effect which is at once cathartic and entertaining.

It is important to note that Brown's selection of "Backwater Blues" is very appropriate. Not only do the lines further the poem thematically; they, like the poems of "New St. Louis Blues," indirectly make a comment on the subject of the blues: that its subject is not limited to love relations. Because several women blues singers had popularized the form with lyrics dealing with love, many people concluded that the blues "are a woman's longing cry for her 'man'. The subject matter," wrote Brown in 1937,

> is not so limited, however, and blues aplenty can be found bewailing tornadoes, high water, hard times in farming, or insisting upon the need for traveling, for leaving this cold-hearted town. As well as self pity there is stoicism in the blues.[27]

Moreover, Brown's selection of "Backwater Blues" gave an air of immediacy to the poem—i.e., his readers were no doubt familiar with Bessie Smith's song and the countless problems caused by floods in the Mississippi Valley, and other river and lowland areas, as recounted in Brown's "Children of the Mississippi," "Foreclosure" and other poems. Therefore, while implying that the range of the subject of the blues is not limited, Brown, in part four of "Ma Rainey," provided his early readers with an experience that was as immediate to them as the threat of air pollution is to us.

Brown's use of other forms of black folk music is similar to his fusion of the blues mode in "Ma Rainey." His fusion of folk music forms with self-conscious literary techniques is thematically functional and constant with the folk and folk life he portrays. In "Strong Men," for example, there are quoted lines from various black folksongs. "Strong Men," it should be noted, is about black people's strength to survive in the face of racism and economic exploitation; the poem is a celebration of the stoicism of black Americans. In other words, in spite of the white man's dehumanization of him from the Middle Passage through the twentieth century, the black man has endured; he has never been completely broken, as it were, for "The strong men keep a-comin' on." In fact, "Gittin' stronger. . . ."

To develop the idea of black stoicism, Brown juxtaposes his catalogue of inhumanities against black people to passages from spirituals and secular songs. The songs Brown quotes bespeak the black man's hope, strength and endurance—his dogged will to survive—born out of the suffering, profitless labor, racial segregation, etc., described in the poem. For centuries these songs and others have served as a solace and a source of strength for black people. As Brown says in "Children's Children," these songs, though unknown or laughed at by first generation Great Migrators, were the "sole comfort" of a suffering Black South people, who have known

> Long days beneath the torrid Dixie sun
> In miasma'd riceswamps;
> The chopping of dried grass, on the third go round
> In strangling cotton;
> Wintry nights in mud-daubed makeshift huts
> With these songs, sole comfort.

The old undefeated black woman in "Virginia Portrait" has her "Old folksongs chanted underneath the stars . . . ," along with her religion and her pleasant memories of times past to help her survive the many problems she faces. Through his use of black folk music in "Strong Men," "Children's Children," and "Virginia Portrait," Brown comments on Black South strength and, indirectly, the function of music in black life and culture. As in "Strong Men," Brown uses excerpts from the spiritual for thematic purposes in "When de Saints Go Ma'ching Home." The lines from the spiritual of the same title are expressive of the dream of the speaker-musician: on Judgment Day he hopes to meet his mother in Heaven and be counted among the saints. The lines from the spiritual also have a technical function; they serve as transitions from one roll call to the next of persons the musician envisions as likely and unlikely saints. Brown's incorporation of passages from black folksongs in his poetry is not unlike a technique T. S. Eliot, Melvin Tolson, Ezra Pound and Robert Hayden employed in their poetry. But Brown's poetry makes fewer demands on the reader.

The stark simplicity and directness of expression in the catalogue of inhumanities in "Strong Men" and, especially, "Old Lem" are akin to those in the following slave secular recorded by Frederick Douglass in *My Bondage and My Freedom* (1853):

> We raise de wheat,
> Dey gib us de corn;
> We bake de bread,
> Dey gib us de crust;
> We sif de meal,
> Dey gib us de huss;
> We peel de meat,
> Dey gib us the skin;

And dat's the way
Dey take us in;
We skim de pot.
Dey gib us de liquor,
And say dat's good enough for nigger.[28]

A passage from "Old Lem" will show Brown's ability to capture that same simplicity and directness of expression through the voice of Old Lem:

"They weigh the cotton
They store the corn
  We only good enough
  To work the rows;
They run the commissary
They keep the books
  We gotta be grateful
  For being cheated;
Whippersnapper clerks
Call us out of our name
  We got to say mister
  To spindling boys
They make our figgers
Turn somersets
  We buck in the middle
  Say, 'Thankyuh, sah.'"[29]

The voice of Old Lem adapts the cadence of the slave secular. Moreover, like the speaker in the slave secular, Old Lem, without resorting to excessive figures of speech or bombastic, emotional language, articulates the powerlessness of his people and the many injustices heaped upon them. No rhetorical tricks becloud his revelation of facts. The clarity and power of the dialect he speaks belie the false image of the black man in the literature of the minstrel and plantation traditions, in which he is represented as a verbose clown, misusing and mutilating polysyllabic words. Using collected folklore, folksongs, and the living speech of the peasant blacks he met and befriended as indices to rural black dialect, Brown, in "Old Lem" and many other poems, attempted to counter the vicious propaganda about black dialect disseminated in American literature. In a word Brown took the dialect of the black peasant and shaped it into consummate art.

Not all of Brown's folk characters speak with the simplicity and directness found in "Old Lem." Like other dialects, black folk speech has its variety, and the form used at a given moment depends upon the occasion as well as the nature of the speaker and his linguistic region. Hence the dialect of the speaker in "Sister Lou" is constant with her Southern character and her vision of Heaven, whereas some of the vocabulary ("down the country," "dicties," "pennies on de numbers") of the speaker's dialect in "Tin Roof Blues" reflects his Northern urban experience. In "Sister Lou," the female speaker's vision of Heaven, that place where she and her auditor hope to be relieved of the troubles of this world, is couched in an idiom that is replete with homely images. Her images and metaphors are reflective of her experience and her status in Southern society. As in spirituals and gospel songs, her God, Jesus, and the saints are seen in anthropomorphic terms. Her Heaven is reflective of places of earthly wealth—places which, from her angle of vision, suggest comfort. The passage from this world to the next will be by train, and, during her auditor's stay in heaven, she should visit "Wid frien' Jesus fo' a spell." God and His saints have human attributes, and her relation to them will be a human relation. Although the organization of this Heaven is reflective of what she knows on earth, God, the Master of the Big House in Heaven, will change her role. No longer will she be the servant; she will become a lady with her own room

> . . . wid windows
> Opening on cherry trees an' plum trees
> Bloomin' everlastin'

She will, moreover, have servants, but they will not disturb her room or her rest. She, a lady in Heaven, will be done with all the rushing imposed on black servants in this world. In short, Brown's poetic idiom of the folk, however secular, is constant with the folk vision of Heaven—a reflection of all that the folk have seen as positive and wanted in this world.

Again in "Memphis Blues," Brown employs the rhythm idiom of black folk church. In fact, he fuses the rhythm and imagery of the black folk sermon with the ejaculatory response of the blues and gospel, and the rhythm of folk rhymes. Parts one and three of "Memphis Blues" employ the rhythm of black folk rhymes. Although part one uses the rhythm of the folk rhyme, underlining its Biblical and historical allusions is the black folk preacher's vision of the threat of destruction. The threat here is not so much "the fire next time" for which the sinner is to prepare his soul, but the destruction of Memphis, Tennessee, by floods and tornadoes. Ultimately the poem is a comment on the transitory nature of all things man-made. In other words, just as great cities of the past fell to decay, so will Memphis. But, because this Memphis does not belong to the black man, the various speakers are indifferent to its inevitable destruction; if Memphis falls, "Nigger won't worry," or if "Memphis come back/Ain' no skin/Off de nigger's back." Rather than prepare for the destruction as the auditors of an exhorting preacher would expect his congregation to do, the speakers stoically accept it without reprimand from the general speaker. Their indifference is summed up in part three, an excellent employment of the rhythm of black folk rhymes:

> Memphis go
> By Flood or Flame;
> Nigger won't worry
> All de same—
> Memphis go

Memphis come back,
Ain' no skin
Off de nigger's back.
All dese cities
Ashes, rust. . . .
De win' sing sperrichals
Through deir dus'.

The rhythm of that stanza is similar to that in the following rhyme entitled "Aunt Kate":

Ole Aunt Date, she died so late
She couldn't get in at the Heaven Gate.
The Angels met her with a great big club,
Knocked her right back in the washin' tub.

And in "Precious Things":

Hold my rooster, hold my hen,
Pray don't touch my Grecian Bend.

Hold my bonnet, hold my shawl,
Pray don't touch my waterfall.

Hold my hands by the finger tips,
But pray don't touch my sweet little lips.[31]

Through the rhythm of folk rhymes, Brown intensifies the black man's indifference toward the destruction of Memphis, for folk rhymes are not only humorous but playful. The threat of the destruction of Memphis is dismissed lightly, for it is of less concern to the black man than it is to the white man, who claims the city as his own.

Presenting each speaker's reaction to the threat of destruction, part two of "Memphis Blues" fuses the voices of the black folk preacher, and the blues and gospel singers. Each stanza is divided into two parts: a call in the voice of the preacher and a response in the voices of musicians. Like the black folk preacher using repetitious, formulaic and rhetorical questions to exhort his congregation to prepare their souls for Judgment Day, the general speaker calls:

Watcha gonna do when de tall flames roar,
Tall flames roar, Mistah Lovin' Man?

And the Loving Man responds:

Gonna love my brownskin better'n before—
Gonna love my baby lak a do right man,
Gonna love my brown baby, oh, my Lawd!

The first two lines, which initiate the last three lines of each stanza, convey the threat of destruction, presented in terms of the traditional fire-water-wind-flame imagery found in the folk sermon. The general speaker's identification or address to each speaker responding by his vocation or avocation recalls the descriptive appellation of the "sinner man" and "gambling man." The repeated, formulaic call ("What you gonna do when . . ."), Presented in a carefully measured rhythm, exemplifies one of the techniques used by the folk preacher to "move" his congregation. Ironically, the response of each speaker in the poem has nothing to do with the impending destruction; while Memphis is being destroyed, each speaker plans to do what he thinks is best for him. On the other hand, the sentiment and repetition of the response recall the blues, but its ejaculatory "oh, my Lawd" is from the tradition of the "shout," and spiritual and gospel singing, which runs throughout "New Steps." "Memphis Blues," then, is not a blues poem in the sense that "New St. Louis Blues," "Kentucky Blues," "Riverbank Blues," and "Ma Rainey" are. But underlining each speaker's indifference in "Memphis Blues" is the sensibility of the blues singer—his stoic ability to transcend his deprived condition.

The dialect of the black folk figures in Brown's poetry is constant with their character. Honed in black folk life, the dialect he employs has none of the "humor and pathos" of the contrived speech used by "black" characters in the literature of the plantation tradition. Neither is the dialect in his poetry a transcription of how blacks supposedly spoke. Although he retains some of the pronunciations common to black speech, Brown does not arbitrarily mutilate the spellings of words to suggest the unlettered character of his folk. At a time when many black poets were avoiding black dialect as a medium for poetry, Brown, wrote Johnson in his Introduction to *Southern Road*, "infused his poetry with genuine characteristic flavor by adopting as his medium the common, racy, living speech of the Negro in certain phases of real life." From that speech, Brown, with a good ear and a sensibility attuned to the folk, selects its varied rhythms, idioms, metaphors and images, and transforms them into conscious art.

Like Euro-American and other Afro-American poets of the twentieth century, Brown has also employed the traditions of the folk ballad in his poetry. Influencing more than fifteen poems in *Southern Road*, the ballad, along with the blues mode, is the most frequently used form in the collection. At times, he adopts the ballad form; at others, he combines the narrative techniques of the ballad with artistic techniques of other forms. "Ma Rainey" and "Georgie Grimes," in which he combines the narrative technique and the stanzaic patterns of the ballad with the ethos of the blues, are excellent examples of the fusion of folk forms. "Ma Rainey" is, says Stephen Henderson, an "invented . . . blues-ballad, which, as a literary phenomenon, is as distinctive as Wordsworth's 'lyrical ballad.'"[32] In other poems, such as "Frankie and Johnny," "The Ballad of Joe Meek," and the Slim Greer series, Brown relies, in the main, on the ballad tradition to interpret the experience of black people.

His poems in the ballad tradition are not confined to the subjects iterated in Gordon Hall Gerould's *The Ballad of Tradition* or those B. Malcolm Laws sees as the prevailing themes of the black folk ballad.[33] Brown's literary ballads, while sometimes adhering closely to the folk ballad form, cover numerous subjects from black folk life. Racial injustice, exploits of folk heroes, tragic love affairs, religion, suffering in poverty, freedom, the need for travel—all of these and many others constitute the subjects of Brown's ballads. His poems in the ballad form alone, more than his poems employing other forms of Afro-American music, give us a broad slice of black life in America.

"Frankie and Johnny" is an example of Brown's use of the subject of a traditional ballad. In this poem, he retains the subject of a love relationship, but he changes the narrative from that found in the traditional ballad, variously called "Frankie and Johnny" to comment on the cruelty, and the sexual racism and fear of the rural South. In the traditional ballad, both lovers are black, but in Brown's poem Frankie is changed to a white girl, "A halfwit" who "Kept a crazy love of torment when she got bigger." Moreover, the source of conflict in the traditional ballad is the unfaithfulness of Frankie's lover, Johnny, whom she, with a thirst for revenge, kills without remorse. The conflict in Brown's poem, on the other hand, is racial and sexual. Sadistic Frankie seduces Johnny, a black plowman, to make love to her. To torment her racist father, a "red-faced cracker, with a cracker's thirst," Frankie spoke to him about her affair with the black plowman. When her "pappy" discovers the truth, the inevitable occurs: Johnny is lynched. The lynching brings pleasure to the sadistic Frankie: "And Frankie yowled hilariously when the thing was done." In spite of Untermeyer's assertion that "Frankie and Johnny" is "a ballad which any genuine lover of folk-songs ought to let alone,"[34] we can argue that Brown's transformation of the story of the traditional ballad is an achievement which points toward one of the major sources of racism—sexual fear.

There is in some of Brown's other ballads a balance between the narrative action and the characters portrayed — i.e., neither the characters nor the action is subordinate to each other. The character portrayal and the action in "The Ballad of Joe Meek"[35] seem to exist as an illustration of the idea embodied in the first two stanzas of part one and part five. In those sections of the poem, Brown, again using the stanzaic pattern of the traditional ballad, exploits the proverbial truth, folk wisdom, of folklore. The truth is this: the external attributes and overt actions of a human being are not always an index to his thoughts or probable actions. So was the case of meek Joe, who, as the narrative progresses, assumes the role of "bad nigger," a black folk hero represented in folklore by Railroad Bill and Stagolee, and in real life by Jack Johnson and Muhammed Ali. The motivation of Joe's "badness" is not akin to that of Stagolee, whose ego is insulted when Billy Lyons steps on his Stetson hat. Joe's change from meekness to badness is motivated by the hot weather (dog days) and police brutality:

> Strolling down Claiborne
>   In the wrong end of town
> Joe saw two policemen
>   Knock a po' gal down
>
> He didn't know her at all,
>   Never saw her befo'
> But that didn't make no difference,
>   To my old boy Joe.

In his revenge of the "po' gal" Joe takes on the qualities of the supernatural hero:

> Shot his way to the station house,
>   Rushed right in,
> Wasn't nothing but space
>   Where the cops had been.
>
> They called the reserves,
>   And the national guard,
> Joe was in a cell
>   Overlooking the yard.
>
> The machine guns sputtered,
>   Didn't faze Joe at all—
> But evvytime *he* fired
>   A cop would fall.
>
> The tear-gas make him laugh
>   When they let it fly,
> Laughing gas made him hang
>   His head an' cry.
>
> He threw the hand grenades back
>   With a outshoot drop,
> An' evvytime he threw
>   They was one less cop.

In the end, Joe, like Railroad Bill, is shot in cold blood. But, as in the legend of Railroad Bill, the white lawmen, in their attempt to capture and subdue Joe, bring out a force larger than the defying black man. From the narrative of "The Ballad of Joe Meek" emerges a well drawn portrait of the "bad man" as hero. Here the motivation for "badness," often absent from the folk ballad about the badman, is explicit. But providing motivation and folk wisdom, Brown raises the folk hero to the level of a living character rather than a type or stereotype.

The tragic and comic are fused in "The Ballad of Joe Meek." In part one of the poem, Joe is represented as a meek creature, whose abnormal humility is foolish.

The narrator humorously tells us how Joe went beyond what was required by the Bible:

> The good book say
> "Turn the other cheek,"
> But that warn't no turning
> To my boy Joe Meek.
>
> He turned up all parts,
>   And baigged you to spank,
> Pulled down his breeches,
>   And supplied the plank.

The incongruity of the early meek Joe, "Soft as pie," in part one and the image of the powerful, defying Joe in the rest of the poem produces a folk humor that is achieved only in the Slim Greer series and "Sporting Beasley."

In addition to providing entertaining action, Brown's ballads paint pictures of numerous folk characters and various aspects of black folk life. There are suffering chain gang Jim in "Convict," protesting Scotty in "Scotty Has His Say," indigent Sam contrasted with wealthy Samuel in "Mister Samuel and Sam," badman Mojo Pete and Deacon Cole in "Checkers," ruined Lulu in "Seeking Religion," wandering working-man Big Boy in "The Odyssey of Big Boy," tragic Johnny in "Johnny Thomas," and many others. The sources of these portraits are not figures in Afro-American folklore. These portraits are informed by the black folk life of the rural South and some of the folk Brown met and befriended.

The series of ballads devoted to the adventures of Slim Greer gives us a highly developed character against a panoramic background of black folk life. The comic ballads are essentially tall tales. In "Slim Greer," the narrator relates Slim's tall tale of how he, who is "no lighter/Than a dark midnight," passes for white. Here he is the trickster or "con man,"[36] who is able, for a while, to deceive "a nice white woman" and her family. "Slim wore the deadpan mask and behind it perpetuated the joke on white society, but his inner nature came out when he played the blues."[37] Slim again assumes, in "Slim Hears 'The Call,'"[38] the role of trickster when he is down and out, when "Big holes is the onlies/Things in" his pockets. He plans to become a bishop in order to get his "cake down here" and his "pie in the sky," a trick he learned from his old buddy. The final stanza of the poem points an accusing finger at the clergy. Having stated his plans to follow the example of his trickster-buddy, Slim concludes:

> An' I says to all de Bishops,
>   What is hearin' my song—
> Ef de cap fits you, brother,
>   Put it on.

In "Slim Greer in Hell,"[39] "Slim in Atlanta," and "Slim Lands a Job?" Brown's traveling epic hero finds himself in humorous situations—but situations which recall the forms of oppression and racism which black people encounter. In addition to the ballad tradition, it is the black tradition of storytelling and folk humor that informs these ballads. Implied in them is the black man's ability to see not only the tragic aspects of his life, but those comic elements also—even in the absurdity of white racism.

The poetry of Sterling A. Brown gives a kaleidoscopic picture of black folk character and life in America—a picture that is constant with the folk themselves. In the main, Brown's are a Black South folk, who, through song, dogged will, ironic laughter, wisdom, "strange legacies," and faith, confront and survive a hostile universe, in spite of the dehumanization they encounter perpetually. "Illiterate, and somehow very wise," Brown's black folk are strong men who "keep-a-comin' on/Gittin' stronger. . . ." Although he concentrates on the folk of the rural South, he gives us a brief picture of the black folk of the urban North in Part Three, "Tin Roof Blues," of *Southern Road*. Like their Southern brothers, they, too, face a hostile universe, but, cut off from their Black South ancestral roots, Brown's Northern black folk act out their illusions of joy and "arrival" in what they thought would be a Promised Land. In his varied portrayals of black folk, Brown makes no apology for them or their lifestyles. Neither does he present distorted pictures of them. To counter the propagandistic images proliferated in American literature, he, with the integrity of the true artist, represents black folk realistically through forms created by them and a spirit that emanates from their lives. In short, his poems eloquently fulfill James Weldon Johnson's request that the black American poet turn inward for an aesthetic that bespeaks the souls of black folk.

NOTES

1. "The New Negro" in *The New Negro*, ed. Alain Locke (New York: Atheneum, 1969), p. 11.
2. Larry Neal, "Eatonville's Zora Neale Hurston: A Profile," *Black Review No. 2*, ed. Mel Watkins (New York: William Morrow, 1979), p. 15. Hereafter referred to as *Black Review No. 2*.
3. *Along This Way* (New York: Viking, 1937), p. 152.
4. For the importance of the folk tradition to the New Negro writer, see Chapter 2, "Folk Art and the Harlem Renaissance," of Bernard Bell's *The Folk Roots of Contemporary Afro-American Poetry* (Detroit: Broadside Press, 1974), pp. 20–31.
5. *Black Review No. 2*, p. 15.
6. "Sterling Brown: A Living Legend," *New Directions: The Howard University Magazine* 1 (Winter 1974): 8–9.
7. Ekaete, "Folk Art and the Harlem Renaissance," p. 9.
8. Ekaete, "Folk Art and the Harlem Renaissance," p. 8.
9. "Negro Literature—Is it True? Complete" in *The Durham Fact-Finding Conference* (1929), p. 27.
10. "Sterling Brown: The New Negro Folk Poet," *Negro Anthology*, ed. Nancy Cunard (London: Wishart, 1934), p. 113.

11. "Folk oriented poems" and poems "in the folk manner" refer to Brown's poems that are about the "folk" or those poems which use some of the technique of folk poetry. The poems in Part Four of *Southern Road* fall into neither of the above classes; the poems in that section are "subjective" or "confessional." After the publication of *Southern Road,* Brown wrote other poems, some of which were published in periodicals, and others were collected in various anthologies.

12. *The Book of American Negro Poetry,* ed. James Weldon Johnson (New York: Harcourt, 1959), pp. 41–42.

13. "Langston Hughes and Afro-American Folk and Cultural Tradition," *Langston Hughes, Black Genius: A Critical Evaluation,* ed. Therman B. O'Daniel (New York: William Morrow, 1971), p. 183.

14. Bruce Jackson, ed., *Wake Up Dead Man: Afro-American Worksongs from Texas Prisons* (Cambridge: Harvard Univ. Press, 1972), pp. 29–30.

15. "Contributions of the American Negro," *One America,* ed. F. J. Brown and J. S. Roucek (New York: Prentice-Hall, 1945), p. 593.

16. Jackson, *Wake Up Dead Man,* pp. 31–33.

17. *The Negro Caravan,* ed. Sterling A. Brown, Arthur P. Davis and Ulysses Lee (New York: Arno, 1970), p. 465. Hereafter referred to as *The Negro Caravan.* Sterling Brown quotes a version of stanza one of the song with "grunts" at the end of the first three lines in his article, "Negro Folk Expression: Spirituals, Seculars, Ballads, and Songs," *Phylon* 14 (1953): 57.

18. *Black Poets of the United States: From Paul Laurence Dunbar to Langston Hughes,* trans. Kenneth Douglas (Chicago: Univ. of Illinois Press, 1973), p. 490. Hereafter referred to as *Black Poets of the United States.*

19. "Black American Poetry, Its Language, and the Folk Tradition," *Black Academy Review* 2 (Spring–Summer 1971): 75.

20. *Self-Conscious Writers and the Black Tradition.* Taped NCTE Distinguished Lecture, Stock No. 77785 (Urbana, Ill.: National Council of Teachers of English).

21. *Black Poets of the United States,* p. 483.

22. Larry Neal, "The Ethos of the Blues," *The Black Scholar* 3 (Summer 1972): 42–48.

23. Neal, "The Ethos of the Blues," pp. 44, 46.

24. Albert Murray, *The Omni-Americans* (New York: Avon, 1971), p. 89.

25. Ralph Ellison, *Shadow and Act* (New York: Random House, 1964), p. 257.

26. Chris Albertson, *Bessie* (New York: Stein & Day, 1972), pp. 127, 131.

27. Sterling Brown, *Negro Poetry and Drama* (Washington, DC: Associates in Negro Folk Education, 1937), p. 27.

28. *My Bondage and My Freedom* (New York: Arno, 1969), pp. 252–53.

29. For the text of "Old Lem," see *The Negro Caravan,* pp. 387–88.

30. Langston Hughes and Arna Bontemps, ed., *The Book of Negro Folklore* (New York: Dodd, Mead, 1958), p. 342.

31. *The Book of Negro Folklore,* p. 334.

32. *Understanding the New Black Poetry* (New York: William Morrow, 1973), p. 51.

33. See Laws's chapter on the Afro-American ballad in his *Native American Balladry* (Philadelphia: The American Folklore Society, 1964).

34. "New Light from an Old Mine," *Opportunity* 10 (Aug. 1932): 250.

35. See the following for the text of "The Ballad of Joe Meek": Bernard W. Bell, ed., *Modern and Contemporary Afro-American Poetry* (Boston: Allyn & Bacon, 1972), pp. 31–35.

36. S. P. Fullinwider, *The Mind and Mood of Black America* (Homewood, Ill.: Dorsey, 1969), p. 215; Stephen A. Henderson, "A Strong Man Called Sterling Brown," *Black World* 29 (Sept. 1970): 9.

37. Fullinwider, *Mind and Mood of Black America,* p. 215.

38. For the text of "Slim Hears 'The Call,'" see Jean Wagner's *Les Poètes Nègres des Etats-Unis* (Paris: Librarie Istra, 1963), pp. 596–600.

39. See B. A. Botkin's *Folk-Say—The Land is Ours* (Norman: Univ. Of Oklahoma Press, 1932), pp. 246–49, for the text of "Slim Greer in Hell."

"THERE'S NO PLACE LIKE HOME":
THE CARNIVAL OF BLACK LIFE IN CLAUDE MCKAY'S
HOME TO HARLEM

ROBERT A. RUSS

"There's no place like home"—this phrase, so much a part of American culture, recalls the schmaltzy "Be it ever so humble" and evokes sentimental images of Dorothy and Glenda, the Good Witch of the North, but it takes on an especially bitter irony when applied to Harlem Renaissance novelist Claude McKay's *Home to Harlem*, for instead of reading it as a sentimental wish to return home because no other place is as good, we read a desperate cry that there *is* no home to return to—it doesn't exist—and no place even "like" a home. Such feelings of homelessness, alienation, and disenfranchisement indeed provided a writer of McKay's vision the vital material necessary for creating art, not polemic, in his analysis and celebration of Black character and culture in America.

The reader of the Harlem Renaissance literature observes that Claude McKay's works were often noticeably more artistically successful than his contemporaries' and less concerned with propagandistic messages and more with the interaction between people and cultures. Indicative of McKay's artistic concerns is the epigram for his *Selected Poems*, a single-couplet poem called "The Word," which echoes St. John's Gospel and rings with spiritual suggestions inherent in language: "Oh spread Thy words like green fields, watered, fresh, / The Word is God and the Word is made flesh!"[1] These lines suggest McKay was a writer who perceived the power in the written word. Therefore in reading McKay's works, Mikhail Bakhtin's literary theories are especially useful. Bakhtin's theories of carnivalization, monologic and dialogic discourse, and "official" and "unofficial" culture have proven useful to today's critics in elucidating the interactive nature of all communication. This proves especially true for an analysis of McKay's first novel, *Home to Harlem*.

The most important Bakhtinian concept, here, is that of "carnival," which Bakhtin poses in *The Problems of Dostoevsky's Poetics*, but which is given full treatment in *Rabelais and His World*, in which Bakhtin discusses the importance of medieval carnival and folk culture, as well as "official" and "unofficial" culture, in Rabelais' *Gargantua and Pantagruel*. The "two-world condition" of "official" and "unofficial" culture may be particularly important in looking at representations of Black culture within white culture, especially in light of the ever-growing moves of black writers and critics to look to their African origins to reclaim their "lost" cultural heritage. The marking off of "official" and "unofficial" segments of society is an essential component of Black life in America. Ironically, Bakhtin's phrase "two-world condition" has often been used, albeit unknowingly, to describe Black Americans' status in this country—"officially" *a part* of it and "unofficially" *apart* from it. It is precisely because of this doubleness of vision that we come to appreciate the complexity of McKay's work.

Bakhtin's discussion of carnival is appropriate for the present analysis because it grows out of the European folk festival, but is found to have wide application to the history of western literature, especially the novel. The qualities inherent in carnival complement Bakhtin's conception of the openness and unfinishedness of the dialogic novel. Carnival is a time of parody, satire, mockery, and inversion. It reverses and debases the forms of "official" culture, mocking freely and celebrating the life of the people in festive laughter. Carnival is also characterized by public feasts, an abundance of food and drink, and life in the public arena. Carnival laughter, Bakhtin observes, is a "festive laughter . . . . the laughter of all the people. . . . it is directed at all and everyone, including the carnival's participants."[2]

Although McKay draws not on the European folk festival of carnival, but on the folk culture—language, stories, behavior, attitudes, and traditions—of Jamaican people, African-American people, and others of African descent, the spirit of the folk culture as imagined is quite consistent, regardless of its origin. "Like Rabelais, Bakhtin throughout this book is exploring an interface between a stasis imposed from above and a desire for change from below, between old and new, official and unofficial."[3]

Such "interface" involves a relationship similar to Bakhtinian "dialogue." And we realize that the "official" culture that carnival reacts against is connected with the "authoritative" discourse that Bakhtin later explored: "The authoritative word demands that we acknowledge it, that we make it our own; it binds us, quite independent of any power it might have to persuade us internally; we encounter it with its authority already fused to it."[4] Bakhtin's method illustrates a basic principle: the "sense of opposition and struggle" that is inherent in communication between individuals but which is also "at the very heart of existence, a ceaseless battle between centrifugal forces that seek to keep things apart, and centripetal forces that strive to make things cohere,"[5] and since it is on the level of language that the "ceaseless battle" of dialogue and interchange is most evident, it is crucial to examine the ways in which a Black artist writes, the ways in which Black characters speak, and the ways in which the "ceaseless battle" manifests itself *between*, to stress one of Bakhtin's recurring terms: *between* characters, between Black characters as well as between Black and white characters. It is also important to note the ways in which Black speech deviates from white speech—deviates not in mangling and distorting the language of white people, although it may do this too, but in making possible a sense of community and a feeling of solidarity among Black people.

Just as Bakhtin approached such diverse topics as psychoanalysis, theology, and linguistics, as well as the writings of Rabelais and Dostoevsky, through his ideas of dialogic discourse, monologic discourse, carnival, and polyphony, so have today's critics found wide application for his theoretical schemata. Especially for the more innovative critics of black literature, most obviously Houston A. Baker, Jr., and Henry Louis Gates, Bakhtin's theories have proven quite useful, probably because the Russian's ideas so well support fundamental questions about Black Americans and Black literature. For good or ill, American society is dominated by "white" Western culture, from which blacks are often excluded, serving to make a "black" culture based on exclusion from "white" culture. That exclusion can perhaps be overcome as we listen closely to the voices created by one of the most complex Black artists of this era.

Although it might be argued that Bakhtin's theories grew out of his reading of Dostoevsky, whom McKay also read, it would be more appropriate to speculate that the dialogical and carnivalesque characteristics of McKay's writing were natural outgrowths of his personality and the social and historical conditions of his time. Although we might wish to know more of McKay's own readings to see their influence on the works he created, in light of what Bakhtin calls the "organic logic" of a genre, it becomes irrelevant to speculate whether McKay himself would have used such terms as "dialogical," "monological," or "carnivalesque" in conjunction with his writings. As Henry Louis Gates has argued, "Black writers, like critics of black literature, learn to write by reading literature, especially the canonical texts of the Western tradition . . . ."[6] Through that reading, the "tradition," the "organic logic" of a genre, and the significance inherent in a particular use of language can take on a life of their own, forming connections of which the author may not have even been aware, but of which he is considered to be the "author." Thus, we can see the validity of Gates' claim "that the literary discourse that is most consistently 'black,' as read against our tradition's own theory of itself, is the most figurative, and that the modes of interpretation most in accord with the vernacular tradition's theory of criticism are those that direct attention to the manner in which language is used."[7]

In *Home to Harlem*, Jake Brown, McKay's hero, is an American Black who, at the outbreak of World War I, enlisted to fight the Germans. Stuck in an unfulfilling non-combat role, he deserts, lives a while in Europe, and finally, homesick, works his way back to America. Jake begins his return by enduring the wretched conditions aboard a freighter and dreaming of the sensuous life of his Harlem "home."[8]

The novel is primarily, though not exclusively, a study in contrasts. First there is the contrast of the two principal characters, Jake, a common working class Black American, and Ray, a cultivated and educated Haitian. The most obvious contrast here is in the fundamental qualities in each character—a dialectic between Ray's intellect and Jake's instinct—representing two aspects of the author himself, but the real drama of the novel "is not between . . . the man of instinct and . . . the man of intellect, but between the capacity of both men to realize their dreams for economic security and human dignity in a parasitic, modern urban society."[9] Also, in the midst of the colorful descriptions and scenes, there is the conflict between order and chaos, with Jake standing "as a symbol of order."[10] And although "order" should be associated with "home," in *Home to Harlem*, the opposite is actually the case. Jake's Harlem has desirable qualities, but is a chaotic place where the desirable is bound together with chaos and frenzy.

Ironically, one theme of *Home to Harlem* is that there is, in the end, no "home" at all, in Harlem or anywhere else, underscoring a dominant theme in Afro-American literature: perpetual homelessness. As Roger Rosenblatt observes, " . . . the true heroes of black fiction . . . never have a home, real or imagined, to turn to." However, a major motif in Black fiction is the Black characters' quest for that non-existent home, and that quest "is peculiarly terrifying, because they are searching not merely for something that does not exist the way they would like it to, in a dreamy sense, but for something that does not exist for them at all . . . ." The home that is sought, as well as all that it represents—peace, security, comfort, order—is perpetually elusive.

While Rosenblatt does observe the frustration inherent in the endless quest, he neglects to point out the hard-won but positive growth therein. He writes, "The act of going home ought ordinarily to be an act of rediscovery, but the paradox is that in black fiction going home becomes an effort at escape from a cycle of punishment, the idea of home itself being unknown and utopian."[11] In a Bakhtinian analysis, however, actually finding a "home" would be more indicative of stagnation than "rediscovery," or at least of "rediscovery" followed by stagnation. For Bakhtin, true "rediscovery" is dependent on continuing dialogue with others and with the world, all of which would be impossible in any finality suggested by "home." However, consistent with Rosenblatt's point, Jake's desertion, in fact, is "an effort at escape," but not from punishment or service in battle, but from the Army's racist practices that kept him out of combat. Hence, in returning to Harlem, Jake seeks to enter a world free from the authority of the "official" culture and to live in the world of "unofficial" carnival culture. Yet however tempting and pleasing that world may be, it is *not home*.

First, although numerous critics have pointed out the circular structure evident in *Home to Harlem*—that of Jake's meeting Felice in the opening section, his losing her and then pursuing a series of picaresque adventure, and his reunion with her in the closing section—a similar circular structure is evident in one of the most revealing aspects of the carnival atmosphere of *Home to Harlem*: the absence of "normal" time, the suspension of the time and logic of everyday reality. Part of this may be explained by the fact that the novel was written not in Harlem, or even the United States, but was the first of McKay's works to be composed during his long years abroad, thus perhaps causing the author to look back on Harlem with the same idealizing memory that he had of Jamaica after leaving there and investing the memory with a timeless quality that ran counter to his efforts at realism. The action of the novel takes place over eight years prior to the writing itself, and as numerous critics have pointed out, the character of Harlem itself had changed by the time McKay wrote of Jake's return "home."

But whatever the effect of McKay's absence from Harlem, the fact is that the novel has very few references to specific dates. We are told that Jake enlisted in the army sometime in 1917, shortly after America declared war on Germany, but the most specific date given is in the first chapter, when McKay reports that Jake was residing in the East End of London when the war ended and that on New Year's Eve, 1919, he went to a dance with the woman with whom he was living. Shortly after, he became homesick and returned to the United States, and in the second chapter, "Arrival," McKay confirms that Jake had been away for two years.

From here on until near the end of the novel, days, weeks, and months pass in a timeless, hazy blur. Events come without concrete ties to the logic and time of everyday reality, emphasizing the fact that the lives of the Harlemites are removed from the ordinary everyday rut of life and are lived in the dreamy, extraordinary, scandalous, festival world of carnival, where anything can happen and the time and logic of everyday life do not apply. To a large extent, this novel's chapters could be read as independent short stories, for they typically contain a unity all their own, focusing on particular places or particular people (such as Gin-head Susy, Miss Curdy and their Myrtle Avenue apartment in chapter six, "Myrtle Avenue"; Zeddy and Gin-head Susy and their relationship in chapter seven, "Zeddy's Rise and Fall"; and the vice cops, the Baltimore club, Madame Suarez, and her buffet flat in chapter eight, "The Raid of the Baltimore"). Each serves as a focal point for a single episode and has little significance outside of its isolated chapter.

Also, numerous chapters begin by defying the logic and time of everyday reality. Chapter nine, "Jake Makes a Move," begins: "Coming home from work one afternoon, Jake remarked a taxicab just driving away from his house" (p. 112). The nebulous reference to "one afternoon" clearly indicates the hazy, indistinct passage of time while Jake lived with Congo Rose. Likewise, chapter thirteen opens: "One night in Philadelphia Jake breezed into the waiters' quarters in Market Street, looking for Ray" (p. 188). Here it is Jake's employment on the railroad that is trapped in the misty passage of time.

In addition to these vague references to time that are evident in numerous chapters, there are also the chapters with abrupt introductions of new places and new events that are unconnected to what has come before—and abrupt conclusions that do not logically lead to what follows. The events in such chapters emerge from the hazy passage of time to chronicle episodic carnivalized adventures of the Black picaro—and then as suddenly recede into the mist, as in the abrupt and unconnected opening of chapter seven, which records the events that led to the closing of the Baltimore and to the raid on Madame Laura's buffet flat: "The blazing lights of the Baltimore were put out and the entrance was padlocked. Fifth Avenue and Lenox talked about nothing else" (p. 102). Unconnected with what had come before, this opening joins with the chapter's concluding paragraph—reporting the effects of the raid and the closing—to form a unified episode in the swirling life of Harlem. Chapter after chapter demonstrates the same narrative strategy, but rather than being a defect in the author's construction of the plot, it underscores the carnivalesque atmosphere that pervades Harlem and Jake's life.

Although such qualities characterize the largest portion of the novel, the third part, the shortest of the three, departs from this narrative strategy and its hazy, disjointed, carnivalesque passage of time. The first chapter in this section, "Spring in Harlem," breaks from the nebulous, hazy passage of time that characterizes the first two sections, and from its opening sentence on to the long passage of Jake's mental reverie associating spring with love, we have the most explicit reference to time, not even the change in seasons being evident throughout the previous sections. Jake's comment, in part two, that "Prohibition is right under our tail" (p. 271) vaguely suggests the year 1920, the story so far having occupied the space of about a year. So only in part three does time become real again, as the first chapter makes clear that the time is indeed the next year, 1920.

In addition, part three in its entirety clearly follows the logic and time of everyday reality. The final three chapters are therefore more rigorously and logically connected than any earlier ones, except the first three. When these three concluding chapters are placed alongside the three opening chapters, a framing symmetry becomes evident. The first aspect of this, already noted, is the framing device of Jake's meeting and losing Felice at the beginning and finding her again at the end. But the symmetrical frame goes far beyond this because of McKay's treatment of the passage of time. Although the first three chapters are not marked off in a separate section, they constitute an entry into the carnival-atmosphere world that characterizes the remainder of the first section and all of the second, just as the final three chapters—"Spring in Harlem," "Felice," and "The Gift That Billy Gave"—which are marked off as a separate section, constitute an exit from that world.

In the opening chapters, outside the carnival world, time and events are coherent, connected, and logical. The first records Jake's journey "home" and describes his life before the war and life in Europe; the second chapter, his first day back, meeting with Felice, and departure the following morning; the third, his finding the note with his money in his pocket, his visit to Uncle Doc's saloon and a pool room, and his realization that he doesn't know her name and address, that he cannot find her, and that he "ain't gwine to know no peace" until he does

(p. 27). What follow until the end of the second part are both random, picaresque adventures and the hazy, illogical, disjointed time of carnival.

As part two begins to emerge from carnival time by the reference to Prohibition, and as "Spring in Harlem" in part three brings into the sunlight, as it were, the nebulous carnival world, what remains to be seen is the return to the logical, connected world of everyday life. At the Sheba Palace Jake is reunited with Felice, and "Spring in Harlem" ends as they leave the Sheba, with the following chapter logically picking up with their conversation outside. "Felice" ends with the visit to the Negro Picture Theater, and the final chapter, "The Gift That Billy Gave," is clearly set a week later, "when Saturday came round again" (p. 315). Thus the novel suggests at least a temporary end to the carnival world as Jake and Felice prepare to leave Harlem. But their departure for Chicago—"a mahvelous place foh niggers" (p. 333)—predicts an eventual renewal of carnival life.

II.

Within this hazy and illogical world that Jake enters on his return from Europe and leaves only at the close of the novel, there are many other characteristics of the carnival spirit—one of the most significant, as Bakhtin points out, being the emphasis on food and eating, especially extravagant, communal feasts and banquets, an aspect that permeates *Home to Harlem*. First noticeable, however, is the absence of the carnival banquet on Jake's ship back to the United States, for the Arabs' washing habits and dietary restrictions mark them off from their fellow sailors, distinguishing them in a way that is at odds with the inclusiveness of the carnival spirit. Not only do we here see the "commonplace, privately consumed food and drink, partaken of by individuals"[12] that is devoid of the communal carnival spirit, but also the absence of celebration in eating, for the ship's food is presented as paltry, ugly, and filthy, devoid of the rich, fruitful abundance characteristic of banquets and feasts, and Jake finally pays the ship's chef to feed him separately from the Arab stokers, thus isolating him from his fellow workers in the taking of meals, which should be, but here is not, a celebration.

In keeping with the carnival spirit and the emphasis on the body, Jake unconsciously associates food and sex. From Jake's thoughts about the food arrangement on board the ship, McKay then goes on to present Jake's revulsion by the smells in his quarters, which are "lousy, and fetid with the mingled smell of stale food and water-closet," with the Arabs "apparently" thinking "that a sleeping quarters could also serve as a garbage can." From all of this that offends him, Jake's thoughts then turn to his destination, Harlem, and the definitive quality about Harlem is sexual: "Roll on, Mister Ship, and stinks all the way as you rolls. Jest take me 'long to Harlem is all I pray. I'm crazy to see again the brown-skin chippies 'long Lenox Avenue. Oh boy!" (p. 3) Indeed, the Harlem that Jake remembers and that lures him back is a Harlem dominated by taunting eroticism: "'Oh, them legs!' Jake thought. 'Them tantalizing brown legs!' . . . Brown lips full and pouted for sweet kissing. Brown breasts throbbing with love" (p. 8).

As soon as he lands back in New York, Jake immerses himself in the sensual pleasures of food and drink and returns to the sensual "home" he had missed while abroad—Harlem, where "[h]is blood was hot" and "[h]is eyes were alert as he sniffed the street like a hound"; Lenox Avenue, with its "girls sipping ice-cream soda through straws" and its cabarets (pp. 10–11). At one of cabarets in this lusty, sensual environment, Jake is immediately attracted to and picked up by a "little brown" Harlem prostitute, who, it is later revealed, is named Felice (meaning "joy" or "happiness"). Her earthy appearance appeals to his sensual nature, and McKay emphasizes Jake's sensual, primitive nature by the emphasis on feelings and sensations. His encounter with Felice is characterized by a sense of drunkenness for both of them: "His flesh tingled. He felt as if his whole body was a flaming wave. She was intoxicated, blinded under the overwhelming force" (p. 12). Along with Jake's sense of being "home," of being where he belongs, is the emphasis on the physical life of this "home"—that physical life being a crucial ingredient in the "unofficial" Black folk culture.

Meditating on the satisfaction of being back in Harlem, Jake sensually refers to it as "Chocolate Harlem" and "Sweet Harlem," and equates this satisfaction of his physical being with "life" itself: "Where else could I have all this life but Harlem?" (p. 14). Jake's feverish revelry becomes an almost Whitmanesque cata-logue of the sensual life of Harlem: "The deep-dyed color, the thickness, the closeness of it. The noises of Harlem. The sugared laughter. The honey-talk on its streets. And all night long, ragtime and 'blues' playing somewhere . . . singing somewhere, dancing somewhere!" And "the contagious fever" that "[b]urn[s] everywhere in dark-eyed Harlem" now burns "in Jake's sweet blood" (p. 15), so overwhelming him that he loses Felice, whose name he doesn't even know at this point, by failing to note her address—and since the Harlem streets all look the same, he can't find her flat again. And Jake feels that he won't find any "happiness" until he finds Felice again: "I ain't gwine to know no peace till I lay these here hands on mah tantalizing brown again" (p. 27). But he cannot find her again and immediately falls back into a free and easy lifestyle, occasionally plagued by thoughts of the "little brown."

The Harlem that Jake does get back "home" to is therefore permeated with both desire of sexuality and carnivalesque banquet feasts, both of which appear in the buffet flats of Harlem, private homes where people eat, drink, gamble, dance, and carouse in an intimate atmosphere. Thus, when Jake and Felice first meet, they appropriately visit a typical buffet flat that virtually oozes with the carnival spirit: shaded windows, alcohol, and music, with couples "dancing, thick as maggots in a vat of sweet liquor, and as wriggling" (pp. 13–14). And among the cabarets, the Congo most embodies the carnival spirit. It is "a real throbbing little Africa in New York" (p. 29)—"African in spirit and color" (p. 30). Barring white customers, it is free of the racial strife of everyday life. It is a place for the Black everyman, an extension of the marketplace or square that Bakhtin associates with carnival: " . . . an amusement place entirely for the unwashed of the Black Belt. Or if they were washed, smells lingered telling the nature of their occupation. Pot-wrestlers, third cooks, W. C. attendants . . . " (p. 29).

Since he is unable to find the "little brown" that has captured his heart, Jake's sensuous nature prompts him to take up temporarily with Congo Rose, a nightclub singer who is as taken with Jake as he is with Felice and who wants to support Jake (have him as a bought "sweetman") and to be beaten by him. But although Jake doesn't love Rose, he won't won't play a sweetman with her or abuse her either, and his personal "code" dampens Rose's interest in him, who she says is "good loving," but "a big Ah-Ah all the same," for she feels "no thrill about the business" of sex with a lover who is "not interested in her earnings" (pp. 113–14).

Immediately thereafter, the first part of this three-section novel ends with Jake leaving Congo Rose, and although he had deserted the Army to return to Harlem, has repeatedly viewed it as a "home," as "God's Country," and has associated it with life itself, he now leaves there. The "home" that he had sought in Harlem, though it is filled with the vitality and sensuality of his fellow Black Americans, was not a truly nourishing home environment. Realizing the need "to get right out of the atmosphere of Harlem," he takes a temporary job as a cook in the dining car of a train "to break the hold that Harlem had upon him" (p. 125). But if he had hopes of some form of unity and community in his employment on the railroad, Jake is soon disillusioned, for there is tension and hatred among the Black workers, and for the most part, the disruptive situation is affected by a racial self-hatred inspired by white prejudice, showing as much of an absence of carnival spirit as was seen on Jake's ship back to the United States. That carnival spirit is seen to be absent in the filthy, bug-infested quarters in which the Black crewmembers must stay and in the lack of community feeling among themselves, who have a color caste system that limits their associations: "There were certain light-skinned ones who went walking with pals of their complexion only in the stop-over cities" (p. 126). Moreover, except for Jake and Ray, who, in spite of their differences, do demonstrate a carnival spirit of fellowship, the train's cooks and waiters "never chummed together, except for gambling" (p. 126).

Moreover, the lack of carnival spirit is more sharply etched because, in spite of the fact that the Black employees are working around food, there is little feasting and celebration for them—little that could qualify as carnival banquet. And an even more sharply defined contrast to carnival spirit is evident in the novel's most pitiful character, the train's Black chef, under whom Jake and the other cooks and waiters have to work, who degrades the Black youths working under him, and who purposely distances himself from things associated with his race. An excellent chef and a valued employee of the railroad, he professes the most exaggerated opinions of himself and continually belittles his fellow employees. But he has lost touch with his racial identity—has become "a great black bundle of consciously suppressed desires" (p. 160). He is both a victim and a tool of prejudice and hatred, and disgraces himself as a servile endorser of an ugly system of prejudice and discrimination. First, the chef is a Black who lives by Booker T. Washington's strategy of racial advancement through professional competence: "His kitchen was well-ordered. The checking up of his provisions always showed a praiseworthy balance. He always had his food ready on time, feeding the heaviest rush of customers as rapidly as the lightest. He fed the steward excellently. He fed the crew well." But in being "one of the model chefs of the service," he does not work for racial advancement, but becomes merely an obsequious puppet for white bosses, doing "his duty as only a martinet can" (pp. 160–61).

Furthermore, the chef, in consciously trying to live counter to racial stereotypes, is actually denying his own racial identity and trying to "be" white. He purposefully rejects all foods "that 'coons' are supposed to like to the point of stealing them," eating neither "watermelon, because white people called it 'The niggers' ice-cream," nor pork chops, nor corn pone. And although the chef makes the crew a delicious chicken stew, he himself cannot stand even "the idea of eating chicken." Of course, these preferences in food are significant because it is ideology rather than taste that determines them. And McKay's representation of the chef's being "big and haughty about not being 'no rugular darky'!" and "pretend[ing] not to know a coon tail from a rabbit foot" (pp. 161–62) is especially double-voiced in conveying both his attitude towards his own race and other Black people's attitude towards his ideology.

Moreover, the chef not only performs his job well because of the fear and intimidation created by the system, but he will not scruple to fawn over his white superiors and put on an "Uncle Tom" act when useful, as when, during a dispute with the pantryman, whom the chef had inflamed by calling him a "bastard-begotten dime-snatcher," he is reported to the steward for threatening to spit in the crew's food. When the steward questions him about the ruckus, the chef assumes the speech of the servile Black who sides with his white "superior" against those of his own race: "Nothing at all, Sah Farrel. I done pull a good bull on them fellars, tha's all. Cause theyse all trying to get mah goat. . . . I don't want no fooling fwom them nigger waiters, nohow" (p. 172). The chef's whole life is based on negative racial self-images. Some actions in themselves, such as denial of stereotypically "Black" foods and the harassing of subordinates, hardly seem harmful, but in the context of the attitudes that bring about the actions, they all dehumanize the individual, and McKay shows that such attitudes and such behavior can, in the end, only be destructive. As Roger Rosenblatt observes, the chef and Gin-head Susy, the "only characters [in the novel] who [really] suffer in any way," are victims of their own attitudes towards their own race and consequently "pay penalties for aspiring to whiteness: Susy because she wants only light-skinned men about her, and the chef because he craves social advancement."[13] Both suffer because they seek the "official" culture and shun the "unofficial" culture.

While carnival is particularly characterized by celebration and joy and the departure from the mundane rut of life, carnival is also ambivalent, its joyful madness often changing into the destructive madness of fights, stabbings, and shootings, even between friends, as when Zeddy confronts Jake about Felice and is ready to "carve any damn-fool nigger for her" (p. 326) until Jake pulls a gun on him. In addition, over the atmosphere of Harlem's "unofficial" culture constantly hangs the threat of the white "official" culture. For Jake, it is most evident in the fact that he is officially a deserter from the Army, making Harlem therefore ambiguous, simultaneously safe and dangerous. Harlem is a different world, a haven outside the reach of white officials, but at the same time, as Zeddy warns, though the inhabitants of Harlem might not turn Jake in for the reward, they might, for other reasons, or no reason, let his secret out. Sensibly warning Jake not to "go shooting off" (p. 22) his mouth about his desertion, Zeddy explains about draft dodgers who had hidden in Harlem in spite of the fifty dollar reward for them: "All their friends knowed it and not a one gived them in. . . . Yet other times, without any natural reason, they will just go vomiting out their guts to the ofays about one another" (p. 23). So Jake appears safe in his Harlem "home" or haven, and the official threat of arrest for desertion is forgotten until the end of the novel. Then, ironically, Zeddy renews the "official" threat when, angered by Jake's relationship with Felice, he falsely accuses Jake of desertion for cowardice and hints of reporting to the authorities. This explosive situation is soon defused when Zeddy apologizes for his behavior and Jake shows that he holds no grudges.

Other threats of the "official" culture include the white interference in the exuberant Harlem entertainments, and it is often the case that the "official" pronouncement against the carnivalesque imbues the forbidden with fresh excitement, as is the case of the song that is sung at the Congo club in spite of the rumored "police ban" on it: "It was an old tune, so far as popular tunes go. But at the Congo it lived fresh and green as grass. Everybody there was giggling and wriggling to it" (p. 36). More importantly, at Madame Laura's buffet flat in Philadelphia, McKay brings into collision a celebration of the carnivalesque character of the buffet flats and the "official" sanctions that threaten it: "Black lovers of life caught up in their own free native rhythm, threaded to a remote scarce-remembered past, celebrating the mid-night hours in themselves, for themselves, of themselves . . . " (p. 197). It is no coincidence that this passage echoes the phrasing "of the people, by the people, for the people" in the American Constitution, for by this repetition with a difference McKay emphasizes the cultural integrity that informs the Harlemite celebrations, but whereas "the people" of the Constitution, and, by implication, America as a whole, seeks a unified nation, a unified culture (including a unified language, or "monoglossia"), and a unified "people" in the great American melting pot, McKay's "themselves" aims for distinctions between peoples and cultures, creating polyglossia, which is antagonistic to any "official" culture.

That antagonism is seen and felt—and carnivalized—in Madame Laura's buffet flat by the intrusion of a policeman, a representative of the "official" culture, in a mock raid of the flat. Also, as Jake points out, the alcohol that is the life and blood of carnival could quickly be taken away because "Prohibition is right under our tail" (p. 271). But no amount of "official" proscription can completely kill the carnival spirit, for as Zeddy observes with the regard to the padlocking of the Baltimore club, "White folks can't padlock niggers outa joy forever" (p. 336). Jake's departure from Harlem and the end of Part One coincide with two significant developments in his life in Harlem: the closing of the Baltimore and his beating of Congo Rose. Both of these are incidents that stifle Jake's life of joy and curtail the carnival atmosphere. Three white vice cops who had begun patronizing the Baltimore and had received an introduction to Madame Suarez's buffet flat "had posed as good fellows, regular guys, looking for a good time only in the Black Belt. They were wearied of the pleasure of the big white world, wanted something new—the primitive joy of Harlem" (p. 109). The object of the investigation is actually Madame Suarez's buffet flat, but for its role "as accessory to the speakeasy crime" (p. 110), the Baltimore is ordered "padlocked" by the "official" culture. The consequences go beyond the mere closing of a cabaret. The Baltimore, after all, is the club in which Jake met Felice and which he returned to in the hope of finding her again. So by its association with her, its closing signals Jake's loss of joy in Harlem. Moreover, when Madame Suarez's buffet flat is raided, the carnivalesque freedom immediately vanishes, and the partiers' status in everyday life brings them shame for their participation in the "unofficial" entertainment: "The women were afraid. Some of them were false grass-widows whose husbands were working somewhere. Some of them were church members. Perhaps one could claim a place in local society!" (p. 110) This is far removed from the classless, shameless, indiscriminate carousing of carnival, and it is the intrusion of "official" culture that destroys the prevailing mood. Nor is this all. The "official" culture also creates a racial barrier in that the judge regrets that he cannot order the two white girls taken in the raid be whipped: whipping being "the only punishment he considered suitable for white women who dishonored their race by associating with colored persons" (p. 110).

In addition, the "official" culture's closing of the Baltimore creates color barriers on the other side as well, first in that the black cabaret begins to turn away white customers and second in that unfamiliar "near-white members of the black race . . . had a difficult time proving their identity" (p. 111). The suspicion cast on light-skinned Blacks is opposed to McKay's joyful and carnivalesque celebrations of the differences in colors that ring throughout *Home to Harlem*, as in Jake's feeling, in chapter one, that the streets of Harlem "with their chocolate-brown and walnut-brown girls, were calling him" (p. 8) and in the catalog of "various and varying pigmentation" along Seventh Avenue in the spring: "dim brown, clear brown, rich brown, chestnut, copper, yellow, near-white, mahogany, and gleaming anthracite" (p. 289). Thus the "official" culture's authority leads to a shattering of Harlem's carnivalesque joy, a characteristic that holds Jake in Harlem and whose destruction is one motivation for his departure.

The second motivation for Jake's move is in his relationship with Congo Rose. Jake had taken up with Congo Rose immediately after losing Felice; significantly, that relationship begins in chapter 4, the first chapter after the time and logic of everyday life in the first three chapters are left behind. The chapter

"Congo Rose," then, constitutes Jake's descent into the hazy, illogical, disjointed time of carnival. The lack of seriousness inherent in such action is evident in Jake's response to Rose's profession of love: "Gwan, tell that to the marines" (p. 40). However, if Jake cannot take Rose's love seriously, he does take his personal code extremely seriously. His independence, self-respect, and abhorrence of brutality are key elements of that code he lives by and, even in the carnival world, he cannot give these up, for they define who he is, and giving them up would mean consigning himself forever to the carnival world, without hope for escape. And this presents a problem, for while the carnival world is characterized by joy, it is an ambivalent world whose joy and riotousness can turn to pain, loss of direction, and loss of self. As McKay's narrator comments on the atmosphere in the Baltimore in the final chapter: "A laugh might finish in a sob. A moan end in hilarity. That gorilla type . . . hugging his mate, may strangle her tonight." (p. 337). Likewise, Jake links up with Rose in spite of the fact that he conceives of the relationship differently than she does. She, in fact, wants to support him, wants him as her sweetman, but this is contrary to Jake's nature. He says, "I've never been a sweetman yet. Never lived off no womens and never will. I always works" (p. 40). And work he does, but for him and Rose disharmony results from his insistence on his independence and self-respect. And Jake's attitude results in Rose's scorn and loss of interest in him by the end of part one: "She felt no thrill about the business when her lover was not interested in her earnings" (p. 114).

Just as he insists on preserving his independence, he refuses to beat Rose, as she is accustomed to because of previous relationships. When finally provoked into beating her at the end of part one, Jake examines himself in a dialogue with his hands, as if they were beings separate from himself, and indeed, they are, in a sense: "' . . . he looked at his palms. "Ahm shame o' you, hands," he murmured. "Mah mother useter tell me, 'Nevah hit no woman,' but that hussy jest made me do it . . . jest made me. . . . It wasn't what I come back to Gawd's own country foh. No, siree!"'" (p. 116) In beating Rose, his hands have responded to the law of Rose's world and have violated his code. His apostrophe to his hands, then, represents a dialogue between conflicting ideologies and a conflict that must be answered by either Jake's capitulation to Rose or his escape from her. His exit from the relationship and from Harlem as well, however, does not include his exit from a carnival world, for though removed from Harlem, Jake's adventures throughout the second part are just as much confined to the shadowy carnival world.

Finally, it must be observed that while the incidents in *Home to Harlem* reveal Harlem not to be a "home," the novel also eschews action within any sort of environment that could be construed as a home, a practice in keeping with the carnivalesque and with Bakhtin's observations about the placement of the action in Dostoevsky's works. That is, as Bakhtin points out, "Action in Dostoevsky's works takes place primarily in . . . 'points' [of crisis]." This means the absence of interior scenes, except, of course, for scandalous scenes and discrownings, when interior space (the drawing room or the hall) becomes a substitute for the square." Instead of the rooms and homes of private life, where people "live a biographical life in biographical time: they are born, they experience childhood and youth, enter into marriage, give birth to children, grow old, and die," Dostoevsky utilizes the public places of the people, of carnival: "On the threshold and on the square the only possible time is crisis time."[14] Hallways, stairs, doorways—these "threshold" spaces are removed from the homey, settled, comfortable interior where all is private. Similarly in *Home to Harlem*, although interior space is the primary setting, it is interior space that is far from the "homey" interior space of biographical life and biographical time. Indeed, McKay's interior spaces are, with few exceptions, public spaces: buffet flats, cabarets, railroad cars, and employees' quarters. Even the private interior spaces (of Jake's flat, for example) are removed from the kind of life that governs the novel, and these spaces are rarely seen, and when they are, they seem extraordinarily temporary, for the changing of residences is part of the life of *Home to Harlem*, and the novel's "homes" are far different from the homes in, say, the novels of Jessie Fausett, in which homey interior space is cojoined with biographical lives and biographical time, far removed from the threshold space and the public arena of carnival.

Just as the novel's first section ends with Jake's departure from the vigorous, enchanting life of Harlem, even though he does periodically return when his train is in town, the second section ends with Ray's fleeing the United States as a mess boy on a freighter. Like Jake, Ray sees some vague something in Harlem from which he must get away, something that is simultaneously attractive and repulsive, for Ray "hates" Harlem's "brutality, gang rowdyism, promiscuous thickness" but is stirred by "[i]ts hot desires" and its "rich blood-red color." Though Harlem is quite different from Ray's home island, its most positive qualities (to him) are reminiscent of his own folk culture: "The warm accent of its composite voice, the fruitiness of its laughter, the trailing rhythm of its 'blues' and the improvised surprises of its jazz" are associated with "happiness" and "joy that glowed gloriously upon him like the high-noon sunlight of his tropic island home" (p. 267).

Like Jake, his counterpart or reverse image, Ray flees Harlem. As an educated Black, he cannot find his place in Harlem, or New York at all, or even in the United States. He is educated, but he doesn't know the purpose of his education, what it is supposed to do for him. He realizes that he is thwarted by some fundamental questions. "All the learning in this world," he tells Jake, "can't answer this little question, Why are we living?" (p. 274) The ability of such people as Jake and Billy Biase—who answers Ray's question with a simple "becas Gawd wants us to"—to simply live, to live without the critical self-examination that Ray finds himself caught up in, makes Ray aware of some shortcoming of his own. His intelligence is not a bad thing, but it is undirected. "Because he is an intellectual, Ray is alone in the novel. To everybody else eroticism means freedom, and civilization, barbarism . . . . Depressed about his future, he acknowledges the wisdom of Jake's happier state of mind, and signs aboard a freighter . . . ."[15]

III.

The novel's third part brings the story full circle. Having recovered from his venereal disease, Jake has returned to Harlem and his free and easy lifestyle. Also, in this section's opening chapter, "Spring in Harlem," Jake's thoughts, celebrating the beauty and richness of life as fully as does the novel's opening chapter of Jake's return from abroad, turn to everything that is "glorious there under the sun in the tender spring grass. Oh, sweet to be alive in that sun beneath that sky! And to be in love—even for one hour of such rare hours!" (p. 280) The meditation continues with Jake recalling, yet again, the "little brown" that he had fallen in love with and lost immediately after returning from Europe: "It was a day like this we romped in the grass . . . a night as soft and intimate as this on which we forgot the world and ourselves. . . . Hours of pagan abandon, celebrating ourselves . . ." (p. 280). And in the closing of this chapter, Jake visits the Sheba Palace, yet another blazing cabaret, and there by chance again meets up with his "little brown," the memory of whom had so haunted him for months. As they are reunited, Felice reveals that she was as taken with Jake as he was with her and that losing him had caused her a similar reaction. Like Jake, she had gotten "sick and tiahd of Harlem" (p. 303) and had taken a job that took her out of town. And like Jake, she had had other relationships in the meantime rather than abstain from sex. But once they are together again, Jake and Felice lose no time. She had come to the Sheba with another man, but she doesn't hesitate to leave with Jake because, as she says, "there ain't no nigger in the wul' I wouldn't ditch foh you, daddy." (p. 399). Some other man may have been acceptable in his absence, but once she finds Jake again, true love has priority, and without "the faintest twinge of conscience," Felice leaves "the one that she was merely makeshifting with" (p. 306).

As the two lovers make their way to Jake's apartment house, McKay injects a description of the Harlem neighborhood they pass through, and it supplies a telling contrast between the austerity of white society and the freer, more loving possibilities of Black society, but also reinforces the awareness of white bigotry that scorns contact between the two worlds. The scene is "the Block Beautiful," an impressive city block that "the whites had not evacuated . . . yet" (p. 300) in their flight from the Black masses. Yet that flight is imminent because "loud-laughing-and-acting black swains and their sweethearts had started in using the block for their afternoon promenade" (p. 301). And that is just too much of an affront to dignified white society: "That was the limit: the desecrating of that atmosphere by black love in the very shadow of the gray, gaunt Protestant church!"

After visiting Jake's apartment, Felice returns to her own, which she was sharing with the man she had abandoned, to get her belongings. There she recalls an incident that foreshadows a coming conflict between Jake and Zeddy, the man, it turns out, that Felice has just deserted. She remembers a fight between two West Indian women over "a vain black bantam, one of the breed that delight in women's scratching over them" (p. 307)—illustrating the primitive nature of human passion as the women undress to fight over the man: "An old custom, perhaps a survival of African tribalism, had been imported from some remote West Indian hillside into a New York back yard" (pp. 308–09).

From this savage display of the "unofficial" culture, McKay brings the "official" and "unofficial" cultures into humorous but revealing collision. The juxtaposition of scenes in Black and white movie houses draws on the parody and travesty nature of carnival. In chapter 20, Jake and Felice visit the Negro Picture Theater and see a movie with Black actors parodying the "official" white culture "in expensive evening clothes, with automobiles, and menials, to imitate white society people." While, the social and economic separation between the "official" white and the "unofficial" Black societies could be viewed with bitterness and anger, the racial and social barriers are instead mocked with carnivalistic laughter, "and the laughter was good on the screen" (p. 314). The ironic element in the performance and the viewing of the performance is multilayered. First, the attitude of the actors—who "pranced and grinned like good-nigger servants, who know that 'mas'r' and 'missus,' intent on being amused, are watching their antics from an upper window"—presupposes the observance by the white "mas'r" and "missus" whose lives are being parodied and who are amused by the carnivalistic incongruity of the Black servants acting like the white employers. Second, although the white society people are not actually shown, through their supposed attitude towards the clowning Black servants, they themselves are being observed by the Black movie audience, so that the white society people who watch the Black servants' "antics from an upper window" are, at another remove, through the racial composition of the audience, themselves watched by those whom they watch.

This scene's irony is heightened in the following chapter, in which Jake and Felice, to celebrate their reunion, go to a nice restaurant and afterwards to a Broadway theater. Now instead of a movie of Black actors for an intended Black audience, they see a movie with a white cast made for an intended white audience. From the "nigger heaven" (Black balcony) of this theater, McKay writes, "they watched high-class people make luxurious love on the screen. They enjoyed the exhibition. There is no better angle from which one can look down on a motion picture than that of the nigger heaven" (p. 315).

In this brief passage's exceptionally double-voiced and ambiguous phrasing, the word choice in saying that Jake and Felice enjoyed the "exhibition"—as opposed to "film," "movie," "show," or even "performance"—suggests an attitude of debasement towards the film, the white audience, and white society in general. The word "exhibition" suggests that the performer—white society in general—is ridiculed and mocked, as in the saying that someone "made a spectacle" of himself. Thus, the white film's attempt to glorify or "crown" white society has the reverse effect with the Black audience.

The next sentence stresses the Black audience's point of view by mentioning the "angle" from which they view the film, and this too is double-voiced. While "angle" denotes the physical point of view—that is, seeing the movie from the balcony—it also connotes the ideology or mental point of view of the Black audience, which is clarified by the fact that the Black audience "can look down on a motion picture." The phrasing here denotes the fact that the "nigger heaven" is the best point from which to see the picture, but the connotation of "look down on" is that the "nigger heaven" is the best vantage point from which to *mock* or *ridicule* the picture and the "official" culture represented. Not only that, but the "nigger heaven" balcony is the best vantage point from which to "look down on" the white audience below, a situation that repeats with a difference the image at the end of the previous chapter. However, in the first situation, the white observers were only imagined; in the second, the Black ones are present. In addition, the imagined whites chose their own vantage point and situated themselves above the Blacks to look down on them to mock and be "amused" by their "antics" and were themselves mocked. While the white theater's policy to restrict Blacks to the "nigger heaven" ostensibly denigrates the Black audience, it ironically situates them above the white audience, making them mocking observers.

After this mocking, carnivalesque, interlude, the primitive emotions of jealous lovers reappear in a showdown involving Zeddy when Jake and Felice run into him at a cabaret and the two male actors in this love triangle learn each other's identity. Although they had been the best of friends, the two come quite close to killing each other, with Zeddy pulling a knife and Jake a gun. Although no one is hurt, harsh words are said, and Jake's freedom is threatened when Zeddy publicly reveals Jake's desertion from the Army. But even if no hard feelings linger between Jake and Zeddy, that does not negate the truth—the dark side of man's animal nature—that the brief conflict reveals. For Jake, the savagery of his confrontation with Zeddy is reminiscent more of the "savagery" of white civilization's "official" culture than the "primitivism" of the Blacks' "unofficial" folk culture, an artistic concept that will be more fully developed in McKay's second novel, *Banjo*. The Black men's fights over women—which Jake perceives as "miserable cock-fights, beastly, tigerish, bloody"—echo white culture's concern with Black sexuality, and Jake is "always sickened, saddened, unmanned" by them.

As in the later *Banjo*, the savagery created by white culture is evaluated against the wholesome primitivism of Black culture, and Jake considers sex in American society as a "wild, shrieking mad woman . . . jeering at him. . . . creat[ing] terror," as opposed to love which in folk culture is a "joy lifting man out of the humdrum ways of life." With regard to his own actions, Jake is shocked and "disgusted with himself," for he had previously succeeded in "delight[ing] in love and yet steer[ing] clear of the hate and violence that govern it in his world. His love nature was generous and warm without any vestige of the diabolical or sadistic," and his confrontation with Zeddy catches him "in the thing that he despised so thoroughly," the "savage emotions" that he had seen in "Brest, London, and his America. . . . the same savage emotions as those vile, vicious, villainous white men who, like hyenas and rattlers, had fought, murdered, and clawed the entrails out of black men over the common, commercial flesh of women" (p. 328).

And in the final passage, Jake and Felice are on their way to Chicago—"I hear it's a mahvelous place foh niggers," Jake says (p. 333)—seeking something that Harlem cannot bring, something that they may not be able to find anywhere, but which they will continue to look for. For all of the "home" that it might be, or at least appear to be, Harlem, as Jake is reminded by his near-fatal quarrel with Zeddy, is just as prone to human vice, rage, violence, and horror as the Europe that he had fled. So at this point, the story has come full circle, from Jake's deserting the army and returning to his imagined "home" of Harlem to his fleeing that corrupted home and setting out to make a new home in Chicago with Felice.

As we have seen, Jake originally flees Europe for his Harlem "home," and at the end of the novel he flees Harlem to make a "happy" "home" with Felice, but this is, finally, an elusive quest, for there is no true home for the displaced, alienated Blacks for whom race is always an issue to be confronted. Therein is both the irony and the tragedy, this "absence of home" being "the reality behind *Home to Harlem*, and . . . the reason that the book's primitivism reaches a dead end." The book's "sense of its own enthusiasm" is balanced "with a sense of dread."[16] But if primitivism itself is "a dead end," rejecting primitive qualities outright is so too. The positive qualities of this primitivism are reinforced by one final aspect of carnival spirit: the animal fable quality, drawn from folklore, in which McKay uses animal characterizations that the characters "wear gracefully."[17] Jake is a goat; Ray, a blue jay; Zeddy, the bear and an ape; the dining car chef, a rhino; Felice, a cat; Nije, a skunk; Billy Biase, The Wolf; and a railroad waiter, a mule. "As in fables, the animal associations indicate character as well as physical appearance. They are either favorable or not, but they are never dehumanizing in the sense of suggesting the brutal." These characterizations are absent from the novel's white characters, who "have left the best aspects of their animalism behind them" and whose "lives are therefore fake."[18]

While Roger Rosenblatt oversimplifies the situation in claiming that "[t]here is little more" to the novel than "enormous pride in, and the celebration of, being black; an assertion of freedom and joy; an easy quest for happiness, achieved," McKay's carnivalization of American culture is an important component of the novel. Indeed, with the name Brown, suggesting an early idea of Black nationalism, Jake "is meant to represent part of the earth itself. . . . resembles the standard natural man of American literature in general . . . . the uncorrupted primitive who has been snatched away from his native land, and from his own nature as well, and who now seeks to return home." But, again, for Jake there is no true home. Although he may share certain characteristics with the "natural man of American literature," such as Natty Bumppo, the "nature" that Black "primitives" are a part of is not American, but African—"the only natural homeland which would have any meaning to them," yet it "may only be returned to within their imaginations."[19] That is, they may not return to that heritage as it was, but they may celebrate what it was and as well as the "unofficial" Black culture that grew from it and exists in counterpoint with the "official" white culture.

McKay's next novel, *Banjo*, presents a sequel not just to the lives of *Home to Harlem*'s main characters, but also to the dialogical interaction, the carnivalesque, and the "unofficial" culture inherent in this first novel. But if the concept of a "home" is ironically fleeting in *Home to Harlem*, it is never even considered in *Banjo*, in which all space is threshold space, public space, the place of interaction, and all time is crisis time. For the displaced Black characters in Marseilles are not even searching for a home, although they do participate in the carnival life that binds them together in the face of the "official" culture and unifies them in a way that could provide a Black nationalist foundation on which "home" could someday stand.

NOTES

1. Claude McKay, "The Word," *Selected Poems of Claude McKay* (New York: Bookman, 1953), p. [10].
2. Mikhail Bakhtin, *Rabelais and His World*, trans. Helene Iswolsky (Cambridge: M.I.T. Press, 1968), p. 11.
3. Katerina Clark and Michael Holquist, *Mikhail Bakhtin* (Cambridge, MA: Belknap, 1984), p. 298.
4. M. M. Bakhtin, *The Dialogic Imagination: Four Essays*, ed. Michael Holquist, trans. Caryl Emerson and Michael Holquist (Austin: Univ. of Texas Press, 1981), p. 342.
5. Michael Holquist, Introduction, *The Dialogic Imagination: Four Essays*, p. xviii.
6. Henry Louis Gates, *The Signifying Monkey: A Theory of Afro-American Literary Criticism* (New York: Oxford Univ. Press, 1988), pp. xxii–xxiii.
7. Gates, *Signifying Monkey*, p. xxvii.
8. Claude McKay, *Home to Harlem* (1928), foreword by Wayne F. Cooper (Boston: Northeastern Univ. Press, 1987), p. 3—hereafter citations in my text are to this edition.
9. Bernard W. Bell, *The Afro-American Novel and Its Tradition* (Amherst: Univ. of Massachusetts Press, 1987), p. 117.
10. Richard K. Barksdale, "Symbolism and Irony in McKay's *Home to Harlem*," *CLA Journal* 15 (1972): 340.
11. Roger Rosenblatt, *Black Fiction* (Cambridge: Harvard Univ. Press, 1974), p. 90.
12. Bakhtin, *Rabelais*, p. 278.
13. Rosenblatt, *Black Fiction*, p. 93.
14. Mikhail Bakhtin, *Problems of Dostoevsky's Poetics*, trans. R. W. Rostel (n.p.: Ardis, 1973), p. 142.
15. Rosenblatt, *Black Fiction*, p. 94–95.
16. Rosenblatt, *Black Fiction*, p. 96.
17. Rosenblatt, *Black Fiction*, p. 92.
18. Rosenblatt, *Black Fiction*, pp. 92–93.
19. Rosenblatt, *Black Fiction*, p. 95.

AFTERWORD

CAROLYN C. DENARD

Few periods in American literary history have been more widely remembered, re-evaluated, re-appraised, or re-examined than that period of intense literary and artistic creativity by Black writers in the 1920s called the Harlem Renaissance. The first such re-evaluation was the publication in 1971 of *The Harlem Renaissance*[1] by noted historian Nathan Huggins. In this controversial study of the Renaissance, Huggins gave the first serious critical appraisal of the writers of the Renaissance and the impact of the social and cultural forces that converged in Harlem in the 1920s. While realizing its lasting merits to the future generations, Huggins criticized the writers of the Renaissance for not being sure enough of their own indigenous expressive culture—particularly the music— in the creation of the art of the Renaissance. Huggins summarized that the effort was mostly one that mimicked Whites rather than one that asserted an independent Black cultural identity.

Closely following Huggins's study was a collection of essays published in 1972 called the *Harlem Renaissance Remembered*[2] edited by Arna Bontemps. Bontemps's review was initiated largely because of his own invaluable role as a participant in that movement. In this lively, informative collection, Bontemps and many notable scholars of the period tried to recapture the feelings, the mood, and the impact of the Renaissance: the excitement it engendered, the promise it offered to budding writers, and the good feeling that it left in the hearts and minds of many, like Bontemps, who participated in it.

A 1974 issue of *Studies in the Literary Imagination*,[3] edited by Victor A. Kramer—the germ of this current study—took a renewed look at the Renaissance. This collection, rather than having the first-hand flavor that characterized the Bontemps collection, took the more scholarly approach of looking at both the contextual and the individual issues: the major theoretical questions and examinations of artistic trends and the works of specific writers. Most notable about this new collection was its focus on the Black and White interrelationship and the racial dynamic that existed between Black writers and their White patrons. It did not judge, as Huggins's study had done; but rather, it sought to explore—regardless of the strengths or weaknesses they revealed—the nature of these relationships.

David Levering Lewis's 1981 study of the Renaissance, *When Harlem was in Vogue*,[4] was a richly layered and highly readable history of the social, political, and cultural forces that converged in Harlem in 1920s to create the fertile ground for its harvest of literary and artistic production. Like Huggins, Lewis also judged the Renaissance a failure—not because of an unrealized artistic integrity but because of a naivete by the participants regarding their ability to effect a wholesale change in American public attitudes about Blacks either during or after the Renaissance. Lewis's detailed engagement in the history of the period, despite his conclusions about its success, reveal the studied attention this moment of intense literary activity commanded even from those looking at the historical and biographical sources which led to its creation.

In 1985, an NEH-sponsored conference on the Harlem Renaissance, "Heritage: A Reappraisal of the Harlem Renaissance," became the basis for Amritjit Singh, William Shiver, and Stanley Brodwin's collection of reflective essays called *The Harlem Renaissance: Revaluations*.[5] Their study assumed yet another analytical posture on the Renaissance, this time endeavoring to see the specific impact of the Harlem Renaissance of the 1920s on the cultural revolution of the 1960s. Singh and his fellow editors "believed there was much to be gained by analyzing in new ways the inner workings of a movement that was doubtless, in many ways, a precursor to the 'black consciousness' strivings of the 1960s."[6]

In 1987, the 1974 journal issue of *Studies in the Literary Imagination* was expanded and issued in book as *The Harlem Renaissance Re-examined*, edited by Victor A. Kramer.[7] That book included many more questions about aesthetics and the complexity of the relationship between Black writers and Whites during the Renaissance, and it also closely examined the role of women and their artistic works. Essays such as Nellie McKay's treatment of women playwrights of the Renaissance and Deborah McDowell's interview with Dorothy West, a surviving writer of the Renaissance, were notable contributions of this volume. Other new pieces examined patronage, the literary marketplace, and the role of writers earlier ignored, such as Rudolph Fisher and Zora Neale Hurston.

Also in 1987, Houston Baker, in *Modernism and the Harlem Renaissance*,[8] tackled the thorny relationship of the work of the Renaissance authors with the High Modernism that influenced many American writers of the early 20th century. Arguing passionately against the Renaissance's failure on any terms, Baker addresses specifically claims that the works of the Renaissance writers held no modernist impulses. Looking back at the moments that preceded the Renaissance of the 1920s all the way to the Cotton Exposition Speech by Booker T.

Washington in 1895, Baker argues for a particularly African American modernism made manifest in both the artistic manipulation of stereotypes (the"mastery of form") and in their radical replacement (the "deformation of mastery"). This dual project—of mastery and deformation—constituted the forms of modernism which characterized the writings of the Harlem Renaissance and which have continued, according to Baker, in one or the other of these forms in African-American literature since.

In 1995, George Hutchinson in *Harlem Renaissance in Black and White*[9] revisited Huggins's earlier interest in the relationship of Black and White writers during the Harlem Renaissance. This time, however, Hutchinson demonstrates, in a thoroughly researched and convincing study, the interdependence of the relationship of Black and White intellectuals in the 1920s. Instead of lamenting their failure to embrace the tenets of the influential European Modernism or celebrating their desire to carve out an African-American modernism of their own, Hutchinson argues that Black intellectuals of the Harlem Renaissance helped shaped—in their writings and in their relationships with White intellectuals in New York—an "American Modernism" characterized by pragmatism, cultural pluralism and cultural nationalism. For Hutchinson the works of the Renaissance are not to be marginalized or placed in a separate category of modernism but offered as integral and necessary components of the American modernism that also emerged in the early 20th century.

The publication of this paperback second edition of *The Harlem Renaissance Re-examined* in an expanded form attests once again to the power of the Renaissance to command attention. This collection adds examinations of race relationships, the complexity of the role of women, and an insightful theoretical analysis of Claude McKay's work by Robert Russ. Russ's essay demonstrates admirably the way in which contemporary theoretical writings like those of Mikhail Bakhtin can, retrospectively, add useful contextual and critical interpretations to the works of the Renaissance. His implications are that McKay's fiction is a paradigm of an artist's struggle with how to craft successful fiction around the dilemma of racism. The chronology and the selected photographs added to this volume indicate a desire by the editors to bring still other facets of the art of the Renaissance into this volume and to shape the book into a valuable teaching tool.

Seeing this long pattern of remembering, re-evaluating, and re-examining the Harlem Renaissance over the past twenty-five years, one is compelled to ask what is there about the Renaissance that merits this kind of continued interest and re-evaluation. What does this desire to look back at the Renaissance, again and again, mean, both in terms of its significance as a literary moment in the 1920s and, perhaps more importantly, as a symbol in American cultural history which has continued to attract scholarly re-examinations over the years.

Editors and writers of these evaluations of the Harlem Renaissance provide a catalog of reasons as to why the Renaissance remains worthy of such continued study. These critics pursue such analyses to review the interplay of social and historical forces which caused it all to come together at the moment that it did: a social and aesthetic attraction to the arts, the value of Harlem real estate, the desire for equality and independence of returning Black war veterans, the migration of Southern Blacks to the urban North, Puritan guilt among many middleclass White Americans, amicable publishers, and a booming economy. They also engage in this recall to explore in detail the way in which the arts offered possibilities and limitations in the dynamic of Black/White race relations. Still other reasons are to understand more fully Harlem as a site for the exploration by Whites of the "cult of the primitive"; or to gain renewed understanding of the methods, themes, and personalities of the individual writers; to study the texts as signs of deeper, buried meanings always waiting to be discovered; or finally, to study it because of its historical manageability as a literary moment, nestled so neatly between the World War I and the Great Depression.

These are all important and valid reasons for studying the Harlem Renaissance, and many of them inform this current re-examination. But the importance of the Harlem Renaissance goes beyond this varied catalog of answers. The meaning is larger still. What is embedded in the questions of scholars and participants in the Renaissance as the greatest cultural import of the Renaissance as a literary and artistic event in American society is that it was a moment, whether naively believed or successfully realized or not, when the creative arts, *not* economic determinism, *nor* political strategy, *nor* constitutional rhetoric, *nor* military strength, but the *arts* were believed to be an agent through which individuals could effect social change.

For Black Americans in the 1920s, it was a move ideologically from a Washingtonian to a Du Boisian moment in the culture. Alain Locke and Charles Johnson generated excitement among young aspiring artists by inviting them to use their brains and not their brawn to achieve respected status in the society. For individuals two generations removed from slavery, whose minds were valued least by society, to gain acceptance through an intellectual aesthetic was a major reorientation regarding personhood and equality.

In invitations and introductions and in the publication space and encouragement given in the *Crisis* and *Opportunity* magazines (not literary magazines, but magazines devoted mainly to historical and social inquiry), Johnson, Locke, and Du Bois encouraged and rewarded service to the cause of liberty and self-respect given through the perfection of literary craft. Langston Hughes, Zora Neale Hurston, Countee Cullen, Dorothy West, and Arna Bontemps all tell memorable and exciting stories about the poem, the story, or the play that became their ticket to Harlem and to membership in its arts corps of the 1920s.[10] Whether naively believed or not, as some historians have suggested, for a time in Harlem in the 1920s, the pen was mightier than the sword in the war to achieve a greater self-definition by Black Americans and a saner, more humane world.

It was clear by virtue of the presence of the many writers who converged on Harlem in the twenties that the challenge these magazines and their editors had offered to young writers had matched their desire for artistic self-expression.

The legitimizing of one's artistry as an indirect way to effect social change was the great magic and magnetism of what happened in Harlem in the 1920s. There was some innocence in such thinking, and there was, to be sure, some disagreement as to what the subject of that art ought to be, but all the Renaissance writers agreed that art was a way to initiate change. The "New Negro," according to Alain Locke, was to be found within the pages of poems, stories, plays and paintings collected in his now famous volume *The New Negro*.[11] The manifesto of those climbing the "racial mountain" for change identified themselves not by social protest or political demands but by their desire for the freedom to write as they chose:

> We younger Negro artists who create now intend to express our individual dark-skinned selves without fear or shame. If white people are pleased we are glad. If they are not, it doesn't matter. We know we are beautiful, and ugly too. The tom tom cries and the tom-tom laughs. If colored people are pleased we are glad. If they are not, their displeasure doesn't matter either. We build our temples for tomorrow as strong as we know how, and we stand on top of the mountain, free within ourselves.[12]

The value of this kind of assertion of cultural independence through the arts is evident in the influence these Harlem writers had on later Black intellectuals also seeking cultural independence. Both the Negritude poets—Léopold Senghor, Aimé Césaire, and Leon Damas[13]—who were fighting for African cultural independence in France in the 1930s, and the Black American writers of that next artistic revolution in the U.S. in the 1960s[14] acknowledged their debts to the example established by the writers of the Harlem Renaissance. What happened in Harlem was triumphant testimony for them that a poet could be called into the service of liberty.

Some have devalued the impact of the Harlem Renaissance.[15] But how successful these writers were at achieving their stated aim in the 1920s is not the real issue in gauging the cultural importance of the Renaissance. What is more important is their joyful and unquestioning belief that they were indeed involved in such a transformation. The primacy of the arts in the vanguard of change lasted as long as it did for a variety of reasons during the 1920s—some admirable, others questionable. But the fact remains that what the Black writers and intellectuals of Harlem saw themselves doing was creating a new cultural and political definition of themselves through their engagement in artistic expression.

It was not, however, just the ethnic cultural consciousness of Black Americans that the arts of the Harlem Renaissance gave rise to in the 1920s. The artistic energy and activity of the Renaissance also provided a way for other Americans to see the world differently and to effect, if only briefly, a vision of racial harmony. For the White intelligentsia genuinely concerned with the arts, even if at times condescendingly, the creative activity of the Renaissance was invigorating and inviting. For those simply drawn by what critics call the "cult of the primitive" and their desire for the exotic, they too, ironically enough, were drawn by the role of art in providing the "feeling" they wanted from the moment. A sometimes "false" religion, or a prescribed patriotism, and even material success had not nourished the soul in the way they believed the arts were capable. In the Harlem of the 1920s, therefore, there seemed to have been a transformative energy given to the arts. And while the rebellious posture of many Whites in Harlem was suspect, being attracted to it as they were because its Black actors seemed distant and "exotic," the *arts* represented the avenue for that rebellion nonetheless—not politics or war or business or any of the avenues they had tried before. In Harlem in the 1920s, literature, music, painting, and drama were the ammunition; and Black Americans, for the possibility of self-redefinition and equality, and White Americans, for intellectual engagement and entertainment, were both drawn to the place where art was the vehicle effecting change.

To use literature in this way strikes a particularly American chord. Americans have always claimed their cultural merit in the world based on the art they produced. Emerson's admonition in 1837 for Americans to turn away from the "courtly muses of Europe" and to create an indigenous art, and the regretful refrain of Washington Irving that America must be more than a "counting house" attest to an early realization that the best and most independent national definition would come from a studied cultivation of artistic expression.[16] "Who can doubt," Emerson proclaimed in 1837, "that poetry will revive and lead in a new age."[17] His proclamation was not much different from the claim of those Black leaders shepherding the artists in Harlem in the 1920s: "There is a spiritual wealth," Alain Locke claimed in 1924, "which if they can properly expound will be ample for a new judgement and re-appraisal of the race."[18] Or as James Weldon Johnson had concluded earlier, "The world does not know that a people is great until that people produces great literature and art."[19] His was a variation of the refrain held by both Blacks and Whites that full cultural independence could not be declared for a society until a respectable art could be mined from its members.

For American intellectuals, cultural independence and vitality have always come in the shape of heightened artistic activity. And thus the reason that the Harlem Renaissance holds a symbolic place in American cultural history is also the reason that scholars are drawn again and again to reexamining this moment. In Harlem in the 1920s, literature mattered; it was in the name of the arts that the credos and the manifestos of independence were sounded.

Nothing has pleased American intellectuals more, our cultural history has shown, than to be defined and validated through artistic achievement. This was no less the case for Black Americans in the 1920s in Harlem. What underlies the desire, then, of American scholars to go back to this period to reexamine and reflect, whether it is a result of wanting to explore its relationship to other literary movements, or being intrigued by a participant who can tell a first-hand account, or being inspired by the sheer outpouring of artistic activity is the same reason that the Renaissance itself is so important to us as a moment in American cultural history. These continuing returns say profoundly that the Harlem Renaissance was most important to us because it affirmed what we continue to value. This engagement by scholars allows them to affirm, again, a moment when the arts were at the vanguard of social and cultural change. The Harlem Renaissance in American scholarship has become like the "American Renaissance" in the 1840s and '50s and in some ways like the Southern Renaissance of the 1920s—a moment of affective, celebratory cultural memory.[20] It represents a place and time which symbolize not only the burgeoning cultural independence of Black Americans in the 1920s, but also what we value in our national, intellectual culture as a whole. Each time that we return to an examination of the Harlem Renaissance, we come not only to understand an earlier time but also to find the clues to how we might recreate the dynamics or this kind of expressive cultural moment again in other circumstances.

Looking back at the Renaissance again and again continues to offer the possibility that we will find one more photograph, relationship, unpublished poem, undocumented contribution, or unrealized literary interpretation that will help inspire us and affirm in us the value of this kind of artistic engagement in the culture. Such continuing studies help us to explain the genesis and the growth of such moments and the true measure and meaning of their failure and success. In so doing, we can analyze, if not celebrate, once more a moment when the arts—literature, painting, drama, and music—brought people together and encouraged optimism and self-affirmation. This was a time when the arts became a concentrated symbol of the energy, the activism, the conflict, the hope, the possibility that artistic involvement by both the artists and the society could produce. In re-examining such moments we keep before us what was the best in us, and in any society: the possibility to redefine ourselves, to reach out to our neighbors, and to influence and inspire successive generations.

NOTES

1. Nathan Huggins, *Harlem Renaissance* (New York: Oxford Univ. Press, 1971).

2. Arna Bontemps, ed., *Harlem Renaissance Remembered* (New York: Dodd Mead, 1972).

3. *Studies in the Literary Imagination.* Georgia State Univ., Atlanta, Georgia, 1974.

4. David Levering Lewis. *When Harlem was in Vogue.* (New Yourk: Knopf, 1981).

5. Amritjit Singh, William S. Shiver, and Stanley Brodwin, eds. *The Harlem Renaissance: Revaluations* (New York: Garland, 1989).

6. Amritjit Singh, Introduction, *The Harlem Renaissance: Revaluations*, p. xi.

7. Victor A. Kramer, ed. *The Harlem Renaissance Re-examined* (New York: AMS Press, 1987).

8. Houston A. Baker, Jr. *Modernism and the Harlem Renaissance.* (Chicago: Univ. of Chicago Press, 1987).

9. George Hutchinson. *The Harlem Renaissance in Black and White.* (Cambridge: Harvard Univ. Press, 1995).

10. See "Conversations With Dorothy West" with Deborah McDowell in this volume, pp. 285–303; Langston Hughes, *The Big Sea* (New York: Hill & Wang, 1940); Zora Neale

Hurston, *Dust Tracks on a Road* (1942; Urbana: Univ. of Illinois Press, 1984); and Arna Bontemps, "The Awakening: A Memoir," in *Harlem Renaissance Remembered.*

11. Alain Locke, ed. *The New Negro* (New York: Atheneum, 1925).

12. Langston Hughes, "The Negro Artist and the Racial Mountain," *Nation* 122 (1926): 694.

13. See Mercer Cook, "Afro-Americans in Senghor's Poetry," in *Hommage á Leopold Sedar Senghor: Homme de Culture* (Paris: Presence Africaine, 1976), p. 154.

14. Singh, Introduction, *The Harlem Renaissance: Revaluations*; Norman Harris, *Connecting Times: Black Writing of the Sixties* (Jackson: Univ. of Mississippi Press, 1988).

15. See Huggins, *Harlem Renaissance*; Harold Cruse, *The Crisis of the Negro Intellectual* (New York: Apollo, 1968); Robert Allen, *Black Awakening in Capitalist America: An Analytic History* (Garden City, NY: Doubleday, 1969).

16. "The American Scholar," 1837; reprint, *American Literature: The Makers and the Making*, Book B, ed. Cleanth Brooks, et.al. (New York: St. Martin's, 1973), pp. 702–17. Washington Irving, *The Sketch Book* (1819).

17. "American Scholar," p. 710.

18. *New Negro*, p. 26.

19. "Preface to *The Book of American Negro Poetry*," Harcourt Brace, 1922, p.vii.

20. See Pierre Nora's discussion of "sites of memory" in his essay "Between Memory and History: *Les Lieux de Memoire*," *Representations* 26 (Spring 1989): 7–25.

THE HARLEM RENAISSANCE:
A SELECTED BIBLIOGRAPHY

ROBERT A. RUSS

The following revised and expanded bibliography does not attempt to be complete. Comprehensive bibliographies are available elsewhere, the most detailed and complete of which is Margaret Perry's *The Harlem Renaissance: An Annotated Bibliography and Commentary* (1982). This work has been one of my major sources, and any student of the period will find it invaluable.

The present bibliography does attempt to provide a manageable and useful first source for those interested in the Harlem Renaissance in general, and in the particular authors and issues addressed in this volume. In selecting the entries, I have attempted to identify major book-length works and significant articles, to update Perry's listings with pertinent materials, to offer listings that fall outside the scope of her study, and to point out even relatively minor works that offer close connections to particular issues examined in this volume.

Since the publication of the first edition of *The Harlem Renaissance Reexamined* in 1987, there has been a swelling tide of new scholarship and criticism about the Harlem Renaissance, making an updated bibliography all the more necessary.

GENERAL STUDIES

Abramson, Doris E. *Negro Playwrights in the American Theatre, 1925–1959*. New York: Columbia Univ. Press, 1969.

Anderson, Jervis. *This Was Harlem: A Cultural Portrait, 1900–1950*. New York: Farrar Straus Giroux, 1981.

Arata, Esther Spring. *More Black American Playwrights: A Bibliography*. Metuchen, NJ: Scarecrow, 1978.

———, and Nicholas John Rotoli. *Black American Playwrights, 1800 to the Present: A Bibliography*. Metuchen, NJ: Scarecrow, 1976.

Baker, Houston A., Jr. *Afro-American Poetics: Revisions of Harlem and the Black Aesthetic*. Madison: Univ. of Wisconsin Press, 1988.

———. *Blues, Ideology, and Afro-American Literature: A Vernacular Theory*. Chicago: Univ. of Chicago Press, 1984.

———. *Modernism and the Harlem Renaissance*. Chicago: Univ. of Chicago Press, 1987.

———. *Workings of the Spirit: The Poetics of Afro-American Women's Writing*. Chicago: Univ. of Chicago Press, 1991.

Bassett, John E. *Harlem in Review: Critical Reactions to Black American Writers, 1917–1939*. Selinsgrove, PA: Susquehanna Univ. Press, 1992.

Bell, Bernard. "Folk Art and the Harlem Renaissance." *Phylon* 36 (1975): 155–63.

Berzon, Judith R. *Neither White Nor Black: The Mulatto Character in American Fiction*. New York: New York Univ. Press, 1978.

Bone, Robert. *Down Home: A History of Afro-American Short Fiction from Its Beginnings to the End of the Harlem Renaissance*. New York: Putnam's, 1975.

———. *The Negro Novel in America*, rev. ed. New Haven: Yale Univ. Press, 1965.

Bontemps, Arna, ed. *The Harlem Renaissance Remembered: Essays*. New York: Dodd, 1972.

Brawley, Benjamin. *The Negro Genius: A New Appraisal of the Achievement of the American Negro in Literature and the Fine Arts*. New York: Dodd, 1937.

Brown, Lloyd W. "The African Heritage and the Harlem Renaissance: A Re-evaluation." *African Literature Today* 9 (1978): 1–9.

Brown, Sterling A. *The Negro in American Fiction*. 1937. New York: Arno, 1969 (with *Negro Poetry and Drama*).

———. *Negro Poetry and Drama*. 1937. New York: Arno, 1969 (with *The Negro in American Fiction*).

Coleman, Floyd, and John Adkins Richardson. "Black Continuities in the Art of the Harlem Renaissance." *Papers on Language and Literature* 12 (1976): 402–21.

Davis, Arthur P. *From the Dark Tower: Afro-American Writers 1900–1960*. Washington, DC: Howard Univ. Press, 1974.

De Jongh, James. *Vicious Modernism: Black Harlem and the Literary Imagination*. New York: Cambridge Univ. Press, 1990.

Dixon, Melvin. *Ride Out the Wilderness: Geography and Identity in Afro-American Literature*. Urbana: Univ. of Illinois Press, 1987. (includes discussions of Jean Toomer, Claude McKay, and Zora Neale Hurston).

Early, Gerald. "Three Notes Towards a Cultural Definition of the Harlem Renaissance." *Callaloo* 14 (1991): 136–49.

Fabre, Michel. *From Harlem to Paris: Black American Writers in France, 1840–1980*. Urbana: Univ. of Illinois Press, 1991.

Floyd, Samuel A., ed. *Black Music in the Harlem Renaissance: A Collection of Essays*. New York: Greenwood Press, 1990.

Ford, Nick Aaron. *The Contemporary Negro Novel: A Study in Race Relations*. 1936. College Park, MD: McGrath, 1968.

Gallagher, Brian. "Explorations of Black Identity from *The New Negro* to *Invisible Man.*" *Perspectives on Contemporary Literature* 8 (1983): 1–9.

Gates, Henry Louis, Jr. *Figures in Black: Words, Signs and the "Racial" Self.* New York: Oxford Univ. Press, 1987.

———. *The Signifying Monkey: A Theory of African-American Literary Criticism.* New York: Oxford Univ. Press, 1988.

Gayle, Addison, Jr. *The Way of the New World: The Black Novel in America.* Garden City, NY: Anchor-Doubleday, 1975.

Gibson, Donald B., ed.. *Modern Black Poets: A Collection of Critical Essays.* Englewood Cliffs, NJ: Prentice-Hall, 1973.

Gloster, Hugh. *Negro Voices in American Fiction.* 1948. New York: Russell, 1965.

Harlem Renaissance: Art of Black America. Intro. by Mary Schmidt Campbell. New York: The Studio Museum of Harlem and Harry N. Abrams, 1987.

Harris, Trudier., ed. *Afro-American Writers from the Harlem Renaissance to 1940.* Detroit: Gale Research, 1987.

Harrison, Paul Carter. *The Drama of Nommo.* New York: Grove, 1972.

Hogue, W. Lawrence. *Discourse and the Other: The Production of the Afro-American Text.* Durham: Duke Univ. Press, 1986.

Huggins, Nathan I. *Harlem Renaissance.* New York: Oxford Univ. Press, 1971.

Hughes, Langston. "Black Renaissance." *The Big Sea: An Autobiography.* 1940. New York: Hill & Wang, 1963. 221–335.

Ikonné, Chidi. *From Du Bois to Van Vechten: The Early New Negro Literature, 1903–1926.* Westport, CT: Greenwood, 1981.

Inge, M. Thomas, Maurice Duke, and Jackson R. Bryer, eds. *Black American Writers: Bibliographical Essays.* 2 vols. New York: St. Martin's, 1978. Vol. 1: The Beginnings through the Harlem Renaissance and Langston Hughes.

Isaacs, Edith J. R. *The Negro in the American Theatre.* New York: Theatre Arts, 1947.

Jackson, Blyden. "The Harlem Renaissance." *The Comic Imagination in American Literature.* Ed. Louis D. Rubin, Jr. New Brunswick, NJ: Rutgers Univ. Press, 1973. 295–303.

———. "Renaissance in the Twenties." *The Twenties: Fiction, Poetry, Drama.* Ed. Warren French. Deland, FL: Everett, 1975.

———. *The Waiting Years: Essays on American Negro Literature.* Baton Rouge: Louisiana State Univ. Press, 1976.

———, and Louis D. Rubin, Jr. *Black Poetry in America: Two Essays in Historical Interpretation.* Baton Rouge: Louisiana State Univ. Press, 1974.

Jones, Gayle. *Liberating Voices: Oral Tradition in African American Literature.* Cambridge: Harvard Univ. Press, 1991.

Kellner, Bruce. *The Harlem Renaissance: An Historical Dictionary for the Era.* Westport, CT: Greenwood, 1984.

Kent, George E. "Patterns of the Harlem Renaissance: The Fork in the Road." *Black World* June 1972: 13–24, 76–80.

Lewis, David Levering. *When Harlem Was in Vogue.* New York: Knopf, 1981.

Littlejohn, David. *Black on White: A Critical Survey of Writing by American Negroes.* New York: Grossman, 1966.

Long, Richard A. "The Genesis of Locke's *The New Negro.*" *Black World* Feb. 1976: 14–20.

Martin, Tony. *Literary Garveyism: Garvey, Black Arts, and the Harlem Renaissance.* Dover, MA: Majority, 1983.

Perry, Margaret. *The Harlem Renaissance: An Annotated Bibliography and Commentary.* New York: Garland, 1982.

———. *Silence to the Drums: A Survey of the Literature of the Harlem Renaissance.* Westport, CT: Greenwood, 1976.

Petesch, Donald A. *A Spy in the Enemy's Country: The Emergence of Modern Black Literature.* Iowa City: Univ. of Iowa Press, 1989.

Redding, J. Saunders. *To Make A Poet Black.* 1939. College Park, MD: McGrath, 1968.

Rosenblatt, Roger. *Black Fiction.* Cambridge: Harvard Univ. Press, 1974.

Rush, Theressa Gunnels, Carol Fairbanks Myers, and Esther Spring Arata. *Black American Writers Past and Present: A Biographical and Bibliographical Dictionary.* 2 vols. Metuchen, NJ: Scarecrow, 1975.

Scruggs, Charles. *The Sage in Harlem: H. L. Mencken and the Black Writers of the 1920s.* Baltimore: Johns Hopkins Univ. Press, 1984.

Singh, Amritjit. *The Novels of the Harlem Renaissance: Twelve Black Writers, 1923–33.* University Park: Pennsylvania State Univ. Press, 1976.

————, William S. Shiver, and Stanley Brodwin, eds. *The Harlem Renaissance: Revaluations.* New York: Garland, 1989.

Singleton, Gregory Holmes. "Birth, Rebirth, and the 'New Negro' of the 1920s." *Phylon* 43 (1982): 29–45.

Starke, Catherine Juanita. *Black Portraiture in American Fiction: Stock Characters, Archetypes, and Individuals.* New York: Basic, 1971.

Turner, Darwin T. "The Harlem Renaissance: One Facet of an Unturned Kaleidoscope." *Toward a New American Literary History: Essays in Honor of Arlin Turner.* Ed. Louis J. Budd, Edwin H. Cady, and Carl L. Anderson. Durham: Duke Univ. Press, 1980. 195–210.

Vincent, Theodore G., ed. *Voices of a Black Nation: Political Journalism in the Harlem Renaissance.* Forestville, CA: Ramparts Press, 1973.

Wagner, Jean. *Black Poets of the United States: From Paul Laurence Dunbar to Langston Hughes.* Urbana: Univ. of Illinois Press, 1973.

Weixlmann, Joe, and Chester J. Fontenot, ed. *Belief vs. Theory in Black American Literary Criticism.* Greenwood, FL: Penkeville Publishing Co., 1986.

Wintz, Gary D. *Black Culture and the Harlem Renaissance.* Houston: Rice Univ. Press, 1988.

Young, James O. *Black Writers of the Thirties.* Baton Rouge: Louisiana State Univ. Press, 1973.

BLACK AESTHETIC

Baker, Houston A. "The Black Spokesman as Critic: Reflections on the Black Aesthetic." *The Journey Back: Issues in Black Literature and Criticism.* Chicago: Univ. of Chicago Press, 1980. 132–43.

Decker, Jeffrey, ed. *The Black Aesthetic Movement; Documentary Series: An Illustrated Chronicle.* Detroit: Bruccoli Clark Layman, 1991.

Dubey, Madhu. *Black Women Novelists and the Nationalist Aesthetic.* Bloomington: Indiana Univ. Press, 1994.

Fowler, Carolyn. *Black Arts and Black Aesthetics: A Bibliography.* Atlanta: First World, 1981.

Gates, Henry Louis, Jr., ed. "The Black Person in Art: How Should S/He Be Portrayed?" *Black American Literature Forum* 21 (1987): 3–24, 317–32.

————, ed. *Black Literature and Literary Theory.* New York: Methuen, 1984.

Gayle, Addison, Jr. *The Black Aesthetic.* New York: Doubleday, 1971.

————. "The Harlem Renaissance: Towards a Black Aesthetic." *Midcontinent American Studies Journal* 11.2 (1970): 78–87.

Jarab, Joseph. "Black Aesthetic: A Cultural or Political Concept?" *Callaloo* 8 (1985): 587–93.

Johnson, Abby Arthur, and Ronald Maberry Johnson. *Propaganda and Aesthetics: The Literary Politics of Afro-American Magazines in the Twentieth Century.* Amherst: Univ. of Massachusetts Press, 1979.

Martin, Tony. *Literary Garveyism: Garvey, Black Arts and the Harlem Renaissance.* Dover, MA: Majority, 1983.

Mason, Ernest D." Black Art and the Configurations of Experience: The Philosophy of the Black Aesthetic." *CLA Journal* 27 (1983): 1–17.

Stern, Frederick C. "Black Lit, White Crit?" *College English* 35 (1974): 637–58.

Tate, Claudia C. "On White Critics and Black Aestheticians." *CLA Journal* 22 (1979): 383–89.
Thomas, Lorenzo. "The Bop Aesthetic and Black Intellectual Tradition." *Library Chronicle of the University of Texas* 24.1–2 (1994): 104–17.

BLACK AND WHITE

Bigsby, C. W. E. "The White Critic in a Black World." *Negro American Literature Forum* 6 (1972): 39–45.
Brown, Sterling A. "Negro Character as Seen by White Authors." *Journal of Negro Education* 2 (1933): 179–203.
Cooley, John. "White Writers and the Harlem Renaissance." *The Harlem Renaissance: Revaluations*. Ed. Amritjit Singh, William S. Shiver, and Stanley Brodwin. New York: Garland, 1989. 13–22.
Feuser, Willfried F. "Black Reflections in a White Mirror: Literature and Culture in the 'Twenties." *Neohelicon* 20 (1993): 289–306.
Fleming, Robert E. "Roots of the White Liberal Stereotype in Black Fiction." *Negro American Literature Forum* 9 (1975): 17–19.
Hart, Robert C. "Black-White Literary Relations in the Harlem Renaissance." *American Literature* 44 (1973): 612–28.
Scruggs, Charles. "'All Dressed Up But No Place to Go': The Black Writer and His Audience During the Harlem Renaissance." *American Literature* 48 (1977): 543–63.
Vacha, J. E. "Black Man on the Great White Way." *Journal of Popular Culture* 7 (1973): 288–301.
Wilentz, Gay. "White Patron and Black Artist: The Correspondence of Fannie Hurst and Zora Neale Hurston." *Library Chronicle of the University of Texas* 35 (1986): 20–43.

WOMEN

Carby, Hazel V. *Reconstructing Womanhood: The Emergence of the Afro-American Woman Novelist*. New York: Oxford Univ. Press, 1987.
Hernton, Calvin C. *The Sexual Mountain and Black Women Writers: Adventures in Sex, Literature, and Real Life*. New York: Anchor, 1987.
Honey, Maureen, ed. *Shadowed Dreams: Women's Poetry of the Harlem Renaissance*. New Brunswick: Rutgers Univ. Press, 1989.
Hull, Gloria T. "The Black Woman Writer and the Diaspora." *Black Scholar* 17.2 (1986): 2–4.
———. *Color, Sex, & Poetry: Three Women Writers of the Harlem Renaissance*. Bloomington: Indiana Univ. Press, 1987. (on Alice Dunbar-Nelson, Angelina Grimké, and Georgia Douglas Johnson).
———, Patricia Bell Scott, Barbara Smith, and Mary Berry. *All the Women Are White, All the Blacks Are Men, But Some of Us Are Brave: Black Women's Studies*. Old Westbury, NY: Feminist Press, 1982.
Kubitschek, Missy Dehn. *Claiming the Heritage: African-American Women Novelists and History*. Jackson: Univ. Press of Mississippi, 1991.
Roses, Lorraine Elena. *Harlem Renaissance and Beyond: Literary Biographies of 100 Black Women Writers, 1900–1945*. Boston: Hall, 1990.
Wall, Cheryl A., ed. *Changing Our Own Words: Essays on Criticism, Theory, and Writing by Black Women*. New Brunswick: Rutgers Univ. Press, 1989.
———. "Poets and Versifiers, Singers and Signifiers: Women of the Harlem Renaissance." *Women, the Arts, and the 1920s in Paris and New York*. Ed. Kenneth W. Wheeler and Virginia Lee Lussier. New Brunswick, NJ: Transaction Books, 1982. 74–98.

Weixlmann, Joe, and Houston A. Baker, Jr., eds. *Black Feminist Criticism and Critical Theory*. Greenwood, FL: Penkeville Publishing Co., 1988.

STUDIES OF SELECTED AUTHORS

Avi-Ram, Amitai F. "The Unreadable Black Body: 'Conventional' Poetic Form in the Harlem Renaissance." *Genders* 7 (1990): 32–46. (Cullen and McKay).

Bronz, Stephen H. *Roots of Negro Racial Consciousness, the 1920's: Three Harlem Renaissance Authors*. New York: Libra, 1964. (Johnson, Cullen and McKay).

Byrd, Rudolph P. "Shared Orientation and Narrative Acts in *Cane, Their Eyes Were Watching God*, and *Meridian*." *MELUS* 17.4 (1991–1992): 41–56. (Toomer, Hurston, and Alice Walker)

Carby, Hazel V. "Policing the Black Woman's Body in an Urban Context." *Critical Inquiry* 18 (1992): 738–55. (Van Vechten and McKay)

Dean, Sharon, and Erlene Stetson. "Flower-Dust and Springtime: Harlem Renaissance Women." *Radical Teacher: A Newsjournal of Socialist Theory and Practice* 18 (1980): 1–8. (Georgia Douglas Johnson and Nella Larsen).

Emanuel, James A. "Renaissance Sonneteers." *Black World* Sept. 1975: 32–45, 92–97. (McKay, Hughes, and Cullen).

Hutchinson, George B. "The Whitman Legacy and the Harlem Renaissance." *Walt Whitman: The Centennial Essays*. Ed. Ed Folsom. Iowa City: Univ. of Iowa Press, 1994. 201–16. (Locke, James Weldon Johnson, Toomer)

Kellner, Bruce. "Langston Hughes's Nigger Heaven Blues." *Langston Hughes Review* 11.1 (1992): 21–27. (Hughes and Van Vechten)

Larson, Charles R. *Invisible Darkness: Jean Toomer & Nella Larsen*. Iowa City: Univ. of Iowa Press, 1993.

———. "Three Harlem Novels of the Jazz Age." *Critique* 11.3 (1969): 66–78. (McKay, Cullen, and Van Vechten)

Lee, A. Robert. "Harlem on My Mind: Fictions of a Black Metropolis." *The American City: Literary and Cultural Perspectives*. Ed. Graham Clarke. New York: St. Martin's, 1988. 62–85. (Alain Locke, McKay, Hughes, Ralph Ellison).

Lupton, Mary Jane. "Black Women and Survival in *Comedy: American Style* and *Their Eyes Were Watching God*." *Zora Neale Hurston Forum* 1.1 (1986): 38–44. (Fauset and Hurston).

Prestianni, Vincent. "Bibliographical Scholarship on Three Black Writers." *Obsidian II: Black Literature in Review* 5.1 (1990): 75–85. (McKay, Brown, and Gwendolyn Brooks).

Rhodes, Chip. "Writing Up the New Negro: The Construction of Consumer Desire in the Twenties." *Journal of American Studies* 28 (1994): 191–207. (Heyward and Larsen)

Sisney, Mary F. "The View from the Outside: Black Novels of Manner." in *Reading and Writing Women's Lives: A Study of the Novel of Manners*. Ed. Bege Bowers and Barbara Brothers. Univ. Microfilms International Research Press, 1990. 171–86. (Fauset, Larsen, and Gloria Naylor).

Smith, Gary. "The Black Protest Sonnet." *American Poetry* 2.1 (1984): 2–12. (McKay and Cullen).

Stadler, Quandra Prettyman. "Visibility and Difference: Black Women in History and Literature: Pieces of a Paper and Some Ruminations." *The Future of Difference*. Ed. Hester Eisenstein and Alice Jardine. Boston: Hall, 1980. 239–46. (Larsen and Hurston).

Story, Ralph D. "Patronage and the Harlem Renaissance: You Get What You Pay For." *CLA Journal* 32 (1989): 284–95. (Hughes, McKay, Hurston, Charlotte Osgood Mason).

Thornton, Jerome E. "'Goin' on de muck': The Paradoxical Journey of the Black American Hero." *CLA Journal* 31 (1988): 261–80. (Hurston and Toomer, as well as Baraka).

Turner, Darwin T. *In a Minor Chord: Three Afro-American Writers and Their Search for Identity.* Carbondale: Southern Illinois Univ. Press, 1971. (Toomer, Cullen, and Hurston)

Turpin, Waters E. "Four Short Fiction Writers of the Harlem Renaissance—Their Legacy of Achievement." *CLA Journal* 11 (1967): 59–72. (Toomer, Fisher, Hughes, and McKay)

STERLING A. BROWN

Alexander, Elizabeth. "Listen Up: Sterling Brown's Folk Remedies." *Village Voice Literary Supplement* May 1990: 23.

Allen, Samuel W. "Sterling Brown: Poems to Endure." *Massachusetts Review* 24 (1983): 649–57.

Benston, Kimberly W. "Sterling Brown's After-Song: 'When de Saints go Ma'ching Home' and the Performances of Afro-American Voice." *Callaloo*, 5.1–2 [14–15] (1982): 33–42.

Callahan, John F. "Sterling Brown Ain't Dead Nothing . . . He Ain't Even Passed." *Black American Literature Forum* 23 (1989): 91–94.

Chamblee, Angela E. "Slim's Heaven and Hell." *CLA Journal* 36 (1993): 339–42.

Gabbin, Joanne V. *Sterling A. Brown: Building the Black Aesthetic Tradition.* Westport, CT: Greenwood, 1985.

Henderson, Stephen A. "A Strong Man Called Sterling Brown." *Black World* Sept. 1970: 5–12.

Henderson, Stephen E. "The Heavy Blues of Sterling Brown: A Study of Craft and Tradition." *Black American Literature Forum* 14 (1980): 32–44.

Kutzinski, Vera M. "The Distant Closeness of Dancing Doubles: Sterling Brown and William Carlos Williams." *Black American Literature Forum* 16 (1982): 19–25.

Nichols, Charles H. "Sterling Brown, Poet, His Place in Afro-American Literary History." *The Harlem Renaissance: Revaluations.* Ed. Amritjit Singh, William S. Shiver, and Stanley Brodwin. New York: Garland, 1989. 91–100.

O'Meally, Robert G. "An Annotated Bibliography of the Works of Sterling A. Brown." *Callaloo* 5.1–2 [14–15] (1982): 90–105.

———. "'Game to the Heart': Sterling Brown and the Badman." *Callaloo* 5.1–2 [14–15] (1982): 43–54.

Rowell, Charles H. "'Let Me Be With Ole Jazz Bo': An Interview with Sterling A. Brown." *Callaloo* 14 (1991): 795–815.

Sanders, Mark A. "The Ballad, the Hero, and the Ride: A Reading of Sterling A. Brown's 'The Ride of Wild Bill.'" *CLA Journal* 38 (1994): 162–82.

Smith, Gary. "The Literary Ballads of Sterling A. Brown." *CLA Journal* 32 (1989): 393–409.

Stepto, Robert B. "Sterling A. Brown: Outsider in the Harlem Renaissance." *The Harlem Renaissance: Revaluations.* Ed. Amritjit Singh, William S. Shiver, and Stanley Brodwin. New York: Garland, 1989. 73–81.

Tidwell, John Edgar. "Sterling A. Brown Remembered." *Black American Literature Forum* 23 (1989): 109–11.

———. "Sterling A. Brown Tribute." *Black American Literature Forum* 23 (1989): 89–112.

Williams, Sherley Anne. "Remembering Prof. Sterling A. Brown, 1901–1989." *Black American Literature Forum* 23 (1989): 106–08.

Wright, John S. "Sterling Brown's Folk Odyssey." *American Literature, Culture, and Ideology: Essays in Memory of Henry Nash Smith.* Ed. Beverly R. Voloshin. New York: Peter Lang, 1990. 331–43.

COUNTEE CULLEN

Baker, Houston A. *A Many-Colored Coat of Dreams: The Poetry of Countee Cullen*. Detroit: Broadside Press, 1974.

Borders, Florence E. *Guide to the Microfilm Edition of the Countee Cullen Papers, 1921–1969*. New Orleans: Armistad Research Center, 1975.

Davis, Arthur P. "The Alien-and-Exile Theme in Countee Cullen's Racial Poems." *Phylon* 14 (1953): 390–400.

Ferguson, Blanche E. *Countee Cullen and the Negro Renaissance*. New York: Dodd, Mead, 1966.

Johnson, Lonnell E. "The Bible and Countee Cullen: Portraying the Outcast and Resolving the Conflict." *Mount Olive Review* 5 (1991): 51–57.

Kirby, David K. "Countee Cullen's 'Heritage': A Black Waste Land." *South Atlantic Bulletin*, 36.4 (1971): 14–20.

Perry, Margaret. *A Bio-Bibliography of Countee P. Cullen, 1903–1946*. Westport, CT: Greenwood, 1971.

Shucard, Alan R. *Countee Cullen*. Boston: Twayne, 1984.

Tuttleton, James W. "Countée Cullen at 'The Heights.'" *The Harlem Renaissance: Revaluations*. Ed. Amritjit Singh, William S. Shiver, and Stanley Brodwin. New York: Garland, 1989. 101–37.

W. E. B. DU BOIS

Andrews, William L., ed. *Critical Essays on W.E.B. Du Bois*. Boston: Hall, 1985.

Aptheker, Herbert. *Annotated Bibliography of the Published Writings of W. E. B. Du Bois*. Millwood, NY: Kraus, 1973.

———, ed. *The Correspondence of W.E.B. Du Bois. Vol. I: Selections, 1877–1934*. Amherst: Univ. of Mass. Press, 1973.

Gibson, Lovie H. "W.E.B. Du Bois as a Propaganda Novelist." *Negro American Literature Forum* 10 (1976): 75–77, 79–82.

Green, Dan S. "Bibliography of Writings about W.E.B. Du Bois." *CLA Journal* 20 (1977): 410–21.

Moore, Jack B. *W.E.B. Du Bois*. Boston: Twayne, 1981.

Rampersad, Arnold. *The Art and Imagination of W.E B. Du Bois*. Cambridge: Harvard Univ. Press, 1976.

———. "W.E.B. Du Bois as a Man of Literature." *American Literature* 51 (1979): 50–68.

RUDOLPH FISHER

Deutsch, Leonard J. "A Corrected Bibliography for Rudolph Fisher." *Bulletin of Bibliography and Magazine Notes* 35 (1978): 30–33.

———. "Rudolph Fisher's Unpublished Manuscripts: Description and Commentary." *Obsidian* 6.1–2 (1980): 82–97.

———. "'The Streets of Harlem': The Short Stories of Rudolph Fisher." *Phylon* 40 (1979): 159–71.

Friedmann, Thomas. "The Good Guys in the Black Hats: Color Coding in Rudolf [*sic*] Fisher's 'Common Meter.'" *Studies in Black Literature* 7.2 (1976), 8–9.

Henry, Oliver Louis. "Rudolph Fisher: An Evaluation." *Crisis* 78 (1971): 149–54.

McCluskey, John, Jr. "'Aim High and Go Straight': The Grandmother Figure in the Short Fiction of Rudolph Fisher." *Black American Literature Forum* 15 (1981): 55–59.

————. "Healing Songs: Secular Music in the Short Fiction of Rudolph Fisher." *CLA Journal* 26 (1982): 191–203.

————. "Introduction." *The City of Refuge: The Collected Stories of Rudolph Fisher*. Columbia: Univ. of Missouri Press, 1987. xi–xxxix.

Tignor, Eleanor Q. "Rudolph Fisher: Harlem Novelist." *Langston Hughes Review* 1.2 (1982): 13–22.

————. "The Short Fiction of Rudolph Fisher." *Langston Hughes Review* 1.1 (1982): 18–24.

DUBOSE HEYWARD

Bokinsky, Caroline. "Dubose Heyward's *Porgy*." *Names in South Carolina* 29 (1982): 23–26.

Durham, Frank. *DuBose Heyward: The Man Who Wrote Porgy*. Columbia: Univ. of South Carolina Press, 1954.

Harrigan, Anthony. "DuBose Heyward: Memorialist and Realist." *Georgia Review* 5 (1951): 335–44.

Shirley, Wayne D. "Reconciliation on Catfish Row: Bess, Serena, and the Short Score of *Porgy and Bess*." *Quarterly Journal of the Library of Congress* 38.3 (1981): 145–65.

Slavick, William H. *DuBose Heyward*. Boston: Twayne, 1981.

LANGSTON HUGHES

Barksdale, Richard K. *Langston Hughes: The Poet and His Critics*. Chicago: American Library Association, 1977.

————. "Langston Hughes and the Blues He Couldn't Lose." *The Harlem Renaissance: Revaluations*. Ed. Amritjit Singh, William S. Shiver, and Stanley Brodwin. New York: Garland, 1989. 83–90.

Berry, Faith. *Langston Hughes: Before and Beyond Harlem*. Westport, CT: Lawrence Hill, 1983.

Bloom, Harold, ed. *Langston Hughes*. New York: Chelsea, 1989.

Dickinson, Donald C. *A Bio-bibliography of Langston Hughes, 1902–1967*. Hamden, CT: Archon Books, 1972.

Emanuel, James A. *Langston Hughes*. New York: Twayne, 1967.

Etheridge, Sharynn O. "Langston Hughes: An Annotated Bibliography (1977–1986)." *Langston Hughes Review* 11.1 (1992): 41–57.

Gates, Henry Louis, Jr., and K. A. Appiah, eds. *Langston Hughes: Critical Perspectives Past and Present*. New York: Amistad, 1993.

Jemie, Onwucheckwa. *Langston Hughes: An Introduction to the Poetry*. New York: Columbia Univ. Press, 1976.

McLaren, Joseph. "Early Recognitions: Duke Ellington and Langston Hughes in New York, 1920–1930." *The Harlem Renaissance: Revaluations*. Ed. Amritjit Singh, William S. Shiver, and Stanley Brodwin. New York: Garland, 1989. 195–208.

Miller, R. Baxter. *The Art and Imagination of Langston Hughes*. Lexington: Univ. Press of Kentucky, 1989.

————. *Langston Hughes and Gwendolyn Brooks: A Reference Guide*. Boston: Hall, 1978.

Mullen, Edward J., ed. *Critical Essays on Langston Hughes*. Boston: Hall, 1986.

Neal, Larry. "Langston Hughes: Black America's Poet Laureate." *American Writing Today*. Ed. Rochard Kostelanetz. Troy, NY: Whitston, 1991. 61–72.

Nichols, Charles H., ed. *Arna Bontemps—Langston Hughes Letters, 1925–1967*. New York: Dodd, 1980.

O'Daniel, Therman B. "Langston Hughes: An Updated Selected Bibliography." *Black American Literature Forum* 15 (1981): 104–07.

————, ed. *Langston Hughes: Black Genius: A Critical Evaluation.* New York: Morrow, 1971.
Ostrom, Hans. *Langston Hughes: A Study of the Short Fiction.* New York: Twayne, 1993.
Rampersad, Arnold. "Langston Hughes and Approaches to Modernism in the Harlem Re-naissance." *The Harlem Renaissance: Revaluations.* Ed. Amritjit Singh, William S. Shiver, and Stanley Brodwin. New York: Garland, 1989. 49–71.
————. *The Life of Langston Hughes.* 2 vol. New York: Oxford Univ. Press, 1986–88.
————. "The Origins of Poetry in Langston Hughes." *Southern Review* 21 (1985): 695–705.
Rollins, Charlemae H. *Black Troubadour: Langston Hughes.* Chicago: Rand, 1970.
Tracy, Steven C. *Langston Hughes & the Blues.* Urbana: Univ. of Illinois Press, 1988.

ZORA NEALE HURSTON

Awkward, Michael, ed. *New Essays on Their Eyes Were Watching God.* New York: Cambridge Univ. Press, 1990.
Bloom, Harold, ed. *Zora Neale Hurston.* New York: Chelsea, 1986.
————, ed. *Zora Neale Hurston's Their Eyes Were Watching God.* New York: Chelsea, 1987.
Boi, Paola. "Zora Neale Hurston's Autobiographic Fictive: Dark Tracks on the Canon of a Female Writer." *The Black Columbiad: Defining Moments in African American Litera-ture and Culture.* Ed. Werner Sollors and Maria Diedrich. Cambridge: Harvard Univ. Press, 1994. 191–200.
Carby, Hazel. "The Politics of Fiction, Anthropology, and the Folk: Zora Neale Hurston." *History and Memory in African-American Culture* . New York: Oxford Univ. Press, 1994. 28–44.
Dance, Daryl C. "Zora Neale Hurston." *American Women Writers: Bibliographical Essays.* Ed. Jackson R. Bryer and M. Thomas Inge. Westport, CT: Greenwood, 1983. 321–51.
Davies, Kathleen. "Zora Neale Hurston's Poetics of Embalmment: Articulating the Rage of Black Women and Narrative Self-Defense." *African American Review* 26.1 (1992): 147–59.
Gates, Henry Louis, Jr. "Zora Neale Hurston and the Speakerly Text." *Southern Literature and Literary Theory.* Ed. Jefferson Humphries. Athens: Univ. of Georgia Press, 1990. 142–69.
————, and K. A. Appiah, eds. *Zora Neale Hurston: Critical Perspectives Past and Present.* New York: Amistad, 1993.
Glassman, Steve, and Kathryn Lee Seidel, eds. *Zora in Florida.* Orlando: Univ. of Central Florida Press, 1991.
Gloster, Hugh M. "Zora Neale Hurston: Novelist and Folklorist." *Phylon* 4 (1943): 153–59.
Hemenway, Robert. *Zora Neale Hurston: A Literary Biography.* Urbana: Univ. of Illinois Press, 1977.
Holloway, Karla F. C. *The Character of the Word: The Texts of Zora Neale Hurston.* Westport, CT: Greenwood, 1987.
Howard, Lillie P. , ed. *Alice Walker and Zora Neale Hurston: The Common Bond.* Westport, CT: Greenwood, 1993.
Howard, Lillie P. *Zora Neale Hurston.* Boston: Twayne, 1980.
Love, Theresa R. "Zora Neale Hurston's America." *Papers on Language and Literature* 12 (1976): 422–37.
Lowe, John. *Jump at the Sun: Zora Neale Hurston's Cosmic Comedy.* Urbana: Univ. of Illinois Press, 1994.
Monroe, Barbara. "Courtship, Comedy, and African-American Expressive Culture in Zora Neale Hurston's Fiction." *Look Who's Laughing: Gender and Comedy.* Ed. Gail Finney. Langhorne, PA: Gordon & Breach, 1994. 173–88.
Newson, Adele S. *Zora Neale Hurston: A Reference Guide.* Boston: Hall, 1987.

Sheffey, Ruthe T., ed. *A Rainbow Round Her Shoulder: The Zora Neale Hurston Symposium Papers.* [Baltimore]: Morgan State Univ. Press, 1982.

Thompson, Gordon E. "Projecting Gender: Personification in the Works of Zora Neale Hurston." *American Literature* 66 (1994): 737–63.

Vickers, Anita M. "The Reaffirmation of African-American Dignity through the Oral Tradition in Zora Neale Hurston's *Their Eyes Were Watching God.*" *CLA Journal* 37 (1994): 303–15.

Wainwright, Mary Katherine. "The Aesthetics of Community: The Insular Black Community as Theme and Focus in Hurston's *Their Eyes Were Watching God.*" *The Harlem Renaissance: Revaluations.* Ed. Amritjit Singh, William S. Shiver, and Stanley Brodwin. New York: Garland, 1989. 233–43.

Wall, Cheryl A. "Zora Neale Hurston: Changing Her Own Words." *American Novelists Revisited: Essays in Feminist Criticism.* Ed. Fritz Fleischmann. Boston: Hall, 1982. 370–93.

Washington, Mary Helen. "I Love the Way Janie Crawford Left Her Husbands: Zora Neale Hurston's Emergent Female Hero." *Invented Lives: Narratives of Black Women, 1860–1960.* New York: Anchor, 1987. 237–54.

NELLA LARSEN

Blackmore, David L. "'That Unreasonable Restless Feeling': The Homosexual Subtexts of Nella Larsen's *Passing.*" *African-American-Review* 26 (1992): 475–84.

Brody, Jennifer DeVere. "Clare Kennedy's 'True' Colors: Race and Class Conflict in Nella Larsen's *Passing.*" *Callaloo* 15 (1992): 1053–65.

Clark, William Bedford. "The Heroine of Mixed Blood in Nella Larsen's *Quicksand.*" *Identity and Awareness in the Minority Experience: Past and Present.* Selected Proceedings of the First and Second Annual Conferences on Minority Studies. March 1973 and April 1974. Ed. George E. Carter and Bruce L. Mouser. La Crosse: Univ. of Wisconsin Press, 1975. 225–38.

———. "The Letters of Nella Larsen to Carl Van Vechten: A Survey." *Resources for American Literary Study* 8 (1978): 193–99.

Conde, Mary "Passing in the Fiction of Jessie Redmon Fauset and Nella Larsen." *Yearbook of English Studies* 24 (1994): 94–104.

Davis, Thadious M. *Nella Larsen, Novelist of the Harlem Renaissance: A Woman's Life Unveiled* Baton Rouge: Louisiana State Univ. Press, 1994.

———. "Nella Larsen's Harlem Aesthetic." in *The Harlem Renaissance: Revaluations.* Ed. Amritjit Singh, William S. Shiver, and Stanley Brodwin. New York: Garland, 1989. 245–56.

Fleming, Robert E. "The Influence of *Main Street* on Nella Larsen's *Quicksand. Modern Fiction Studies* 31 (1985): 547–53.

Johnson, Barbara. "The Quicksands of the Self: Nella Larsen and Heinz Kohut." *Telling Facts: History and Narration in Psychoanalysis.* Ed. Joseph H. Smith and Humphrey Morris. Baltimore: Johns Hopkins Univ. Press, 1992. 184–99.

Lay, Mary M. "Parallels: Henry James's *The Portrait of a Lady* and Nella Larsen's *Quicksand.*" *CLA Journal* 20 (1977): 475–86.

Lewis, Vashti. "Nella Larsen's Use of the Near-White Female in *Quicksand* and *Passing.*" *Western Journal of Black Studies* 10 (1986): 137–42.

Madigan, Mark J. "'Then Everything Was Dark'?: The Two Endings of Nella Larsen's *Passing.*" *Papers of the Bibliographical Society of America* 83 (1989): 521–23.

McDowell, Deborah E. "'That nameless . . . shameful impulse': Sexuality in Nella Larsen's *Quicksand* and *Passing.* in *Black Feminist Criticism and Critical Theory.* Ed. Joe Weixlmann and Houston A. Baker, Jr. Greenwood, FL: Penkeville, 1988. 139–67.

McLendon, Jacquelyn Y. "Self-Representation and Art in the Novels of Nella Larsen." in *Redefining Autobiography in Twentieth-Century Women's Fiction: An Essay Collection*. Ed. Janice Morgan, Colette T. Hall, and Carol L. Snyder. Forward by Molly Hite. New York: Garland, 1991. 149–68.

McMillan, T. S. "Passing Beyond: The Novels of Nella Larsen." *West Virginia University Philological Papers* 38 (1992): 134–46.

Horton, Merrill. "Blackness, Betrayal, and Childhood: Race and Identity in Nella Larsen's *Passing*." *CLA Journal* 28 (1994): 31–45.

Hostetler, Ann E. "The Aesthetics of Race and Gender in Nella Larsen's *Quicksand*." *PMLA* 105 (1990): 35–46.

Rabinowitz, Peter J. " 'Betraying the Sender': The Rhetoric and Ethics of Fragile Texts." *Narrative* 2 (1994): 201–13.

Silverman, Debra B. "Nella Larsen's *Quicksand*: Untangling the Webs of Exoticism." *African-American-Review* 27 (1993): 599–614.

Thornton, Hortense. "Sexism and Quagmire: Nella Larsen's *Quicksand*." *CLA Journal* 16 (1973): 285–301.

Wall, Cheryl A. "Passing for What? Aspects of Identity in Nella Larsen's Novels." *Black American Literature Forum* 20 (1986): 97–111.

Washington, Mary Helen. "The Mulatto Trap: Nella Larsen's Women of the 1920's." *Invented Lives: Narratives of Black Women, 1860–1960*. New York: Anchor, 1987. 159–67.

CLAUDE MCKAY

Binder, Wolfgang. "'A Black Icon in the Flesh': The Afroamerican Writer in Europe: The Case of Claude McKay." in *L'Amerérique et l'Europe: Réalités et représentations*. Pref. by Neil Larry Shumsky. I. Aix-en-Provence: Univ de Provence; 1985. 137–51. [disc. *Long Way from Home* and *Home to Harlem*]

Chauhan, P. S. "Rereading Claude McKay." *CLA Journal* 34 (1990): 68–80.

Chi, Yuan Wen. "In Search of Black Identity: Claude McKay's *Home to Harlem*." *American Studies* 21 (1991): 103–22.

Collier, Eugenia W. "The Four-Way Dilemma of Claude McKay." *CLA Journal* 15 (1972): 345–53.

Conroy, Mary. "The Vagabond Motif in the Writings of Claude McKay." *Negro American Literature Forum* 5 (1971): 15–23.

Cooper, Wayne. "Claude McKay and the New Negro of the 1920's." *Phylon* (1964): 297–306.

———. *Claude McKay—Rebel Sojourner in the Harlem Renaissance*. Baton Rouge: Louisiana State Univ. Press, 1987.

Dorris, Ronald. "Claude McKay's *Home to Harlem*: A Social Commentary." *McNeese Review* 29 (1982–83): 53–62.

Giles, James. *Claude McKay*. Boston: Twayne, 1976.

Greenberg, Robert M. "Idealism and Realism in the Fiction of Claude McKay." *CLA Journal* 24 (1981): 237–61.

Griffin, Barbara J. "Claude McKay: The Evolution of a Conservative." *CLA Journal* 36 (1992): 157–70.

Kent, George E. "The Soulful Way of Claude McKay." *Blackness and the Adventures of Western Culture*. Chicago: Third World Press, 1972. 36–52.

LeSeur, Geta. "Claude McKay's Marxism." *The Harlem Renaissance: Revaluations*. Ed. Amritjit Singh, William S. Shiver, and Stanley Brodwin. New York: Garland, 1989. 219–31.

———. "Claude McKay's Romanticism." *CLA Journal* 32 (1989): 296–308.

Lively, Adam. "Continuity and Radicalism in American Black Nationalist Thought, 1914–1929." *Journal of American Studies* 18 (1984): 207–35. [*Banjo, Banana Bottom*, Garvey, DuBois]

Lueth, Elmer. "The Scope of Black Life in Claude McKay's *Home to Harlem*." *Obsidian II* 5.3 (1990): 43–52.

McLeod, A. L. "Claude McKay, Alain Locke, and the Harlem Renaissance." *Literary Half-Yearly* 27.2 (1986): 65–75.

———. "Claude McKay as Historical Witness." *Subjects Worthy of Fame: Essays on Commonwealth Literature in Honour of H. H. Anniah Gowda*. Ed. A. L. McLeod. New Delhi: Sterling, 1989. 62–71.

Nelson, Emmanuel S. "Community and Individual Identity in the Novels of Claude McKay." *Claude McKay: Centennial Studies*. Ed. A. L. McLeod. New Delhi: Sterling, 1992. 106–13.

Sen, Sarbani. "How 'Red' Is 'Black'? An Analysis of the Relationship of the African-American Movement with Marxism." *Literature and Politics in Twentieth Century America*. Ed. J. L. Plakkoottam and Prashant K. Sinha. Hyderabad: American Studies Research Centre, 1993. 32–40.

Priebe, Richard. "The Search for Community in the Novels of Claude McKay." *Studies in Black Literature* 3.2 (1972): 22–30.

Pyne-Timothy, Helen. "Claude McKay: Individualism and Group Consciousness." in *A Celebration of Black and African Writing*. Ed. Bruce King and Kolawole Ogungbesan. Zaria: Ahmadu Bello Univ. Press; and London: Oxford Univ. Press, 1975. 15–29.

Smith, Robert A. "Claude McKay: An Essay in Criticism." *Phylon* 9 (1948): 270–73.

Stoff, Michael B. "Claude McKay and the Cult of Primitivism." *The Harlem Renaissance Remembered*. Ed. Arna Bontemps. New York: Dodd, Mead, 1972. 126–46.

Tillery, Tyrone. *Claude McKay: A Black Poet's Struggle for Identity*. Amherst: Univ. of Massachusetts Press, 1992.

Tolson, Melvin B. "Claude McKay's Art." *Poetry* 83 (1954): 287–90.

Warren, Stanley. "Claude McKay as an Artist." *Negro History Bulletin* 40 (1977): 685–87.

EUGENE O'NEILL

Bordewyk, Gordon, and Michael McGowan. "Another Source of Eugene O'Neill's *The Emperor Jones*." *Notes on Modern American Literature* 6.2 (1982): Item 10.

Carpenter, Frederic I. *Eugene O'Neill*. Rev. ed. Boston: Twayne, 1979.

Colakis, Marianthe. "Eugene O'Neill's *The Emperor Jones* as Senecan Tragedy." *Classical and Modern Literature: A Quarterly* 10.2 (1990): 153–59.

Conklin, Robert. "The Expression of Character in O'Neill's *The Emperor Jones* and *The Hairy Ape*." *West Virginia University Philological Papers* 39 (1993): 101–07.

Corey, James. "O'Neill's *The Emperor Jones*." *American Notes and Queries* 12 (1974): 156–57.

Engel, Edwin A. *The Haunted Heroes of Eugene O'Neill*. Cambridge: Harvard Univ. Press, 1953.

Gelb, Arthur, and Barbara Gelb. *O'Neill*. New York: Harper, 1962.

Gillett, Peter J. "O'Neill and the Racial Myths." *Twentieth Century Literature* 18 (1972): 111–20.

Hamner, Robert. "Dramatizing the New World's African King: O'Neill, Walcott and Cesaire on Christophe." *Journal of West Indian Literature* 5.1–2 (1992): 30–47.

Londre, Felicia Hardison. "Dramatic Tension between Expressionistic Design and Naturalistic Acting in *The Emperor Jones*." *Eugene O'Neill in China: An International Centenary Celebration*. Ed. Haiping Liu and Lowell Swortzell. New York: Greenwood, 1992. 183–97.

Hinden, Michael. "*The Emperor Jones*: O'Neill, Nietzsche, and the American Past." *Eugene O'Neill Newsletter* 3.3 (1980): 2–4.

Kagan, Norman. "The Return of *The Emperor Jones*." *Negro History Bulletin* 34 (1971): 160–62.

Krimsky, John. "*The Emperor Jones*: Robeson and O'Neill on Film." *Connecticut Review* 7.2 (1974): 94–99.

Nolan, Patrick J. "*The Emperor Jones*: A Jungian View of the Origin of Fear in the Black Race." *Eugene O'Neill Newsletter* 4.1–2 (1980): 6–9.

Orlandello, John. "*The Emperor Jones*." *O'Neill on Film*. Rutherford, NJ: Fairleigh Dickinson Univ. Press, 1982. 51–65.

Pawley, Thomas D. "The Black World of Eugene O'Neill." *Eugene O'Neill in China: An International Centenary Celebration*. Ed. Haiping Liu and Lowell Swortzell. New York: Greenwood, 1992. 137–48.

Schwerdt, Lisa M. "Blueprint for the Future: *The Emperor Jones*." *Critical Essays on Eugene O'Neill*. Ed. James J. Martine. Boston: Hall, 1984. 72–77.

Singh, Veena. "O'Neill's Yank and Jones: The Dislocated Characters." *Panjab University Research Bulletin* 18.1 (1987): 45–54.

Smith, Madeline. "*The Emperor Jones* and Confession." *Bulletin of the West Virginia Association of College English Teachers* 8 (1983): 17–22.

———, and Richard Eaton. *Eugene O'Neill: An Annotated Bibliography*. New York: Garland, 1988.

Stroupe, John H., ed. *Critical Approaches to O'Neill*. New York: AMS Press, 1988.

Swortzell, Lowell. "*The Emperor Jones* as a Source of Theatrical Experimentation, 1920s–1980s." *Eugene O'Neill in China: An International Centenary Celebration*. Ed. Haiping Liu and Lowell Swortzell. New York: Greenwood, 1992. 199–209.

Viswanathan, R. "The Ship Scene in *The Emperor Jones*." *Eugene O'Neill Newsletter* 4.3 (1980): 3–5.

Watt, Stephen M. "The 'Formless Fear' of O'Neill's Emperor and Tennyson's King." *Eugene O'Neill Newsletter* 6.3 (1983): 14–15.

Zucker, Wolfgang M. "The Return of the Demons." *Continuities and Discontinuities: Essays in Psychohistory*. Ed. Shirley Sugerman. Madison, NJ: Drew Univ. Press, 1978. 44–57.

GEORGE SCHUYLER

Faulkner, Howard J. "A Vanishing Race." *CLA Journal* 37 (1994): 274–92.

Gates, Henry Louis, Jr. "A Fragmented Man: George Schuyler and the Claims of Race." *New York Times Book Review* 20 Sept. 1992: 31, 42–43.

Peplow, Michael W. *George S. Schuyler*. Boston: Twayne: 1980.

Rayson, Ann. "George Schuyler: Paradox among 'Assimilationist' Writers." *Black American Literature Forum* 12 (1978): 102–06.

Reilly, John M. "The Black Anti-Utopia." *Black American Literature Forum* 12 (1978): 107–09.

Singh, Amritjit. "Racial Politics in Afro-American Literature: Reflections in a Cross-Continental Context." *Journal of the School of Languages* 8.1–2 (Monsoon-Winter 1981–82):136–148.

WALLACE THURMAN

Gaither, Renoir W. "The Moment of Revision: A Reappraisal of Wallace Thurman's Aesthetics in *The Blacker the Berry* and *Infants of the Spring*." *CLA Journal* 37 (1993): 81–93.

Haslam, Gerald. "Wallace Thurman: A Western Renaissance Man." *Western American Literature* 6 (1971): 53–59.

Klotman, Phyllis. "The Black Writer in Hollywood, Circa 1930: The Case of Wallace Thurman." in *Black American Cinema*. Ed. Manthia Diawara. London: Routledge, 1993. 80–92.

Notten, Eleonore van. *Wallace Thurman's Harlem Renaissance*. Amsterdam: Rodopi, 1994.
West, Dorothy. "Elephant's Dance: A Memoir of Wallace Thurman." *Black World* Nov.
  1970: 77–85.

JEAN TOOMER

Baker, Houston. "Journey Toward Black Art: Jean Toomer's *Cane*." *Singers of Daybreak*.
  Washington, D.C.: Howard Univ. Press, 1974. 53–80.
Bell, Bernard W. "A Key to the Poems in *Cane*." *CLA Journal* 14 (1971): 251–58.
Benson, Brian Joseph, and Mabel Mayle Dillard. *Jean Toomer*. Boston: Twayne, 1980.
Bradley, David. "Looking Behind Cane." *Southern Review* 21 (1985): 682–94.
Brinkmeyer, Robert H., Jr. "Wasted Talent, Wasted Art: The Literary Career of Jean Toomer."
  Southern Quarterly 20.1 (1981): 75–84.
Bus, Heiner. "Jean Toomer and the Black Heritage." *History and Tradition in Afro-American
  Culture*. Ed. Gunter H. Lenz. Frankfurt: Campus, 1984.
Byrd, Rudolph P. "Jean Toomer and the Writers of the Harlem Renaissance: Was He There
  with Them?" *The Harlem Renaissance: Revaluations*. Ed. Amritjit Singh, William S.
  Shiver, and Stanley Brodwin. New York: Garland, 1989. 209–18.
———. *Jean Toomer's Years with Gurdjieff: A Portrait of an Artist, 1923–1936*. Athens:
  Univ. of Georgia Press, 1990.
Durham, Frank, comp. *The Merrill Studies in* Cane. Columbus, OH: Merrill, 1971.
Golding, Alan. "Jean Toomer's *Cane*: The Search for Identity through Form." *Arizona
  Quarterly* 39 (1983): 197–214.
Hajek, Friederike. "The Change of Literary Authority in the Harlem Renaissance: Jean
  Toomer's *Cane*." *The Black Columbiad: Defining Moments in African American Lit-
  erature and Culture*. Ed. Werner Sollors and Maria Diedrich. Cambridge: Harvard Univ.
  Press, 1994. 185–90.
Hutchinson, George B. "Jean Toomer and the 'New Negroes' of Washington." *American
  Literature* 63 (1991): 683–92.
Kerman, Cynthia Earl and Richard Eldridge. *The Lives of Jean Toomer: A Hunger for
  Wholeness*. Baton Rouge: Louisiana State Univ. Press, 1987.
Lieber, Todd. "Design and Movement in *Cane*." *CLA Journal* 13 (1969): 35–50.
Martin, Odette C. "*Cane*: Method and Myth." *Obsidian: Black Literature in Review* 2.1
  (1976): 5–20.
Matthews, George C. "Toomer's 'Cane': The Artist and His World." *CLA Journal* 17 (1974):
  543–59.
McKay, Nellie Y. *Jean Toomer, Artist: A Study of His Literary Life and Work, 1894–1936*.
  Chapel Hill: Univ. of North Carolina Press, 1984.
Munro, C. Lynn. "Jean Toomer: A Bibliography of Secondary Sources." *Black American
  Literature Forum* 21 (1987): 275–87.
O'Daniel, Thurman, ed. *Jean Toomer: A Critical Evaluation*. Washington: Howard Univ.
  Press, 1988.
Reilly, John M. "The Search for Black Redemption: Jean Toomer's *Cane*." *Studies in the
  Novel* 2 (1970): 312–24.
Rohrberger, Mary. "The Question of Regionalism: Limitation and Transcendence." *The
  American Short Story: 1900–1945: A Critical History*. Ed. Philip Stevick. Boston:
  Twayne, 1984. 147–82.
Scruggs, Charles W. "The Mark of Cain and the Redemption of Art: A Study in Theme and
  Structure of Jean Toomer's *Cane*." *American Literature* 44 (1972): 276–91.
———. "Textuality and Vision in Jean Toomer's *Cane*." *Journal of the Short Story in
  English* 10 (1988): 93–114.

Taylor, Clyde. "The Second Coming of Jean Toomer." *Obsidian: Black Literature in Review* 1.3 (1975): 37–57.
Twombly, Robert C. "A Disciple's Odyssey: Jean Toomer's Gurdjieffian Career." *Prospects: An Annual of American Cultural Studies*. Vol 2. Ed. Jack Salzman. New York: Burt Franklin, 1976. 437–62.

CARL VAN VECHTEN

Helbling, Mark. "Carl Van Vechten and the Harlem Renaissance." *Negro American Literature Forum* 10 (1976): 39–47.
Kellner, Bruce. *A Bibliography of the Work of Carl Van Vechten*. Westport, CT: Greenwood, 1980.
———. *Carl Van Vechten and the Irreverent Decades*. Norman: Univ. of Oklahoma Press, 1968.
———. "Carl Van Vechten's Black Renaissance." *The Harlem Renaissance: Revaluations*. Ed. Amritjit Singh, William S. Shiver, and Stanley Brodwin. New York: Garland, 1989. 23–33.
———. *"Keep A-Inchin' Along": Selected Writings of Carl Van Vechten About Black Art and Letters*. Westport, CT: Greenwood, 1979.
———, ed. *Letters of Carl Van Vechten*. New Haven: Yale Univ. Press, 1987.
Kishimoto, Hisao. *Carl Van Vechten: The Man and His Role in the Harlem Renaissance*. Tokyo: Seibido, 1983.
Lueders, Edward G. *Carl Van Vechten*. New York: Twayne, 1965.
———. *Carl Van Vechten and The Twenties*. Albuquerque: Univ. of New Mexico Press, 1955.
Perényi, Eleanor. "Carl Van Vechten." *The Yale Review* 77 (1988): 537–43.
Pizer, Donald. "The Novels of Carl Van Vechten and the Spirit of the Age." *Toward a New American Literary History: Essays in Honor of Arlin Turner*. Ed. Louis J. Budd, Edwin H. Cady, and Carl L. Anderson. Durham: Duke Univ. Press, 1980. 211–29.
Schuyler, George. "The Van Vechten Revolution." *Phylon* 11 (1950): 362–68.

DOROTHY WEST

Dalsbard, Katrine. "Alive and Well and Living on the Island of Martha's Vineyard: An Interview with Dorothy West, October 29, 1988." *Langston Hughes Review* 12.2 (1993): 28–44.
Ferguson, SallyAnn H. "Dorothy and Helene Johnson in *Infants of the Spring*." *Langston Hughes Review* 2.2 (1983): 22–24.
Roses, Lorraine Elena. "Interviews with Black Women Writers: Dorothy West at Oak Bluffs, Massachusetts, July 1984." *SAGE: A Scholarly Journal on Black Women*, 2.1 (1985): 47–49.
Rueschmann, Eva. "Sister Bonds: Intersections of Family and Race in Jessie Redmon Fauset's *Plum Bun* and Dorothy West's *The Living Is Easy*." *The Significance of Sibling Relationships in Literature*. Ed. JoAnna Stephens Mink and Janet Doubler Ward. Bowling Green, OH: Popular, 1992. 120–31.
Wade-Gayles, Gloria. "The Truths of Our Mothers' Lives: Mother-Daughter Relationships in Black Women's Fiction." *SAGE: A Scholarly Journal on Black Women* 1.2 (1984): 8–12.
Washington, Mary Helen. "I Sign My Mother's Name: Alice Walker, Dorothy West, Paule Marshall." in *Mothering the Mind: Twelve Studies of Writers and Their Silent Partners*. Ed. Ruth Perry and Martine Watson Brownley. New York: Holmes & Meier: 1984. 142–63.

NOTES ON CONTRIBUTORS

LEON COLEMAN is Professor of English Studies at the University of the District of Columbia. He holds the Doctor of Philosophy in American Studies and has been a consultant and lecturer in Afro-American Literature for twenty years.

JOHN COOLEY, Professor of English at Western Michigan University, has been a visiting professor of American Studies at the universities of Sussex and Exeter. His article in this book emerged from his research for *Savages and Naturals: Black Portraits By White Writers in Modern American Literature* (1982). His articles on American literature have appeared in *Mississippi Quarterly*, *Journal of Modern Literature*, and *Southern Humanities Review*.

The late CHARLES T. DAVIS was Master of Calhoun College and Professor of English at Yale University as well as chairman of the Afro-American Studies Program. His books included *Walt Whitman's Poems: Selections with Critical Aids* (with Gay Wilson Allen), *E. A. Robinson: Selected Early Poems and Letters*, and *On Being Black* (with Daniel Walden). Professor Davis led the symposium on the Harlem Renaissance held at the University of Iowa in 1970, which served as a stimulus for the 1974 issue of *Studies in the Literary Imagination*, *The Harlem Renaissance*, and indirectly, therefore, he is responsible for this new edition.

CAROLYN C. DENARD is Associate Professor of American Literature at Georgia State University. Her general research interest is in cultural, historical, and ethical approaches to literature. Her published work includes critical articles on Toni Morrison, William Faulkner, and a historical introduction to the works of Charlotte Hawkins Brown. She is also president of the Toni Morrison Society.

LILLIE P. HOWARD is Professor of English and Associate Provost for Academic Affairs (including Undergraduate Education) at Wright State University, Dayton, Ohio. She has published two books, *Zora Neale Hurston* (1980) and *Alice Walker and Zora Neale Hurston: The Common Bond* (1993) as well as numerous articles on African American literature.

BRUCE KELLNER is Professor of English at Millersville University in Pennsylvania, where he teaches courses in poetry, Shakespeare, and literary research. In addition to many essays and reviews, he has published books including *Carl Van Vechten and the Irreverent Decades* (1968), *The Harlem Renaissance: A Historical Dictionary for the Era* (1984), *The Letters of Carl Van Vechten* (1987), *A Gertrude Stein Companion: Content with the Example* (1988), and *The Last Dandy, Ralph Barton: American Artist, 1891–1931* (1991).

VICTOR A. KRAMER, Professor of English at Georgia State University, was named Senior Fulbright Lecturer at the University of Heidelberg, Germany, 1996–97. He served as General Editor of the Georgia State Literary Studies Series and has written and edited books about both James Agee and Thomas Merton. His edited volume of Merton's complete journal, *Turning Toward the World (1960–1963)*, was published in 1996, as well as his *Agee: Selected Literary Documents*.

JANE KUENZ is Assistant Professor of English at Georgia State University where she writes about and teaches American literature and culture. She is coauthor of *Inside the Mouse: Work and Play at Disney World* (1995). Her essays and reviews have appeared in *South Atlantic Quarterly, African American Review*, and *American Literature*. She is currently finishing a study of the cultural production of the New Negro in the Harlem Renaissance called "Producing the New Negro: The Work of Art in the Harlem Renaissance."

MICHAEL L. LOMAX was Associate Professor of English at Spelman College and an adjunct Associate Professor of English at the University of Georgia. He writes and speaks frequently on African American literature and culture. His essay included in this book sprung from his research for his Master's Thesis, entitled "Countee Cullen, from the Dark Tower."

RICHARD A. LONG was Professor at Atlanta University and is now Adjunct Professor in the Graduate Institute of Liberal Arts at Emory University. A well-known specialist on the Harlem Renaissance, he is co-editor of an illustrative cultural history, *Black Americana* (1985) and *Afro-American Writing: An Anthology of Prose and Poetry* (1985). In 1989 he also authored *The Black Tradition in American Dance*.

JOHN LOWE was Senior Fulbright Professor at the Amerika Institut, Universität München in 1995–96 and is Professor of English at Louisiana State University. Professor Lowe is the author of *Jump at the Sun: Zora Neale Hurston's Cosmic Comedy* (1994), editor of *Conversations with Ernest Gaines* (1995), and co-editor (with Jefferson Humphries) of *The Future of Southern Letters* (1996). He is currently completing a book entitled "The Americanization of Ethnic Humor," a cross-cultural, multidisciplinary examination of changing patterns in American comic literature.

DEBORAH E. MCDOWELL is Professor of English at the University of Virginia, and has published a number of articles and reviews on the literature of black women novelists that have appeared in journals such as *Black American Literature Forum* and *Women's Review of Books*. She also co-edited *Slavery and the Literary Imagination* (with Arnold Rampersad) in 1989 and authored *"The Changing Same": Black Women's Literature, Criticism, and Theory* (1995).

NELLIE Y. MCKAY is Professor of Afro-American and American literature at the University of Wisconsin, Madison. Her book, *Jean Toomer, Artist: A Study of His Literary Life and Work*, the first full-length study on Toomer, appeared in 1984. She is editor of *Critical Essays on Toni Morrison*, which appeared in 1988; general co-editor of *The Norton Anthology of African American Literature* (1996), and has written extensively on black women's writings.

MARGARET PERRY has taught African American literature at the University of Rochester and Valparaiso University. She has published four books on the Harlem Renaissance: *A Bio-bibliography of Countee Cullen, 1903–1946* (1971); *Silence to the Drums* (1976); *The Harlem Renaissance: An Annotated Bibliography and Commentary* (1982), and *The Short Fiction of Rudolph Fisher* (1987). She is also the author of poetry and short stories.

CHARLES H. ROWELL, Professor of English at the University of Virginia, is the founder of *Callaloo: An Afro-American and African Journal of Arts and Letters*. His publications include poems, articles, and interviews in such periodicals as *Southern Humanities Review* and *The Southern Review* as well as his 1995 book *Ancestral House: The Black Short Story in the Americas and Europe*.

ROBERT RUSS, an Associate Professor of English at Livingstone College, Salisbury, North Carolina, has also taught at Georgia State University and West Georgia College. His article in this book grew out of his doctoral dissertation on Claude McKay. He is currently continuing his research on McKay and is coauthoring a novel. His primary interests are modern American literature, African American literature, and philosophy.

CHARLES SCRUGGS is Professor of English at the University of Arizona. In addition to writing articles on both American and English literature, he is the author of *The Sage in Harlem: H. L. Mencken and the Black Writers of the 1920's* (1984), and most recently, *Sweet Home: Invisible Cities in the Afro-American Novel* (1993).

AMRITJIT SINGH, Professor of English and African American Studies at Rhode Island College, is currently at work on an intellectual biography of Richard Wright's final phase. Books written and edited by him include *The Novels of the Harlem Renaissance* (1976; rev. ed., 1996); *The Harlem Renaissance: Revaluations* (1989); *American Studies Today* (1995); *Conversations with Ralph Ellison* (1995); *Memory, Narrative, and Identity* (1994); *Conversations with Ishamel Reed* (1995), and *Memory and Cultural Politics* (1996).

WILLIAM H. SLAVICK is Professor Emeritus at the University of Southern Maine and author of *Dubose Heyward: The Rhythms of Charleston* (1971). He has also published widely on Elizabeth Madox Roberts—including a collection of her unpublished poetry, an Introduction to *The Time of Man*, and Afterword for *Under the Tree*, and a discussion of her papers in *The Southern Review*. He has also produced a television documentary on Roberts.

RAYMOND W. SMITH received his M.A. and his M.Phil. from Yale University in American Studies. He is a member of the Antiquarian Booksellers of America. As *R. W. Smith—Booksellers* (est. 1975), he has specialized in out-of-print reference material on American art and architecture.

DARWIN T. TURNER was University of Iowa Foundation Professor of English and Head of the African-American World Studies Program. He was a prolific writer and editor in the field of African American culture, literature, and the humanities. His work includes *The Wayward and the Seeking: Selected Writings of Jean Toomer* (1980); *The Art of Slave Narratives* (1982); *Black American Culture in the Second Renaissance, 1954–1970*; a Norton Critical Edition of Jean Toomer's *Cane* (1988), and *Black Drama in America: An Anthology* (1994).

DANIEL WALDEN, Professor of American Studies and Director of the American Studies Program at Pennsylvania State University, published *On Being Black* in 1970 (with Charles T. Davis); *W. E. B. Du Bois: The Crisis Writings* (1972); *Bernard Malamud's Literary Imagination: A New Look* (1995); as well as several articles on Du Bois, Richard Wright, Henry Roth, Philip Roth, Chaim Potok, and Saul Bellow. Professor Walden's *Eclectic and Jewish American*, an issue of *Studies in American Jewish Literature* 15, is forthcoming.

INDEX